Father Leopold Sabourin, S.J. was born and educated in Canada and is currently professor of exegesis and biblical theology of the Pontifical Biblical Institute in Rome and in Jerusalem. He previously taught Scripture in the Jesuit House of Studies at Montreal as well as in the major theological seminary at Port-au-Prince, Haiti. Father Sabourin studied at Rome's Pontifical Biblical Institute from 1954 to 1957 and dedicated several more years to research in Montreal, Rome and Jerusalem. Among his previously published books, now available in three languages, are *Redemption as Sacrifice* and *The Names and Titles of Jesus*. Father Sabourin is a member of the Catholic Biblical Association of America.

What the critics are saying...

"The most complete, up-to-date, and reliable study of the Psalms in English.... an over-all presentation of important trends in understanding the Psalms today." —CARROLL STUHLMUELLER, C.P., *Theological Studies*

"An elaborate treatment of the major problems of the Psalter. This work provides the scholar with a reliable and comprehensive orientation." —HANS BARDTKE, *Theologische Literaturzeitung*

"In Sabourin's work the clergy, theological students, and qualified laity have a knowledgeable and reliable guide." —MITCHELL DAHOOD, S.J., *Catholic Biblical Quarterly*

"The fruit of great erudition and painstaking mastery of contemporary scholarship....who desires an intellectual challenge will be much indebted to the thoroughness and expertise of Fr. Sabourin." —DAVID STANLEY, S.J.

"Only gratitude to Fr. Sabourin for his invaluable work can be the sentiment of seminary professors, preachers, teachers, catechists and liturgists, and all who wish ready access to the Word of God as it is enshrined in the perennial and universal songs of God's people." —P. J. CALDERONE, S.J.

THE PSALMS

LEOPOLD SABOURIN, S.J.

THE PSALMS

THEIR ORIGIN AND MEANING
NEW, ENLARGED, UPDATED EDITION

ALBA · HOUSE   NEW · YORK

SOCIETY OF ST. PAUL, 2187 VICTORY BLVD., STATEN ISLAND, NEW YORK 10314

Psalm references from the New American Bible © 1970
used herein by permission of the Confraternity of Christian Doctrine, copyright owner.

Library of Congress Cataloging in Publication Data

Sabourin, Leopold.
  The Psalms: their origin and meaning.

  Bibliography: v.2, p.
  1. Bible. O.T. Psalms-Criticism, interpretation, etc.
I. Title.
BS1430.2.S23   1974   223'.2066   73-16459
ISBN 0-8189-0121-7

Designed, printed and bound in the United States of
America by the Fathers and Brothers of the Society of St. Paul,
2187 Victory Boulevard, Staten Island, New York, 10314,
as part of their communications apostolate.

` 3 4 5 6 7 8 9 (*Current Printing: first digit*).

Foreword

Seper tehillim, the Book of Psalms, has had a privileged history, among all existing collections of prayer-texts. Some of its 150 numbers date from 1000 years before the Christian era; the collection was completed and "closed" probably in the fourth or third century B.C. All its contents, from the times of their respective creations down to the present day, have been in uninterrupted regular use, first in Jerusalem, then in Palestine, in the Near East, and now all over the world. First the Jewish people, then the Christian church in its worldwide expansion, have carried with them, as a precious ancestral heritage, this treasury of sacred song. If ever men could apply to themselves what one of them said about the heavens—"through all the earth their voice resounds, and to the ends of the world, their message"—surely those men were the psalmists of Israel.

Many other prayers, from many ancient cults and religions, are known to us, some of them even older than the psalms. But those texts are museum-pieces, relics of a dead past, addressed to divinities long since deserted by men and almost forgotten. No religious community of today uses an Egyptian hymn to the Sun-god, or Babylonian prayers to Marduk, or the Stoics' Hymn to Zeus, as expressions of modern faith and worship. But Israel's hymns and supplications to YHWH are still a living language of prayer, used by millions in the modern world to address the One God whom they worship.

In this millennial tradition of the Psalter's use, successive generations and various cultures have had the problem of making the psalms accessible and comprehensible to their members, in the first place by translation into whatever language was their own. Already in pre-Christian times the text, along with the rest of the Hebrew scriptures, was rendered into Greek and into Aramaic, by the Jews themselves. Since then, such work has been continually repeated, as indeed it must ever be.

In the Catholic Church of today, there has been a marked revival of interest in the liturgy, a renewed understanding of the vital importance of meaningful and comprehensible public worship. This movement was sanctioned and powerfully promoted by Vatican Council II. Automatically, it has awakened among Catholics fresh interest in the psalms. All existing Christian liturgies, some of them very ancient, have given the psalms pride of place. They make up a large part of the prayer-texts used by the Church, they supply much of her dialogue with her Creator and Redeemer. Any revitalizing of the liturgy, therefore, necessarily involves a re-examination and *re-valuing* of the psalms. Even if (and this is a moot point) they are to have a smaller part in the liturgy of the future, to make intelligent changes we must first discover and understand why they have had such a predominant position in the liturgies of the past.

To make the psalms "accessible," therefore, to modern man, to help him to understand them as expressive of his needs and aspirations, is an important and not altogether an easy task. Much has been accomplished, much more remains to be done. For users of the English language, there is certainly room, and need, for new translations, perhaps, still more for new commentaries, which will help pastors, preachers, catechists and liturgists, to experience for themselves the religious value of the psalms and to facilitate that experience for others.

It is to such a task that Father Sabourin has addressed himself in this book. He tells us that his purpose was "to present in readable form the best material now available on the biblical psalms." That means especially the results of modern literary and historical studies, which have so greatly enlarged our understanding of the historical setting and original function of the psalms. They have illuminated also the thought-world of the psalmists, and analyzed the beliefs and doctrines which they held and expressed.

In this book the author has digested and summarized the results of an immense amount of labor devoted to the text of the psalms, in modern times, mostly by Protestant and Catholic scholars. A glance at the Bibliography, limited to "works to which the present writer had direct access," will attest the thoroughness of his researches and his mastery of the vast field. The reader will see that the fundamental achievement of this "modern approach" has been the classification of the psalms in terms of their original functions, the *Gattungsforschung* pioneered by Hermann Gunkel and refined by his successors.

There is also the question of the Christian interpretation of the psalms. They are presented to us in the liturgy, enriched by a whole tradition, which starts with the quotations in the New Testament and continues through the patristic and mediaeval usage, in both Eastern and Western churches. Modern Christian interpreters cannot ignore the wealth of Christian signification which our predecessors have found in the Psalter. In the present work, this important question is discussed at the end of the third chapter.

One may hope and expect that Father Sabourin's devoted labors will make easier and more effective the work of many other popularizers of these inspired praises of God.

Rome   *R.A.F. MacKenzie, S.J.*

Preface

To make available to a larger readership this work, which has been received so favorably, a new, revised, augmented, but more economical edition in one volume has been produced. It should thus be possible to use it as textbook for students of theology and religion and for study and discussion groups. To reduce the cost of production we have not included the text itself of the psalms, leaving the reader to choose the edition he prefers (more often than not our quotations are taken from *The New American Bible or The Revised Standard Version*). The new material of this second edition will be found mostly in the introductions to Pss 51-150, since it discusses mainly the distinctive contributions of Fr. Mitchell Dahood's *Psalms* II and III of the Anchor Bible (not available to the present writer for the first edition). As any attentive reader will see, Dahood's often controversial suggestions have been carefully selected, and at times criticized in our work. We owe him special thanks for the new avenues he opens towards understanding hitherto obscure passages. The main additions will be found on Pss 22, 55, 63, 74, 83, 84, 86, 89, 102, 106, 109, 114, 119, 132, 139, 142. The general bibliography has also been updated but it does not include all the new titles which have been added in the introduction itself to the psalms or to the matter with which they are specifically concerned. Some of the corrections made have been suggested by reviewers, among whom I gratefully mention C. Stuhlmueller (*TS* 1970, 582f and *The Bible Today*, April 1971, 397), Ph. J. Calderone (*Philippine Studies* 1971, 243-46), R. Murphy (*Bib* 1971, 145f), J. Coppens (*ETL* 1970, *75f), and the German scholar Hans Bardtke (*TLZ* 1971, 898ff), the main editor of the new completely revised *Liber Psalmorum* of the (R. Kittel) *Biblica Hebraica* (Stuttgart 1969). Above all, I wish to express my thanks to Fr. Bernard J. Shields, S.J., from Wah Yan College, Hong Kong, who has sent me an extensive and accurate list of misprints and other mistakes, all of which I have corrected in this new edition. What follows in this Preface mainly reproduces the text of the first edition.

Not a detailed commentary but a substantial introduction to the

Psalter and to each psalm will be found in this work. A special attention is paid to the original setting of the poems and to their essential message. As a rule, the more common or traditional opinion is first expressed, then other views are exposed and appraised. This explains that the introduction to Psalms 2, 18, 22, 51, 68, 73, 110, for example, is much more extensive than for other psalms rarely studied. The main purpose of the present work is in fact to present in readable form the best material now available on the biblical psalms. Too many sound results of scholarly investigations remain unnoticed by readers who would have the necessary preparation for understanding them. It is not enough to read about them in periodical "abstracts." They appear in their proper light when seen against the complex background of research. Impressions and convictions need to be tempered and matured against divergent opinion. Not a few commentaries of the psalms or introductions to them have been written, it would seem, to prove a thesis rather than to help the reader understand the text. It is hoped that the present work will offer to the clergy, to the theological students and to a qualified laity what they need at the present time to update their knowledge of a biblical book so widely used in the Jewish as well as in the Christian liturgy and so expressive of mankind's religious sentiment.

The fruits of serious biblical research have also been drawn upon in the general introduction which consists of the first three chapters. It will be noticed that several sections are devoted to the contribution of modern interpreters like Hermann Gunkel and Sigmund Mowinckel. New trends are also noted: that, for example, represented by the Myth and Ritual School, that also which results from the impact produced on psalm study by the discoveries of Ras-Shamra-Ugarit. The chapter entitled "The Beliefs of Piety" analyzes the main points of the teachings of the psalmists, exposes their biblical background and sets forth great themes of the religious thought of the Old Testament. Messianism in the Psalter receives proper attention, as does also the significance of the psalms for Christ and the Christian.

Classification, an essential element in any knowledge, is especially relevant for the study of a book consisting of 150 poems. It is not surprising therefore that their classification in "types" has received special attention since the basic work of Hermann Gunkel (cf. §7a). The grouping of the psalms into their literary categories also facilitates exposition and adds to clarity. A numerical index (§34) will tell the reader where a given psalm is treated *ex professo* in this work. The special introduction which presents each category increases perceptiveness in regard to the individual compositions. Tedious repetitions of common features is also thus avoided without weakening information.

In the beginning of this century C.A. Briggs referred to the "vast amount of literature" devoted to the Psalms. How would he characterize the present situation? A complete bibliography extending from 1929 has been published in 1955 by J. J. Stamm in *Theologische Rundschau* 23 (1955), pp. 1-68. A good survey, which gives due credit to Catholic authors, is that of J. Coppens in *Le Psautier* (Louvain, 1926), pp. 1-71. Previously A. R. Johnson had done a similar work in *The Old Testament and Modern Study* (H. H. Rowley, edit.: Oxford, 1951), pp. 162-209.

The bibliography offered in the present book is extensive, although it includes only works to which the present writer had direct access. The majority of the authors mentioned are quoted or referred to in some instance, generally by a simple indication of the name and page (or simply the name, if it is a commentary or a short article). For practical reasons the bibliography follows the alphabetical order, but studies relevant to a given psalm or subject will be opportunely indicated. In the bibliography itself references to particularly relevant paragraphs (§ ...) are appended to the main work of some prominent authors. A good bibliography of the ancient commentators, omitted here, will be found in G. Castellino, *Libro dei Salmi* (Roma, 1955) 34-38. See also R. Devreesse, *Les anciens commentateurs grecs des Psaumes* (Città del Vaticano 1970).

Items treated explicitly in one of the first three chapters or elsewhere are also referred to by indicating the paragraph and, in most cases, its sub-division, like §5b, 10d (the pages are given in the Contents). Readings like cf. Ps *52 or cf. *Ps 110:7 indicate that in the introduction to this particular psalm or verse, offered in the present work, the reader will find additional relevant material. The subtitles for each psalm are borrowed from the *NAB*.

From the unpublished chapter of thanks the present writer wishes to single out authors of studies which have proved particularly useful to him: M. Dahood, H.-J. Kraus, S. Mowinckel, R. Tournay (*BJ*), A. Weiser. He owes a special gratitude to an emeritus professor of Hebrew language, Father Louis Semkowski, S.J., who has reviewed the manuscript.

Leopold Sabourin, S.J.
Piazza del Gesù, 45
00186 Rome, Italy

Contents

Abbreviations

ANEP	Ancient Near East in Pictures (J. B. Pritchard)
ANET	Ancient Near Eastern Texts (J. B. Pritchard)
AssSeign	Assemblées du Seigneur
BA	Biblical Archaeologist
BASOR	Bulletin of the American Schools of Oriental Research
Bib	Biblica
BibOr	Bibbia e Oriente
BibTB	Biblical Theology Bulletin
BiLeb	Bibel und Leben
BiLit	Bibel und Liturgie
BiViChr	Bible et Vie Chrétienne
BJ	Bible de Jérusalem [=R. Tournay-R. Schwab, *Les Psaumes*]
BZ	Biblische Zeitschrift
BZAW	Beihefte zum *ZAW*
CBQ	Catholic Biblical Quarterly
ColBibLat	Collectanea Biblica Latina (Roma)
CV	Confraternity Version [=text of the Confraternity of Christian Doctrine]. Same as NAB.
EncBib	Enciclopedia de la Biblia (Barcelona)
EstBib	Estudios Biblicos
EstE	Estudios Eclesiasticos
ETL	Ephemerides Theologicae Lovanienses
ExpT	Expository Times
FRLANT	Forschungen zur Religion und Literatur d. Alten u. Neuen Testa-

	ments
Greg	Gregorianum
HUCA	Hebrew Union College Annual
IEJ	Israel Exploration Journal
JB	Jerusalem Bible
JBL	Journal of Biblical Literature
JEOL	Jaarbericht...ex Oriente Lux
JNES	Journal of Near Eastern Studies
JQR	Jewish Quarterly Review
JSS	Journal of Semitic Studies
JTS	Journal of Theological Studies
Liber Annuus	Studii Biblici Franciscani Liber Annuus (Jerusalem)
MT	Massoretic Text (cf. §2a)
MüTZ	Münchener Theologische Zeitschrift
NAB	New American Bible
NRT	Nouvelle Revue Théologique
OABA	Oxford Annotated Bible with the Apocrypha
OTS	Oudtestamentische Studien
PEQ	Palestine Exploration Quarterly
RB	Revue Biblique
RBibIt	Rivista Biblica [Italiana]
RQum	Revue de Qumran
RSR	Recherches de Science Religieuse
RSV	Revised Standard Version
ScEcc	Sciences Ecclésiastiques
SDB	Supplément au Dictionnaire de la Bible
TGl	Theologie und Glaube
TLZ	Theologische Literaturzeitung
TS	Theological Studies
TZBas	Theologische Zeitschrift (Basel)
UT	Ugaritic Texts
VD	Verbum Domini
VT	Vetus Testamentum
ZAW	Zeitschrift für die Alttestamentliche Wissenschaft

THE PSALMS

I.   The Book of Psalms

This first chapter includes much material which can be found in any one of the major commentaries, in those, for example, of A. F. Kirkpatrick, C. A. Briggs, E. J. Kissane and A. Weiser, to mention only works published in English. Some aspects have been clarified in recent studies.

§1. THE PSALTER AND THE BIBLE

Of all the books of the Old Testament it is the Psalter which the Christian community found the easiest to approach in a direct and personal way (Weiser, p. 19). It is through the New Testament use (cf. Lk 20:42;   24:44; Ac 1:20;   13:33) that "Psalms" has become the regular designation of this book of religious lyrics. The name originated in the Greek translation of the Old Testament, the Septuagint, produced by the Jewish Diaspora of Alexandria in the third century before Christ. In the fourth century A.D. Codex Vaticanus of the LXX, the title *Psalmoi* and the subtitle *Biblos psalmôn* (Book of Psalms: cf. Lk 20:42; Ac 1: 20) are transmitted, while in the fifth century Codex Alexandrinus the name *Psaltèrion* is used. This word originally meant a "stringed instrument" (cf. Dn 3:5), but also "a collection of songs." The Hebrew term *mizmôr*, "hymn," which features in the heading of 57 psalms, suggested the title "Psalms" for the whole collection.

In the Hebrew Bible, Weiser notes, the Book of Psalms originally lacked a general title, but the Jews called the psalms *tᵉhillîm*, "hymns" (cf. *tᵉhillâh*, "praise" in Ps 145:1). At an early stage in the composition of the psalms, the term *tᵉphillôt*, "prayers," appears to have been in use, as the subtitle given to the Davidic Psalter (cf. §3b) in Ps 72: 20 (cf. also the headings of the Pss 17, 90, 102, 142) would testify. Hanna's thanksgiving and Habakkuk's ode are both described as prayers (1 Sm 2:1; Hb 3:1). On *tᵉfillā* as denoting a category see Heinen's remarks in *BZ* 1973, 103-105.

The Hebrew Old Testament consists of three parts: the Law, the Prophets and the Writings, or Hagiographa. The modern Hebrew name for the Bible, *tanak*, combines the Hebrew initials of these three sections: *tôrâh, nᵉbî'îm, kᵉtûbim*. Among the Writings (cf. Sir, prol. 10) were numbered the Psalms, Job, Proverbs, then five *mᵉgillôt* ("rolls"), Ruth the Canticle, Qohēlet (=Ecclesiastes), Lamentations, Esther, and finally a group of three books considered more recent: Daniel, Ezra-Nehemiah and Chronicles (=Paralipomena). In Lk 24:44, "the Psalms" seems to be used as the title of the Writings in general. This is more easily understood if Psalms were considered to be the first of the Hagiographa.

The Psalter has been called "a microcosm of the whole Old Testament" (cf. H. McKeating) or "the epitome of Israel's spiritual experience." It is a fact that the great themes of the Old Testament are recapitulated in the psalms under the form of prayer. This is also true of the main events of salvation history, from creation to exodus, from the conquest to the restoration, when the messianic hope for the definitive establishment of God's kingdom came to maturity. The best commentary of the psalms is the Bible itself, not excluding the New Testament, in which so much that was obscure is seen in a new light.

§2. THE TEXT AND THE ANCIENT VERSIONS OF THE PSALTER

(a) *The Hebrew text*

In their written form, Semitic languages are seldom vocalized. The division, pronunciation, and precise meaning of the original Hebrew text of the Psalms was transmitted by oral tradition (*massôrâh*) for over a thousand years. The text of our Hebrew Bibles is the Massoretic Text (MT). It results from the work of rabbis called Massoretes, who, about the tenth century A.D., had accomplished the task of fixing the traditional pronunciations, the synagogal method of recitation and the division of the written text, by means of vowel points, accents and other signs. In spite of this careful work, carried out too late, the text is not entirely satisfactory (cf. K. Budde, G.R. Driver). Often the Massoretes blundered, because in their time the text already featured corruptions and alterations, or because they lacked the insight or the training required to understand it. In recent years, however, critics have succeeded in correcting some passages of the "received" text by restoring the original one.

The study of comparative Semitic languages and a better knowledge of contemporary literatures favor this new achievement. The best scholars very rarely resort to emendations which affect the consonantal text. The number and importance of the places where the MT has failed to preserve the original are indeed small. This is confirmed by the discovery at Qumrân of Hebrew manuscripts (MSS) dating from the first and second centuries B.C. (cf. §3a).

(b) Greek versions, Targum and Peshitto

The Qumrân MSS of biblical texts seem to indicate that the Septuagint (LXX: cf. §1) is the translation of a Hebrew text slightly different from the MT. In relation to the MT, the LXX text of Psalms (cf. M. Flashar) and of Prophets (except Daniel) can be considered as a literal translation. Yet, as a whole, the Septuagint is regarded as the first *interpretation* of the Old Testament. The Greek Bible was adopted by the first Christians, when they began to evangelize the Hellenistic world. Thus it happened that 300 of the 350 citations from the Old Testament are quoted according to the LXX. This usage naturally had exegetical and even theological repercussions (see on *Ps 16:10). It is probable that YHWH was pronounced "Yahweh," certainly not "Jehovah" (cf. the testimony of Clement of Alexandria: *Stromata V*, ch. 6, n. 34). To avoid pronouncing the sacred tetragram the name *Adonai* was read in its stead. This became *kyrios* in the LXX, and "the Lord" in modern translations.

From the beginning of the second century A.D. other Greek translations made their appearance, at a time when the Septuagint suffered discredit, during the Christian-Jewish controversy. The version of Aquila, of Theodotion, and of Symmachus are the principal ones. While the first is slavishly close to the Hebrew, the second is little more than a revision of the LXX, while that of Symmachus, also based on the LXX, is the best of the three. These versions and later ones were incorporated in Origen's *Hexapla* which gave, in six parallel columns, the original Hebrew text, the same transliterated, a purified text of the LXX, and the other Greek versions. Unfortunately, the greater part of the *Hexapla* has perished, but St. Jerome had access to it.

The *Peshitto* ("simple"), the oldest Syriac version of the Bible, was composed for Christians in the first centuries A.D. It is a translation of the unvocalized Hebrew text and is not too dependent on the Greek texts.

(c) *The Latin versions*

The oldest Latin version of the Psalms is that of the *Vetus Itala,* a translation of the Septuagint. It originated in Africa about the end of the second century A.D. (cf. A. Allgeier). Revised by St. Jerome about 383, it became known as the Roman Psalter (cf. D. R. Weber). Some years later (after 387), St. Jerome prepared another revision based on the Greek of Origen's Hexapla (cf. J. Mercati). This is known as the Gallican Psalter, which is incorporated in the Vulgate and used in the Divine Office. This text has been revised recently by the professors of the Pontifical Biblical Institute and published as the *Liber Psalmorum* (see bibliog.) From 390 to 405, St. Jerome worked in Bethlehem on a Latin translation of the entire Old Testament from the original Hebrew. This version gradually replaced the old Latin versions in all the books except the Psalter, and is known as the Vulgate. Jerome's *Psalterium juxta Hebraeos* (cf. D. H. de Sainte-Marie) failed to dislodge the Gallican Psalter in the usage of the Church, but it has the same qualities as the translation of the other books of the Vulgate (cf. A. Vaccari). Extensive bibliographies on the text and versions of the Psalter will be found in G. Castellino, *Libro dei Salmi,* p. 33f. and in H.-J. Kraus, Psalmen, p. 82.

§3. THE FORMATION OF THE PSALTER

(a) *The books of the Psalter*

In its present state the Psalter comprises 150 psalms divided into five books (1-41; 42-72; 73-89; 90-106; 107-150), each ending with a doxology. The enumeration of the psalms is not exactly the same in the Hebrew and the Greek (=also Vulgate and Douay versions). This is because the Hebrew divides the text so as to form two poems where the Greek has only one (9-10, 114-115), or combines into a single poem what forms two in the Greek (116, 147). In the present work the Hebrew numbering is followed, but the Greek-Vulgate enumeration appears between parentheses in the title number of each psalm and in the complete numerical list of the Appendix. The following table shows how the two numberings correspond:

HEBREW	GREEK
1-8	1-8

9-10	9
11-113	10-112
114-115	113
116	114-115
117-146	116-145
147	146-147
148-150	148-150

There are some instances in which both the Hebrew and the Greek have combined into one composition what was originally written, it seems, as two or more distinct poems or fragments (cf. Ps 27: 1-6 and 7-14). It can happen, too, that a composition originally one appears as two psalms (42-43). In other cases, the same psalm is repeated in a variant form (14 and 53: see below), or a psalm is found to be made up of fragments from other psalms (70, 108). Some MSS of Ac 13.33 combine Pss 1 and 2 (cf. A. Bentzen, II, p. 164).

The five-fold division, Kirkpatrick asserts (vol. 3, p. 13), is earlier than the Septuagint, which contains the doxologies. It is often referred to by Jewish and Christian authorities, and compared to the five books of the Pentateuch. A. Arens discovers a similarity of thought in the first readings of the books of the two collections, the Pentateuch and the Psalter. Reviewing Arens' book (*Die Psalmen...*) H. Schneider adds remarks on the five-fold division (cf. *Theol. Revue,* 1962, c. 232ff). Although the doxologies are usually given only at the close of the book, notes Briggs (I: p. 83), they were really used at the conclusion of every psalm or part of psalm sung in the liturgy, much like the *Gloria Patri...* of the Roman Office (cf. Ps 135:21). The fourth doxology (Ps 106:48) apparently belongs to the psalm and is not merely an editor's addition to mark the end of a book. Some views of J. Enciso on the formation of the Psalter will be mentioned in connection with Pss 2, 119, 137 (cf. §4a).

The Psalms Scroll of Qumrân Cave 11 (11 QPs^a) has just been published by J. A. Sanders (Oxford, 1965). The scroll contains apocryphal compositions, of which can be mentioned here No. I, II and III of the five Syriac apocryphal psalms. The first of these corresponds to apocryphal Ps 151, preserved also by the LXX and the Vetus Latina (=Itala). The Qumrân find indicates that LXX Ps 151 condenses the two Hebrew apocryphal psalms originally reflecting an Hellenistic interpretation of 1 Sm 16-17. The epitomist probably wrote in Hebrew and LXX Ps 151 is the translation of the amalgam. Although the amalgamist carefully

THE PSALMS

excised the orphic elements (cf. ZAW 75, 1963, 81 ff) from his poem memory of its original Hellenism may have served to exclude it from the canon of the Hagiographa (cf. §2a). In the amalgam the beauty and the artistry, as well as the meaning of the original compositions are sacrificed. The scroll 11QPss closes with (apocryphal) psalms celebrating David as musician and leader of the people. This can be taken as evidence of the belief in Davidic authorship of the Psalms (cf. §4g). Recent literature on "psalms" at Qumrân concerns mostly apocryphal, not canonical compositions: see the studies of J. Allegro, M. Baillet, J. Carmignac, M. Delcor, M. Philonenko, I. Rabinowitz, J. Sanders, P. W. Skehan, J. Strugnell, J. Van der Ploeg (cf. bibliog.). On the canonical Qumrân Psalm scrolls see *BJ* 65f.

(b) Collections in the Psalter

The division of the Psalter into five books marks the end of a long period of evolution. It is not difficult, Kissane believes (p. 10), to detect the marks of an earlier stage, in which there were three collections, each in turn composed of psalms drawn from smaller and earlier collections. This would explain that the same psalm does appear twice in the present Psalter (cf. above). It had been incorporated in two of the smaller collections. The three main collections are the following:

1) The Yahwistic Psalter (3-41), in which the name "Yahweh" is generally used (273 times, against 15 times for "Elohim"). The name of David appears in the title of each psalm, Ps 33 excepted.
2) The Elohistic Psalter (42-89). The name "Elohim" is used five times more often than "Yahweh" in Pss 42-83. It is believed that the change from "Yahweh," "the Lord," to "Elohim," "God" is the work of an early scribe. Thus we have the strange phrase, "O God, my God," instead of the original, "O Lord, my God" (e.g., Pss 43:4; 45:8, 51:14; 63:1). R. Boling argues, however (cf. p. 253ff.), that the frequencies of "Yahweh" and "Elohim" in the Yahwistic and Elohistic psalms represent opposing stylistic preferences. B.D. Eerdmans maintains that "there is no evidence of a definite attempt to avoid the name "Jahu (=Yahweh) for some dogmatical reason" (*OTS* I, p. 265). Consequently he denies the existence of an "Elohistic Psalter" and believes "that the singers used the names of God arbitrarily" (p. 267; see on °Ps 53). Pss 84-89 use the name "Yahweh" and all assigned to the sons of Korah, except Pss 86 (David) and 89 (Ethan). The note at the end of Ps 72, "the prayers of David the son of Jesse are ended" suggests that at an early stage all the Davidic psalms formed a single collection.
3) The later Yahwistic collection (90-150). The name "Yahweh" is always used, ex-

cept in Ps 108 and in Ps 144:9, quoted from the Elohistic collection. In this collection, 17 psalms are attributed to David, one (90) to Moses and one (127) to Solomon. The rest are without title of authorship.

According to Kissane, the first of these three collections was formed probably in the period of the kings (before 586 B.C.), while the third is certainly post-exilic in origin (after 536 B.C.) though it may contain some psalms of earlier date. The formation of the Psalms is a complex question which other authors have examined carefully; cf. apart from the major commentaries: M.J. Buss, G. Wankle, C. Westermann, J. Enciso, H. Schneider (cf. §17a). On the Hallel psalms, cf. L. Finkelstein, T. F. Torrance, and on the "Pilgrim Psalms": B. D. Eerdmans, P. Guichou and L. J. Liebreich.

The following conspectus of the partial collections can be drawn up, for the purpose of greater clarity:

A. Yahwistic series of the "prayers of David" (3-41: homogeneous collection).
B. The Elohistic Psalter (42-89: unified collection):
    a) The Psalter of the sons of Core (42-49).
    b) Elohistic series of the "prayers of David" (51-72).
    c) The psalms of Asaph (50:73-83).
    d) Yahwistic supplement to the Elohistic Psalter (84-89).
C. Later Yahwistic collection (90-150: without real unity):
    a) Psalms in praise of Yahweh's kingship (93-99).
    b) The alleluia-psalms (104-106; 111-117; 135; 146-150). [Pss 113-118 form the Hallel of the ancient synagogue; cf. on °Pss 111, 136].
    c) The "Pilgrim Psalms" (120-134).
    d) Other "Davidic psalms" (101, 103, 108-110, 138-145).
    e) Ten other isolated psalms.

The attribution of psalms to Core, Asaph and others will be discussed in connection with the "titles" of the psalms (see §4ef). The "psalms in praise of Yahweh's kingship" form a sub-category of the "hymns" (cf. §18). The "alphabetic psalms" will be mentioned again in the remarks on metrical structure of the psalms (§6d). There remains to examine here some common characteristics of the "Pilgrim Songs," although the individual psalms of this group are studied with the others of the same literary category.

(c) *The "Pilgrim Psalms"* (120-134)

In the title of each of these psalms the following notation appears: "A song of ascents." The "Pilgrim Psalms" do not constitute a literary type, and, Ps 122 excepted, are not among the "Canticles of Zion" (cf. §19), although in them also would naturally feature themes connected with the Holy City. The "Pilgrim Songs" were in fact meant to provide devotional inspiration to those on pilgrimage (cf. Ps 84).

According to H.-J. Kraus (*Psalmen*, p. 20f), five main explanations have been proposed for the expression *šîr hamma'alôt*, "song of ascents":

1) "Serial songs"; it is a purely formal or extrinsic explanation.
2) Songs built according to the "gradual rhythm," which follows a literary device called *anadiplosis*: the last word of a verse or half-verse recurs in the beginning of the next literary unit (cf. Ps 121). But this stylistic particularity is not proper to the "songs of ascents," also called "gradual psalms."
3) Songs of the repatriated, when they *ascended* to Jerusalem after the captivity (cf. Ezr 2:1; 7:7).
4) "Songs of degrees," by reference to the place where they were sung (altar, throne or porch). According to *Middôt* (II:6), a Mishnic treatise, the levites performed their songs on the fifteen steps of the portal of Nicanor. But this obscure text could well mean something else (cf. Kirkpatrick, vol. 3, p. XXVIII).
5) "Pilgrim songs," The verb *'âlâh*, "to ascend," could apply to the last stretch of the ascent to Jerusalem (cf. 2 S 6:2; 2 K 23:2) or to the pilgrimage as a whole (cf. Pss 24:3; 122:4; Mk 10:33; Lk 2:42). This is the most probable interpretation. The pilgrims did go up (Jr 31:6; Mi 4:2) with singing, "toward the mountain of the Lord" (Is 30:29), and many of the "Pilgrim Songs" are well suited for the occasion (esp. 121, 123, 125, 128, 132, 133, 134).

The textual discoveries at Qumran suggest a new possibility, explained by M. Dahood, in *Bib* 1966, p. 143, and in *Psalms* III, p. 195. In *11-QPsᵃ Zion*, 14, we read: "May your praise, O Zion, enter into his presence, extolment (*m'lh*) from all the world." Thus *šîr hamma'alôt* could mean "song of extolments," although this description does not fit all the "Pilgrim Psalms."

L. J. Liebreich maintains that the "Songs of Ascents" are related to four key words (italicized) of the Priestly Blessing: "The Lord *bless* you and *keep* you! The Lord let his face shine upon you, and be *gracious* to you! The Lord look upon you kindly and give you *peace!*" (Nm 6:24 f). All but three of the "Pilgrim Psalms" (124, 126, 131) contain one or more of these key words: bless, keep, be gracious, peace (comparing the Hebrew texts). But aren't some of the words found in many psalms? According to the treatise *Tosephta Sotah* (VII, 7: ed. Zuckermandel, p. 307), Liebreich adds, the priest pronounced the Aaronic Blessing *on the steps* of the hall which led to the interior of the temple. Consequently, *šîr hamma'alôt* would mean: "a Song rendered in connection with the Priestly Blessing which was pronounced on the steps of the temple hall."

Thus, he concludes, "each of the Songs of Ascents was in the nature of a response following the Priestly Blessing."

Joyful confidence in God, hopeful requests of forgiveness, expressions of thanksgiving for the Lord's kindness towards Israel, some wisdom sayings on the blessing of piety, and a few moderate complaints, feature among the main thoughts voiced in these psalms which, more than others, reveal intimate aspects of the pious Israelite's social and devotional life.

§4. THE TITLES OF THE PSALMS

(a) *Their general character*

The words or phrases prefixed to all but 34 of the psalms are known as their "titles." Since the eighteenth century the critics have willingly minimized the value of these headings. The Gunkel school ignored them. It is not so today. A. Ahlström, a Scandinavian scholar, claims that they reveal the cultic origin of the psalms. J. Enciso finds in the omission or the presence of the titles early indications as to the history and growth of the Psalter. It is true that many elements of these headings can be linked to the liturgical traditions attested by Chronicles (cf. H.-J. Kraus, *Psalmen,* p. 30 and §7a).

The titles are not an integral part of the psalms although they were known, but not understood, by the Septuagint interpreters. They reflect traditions much older still, even Davidic, the meaning of which was already lost in the days of the Chronicler (fourth cent.). This would explain that some titles seem to introduce the wrong psalm. Thus Ps. 30, originally a private thanksgiving, was associated with the Dedication liturgy. It is not easier to understand these headings today. J. J. Glueck writes: "Two fine commentaries on the Psalms [A. Briggs and H.-J. Kraus], separated by some sixty years, reveal that the twentieth century added nothing to our knowledge about the proems to the Psalms" (p. 30). It is true that despite all the scholarly work the meanings attached to many of them are largely conjectural (on the "titles" see the studies of L. Delekat, J. Enciso, H. I. Ginsberg, J. J. Glueck, P. Salmon, J.-M. Vosté, R. Tournay). In view of this fact, and because "the matter is not of much practical importance," Kissane does not discuss it in detail. What is proposed here is based partly on his exposition (I. p. 22ff). The various elements forming the titles can be classified according to their apparent function (the *NAB* or *CV* translation is generally used).

(b) *Terms indicating the nature of the psalms*

:*šîr* (30 times: "song"); *mizmôr* (57 times: "psalm"), probably "a song with accompaniment."

:*maškil* (13 times): perhaps (cf. *BJ*, p. 9) "a didactic psalm" (cf. Pss 32, 47, 78) or "an artistic psalm" (cf. Ps 47:8 and 2 Ch 30:22).

:*miktam,* occurring in Pss 16 and 56-60, may allude to a hidden (*kātam*) or mysterious meaning, or suggest a "golden (*ketem*) poem." The relevance of either meaning to particular psalms is not discernible. According to H. I. Ginsberg, whether or not the words *miktāb* ("writing") and *miktām* are related etymologically, their use indicates that the authors of some verses did not hesitate to attribute to pious kings of Judah the practice so well attested for other nations of the Ancient Orient of setting up inscriptions of petition and acknowledgment. *Miktām* is interpreted by the LXX as "(a poem) to be inscribed on a stele" (cf. Is 38:9, corr.).

:*šiggāyôn* (Ps 7 only): the name (cf. Hb 3:1) seems akin to Assyrian *shegu,* a complaint or a penitential psalm.

:*tehillâh,* a song of praise, occurs only once (Ps 145). But the same word in the masculine plural is used to describe the whole collection of psalms. On the use of *tephillâh,* "prayer," cf. §1.

(c) *Liturgical rubrics*

In the Hebrew, only *Ps 92 is assigned to a *special day* (Sabbath). In the Septuagint, however, other psalms are assigned to one of the days of the week: Ps 24 (1st), Ps 48 (2nd), Ps 94 (3rd), Ps 93 (6th). The Vulgate assigns Ps 81 to the fifth day and the Mishna assigns Ps 82 to the third day. The rubric "for remembrance" (Pss 38, 70; cf. Si 50:16) would refer to the *'azkārâh* or portion of the meal-offering which was anointed with oil and burned (cf. Lv 2:2ff). The note "for thanksgiving" in Ps 100 probably refers to the sacrifice of thanksgiving (Lv 7:12; 22:29). The meaning of other liturgical rubrics is self-evident.

(d) *Musical annotations*

Their interpretation is not easy because we know very little about ancient Israelite music. Broadly speaking these headings belong to two groups.

A first category of headings refer to the instruments which are to accompany the voices: "stringed instruments" (cf. Pss 4, 6, 54, 55, 61, 67, 76) and "wind instruments" (flute? Ps 5). "Upon the gittith" (8, 81, 84) can indicate a kind of harp (from Gath?) or a tune ("the woman of Gath"). " 'al haŝŝᵉmînît" (6; 12; CV: "upon the eighth") and " 'al 'alāmôt" (46; CV: "according to Virgins") might mean "with soprano voices" and "with bass voices," respectively (cf. 1 Chr 15: 20f); but the former, Kissane believes, more probably means "with the eight-stringed harp" (on the meaning of 'al in these headings, cf. L. Delekat).

A second category of rubrics probably allude to popular songs to the air of which the psalms were to be sung: "Do not destroy" (57, 58, 59, 75; cf. Is 65:8), "The hind of the dawn" (22), "The dove of the distant terebinths" (56), "According to Muth Labben" (9:? "the death of the son," perhaps an Egyptian harp: BJ), "According to Mahalath" (53, 8: "for the illness"?). "According to Lilies" (45, 69), "The law is a lily" (60), "The law is lilies" (80) could refer to a popular song extolling the Law.

An obscure term "selah" is often inserted in the body of a psalm at the end of a verse: 71 times in 39 psalms, all of which are in the first three books (Pss 3-89), except two (Pss 140 and 143). It is usually found at the end of a strophe and would indicate a pause in the singing, while the people prostrate in prayer. Other authors, however, hold that it indicates a "raising" of the voices or a musical interlude (see also: N. H. Snaith and L. Kunz).

(e) *Headings with proper names*

These names, to which a *lamed* is usually perfixed, could indicate authors or collections (see below). The attributions are as follows: one to Moses (90), two to Solomon (72, 127), 12 to Asaph (50, 73-83), 11 to the sons of Core (42-43; 44-49, 84, 85, 87, 88), one each to Heman (88) and to Ethan (89 + yᵉdûtûn: 39?). 73 psalms bear the name of David: in book I, all except 1, 2, 9-10, 33; in book II: 51-65, 68-70; in book III, 86 only; in book IV, 101-103; in book V, 108-110, 122, 124, 131, 133, 138-145. The LXX adds to the list: 33, 43, 67, 71, 91, 93, 101, 104, 137. A particular occasion of David's life is sometimes associated with a psalm by the headings: his persecution by Saul (7, 32, 52, 56, 57, 59, 142), his adultery (51), his victory over Edom (60), his flight from Absalom

(3, 63). In the introduction to these psalms the assumed reason of the association will often be indicated (see on *Pss 34, 52, 54, 56, 59). E. R. Dalglish is willing to give some credit to the 13 historical notices in the titles of Pss 3, 7, 18, 34, 51, 52, 54, 56, 57, 59, 60, 63, 92: "While one may frankly admit that the historical reliability of the occasions mentioned in the superscriptions is negligible, the historical notices...may be considered from a totally different point of view...as a part of the rubrics of the lamentations used in the liturgical services of the fasts of the exile or later period" (*The Hebrew Penitential Psalms*...p. 233)

An attribution (*lmnṣḥ*) translated "for the leader" in *CV*, "to the choirmaster" by others, occurs 55 times, but only in the first three books and in Pss 109, 139, 140. The term, writes Kissane (p. 24), is probably to be derived from a root *naṣaḥ*, used in Chronicles in the sense of "supervise" the construction or the functions of the temple (cf. 1 Ch 23:4; 2 Ch 2:1-17; 34:12-13; Ezr 3:8f). In 1 Chronicles 15:21, the same word is used in reference to the direction of the singing. The translation of the title in the Greek and in the Latin (*"in finem"*) is based on another root *naṣaḥ*, meaning "to end." Since the title is usually prefixed to psalms which have also a title of authorship (?), it is assumed that it indicates a collection in the possession of the choir-leader (on *lmnṣḥ* see also L. Delekat).

(f) *Lamed of authorship or of attribution*

To the proper names mentioned in the preceding paragraph is generally prefixed the Hebrew preposition *lamed*. It is now known (cf. M. Dahood, Psalms, I, p. 26 and *BJ*, p. 15) that in the Canaanite poetry the preposition *min* (in Hebrew: "from," "by") was unknown and that its function was filled by *b* and *l*. In the Ras-Shamra-Ugarit tablets (see §9d) the poem heading, *lb'l*, "to Ba'al," *lkrt*, "to Keret," indicates the "cycle" or literary serial to which the compositions are attributed. In the same way, psalms are said "of the sons of Core" or of Asaph, because they belonged *to* their collection or were drawn *from* their collection. Even after *min* was introduced into biblical Hebrew the prepositions *b* and *l* continued in many cases to retain the meaning "from" (cf. on *Ps 33:19). This being the case, *ledawid* in 73 psalm headings can mean either "from David" or concerning David" (cf. Dahood, I, p. 15).

Almost twenty years ago, H. Cazelles had expressed a view which is still sound and can be summarized as follows. The *lamed* prefixed to proper names in the psalms' headings was probably understood at first as a *lamed* of *attribution* or of *classification,* not of author. Towards the end of the monarchy and after the exile, it began to be interpreted as a *lamed auctoris,* as in Hab 3:1. When they rendered *lamed* by a dative the LXX interpreters indicated a reluctance to accept the *lamed auctoris,* whereas the Vulgate, with its genitive, confirmed the validity of the authorship interpretation.

"The headings," writes J.J. Glueck, "are rightly regarded as later additions, but in contrast with others found in the Bible, they were not added by scribes but by professional musicians whose duty it was to present the Psalms in the precincts of the temple—the presentation being vocal, instrumental and probably also dramatic. The headings should be regarded as the private notes of those who used the psalms daily, being the property, or in the possession, of family guilds of temple musicians. Copies probably without headings, were undoubtedly also kept in the temple archives, but when these were not available, owing to national calamities such as the destruction of the temple or the Exile, compilers had of necessity to look for the nearest authoritative copies, which were, of course, those belonging to the families of singers and musicians of the Judean and Israeli [*sic!*] sanctuaries with the professional remarks interpolated and prefixed. It is doubtful whether the early scribes understood the meaning of these professional remarks; the later scribes did not, as is evident from their persistent mistranslation in the Septuaginta and onwards" (p. 30). According to J. A. Sanders ("Variorum..." p. 88), "the attribution of Davidic authorship did not come after the Psalter was fixed, but was applied to smaller collections of psalms and to individual psalms over a long period of time."

The attribution of the psalms to Asaph, Heman, Ethan and the sons of Korah, Mowinckel (II, 96) believes, reflects "a dependable tradition concerning the circles in which these psalms came into being. They are the names of such person—historical or legendary—as were supposed to be the ancestors of the guilds of temple singers." The Chronicler often mentions these names: "The singers, Heman, Asaph, and Ethan, were to sound bronze cymbals" (1 Ch 15:19). "And Hezekiah the king and the princes commanded the Levites to sing praises to the Lord with the words of David and of Asaph the seer. And they sang praises with gladness, and they bowed down and worshipped" (2 Ch 29:30). Among the repatriates are numbered "the singers: the sons of Asaph, one hundred and twenty-eight" (Ezr 2:41). It is then noted: "And when the builders laid the foundation of the temple of the Lord, the priests in their vestments came forward with trumpets, and the Levites, the sons of Asaph, with cymbals, to praise the Lord, according to the directions of David king of Israel" (3: 10). It would seem (cf. *BJ*, p. 12) that Ethan (1 Ch 15:17) is called Y^e*dûtûn* from 1 Ch 16:38 (cf. 25:1). Mowinckel (II, 95), however, understands Y^e*dûtûn* (*CV: Idithun*) as "a liturgical technical term." It features in the heading of three psalms (39, 62, 77).

It is quite certain that the same author wrote Chronicles, Ezra and Nehemiah. The interest of the Chronicler for liturgy is better understood in the background thus presented by *The Oxford Annotated Bible* (p. 495): "The purpose of 1 and 2 Chronicles, like that of 1 and 2 Kings, is theological and idealistic. There is practically no attempt to present history as we understand the word. The Chronicler wishes to advocate a certain pattern of religious life for his own day, and to indicate what a proper kingdom of his people under God would be like. He does this by describing the reigns of David and Solomon in particular, not as they actually had been, but as they ought to have been. David, especially, is highly idealized, and becomes the real founder of the temple and its ritual. A primary interest of the Chronicler is in the staff of the post-exilic temple, the organization of the priests, Levites, musicians, custodians, and others. Because of his manifest concern with Levites and singers in particular, it has been conjectured that the Chronicler was both a Levite and a singer.

(g) Davidic authorship

With this in mind it is easier to see why such a role is assigned to David in the liturgy and why he was traditionally held to be the author of so many psalms. The difficult and delicate question of the Davidic authorship of the psalms is well presented by the *Jerusalem Bible*. It would be wrong, it says, "to neglect the ancient and valuable information embodied in the inscriptions. It is reasonable to admit that the collections of Asaph and the sons of Korah were composed by poets attached to the temple. It is equally reasonable to hold that there must be some connection between the Davidic collection and David himself. Taking into account what the historical books have to say of his musical talent, 1 S 16:16-18; cf. Am 6:5, his poetic gifts, 2 S 1:19-27; 3:33f., and his love of the liturgy, 2 S 6:5, 15f., it would seem inevitable that the Psalter should contain some of David's compositions. Indeed Ps 18 is simply a different edition of a poem attributed to David in 2 Sm 22. Not all the psalms of the Davidic collections are by him, no doubt, but the collection must have had a few of these for a nucleus. It is difficult, however, to be more definite than this. The Hebrew inscriptions are not decisive, as we have seen, and when the New Testament writers quote a psalm as being by David they are speaking as their contemporaries spoke. Even so, the evidence should not be rejected without good reason, and David, who "sang the song of Irsael," 2 S 23:1, "must be conceded an essential part in the formation of the religious poetry of the Chosen People" (p. 784).

§5. DATING THE PSALMS

To very few psalms can be assigned with certainty even an approximate date. Serious authors are known to have assigned a given psalm (e.g., Ps 68) to the period of the Judges and to that of the Maccabees, a difference of one thousand years; almost every possible date, from the tenth to the second centuries B.C., has been proposed for *Ps 80. B. Duhm believed that the majority of the psalms originated under the Maccabees or Hasmoneans. Wellhausen was not sure if there exists any pre-exilic psalm, while I. Engell, of the "Myth and Ritual School" (cf. §8d), cannot affirm that more than one psalm has been written after the exile. As for S. Mowinckel, he believes that the golden age of psalm writing was the time of the monarchy.

The methods used for dating the psalms also differ widely (cf. C. Hauret). Some rely on supposed allusions to historical events in the psalms themselves, while others consider liturgical factors, or, better yet, look for literary and theological relations with other biblical passages more easily dated. This has been done in detail by R. Tournay for *Pss 20 and 21 (RB 1959, pp. 161-190). Mowinckel believes (II, 146) that progress will be made in dating the psalms if the types are considered first, and then the individual poems.

(a) "Rereadings" in the psalms

"There is a special difficulty," writes John L. McKenzie, "in handling the psalms, because the book was obviously submitted to *an unceasing process of development and adaptation*: individual psalms become collective, private prayers become liturgical, songs of local sanctuaries are adapted to the temple of Jerusalem, royal psalms become messianic, historical psalms become eschatological. Modern interpreters speak of the 'rereadings' of the psalms; an earlier psalm which has in some way become antiquated (e.g. by the fall of the monarchy, the destruction of Jerusalem and the temple, the loss of political independence) is reworked to fit a contemporary situation and given a direction to the future which was not present in the original composition" (*Dict. of the Bible*, p. 703). Many authors do in fact introduce a distinction between original and extant texts, loaded, they say, with additions and obscured by new readings (see on *Ps 60 and A. Gelin's "relectures"). A good survey of the relevant literature on the dating of the psalms has been made by J. Coppens in *Le Psautier*, pp. 7f, 57ff (see also the studies of M. Buttenweiser, M. Dahood, A. Deissler, C. Hauret and R. Tournay).

(b) *Any Maccabean Psalms?*

The authors who ceased to maintain a Davidic authorship for the psalms favored at first an exilic or post-exilic dating. E. Sellin held on, however, for a pre-exilic date of the first book of psalms (1-41). The reign of Hezekiah (716-687) was considered by some as having been particularly suitable for the composition of lyrics. Then, quite a few of the older generation of critics (c. 1850-1950) ascribed a great number of psalms to the Maccabean period (2nd cent. B.C.): J. Olshausen, F. Hitzig, J. Wellhausen, B. Duhm, T. K. Cheyne, E. Kautsch, A. Bertholet, E. König retained only Ps 74 for that period, while R. Kittel admitted about five psalms. W. O. Oesterley, M. Buttenweiser and the majority of recent interpreters refuse Maccabean dating to any canonical psalms. Some consider as significant the use of existing *Ps 30 for the new festival instituted in that period.

Psalms 44, 74, 79, 83 were those most often cited as Maccabean (also 46-48, 66-68, 76, 87, 93, 124-126, 129, 144). In his *Introduction to the Old Testament* (New York, 1948), R. H. Pfeiffer considers Ps 79 as "a typical example of Maccabean complaint." "The great majority of psalms," he writes, "were presumably written during the assembling of the Psalter, between 400 and 100 B.C., and shortly before, in the fifth century" (p. 629). The prevailing tendency is to make them much older. Not many though would accept I. Engnell's position: "Speaking candidly, there is merely one psalm in the whole Psalter of which I am quite convinced that it is post-exilic: Ps 137. And as far as I can ascertain, no other psalm is comparable with it in content and style" (*Studies...*p.

176, n. 2). "As a rule," writes A. Bentzen, "we must keep in mind the psalms may date from *all periods* in the history of Israel and Judaism, but *the classical period of this poetry* is the ancient times, when the poems were expressions of the relations of men and God" (Introduction...II, p. 168). Royal psalms concerned with a living monarch must, of course, be pre-exilic, if they are not Maccabean.

(c) *Ancient (cultic) psalms and the prophets*

What D. C. Simpson wrote in introducing *The Psalmists* (Oxford, 1926) is intended to reflect the common opinion expressed in the book: "The *immediate background* of the extant psalms was Palestinian, and though, in their origin, they were pre-exilic, most of them, in the form in which they have been preserved, are best understood as reflecting the social and religious problems of the earlier and middle periods of post-exilic and pre-Christian Judaism" (p. 14). According to one of the contributors of *The Psalmists,* H. Gressman, the prophets occasionally imitate the lyrics of the Psalter. These prophetic psalms always form part of an oracle and naturally concern the future. There are only a few examples in the pre-exilic prophecies, but plenty in Deutero-Isaiah [ch. 40-55: 6th cent. B.C.; cf. §14c]. Hosea 6: 1-3, a sort of psalm of repentance (cf. Ps 51), would contain an allusion to the dying and rising of Adonis (Phoenician male diety). Isaiah 2:2 [=Mi 4:2] applies to the "nations" what Ps 122:1, or another pilgrimage-psalm, said of the individual. The ethical duties required of the future community proselytes are also alluded to (comp. Ps 15:2-4). The mention in Amos (cf. 5:23; 6:5), and in other prophets (cf. Is 30:29), of the musical accompaniment of sacrifices seems to suggest that they had knowledge of some psalms.

If David was the promoter of psalmody, he was not necessarily its initiator. The song of Miriam (Ex 15:21) and the song of Deborah (Jg 5) probably originated before his time. The longer exodus song (Ex 15:1-18) dates perhaps to the time of Solomon. The destruction of the Egyptians became a favorite hymnic theme at the passover festivals (cf. Pss 106:11; 135:15). If the psalms were originally connected with sacrificial worship, then psalmody is as old as sacrificial worship itself. It is Gressman's view (p. 11) that the older psalms are more closely connected with the ritual of Divine Service than are the later ones. Like Mowinckel (cf. next parag.), he maintains that psalms did accompany sacrificial worship, since word and ritual-act cannot be separated in the sphere of religion any more than in that of magic. But under the influence of the prophets many psalms lost their original connection with the temple and even became an expression of opposition to sacrifices (cf. Pss 40:7; 50:8ff; 51:18). The psalms composed in the Diaspora were intended for private edification. Only afterwards were they received into the prayer-book of the community. The addition of prayers for the king in some psalms must of course have taken place in pre-exilic times. H.-J. Kraus, however, warns against assuming too hastily that "prayers for the king" are later additions (on Ps 61:7f; cf. Pss 28:8ff; 63:12; 72:15; 84:9f). The psalms were ascribed to David, Gressman believes, mainly because the king in the ancient Oriental world was considered the head of the professional offerers of prayers. The title Messiah designated him as the priest-king, at least from the time of Melchizedek (but see on *Ps 110). Only a few psalms are concerned with the reigning king, argues Gressmann, and none is a psalm of the messianic king, "as is often wrongly supposed" (p. 15). But Gressmann, as a critic, is not always free of arbitrary preconceptions (cf. §11b). This is apparent also in some of his views concerning the dependence of the prophets in regard to the psalmists (comp., in §13a, C. Westermann's views versus Mowinckel's).

(d) *Antiquity of psalmography*

Mowinckel also stresses the antiquity of psalmography (II, 146-158). The angelic hymn heard by Isaiah at his inaugural vision (Is 6:3) seems to be, in form and substance, an echo of the hymns of the cult. In a similar way, A. Gelin wrote about Rv 1:5-7: "The Apocalypse contains a certain number of heavenly *carmina* which could easily be specimens and transportations of earthly acclamations" (*La Sainte Bible*, L. Pirot, XII, p. 597). The hymn of Habakkuk (cf. below) has in all probability really been composed as the prophetical part of an actual temple liturgy. "Even Jeremiah, adds Mowinckel, was attached to the temple of Jerusalem, and in him, too, we find hymnic motives and forms used as elements of the prophetic word (5:22, 29) —evidence that he was so familiar with the hymnic style that he would unconsciously have recourse to it, for instance when wanting to motivate the message by pointing to the authority and power of God underlying it" (p. 147). Deutero-Isaiah abounds in hymnic elements (42:10-13; 44:23; 49:13; 52:9f) and in hymnic motifs (40:22-31; 44:25-28; 45:18; 46:10f) which would be this prophet's expression of ideas and forms linked to the enthronement ideology and to the ancient creation myths (see §13a).

"From the period of the monarchy we have unmistakable evidence also for the psalm of lamentation, namely in the imitations of its form and substance by the prophets as a vehicle for their message" (p. 148): cf. Jer 3:22b-25; 4:10; 14:2-6, 19-22; 31:18ff; Hos 6:1-3; Is 40: 27; 49:14, 24; 51:9ff. In the "prophetic poetry" of Jeremiah especially are found all the features of that type of psalm. But Jeremiah is not the originator of the form, since the oracular answers to the lament often contradict what the worshippers were expected to hear. In other instances Jeremiah uses the individual psalm of lamentation for his personal "confessions": cf. 11:18-20; 15:15:21; 18:18-23; 20:10-13; 12:1-6; 15:10-12; 20:7-9, 14-18 (cf. Mowinckel, p. 149 and W. Baumgartner, *Die Klagegedichte des Jeremia*, Stuttgart, 1917). Pierre E. Bonnard, however, in his work *Le Psautier selon Jérémie* (Paris, 1960), finds the influence of Jeremiah on 33 psalms, 12 from a literary viewpoint and the others from the standpoint of a "spirituality." These psalms, which would be contemporaneous or later than Jeremiah are: Pss 1, 6, 7, 16, 17, 22, 26, 31, 35, 36, 38, 40, 41, 44, 51, 55, 69, 71, 73, 74, 75, 76, 78, 79, 81, 83, 86, 99, 106, 109, 119, 135, 139, (cf. on *Ps 6).

The antiquity of Israelite psalmography is also implied in Mowinckel's basic assumption that "the temples are the homes of psalmography" (II, 151). The art of writing psalms in Israel would then have originated with the relatively ancient founding of various "permanent temples" at Shiloh, Mount Zion, Bethel and Dan (cf. Jg 21:19ff; 1 K 5 and 12).

(e) *A method in psalm chronology*

The method applied by R. Tournay to psalm chronology can be illustrated by the following reasonings (cf. *RB* 1958, p. 321ff). The mentality of the 'anāwîm (cf. §12a), prepared by Isaiah 14:30-32, is clearly expressed for the first time in Zephaniah (2:3; 3:12), around 630 B.C. Some thirty psalms which originated in the circle of these pious seekers of God cannot have preceded Josiah's reform (621). The phrase, "for his name's sake," used in eight psalms (23:3; 25:11; 31:4; 79:9; 106:8; 109:21; 115:1; 143:11) is not used before Jeremiah (14:7,21), Ezekiel (cf. 20:9, 14) and Deutero-Isaiah (48:9; 11). Other indications assign these psalms to the Persian period (5th-4th cent.).

There exists, besides, a close relation between *the psalms of God's kingship* and the Isaian apocalypse (Is 24-27), which mentions the destruction of a godless "city of chaos" (24:10), identified by Tournay and others (cf. *RB* 1958, p. 323f) as the capital of Moab (cf. Sir 36: 7-10). So Pss (47), 93, 95-100 would have been written as late as the beginning of the third century (comp. with §13a). Psalm 29 could also be of the Hellenistic period (4th-3rd cent.). *OABA*, however, regards the "Isaiah Apocalypse" as a transitional form between traditional prophetic and apocalyptic materials, dating between 540 and 425 B.C. (p. 849). Yet for Tournay the third conquest of Moab by the Nabateans constitutes an important landmark for psalm chronology, much more precise, he adds, than the doubtful enthronement of Yahweh (cf. §13a), proposed by the Scandinavian school (*RB* 1958, p. 324f). Shortly after the exile grew the eschatological hope which would express itself in the psalms of Yahweh's kingship (cf. §14c).

The incomplete acrostic psalm which opens Nahum's booklet (1:2-11) apparently proves the existence of a *psalmic genre before the exile* (cf.*RB* 1958, p. 326). The same could be said of the hymnic "prayer of Habakkuk" (Hab 3:1-19; end of 6th cent.) Yet *OABA* considers it probable that these poems were added later by editors. The thanksgiving psalm of Ex 15:1-18 reflects other writings of Josiah's time (628-609) and could have been composed for the exceptional passover-feast of 622 (2 K 23:22), perhaps ten years before the Nahum psalm. These three psalms, Tournay believes, constitute important landmarks for psalm chronology.

The royal psalms, 20 and 21, are assigned by Tournay to *the reign of Josiah,* and are believed to originate from *Deuteronomic circles.* Indications for this include the theology of the divine name (Ps 20: 2, 6, 8; cf. §10b), Deuteronomic sayings (cf. Ps 20:5), the use of expressions characteristic of that period and affinity with other writings of the same time, like Ex 15:1-18. The king of these psalms could be Josiah himself. The extravagant praise of Ps 21:6f should not surprise since each anointed king was in a way a messiah, a new David, a type of promised Emmanuel (Is 6-12; cf. §15c). In these two psalms, liturgy and prophecy blend to form a mixed type. Psalms 20 and 21 would have been recited at the anniversary of the king's coronation, Ps 20 during the holocaust, Ps 21 at the end of the ceremony (*RB* 1959, p. 166). It is Tournay's conclusion that the reign of Josiah is an important landmark in the development of the inspired writings: the royal (Pss 20, 21) and paschal (Ex 15) liturgies, the prophetic psalm (Na 1) testify to the lyric and psalmic activity of the levitical circles from which would emerge also the prayer of Habakkuk (Hab 3) and Ps 61. Responding to this literary movement, the royal scribes instruct younger members of the ruling class in all the wisdom and didactic literature, that of Egypt not excluded. For Tournay one of the guiding principles in dating the psalms is stress on intra-biblical comparisons rather than on the extra-biblical ones (cf. *RB* 1956, p. 125f).

(f) *Various suggestions*

In *"Les saints dans le psautier"* (ETL 1963, p. 493f), J. Coppens applies specific criteria to the dating of two psalms. For a rather recent date, certainly post-exilic, of Ps 34, the following reasons can be invoked: the presence of the acrostic device, the developed form of the thanksgiving, the sapiential and didactic style (cf. v 12), notions of angelology (v 8), unlimited confidence in God, almost suppressing the agonizing problem of evil. As for Ps 106, the following indications point also to a post-exilic date: part of Israel lives in the Diaspora (v 47), Deuteronomic theology is reflected in various ways: divine saving deeds are contrasted to the infidelity of the people; the psalmist expresses repentance and adopts the penitential thought-pattern of the exilic and post-exilic periods; the historical data of the psalm presuppose, it seems, the existence of the Pentateuch; finally, the insistence on Moses' and Phinees' mediating roles (vv 23, 30) reflect the theology of later Judaism, which praised Tôrâh and its mediator, the priesthood and its main representatives.

Psalm 16:3 belongs, on the other hand, to a pre-exilic composition, Coppens believes, while Ps 89, although post-exilic in its present form, is based on pre-exilic traditions. In another article, *"Les Psaumes des hasidim"* (cf. §12c), Coppens dates after the exile Pss 31, 32, 37, 79, 85, 86, 89, 97, 116, 132, 145, 148, 149 but sees no compelling reason to refuse a pre-exilic origin for Pss 4, 12, 16, 30, 43, 50, 52. The almost complete absence of Exodus typology in the Psalter represents in J. Harvey's view an additional indication suggesting that very few in number are the exilic and post-exilic psalms (*ScEcc* 1963, p. 399; cf. §14a). It will be seen (cf. §9d, c. fi.) that the end of the sixth century (soon after the exile) is considered by some as "an archaizing age." Pss 48, 118, 128 would betray this tendency.

M. Buttenweiser, known for his sustained interest in psalm chronology, assigns a pre-exilic date to Pss 8, 15, 19A, 20, 21, 24, 29, 45,

48, 50, 51, 76, 78, 81, 95, 100, 105, 114, 127, 128, 133, 136 and to parts of Pss 57, 60, 65, 68, while he dates from the period of the exile Pss 42-43, 80, 85, 89, 126, 137 and the first part of Ps 68. The other psalms, he thinks, are post-exilic. H.-J. Kraus would date the origin of the royal psalms (cf. §28) to the period of the monarchy while he considers Pss 29 and 68 as very ancient. Pss. 44, 74, 79 and 137 seem to have been written during the exile. G. Castellino would grant Davidic authenticity to Pss 2, 7, 16, 17, 18, 23, 24, 35, 51, 54, 56, 57, 60, 69, 101, 110. As for Podechard, he finds many pre-exilic psalms in the group 1-75: Pss: 2, 4, 8, 13, 14 (=53), 18, 20, 21, 24B, 28, 29, 42-43, 44, 45, 46, 47, 48, 52, 60, 63, 72. In *Psalms III*, pp. XXXIVff, Dahood presents arguments in support of an early date for the psalms.

(g) *Tentative conclusion*

To conclude, it can be stated that in spite of wide divergences of views there is some kind of consensus on a certain number of psalms as to whether they belong to the pre-exilic or to the post-exilic periods. The case of some of them is discussed in this general introduction (ch I-III), the dating of others (to which an asterisk is prefixed) will be at least mentioned in the special introduction to the individual psalms (the relevance of Ugaritic material for dating will be considered in §9d). Pss 44, 74, 79, 92, 137 are, more often than not, dated during the exile. In the following list the numbers in brackets indicate the psalms which have been seriously assigned by various authors both to the pre-exilic or to the post-exilic periods. The psalms not mentioned have not been the object of significant discussion:

Pre-exilic: *(2), *(4), 7, 12, *(16), *18, 20, *21, 29, 30, 42/43, 45, *47, 50, *(51), 52, *(60), *68, *(72), *(76), *78, *(80), *(82), *(83), *(89), *(93), 99, 101, 108, *(110), (132), 144.

Post-exilic: 1, *(2), *(4), *8, *(16), *19, 23, 25, 31, 32, *33, 34, 37, *46, 48, *(51), *(60), *66, *(72), 74, *75, *(76), *77, 79, *(80), *(82), *(83), *85, 86, (89), *90, *(93), 96, 97, 98, 100, 102, 103, 106, 109, *(110), *111, *115, 116, 118, *119, *122, *123, 125, *126, 128, (132), 135, 137, 143, *145, *146, 148, *149, 150.

§6. RHYTHM AND METRE IN THE PSALTER

"To appreciate the general principles of Hebrew metrical structure, it is not necessary for the student to reach a definite conclusion on the details which are still a subject of controversy among scholars. There is a sufficient measure of agreement on the broad general principles to enable him to grasp the essentials, and the details which are still a matter controversy have not an important bearing on the interpretation of the text." With these remarks Kissane opened his brief but substantial treatment of the "metrical structure of the Psalms" (vol. I, pp. XXXV-XLII). Since Hebrew prosody has no rigid scheme and constant patterns, it is always risky to emend the text on metrical grounds alone. Reviewing C. Lattey's *The Psalter in the Westminster Version of the Sacred Scriptures* (London, 1945), T. E. Bird asked the "convinced metricist": is it plausible that the text should need emendation in more than a hundred places simply to satisfy meter? In drawing up the New Psalter, he adds, "the professors of the Biblical Institute, to our great satisfaction, steered clear of metrical theories" (*Scripture* 1, 1946, p. 16f). It seems appropriate and sufficient to present here a short explanation of the various metrical elements used in the Psalter.

(a) The *verse line* is the metrical unit. It is generally a bicolon, couplet, or distich, consisting of two clauses; it is rarely a tricolon, triplet or tristich, consisting of three clauses. The measure or length of the clauses does not depend on the number of syllables (as in English), nor on their quantity (as in Latin), but on the number of tonic accents (from two to four in each colon). Some kind of rhyme or alliteration (mainly from pronominal suffixes) is perceived by *BJ* (p. 50) in Pss 2, 7, 45, 54, 110, 124. The simplest Hebrew verse clause or colon contains two significant words, each with an accent:

With their mou´th they ble´ss,
But with their he´art they cu´rse. (62:5)

Much more common is the Qina-rhythm, characteristic of lamentations. The verse line then consists of 3+2 accented clauses:

Ya´hweh is my li´ght and my salv´ation,
Who´m shall I fe´ar? (Ps 21:1)

But the more common form of the Hebrew verse is 3+3:

> Ya′hweh, how num′erous are my adv′ersaries,
> How ma′ny they that ri′se up agai′nst me. (Ps 3:1)

All these forms can be varied by a change in the number of accents: 3+4 (cf. Ps 18:7); 4+4 (Ps 13:1); 4+3 (Ps 17:3). Some psalms are entirely composed of tricola verses (e.g., Pss 45, 93, 100). Abrupt changes in the same psalm from one form to another, as from "couplet" to "triplet," usually points to a new thought pattern, not necessarily to a new author.

(b) The essential feature of the Hebrew verse, its rhythm, rests in a balance of thought (*parallelismus membrorum*). Rhythm can be grasped to a certain degree even in the translations. *Synonymous* parallelism is observed in verse 1 of Ps 114 and in the rest of the poem:

> When Israel came forth from Egypt,
>   the house of Jacob from a people of alien tongue.

Sometimes such parallelism is maintained over several lines (cf. Pss 6:7-8; 7:13-14; 17:13-14a; 19:8-10). Thought rhyme is a fundamental law of style and poetry to such an extent, writes Mowinckel (II, 167), that we often meet with parallel bicola in which the two cola of each bicolon are parallel *inter se;* this means that we get a double thought rhyme with the pair of bicola:

> A (a) Show me favor, oh God, in accord with thy mercy,
>   (b) in thy fullness of sympathy wipe out my trespass.
> B (a) Truly wash me free of guilt,
>   (b) and from my sin do thou me cleanse (Ps 51:3f).

Antithetic or contrasted parallelism, suited for gnomic poetry (cf. Prv 10-22), is also used in the psalms:

> For the Lord watches over the way of the just,
>   but the way of the wicked vanishes (Ps 1:6; cf. 18; 28).

In a verse structure improperly called *synthetic parallelism* the second clause merely completes the first: "I myself have set up my king on Sion, my holy mountain" (Ps 2:6). It is the form most commonly used in the psalms (cf. Pss 14:2; 17:11f; 23:5f, 40:2ff). Sometimes, however, a part of the first clause is repeated (repetitive or *climactic* parallelism):

Yahweh, strong and mighty,
the Lord, mighty in battle (24: 8bc).

Give to the Lord, you sons of God,
give to the Lord glory and praise (29:1).

This type of Parallelism occurs in Ugaritic (see on *Ps 92).

(c) *Strophes* or *stanzas* are logical units, each of which generally contain the same number of verses (rhythmical units). They are indicated by Roman numbers in *CV* (as in *Liber Psalm*). In Ps 119 there are as many 8-verse stanzas as letters in the Hebrew alphabet. Other psalms are known to be divided into strophes by the presence of refrains or other literary devices (cf. Pss 20, 21, 27b, 42-43, 46, 49, 56, 57, 59, 67, 80, 88, 99, 148). The existence of strophic structure is generally admitted but its application to individual psalms is more often than not a matter of controversy (see the studies of E. Baumann, R. Galdos, H. Möller, J. A. Montgomery, J. Schildenberger).

(d) The *alphabetic psalms* are 9-10, 25, 34, 37, 111, 112, 119, 145. They follow a literary device in which half-lines, lines, verses or stanzas begin successively with a different letter of the Hebrew alphabet. In Ps 119 the letter is repeated eight times throughout the 22 alphabetical stanzas. "Pss 9-10, writes Dahood (on Ps 9), originally formed a single alphabetical poem in which every second, third, or fourth verse began with a successive letter of the Hebrew alphabet. M. Löhr once proposed that the letters of the alphabet possessed magical significance, but the discovery at Ras Shamra of several tablets inscribed with just the alphabet confutes the theory of Löhr. The acrostic arrangement served rather as an aid to the memory of the learner and provided a framework, like the sonnet, within which the poet could work." (On the date of the alphabetic psalms see *Ps 34.)

(e) A scholarly study of ancient Hebrew poetry has been published recently: Luís Alonso Schökel, *Estudios de Poética Hebrea* (Barcelona, 1963), 550 pp. It contains all the bibliographical annotations desired, mainly on pp. 3-54 and 121-129. Recent studies on metrical and poetic problems of the Psalter include those of E. Baumann (structure of Pss 4, 8, 13, 18, 26, 32, 36, 39, 40, 50, 56, 57 investigated), of R. G. Boling (Synonymous parallelism), of W. Grosmann (euphony and poetic devices), of L. Kunz (psalm structure), of J. Magne and J. Muilenburg (word repetition), of S. Mowinckel (tricola and meter), of N. H. Ridderbos (style-figures and structures), of T. H. Robinson (Hebrew poetry), of D. Michel (tenses and clause arrangement), of M. Weiss (survey of relevant literature). See also the bibliography under the names of G. Bickel, R. Lowth, E. Sievers, F. Zorrell. On grammar philology, cf. C. Brekelmans, M. Dahood, H. Jänicke, D. Michel, M. Tsevat. On "poetic techniques" in the Psalter and comparative literature see M. Dahood, *Psalms* III, pp. XXVff. At the end of this volume he and T. Penar draw from a mass of examples what they call "The Grammar of the Psalter" (pp. 361-456).

II. The Original Setting of the Psalms

§7. LITERARY FORMS IN THE PSALTER

(a) Gunkel and the "Gattungsforschung"

"In so far as the study of the Psalter has made any progress during the generation which has passed since the foundation of the Society for Old Testament Study, it is largely due to the influence of one man— Hermann Gunkel." These words A. R. Johnson pronounced in 1950 about the preceding half-century. Johnson has well expressed the importance of Gunkel's work in his survey of the studies on the psalms during the period mentioned (*The Old Testament and Modern Study*, H. H. Rowley edit., pp. 162-209). The present more modest introduction to Gunkel and the literary forms of the psalms completes the contents of an article published in 1964 (cf. L. Sabourin in bibliog.). Gunkel's *Gattungsforschung*, his investigation of literary types, was conducted in the light of a few guiding principles which we shall attempt to set forth in readable form.

Literary forms

A piece of literature, Gunkel held, must be studied *formgeschichtlich*, according, that is, to the history of the literary forms to which it belongs. A study of the *Gattungen*, the literary types, naturally precedes any attempt to classify. The *Gattungen* consist of literary units which draw from a common stock of words, formulas and images to express concepts and sentiments associated with one same situation in life (*Sitz in Leben*). A fixed pattern of expression is not abnormal in biblical literature, since religious experience will likely be couched in traditional or conventional phraseology. A cultic setting helps also to constitute the fixed pattern (*feste Gestalt*) of the psalms' *Gattungen*. The phraseology involved can become as invariable as a formulary. The *formgeschichtliche* study of a psalm consists in investigating the interrelation of its three constituting elements: content, setting in life, stylistic form. In this last element a clear distinction is to be made between the secondary data, useless in the inquiry, and the essential data, those, that is, which reflect a concrete situation or render possible its reconstitution. A "form," according to Gunkel, is that by which a text belongs to a given literary type or category. Content and form belong together.

Sitz im Leben and cultic setting

Any literary work originates in a precise *Sitz im Leben,* an important factor for the choice of the form of expression. This "setting in life" was, for the ancients, that of the community rather than of the individual. In that respect the psalms constitute for the *formgeschichtler* an exceptional field of inquiry. "Gunkel assumed," writes H. Ringgren, "that each type of psalm had originally a specific function, and this function had to do with certain ceremonies of the temple cult. A psalm of thanksgiving, for instance, was presumably written to accompany a sacrifice of thanksgiving. Such a psalm did not reflect a specific situation, but was meant for use by any individual who wanted to offer a thanksgiving sacrifice. Since it was written to meet the needs of many, it reflected that which was typical of the many situations in which thanksgiving was offered" (*The Faith...p.* XII). Mowinckel would propose for the cultic setting of the psalms other ceremonies beside the sacrificial cult, the "enthronement festival" for example (cf. §13a; on the psalms and the cult see also §8).

Concerning the psalms, a capital question has to be answered: is their *Sitz im Leben* generally communal, even though the texts, as transmitted, seem to reflect, more often than not, individual interests? Gunkel would answer by saying that evolution, which affects all human realities, has also modified the course of the psalmic tradition. The cultic setting constitutes the original soil (*Mutterboden*), in which psalmody in Israel took shape and developed (cf. A. Weiser, "Zur Frage...," p. 526). This is not unexpected since collective authorship was, in ancient times, the rule, and, in Israel, communal religious life found its expression in the cult. Many psalms have preserved their primitive cultic physiognomy, but others have been reshaped, adapted to new situations and often left with very little of their initial destination. Besides, a number of psalms were never associated with the cult. The individual laments, for example, were dissociated from the cult very likely before the exile, to serve as the expression of individual pity and of interior religion. This new situation, Gunkel believed, became, in respect to the cult, a rival *Sitz im Leben*.

The literary context

A literary study of the psalms, Gunkel affirmed, includes an investigation, as thorough as possible, of all the biblical and extrabiblical data available. Hymns feature among the most ancient of the biblical writings (e.g., Ex 15; cf. §5c and 17a). The Book of Job, some passages of the post-exilic Prophets, the Lamentations, the apocrypha [=deuterocanonica] and the pseudepigrapha (e.g., the non-canonical psalms of Solomon), even some New Testament compositions can be illuminating. The biblical psalms have to be studied, in Gunkel's view, against an even broader background, which will include the comparative literatures of the ancient Middle East countries. This important aspect of the question will be examined below (§9).

By its very existence such an extensive literary activity, both inside and outside Israel, implies the presence of a poetical art, whose laws can be determined and whose creations can be classified. Another equally important field of investigation concerns the history of psalmic literature. This is likely to reveal in our psalms the literary activity of many generations, expressed in revisions and recensions of the primitive texts (cf. §5a). Since, however, the literary form reflects the initial function of a genre, it will usually be possible and desirable to reconstitute the original composition and its primitive setting.

Gunkel's classification of the psalms

The main practical results of Gunkel's *Gattungsforschung* are laid out in a book published after his death by J. Begrich: *Einleitung in die Psalmen* (Göttingen, 1933). As early as 1904, the main lines of Gunkel's classification were made known in his *Ausgewählte Psalmen*. In the complete commentary, *Die Psalmen* (Göttingen, 1926), p. 9f., appears a list of the literary types which would be fully explained in the *Einleitung...*(see also A. R. Johnson, op. cit., pp. 166ff. and A. Descamps).

The five main categories (*Hauptgattungen*) of Gunkel's classification are the following:

1) Hymns: 8,   19,   29,   33,   65,   68,   96,   98,   100,   103,
104,   105,   111,   113,   114,   115,   117,   135,   136,
145-150. To these he adds the "Songs of Sion" (46, 48,
76,   87) and the "Enthronement Psalms" (47,   93,   97,
99 + Ps 96:10ff and 98, mentioned previously).

2) Communal Laments (Klagelieder des Volkes): mainly Pss 44,   74,
79,   80,   83, but also 58,   106,   135.

3) Royal Psalms: Pss 2,   18,   20,   21,   45,   72,   101,   132.

4) Individual Laments (Klagelieder des Einzelnen): same list as below
(§20b), but Gunkel includes also Pss 3, 27 (vv 7-14) and omits Ps
36.

5) Individual Songs of Thanksgiving (Danklieder des Einzelnen):
Pss 18 (also a royal psalm), 30,   32,   34,   41,   66,   92,   116,   118,
138.

Of other categories recognized by Gunkel, there are only four,
Johnson believes (p. 176), which merit serious consideration, as being
clearly defined types. The first two are small categories, including only
two psalms each: Songs of Pilgrimage (Pss 84 and 122) and the Communal Songs of Thanksgiving (Pss 67 and 124 are the only full examples). The third of the minor types is called Wisdom Poetry. In this
category only two psalms (127 and 133) are of the simple proverbial
type, while Pss 1,   37,   49,   73,   112,   128 belong to the more developed class of wisdom poetry.

The fourth minor type deserves special mention. The presence of
antiphonal elements, of refrains and of oracular responses in several
psalms suggested to Gunkel that some of the compositions can in full or
in part be classed as liturgies: Pss 15 and 24 he called Torah Liturgies
(cf. §32); Ps 134 he explained as a combination of hymn and priestly
blessing; in Pss 12,   75,   85,   126 he discovered Prophetic Liturgies;
to these must be added Pss 14,   81,   82,   95,   in which also appears
the influence of the canonical prophets in the blending of hymn and
oracle. Finally, Gunkel easily admitted that a number of psalms cannot
be simply classified in any of his categories, since they borrow elements
from two or more types. These he called Mischungen or Mischgedichte,
"Mixed Poems": Pss 9-10,   36,   40,   77,   78,   89,   90,   94,   107,
108,   119,   123,   129,   137,   139,   144.

Gunkel's method of classification, his insights in the history of the
forms, their application to the psalms, will remain the basis of all further

studies. The present writer's detailed introduction to each type and in fact to each psalm, as will be seen, does follow *the new approach* initiated by Gunkel. This is true also of the next chapter, which attempts to bring out the main thought patterns and the great themes of the psalms. Much, besides, of what follows, in this chapter can be referred to one or another aspect of Gunkel's contribution. It should surprise no one then that in this *ex professo* treatment of his great work so much has been omitted and the rest so briefly stated.

(b) *Divergent and complementary trends*

Gunkel's method has imperfections and some of his conclusions are tainted with arbitrariness. This is especially true of his attempt to trace the inner history of the types: the shorter and more simple psalms are more ancient than the longer more complex ones; the community inspired compositions preceded those of a private character; the thanksgiving is a more "primitive" type than the lament. There may be some truth in these principles, but their use in the chronology of the psalms is highly problematic. Besides, Gunkel's textual criticism of the psalms has been under heavy fire. Even his most ardent admirer, A. R. Johnson writes, "can hardly acquit him of a supreme manifestation of arbitrariness in his attempted emendations of the text, which are on such a scale that they would have made the work of a lesser man appear almost ridiculous" (p. 181).

Leaving aside for the moment Sigmund Mowinckel's work, we can devote some lines to a few other authors who had their say about the Gunkel approach to psalmic literature. The French scholar, A. Robert, to whom an important *Festchrift* has been dedicated (cf. *Mélanges bibliques...*), expressed the view that Gunkel had exaggerated the importance of extrabiblical sources and neglected the comparative material of the Bible itself. On better grounds it would seem, he censured his way of distinguishing too insistently, of opposing even, communal cultic piety, allegedly more "primitive," and personal piety, more recent, associated with a purified and spiritual religion, influenced by the preaching of the prophets (cf. also §12f). H.-J. Kraus believes that the individual piety of the psalmists was not subject to strict literary categories of expression. He himself, in his commentary, proceeds *konsequent-formgeschichtlich* (cf. *Psalmen*, p. XLf), in the sense presumably that no fixed pattern of interpretation is followed, but each psalm or group of psalms are examined in their own light.

G. W. Ahlström suggested that Gunkel's classification of the psalms be radically revised (*Psalm* 89. . . , p. 10). He seems to have a better point when he states that a composite psalm is not necessarily without unity (p. 9). Other authors propose to revise partially the literary categories set out by Gunkel. A. Weiser considers the lament and the thanksgiving as closely related in the setting of the cult community. It will be seen (§13c) what importance Weiser attributes to the cult and to the Covenant festival for the correct understanding of the psalms. C. Westermann's own views on the cult will be discussed below (cf. §13ad). Gunkel's method is sound, he believes, but his work has to be completed. For Westermann there exist two basic psalm categories: laments and psalms of praise. These he divides into "declarative" psalms of praise and "descriptive" psalms of praise. Some reviewers, not all (cf. *CBQ* 1959, pp. 83-87), think that this distinction is new in form only. Praise and prayer, in Westermann's view, constitute the two fundamental attitudes on which converge the whole content of the psalms (see §22).

Other important names will be mentioned in the course of this chapter and elsewhere, names particularly associated with more limited problems. Yet there is an author whose single contribution during the past fifty years has influenced the course of nearly every aspect of psalm research. Sigmund Mowinckel's first work on the psalms appeared in 1916; then there was *Psalmen-Studien* I-VI (1912-1924) and *Offersang og Sangoffer* (1951), now published in English in a revised form: *The Psalms in Israel's Worship*, vol. I-II, translated by D. R. Ap-Thomas (Oxford, 1962). This work is not a commentary of the psalms, but a series of studies on the psalms. It will be henceforth quoted as Mowinckel I or II (see II, p. 282ff: the bibliography of Mowinckel's works; cf. §5d, 8a, 13a, 14d on some of his central views).

§.8 THE   PSALMS   AND   THE   CULT

(a) *The psalms' origin and the cultic realities*

Mowinckel's definition of the cult may be accepted as a working basis: "Cult or ritual may be defined as the socially established and regulated holy acts and words in which the encounter and communion of the Deity with the congregation is established, developed, and brought to its ultimate goal." In other words, cult is "the visible and audible expression of the relation between the congregation and the Deity" (I, p. 15f).

Through the cult, through sacrifice especially, the power of the Holy, its life or blessing, are bestowed upon the partakers, and a relationship is established or renewed between them and the deity. The "fact of salvation" is actualized in the cult, mainly when the reality of the divine saving deeds is symbolically re-presented by a "dramatic" re-enactment of the past. Originally, it seems, the *words* of the cult belonged to the acts as interpretations and complement. In their proper setting words produce the blessings pronounced, just as the curse brings malediction. The "sacramental" words "express what is to happen to the congregation or to an individual member by an act of the diety" (I, p. 21). So does the "cultic oracle," sometimes connected with the "augural sacrifice." The natural form of the cultic prayer is the *psalm*, Mowinckel writes (I, 22), and the rhythmic form adds stress and strength to the words.

Cultic origin

It is Mowinckel's view that the great majority of the psalms do not simply derive, as a matter of form history or literary history, from ancient cult poetry (cf. §5d). They are "real cult psalms *composed for* and used in the actual services of the temple. Private and more personal psalm poetry first occurs in the late Jewish period. In the Psalter such psalms constitute a minority" (I p. 23). It was, however, the traditional Jewish and Christian view that the psalms were originally private, individual psalms. Ancient scholars and the older generation of modern psalm interpreters also generally shared this opinion, adding only that at a later stage these private lyrics were given a secondary use as songs for the temple service. The traditional assumption that the psalms originated as private compositions can be explained by the generalized belief "that most of the psalms had been composed by David and some of his supposed contemporaries, such as Asaph, Heman, etc." But even Mowinckel would not simply call the Psalter (as a collection) "the hymnbook of the Second Temple," which perhaps it became, but was scarcely made with that end in view (cf. I, p. 2, 5). As non-cultic psalms Mowinckel suggests: Pss 1, 19B, 34, 37, 49, 78, 105, 106, 111, 112, 127. They consist mainly of sapiential and historical psalms (cf. II p. 111; comp. with G. Quell in §8f).

For those not restricted by an authorship dogma, for certain Protestant scholars, the failure to appreciate the cultic origin of the psalms lay in the low estimate they had of the value of cult and liturgy. Even those, like R.

Smend, who found in the "I" of the psalms a poetical personifiation of the Jewish congregation (cf. §23a), even they did not discuss a real cultic destination of the psalms. For them "the congregation" meant the pious "private" lay circles supposed to exist within it and to which they applied the expressions 'anāwîm, ḥasîdîm, ṣaddîqîm, the "poor," the "righteous," the "just," occurring in the psalms (I, p. 12; cf. below §12a-d). Circles of pietists, known to the modern revival movements, were believed to have existed also in ancient Israel. Such "private religious lyrics," independent of the temple cult, and emanating from certain "pious circles" of later Judaism do exist; they are found in the so-called Psalms of Solomon, and in the newly discovered Essenian Hôdāyôt from the Qumrân caves. These psalms were indeed also composed in the old style, though no longer for cultic use (Mowinckel I, pp. 30, 41).

"In the meantime, the comparative study of religions had brought to the fore the important place of the cult in religion in general" (I, p. 13), and in Israel in particular. Like A. Bentzen and T.H. Gaster, Mowinckel follows a path opened by V. Groenbech (see §8d). For them the realities of salvation are actualized and lived through the symbols and rites. A better appreciation, even in Protestant Christianity, of cult values helped produce a change in the interpretation of the psalms. By his "form-critical" or "form-historical" (formgeschichtliche) and "type-critical" (gattungsgeschichtliche) methods, Gunkel, Mowinckel believes, "has proved beyond doubt that in Israel also the origin of psalm poetry is to be found in the public cult" (ibid).

Traditionalism   versus   Personality

Yet Gunkel believed that this was true only of the original, *now mostly lost*, psalm poetry, and that "the now extant psalms were to be considered as a later [mainly post-exilic] evolution, a free private poetry, unconnected with the cultic situation, but *imitating* (cf. §5c) the style and the motifs of the older one" (p. 14). If, however, as the Jewish sources seem to testify, our psalms were used in the cult, it is hardly conceivable, as noted by Mowinckel, "how any younger, private, lay poetry could possibly have made its way into the cult, and even supplanted most of the genuine old ritual poetry" (I, p. 30). The cultic sphere is indeed known to be a closed, almost intangible world.

Gunkel based his assumption mainly on an alleged incompatibility between the personal religious note in so many of the psalms, and the impersonal character of the liturgical formulas. Mowinckel has, however, attempted to prove that there is no real incompatibility between "traditionalism" and "personality" in religious poetry, that sacred forms and expressions may often carry a rich personal content (II, p. 126-145). Yet the problem remains and it has been clearly proposed by Mowinckel himself (I, 30f): "What strikes us in the biblical psalms is the uniformity and formality which characterize most of them. One is often so like another that they are difficult to differentiate. The personal individual element is pushed into the background. Imagery and phraseology are often stereotyped traditional ones. Rarely is there a clear allusion to the poet's personal situation, rarely anything definite and concrete, almost invariably only what is typical of a whole circle, in the most general terms. The set formality of the psalms can only be explained on the basis that they are not primarily meant to be personal effusions, but are, in accordance with their type and origin, ritual lyrics. It is of the nature of the cultic psalm that it cannot express the individual's definite, once-for-all, experiences and emotions. It voices these moods and experiences which have common currency with the cult community."

Content and form

Besides, according to Mowinckel, Gunkel failed to admit that the rule "content and form go together," as applied to the psalms, suffers exceptions. "An alien form may have been used as an effective means of expressing the content. Thus, although the prophets often used the psalm-style to underline and emphasize their message, nevertheless their utterances are prophecies and neither hymns nor lamentations. And the psalm-writer may use the form of the 'wisdom-poetry' for his personal expression of the praise of God, or thanksgiving for a blessing received—without his psalm becoming a wisdom or problem poem" (I, 31). Thus also, a psalm may consist of parts belonging to different form types: hymn, praise, lamentation. This variety may correspond to the liturgical setting.

So the form-historical method has to be complemented by the cult-functional method. Various sentiments could be expressed in the course of the same festival, and these are reflected in the "compound" psalms. To understand a psalm cult-functionally means to see it in the right cultic situation. This is no doubt important, if it can be done. Everybody will agree, writes Mowinckel, "that a Christian baptismal hymn or a communion hymn acquires full significance only when seen in connection with the holy act to which it belongs" (I, 34). To concentrate the attention on the form could lead to other misinterpretations, that, for example, of equating "I" -psalms with private psalms and "We" psalms with congregational psalms (cf. §23a).

Mowinckel's categories

Few will doubt that Mowinckel's theory of interpretation is basically sound. Whether it is as useful as he says for interpreting the psalms still has to be seen, since it is usually very difficult to get a clear picture of the original liturgical set up. Mowinckel himself, it seems, concludes too easily from vague allusions or hypothetical connections. For him there are four main types of psalms:

I. Praise and thanksgiving psalms of the congregation:
   a) the common praises or *hymns,* about God's excellence and benefactions in general.
   b) the special thanksgiving psalms, giving thanks for a particular, just experienced, salvation.
II. Private (that is, individual) thanksgivings.
III. Congregational lamentation and prayer psalms:
   a) for common and general situations.
   b) for a special occasion
      :after a catastrophe (real lamentations).
      :in face of a threatening danger (*protective* psalms: cf. on *71).
IV. Individual lamentation and prayer psalms.

(b) *The psalms and the cult: biblical evidence*

Evidence for the cultic use of the psalms can be drawn from various sources: the headings of the psalms (see §4c), allusions in the psalms themselves, the liturgical annotations of the Chronicler (cf. §4e), and the testimony of the Mishna and Talmud regarding a series of psalms which were used on different occasions in the temple cult (cf. Mowinckel I, p. 2f).

The Priestly Code

The most extensive information we have on the cult in Israel is found in the "Priestly Document," the latest of the Pentateuchal sources, collected in the post-exilic, Jewish times (*Id.* I, p. 35). It presents ritual and other features of the service from the priests' own technical point of view (cf. Ex 24-31; 34-40; Lv 1-26). The picture which results is "both one-sided and fragmentary." Little is said of the ritual festivals as a whole and practically nothing about the part played by the congregation, about the words belonging to the cult, about the prayers or the psalms that accompanied the cultic actions. Besides, there is little doubt that a large number of the psalms are much older than the "Priestly Document" and date from the time of the monarchy (before the exile). To a certain extent, then, concludes Mowinckel, "the situations can and must be pictured from hints in the psalms themselves" (p. 36).

Cultic acts

There are psalms, Mowinckel notes, "that obviously presuppose, and are made for, a festal procession, such as Pss 24, 68, 118, 132. They can only be understood in connexion with a vision of the procession itself and its different acts and scenes" (I, p. 5). In other psalms are found allusions to what can only be understood as acts of the cult: intention to worship (5:7), to fulfill vows (7: 18; 22:26; 50:14; 56:13; 61: 6-9; 65:2; 66:13f; 76:12; 116:14, 18), to offer sacrifices (27:6; 54:8; 66:15; 96:8; 116:17), to sing praises "in the vast assembly" 22:23ff; 35:18; 40:11; 68:27; 89:6; 111:1; 150:1), to walk around the altar (26:5; 43:4), to join in the procession (42:5; 68:25f; 118:19-27), to offer prayers like an evening sacrifice (141:2), to undergo purification ceremonies (51:9), to receive or pronounce blessings (often). The frequent allusions to Jerusalem, to the temple, to the sanctuary, to God's mountain, to his abode, to his footstool and to the holy feasts indicate that, in one way or another, a great number of the psalms originated in relationship with the temple (see on *Ps 66).

A cultic setting is also presupposed by the association of the psalms, the hymns mainly, with song and music. The tune in Israel's cult was seemingly a simple one, "more like a sort of recitative." Mowinckel adds that "the first task of the musical accompaniment was undoubtedly to stress the rhythm, to keep time. . . . The temple music had no independent significance. It was meant to accompany the song, the chanting recitation of prayers and hymns" (I, p. 9f). Some allusions to the cultic dance can be found in the psalms (30:12;   87:17;   149:3   150:4) as elsewhere in the Bible (cf. Ex 15:20;   2 S 6:16;   Jdt 15:12).

Qualified inferences

The authors of *BJ* (Psalms), R. Tournay and R. Schwab, have proposed various remarks and suggestions concerning the cultic origin of the psalms as supposedly indicated by the biblical data (cf. pp. 44-49). The presence of liturgical rubrics in a psalm's heading, the use of traditional, perhaps cultic formulas, and the mention of musical instruments in the psalm itself, do not necessarily imply that a psalm has been directly composed for the cult. These indications can point simply to a later use of the psalm or can be referred to conventional accompaniments of the hymnic genre. Refrains (Pss 56 and 80), dialogues (91, 122), quotations and oracles (50,   60,   82 etc.) can be mere literary devices. The use of Pss 95, 105, 106 in 1 Ch does not prove their cultic origin. This is true also of Ps 132 in respect to 2 Ch 6:41. It is not sure that Ps 24:7f featured in the transfer of the ark under David (2 S 6).

Although a change of (pronominal) persons does not necessarily point to a real dialogue or to the presence of a choir and a soloist, this is implied by a litany, as in Ps 136, and by antiphons (Pss 106, 107,   115, 118) as, also, presumably, in Pss 20,   75,   85,   134. The liturgical character of a prayer is manifest when the worshiper performs in the temple a distinct rite, in a precise setting: cf. 20:4;   26:6: 66:13;   81:4;   116: 17;   134:2;   135:2. In some cases the cultic adaptation of a psalm seems reflected in the addition of a final blessing (cf. Pss 118,   125,   128,   129, 134), or in other less conspicuous changes. This is but one type of "relectures" cf. §5a) introduced during the psalms' long history. It is rarely easy to distinguish in the Hebrew text the primitive from the subsequent layers.

(c) *The Psalter in the Jewish cycle reading*

"The reading of the Law and Prophets in a Triennial Cycle" had been studied by A. Büchler a long time ago (cf. *JQR* 5, 1893, pp. 420-468; 6, 1894, pp. 1-73). Other scholars, E. G. King, I. Abrahams, L.

Rabinowitz and N. H. Snaith (cf. bibliog.) have later discussed the possibility that a similar arrangement applied to the Psalter (cf. also A. Arens, *Le Psautier*, p. 107ff). A. Guilding has reopened the debate, first in "Some obscured Rubrics and Lectionary Allusions in the Psalter" (*JTS* 3, 1952, pp. 41-55), then in her book, *The Fourth Gospel and Jewish Worship*... (Oxford, 1960). The name "triennial cycle," as she explains it in the book (p. 6), "is given to the early Palestinian system of reading the whole of the Pentateuch through once on the consecutive sabbaths of three lunar years. The Pentateuch was divided for this purpose into rather more than 150 sections, known as *sedarim*. In course of time there grew up the habit of adding a second lesson from the Prophets, known as a *haphtorah* or 'concluding passage. It seems possible also that the Psalms were recited over a three-year period: the number of Psalms corresponds to the number of sabbaths in three lunar years, and the arrangement of the Psalter seems to have been influenced by liturgical considerations."

Evidence of cycle reading

A cycle reading of the Psalms seems attested by the Talmud and also suggested by the comparison of the five books of Moses with the five books of the Psalter. Besides, adds Guilding (p. 39), "the fact that just as the Midrashim [Jewish commentaries] to the Pentateuch are homilies based on the pericopes of the Torah read during the triennial cycle, so an examination of Midrash *Tehillim* [of the Psalms] ...established beyond doubt that part of its exposition was influenced by the custom of reading the Psalm in a certain triennial cycle." Finally "it is suggested that this theory is supported by the internal evidence of the Psalter: certain obscure passages in some of the Psalms are really rubrics which have later been incorporated in the text of the Psalm, and when these rubrics are examined they are found to consist of strings of three words or phrases—the catchwords to the Torah lesson for each of the three years of the triennial cycle for the particular sabbath to which the Psalm was allocated." The author illustrates the theory with examples, mainly Ps 81, "a psalm for New Year's day" and Ps 11:6 (pp. 39:44). The origin of the triennial cycle could be traced back to approximately 400 B.C. (p. 24). For Sabbath reading see on *Ps 92.

In a study devoted to the psalms in Old Testament worship, A. Arens (*Die Psalmen*...) discovers parallel thought patterns in the corresponding three-year cycle readings: Gn 1-2 and Pss 1-2; Gn 49-50 and Ps 41; Ex

1-2 and Ps 42-43; Ex 39-40 and Ps 72; Lv 1-2 and Ps 73; Lv 26-27 and Ps 89; Nb 1-2 and Ps 90; Nb 35-36 and Ps 118; Dt 1-2 and Ps 119; Dt 33-34 and Ps 150 (cf. pp. 169-177). R. Tournay thinks that the correspondence proposed for Pss 118 and 90 is either not apparent or too subtle (*RB* 1962, p. 611).

Liturgy spiritualized

A remark of H. Gressmann in The Psalmists (Oxford, 1926) reflects an opinion current at that time among exegetes of a certain tendency. Commenting on what he calls "the transfer of the psalms from the temple to the synagogue," he writes: "It meant a great step forward in the religious history of the Jewish people. They formed henceforth a spiritual liturgy adequate to the worship of God in spirit and in truth" (p. 13). The same idea had been expressed before him by I. Elbogen, in his book *Der jüdische Gottesdienst in seiner geschichtlichen Entwicklung* (Frankfurt, 1913; ed. 3:1931), where he maintains (p. 233f) that the introduction of the synagogal liturgy marked an abandonment of and a reaction against the sacrificial cult of the temple and of the priestly mediation. Arens questions this view (p. 55f) and discovers, on the contrary, a continuity between Ex 24, 1 Ch 21 and Ezr 3, between Ex 40, 2 Ch 5-7 and Ne 8, between the Dwelling (cf. Ex 25:9) and the synagogue, preserving the past in a new light (cf. *Bib* 1962, pp. 226-229). The probem of the prophetic attitude to the sacrificial worship, as reflected in some psalms, will be examined elsewhere (see on *Ps 51:18).

(d) *Myth and Ritual*

A number of modern scholars, mainly Scandinavian, have attempted to use in the interpretation of the Bible and of the Psalms some of the ideas proposed for the history of religions by anthropologist V. Groenbech. In the second volume of *The Culture of the Teutons* I-III (London, 1930-1931), Groenbech had exposed his views on ritual drama. A. Bentzen, S. Mowinckel, T. H. Gaster, J. Pedersen and others have, in varying degree, followed his line of thought: rites are not mere symbols; they produce what they signify. Drama can be creative and the realities of salvation are re-presented, actualized, re-enacted and lived in the cult.

The name of S. H. Hooke is linked with the so-called "Myth and Ritual School," since he has been the editor of various collections of essays entitled: *Myth and Ritual. Essays on the Myth and Ritual of the Hebrews in Relation to the Cultic Pattern of the Ancient East* (Oxford, 1933); *The Labyrinth. Further Studies in the Relation between Myth and Ritual in the Ancient World* (London, 1935); *Myth, Ritual and Kingship. Essays on the Theory and Practice of Kingship in the Ancient Near East and in Israel* (Oxford, 1958). See also now T. H. Gaster, *Myth, Legend and Custom in the OT* (New York, 1969) 741-783, on the psalms.

These titles tell us something about the new trend. What is meant by myth and ritual S. H. Hooke attempts to describe in the introduction of the first of these works: "In general the spoken part of ritual consists of a description of what is being done, it is the story which the ritual inacts. This is the sense in which the term myth is used in our discussion. The original myth, inseparable in the first instance from its ritual, embodies in more or less symbolic fashion the original situation which is seasonally re-enacted in the ritual" (p. 3).

H. Ringgren's description of "myth" is still more explicit and clear. "In everyday speech a myth often means a story in which gods (and goddesses) appear as acting characters. It is also generally understood that a myth is not true. Modern writers on comparative religion, however, tend to use the word 'myth' in a very specific sense. They define 'myth' as 'the spoken part of a ritual': in a cultic celebration the myth explains the rite, and the rite visualizes or enacts the myth. According to this definition, such a story as the account of Israel's exodus from Egypt would be a myth, since the Lord appears as one of the main characters, and the story forms an integrating part of the celebration of Passover. At the same time the majority of scholars maintain that this narrative reflects a real historical event" (*The Faith of the Psalmists*, p. 94; see also below: §11a).

A privileged area for the application of these principles is that of kingship in Israel. A. R. Johnson, the author of *Sacral Kingship in Ancient Israel* (Cardiff, 1955), offers in *The Old Testament and Modern Study* an outline of the complex ideology involving kingship in the ritual drama. "Here the argument is that in the ritual drama the kings or nations of the earth, representing the forces of darkness and death as opposed to those of light and life, unite in an attempt to destroy Yahweh's chosen people by attacking the Davidic king upon whom its vitality as a social body is peculiarly dependent. At first the king, who is referred to from time to time as the Son, the Servant and the Messiah of Yahweh, suffers humiliation and defeat, and is nearly swallowed up by the chaos of waters which lead to the underworld of Sheol; but ultimately, in virtue of his protestation of devotion and his claim to righteousness, he is delivered by Yahweh from this threat of death. Such a renewal of life on the part of the king, however, is nothing less than a ritual re-birth; it is an indication that the suffering Servant and duly humble Messiah has been adopted once more as the Son of the Most High or, to express this mediatory role in different terms, that he has been renewed in office as priest 'after the order of Melchizedek.' In this way the life or well-being of the nation, for which the king is directly responsible, receives provisional guarantee for another year" (p. 196f).

"The reader should be warned," adds Johnson, "against exaggerating the degree to which this theory fits into that of a general myth and ritual pattern common to the ancient Near East, which is advocated by S. H. Hooke, the founder of the so-called Myth and Ritual School. There is certainly no suggestion in all this that Yahweh was ever thought of as a type of divine king" (references to G. Widengren and A. Haldar).

The Johnson drama represents the king's cultic struggle and triumph, re-enacting the nature-religion myth of dying and rising divinities. Traces of the ritual drama, Johnson claims, can be found in Pss 46, 48, 68, 82, 84, 89, 97, 98, 101, 149.

In "Additional Notes" of *The Psalms in Israel's Worship*, Mowinckel has presented his observations on Johnson's theory. He writes, *inter alia*: "Johnson is perfectly right in saying that the dramatic presentation of Yahweh's victory over the 'nations' in the cult played a part in the Israelite new year festival. But there is nothing to prove that the king was looked upon as the leader of the struggle on behalf of Yahweh, nor that Israel had anything corresponding to the Babylonian rite with the atoning humiliation of the kings. . . . Beyond the supposed fundamental evidence of Pss 18, 89, and 118, to which Johnson has drawn attention, and Ps 116, Engnell has not been able to provide any proofs of the 'cultic suffering' of the king. . . Without giving any ground whatever he adds Pss 22 and 49 and Is 38:9ff and—apparently joining Widengren—Ps 88" (II, p. 254f). Various other examples of "Myth and Ritual School" exegesis will be given in the introductions to Pss 1, 44, 74, 89 (on the respective positions of Ahlström, Engnell, Widengren, Bentzen, Johnson, H. Schmidt, Mowinckel, see on *Ps 89).

The "Myth and Ritual" books edited by Hooke can be considered as "programme writings" and as such do not offer much guarantee of solidity and judiciousness. What has the Yahwist religion to do with hierogamy and with vegetation and fertility cults of the nature-religions? A sharp distinction has to be drawn between literary and ideological patterns. A. R. Johnson and I. Engnell, even though favorable to the myth and ritual trend, reject the idea that Yahweh could ever have been considered a dying and rising God (a Widengren postulate: see on *Ps 44: 24). The importance attached to temporal royalty by the Myth and Ritual School appears also in this quite apodictic statement of I. Engnell: "The *Messiah* we meet with in the Psalms is without the slightest doubt the 'historical' and living 'Messiah' of the Davidic dynasty, the sacral king and savior, whether we meet him in the positive aspect of the ritual, as victorious and exalted, or in its negative aspect, as humiliated and suffering, expiating his own and his people's sins, that is to say, in the role of the Suffering Servant" ("Planted. . ." p. 86).

In two well documented articles C. Hauret has presented and criticized the "Interpretation of the Psalms according to the Myth and Ritual School" (*Rev.Sc.Rel.*, 1959, pp. 321-346; 1960, pp. 1-34). The complexity of the problems involved and the importance of the debate are also reflected in the extensive notes appended to Mowinckel's own treatment of related subjects (cf. II, pp. 240-255). Some additional light on the subject will hopefully result from what remains to be said in connection with the "Enthronement festival of Yahweh" (§13c) and the royal Psalms (§26-27).

(e) *The cult oracle*

Gunkel had attributed to the influence of the canonical prophets the presence in many psalms of oracular elements. Other authors prefer to say that the prophets imitated the psalmists (cf. §5c). A. R. Johnson sets the problem in its proper perspective. "There is ample evidence outside the Psalter to prove that during the monarchy and until well into the post-exilic period there were prophets who had as close a connexion with the formal religion of Israel as the priests themselves and were only quite late in this period absorbed, like the singers, into the Levitical orders. This being the case, the question arises as to whether or not the oracular element in the Psalter and indeed some of the prayers themselves should not be ascribed to such cultic prophets, who from the first show themselves to have been subject to the inspirational power of music" (*The Old Testament and Modern Study*, p. 206). Biblical references to this subject include: Nb 11:24-30; 1 S 10:5-13; 1 K 18:30ff; 19:10, 14; 22:

5-28; 2 K 4:23; Jr 5:30f; 23:11; 25:14; Lm 3:20; 1 Ch 25:1-6; 2 Ch 20:1-30; 34: 30 (comp. with 2 K 23:2).

Several passages of the psalms seem to imply that some kind of oracle has made known to the worshiper that his prayer has been heard (cf. Ps 6:9f; 22:25; 28:6; 34:7; 66:19). Such reassuring oracles (*Heils-orakeln*) would explain that some laments end on a tone of triumph or of full confidence and even include an anticipated thanksgiving (cf. Pss 6:9; 31:20-25). That God was ritually consulted seems implied in expressions like the following: "Say to my soul, I am your salvation" (Ps 35:3). Allusions to various kinds of oracles can be read in Pss 2:7; 12:6; 13:4ff; 20:7; 21:9-13; 27:7; 38:16; 46:11; 49:17ff; 55:23; 60:8-10; 62:12f; 68:12ff, 23ff; 75:3f; 89:20-38; 91:14ff; 95:7-11; 102:3; 107:20; 108:8-10; 110:1-7.

Some authors then would say that a cultic prophet pronounced the oracle. See: A. R. Johnson, *The Cultic Prophet in Ancient Israel* (Cardiff, 1944 and 1962); A. Haldar, *Associations of Cult Prophets among the Ancient Semites* (Uppsala, 1945); S. Mowinckel, *The Psalms in Israel's Worship*, II pp. 53-73. According to G. Pidoux, the *oracle d'exaucement* was pronounced by a priest (or a cult prophet) from the sacrifice (*Du Portique à l'autel*, p. 97). Such oracles are not explicitly mentioned in the psalms because they were not part of the prayers. R. de Vaux writes: "In ancient Israel men went to a sanctuary 'to consult Yahweh,' and the priest gave oracles" (*Ancient Israel...*p. 454; the French edition has : "Le prêtre était un donneur d'oracles," II, p. 200). The cult oracle was of current use, Tournay notes, at the ceremonies attended by the Egyptian Pharaoh. From the 21st Dynasty (1085-950) onwards the oracle took in Egypt an official character. Before an expedition the king would consult the oracle and offer thanks at his return (*RB* 1959, pp. 166, 182).

Rabbinism attributed a prophetic character to the function of High-Priest (cf. Ex 28:30; Lv 8:8; Ezr 2:63; Ne 7:65; Jn 11:52 and E. Bammel, in *TLZ*, n. 79, 1954, pp. 351-356). On the priestly oracle see the articles of J. Begrich in *ZAW* 52 (1934), 81-92 and of F. Küchler in *Fs. W .G. von Baudissin: BZAW* 33 (1918) 285-301; cf. on *Pss 12 and 86; also §31a.

In his *Introduction to the Old Testament*, I, pp. 185-202, A. Bentzen treats of both the priestly and the prophetic oracles, including also remarks on the "Benediction" and the "Curse," the liturgical *tôrâh* and the ordeal. "Cursing" and "blessing" are subjects for which Mowinckel shows a striking interest (cf. II, 1-8; 44-52). He believed that the "enemies" and "evildoers" of the psalms are to be identified mainly with sorcerers and their demonic allies, operating with an antisocial magical power (cf. § 14d on "imprecations" and also §12g). In this also the Norwegian scholar reflects the current tendency to import into the biblical world data collected by anthropologists in the broader field of foreign and often primitive beliefs.

(f) *Various studies on the cultic background of the psalms*

G. Quell divides the psalms into three main groups: to *Kultusgruppe* A belong 62 psalms, dominated by cultic ideas or belonging to liturgical patterns: Pss 1, 2, 12, 14, 15, 20/21, 24, 29, 33, 44-48, 50, 58, 60, 65, 67, 68, 72, 74, 76, 78-83, 85, 87, 90, 93, 95-100, 102, 105, 107, 110, 112-114, 117, 124-126, 128, 129, 132-136, 147-150. To *kultisch-religiöse Mischgruppe* B belongs 75 psalms, in which cultic elements are mixed with non-cultic religious sentiments (all the psalms not included in groups A and C). To *religiöse Gruppe* C belongs 13 psalms, in which only cult-free religious expression is to be found: Pss 6, 19:1-7, 38, 39, 41, 88, 91, 102A, 120, 127, 131, 139, 143 (comp. with Mowinckel's non-cultic psalms; only Ps 127 is common!).

A. C. Welch follows Gunkel's lead in claiming that although the psalms were intended for use in the temple worship, they have been later detached from their original setting while maintaining their place in the community's religious life after the destruction of the temple and the continuance of its services. J. P. Peters stressed that the psalms are not occasional poems nor occasional lyrics. They can be studied only within the framework of the history of the liturgies. C. L. Feinberg ("The uses ..."), on the other hand, warns that insistence on the liturgy risks to obscure "the devotional purpose of the psalms." He mentions that B. Duhm understood the Psalter as a manual for devotional reading and meditation. R. H. Pfeiffer views it as a devotional anthology of religious poems, meant for the uplift of the general public. A cultic origin requires a pre-exilic date for many psalms, and this can hardly be admitted, Pfeiffer claims (cf. §5b).

The truth presumably lies *in medio*. Some psalms are *cultic*, others are not. Already in 1942 A. Szörenyi had proposed criteria for discerning which psalms had been composed for liturgical use. Twenty years later he publishes a new, comprehensive study along the same lines, and rejects, *inter alia*, as a Mowinckel myth, the so-called "Feast of the Enthronement of Yahweh" (cf. §13a). A. L. Ricotti has investigated the use of the psalms in the Jewish cult up to the New Testament times. She based her study on the Bible, the Mishnâ, the Talmud, the Toseftâ and the treatise Soferîm. K. Koch has studied the role of the decalogue in the liturgies of entry, not only in *Ps 15 and *Ps 24:4:6, but also in Is 33:14ff; Mi 6:6ff; 18:5ff. A good bibliography of the Old Testament cult can be found in H.-J. Kraus, *Psalmen*, p. LXXXIVff and a good treatment of the subject in his *Worship in Israel.* "The cultic element" in the Psalms is clearly presented by H. Ringgren in *The Faith of the Psalmists*, pp. 1-9 (see also the studies of C. C. Keet, J. P. Peters, N. H. Ridderbos, N. H. Snaith, A. Weiser, H. Zirker, V. Schönbächler).

§9. FOREIGN INFLUENCES ON THE PSALTER

Hermann Gunkel stressed the primary importance of studying the comparative material from ancient Mesopotamia and Egypt for the interpretation of the Psalms His claim that too little was made of this would hardly be true today, when oriental studies have invaded the biblical field to the degree we know. Some significant parallels will be mentioned in the introduction to the individual psalms. These particular data will be, it is hoped, better understood against the broader background presented in the next paragraphs. General observations on the subject will be followed by particular ones regarding the various cultures involved.

(a) *Two complementary views*

Being especially interested in the cult and in the study of comparative religions, Mowinckel claims that the association of the psalms with the cult can be confirmed by analogies from neighboring oriental civilizations. In both form and thought the Israelites were borrowers. In his own words: "We must realize that in matters of the framework of the cult, incidentally, of many of the ideas expressed through it, the partially Cannaanized Israelites took as models the temple cults of the neighboring peoples.... The religious history of Israel in the following period [after the rise of the monarchy] largely consists of a dramatic struggle to expel the obviously syncretistic, and to work out the peculiar historical significance of the Yahweh religion" (I, 36: the main religious feasts, the temple and the divine name *El Elyôn* are cited as examples of the influence exercised on yahwism by the environment). For Mowinckel, "it becomes evident that most of the stylistic and formal elements, and quite a number of details of content in general oriental cult poetry are either the same as the biblical ones, or at least show great similarities to it. Undoubtedly there is here a great cult-historical connexion.... The special characteristics of Israel's religious poetry developed against a background of general oriental culture. This is all the more probable as the Israelite liturgy to a large extent adopted the older cultic patterns of the East, with Canaan as intermediary" (I, p. 41). "Babylonian-Assyrian and Egyptian, and for all we know even Canaanite psalmography, "he claims," was fully developed even before it started in Israel, and it is a fact that Israel has used these foreign patterns" (II, 157).

A more discerning appraisal and one, it seems, closer to the truth, is offered by the authors of the *BJ* fascicule on the Psalms (cf, pp. 58-64). For what regards doctrine, they think, affinities are scarce while discrepancies abound. True, the Egyptians knew one God, almighty providence and judge. In Egypt also, the scribes exhorted their disciples to "be upright of heart" (Ps 7:11) for the sake of God, hidden and near. They seem to have had a certain knowledge of values related to interior life: the presence of the divine spirit in the heart of the just, the craving for God, submission to his will, the meaning of silence. Henotheism, represented in one way or another, in different periods, coexisted, however, with the polytheist cult, while in Israel opposition to idolatry never failed.

It can be conceded that the Israelite's representation of the after-life (cf. §14d) reflects common Semitic belief. As a consequence, the system of temporal retribution was maintained in spite of its obvious shortcomings. It prevented also the spread in Israel of necromancy, of magic and of superstitious cults of the dead, by blocking belief in the Osiris type of judgment. In Oriental paganism sin was viewed primarily as a physical stain, to be eliminated by magic rites. Evil spirits were expelled with incantations, and omens were believed to reveal the future. Complicated myths accounted for the origin and order or disorder of the physical world and a system of nature rites was believed to assure national prosperity. In contrast, the Psalms picture sin as a violation of the moral order. Only repentance can erase it; idolatry and paganism are condemned; magic is not even mentioned.

(b) Comparative material from Mesopotamia

In 1875 E. Schrader published the first critical edition of Assyro-Babylonian texts related to the Bible. Ten years later it appeared in English: *The Cuneiform Inscriptions and the Old Testament*, vols. I-II (London, 1885-1888), translated from the second enlarged edition. At the end of the nineteenth century A. Jeremias edited *Der alte Orient* in several volumes, containing a mass of data on the ancient Near-East cultures. A few years later he brought to light a very informative work (in German) on the Old Testament in the light of the ancient Orient. About the same period F. Winkler was also active in a similar field. He is, with Jeremias, a leading representative of the so-called "pan-Babylonian school," which proclaimed the existence of a uniform pattern of religion and cult, dominating in all essentials the whole civilization of the ancient East. "According to the pan-Babylonians," writes Mowinckel (II, p. 240), "it was the supposed old-Babylonian *Weltanschauung* and culture developed on an astronomical and scientific basis which always underlay religious and cultic symbolism." This reflects quite exactly the sonorous title of one of Winckler's essays: *Himmels- und Weltenbild der Babylonier als Grundlage der Weltanschauung und Mythologie aller Völker*. The great Babylonian vogue subsided and the idea of a common ritual pattern was put forward by the "Myth and Ritual School" (cf. §8d). With the discovery of *Ras Shamra*, a new trend, a very serious one indeed, has developed, in which Canaanite-Ugaritic patterns of thought and expression are scientifically investigated and applied to biblical research (see below).

In the beginning of this century H. Zimmern published in *Der alte Orient* collection (1905 and 1911) two anthologies *Babylonian hymns and prayers*. P. Dhorme was not far behind in the *Etudes Bibliques*, with *Choix de textes religieux Assyro-Babyloniens* (Paris, 1907). Then in 1912 A. Schollmeyer edited Sumerian-Babylonian hymns and prayers to the Sun-god Shamash. Ten years later, F. Stummer made a detailed comparison of the formal similaritiees between the Sumerian and Akkadian hymns and the Hebrew psalms, and concluded that "although the latter showed considerable freedom in their development, they must be regarded as dependent in origin upon the former either directly or indirectly through the culture of Canaan" (A.R. Johnson, *The Old Testament and Modern Study*, p. 187). In the first extensive study of the subject published in English, G. R. Driver examined "The Psalms in the

Light of Babylonian research" (*The Psalmists,* Oxford 1926, pp. 109-175) and came to the conclusion that the discovery of such analogies does not in itself constitute proof of direct dependence. In fact, he held, notes Johnson, that these analogies "may well be due to a quite independent functioning of the human mind or even to a common heritage, and that, if there was any Babylonian influence, this must have been conveyed through the Canaanite channels" (*ibid.*). This judgment would be confirmed by the later studies of J. Begrich, in ZAW 46, 1928, p. 221ff (on the expression of confidence in the Israelite and Babylonian individual laments), of C. G. Cumming, *The Assyrian and Hebrew Hymns of Praise* (New York, 1934), of G. Widengren, *The Accadian and the Hebrew Psalms of Lamentation as Religious Documents* (Stockholm, 1937), of R. G. Castellino, *Le lamentazioni individuali e gli inni in Babilonia e in Israele* (Torino, 1939), of C. Westermann, *The Praise of God in the Psalms* (Richmond, 1965), p. 36-51. Among the latest publications of Sumerian and Akkadian hymns and prayers may be mentioned: A. Falkenstein and W. von Soden, *Sumerische und Akkadische Hymnen und Gebete* (Zurich-Stuttgart, 1953) and W. H. Ph. Römer, *Sumerische "Königs-hymnen" der Isin-Zeit* (Leiden, 1965). G. Widengren believes that the Israelite laments have developed under the influence of their Akkadian counterpart, "though not directly, but by the way of a Canaanitic cult-literature whose existence we are compelled to assume" (*op. cit.,* p. 315). Cf. also J. Krecher, *Sumerische Kultlyric* (Wiesbaden, 1966).

Of *various similarities* usually quoted only a few can be recalled here (the exact referenes can be found in almost any of the works mentioned). The Babylonian psalms, very often literal translations of Sumerian originals, are also characterized by the use of parallelism. A Babylonian psalmist complains:

> "I cried unto my god, but he showed me not his face;
> I implored my goddess, but her head is not lifted up."

This can be compared with the prayer of the Hebrew psalmist:

> "Hide not your face from me:
>   do not in anger repel your servant" (27:9).

The *NAB* translation of Ps 16:9 is: "Therefore my heart is glad and my soul rejoices." "My soul" here has been substituted for the MT "my glory." What should be read in fact is "my liver" (similar word in Hebrew and Babylonian: root *kbd* meaning also "glory"). In Babylonian poetry the liver is often regarded as an organ of emotion and gives a good sense here. Besides, there is a Babylonian saying: "May thy heart be at ease, may thy liver be appeased!" (cf. G. R. Driver, *op. cit.*, p. 123).

A Babylonian could address his god as *shadū rabū*, "great mountain." For this and other reasons, modern commentators understand the divine title *El Shaddai*, current in patriarchal times (cf. Gn 17:1), as meaning "the Mountain God" (cf. Pss 68:15; 91:1; CV="the Almighty"). Much has been made of the fact that the cry "how long?" with which the psalmists sometimes open their prayer (cf. Ps 79:5), is of frequent occurrence also in Babylonian prayers, often repeated several times (see in *Ps 13). The same is true of various anthropomorphisms said of the divinity, like "Arouse Thyself...awake." But in all these instances, Driver observes (p. 131), the resemblances are hardly more than verbal. Parallels are sometimes invoked which rest on expressions that can hardly be avoided in speech! "The close formal affinity between the Babylonian and the Old Testament psalms...is due primarily to the fact that the poetic canons were the same all over the ancient Near East," H. Ringgren believes (*The Faith of the Psalmists*, p. 116).

We read in a royal psalm: "May he rule from sea to sea, and from the River to the ends of the earth" (72:8). The same maximal boundaries are assigned to Abraham's descendants in Si 44:21. Another version, also idealized, of the ambitious claims, can be read in Deuteronomy: "Every place where you set foot shall be yours: from the desert and from Lebanon, from the Euphrates River to the Western Sea, shall be your territory" (11:24). The two interior seas of Israel, *yam kinneret* (the lake of Galilee) and *yam hammelaḥ* (the sea of salt), as also *hayyam haggadôl* (the great sea) are mentioned as boundaries (cf. Nb 34:6, 11f; Jos 15:2, 5). Yet geographical expressions like those read in Ps 72:8, even in the figurative, came to Palestine from Mesopotamia.

Divine myth patterns

The Babylonian *Epic of Creation* "tells how Marduk after a long struggle defeated *Tiamat*, who personified the formless, watery chaos which preceded the making of the universe, and her fearful brood of monsters and, having cut her into two halves, made of them the upper and lower firmaments; half he spread above to form the heavens and half be-low to become the earth" (Driver, p. 140). Demythologized elements of the Epic have been pointed out in the Genesis narrative of creation and in other biblical passages (cf. §11a). The *Tᵉhôm*, "the Deep" (CV: "the ocean") of Ps 104:6 and Gn 1:2 recall philologically the Babylonian *Tiamat* (feminine personification), while the action of Marduk seems reflected in the smashing of the dragon's heads and in the crushing of Leviathan and Rahab (Pss 74:13, 14; 89:11). In other passages the awesome might of the waters, almost personified, only vaguely alludes to the primeval rebellious ocean (cf. Pss 18:16; 33:7; 46:3f; 77:17; 93:3f; 104:5-9). In Babylonian legend the Sheol was guarded by seven or even fourteen gates. This imagery could be reflected in the psalmist's call to Yahweh, "you who have raised me up from the gates of death" (Ps 9:14).

"Yahweh and Marduk," writes Driver, "are both portrayed as equip-ped with the panoply of thunder and lightning and riding upon the storm-winds. While, however, to the monotheistic Hebrew it was Yahweh alone who controlled the forces of nature, the Babylonian as-cribed different spheres of influence to different gods" (p. 151). The "sons of God" or the "gods," mentioned in the psalms (cf. 29:1; 58:1; 82:1, 6; 89:8) are represented, it seems, as performing for Yahweh functions analogous to those which the Igigi, "the gods of the upper world" (who represented the host of visible stars) and the Anunnaki, "the gods of the lower world", performed for the principal deities of the Babylonian Pantheon (cf. Driver, p. 153; also below §10g).

According to Ps 19:5f, God "has pitched a tent there for the sun, which comes forth like the groom from his bridal chamber and, like a giant, joyfully runs its course." Although the poet probably understood the "sun" in its natural meaning, the imagery could have been originally associated with the sun-god *Shamash*. A stone tablet represents the As-syrian divinity enthroned in the tabernacle floating on the heavenly ocean (*ANEP*, n. 529). King Nabuapaliddin (Middle of the 9th cent. B.C.) stands before the god, in whose tabernacle also dwelled the bride. The divine bridegroom was known to come forth out of the sea to pur-sue his enemies. During Manasseh's long reign (c. 687-642), the syncre-tist cult he supported included worship of "all the host of heaven" (2 K 21:3). Exampes of Mesopotamian influence on the psalms will be given in the introduction to Pss 13, 18, 21, 101, 124 and others (cf. also the bibliog., under the name **B. Bonkamp).**

(c) *Egyptian hymnology and the Psalter*

Although Egyptology has grown into a science of its own, with numerous and outstanding contributors, very few comprehensive studies have been published on the possible relations between Egyptian and Hebrew psalmody. Fortunately we have one now: the monumental work of A. Barucq, *L' expression de la louange divine et de la prière dans la Bible et en Égypte* (Le Caire, 1962), 586 pp. In the Introduction Barucq reveals that his work intends to be for the Egyptian what R. G. Castellino's has been for the Babylonian literature. What he does in fact is to examine one by one the various elements of the biblical psalms (beginning, development, conclusion) or their many categories, and to compare them, in structure and content, with their Egyptian counterpart. The bibliography (10 pages), the footnotes and the reference tables indicate what amount of work has been spent on the composition of this study: "The expression of divine praise and of prayer in the Bible and in Egypt." Some of the conclusions Barucq has drawn at the end of his book (pp. 502-512) can be useful to our limited purpose.

These conclusions are derived from the examination of various hymnal elements:

I. No significant analogies can be reported in respect to the *initial elements* (title, introduction, salutation, invocation).

II. As for the *central element* of the poems:

1) Similarities are discernible in the *laudatory developments,* but no significant divergence or resemblance in the prayers. Not enough is known yet of Egyptian *poetic devices* to prove affinities of psalmography between Egypt and Israel.

2) With respect to *ideas* the Egyptian writers sing the names of the gods, their sanctuaries, their genealogies and their mythic performances. Nothing of that, of course, in Israel, where the attributes of God are praised, mainly his kindness and transcendence. In his stand on God's unicity the Israelite psalmist seems closer to the Semitic than to the Egyptian viewpoint. But *fellowship* of man with God is stressed in the laudatory developments of the Hebrew and Egyptian poems. There may have been literary contacts, but neither imitation nor borrowing can be substantiated. The Israelite psalmist has clearly kept his originality in his treatment of divine glorification by the universe and man. A special case, however, can be made of °Ps 33 and °Ps 104. The possibility of *dependence* towards Egypt cannot be excluded in the development of themes emanating from wisdom and royal circles or from El Amarna (see next section).

III. Other results have appeared in these psalmic elements where the singer or writer gives a more *personal expression* of his religious sentiments.

1) The protestation of confidence, a theme of royal praise, and the writings of the "poor" are areas of Egyptian literature which may be related to Israelite counterpart. In Israel, however, the expression is more explicit.

2) The possibility of comparison is also attested in the themes related to self-presentation: declaration of innocence and of good conduct, negative confessions (see on °Ps 101) and also confessions of guilt. In this also the Israelite is more personal, and he follows his own tradition, so that a borrowing from Egypt seems improbable.

3) As for the lament theme, it is in Egypt, as in Assyria and Israel, the normal reaction to particular situations. The expression of the natural feelings corresponds to the respective religious conceptions.

4) In the sphere of *personal prayers,* few biblical psalms (cf. Pss 14:7; 20: 10; 25:22) show any affinity to the Egyptian cultic prayers sometimes joined to the hymns. Similarities abound, however, in the *demands* expressed by the "poor" and in the motives set forth to obtain divine favor. No real imitation though is necessarily indicated in these cases, no more than in the prayers for the king, except perhaps in °Ps 72.

IV. Examined in the light of *Egyptian literature* in general, the biblical psalms suggest that the Psalmographers of Israel, the Professional at least, could have known in Egypt or at home from Egyptian scribes (cf. *RB* 1939, pp. 394-405) the classics of Egypt's sapiential, royal and religious literature. Texts related to wisdom and royal thought pattern are siginificant enough to indicate an Egyptian influence on the redaction of Pss 1, 2, 33, 34, 104 and 110. Similarities have been pointed out between some expressions of Pss 34, 112, 119, 128 and texts of the tomb of Petosiris (cf. G. Lefebvre in *RB* 122, pp. 481-488).

How the Israelites came into contact with the Egyptian hymnology is for us a question of lesser importance. Indirect contact through Phoenicia is likely, Barucq believes, for the period which extends from David to Ahab (c. 1000-850), while direct contact becomes possible with the accession of Solomon. R. Tournay (*RB* 1959, p. 179) reads in a convergence of allusions that the influence of Egypt on Israel was greater around the end of the monarchy (6th cent. B.C.) while the Babylonian influence would spread from the period of the first exile (in 596). The Israelite *intelligentsia* of scribes and annalists seems to have functioned according to an Egyptian pattern and the story of Joseph in Egypt reflects the writer's good knowledge of Egyptian administration.

Some years ago, Barucq notes, the ark of the covenant, the temple, the altar, the priestly vestments of the Israelite cult were declared related to Egyptian patterns. More recently, however, the attention is drawn to Phoenician and Canaanite models. The presence of Lebanese among the builders of the temple would in fact favor the second hypothesis. Indications from various sources, like the burial narratives of Jacob and Joseph, seem to confirm that Israel accepted cultural ties with Egypt but firmly resisted any influence properly religious. If Israelite scribes were trained in Egypt, it would have been in the profane type of schools, not in the religious ones, associated with the temple (cf. B. Van der Walle, *La transmission des textes littéraires égyptiens*, Bruxelles, 1948, p. 13ff).

Finally, Barucq stresses in his conclusions the originality of the Israelite expression of prayer and praise. Any foreign element used has been assimilated, reorientated and transformed to fit a particular thought pattern on God, man, the universe and their mutual relations. Racial diversity characterized the origins of Israel: "Thus says the Lord God to Jerusalem: By origin and birth you are of the land of Canaan; your father was an Amorite and your mother a Hittite" (Ez 16:3). But God's own people developed its own religious personality and centuries later foreign influence appeared like a fading souvenir. It is a difficult task to distinguish the contributions of so many diverse generations.

In *The Psalmists* (Oxford, 1926) H. Gressmann had a word to say about the origin of *Ps 104. "Just as the temple of Jerusalem was modelled on an Egyptian-Phoenician sanctuary, so behind Ps 104 we sense an Egyptian-Phoenician original, not specifically the psalm of Ikhnaton (as is often urged), but more generally an Egyptian psalm in Phoenician guise" (p. 20). When, in verse 16, the Lord is said to have planted the cedars of Lebanon, it is, seemingly, as substituted to Adonis, the Baal of Lebanon (p. 19). The mention in the same verse of "ships" and crocodiles (cf. "Leviathan") would also suggest an Egyptian prototype. Phoenician geography, it seems, is alluded to in verse 18: "The high mountains are for wild goats; the cliffs are a refuge for rock-badgers."

In his contribution to *The Psalmists*, A. M. Blackman has examined "The Psalms in the Light of Egyptian Research" (pp. 177-197). The group of the 19th Dynasty (1320-1200) hymns, he writes, are imbued with the same spirit as many of the Hebrew psalms. In these hymns the sun-god appears as the good herdsman and as the judge of the poor, two titles frequently assigned to Yahweh in the psalms (cf. §11c). In two hymns god Amun is the judge who defends the cause of the poor (p. 182). Most of his other remarks concern analogies which will be noted in the present work (see on *Pss 1, 18, 21, 23, 30, 34, 101, 104, 110, 141 and others). In both the Hebrew psalms and the Egyptian hymns or prayers, Blackman concludes, "great emphasis is laid on justice and judgment as qualities alike of their deity and of the king. Both teach God's hatred of sin. His forgiveness of sins repented of, His preferring righteousness to sacrifice, His love and care for mankind and all His creatures, and His solicitude for the poor and distressed; both represent God in the rôle of the good shepherd or herdsman; and both, though the Hebrew writings much more frequently and emphatically, foretell the coming of the king who will reign in righteousness" (p. 190f; see on *Ps 23).

(d) The relevance of Canaanite-Ugaritic literature

Almost twenty years ago, when the present writer was studying Ugaritic under the able direction of Fr. Mitchell Dahood, the discoveries of Ras Shamra were still mostly the concern of a few orientalists. Now very few scholars will dare write anything on the Bible without at least a passing reference to the new data from Ugarit. In 1941 already, W. F. Albright could write: "It is not too much to say that all future investigations of the Book of Psalms must deal intensively with the Ugaritic texts" (*JBL* 1941, p. 438). Dahood has well followed this advice. In the Introduction to *Psalms I* of *The Anchor Bible* (New York, 1966), he writes: "...the primary scope of this study [is]... a translation and philological commentary which utilizes the linguistic information offered by Ras Shamra tablets" (p. XVII; cf. p. XV and 20). This, in spite of the fact that "psalms as such have not yet been unearthed at Ras Shamra" (p. XVII). In the Introduction to Dahood's *Psalms* can be read first hand information on the discoveries of Ras Shamra-Ugarit and up-to-date insights of their value for biblical studies. This has also been expressed by W. L. Moran. Having recalled that the decipherment of the Ras Shamra tablets disclosed a hitherto unknown Northwest Semitic dialect, he writes: "More important, the contents of the tablets were principally epic literature. Contacts with biblical literature were immediately apparent, and today there are few areas of biblical studies unaffected by the discoveries at Ugarit. Prosody, textual criticisms, literary history, biblical theology—all have a pre-and post-Ugaritic date" ("The Hebrew Language in its Northwest Semitic Background," in *The Bible and the Ancient Near-East*, New York, 1965, p. 64).

The Ras Shamra-Ugarit discoveries

Ras Shamra or "Fennel Promontory" (Dahood, p. XVIII) is the mound on the north Syrian coast which concealed the ancient city of

Ugarit, where C. F. A. Schaeffer of Strasbourg has been excavating since 1929. "The discoveries," writes Dahood, "include enormous quantities of pottery, weights, bronzes, jewelry, statuary, stelae, tombs, constructions such as temples, palaces, private homes, sanitation systems and, above all, texts" (p. XVIII). Most of the tablets are written in a previously unknown cuneiform alphabet of 29 or 30 signs. "The widely held view that Ugaritic is a Canaanite dialect whose closest affinity is to biblical Hebrew, especially in the poetic books, has been winning the day," thinks Dahood (p. IX).

According to C. R. Gordon, "the tablets start in the first half of the fourteenth century B.C., though the oral composition of the literary texts generally goes back to earlier periods. Ugaritic texts continued to be written down to the latter part of the thirteenth century" (*Ugaritic Textbook*, Rome, 1965, p. 1). Gordon explains the special importance of Ugaritic in cultural studies mainly from the fact that "Ugaritic literature was produced at the crossroads of the Cuneiform and East Mediterranean Worlds, and of Canaan and Anatolia, during the pivotal era of ancient Near East history: the Amarna age" (p. 2). The longest and most important composition of the Ugaritic texts is the Baal cycle, a collection of episodes about the Canaanite gods (about 2000 lines). On Baal see W. F. Albright, *Yahweh and the Gods of Canaan* (London, 1968) 108-112. Next in importance are the *Legend of King Keret*, a semi-historical poem (about 500 lines) and the *Epic of Aqhat* (about 400 lines). One of two other mythological poems is named after its invocation, *The Beautiful and Gracious Gods*, and describes the birth of the twin deities Dawn and Dusk. The other tablets treat of a variety of subjects (cf. Dahood, p. XIX).

Phoenicia   and   Canaan

Ugaritic has much in common with Phoenician and Canaanite under various aspects: language, literature, culture. The Canaanites are known to most people only as the unhappy precursors of Israel in Palestine. Albright contributes some clarity to the subject in introducing an article of his: "However, if we remember that the word 'Canaanite' is historically, geographically, and culturally synonymous with 'Phoenician,' the title [of his article] immediately becomes more impressive, since it also deals with the role of the Phoenicians in the history of civilization. For convenience we shall employ 'Canaanite' below to designate the Northwest

Semitic people and culture of western Syria and Palestine before the twelfth century B.C. and the term 'Phoenician' to indicate the same people and culture after this date" ("The Role of the Canaanites in the History of Civilization," in *The Bible and the Ancient Near-East*, p. 438). The name "Canaan" is a West Semitic expression meaning "belonging to [the land of] Purple," and the Greek name "Phoenicia" probably refers to the "purple" industry. "Through the conquest of Palestine by Israel and of Syria by the Aramaeans, these two peoples became in large measure the heirs of Canaanite culture." This is one aspect of Albright's view of the important part played by the Canaanites in the ancient Near East. The Canaanite background of Phoenician civilization has been enormously broadened by the discoveries at Ugarit. "C. Virolleaud," notes Albright (p. 44f) "has now published the overwhelming majority of the alphabetic tablets, which are written in a script strongly influenced by the Linear "Phoenician alphabet and in a dialect closely related to the ancestral Canaanite of Phoenicia and Palestine."

Our knowledge of the "Canaanite" language has greatly increased with the discoveries of Ras Shamra. It was partly known by the Amarna letters. As is well known, Amarna, about 200 miles south of Cairo, was the capital of Egypt during the later years of the reign of "monotheist" Akhnaton (Amenophis IV: c. 1364-1347). "Over 200 of these letters were sent by vassal Canaanite kings to the Egyptian court in the early fourteenth century B.C. Composed by Canaanite scribes little conversant with the Babylonian language they were employing, besides containing numerous Canaanite glosses to Babylonian words, they constantly betray in form and idiom the native Canaanite speech of their writers" (W. L. Moran, *art. cit.*, p. 60). The language of these letters has advanced greatly our understanding of the early history of Hebrew and their content throws light on life in Palestine at that period. New data from Mari and Ugarit indicate, on the other hand, that Manetho (3rd cent. A.D.) was probably right in designating as "Phoenicians" the Hyksos conquerors of Egypt (c. 1720-1560 B.C. On Canaanite influence see also §13b).

Canaanite literature and the Psalms

Some areas of comparison between the Bible and the Canaanite literature as reflected in the Ugaritic texts have been singled out by Albright: "Verbally and stylistically these specimens of Canaanite literature show striking similarity to Hebrew poetry, especially to such early poems as the Song of Miriam (Ex 15), the Song of Deborah (Jg 5), the Blessing of Moses (Dt 33), the 29th and 68th Psalms. There is somewhat less influence in many other early poems, in the Psalter and outside it. There is also a great deal of less direct influence on didactic literature, as well as some striking direct influence on archaistic compositions such as the first two thirds of the Psalm of Habakkuk. This influence is particularly clear in the early repetitive style as first isolated by C. F. Burney, as compared directly with Ugaritic style by H. L. Ginsberg, and as first utilized for the chronology of literary style by the writer and his pupils. There is no doubt whatever that Hebrew poetic literature was under immeasurable obligation to Canaanite poets of the Bronze Age, who fashioned the vehicle and cultivated the style which have given biblical verse most of its formal appeal. There are striking parallels between the prosody and the style of Canaanite and of early Akkadian poetry, especially Akkadian poetry of the so-called hymnal-epic category, which clearly goes back to pre-Sumerian time for its roots" (art. cit., p: 453).

Ras Shamra and the Bible is a subject that has received considerable attention. Only a few studies can be singled out: W. Baumgartner, "Ras Shamra und das Alte Testament," *Th. Revue* 12 (1940) 163ff; 13 (1941) 1ff; 85ff; 157ff; W. F. Albright, "The Old Testament and the Canaanite Language and Literature," *CBQ* 7 (1945) 5-31; R. De Langhe, *Les textes de Ras Shamra-Ugarit et leurs rapports avec le milieu biblique de l'Ancien Testament,* I-II (Gembloux-Paris, 1945); J. Gray, *The Legacy of Canaan: the Ras Shamra Texts and their Relevance to the Old Testament* (Leiden, 1957 and 1965); M. Dahood, "Ugaritic Studies and the Bible," *Greg* 43 (1962) 55-79; A. S. Kapelrud, *The Ras Shamra Discoveries and the Old Testament* (Noran, Okla, 1963). Other studies concern the Psalter: see the bibliography under the names of J. Coppens, F. M. Cross, F. C. Fensham, H. L. Ginsberg, C. H. Gordon, H. G. Jefferson, L. M. Muntingh, J. Obermann, R. T. O'Callaghan, J. H. Patton, R. Rendtorff, C. Schedl, and M. Dahood, *Psalms* III, pp. XXIIff. That multiple factors have to be considered in evaluating extrabiblical influence in the composition of the Old Testament is illustrated by R. Gordis, "Was Koheleth a Phoenician? Some Obesrvations on Methods in Research," *JBL* 74 (1955) 103-114. See H. Donner for the use of Ugaritic in Pss 8:2; 19:25a; 29:2; 42:2; 73:9; 74:13f; 92: 10; 93:3.

Psalm 29, in particular, has been the object of various studies. Back in 1950, F. M. Cross could write: "In 1936, H. L. Ginsberg drew up conclusive evidence that Ps 29 is an ancient Canaanite Baal hymn, only slightly modified for use in the cultus of Yahweh. Accordingly, Ps 29 takes on a rare new importance for the analysis of Canaanite prosodic canons and their influence on Israelite psalmody. The Ugaritic literature is largely epic, and while refrains and lyric or odic passages appear, we do not have from Ugarit a clear cut example of the Canaanite cultic psalm. Thus Ps 29 fills a real gap in the extant Canaanite literature" (*BASOR* 117, 1950, p. 19). Yet it must be noted that as yet no Canaanite psalm comparable to the biblical psalms has been found, in spite of B. Margulis, "A Ugaritic Psalm (*RS* 24.252)," *JBL* 89 (1970) 303-12. The somewhat extravagant language which is occasionally used in the Amarna letters in addressing the Pharaoh (see on *Ps 139) may be derived from Canaanite hymnology, and so may point to the existence of Canaanite prototypes for the Hebrew psalms (cf. A. R. Johnson, art. cit., p. 188). Virtually every word of Ps 29 can now be duplicated in older Canaanite texts (Dahood, p. 175).

Canaanite "archaisms" in the Psalms

Having noted the tendency of prayer to perpetuate the common language, secular or sacred, of an earlier period, M. Tsevat sees this confirmed indirectly by a study of the Psalms. "If one can find linguistic features which are common to the biblical psalms and Canaanite dialects but which are not at all or only to a limited extent shared by the rest of the Bible, one may safely infer that this is a common heritage from a time when Hebrew and other branches of Canaanite were not yet separated. The language of Hebrew devotional poetry, one would conclude, has preserved remnants of an earlier linguistic stage which has been lost or almost lost in common contemporary Hebrew" (*A Study...*p. 47).

Such principles would seem to corroborate the new tendency to assign earlier rather than later dates to psalms reputed to have Canaanite associations. The Ugaritic texts would show that much of the phraseology of the Psalter was current in Palestine long before the writing prophets and that intrabiblical literary dependence becomes difficult to handle (cf. Dahood, p. XXX). Linguistic observations, for example, would help in fixing the general date of Ps 48: "From the distinct archaizing tendency of this psalm, it is not unreasonable to suggest the end of the sixth century B.C., as a likely period for its composition. This was an archaizing age, and the hymn is replete with archaisms. Recent studies in Deutero-Isaiah, Ezekiel, Job and Proverbs have shown that most of 'the close stylistic and verbal parallels between Israelite and Canaanite literature belong to the Exilic and early post-exilic periods'" (CBQ 1954, p. 19). Tournay notes also that with the exile learned Jews, scattered in various areas, came into contact with the neighboring cultures (RB 1956, p. 125). The dangers of syncretism having subsided with a strengthened Yahwism, foreign elements could be more freely admitted in the literary and even in the religious circles. Albright discovers in Pss 118 and 128 archaizing phrases and a tendency to imitate ancient repetitive forms (in *Fs. Mowinckel*, p. 8f). *Deliberate archaizing* is certainly a feature of some biblical books, of Job especially, in which the "archaic" divine title *Shaddai* is continuously used. So the use of "archaisms" to date a psalm presents its problems, as also the use of Ugaritic vocabulary (cf. *JBL* 1955, pp. 103-114; about Koheleth). Tournay believes that intrabiblical comparison is the safest method (RB 1956, p. 125; cf. §5e).

Not many specific affinities have been noted here between Ugaritic or Canaanite material and the biblical psalms. The reason is that details will be mentioned in the study of the psalms themselves (see on *Pss 18, 29, 48, 67, 68, 73, 92, 93, 139, and others).

III.   The Beliefs of Piety

In his *Das kultische Problem der Psalmen* (Stuttgart, 1936), G. Quell postulated a basic and essential difference between cult and piety (cf. §7b, 8b). H. Ringgren rejects such a sharp distinction and considers it unfair "to regard the psalmists as lacking in religious experience or personal piety on the grounds that they nourished their religious life with that which they experienced in the cult. Instead we have to try to understanding their religious experience in precisely this cultic setting" (*The Faith*...p. 21). In any case very few will put in doubt the fact that the Psalms represent a summit in the expression of religious experience, of praise and of prayer. No systematic exposition of religion or of doctrine will be found in the Psalter. The psalmists speak to God rather than of God. But their piety (understood in its broadest sense) is formulated in the context of the Israelite religion and cult, which it reflects in part. Although one could hardly speak of a theology of the Psalms, it is obvious that in them are found dominant themes and patterns of religious thought consistent enough to be called "the beliefs of piety." Not all of these will be recorded here, since our intention is to suggest rather than to achieve what could be done in this domain. Neither will all the items be seen to fit equally well in the classification proposed. Yet a special effort has been made to avoid reducing the material assembled to modern thought patterns.

The psalmists' interests are centered on God, obviously in the hymns, but also, indirectly at least, in the other psalms, since the main concern always remains the glory of God, not the welfare of the psalmist or even of the nation. If, on the other hand, religion is man's response to his God, then the character of a religion is determined by the nature of the God worshipped. It would seem then that a classification centered on God would have a better chance of reflecting the psalmists' own frame of mind.

§10. THE GOD OF THE PSALMISTS

Typical formulations of the *main interest* of the psalmists are found in the hymns: "Enter his gates with thanksgiving, his courts with praise" (100:4); "With the ten-stringed lyre chant his praises" (33:2); "Give to the Lord glory and praise" (29:1); "Give to the Lord the glory due his name" (29:2); "Sing to him a new song" (33:3); "Proclaim among the nations his deeds" (9:12); "Sing joyfully to the Lord, all you lands" (100:1). Two passages have here a particular relevance:

I will give thanks to you, O Lord, with all my heart;
 I will declare all your wondrous deeds.
I will be glad and exult in you;
 I will sing praise to your name, Most High (9:2f).

Give thanks to him; bless his name, for he is good:
 the Lord, whose kindness endures forever,
 and his faithfulness, to all generations (100:4f).

The *motives for praise* expressed in this last text include the goodness, the kindness and the faithfulness of God. These and other *divine attributes* to be praised figure among the basic "beliefs of piety" which form the background of so many psalms. Although these beliefs do not contradict the dictates of reason and of theology, their reality is suggested to the psalmists' faith from other sources: cultic traditions, history of Israel, personal religious experience and common ancient Oriental thought patterns. From the psalmists' way of speaking to God we learn much about what they thought their God was. Any attempt to present *the God of the Psalmists* involves a choice of topics which might seem arbitrary. Those proposed for exposition reflect the more dominant themes and the more characteristic ones.

(a) "Where is their God?"

Certainly at the time of Thomas Aquinas (13th cent.) and in the centuries that followed, the problem of the *existence of* God has been posed in terms both of theory and of practice. Reflecting the mood of his times the biblical man had little concern for the question, "Does God exist?" Theoretical atheists were few. But two questions were likely to be asked, one by the non-Israelites: "Which God is the strongest?" another by the "godless": "Is God concerned with us?" The psalmists' prime interest for the glory of God is reflected in the motivations put forward in their cry for help: "Why should the nations say, Where is their God?" (79:10) and "Why should the pagans say, Where is their God?" (115: 2). The answer of the psalmists: "Our God is in heaven; whatever he will, he does" (115:3). Another answer is even more explicit: "All that the Lord wills he does in heaven and on earth, in the seas and in all the deeps" (135:6; cf. Ps 10:4; 11-14).

The practical atheists—there were perhaps relatively as many then as today—live and act as if God did not exist (see on *Ps 14). This is what the Babylonians used to call "living *ina ramânishu*," i.e., living by oneself, on one's own resources, without dependence on God (Ringgren, p. 35). This is the essence of sin and for that reason, because he attributed to himself what God has done by him, was the king of Assyria condemned with his nation (Is 10:12-19). Another prophet formulates a similar reaction as regards evildoers:

> You have worried the Lord with your words,
>   yet you say, "How have we wearied him?"
> By your saying, "Every evildoer
>   is good in the sight of the Lord,
> And he is pleased with him";
>   or else, "Where is the just God?" (Ml 2:17)

On the practical acknowledgment or denial of God's existence wisdom stands or falls: "The fool says in his heart, There is no God" (Ps 53:2; cf. Jb 2:10); "The fear of the Lord is the beginning of wisdom; prudent are we all who live by it" (111:10).

(b) Praise of the Name

The praise of the psalmists often goes to the *name of God* (cf. 18:50; 61:9). God had various names, which have been studied over and over again (cf. P. Van Imschoot, *Theology of the Od Testament*, ch. I, §2). Many of these names appear in the Psalms (cf. H. J. Kraus, *Psalmen*, pp. 197-201) and will be analyzed at the opportune moment. In antiquity it was believed that a person's self was concentrated in its name (cf. Ex 3: 13f; Jg 13:17). The name would give meaning and bestow full existence to its bearer (cf. Gn 2:19f, 23). To know somebody's name was to gain power over him (cf. Gn 32:29), because a power, a *dunamis* was supposed to rest in the name: "O God, by your name save me, and by your might defend my cause" (Ps 54:3). This striking formulation, Weiser writes, presupposes "that the divine name possesses a special miraculous power, a conception whose roots reach down to ideas about magic."

A theology of God's name found clear expression shortly before and during the exile. With Deuteronomy, writes E. Jacob, we are on the road to the hypostatizing of the name of Yahweh, the granting it an independent existence (*Theology of the Old Testament*, p. 83). Texts like Zech 14:9 and Ps 8:2 (cf. Ps 48:11) reflect this tendency. A theology of the Name is also found in Ezekiel and Deutero-Isaiah. Psalm 20, which repeatedly mentions the "name of God" (vv 2, 6, 8), would belong to that period (cf. *RB* 1959, p. 162). In many other passages, however, even in Is 56:6 and Ps 103:1, the name is only a synonym for Yahweh himself. The phrase "name of the Lord" occurs about 100 times in 67 different psalms. The systematic study of these occurrences would be a worthwhile undertaking which we leave to others.

W. I. Wolverton (p. 28f) states that the "Deuteronomist historian" was aware of a problem: can God be localized in a temple? He resolved in a unique manner (cf. 1 K 8:27ff): God will not dwell in the temple but his name will (cf. Dt 12:5; 14:23; 16:2). But "there is little regard for this theological nicety in the Psalms" (expect perhaps Ps 74:7).

(c) *The living God, Eternal and Omnipresent*

That Yahweh is *the living God* figures among the very first beliefs of the Israelite. Even before monotheism was clearly formulated, life differentiated Yahweh from the other gods. Life is a mysterious reality which invades man with its power. So also, God the source of life. "Strongly typical in this respect is the sudden and unexpected appearance on the scene of history of the prophet Elijah, who justifies his interventions simply by the words, 'Yahweh is living' (1 K 17:1).... It is because they see in the Living One essentially the source of life that believers regard as the supreme aspiration of piety the ability to approach the living God (Pss 42:3; 84:3)," writes E. Jacob (p. 38f). The psalmist's conviction that with Yahweh "is the fountain of life" (36:10; cf. 85:7) is shared also by Jeremiah, revealing God's complaint: "They have forsaken me, the source of living waters" (2: 13; cf 17:13). In Proverbs the "fountain of life" is wisdom (13: 14; 16:22) or the fear of God (14: 27).

Because Yahweh is in the full sense "living," the "source of life," he is also *eternal*. It is another testimony to the theocentric thought of the psalmists, that they should contrast man's mortality with God's eternal being:

> Before the mountains were begotten
>> and the earth and the world were brought forth
>> from everlasting to everlasting you are God.
> You turn man back to dust,
>> saying, "Return, O children of men."
> For a thousand years in your sight
>> are as yesterday, now that it is past,
>> or as the watch of the night.
> You make an end of them in their sleep;
>> the next morning they are like the changing grass,
> Which at dawn springs up anew,
>> but by evening wilts and fades (90:2-6).

"God forever and ever" (48:15), "The Most High forever" (92:9), his name (135:13) and mercy (136:1) endure forever. Both "now and forever" the Lord is around his people (125:2). There is no speculation here on endless time or timeless being. Immutability rather seems to be meant, as in the following passage:

> My days are like a lengthening shadow,
>> and I wither like grass.
> But you, O Lord, abide forever,
>> and your name through all generations.
> I say: O my God,
> Take me not hence in the midst of my days;
>> through all generations your years endure,
> Of old you established the earth,
>> and the heavens are the work of your hands.
> They shall perish, but you remain
>> though all of them grow old like a garment (Ps 102: 12f, 25-27).

Eternity places God outside the limits of time. Yet both an accurate

notion of God's transcendence and the reality of his intervention in
history are maintained in the Bible. The clearest formulations of God's
eternity are found in the more recent biblical writings.

Like Ps 90, quoted above, Ps 139 displays its sapiential character
when it states that God is everywhere and knows everything. Such qualities of God's eternal being had been alluded to by the prophets (cf. Am
4:13; 9:2f; Jr 23:24). God who fashioned the heart of each, say the
psalmists, knows the secrets of the heart and all the works of men (Pss
33:15; 44:22). But the wicked man says in his heart, "God has forgotten;
he hides his face, he never sees" (Ps 10:11). To the godless who say,
"The Lord sees not; the God of Jacob perceives not," the psalmist re-
torts:

> Understand, you senseless ones among the people;
>   and, you fools, when will you be wise?
> Shall he who shaped the ear not hear?
>   or he who formed the eye not see?
> Shall he who instructs nations not chastise,
>   he who teaches men knowledge?
> The Lord knows the thoughts of men,
>   and that they are vain (94:8-11).

In the second century B.C. the belief in the *omnipresence and omniscience* could be expressed with all the desired clarity:

> He plumbs the depths and penetrates the heart;
>   their innermost being he understands.
> The Lord possesses all knowledge,
>   and sees from of old the things that are to come:
> He makes known the past and the future,
>   and reveals the deepest secrets.
> No understanding does he lack;
>   no single thing escapes him (Si 42:18-20).

(d) *The Holy One*

Some of the divine attributes are more closely linked to *the holiness of
God*. In its primitive notion holiness implies a concentration of power
and life. The person or object removed from normal usage is under the

dominion of a power which, like that of *mana* and *tabu,* can be either dangerous or beneficent (cf. E. Jacob, p. 86). An allusion to this primitive notion can be read in what happened to Uzzah when he tried to steady the sacred ark during its transfer to Jerusalem (2 S 6:6ff). This concentration of life and power accompanies the removal of the person or thing from ordinary life and normal usage. This idea of "separation" is implied in *qdš,* the basic root for the words meaning "sacred" or "holy." As expressing "fullness of power and life," holiness is rightly considered the main characteristic of Yahweh's deity.

"In the Old Testament religion," writes Jacob, "the power of holiness no more consists in prohibition, in the limitation of the sacred sphere, but in the power which communicates itself in order to bestow life" (p. 87; the sacred enclosure idea is not, however, absent from texts like Ex 19: 12f; cf. ScEcc, 1966, pp. 32, 41f). The subjection of holiness to Yahweh was so complete, he adds, that very often Yahweh is defined as "the holy one," the term holy being synonymous with the divine (Is 40:25; Ho 11:9); in other instances the terms God and holy are put in parallel (Is 5:24; Hab 3:3; Ps 71:22). God swears by his holiness (Am 4:2; Ps 89: 36) as he swears "by his very self" (Am 6:8).

Is it significant that Ps 111:9 should recall that God's name is "holy and awesome (=*nôrā':* 'terrible'), and that the inhabitants of Beth-Shemesh exclaimed: "Who can survive before Yahweh, the holy God"? (1 S 6:20). A tendency to identify holiness and deity can be read in the current phrase "in my holy name": Lv 20:3; Am 2:7; Pss 33:21; 103:1; 105:3; 106:47. Name, holiness and sacred fear appear together in the scene of the burning bush (Ex 3:11-15), and from this episode could well have originated the biblical association of the three notions, also illustrated by Ps 99:3: "Let them praise your great and awesome name; holy is he!" In this psalm, the refrain "holy is he" accompanies the invitation to tremble and prostrate before Yahweh, who in the sanctuary appears "in holy attire" (Pss 29:2; 96:9; 110:3). There is no clear distinction between holiness and glory (*kābôd*) as *predicated* of God. Whereas glory is more a terrifying manifestation (cf. Ps 29), holiness is a life-giving power, it "not only presents but gives itself" (E. Jacob, p. 88).

It is as *God of the covenant* (cf. §13c) that Yahweh manifests his holiness to his people in various acts of deliverance. The title *Holy One of Israel* is applied to God by Isaiah and Deutero-Isaiah, respectively 14 and 16 times. From Isaiah the expression spread to other writings: Pss 71:22;

78:41; 89:19; Jr 50:29; 51:6 and Ex 39:7. "Yahweh is the Holy One of Israel, notes Jacob, not because he is consecrated to Israel but because he has consecrated Israel to himself, and Israel itself is holy only because of this consecration to Yahweh" (p. 89).

(e) *Glorious and Great*

The *glory of God* then (see above) has close affinities with his holiness. The psalmists praise divine glory as the divine person itself:

High above all nations is the Lord;
    above the heavens is his glory (113:4).

Be exalted above the heavens, O God;
    above all the earth be your glory! (57:6).

In this last text and in Ps 72:19 (cf. Is 40:5; Hab 2:14) the *kābôd* is associated with the eschatological hope (cf. Ps 86:9 and §14). Glory, like holiness, befits the name of Yahweh (Pss 29:2; 66:2; 72:19): "Not to us, O Lord, not to us but to your name give glory because of your kindness, because of your truth" (Ps 115:1). "I *will glorify* your name forever," says another psalmist (86:12). God is holy in all his works (Ps 145:17), his glory is proclaimed by his wonderous deeds (96:3). But before coming to the "deeds of the Lord" it seems apposite to say something about the *greatness of God*.

It has been noted that the concept of holiness involves that of power. The "Holy One of Israel!" is also called "the Mighty One of Jacob" in the ancient oracles of Jacob (Gn 49:24) and in Ps 132:2, 5. God's power reveals itself especially in dominating the mighty waters (Pss 29:3; 65:8, 93:4; 104:7) and the effects it produces are described in the theophany themes (cf. §13d). In one of these a peculiar prayer is addressed to God: "Show forth, O God, your power, the power, O God, with which you took our part" (Ps 68:29).

When Jethro heard from the mouth of Moses what Yahweh had done for the Hebrews he declared: "Now I know that the Lord is a deity great beyond any other" (Ex 18:11). A psalmist formulated a similar "confession": "For I know that the Lord is great (*gdl*); our Lord is greater than all gods" (135:5). The *greatness of Yahweh* in relation to other gods is often proclaimed in the psalms (cf. 77:14; 86:8; 95:3; 96:4). In other psalms this greatness is implied by the praise addressed to the Lord: "Who is like you?" (35:10; 71:19; 89:9; 113:5; Ex 15:11). In the song of Hannah (1 S 2:2) and in Deuteronomy (32:31), the same idea occurs in a slightly different form: "There is no rock like our God." The worshiping congregation is often invited to *magnify* (*gdl*) the Lord, to proclaim his greatness: Pss 34:4; 35:27; 40:17; 69:31; 70:5; 96:3. The song of Hannah and innumerable praises have been recapitulated in this new and greater *magnificat* (Lk 1:46-55) which proclaimed, at the advent of the Kingdom, that the Lord is mighty, that holy is his name and that his mercy is for generation upon generation to those who fear him.

(f) *Of wondrous deeds*

God's greatness is manifested in his *wondrous deeds* (Ps 86:10), also called "glorious" (78:4), "awe-inspiring" (65:6), "tremendous" (66:3), "great wonders" (136:4; cf. 139:14) and "mighty words" (26:7; 71:17; 75:2; 96:3; 105:2). The greatness of God, the "wonderful" character of his works David extolled after receiving the promises through Nathan the prophet (see on *Ps 89 and §13b):

> Therefore you are magnified, O Lord God, because there is none like you: neither is there any God besides you, in all the things that we have heard with our ears. And what nation is there upon earth, as your people Israel, whom God went to redeem for a people to himself, and to make him a name, and to do for them great and terrible things, upon the earth, before the face of your people, whom you redeemed to yourself out of Egypt, from the nations and their gods? (2 S 7:22f).

The Lord alone is God (Ps 86:10), who alone does wondrous deeds (Ps 72:18), declare the psalmists. His works and his might are again mentioned in Ps 145, which shows a peculiar interest for the kingdom of God:

> Great is the Lord and highly to be praised;
>   his greatness is unsearchable.
> Generation after generation praises your works
>   and proclaims your might.
> They speak of the splendour of your glorious majesty
>   and tell of your wondrous works.

They discourse of the power of your terrible deeds
and declare your greatness (vv 3-6)

(g) Beyond all gods

If the NAB's "you alone are God," the RSV's "thou alone art God,"
the New Latin Psalter's *"tu solus es Deus"* do render correctly the original
Hebrew of Ps 86:10, then we have a remarkable affirmation of *pure
monotheism* (cf. 32:39). The *Jerusalem Bible,* however, translates the
verse a little differently: "All the pagans will come and adore you, Lord,
all will glorify your name; since you alone are great, you perform mar-
vels, you God, you alone." Nothing decisive can be drawn from the text
but it can serve to introduce a problem. In his contribution to *The
Psalmists* (Oxford, 1926), T. H. Robinson wrote on "The God of the
Psalmists" (pp. 23-44). Some of his reflections can be of interest to the
general reader. Although "there is no book in the Bible about which it is
harder to generalize than the Book of Psalms," certain elements of belief
do emerge as common to most psalmists, as is apparent from the preceding paragraphs. Besides, all the psalmists consider God as a person
above all other beings in status and power. Some questions can be asked
in connection with the following passages:

There is none like you among the gods, O Lord,
    and there are no works like yours (86:8).
For the Lord is a great God,
    and a great king above all gods (95:3).
For great is the Lord and highly to be praised;
    awesome is he, beyond all gods (96:4).
For I know that the Lord is great;
    our Lord is greater than all gods (135:5).

Read independently of any context these statements clearly imply that
the psalmists were not pure monotheists, that they admitted the existence of other deities of lower status, above whom Yahweh stood as
"supreme over all rivals." It is probable that in these passages the psalmists
did not intend to speculate on the reality of these other gods but simply
mentioned them as an element of praise: "It is, from some points of view,
a greater thing to be the master and Lord of all gods then to be master
and Lord of lower orders of being only" (T. H. Robinson, *art. cit.,* p.

27). That the mention of the "gods" is partly at least literary seems to be confirmed by the contexts in which the $b^e n \hat{e}$ 'elîm, the "sons of the gods," of the Canaanite pantheon, appear in a demythologized form as "spiritual beings" of Yahweh's celestial court (see on *Pss 29:1; 82:6; 89:6ff). In other psalms the "idols of the nations" are described as lifeless and without substance or final reality (Pss 115:2-7; 135:15-18). The conclusion is that no hasty judgment can be passed on the monotheism of the psalmists (see on *Ps 82).

In his article "The Sons of (the) God (s)" (ZAW 1964, 22-47), G. Cooke concentrates his attention on the following passages: Gn 1:26f, 3:22, 6:1-4, 11:7; Pss 29:1; 82:1b, 6 (with excursus on Dt 32:8f); 89:5-7; 1K 22:19; Is 6:2-4, 7f; Dt 33:2f; Jb 1:6; 2:1; 38:7; Dn 3: 25; 10:13, 20f. He finds a strong possibility that in Gn 1:26f; 3:22; 11:7 a conception of plurality of divine beings rather than "plural of majesty" is meant. In Ps 8:6 he woud read: "You have made him little less than gods." He has this to say about the 'elōhîm and the $b^e n \hat{e}$ elyôn of Ps 82:6f: "The statement that those who are gods shall nevertheless die like men appears to us to be an undeniable indication of the divine status of those who are so addressed; their (former) immortality is clearly presupposed" (p. 31). So not Israelite judges or rulers are meant. "It seems," he thinks, "that at some time an ancient mythological fragment dscribing 'Elyôn's lordship over the world was taken into Israelite tradition to express the same position of Yahweh vis-à-vis the peoples and the sons of God" (p. 34). In one of his conclusions Cooke affirms that in his opinion "the conception of a heavenly assembly" is not a purely literary from taken over by Israel but is "an element of the living pattern of Israelite faith." One reason for that is that "the Hebrews were practical monotheists or monolatrists rather than theoretical monotheists throughout most of the biblical period. The existence of gods other than Yahweh, gods of other nations, is frequently acknowledged in Old Testament writings (Jg 11:24 [?]; 1 S 26:19f; 1 K 11:5, 7 etc.). An explicit or theoretical monotheism is not reached until Jeremiah (e.g., 5:7; 10:2ff; 16:20) or Deutero-Isaiah (e.g., Is 41:21ff; 44: 9ff). Even in the books of these prophets the conception of a heavenly company finds expression" (p. 45). Finally, Cooke can conclude from the texts analyzed (see above) that "the true prophet. . . has access to the heavenly assembly's deliberations, acts as messenger and bearer of the divine counsel to the people, and is a representative of Yahweh who exhibits a kind of psychic identity with Yahweh" (p. 47).

In *The Old Testament against its Environment* (London, 1950), G. E. Wright has a chapter entitled "What great Nation hath a God like the Lord?" (Dt 4:7). It contains valuable insights on the Israelite belief in God against its environment. Introducing a quotation from Albright, he writes: "I know of no better summary in abstract terms of the conception of God in early Israel" (p. 29). This is the quotation: "The belief in the existence of only one God, who is the Creator of the world and the giver of all life; the belief that God is holy and just, without sexuality or mythology; the belief that God is invisible to man except under special conditions and that no graphic nor plastic representation of Him is permissible; the belief that God is not restricted to any part of His creation, but is equally at home in heaven, in the desert, or in Palestine; the belief that God is so far superior to all created beings, whether heavenly bodies, angelic messengers, demons, or false gods, that He remains absolutely unique; the belief that God has chosen Israel by formal compact to be His favored people, guided exclusively by laws imposed by Him" (W. F. Albright, *Archeology and the Religion of Israel*, Baltimore, 1942, p. 116).

§11. GOD AND MAN

The God of the psalmists is a personal being known also as the Creator, the Providence and the Savior of man. Justice and kindness characterize his divine rule and his attitude to all human beings, particularly to the worshipers of his name.

(a) *Creation and myth*

Karl Barth is quoted by E. Jacob as having written: "The covenant is the goal of creation, creation is the way to the covenant" (*Theology of the Old Testament*, p. 136). As a consequence, the idea of creation is secondary to that of the covenant; faith in God the Savior is more important than belief in God the Creator. Old Testament thought, it is noted, carefully avoids confusing the creation with the Creator, author of the *cosmos*, "a universe organized with wisdom where each thing has its place and is produced in its own time" (*ibid.*). God made the universe as an architect builds a house (Jb 38:4-7) or a temple (cf. Gn 1, 1-2, 4).

The relevance of the material universe to biblical thought is also apparent from *the cosmical background* of God's interventions: deliverance from Egypt, conquests of Joshua, victory over the Canaanites (cf. Jg 4-5). Deutero-Isaiah much later spoke of transformations on a cosmic scale which would precede or accompany the return of the exiles (cf. Is 49:8-26). The *cosmos* will be involved also in the events of the last days (cf. §14). The psalmists, like other biblical writers, have described what repercussions on nature produce the interventions or judgments of the theophany God (see §13d).

If there is a *"creation myth"* in the Old Testament (cf. §9b) it does not have the same meaning as in other religions. "Ancient Israel knew one or perhaps several creation myths whose traces can be detected less in the Genesis narratives than in certain passages of the prophets and of the poetic books. In texts such as Jb 7:12ff; 26:10-13; 38:8-11; Pss 74; 89:11ff; Is 51:9ff, we can gather that these ancient myths told of Yahweh's struggle with rival powers, with sea monsters like Rahab and Leviathan, and doubtless Babylonian traditions of the struggle of Baal with the sea were not alien to the composition of these myths. But in the narratives of Genesis and their poetic parallel in Ps 104, which are the only passages where theological reflection about the creation is exercised, mythological elements are clearly subordinated to history, so that we are here in the presence of a *history of creation* and not of a myth of creation; the features characteristic of myth are absent from it" (E. Jacob, p. 138). For example, "there is no trace in the Old Testament of theogony or theomachy" and "there is a lack of what is increasingly considered to be the essence of myth, namely repetition. A myth only lives in the measure in which it is repeated and actualized in ritual; thus the Babylonian myth of creation was recited and represented in the New Year festival, because each year it was necessary to celebrate the cosmic power of Marduk if one wished to assure the prosperity of men and things and above all that of Babylon, of which Marduk was the national god" (*ibid.*) Aspects of this problem will be examined in connection with the "Enthronement Psalms" (vf. §13a, 18).

Creation, when limited to the domain of myth and ritual, as in Babylon, cannot have a sequel in history, but in the biblical interpretation it marks *the beginning of history*. This is indicated also by the use of two terms: *rēš'ît*, "beginning," to introduce the first creation narrative (Gn 1: 1-2:4a; priestly tradition) and *tôlᵉdôt* (2: 4a), "generations," to express the story of creation, the very term used for the genealogy of the patriarchs (5:1). As for the yahwist author of the sacred creation narratives (2:4b-25), he presents the early ages of mankind according to the reli–

gious pattern of the covenant: a "succession of judgments and restorations" which was to characterize the history of Israel (cf. Jacob, p. 139). The problem of "Myth in the Old Testament" is clearly presented by A. Strobel in *Theology Digest* 14 (1966) 218-222. The views of leading scholars are briefly analyzed. H. Cazelles' "practical solution" is retained: use the word "myth" for the literary genre but not for the doctrinal content. Strobel concludes: "Myth, too, was one of those forms of speech in which the ancients were accustomed to express their thoughts. Hence it need not be foreign to the Word of God. If myth is the means of expressing religious knowledge in antiquity, then it seems a natural demand that God, at least in the beginning, use the language of myth. Revelation progresses, and moves from myth to *logos*. The course from the heavily mythic language of the Yahwistic tradition through the demythologizing attempts of the Elohistic and especially the priestly tradition is long. But it runs in a straight line" (p. 221f).

Some texts imply that the universe is ruled by decrees or *laws of nature* established once and for all: the earth will yield its produce (Gn 1: 11), the span of man's life is limited (Jb 14:5), the boundaries of the sea are set (Jb 38:10f; Ps 104:9), and the fixity of "natural laws" serves Jeremiah as points of comparison (31:36; cf. 33:20, 25). But more generally, and in older texts perhaps, creation appears as *being continued* in the conservation of the world (see next section). God remains master of the material universe and of the "laws of nature." On the "day of the Lord" (cf. §14b) the order of nature will be altered to punish the wicked. The consequences of sin, felt at the fall (cf. Gn 3:17ff), remain a threat to man's peaceful survival in the universe. Was this in the psalmist's mind when he concluded his praise of the creator and of creation with the surprising wish: "May sinners cease from the earth, and may the wicked be no more"? (104: 35).

The direct intervention of God in nature proves his lordship over the elements, but it sometimes takes the form of a veritable struggle, "because in spite of its perfection, creation is unceasingly menaced by two forces which have not been created by Yahweh but have simply been subjected to him, namely darkness and the sea, residues of the chaos which existed before creation" (Jacob, p. 140). A negative answer is suggested by the psalmist to the question: "Are your wonders made known in the darkness, or your justice in the land of oblivion?" (88:13). It almost seems that the vast domain of the waters was neutralized rather than conquered when limits were assigned to them (Ps 104:7ff). The figure of "the chained rebellious sea" could easily serve to describe the restless and powerful enemies of Israel (cf. Is 17:12; Jr 6:23). "Without doubt, writes Jacob, it is no mere chance that the great miracles of Yahweh in the world of nature are victories won over the waters (the Red Sea, the Jordan, and in some measure Jonah's fish": p. 141). A significant literary personification is used in Ps 77:17:

> The waters saw you, O God;
>> the waters saw you and shuddered;
>> the very depths were troubled.

With the final divine victory over organized evil and with the advent of the New Heaven and of the New Earth the sea and the night will be no more (Rv 21:1; 22:5).

Various terms are used by the psalmists to describe the act of creation: God made (*'āśâh*) the sea (95:5), the heavens (96:5; 33:6), the moon to mark the seasons (104:19), and he has made us (100:3), he has formed or fashioned (*yāṣar*) the dry land, the heart of each one (33:15), he has established (*hēkīn*) the moon and the sun (74:16) and has spread the heavens like a tent-cloth (104:2). In Ps 136:4-9, God's work at the creation is told in lines alternating with the refrain: "for his mercy endures forever":

> Who alone does great wonders
> Who made the heavens in wisdom
> Who spread out the earth upon the waters,
> Who made the great lights,
> The sun to rule over the day,
> The moon and the stars to rule over the night.

Psalm 33 stresses the role of the word in creation:
> By the word (*dābār*) of the Lord the heavens were made;
>> by the breath (*rûaḥ*) of his mouth all their host (v 6).
> Let all the earth fear the Lord;
>> let all who dwell in the world revere him.
> For he spoke, and it was (made);
>> he commanded, and it stood forth (vv 8f).

In connection with verse 6 Jacob notes: "Originally the *spirit* was a force more dynamic than moral, more destructive than constructive; so, to become a power serviceable in creation it had to be subjected to the word" (p. 144).

The psalmists use also the word *bārā'*, "create" (cf. Gn 1:1) in different contexts: "Remember how short my life is; how frail you *created* all the children of men!" (89:48); "When you send forth your spirit, they are *created,* and you renew the face of the earth" (104:30); "Let them praise the name of the Lord, for he commanded and they *were created*" (148:5). Psalm 102:19 speaks of a people (to be) created who will praise *yâh*. Although *creatio ex nihilo* (creation out of nothing) is implied in the act of creation by the word, the concept is explicit only in 2 M 7:28: the youngest brother is exhorted by his mother to look at the heavens and the earth and to "recognize that God did not make them out of things that existed" (Greek), or, in Latin: *"ex nihilo fecit illa Deus et hominum genus."*

The *unity of the universe* is expressed in the first and in the second accounts of creation, that of the priestly writer and that of the Yahwist. "The third account, which in some respects is the most complete and which equally emphasizes the unity of the creation, is in *Ps 104, which expresses in less solemn but much more picturesque language the interdependence binding together the various parts of the cosmos. For this poet the antinomies still apparent in the first chapter of Genesis are resolved, there is no more opposition between the earth and the sea; the latter, personified by Leviathan, is no more than a plaything with which Yahweh amuses himself and the ships ply there without risk of being swallowed up by chaos. The universe is not only a house solidly built, it is also a work of art" (Jacob, p. 147). For the Israelites creation is an eschatological concept (cf. §14a), in the sense that its final aim is the salvation of humanity. This is especially apparent in the theology of Deutero-Isaiah, which presents the covenant in the language of creation rather than in that of election: "God is the creator God because he is the God of the covenant and he is the God of the covenant because he is the creator God" (*id.,* p. 148). For the psalmists the heavens declare the glory of God because they are a visible form of his presence (cf. Pss 8 and 19).

(b) Providence and the just

The Providence of God is a *creatio continua* which preserves and governs men and the world (but see §14c). About the middle of the first century B.C., the author of Wisdom, for the first time in the Bible, mentioned the word *pronoia*, "providence" (14:3). The term "is borrowed from Greek philosophy and literature. The idea, however, is biblical" (*JB*). In ancient Israel everything that happened was attributed to God as to the ultimate cause. The whole story of Joseph in Genesis implicitly demonstrates how divine providence protects the just against the plots of the wicked: "The evil you planned to do me, Joseph says, has by God's design turned to good, that he might bring about, as indeed he has, the deliverance of a numerous people" (Gn 50:20). Previously he had told his brothers twice: it is God who had sent me to Egypt for your sake (45: 5-8); human failure God uses to attain his ends. Accidents and calamities also were attributed to God (*actio Dei*): "If evil befalls a city, has not the Lord caused it?" (Am 3:6). Places of refuge are provided for those who have killed anyone, not intentionally but whom God "has delivered into his hands" (Ex 21:13). An action considered by David as sinful is attributed to "the anger of Yahweh" (2 S 24:1), as to the ultimate cause. But further revelation and reflection would suggest to the Chronicler that the temptation came from Satan, the enemy of human nature (1 Ch 21: 1). Job has asked many questions regarding the ways of God with men. One of them was: is God responsible for the failures of human conduct: "If it is not he, who then is it?" (9:24). It is a wisdom writer also who states: "For neither is there any god besides you who have the care of all..." (Ws 12:13).

G. S. Gunn has found that the two structural ideas on which the whole religious thought of the Psalter converges are "that God exercises a providential control in history as a whole and that he has graciously made Himself available in the personal experience of men" (*God in the Psalms*, p. 152). For Deutero-Isaiah, notes G. von Rad (II, p. 242), the "Lord of history" is "he who can allow the future to be told in advance (cf. Is 41:25ff; 48:14). This is something the gods of the heathen cannot do.... The power of Yahweh's word in history is shown particularly in the shaping of the future of God's people" (Is 55:10f). What the prophets reveal in fact is less the future as such than the configuration of the future; from them we learn that the pattern of saving history followed in the past has a permanent meaning, or to put it in G. von Rad's words: "Even prophetic predictions cannot be called predictions in a direct sense, but only the prediction of a *prefiguration,* in so far as what the prophets say about the future of God's chosen people does not in principle depart from the specific Old Testament concepts of the saving blessings..." (II, p. 384).

The psalmists' personal and direct experience of God's providence is reflected in the way they describe, for example, how he provides shelter, food, and drink:

> How precious is your kindness, O God!
>   The children of men take refuge in the shadow
>   of your wings.
> They have their fill of the prime gifts of your house;
>   from your delightful stream you give them to drink.
> For with you is the fountain of life,
>   and in your light we see light (36:8ff).

It is God himself, the psalmists say, who through nature provides for men and beasts alike: he supplies the seeds, prepares the soil, brings the harvests, causes the flocks to multiply, assures shelter and food to the birds, the beasts and men, regulates the changes of time and season (cf. Pss 65: 10-14; 104:10-30; 147:8ff). Speaking to Jonah, with some irony, God expressed his concern over both men and cattle (Jon 4:11).

God's special providence goes to man and the just. This is one of the psalmists' main beliefs and they express it in a variety of ways. Psalm 121 is a hymn to the Lord's watchfulness:

> Indeed he neither slumbers nor sleeps,
>   the guardian of Israel.
> The Lord will guard you from all evil;
>   he will guard your life (vv 4, 7).

From on high God beholds and watches the earth, mankind (11:4; 33: 13f; 102:20) and the nations (66:7). His eyes of benevolence are for man (32:8), for those who fear him (33:18) and for the just (34:6; cf. 101:6). Although Providence intervenes more manifestly at certain crucial moments, the whole life of individuals is the object of its care:

> O Lord, you have probed me and you know me;
>   you know when I sit and when I stand;

you understand my thoughts from afar.
My journeys and my rest you scrutinize,
    with all my ways you are familiar.
Even before a word is on my tongue,
    behold, O Lord, you know the whole of it.
Behind me and before, you hem me in
    and rest your hand upon me.
Such knowledge is too wonderful for me;
    too lofty for me to attain (Ps 139:1-6).

The whole being of man, his mysterious growth in the womb, his activity and destination, his life's span, all this has received divine attention, all is recorded in *the book of life* (139:13-16; see §14d on the "book of life").

    The Lord is the just man's *refuge,* his salvation, in the time of distress (37:39; 57:2; 64:11), when his life is threatened (27: 1; 142:6).

This refuge he seeks mostly in the temple under the wings of the Cherubim, where the Lord has his abode, enthroned on the mercy-seat:
You who dwell in the shelter of the Most High,
    who abide in the shadow of the Almighty,
Say to the Lord, "My refuge and my fortress,
    my God, in whom I trust."
For he will rescue you from the snare of the fowler,
    from the destroying pestilence.
With his pinions he will cover you.
    and under his wings you shall take refuge;
his faithfulness is a buckler and a shield (91:1-4).

Several terms of this passage evoke themes which in the psalms praise the Providence of God: shelter, refuge, fortress, trust, rescue, wings, faithfulness, shield. We read in Ps 61:5: "Oh, that I might lodge in your tent forever, take refuge in the shelter of your wings!" The shelter under the wings is mentioned often (cf. 17:8; 36:8; 57:2; 63:8) and alludes as we have said, to God's *locum praesentiae* in the temple. But the theme has other implications, since in three texts at least the image of the bird carrying or protecting its young has been applied to the care of God for his people. Moses is to tell the people: "You have seen for yourselves how

I treated the Egyptians and how I bore you up on eagle wings and brought you here to myself" (Ex 19:4). The same idea recurs in the "song of Moses":

> As an eagle incites its nestlings forth
>   by hovering over its brood,
> So he spreads his wings to receive them
>   and bore them up on his pinions (Dt 32:11).

The idea of protection is put forth in Isaiah's metaphor: "Like hovering birds so the Lord of hosts shall shield Jerusalem, to protect and deliver, to spare and rescue it" (31:5; cf. Mt 23:37). That H. Gressmann easily constructs on insufficient or misinterpreted evidence appears from his assertion about the prayer, "hide me in the shadow of your wings" (Ps 17:8; cf. 36:8; 57:2): "Wings of Yahweh are never heard of, but we know of the wings of the sun-god which hide the king under their shadow. This figure originated in Egypt where the hawk of Horus stretched out his wings over the king" (*The Psalmists*, p. 14). Cherubim and Seraphim are, of course, Israelite versions of various winged creatures known in the ancient Middle-East as guardian genii at the gates of temples and palaces (cf Gn 3:24 and *ANEP*, nn. 644, 646f, 652ff). But Gressmann could have paid more attention to the biblical texts cited above. Besides, is not God represented by *Ps 18:11 as: "mounted on a Cherub," and did not the cherubim of glory overshadow the mercy-seat (Heb 9:5)? The statement of Ps 80:2, "From your throne upon the cherubim shine forth" has been illustrated by a picture of King Ahiram who ruled in Byblos at the time of the Judges. On his sarcophagus he is represented seated on a throne flanked by winged sphinxes (see *ANEP*, nn. 456, 458).

(c) Rock and Fortress; Guardian of the little ones

The idea of *strength* is often linked by the psalmists to that of refuge: "With God is my safety and my glory, he is the rock of my strength; my refuge is in God" (62:8; cf. 46:2; 71:7). Few passages have more synonyms than Ps 18:2f to express confidence in the strong refuge that is God:

> I love you, O Lord, my strength,

O Lord, my rock, my fortress, my deliverer.
My God, my rock of refuge,
    my shield, the horn of my salvation, my stronghold.

The metaphor of the *Rock*, when applied to God, accompanies different concepts: refuge (31:3; 71:3; 94:22), salvation (62:7; 95:1, Dt 32:15; 1 S 2:2), redemption (89:27), holy war (144:1). The concept of God as Rock can perhaps be linked with the episode of the miraculous spring (Ex 17:1ff; Nb 20:8f; 1 Cor 10:4) or with the rock on which the temple was built (2 S 24:18ff). Some texts suggest that God is the Rock when he saves from the slippery road leading to Sheol: "To you, O Lord, I call; O my Rock, be not deaf to me, lest, if you heed me not, I become one of these going down into the pit" (28:1; cf. §14d and *Ps 61). W. I. Wolverton notes: "Our tradition has it that the threshing floor of Araunah (2 S 24:16) became the base for the altar in Solomon's temple. It is probably this rock which in earlier days gave rise to the notion of the earth-pillar in the holy city, and to the figure of God as the Rock which appears so often in the Psalms (*sur*: 18:3, 47; 19:15; 27:5; 31:3, 4; 62:3, 7, 8; 71:3; 78:35), although in the latter case simple poetic imagery would account for many users of the word. However, the notion of stability suggested by the Rock, the earth-pillar, must surely have promoted the belief in the asylum character of Zion."

To call God the Rock (or "the Crag," *sela'*: cf. Pss 18:3; 31:4; 42:10; 71:3), is the concrete way of saying that his is the attribute of immutability, involving firmness, constancy, stability and permanence. The psalmists say it in various ways: "The plan of the Lord stands forever, the design of his heart, through all generations" (31:11); "They who trust in the Lord are like Mount Zion, which is immovable; which forever stands" (125:1; cf. 16:8; 21:8; 112:6): God is a *stronghold*, a fortress, a shield for those who put in him their faith: 31:3f; 48:4; 94:22; 114:2. He has made the world *firm*, not to be moved (93:1; 96:10). To God the psalmists says: "Through all generations your truth endures; you have established the earth, and it stands firm" (119:90). His *kingship* is just as firm; he is king forever (29:10), from of old (74:12), sitting on a throne: fixed (33:14), firm (93:2), and eternal (55:20). God shall reign forever (146:10).

Yahweh is in a special way *the God of his humbler subjects* (cf. *Ps 113). He rescues the afflicted (25:16), the needy (35:10), the lowly

(147:6), the *poor* (40:18; 69:34; 82:4; 86:1). He is the father of orphans and the defender of widows (68:6; 146:9), he keeps the little ones (116:6) and "established in her home the barren wife as the joyful mother of children" (113:9). In words very similar to those of "the song of Hannah" (1 S 2:8; cf. Lk 1:52) a psalmist has expressed the special solicitude of God for the lowly ones:

> He raises up the lowly from the dust;
> from the dunghill he lifts up the poor.
> To seat them with princes,
> with the princes of his own people (113:7f).

A special blessing awaits those who imitate God's solicitude for the lowly and the poor:

> Happy is he who has regard for the lowly and the poor;
> in the day of misfortune the Lord will deliver him.
> The Lord will keep and preserve him;
> he will make him happy on the earth,
> and not give him over to the will of his enemies (41:2).

G. Widengren writes: "A characteristic feature of the idea of God in urban Semitic religion was that God took especial care of the socially oppressed categories" (*The Accadian...* p. 317; cf. F. C. Fensham).

(d) *Savior and Redeemer*

God created the universe and man, his Providence rules and preserves both. Of man and of Israel he is also the *savior and the redeemer*. Môšia', a word peculiar to Hebrew, usually translated "savior," invariably implies, writes J. Sawyer (*VT* 1965, p. 475ff) a champion of justice in a situation of controversy, battle or oppression. In the language of the prophets (especially Deutero-Isaiah) and in the psalms it is one of the titles of the God of Israel: Is 43:3, 11; 45:15, 21; 49:26=60:16; Jr 14:8; Ho 13:4; Pss 7:11; 17:7; 18:3; 106:21. Anciently, it seems, môšia' designated a definite office, as an "advocate" or "witness for the defense." Then the appellation was applied to God, first with the same connotation, and finally in any general context. In the CV translation other derivatives of the root $y\check{s}'$ are used by the psalmist to call God "my Savior" (27:9; 42:12; 65:6; 79:9; 118:14) or "my salvation" (at least 14 times: cf. 18:3; 25:5; 27:1).

The notions of "salvation" and of "Savior" do not have to be exposed here (see *The Names and Titles of Jesus,* p. 133f). Salvation can refer, as often in the psalms, to mere deliverance from temporal evils (cf. 1 S 10:19), or to a higher, spiritualized meaning: the salvation of the chosen people worked, for example, on the occasion of their passage through the Red Sea (Ex 14:13) or their return from Babylon: "Israel, you are saved by the Lord, saved forever" (Is 45: 17). In biblical thought the places of servitude or exile represented lands of sin, for idolatry and vice flourished there. If "liberations" from such lands did prefigure messianic salvation, then the more perfect notion of salvation as "deliverance from sin" is not far off. We read in the Septuagint: "God shall save us... for their sin will be pardoned" (Is 53:22, 24); "You shall be my people, and I will be your God. I will save you from all your iniquities" (Ezk 36:28f; cf. 37:23). Successive deceptions carried the perspectives of salvation forward to the end of time. According to the *prophetic notion,* such an eschatological salvation will entail the establishment of the chosen people in Palestine and the inauguration of the messianic kingdom (cf. Is 11:1-10). In the apocalyptic perspective of eschatological salvation the messianic era shall have for theater "new heavens and a new earth" (Is 45: 17), after the old universe has been crushed under the devastating judgments of Yahweh (cf. 24:4, 19f, 23). The apocalyptic notion of salvation dominates paracanonical Judaic literature.

Those liberators of the people of God whom we call "Judges" are called "Saviors" in three texts from the Septuagint (Jg 3:9, 15; Ne 9: 27). Although Scripture does not call Moses "Savior," the role assigned to him by God is certainly that of a savior (cf. Is 19:20). If the function of Savior is rarely attributed to the Messiah (cf. Zech 9:9, Greek), it is doubtless due to the Old Testament custom of reserving the title and role of Savior to God himself (mainly in Isaiah: cf. 12:2; 45:21f and in the Psalms). For the biblical writers, only God truly saves (cf. Jdt 9:14). Isolated or collectively, human forces could not save the king (Ps 32:16) or the people (Is 31:1; Ho 5:13). The divine title Savior is applied to Jesus by several New Testament texts.

God's *redeeming role* is expressed in the psalms mainly with words derived from *gā'al,* to redeem, ransom or avenge, and *pādâh,* to redeem, ransom, deliver. It was the duty of the *gô'ēl* (the next of kin) to uphold the rights of a family member by appropriate means, provided by the law: redeeming the property (Lv 25:25ff; Rt 4:4), marrying the widow of the deceased relative (Dt 25:5-10), avenging the blood (Nb 35:12). Cities of refuge were selected as an attempt to restrain the tribal law of blood revenge (cf. Nb 35:9-15). This redeeming, *"protective right,"* God has exercised it in favor of Israel, especially at the time of the exodus from Egypt and the return from exile in Babylon (cf. Pss 74:2; 77:15; 78: 35; 106:10; Ex 6:6; 15:13; Is 43:1; 44:22; 52:9). The function of *gôʾēl* can also be exercised by Yahweh for the benefit of the individuals: Pss 69:18; 103:4; Gn 48:16; Jb 19:26. The term *pādâh*, originally meant to express the payment of the ransom of the firstborn (Ex 13:13; Nb 3:46) or of the slave (Ex 21:8; Lv 19:26), came to be used like *gāʾal*, to denote the liberation of the people from the Egyptian servitude (Ps 78: 42; Dt 7:8; 1 Ch 17:21) or even deliverance from enemies, sickness and death (Pss 44:27; 49:16; 2 S 4:9; Jb 33:28). In Deutero-Isaiah, writes G. von Rad, "to create" and "to redeem" (*gʾl*) can be used as entirely synonymous (II, p. 241).

The psalmists call on God to redeem (*pādâh*) them from the company of sinners (26:11), from the snares of the enemy (31:6; 71:23), from the power of the nether world (49:16). The Lord redeems from death the lives of his servants (34:23) and the whole nation from disaster (44: 27), "for with the Lord is kindness and with him is plenteous redemption" (130:7: *pᵉdût*). Deutero-Isaiah had said: "Fear not, O worm Jacob, O maggot Israel; I will help you, says the Lord; your redeemer (*gôʾēl*) is the Holy One of Israel" (41:14). After an educative punishment, the rebellious tribes, says the psalmist (78:35), remembered "that God was their Rock and the Most High God (*ʾēl ʿelyôn*) their redeemer (*gôʾēl*)". With your strong arm, says another psalmist to God, you redeemed your people, the sons of Jacob and Joseph (77:16; cf. 74:2). The life of individuals also God redeems (*gôʾēl*) from destruction (103:4) and from the hand of the foe (107:2). Both words for "redeem" are used in the following verse: "Come and ransom (*gāʾal*) my life; as an answer for my enemies, redeem (*pādâh*) me" (69:19). Redemption or liberation (*pidyôn*) from death penalty could in some cases be obtained by paying ransom called *kôpher* (Ex 21:30). The *kôpher* is mentioned in many other cases. A psalmist notes that no man can ransom himself (or his brother), or give to God the required *kôpher*, for ransom (*pidyôn*) for his (their) life is costly and can never suffice (49:7f; cf. v 16).

(e) *His are justice, kindness, truth*

Justice and kindness characterize God's dealings with man in the religious experience of the psalmists. They are not to be opposed, as is sometimes believed, but are to each other in a relation which will have to be determined: "In your justice free me from distress, and in your kindness destroy my enemies" (Ps 143:11f).

Justice: punitive or saving?

God's justice (ṣedeq or ṣᵉdāqâh) is generally understood by the Old Testament in the framework of the covenant, but with a variety of meanings: "Just" or "righteous" is God who commits no iniquity, who leaves not wickedness unpunished nor good unrecognized, who is merciful and slow to anger, "who takes no pleasure in the death of the wicked man, but rather in the wicked man's conversion, that he may live" (Ezk 33:11), who procures the salvation of his people, who communicates his righteousness to the sinner and justifies him (cf. E. Jacob, p. 96). "It is incorrect," notes Jacob, "to see in righteousness (="justice") the sequence of God's plans for the salvation of believers, the punishment of the wicked being the work of his wrath (§11h), which some texts indeed contrast with his righteousness" (cf. Jr 10:24; Mi 7:9). In Isaiah 10:22, for example, justice seems associated with punishment: "For though your people, Israel, were the sand of the sea, only a remnant of them will return; their destruction is decreed as overwhelming justice (ṣᵉdāqâh) demands" (Is 10:22). In the "confession of Ezra," however, the fact of the Remnant is called a "grace" (ḥesed: 9:8f), or an effect of God's saving justice: "O Lord, the God of Israel, thou art just (ṣaddîq); for we are left a remnant that has escaped, as at this day" (9:15 RSV; the Vulgate-Douay translation is here misleading and JB is not precise).

"Righteousness as the free and saving favor of God has many echoes in the Old Testament, particularly in the Psalms where the righteousness of God is presented as the refuge of the faithful and as the source of pardon. . . . If from the time of Jeremiah the punitive aspect of righteousness passes more and more into the background it is doubtless because the just judgment of Yahweh was thought to have been accomplished by the exile. It is above all with Second Isaiah that righteousness becomes synonymous with grace and salvation" (Jacob, p. 101). In his messianic and eschatological perspective "the framework of the covenant is widened because righteousness will extend not only to the Israelites but to all peoples." So Deutero-Isaiah can be called a "universalist," in that sense that foreigners, in his view, will be admitted in the covenant. The beneficiary of this saving justice will not be the innocent and the oppressed "but the people who have no other merits than being the elect of Yahweh" (*ibid.*).

Justice and mercy

The association of the meaning of *ṣᵉdāqâh* away from its association with God the Judge (cf. I. H. Eybers) towards a closer affinity with mercy, could be linked, Jacob believes, with the new meaning of the words for "poor" and "unfortunate": "following a line of thought whose origin is found with Jeremiah and Zephaniah, the poor is no longer, or not merely, the unfortunate one, the victim of an injustice, awaiting the re-establishment of his rights, but every believer has before God the attitude of a suppliant, of an *'ebyôn* who begs for a decision in his favor, not in order to be justified against an adversary but in an absolute manner" (p. 102; on the "justice" and "mercy" of God, cf. also G. Bernini, pp. 222-237). Effectively, *ṣᵉdāqāh* in later Judaism took the meaning of mercy, of alms-giving especially: "Therefore, O king, let my counsel be acceptable to you; break off your sins by practicing (*ṣidᵉqâh*:aram.), and your iniquities by showing mercy to the oppressed..." (Dn 4:24=27 *RSV*).

Saving justice in the Psalms

In the second part of his *Die Gerechtigkeit in den Psalmen,* A. H. Van der Weijden deals with *righteousness* or *justice,* as related to God. Some aspects of his research can be noted here profitably. The mention of the Hebrew terms is not superfluous since too often their translation is unduly adapted to the context. *JB* for example translates *ṣᵉdāqâh* "integrity" in Is 10:22, "virtuous actions" in Dn 4:24, "kindness" in Ps 40:11, "virtue" in Ps 33:5, "vindication" in Ps 24:5. *CV,* on the other hand, translates *mišpat* as "right" in Ps 33:5, "justice" in 99:4 and "judgment" in 97:2. Some translators will want to use "justice" according to the meaning it generally has today; if the biblical context does not suit this, they use another word, but this can be very misleading.

The psalmists, according to Van der Weijden, either appeal to God's righteousness or they praise it. From God's justice (=righteousness) *they hope to obtain* rescue from the enemies (31:2; 71:2; 143:1, 11), proper guidance (5:9) or life (119:40; 143:11). Their hope rests on the belief that God's justice means salvation: "Vindicate me, O Lord, my God, according to thy righteousness" (35:24 *RSV*), not according to our merit, because "before you no living man is just" (143:2). It is noteworthy that the favors expected from God's justice (*ṣᵉdāqâh* or *Ṣedeq*) are also associated sometimes in the same psalm, with God's truth ('*emet*: comp. 31:2 and 6; 71:2 and 22:5:9 and 43:3), with God's faithfulness ('*emûnâh*: comp. 143:1 a and b), with God's mercy (*hesed*: comp. 31:2 and 8, 17, 22; 143: 1, 11 and 8; 5:9 and 8; 119:40 and 88, 149, 150), with God's compassion (*rahamîm*: comp. 119:40 and 77, 156). This language indicates that in some circles at least *sedeq* or *s*e*dāqâh* meant "saving justice." The following parallels are particularly significant:

> Prolong your kindness (*hesed*) to those who know you;
>   and your justice (*s*e*dāqâh*) to the upright of heart (36:11).
> In your justice (*s*e*dāqâh*) free me from distress,
>   and in your kindness (*hesed*) destroy my enemies (143:11f).
> I will make my justice come speedily;
>   my salvation shall go forth (Is 51:5).

It is found secondly that the psalmists *praise* God's justice when they have obtained from it the following favors: deliverance from enemies (17:15f, 19, 24; 22:32); rescue from an undetermined necessity, presumably also from enemy danger (40:10f); remission of blood guilt (51:16). God's justice is also praised disinterestedly, in connection, however, with his kindness (88:13; 145:7) or in legalistic context (7:18; 35:28; 50:6; 89:17; 97:6). Here again then is God's justice mainly presented as beneficent not punitive (for this, cf. G. Sauer). This appears also in the fact that in the same context as God's justice are also praised his truth ('*emet*: cf. 40:11), his faithfulness ('*emûnâh*: cf. 40:11; 88:13 and 12; 89:17 and 2, 3, 6, 9), his mercy *hesed*: cf. 40:11; 88:13 and 12; 89:17and 2. 3), and his goodness (*tûb*: 145:7). Especially noteworthy in that respect is the following verse:

> Your justice I kept not hid within my heart;
>   your faithfulness and your salvation I have spoken of;
> I have made no secret of your kindness and your truth
>   in the vast assembly (40:11).

Justice and judgment

Divine justice is also mentioned by the psalmists in connection with God's role as judge. The phrase, "Yahweh judges the word with justice" (*ṣedeq*: 9:9; 96:13; 98:9), refers to the great judgment of *Endzeit* (cf. §14a). In that context the idea of retribution is naturally present, but Ps 98:2f shows that even there the other aspects are not forgotten:

> The Lord has made his salvation known:
>> in the sight of the nations he has revealed his justice.
> He has remembered his kindness and his faithfulness
>> toward the house of Israel.
> All the ends of the earth have seen
>> the salvation by our Lord.

In Pss 89:15 and 97:2 justice and judgment are seen as attributes of divine kingship. *Saving justice* is implied in the first of these verses:

> Justice and judgment are the foundations of your throne;
>> kindness and truth go before you.

In other passages God's justice brings salvation to the faithful, shame to their enemies: 35:24ff; 48:5ff, 11; 50:6; 89:17; 99:6. The same notions are alluded to in a few texts which speak of the "just" God and the "just" judge: 7:10; 9:5.

Attributes personified

Many other texts could be cited in which justice is mentioned in parallel to faithfulness (*'emûnâh*: 36:6f; 96:13; 98:2f), to mercy (*hesed*: 33:5; 36:6f, 11; 48:10f; 85:11; 89:15; 98:2f), to peace (*šalôm*: 72:3, 7). The following verses illustrate the psalmists' understanding of God's justice:

> Kindness and truth shall meet;
>> justice and peace shall kiss.
> Truth shall spring out of the earth,
>> and justice shall look down from heaven.
> Justice shall walk before him,
>> and salvation, along the way of his steps (85:11; 12, 14).

Concerning the active and personal role of *ṣedeq*, Jacob notes the following: "*Tsedeq* goes before Yahweh (Ps 85:14), it looks down from the

height of heaven (Ps 85:12), along with *mishpat* it is the foundation of
Yahweh's throne (Pss 89;15; 97:2); *Tsedeq* and *Shalom,* another Jeru-
salemite deity, embrace each other (Ps 85:11). Whether this refers to
primitive gods become servants of Yahweh or to the hypostatization of the
attributes of one great god, it shows that righteousness was always regarded in the Old Testament and in the surrounding world as one of the
principle attributes of deity" (p. 98). "Justice," he adds (note 2), "is less
an attribute peculiar to Yahweh than his holiness. Justice was characteristic of gods by and large...but Yahweh alone is the Holy One" (see
also on *Ps 57).

A well known saying of the *Miserere* has been translated and interpreted in various ways: "You are just when you pass sentence on me, blameless when you give judgment" (*JB*). This text will be discussed *in loco*
(cf. *Ps 51:6). Van der Weijden (p. 171) says that more probably it
means simply that God shows his justice (his saving justice) when he
forgives (cf. v 16; also Is 56:1; Rm 1:17; 3:26). Saint John could write:
"If we acknowledge our sins, he is *faithful and just* to forgive us our
sins and to cleanse us from all iniquity" (1 Jn 1:9). On "kindness and
fidelity," cf. *Ps 138.

(f) God's mercy (*ḥesed*)

The Hebrew word *ḥesed* is usually rendered by the Septuagint as
éleos, "mercy" and by modern translators as "kindness," "grace," or fidelity." The idea of "strength" belongs, it seems, to the notion of *ḥesed*:
"Strength ('*ōz*) belongs to God, and yours, O Lord, is *ḥesed*" (Ps 62:
12f). [God is] "my *ḥesed* and my fortress, my stronghold, my deliverer,
my shield..." (144:2). Besides, God's *ḥesed* is often associated with his
'emet, "truth," implying the idea of firmness, stability, security: "All the
paths of the Lord are *ḥesed* and *'emet*" (25:10; cf. 40:11); "I will worship
at your holy temple and give thanks to your name, because of your *ḥesed*
and your *'emet*" (138:2).

In *Hesed in the Bible* (Cincinnati, 1967; first German edit., 1927),
Nelson Glueck showed the link existing between *ḥesed* and the covenant.
Along that line Jacob remarks: "The use of the term *ḥesed* for human
relationships shows clearly that the meaning of benevolence and mercy is
secondary to that of solidarity or simply of loyalty" (cf. Gn 19:19; 2
S 10:2), qualities associated with covenants (*bᵉrît*) or treaties (cf. §13c).
In fact the terms *ḥesed* and *bᵉrît* are found together in many texts (Dt

7:2, 9, 12; Pss 50:5, 36; 89:29, 34), and Jacob would define *hesed* as "the power which guarantees a covenant and makes it strong and durable" (p. 104). For the prophets the breaking of the covenant *hesed* on the part of Israel does not suppress the activity of divine *hesed*. Hosea especially has stressed the ever present initiative of God's *hesed*: "And I will betroth you to me forever; I will betroth you to me in righteousness (*sedeq*) and in justice (*mišpat*), in steadfast love (*hesed*) and in mercy (*rahamin*); I will betroth you to me in faithfulness ('*emûnâh*); and you shall know the Lord" (2:21f; *RSV*). "In teaching of the prophets about human relations *hesed* is conceived after the pattern of the divine *hesed* and a summary of obligations like that of Micah 6:8 shows that the imitation of God is the mainspring of all the religion and ethics of the Old Testament" (Jacob, p. 105): "You have been told, O man, what is good, and what the Lord requires of you; only to do the right and to love *hesed*, and to walk humbly with your God." *Hesed* in that context obviously embodies a number of social virtues required of the members of the covenant.

The meaning of *hesed* is, however, far from being exhausted with the legal aspect, set forth by Glueck, since Yahweh is not bound by any pattern of action and is known for his merciful initative in entering into or in renewing fellowship with man: "Return, rebel Israel, says the Lord, I will not remain angry with you; for I am merciful (*hāsîd*), says the Lord, I will not continue my wrath forever" (Jr 3:12; cf. Is 54:7f). "The Lord is *saddîq* in all his ways, and *hāsîd* in all his works," says a psalmist (145:17). The unexpected deeds of divine *hesed* are celebrated as wonder by the psalmists: "Blessed be the Lord whose wondrous *hesed* he has shown me from the fortified city" (31:22; cf. 4:4; 17:1); "Let them give thanks to the Lord for his *hesed* and his wondrous deeds to the children of men" (107:8; 15, 21, 31).

Divine *hesed* extends to the whole creation: "Of the Lord's *hesed* the earth is full" (33:5; 119:64). In "the great liturgy of Ps 136" (Jacob, p. 107), the refrain, "for his *hesed* endures forever" (cf. 100:5; 106:1; 107:1), scans the review of the Lord's marvellous deeds, in creating the universe (4-9), in bringing Israel to the Promised Land (10-22) and in having pity on the misery of the people (23-25). In the following passage *hesed*'s range of action is compared to other manifestations of divine power and kindness:

O Lord, your *hesed* reaches to heaven;

your faithfulness (*'emûnâh*), to the clouds.
Your justice (*ṣedâqâh*) is like the mountains of God;
   your judgments (*mišpat*), like the mighty deep;
   man and beast you save, O Lord.
How precious is your *ḥesed*, O God!
The children of man take refuge in the shadow
   of your wings (36:6-8).

(g) God's love

The prophet Jeremiah reveals that God appeared to his people saying: "I have loved you with an everlasting love; therefore I have continued my *ḥesed* to you" (31:3). It is the Hebrew *'āhab* which is used here for "love." In most cases the object of God's love, in the Old Testament writings, is the nation of Israel. Three times only, Jacob notes (p. 109), we are told that God "loves" individuals: twice Solomon (2 S 12:24; Ne 13:26) and once Cyrus (Is 48:14), presumably in their role as royal personages.

Using the term *'āhab*, "love" the psalmists tell us that God loves "the glory of Jacob" (47:5), the righteous (*ṣaddîqîm*: 146:8), Mount Zion (78:68) and Zion (87:2), justice (*mišpat*: 33:5; 37:28; 99:4; cf. 45:8), righteousness (*ṣedâqâh*: 33:5) and just deeds (*ṣedâqôt*: 11:7). Another term, from the root *ḥpṣ*, is used to express divine love, but it is generally translated "to delight in." Thus a psalmist confesses: "He set me free in the open, and rescued me, because he loves me" (18:20). "That you love me, says another, I know by this, that my enemy does not triumph over me" (41:12). The enemies of the author of Ps 22 mock him saying: "He relied on the Lord... let him rescue him, if he loves him" (v 9). Besides, God "loves the truth (*'emet*) in the inward being" (51:8), takes delight in the welfare of his servant (32:27), and will take pleasure in right sacrifices (37:23). We read in Ps 37:23: "The steps of a man are from the Lord, and he establishes him in whose way he delights." In Ps 115:3, finally, it is said: "Our God is in the heavens; he does whatever he pleases" (*ḥāpēṣ;* cf. 135:6). This becomes in JB: "Ours is the God whose will is sovereign in the heavens and on earth."

Numerous biblical passages concerned with God's loving care for man have been influenced and inspired by a declaration of God himself on Mount Sinai. It is a sort of summary, probably an old cultic confession, the contents of which are alluded to quite explicitly in Nb 14:18; Ne

9:17, 31; Jr 32:18; Jon 4:7 and Ps 103:8. In this definition of himself the loving God does not exclude severity implied in collective punishment.

> Having come down in a cloud, the Lord stood with him [Moses] there
> and proclaimed his name, "Lord." Thus the Lord passed before him
> and cried out, "The Lord, the Lord, a merciful and gracious God,
> slow to anger and rich in kindness and fidelity, continuing his kind-
> ness for a thousand generations, and forgiving wickedness and crime
> and sin; yet not declaring the guilty guiltless, but punishing children
> and grandchildren to the third and fourth generation for their fathers'
> wickedness!" (Ex 34:6f).

(h) *God's wrath*

In their metaphorical and anthropomorphic language biblical writers
present as *wrath* a reaction of God which in some texts appears as the
opposite of *hesed*. Sometimes God's wrath is kindled without apparent
motivation, mostly when the sphere of his holiness is threatened with
profanation (cf. 2 S 6:7; Ex 19:3; 33:20; 2 S 24:1). Usually, however, God's wrath comes in reaction to sin (cf. Mi 7:9), especially to will-
ful transgressions of the Covenant (Dt 6:15). The "day of Yahweh" (cf
§14b) will also be a "day of wrath" (Is 13:13; Zp 1:15; Hab 3:13),
when the sinners' or the nations' rebellion will be consummated. The
"wrath of God" appears in many cases to be a theological explanation of
the defeats of Israel and of the disasters which fell on God's chosen people. This, some authors like W. I. Wolverton (see §13b), would presumably call a mythologizing presentation of history: when human action or
failure is attributed to the divinity.
    For the New Testament, in St. Paul especially, God's wrath coincides
with the spread of sin (Rm 1:18ff), while the effects of his (saving)
justice are seen in the dispensation of grace (Rm 3:21ff). The same
pattern of anger and grace is illustrated in the prodigal son's straying and
return (Lk 15:11ff).
    The psalmists implore God: "Do not punish me in your anger!"
(6:2; cf. 27:9; 38:2; 74:1) or say to him: Do not be forever angry
with Israel (79:5; 85:6), but pour your wrath upon the nations (79:6;
cf. 56:8), as you did against the Egyptians (78:49ff). But the formula
of Ex 34:6, "slow to anger and rich in kindness and fidelity," repeated

by the psalmists (86:15; 103:8f; 145:8), indicates that for the Old Testament anger is secondary as an expression of God's ways, and stands no comparison with *ḥesed*. The psalmists certainly agreed: "For his anger lasts but a moment; a lifetime, his favor" (30:6).

§12. MAN AND GOD

The psalms are very theocentric in character. Their authors praise the living and eternal God as great and holy in himself, as the Creator and Providence of the universe, as the Savior who redeems man in justice and in mercy. Turning now our look from God to the psalmists we shall try to learn what they reveal about themselves in their songs.

(a) *Who are the 'anāwîm?*

The speakers of several psalms are referred to as "poor," "needy," "afflicted," or "humble." The exact meaning of the corresponding Hebrew words, mainly *'ānî* and *'ānāw,* the semantic evolution of the concepts involved have been the subject of controversy for many decades. On the meaning of these words depends also in part the solution of another problem: who are the "enemies" and the "evildoers" in the Book of Psalms? (see §12g). It happens that there are about as many occurrences of *'ānî* and *'ānāw* in the Psalter as in the rest of the whole Bible. It seems then appropriate to give special attention to these issues. In a recent article, P. Van den Berghe has reviewed the history of the debate on the vocabulary of the "poor"; "*'Ani et 'Anaw dans les psaumes,*" in *Le Psautier,* pp. 273-295.

Ten years after the problem about the terms had been seriously raised, A. Rahlfs published his basic study *'Ani und 'Anaw in den Psalmen* (Göttingen, 1892). He claimed that the terms were two different forms of the same root. The *'ānî* is the one depressed, afflicted by distress or misery. The *'ānāw,* on the contrary, is one who stands before God as a servant before his master, one who makes himself humble before the Lord. The *'anāwîm* are the faithful yahwists grouped in a party during and after the exile.

Over a long period the controversy centered on the respective meanings of *'ānî* and *'ānāw.* Is *'ānî* morally neutral as referring to a social condition of humility or poverty, while *'ānāw* would express the corresponding religious attitude? Others denied any difference of meaning between the two words, 'aniyyîm, more common, being the main form, and 'anāwîm, also "the poor" (plural), a secondary one. These authors admitted that a moral connotation had been added to the meaning of the two terms when the poorer and humbler class of Israel began to be considered as the special object of divine care and mercy. Consequently more recent scholars left aside the study of a doubtful distinction between the two terms and concentrated their attention on explaining how 'ānî and 'ānāw had come to express a moral and religious ideal after having been used to denote the social conditions proper to poverty and distress. Various factors contributed to this, claimed R. Kittel in Die Psalmen (Leipzig, 1929). First, the preaching of the prophets who, as defenders of the poor, tended to present them as the real friends of God, as the pious and the saints. Then, also, with the exile, the pious Israelites became socially poor. Their poverty figures in second Isaiah among the titles of honor applied to the people of God. Finally, among the repatriates, the name "poor of Yahweh" was claimed especially by the faithful yahwists, as contrasted with those who had become worldly unbelievers.

Kittel's explanation was accepted in its main lines by Catholic authors as well. More even than A. Robert and P. Humbert, A. Gelin discovered a treasure of spirituality in the vocabulary of poverty. He published his findings in Les Pauvres de Yahvé (Paris, 1953). Other authors though have singled out weak points in Kittel's reasoning. The religious meaning of the terms, they claimed, is attested before the exile, while 'ānāw is absent from some postbiblical prophetic writings.

During the debate on the semantic evolution of the terms of poverty a number of authors, after A. Rahlfs, went their own way to find evidence that there existed a "party of the poor," not socially poor necessarily but devoted to a pious, prayerful and humble life before God. These 'anāwim claimed as their spiritual ancestors all those who in the past had lived the ideal of a simple society, practicing justice as in the patriarchal period. Included also were the more recent faithful who, like the prophets, had opposed the law of God to the deviations of a corrupt society. In his book, Les Pauvres d'Israel, Prophètes, Psalmistes, Messianistes, (Paris, 1922), A. Causse considers the psalmists as the representatives par excellence of this party of the poor. In his Geschichte des Volkes Israels (vol. III, 1, p. 702ff), R. Kittel admitted the existence of such a party, but claimed that it consisted of traditionalist Jews (Altgläubigen) who belonged to the lower social classes at the time of the Greek domination (333-63 B.C.). A. Robert favored an earlier date, that of the Persian period (550-330), while A. Gelin traced the origin of the spiritual movement of "poverty" to prophet Zephaniah (640-630), its great representatives being Jeremiah and two figurative personages: Job and the Isaian Servant of God.

To present the psalmists as belonging generally to a socially inferior and somewhat outcast class does not favor a cultic interpretation of the psalms. Mowinckel rejects the idea that there existed "a community of the poor" (A. Causse) and writes: "The thesis of Causse is held by Gelin ...who fancies that even the psalmists belong to 'the poor' as a spiritual community of righteous persons" (II, p. 251). In the National Psalms of Lamentation, he writes, "the 'oppressed' or 'humble'...are no party nor class, but Israel, or her representative men in times of emergency, 'oppressed' by external enemies, 'helpless' in their own power... and "humbly' hoping for the interference of Yahweh" (I: 229; Pss 12:6; 74:19--21 are quoted as examples, p. 196). That type of "poor" can be found in the courts of the temple waiting to seek the Lord's help in the cult. In favor of a "community of the poor," however, stands the fact that 'anāwim is practically used only in the plural: the only exception could be Nb 12:3, but even there the reading is doubtful. In 'Ani und 'Anaw in den Psalmen (Oslo, 1932), H. Birkeland showed that in the majority of cases the "poor" in the psalms are real "sufferers." This was not unexpected since the 'anāwim are mentioned mainly in the laments. These "sufferers", he found, are generally affected by a state of weakness, of reduced energy. In fact the terms have more than one meaning in different contexts. (On the "poor" see also the studies of P. A. Munch and H. J. Kraus, Psalmen, p. 82f; cf. EstBib 1966, pp. 117-168.)

The terms 'ānî, 'ānāw and related expressions occur mainly in Pss 9, 10 (8 times), 14, 18, 22, 25, 34, 35, 40, 41, 69, 72, 74, 82, 86, 88, 102, 109, 113, 140, 147, 149. A. Rahlfs and H. Ewald thought that a distinct category of psalms was constituted by Pss 22, 25, 34, 35, 40, 69, 102, 109 and other psalms in which the notion of poverty is represented: 31, 38, 51, 70, 71. The studies of H. Gunkel have shown that most of these psalms are to be classified as laments.

Among the other terms used in this vocabulary of the "poor" can be mentioned: 'ebyôn, "needy," dal, "lowly," rāš "destitute," dak, "downtrodden," šāfāl, "humble," miskēn, "poor." Understandably enough, modern translators do not quite agree on the English equivalents of 'ānî. In Ps 74:21, for example, it is rendered "afflicted" by Briggs and CV, "poor" by RSV and JB. In Ps 82:3 it is translated "afflicted" by Briggs, CV, RSV and "wretched by JB. The meaning of 'anāwim (twice) in

25:9 is given as "the humble" by CV and RSV, as "the afflicted" by Briggs, and by JB as "the humble" and "the poor."

If we examine now the use of the words in the Psalms, we find that God is said to protect, defend, save and rescue the 'ānî: 18:28;   22:25; 34:7; 35:10; 69:30; 72:4, 12; 82:3. God does not forget him (40: 18=70:6) but does him justice (140:13). The 'ānî praises God's name (74:21) and implores the Lord to listen to him: 25:16;   74:19;   86:1; 109:22. One psalmist confesses he has been 'ānî and "in agony" since his youth (88:16). In two instances 'ānî can refer to the nation: God has provided soil with rain for the 'ānî (68:11) and a hope is expressed: that the king will judge (yādîn, govern?) God's people with righteousness and his "poor" ('aniyyîm) with justice! (72:2). As for the 'anāwîm, God has not forgotten them (9:13,   19;   10:12), he guides and teaches them (25:9), hears their desires (10:17), sustains them (147:6). They shall have their fill and rejoice (22:27;   34:3; 69:33). The 'anāwîm also can be identified with the nation in Ps 149:4: "For the Lord loves his people, and he adorns the 'anāwîm with victory" (149:4). According to BJ, "Israel" in "Peace be upon Israel!" (125:5) could designate the group of the "poor," "L'Israel qualitatif" (cf. 73:1; 102:1, 128:6; 130:7f).

"Poverty," a social factor in the beginning, writes A. Gelin (Les pauvres... p. 28f), gradually came to express an attitude of the soul. The "poor" became the "client" of God, receptive to his grace and disposed to accomplish his will. The vocabulary of poverty took a religious significance and "poor" became, like "servant," a title of honor (cf. E. Sachsse in Sellin Festschrift, pp. 105-110). Poverty provided in fact the ideal condition in which humility and faith could grow into a mystique. It will be seen that another group, the "just ones" or the "saints", were recruited mainly among the "poor." The spiritual movement grew with the approach of the messianic age. Jesus, who was poor (Mt 8:20) and called himself "meek and humble of heart" (Mt 11:29), opened his inaugural discourse with the words: "Blessed are the poor in spirit, for theirs is the kingdom of heaven" (Mt 5:3). Mary, his Mother, had anticipated the good news in her Magnificat, saying: "'He has put down the mighty from their thrones, and has exalted the lowly" (Lk 1:52).

(b) Distinctive features of the saddîqîm

Between the "poor" and the "just" there is in the Psalter a distinction which has to be determined in every context. Yet the two concepts have more than one aspect in common. Both the "poor" and the "just" are harassed by the wicked; both are under a special protection of God and not forgotten by him; both rejoice in the Lord and to both God grants victory. The words for "poor" and the terms *ṣāddîq* or *ṣaddîqîm*, "the just" (sing. and pl.) are often used in the same psalms and similar contexts. Ps 34 provides a good example of the variety of appellations applicable to the just:

3. The *'anāwîm* will hear me and be glad.
7. When the *'ānî* called out, the Lord heard.
10. Fear the Lord, you his holy ones (*qᵉdôšîm*).
16. The Lord has eyes for the *ṣaddîqîm*.
19. The Lord is close to the brokenhearted;
    and those who are crushed in spirit he saves.
20. Many are the troubles of the *ṣāddîq*,
    but out of them all the Lord delivers him.
22. Vice slays the wicked,
    and the enemies of the *ṣāddîq* pay for their guilt.
23. But the Lord redeems the lives of his servants (*'abādîm*).

Nowhere is the *ṣāddîq* defined in the psalms, but the contexts in which the term is used present a consistent picture of him. The Lord loves the *ṣāddîq* (146:8), sees him and listens to him (34:16), never forsakes him (37:25) but watches over his ways (5:13; 34:21), surrounds him with his protection (5:13), sustains and saves him (7:10; 34:20; 37:17, 39; 55:23). The *ṣaddîqîm* rejoice in the Lord (32:11; 64:11; 68:4; 97:12), their destiny is a blessed one (1:1; 37:16; 58:12): they will bear fruit (1:3; 92:13), will possess the land (37:29; cf. Mt 5:4), will see light (97:11) and will be in everlasting remembrance (112:6). The just is charitable (37:21) and speaks wisdom (37:30). The wicked who harass the just (37:12, 32; 94:21) will be punished (31:19; 34:22); they will not sit in the assembly of the just (1:5; 69:29; 111:1) but the just will triumph over them (52:8; 58:11; 75:11; 118:15). In some cases, it seems, the *ṣaddîqîm* could refer to "qualitative Israel," to Israel as the holy people (cf. below), with a sacred destiny: "For the scepter of wickedness shall not rest upon the land allotted to the *ṣaddîqîm*, lest the *ṣaddîqîm* put forth their hands to do wrong" (125:3 RSV).

The Hebrew *yāšār*, "upright," also designates the just man in the psalms:

33:1. Exalt you *ṣaddîqîm*, in the Lord;
      praise for the *yᵉsārîm* is fitting.
64:11. The *ṣāddîq* is glad in the Lord and takes refuge in him;
      in his glory all the upright of heart.
97:11. Light dawns for the *ṣāddîq;*
      and gladness, for the upright of heart.
140:14. Surely the *ṣaddîqîm* shall give thanks to your name;
      the *yᵉšārîm* shall dwell in your presence.

(c) *Can the ḥasîdîm be identified?*

Very often in the Psalter the pious people are referred to as *ḥasîdîm*: 4:4; 12:2; 16:10; 18:26; 30:5; 31:24; 32:6; 34:10; 37:28; 43:1; 50:5; 52:11; 79:2; 85:9; 86:2; 89:20; 97:10; 116:15; 132:9, 16; 145:10; 148:14; 149:1, 5, 9. The term is translated "the faithful" by CV, "the saints" by the Vulgate and the New Latin Psalter. J. Coppens, investigating "Les psaumes des *ḥasîdîm,*" has discovered in the use of *ḥāsîd* various shades of meanings corresponding to the categories of the relevant psalms. The *pietist* nuance appears mostly in the psalms of individuals, where personal relations with Yahweh are stressed: Pss 12, 16, 18, 30, 31, 43, 86, 116. The *sapiential* note occurs in those psalms which oppose the community of the faithful to the council of the wicked, mainly Pss 32, 37, 97, but also, it seems, Pss 4 and 52. The national sentiment is more apparent where the *ḥasîdîm* refer to persons who are such by *profession,* namely the *ḥasîdîm* refer to the nation as a whole, considered as the Remnant, the beneficiary of salvation. This meaning, particularly verified in Ps 79, is not absent from the hymns of recent date: Pss 145, 148, 149. Finally, it may be that in Pss 50, 85, and 132 the *ḥasîdîm* refer to persons who are such by *profession,* namely the Levites.

No real evidence can be produced to prove that there existed before the Maccabees a class of *ḥasîdîm* distinct socially or professionally. Nor were they different from the other Israelites cultually, as active participants of the covenant festivals. This is not to deny that the *ḥasîdîm* constituted *de facto* a moral body comprising all the faithful yahwists. This argumentation has in view, partly at least, the claims of B.D. Eerdmans who has treated of *The Chasidim* in 1942 and analyzed for this purpose Pss 4, 16, 26, 29, 31, 32, 44, 46, 47, 48, 50, 60, 69, 74, 79, 94, 95, 99, 141, 145. In some passages, he writes, the *chasidim* "appear to be a group in themselves, consisting of pious, upright and righteous men...but every righteous man was not a *chasid*," because the *chasid* was elected by God (p. 177). Ps 149:5-9 describes "a gathering of *chasidim*, lying on couches, uttering threats and longing to take revenge on enemies, like dervishes used to meet, or is it a picture of their triumphant mood after successful raids?" (p. 194). "We" in Ps 44:21 "appear to have been defeated by their adversaries and to have been a body of warriors.... The word *chasidim* does not appear in the psalm. Yet we cannot suppose another *bodyguard of Jahu* [=Yahweh] to have existed" (p. 197). "The *chasidim* were laymen of erudition, knowing the historical traditions of Israel, capable of playing instruments and composing songs. Being reputable for their piety they held a position between the priests and the great prophets of the eighth century b.c." (p. 254). They existed before the exile and appear to have survived through all the political changes, "without losing the old spirit" (p. 206f).

But Coppens challenges the validity of the evidence produced by Eerdmans and others about the *early* existence of a professional body of *ḥasîdîm* (p. 223f). One argument is that a suffix (like "his," "your") almost always accompanies *ḥasîdîm* referring them to Yahweh. Psalm 132:16, however, speaks of the "*ḥasîdîm* of Zion," while Ps 149:1, 5 simply of "the *ḥasîdîm*." Besides, other terms having a similar meaning also carry the suffix, the term *'ebed* mainly, meaning "servant": Pss 19:12;   27:9;   31:17;   34:23;   69:37;   89:40;   116:16;   119:17, 23, 65, 84, 122, 124, 176;   135:14. The "*ḥasîdîm* of Yahweh" are the beneficiaries *par excellence* of divine *ḥesed* (see §11f). Other texts cited are not more convincing. Dt 33:8 and 2 Ch 6:41 concern the Levites. In 1 S 2:9; Mi 7:2; Pr 2:8, the *ḥasîdîm* are the righteous ones and the faithful in general. But the term "*ḥasîdîm*" was striking, and with *Maccabees* it was taken up to designate a *distinct body of persons*. They remembered that the death of the *ḥasîdîm* is precious in the eyes of the Lord (Ps 116:15), that Yahweh does not abandon the *ḥasîdîm* (16:10;   37:28), that he defends and protects them (86:2;   97:10;   1 S 2:9; Pr 2:8) and that in certain cases he will produce wonders for them (Pss 4:4;   31:22;   86:10;   145:5). The Assideans (Douay) or Hasidaeans (*JB*) mentioned in 1 M 7:12ff are probably to be identified with the "group of scribes," but they are clearly defined by Alcimus: "Those of the Jews who are called

Hasidaeans, whose leader is Judas Maccabeus, are keeping up war and stirring up sedition, and will not let the kingdom attain tranquillity" (2 M 14:6).

Coppens has noted that the *hasîdim* of the psalms are described as "faithful" (12:2; 31:24), "righteous" (31:19...), "perfect" (*tāmîm*: 18:26, 33; 37:18), "upright" (32:11...), as loving (97:10; 145: 20) and serving God (31:20...), as taking refuge in him (18:3, 31...) or placing their trust (4:6...) and hope (43:5...) in him. These are much the same characteristics as can be found in connection with any vocabulary of the just in the psalms.

(d) *Saints and holy ones*

Psalm 89:6-8 provides a good example of the use in the Bible of the term *qᵉdōšim*, "holy ones," to designate God's celestial attendants:

The heavens proclaim your wonders, O Lord,
  and your faithfulness in the assembly of the holy ones.
For who in the skies can rank with the Lord?
  Who is like the Lord among the sons of God?
God is terrible in the council of the holy ones;
  he is great and awesome beyond all round about him.

If the question of the *qᵉdōšim* is raised here, it is because the term is used in the psalms to designate also the faithful on earth. According to recent research, writes Coppens, the noun *qᵉdōšim* generally designates in the Massoretic text the supraterrestrial beings who form the court of Yahweh (in *ETL* 1963, pp. 485-500). These beings the Old Testament also calls *bᵉnê 'Elôhîm*, "sons of God." In the Christian tradition they are "angels." The *qᵉdōšim* of Ps 89:6 and 8 form a group, a collectivity, called *qāhāl*, "assembly" and *sôd*, "council." These *qᵉdōšim* are mentioned in parallel to *bᵉnê 'ēlîm*, "sons of the gods" (v 7), who figure in Ps 29: 1, and probably in Jb 1:6; 2:1; 38:7 as *bᵉnê (hā)'elôhîm*, and in Pss 82:1, 6; 97:7, 9 as *'elôhîm*. The "council of Yahweh" is mentioned in Jr 23:18, 22 and Jb 15:8.

It has been proposed to see in the *qᵉdōšim* of Ps 89 not "angels," but gods (see on *Ps 29:1), brought to subjection by Yahweh (see §10g). This interpretation would be suggested by other texts where the false gods are alluded to Pss 82:1; 95:3; 96:7, 9; 135:5; Ex 15:11 and

Dn 11:36. Coppens, however, observes that in Ps 89 there is no trace of a polemic against false gods. Celestial beings are meant, who form Yahweh's court and act as his *māl'ākîm*, "messengers": cf. Dt 33:2f; 1 K 22:19; Jr 23:18, 22; Zc 14:5; Dn 4:10, 14, 20; 8:13; Jb 4:17-19; 5:1; 15:15; Pr 9:10; 30:3; Ws 5:5; 10:10; Si 24:2; 42:17 (on "angels," cf. L. Dequeker, p. 484).

Another subject of debate is the meaning of *q^edōšîm* is Ps 16:3: "How wonderfully has he made me cherish *the holy ones* who are in the land." It is not probable that they are "the souls of the deceased." To understand them as "the saints of Israel" does not explain the mention of idols in the next verse. *Q^edōšîm* then probably refers to "false divinities." In *The Jerusalem Bible* verses 2-3 are translated thus:

> To Yahweh you say, "My Lord,
> you are my fortune, nothing else but you,"
> yet to those pagan deities in the land,
> "My princes, all my pleasure is in you."
> Their idols teem, after these they run:
> shall I pour their blood-libations?-not I!
> Take their names on my lips?—never!

The following commentary is added: "Verse 2-3 are addressed to the psalmist's contemporaries who thought they could combine the worship of Yahweh as supreme god, verse 2, with that of local deities (lit. holy ones cf. 1 S 2:2), verse 3; such syncretism was Israel's great and persistent temptation. The translation changes (supported by the versions) only two vowels of the Hebrew text, keeping all the consonants." The *q^edōšîm* are said to be on earth presumably in contrast to the true God, Yahweh, who lives in heaven. According to Dahood, as we shall see (cf. *Ps 16:3), verse 3 is part of the *professio fidei* of "a Canaanite convert to Yahwism."

The "holy one of the Lord" in Ps 106:16 is clearly identified as Aaron. A special holiness, mostly cultic in character, was attributed to the high-priest (Ex 28:36; 39:30), to the priests (Lv 21:6-23; 22:9, 16, 32), to the levites (2 Ch 35:3). In Ps 34:10, however, the title *q^edōšîm* is attributed to all the faithful Israelites: "Fear the Lord, you *his holy ones*, for nought is lacking to those who fear him." Coppens would read two compositions in Ps 34: one is a thanksgiving of a *'ānî-'ānāw* (vv 2-7), the other (8-23) is a didactic and sapiential piece celebrating God's special providence towards the just. Numerous biblical texts do in fact call "holy" the children of Israel: Ne 2:20; Is 54:17; 63:17; 65:8-14 (cf. Pss 69:37; 135:14). In Ws 18:9, as in Ps 34:10, the appellation "holy" is applied to all the faithful servants of Yahweh.

It seems that the sacred writers, following the tradition, transferred to the individuals what had been said of God's people as such. That holiness characterizes the chosen people appears in numerous texts setting forth various aspects. This holiness derives from divine election (Ex 19:6; Dt 7:6; 14:2; 26:19; 28:9). In some texts of Isaiah the eschatological or messianic people of God are the subject of that holiness (4:3; 6:13; 62:12; cf. Dn 12:7) but elsewhere it is attributed to historic Israel (cf. Lv 19:2; 20:7, 26; Nb 16:3).

Coppens concludes his study with some observations designed to explain (1) how the concept of holiness was extended to the ordinary faithful, as in Ps 34:10 and (2) how the moral or ethical aspect of holiness superseded its cultic or angelical notion. The just, he thinks, would have been assimilated to the angelic condition through the "son of God" concept applied to the nation (Ex 4:22; Dt 32:5f; Ho 11:1; Jr 3:19; Ws 12:19) and to individuals (Is 63:16; Ws 2:18; Si 4:10). Or else the cultic notion of holiness proper to priests was extended to all the faithful. Then, in a third stage, the concept of sacred and cultic holiness was spiritualized and transferred to the ethical level, leaving behind the cultic implications. These reflections will help, it is hoped, to understand the vocabulary of the "just" in the Psalms.

(e) Sin and forgiveness

The "man to God" relations are conditioned in great part by *sin and forgiveness*. Though the man who trusts in God may fall, "he does not lie prostrate, for the hand of the Lord sustains him" (Ps 37:24). Not all the psalmists proclaim themselves righteous. One is overwhelmed by his sins:

> Withhold not, O Lord, your compassion from me;
>   may your kindness and your truth ever preserve me.
> For all about me are evils beyond reckoning;
>   my sins so overcome me that I cannot see;
> They are more numerous than the hairs of my head,
>   and my heart fails me (40:12f).

The remedy to sin is repentance and God's forgiveness.

Sin and mercy

A well known antiphony, "his *ḥesed* is everlasting" (cf. §11f), praises in Pss 106, 107, 118, and 136 the mercy and the love of God, as it did at the dedication of the first and second temples (2 Ch 7:3; Ezr 3:11). Elsewhere Yahweh is called "merciful and gracious" (Ex 34:6; Pss 86:15; 103:8; 111:4; 112:4; 145:8). God's dealings with man are marked by mercy and equity. How these two attitudes can be reconciled is a puzzling question for the religious man. Ps. 99:8 illustrates this "unity of opposites" which seems to characterize some aspects of the Old Testament concept of God:

O Lord, our God, you answered them;
   a forgiving God you were to them,
   though requiting their misdeeds.

Thus God dealt with Israel's great leaders. He acted in the same way with the rebellious generation of the Sinai wilderness: "Being merciful, he forgave their sin....remembered that they were flesh, a passing breath that returns not" (78:38f). There is a plea often heard in the psalms: "Remember not against us the iniquities of the past...deliver us and pardon our sins for your names' sake" (79:8f), "for you, O Lord, are good and forgiving" (86:5).

Sinfulness versus innocence

Because the psalms reflect different stages of biblical thought, it is always necessary to study the general background of any given theme. There are different views on sin in the Old Testament (cf. *SDB, VII,* c. 407-471). In some texts sin appears almost as a congenital, incurable illness. According to the Yahwist (one of the Pentateuchal traditions), "the inclination of man's heart is evil from his youth" (8:21; cf. 6:5). Jeremiah would say: "More tortuous than all else is the human heart beyond remedy" (17:9); "Can the Ethiopian change his skin? the leopard his spots? As easily would you be able to do good, accustomed to evil as you are" (13:23); "From the womb the wicked are perverted; astray from birth have the liars gone" (Ps 58:4); "There is no man who does not sin," stated Solomon at the temple's dedication (1 K 8:46). Ecclesiastes is of the same opinion (7:20) and the author of Proverbs declares: Who can say, "I have made my heart clean, I am cleansed of my sin?" (20: 9). Eliphaz' question is well known: "Can a man be righteous as against God? Can a mortal be blameless against his Maker?" (Jb 4:17). The author of the *Miserere* reflects this tradition: "Indeed, in guilt was I born, and in sin my mother conceived me" (Pss 51:7; 58:4). This confession of a congenital inclination to sin attenuates guilt and appeals to God's mercy, as in other psalms: "Enter not into judgment with your servant, for before you no living man is just" (143:2). God does not in fact requite men according to their crimes (103:10; 130:4), because he is merciful (78:38) and because "their spirits would faint before me, the souls that I have made" (Is 57:16). There will be more to say about verse 7 in the introduction to *Ps 51. H. W. Robinson does not find there "the doctrine of original sin" but only "the doctrine of racial evil," the universal tendency that is expressed in Isaiah (6:5) also: "Woe is me, I am doomed! For I am a man of unclean lips, living among people of unclean lips'" (*The Psalmists*, p. 61).

Several psalmists, on the other hand, claim to have "walked in integrity" (26:1, 11; 41:13), to have kept their heart clean (73:13). They produce formal attestations of innocence (18:21ff; 26:1-8; 101: 2-8) and go as far as telling God: "Do me justice, O Lord, because I am just and because of the innocence that is mine" (7:8; comp, 35:24); "The Lord has rewarded me according to my justice..." (18:21, 25). Dahood would classify as "Psalms of innocence": Pss 5, 17, 26, 139 (on "negative confessions," see *Ps 101). In Elihu's words Job had repeatedly said: "I am clean and without transgression; I am innocent; there is no guilt in me" (33:9). The prophets, however, never thought of denying their own sin, but they asked to be delivered from it. At the time of the Flood it is not said that Noah was sinless, but that he had found grace before God. The Remnant, who will be saved from the eschatological judgment, is not the community of the just but that of the elect (for the Remnant see §15a). Full cleansing from sin is hoped for by Isaiah (1:18) and the *Miserere*: "Cleanse me of sin with hyssop, that I may be purified; wash me, and I shall be whiter than snow" (Ps 51:9; on the so-called "oaths of exculpation or of purgation," see on *Pss 7, 26, 139).

Notions of sin

More generally sin is considered by Old Testament writers as a refusal of God, as a rebellion against him, as a breaking of communion between Yahweh and a member of the covenant: "It is your crimes that
separate you from your God" (Is 59:2). Although the "hardening of
the heart" comes from God (cf. Is 6:10; 29:10) the sinner bears full
responsibility for the rupture with him, and for not listening to his repeated appeals: "Oh, that today you would hear his voice: Harden not
your hearts as at Meriba, as in the day of Massa in the desert, where
your fathers tempted me" (Ps 95:8f). This refusal of God, according
to the prophets, include different aspects: "for Amos, it is *ingratitude,*
for Hosea, *unfriendliness,* for Isaiah, *pride,* for Jeremiah, *falseness* concealed in the heart, for Ezekiel, open *rebellion*—but always the breaking
of a bond" (Jacob, p. 285: my italics). The sayings of the psalmists on
sin reflect one or another of these aspects.

Lex talionis

Although God can grant mercy to sinners and often does, sin is
generally considered as having a sequel, *lex talionis* (cf. §14d): the sinner's conduct does no harm to God but falls back upon the sinner's own
head: "They deal out evil to themselves" (Is 3:9); "Is it I whom they
hurt, says the Lord; is it not rather themselves, to their own confusion?"
(Jr 7:19); "I have brought down their conduct upon their heads" (Ezk
22:31), says the Lord God. *Lex talionis,* understood in this sense, finds
numerous echoes in the psalms, when they speak of the wicked: they
fall into the pit they have themselves dug (7:16; 9:16;. 35:8; 57:7;
cf. Pr 26:27; Ec 10:8; Si 27:26), they are caught in their own net
(141:10) and their own snare (9:16; 35:8; 69:23), they will be
pierced by their own swords (37:15) and fall victims of their own lies
(59:13; 64:9; cf. Jr 18:18). This law of retribution (see §14d) was
a dictum of wisdom: "By his own iniquities the wicked man will be
caught, in the meshes of his own sin he will be held fast" (Pr 5:22;
cf. 12:13; see on *Ps 37). The just are rewarded in the same way (Pr
12:14). On *Lex talionis* as a legal maxim see *Ps 7.

Purification from sin

We read then in Ps 51:9: "Cleanse me of sin with hyssop, that I may be purified; wash me, and I shall be whiter than snow." If we grant that *rites of purification* did occur in Israel, "we shall not immediately depreciate them as mere externalism," writes H. Ringgren (*The Faith* ...p. 69): "The deep insight into the essence and nature of sin which is found in Ps 51 could obviously exist alongside outward rites which served as visible signs of the forgiveness of sins, namely, washing hyssop, and the wiping out of sins written on a tablet. Such a rite is known in Babylonia. The existence of outward signs does not necessarily make the religious experience less 'spiritual'; it only serves to reinforce the experience. Religion occupies the whole man, and the religious life is accordingly influenced by sense impressions called forth by symbolic actions" (*ibid.*). Mainly, however, the psalmists look directly to God to have their sins removed through divine forgiveness: "All flesh must come to you with all its sins; though our faults overpower us, you blot them out" (Ps 65:3f; cf. 130:4). With examples drawn from Babylonia, W. F. Forrester states that the pagan sought to be delivered from his misfortune by appropriate superstitious rites. He did not, like the psalmist (cf. Ps 32:3-5), seek forgiveness for a fault for which he was sorry. The verb *kapper,* translated "to blot out" by JB in Ps 65:4, literally means "to cover." The expression is used in the "Priestly" vocabulary to designate "pardon," granted especially on the Day of Atonement (cf. Lv 16 and Pss 78:38; 79:9). Elsewhere in the psalms, the forgiven sins are explicitly described as covered: "Happy is he whose fault is taken away, whose sin is covered" (32:1; cf. Rm 4:7; Ps 85:3). An abundant and well documented treatment of "remission of sin" in the psalms will be found in G. Bernini, pp. 247-284 (see also the studies of E. Beaucamp on Ps 51:6 and of H. Bückers, E. R. Dalglish, H. McKeating).

Hidden sins

Some paslmists worry about *unknown or hidden* sins: "Though your servant is careful of them, very diligent in keeping them [the commandments], yet who can detect failings? Cleanse me from my unknown faults!" (19:12f). In Ps 90:8 it is apparently said that God has summoned man's iniquities, inspected his secret (sins) in his own light.

These sins could be unintentional faults, like those of Ps 19, or they could be sins hidden from others. Such allusions to secret sins are rare in the Bible, but "in Babylonian psalms of lament the fact that a man has suffered misfortune is frequently taken to mean that he must have sinned in some way even without knowing it, so that it is necessary to find out what his sin is. Accordingly, it is not unusual that forgiveness is asked for sins which are unknown to the speaker. This presupposes a rather mechanical conception of sin: if man has transgressed some of the precepts of the gods, whether he is aware of his transgressions or not, punishment will necessarily come" (H. Ringgren, *The Faith...*p. 70).

On the other hand, the personal and moral aspects of sin are implied in almost every line of Ps 51:

> For I acknowledge my offense,
>   and my sin is before me always:
> "Against you only have I sinned,
>   and done what is evil in your sight" (vv 5-6; cf. 38:19).

One psalmist reveals the benefit brought to him by the *confession of his sins*:

> As long as I would not speak, my bones wasted away
>   with my groaning all the day,
> For day and night your hand was heavy upon me;
>   my strength was dried up as by the heat of summer.
> Then I acknowledged my sin to you,
>   my guilt covered not.
> I said, "I confess my faults to the Lord,"
>   and you took away the guilt of my sin (32:3-5).

It is hard to say what produced the change. Is it physical pain he was relieved of when God removed his hand, cured him of his well deserved illness, or was the anguish of a bad conscience that which made him suffer? In any case the psalmist believed that sin and suffering are related and that the way out of both was the return to God through penitence and confession (see on *Ps 51): God pardons when man repents (cf. Jr 3:12; 18:7-11; Jl 2:13).

Sin and suffering

The relation of sin with physical suffering, caused mostly by illness, did raise problems to the mind of the religiously conscious Israelite. In the yahwist's etiological account of the fall, there are traces of an attempt to link suffering with sin (Gn 3:16-19). Job could not understand that calamities should plague an innocent man. He found that he was not as guiltless as he thought he was: "Therefore I disown what I have said, and repent in dust and ashes" (Jb 42:6). One psalmist could only state that somehow God is responsible:

> I was speechless and opened not my mouth,
> because it was your doing;
> Take away your scourge from me;
> at the blow of your hand I wasted away (39:10f).

The suppliant of an individual lament speaks of the anger of God (cf. §11h) and of his arrows, a metaphor meaning the trials of the just:

> O Lord, in your anger punish me not,
> in your wrath chastise me not;
> For your arrows have sunk deep in me,
> and your hands come down upon me.
> There is no health in my flesh because of your indignation;
> there is no wholeness in my bones because of my sins,
> For my iniquities have overwhelmed me;
> they are like a heavy burden beyond my strength (38:2-5).

Not all the afflicted immediately understood the merciful aspect of divine action: "But he saves the unfortunate through their affliction, and instructs them through distress" (Jb 36:15).

(f) *The inner life of the psalmists*

Writing on the inner life of the psalmists, H. W. Robinson notes that in the psalms "man looks up to God through four concentric circles of human experience": the temple and its worship, the circle of Jewish society, the arena of history and nature itself. Concerning temple worship we need only add here a word to what has been said about "the psalms and the cult" (cf. §8ab). H. Ringgren rightly denies, against G. Quell, that piety is essentially different from cult. "It is not fair," he writes, "to regard the psalmists as lacking in religious experience or personal piety on the ground that they nourished their religious life with that which they experienced in the cult. Instead we have to try to understand their religious experience in precisely this cultic setting.... We must analyze the religion of the Psalms as cultic religion, as piety nourished by the cult and expressed in cultic acts" (p. 21f; see on *Ps 86).

This can be illustrated in many ways. Before enumerating the saving deeds of Yahweh Ps 66 extends an invitation to all believers:

Let all on earth worship and sing praise to you,
      sing praise to your name!
Come and see the works of God,
      his tremendous deeds among men (vv 4f).

This needs not refer to "cultic drama," but some worshippers at least underwent in the temple an experience which was equivalent to "seeing God's mighty deeds." Another psalmist was troubled by the prosperity of the wicked, until he entered the sanctuary of God "and considered their final destiny" (73:17). These examples — there are many others — tend to show that cultic experience did nourish piety and strengthen the faith of the worshippers and presumably, of the psalmists themselves.

A. Gelin has written excellently on the concept of "faith" as illustrated in Job and some psalms. He had explained the *signs of God*: the sign of *creation*, re-enacted in the theophanies, the sign of *history*, which is also an epiphany of God (God speaking through the events), the *temple* as sign (cf. Ezk 48:35), and finally *Israel*, who, in a way, was also a sign. But God has been met also beyond or without signs by some men, already in the Old Testament. Job is an illustration... "He had lost everything and even his last sign, his theology... He finds himself in God's presence as if in the presence of a blind force that will not let him eat or breathe, whose power he can indeed see but not its rightness. Yet all these facts cannot break the contact with God established by faith. In praying, in hoping, Job comes to realize that God's justice is a mystery, that the categories in which we try to enclose Him are inadequate. His friends are angry with him on this account because, they say, 'he is destroying piety,' when really he is saving it by living its essential dimension: the approach to God Himself, beyond all supports, all representations, all images, all signs" (*The Psalms are our Prayers*, p. 35). In the Psalms, adds Gelin, we find this silence of Job reproduced in warmer, less abrupt terms, in terms of a communion in which the contact with God is established on the ruins of a former rigidity, a self-sufficiency that had to be broken up. This communion has a degree of intimacy that corresponds to the intensity of the responses (cf. Ps 130). "Another psalmist [Ps 73:21-26] has been scandalized by the absence of signs of God: the world seems to be ruled by a series of blunders. But he takes hold of himself, prays in silence in the Temple, and finally discovers that God is more valuable than His gifts, that His dealings have the air of eternity" (p. 36).

The main elements of the *psalmists' interior life* are no doubt reflected in the description they give of the life-situations, praises and prayers of the "poor" and the "just," presented above. The limits of their "inner life" have been a subject of speculation with the publication of H. J. Franken's *The mystical Communion with YHWH in the Book of Psalms* (Leiden, 1954). If "mysticism," writes H. Ringgren, "is taken to denote 'the experience of union or identification with the deity,' as is often the case, 'there is certainly no mysticism in the Psalms.' But if it is employed in the sense of an 'intimate and immediate communion with God,' then some expressions deserve consideration" (*The Faith...p.* 56) Franken concludes his study with the following reflections: "The oriental way of meditation, the ecstasy in the sanctuary, the perfect peace with the world of God expressed in praise, the lifting up of the hands and blessings, and finally the experience of seeing God point to *the mystical tendency* in the piety of the psalms" (p. 92).

The psalmists often speak of "meditating" (*śiaḥ*) on the law of God (119:78), on his wondrous works (143:5; 145:5) or his mighty deeds (77:13). One says he "reflects" on God in the watches of the night (63: 7). The verb used here is *hāgâh*, "to murmur religious phrases," also translated "meditate" or "muse" (*RSV*): "Happy the man who meditates (*hāgâh*) day and night on the law of the Lord" (1:2). The psalmists also "reflect" on God's work and deeds (77:13; 143:5) and their silent or murmuring prayer they call *hegyôn lēb* (19:15) or *hāgût lēb* (49:4), "whispering of the heart." The meaning conveyed by *hgh*, writes Franken, "is not the same as the Western way of meditation which is interested in the contents of texts, studying them with the heart as with the intellect, but it is the repeated recollection of well known texts, looking for arbitrary associations while reciting and hearing the sound of the words. It is the activity of muttering, hearing and reading the sacred texts, by which the memory and the heart become full of contents" (p. 21).

Other aspects of the psalmists' inner life are suggested by what they practice and recommend: "Be still (*dûm*) before the Lord, and wait patiently for him" (37:7); "For God alone my soul waits in silence" (*dûmiyyâh*: 62:1); "To you, O Lord, I lift up my soul" (86:4); "My soul thirsts for you" (143:16; cf. 42:2; 63:1); "The close secret of Yahweh belongs to them who fear him" (25:14 JB); "But for me it is good to be near God" (73:28); "There is nothing upon earth that I desire besides thee" (73:25; "Into your hands I commend my spirit" (31: 6); "My soul waits for the Lord more than sentinels wait for the dawn" (130:6). In some cases at least, "my soul" simply means "myself" but the significance for our purpose is the same. "Love for God" is obviously implied in these declarations of the psalmists. Yet it is rarely explicitly mentioned: "I love thee, O Lord, my strength" (18:2, *rāḥam*); "I love the Lord because he has heard my voice in supplication" (116:1, *'āhab*). Besides, the psalmists speak of loving God's name (5:11; 69:36). The psalmists' love for God or their devotion to him is also reflected in the way they proclaim their joy in the Lord or exhort others to holy rejoicing: 33: 1; 35:9; 40:17; 70:5; 71:23; 75:10; 89:17, 97:12. The reasons for rejoicing generally refer to what God has done, rather than to what he is: "For you make me glad, O Lord, by your deeds; at the works of your hands I rejoice" (92:5). All these declarations certainly reflect an intimate fellowship with God. Only by reading beyond the words can the concept of "mystical communion" be discovered in these and in other statements of the psalmists.

It is significant that a psalmist should confess: "Therefore my heart is glad and my soul rejoices; my body, too, abides in confidence" (16:9). God provides for the body as well as for the soul; he dispenses the gifts to all living things (see §11b):

The eyes of all look hopefully for you,
  and you give them their food in due season:
You open your hand
  and satisfy the desire of every living thing (145:15f; cf. 136:25).

"God satisfies him (*nefesh!*) who is thirsty, and the hungry he fills with good things" (107:9; cf. 65:5; 104:27), "with the riches of a banquet (63:6; cf. 22:27). The divine Shepherd leads to "restful waters" and refreshes the soul (23:2; cf. Is 49:10; Jr 31:12). Attention to both man's physical and spiritual desires is recalled under this variety of metaphors. One psalmist has ably described the fortune of the "children of men" who seek refuge from Yahweh, in the shadow of his wings:

> They have their fill of the prime gifts of your house;
>> from your delightful stream you give them to drink.
> For with you is the fountain of life,
>> and in your light we see light (36:9f).

(g) *Enemies and evildoers*

The identity of the "enemies" and "evildoers" in the psalms will presumably vary with the identity of the psalmist who complains about them. In that respect there are three possibilities: the speaking subject is expressly plural ("We"), expressly singular ("I") and referring to a private individual, or singular but representing the king or a leader of the nation (collective "I"). The "enemies" of the king or of his representative can of course be identified with the enemies of the nation. Complicating factors do, however, intervene, to disturb this simple pattern and constitute the issues of a debate. The surprising monotony which characterizes the description of the "enemies" can be ascribed to the generous use in psalmography of conventional expressions and formulas. The important role played by the "enemies" in the individual laments is more difficult to explain. Some scholars believe (d) that the "I" of the psalms rarely or never represents a private individual (see §23a). In 1888 already, R. Smend argued that the "I" is the community. "Nearly a quarter of a century later, Emile Balla contended that the 'I' should be taken in a genuinely individual sense, except in those psalms where there are clear indications that the reference is collective, a view which, on the whole, was endorsed by Herrmann Gunkel and his disciples" (G. W. Anderson, p. 20). The problem is neither simple, nor easy. Before consulting other authorities it is advisable to interrogate the psalmists themselves.

The "enemies" (*'ōyēb*) or "adversaries" (*sār*) are generally called "evil-doers" (*pō'alê 'āwen*): 5:6;   6:9;   14:4 [=53:4]; 28:3;   36:13; 59:3;   64:3;   92:8, 10;   94:4, 16;   101:8;   125:5;   141:4, 9 (cf. Is 31:2;   Ho 6:8;   Jb 34:8, 22). More specific appellations describe the wicked or the enemies as persecutors (7:2;   31:16;   55:4), as false witnesses (27:12;   35:11), as insolent (31:19;   54:5), proud (36:12), bloodthirsty men (54:24; 59:3; 139:19). In the figurative they are compared to roaring beasts (35:17; 55:11; 58:7), lions (17:12; 35: 17; 57:5; 58:7) or bulls (68:31; 75:11). As for the terms *rešā'îm*, "wicked," is occurs more than 40 times. One psalmist at least complains that a friend who had his trust has joined the ranks of his enemies (41: 10). Several suppliants suffer from having become a laughingstock to their neighbors (30:12; 44:14; 79:4), a dread to their friends (30: 12; 38:12), outcasts for their family (69:9).

Conventional language is also used to describe the hostile activity of the evildoers. The psalmist will say: they seek my life (35:4; 38:13; 40:15; 54:5; 59:4), they mock me (31:12; 35:16; 40:16; 70:4), they plot against me (37:12; 71:10; 83:4), they lay snares (31:5; 57: 7; 140:6), they trample upon me (56:3; 57:4; 62:4), they repay evil for good (35:12; 38:21), they hate me and attack me without cause (59:5; 69:5). The evildoers are mainly false accusers: their lying (109:2; 120: 3f), treacherous tongues (55:22) are compared to sharp swords and arrows (57:5; 64:4; cf. Jr 9:2, 7; Pr 30:14). The slanders (41:8f) bend their bow against their victims (7:13; 11:2; 37:14).

Having examined "the prayer of the accused," H. Schmidt concluded that the false accusations of which the sick suppliants complain must be inferences drawn by their enemies: they are ill, therefore they are guilty. One way of refuting the slanders was to submit to a test of innocence or to oaths of exculpation (cf. *Pss 7, 26). Consistent with his views on the "party of the poor" (cf. §12a), A. Rahlfs held that the "enemies" were a group or party of godless Jews in the post-exilic period. But Gunkel pointed out, rightly it seems, that socially and religiously diverging parties existed in pre-exilic times. A. Puukko has identified national and other enemies in a number of psalms, for example the Philistines (Ps 78), the Assyrians (46), the Babylonians (137), enemies of Maccabean times (44, 74, 79, 80, 83), mythical enemies, like Rahab (89:11) and Leviathan (74:13f), and also Pestilence (91:1-8).

As early as 1921, in the first of his *Psalmenstudien*, Mowinckel wrote on "*'āwen* und die individuellen Klagepsalmen." He argued that in the expression *pō'alê 'āwen*, *'āwen* ("wickedness") "indicates supernatural or magical power, that the '*pō'alê 'āwen*' [see above] were sorcerers who by their potent spells, brought about the affliction of the pious sufferers, and that the psalms in question [individual laments] were used to ward off or counteract the evil effects of the black arts practiced by the *pō'alê 'āwen*" (G. Anderson, p. 24). These views were challenged by several scholars.

There is no evidence. A. Hjelt thought, that the psalmists looked upon the evildoers as the cause of their illness. He observed, besides, that "the terms which Mowinckel had regarded as referring to magical practices need not, or do not normally and naturally, carry such a sense" (Anderson, p. 24). G. R. Driver would not easily admit that the "workers of mischief" can be taken as sorcerers or that Ps 51 can be understood as an anti-magical prayer, directed against an enemy who seeks to procure his victim's death by magical means (*The Psalmists*, p. 112). Comparison with Babylonian practices did not constitute proof, Driver thought, and Mowinckel's theory seemed to him "intrinsically highly improbable in view of the Jewish attitude towards sorcerers and witches" (p. 113). In *"De Werkers der Angerechtigheid,"* N. H. Ridderbos offered additional support to the objections raised by Hjelt and Driver. While rejecting Mowinckel's interpretation of the term *'āwen,* A. Guillaume strongly favored his idea of interpreting the individual laments in terms of magical practice (*Prophecy* . . . pp. 272-289).

In the meantime, however, Mowinckel had modified some of his views (see below §14d), in accordance with new evidence supplied by his disciple, H. Birkeland, who claimed in 1955: "Mowinckel. . .founded his interpretation of the individual psalms on my studies" (*ZAW* 1955, p. 99, note). In *The Evildoers*. . .Birkeland argued that the "I" speaking in the individual as well as in the national psalms of lamentation is a king or a national leader, that the "enemies" are foreign nations, that the situations are national calamities. The presence of "enemies" within Israel reflects periods when Israel was subjected to foreign powers. Birkeland starts with indubitable national psalms in the "We" form (44, 60, 79, 80, 83, 124, 125). Foreign enemies are also referred to, he thinks, in the royal psalms, mainly in Pss 18, 20, 21, 89, 144, and even in a third group, composed of "I" psalms: Pss 28, 61, 73 and 1 S 2:1-10. In the psalms the enemies are described in the same way as in the national laments: they are foreign foes and the affliction is war. There is no gap then between the individual and the national psalms. For Birkeland, in fact, practically all individual psalms are royal psalms. Against the king, as representative of the people, the (foreign) enemies directed their attacks. Their strength could consist in military might or in potent words endowed with magical power.

In a few psalms only can in fact the "enemies" be with certainty identified as *gôyîm* (cf. 79:6; 106:17; 115:2). M. Tsevat discovered an "intrinsic fallacy" in Birkeland's methodology (cf. *JBL* 1957, p. 162): the psalms being "stylistically highly patternized" it is likely that aggressive and military phraseology could be used throughout even when the "enemies" are no longer nations or *gôyim* but individual accusers or dangerous personal foes. Birkeland also seems to have succumbed to the temptation of reducing diversity to a single pattern, even against contrary evidence. It is hardly possible to grant credit to an hypothesis which implicity denies the existence of genuinely individual psalms of lamentation. Why should it be insisted, asks Anderson, that "an impious nation" in Ps 43:1 must refer to a foreign power, when a "sinful nation" in Is 1:4 unquestionably refers to Judah? (p. 29). It is on a broader scope and a higher level that a kind of unity relates the descriptions which the psalmists give of affliction and conflict. It has been expressed by H. Ringgren: "What is important for our study is the fact that the opposition between the righteous and their enemies—whether they are called 'the wicked' or something else—is lifted up to a higher mythological or metaphysical level and related to the opposition between cosmos and chaos, or life and death, which, according to Pedersen, is so typical of the ancient Israelitic view of life" (*The Faith...*, p. 46; cf. J. Pedersen, I-II, pp. 453-496). More will be said below on the role of "enemies" in the individual laments (§20a).

§13. CULT FESTIVALS AND PSALMS

God's kingship, the role of the sacred Ark, the election of David and of Jerusalem, life within the covenant: these are themes which it is appropriate to examine in connection with the psalms and with "the beliefs of piety." The discussion of the problems they raise coincides mainly with that of three cult festivals brought into view by leading scholars.

(a) *The enthronement festival of Yahweh*

A number of hymns celebrate Yahweh's kingship, mainly Pss 47, 93, 96, 97, 98. With these "enthronement psalms," S. Mowinckel, the leading scholar in the field, associates Pss 81 and 95. All of them, he claims, are connected with the harvest and new year festival. "Characteristic of this group is that they salute Yahweh as the king, who has just ascended his royal throne to wield his royal power. The situation envisaged in the poet's imagination, is Yahweh's ascent to the throne and the acclamation of Yahweh as king; the psalm is meant as the song of praise which is to meet Yahweh on his 'epiphany,' his appearance as the new, victorious, king" (I, p. 106). The phrase *Yhwh mālak* in Pss 47:8; 93: 1; 96:10; 97:1 is to be translated "Yahweh has become king." "The picture seen by the poets is that of a great celebration which they present with the same features as that of the enthronement of a terrestrial monarch, only on a magnified mythical scale and with unearthly splendor" (p. 107). This event is mythically presented but is viewed as real, for, writes Mowinckel, "the myth is the genuine form of the religious conception" (*ibid.*; cf. §8d, 9b, 11a).

Myth, not history or eschatology

Yahweh has become King, not only of Israel, but of the whole earth. Other ideas, explains Mowinckel, are connected with the enthronement psalms: the mythical conception of creation [cf.§11a] as a primeval struggle against the watery chaos; victory over the gods; Yahweh's act of judgment (or "rule"), on his enemies or on the gods; the creation of Israel and all the events that followed, in its ancient history. But Mowinckel rejects any attempt to link Yahweh's enthronement with some historical event. "They are not actual and historical, but mythical, unearthly events, to which the enthronement psalms refer" (I, p. 110).

Others, Mowinckel writes, have tried to interpret these psalms *eschatologically* (cf. §14): "The poet and the congregation sing in advance the poem regarding the final salvation, when Yahweh shall annihilate the power of evil and deliver his people and establish the eschatological kingdom of God, when he wholly and absolutely shall become king and be recognized as such by the whole world" (p. 110f). Mowinckel admits that there exist "anticipatory salvation songs" in which prophecy is expressed (cf. Is 12:1-4; Jr 31:6). But in a separate individual psalm, he claims, there is no indication that it concerns the future. The fact is, he thinks, that prophecy has reinterpreted for its own purpose material drawn from the same source as the enthronement psalms (cf. §5c). There are no "eschatological" psalms proper in the whole Psalter, he believes, only eschatological motifs (cf. I, p. 11; II, p. 225f). The psalmists, he explains, do not describe Yahweh's enthronement as they would if it were a furture event; they merely rejoice that it has taken place. The "acts of salvation" referred to in the enthronement psalms belong both to the past and to the present. This can be explained only against a cultic background. In fact, the main elements of Mowinckel's explanation can be understood only if the enthronement psalms "from their very nature sprung from and belong to, a festival, which has, at least from one point of view, been celebrated as a *festival of enthronement of Yahweh*. At this festival the congregation has most vividly experienced the personal coming of the Lord to save his people—his epiphany" (I, p. 112f).

New Year-Harvest festival

Mowinckel admits that *no particular day* named after the feast of Yahweh's enthronement is expressly mentioned in the texts. It could be that the ethronement idea was only one of many aspects of the festival. He attempts, however, to determine on which of the great feast days of the year the enthronement is most likely to have taken place: "Yahweh's enthronement day is the day when he 'comes' (96:13; 98:9) and 'makes himself known' (98:2), reveals himself and his 'salvation' and his will (93:5; 99:7), when he repeats the theophany of Mount Sinai (97:3ff; 99:7f), and renews the election (47:5) of Israel, and the covenant with his people (95:6ff; 99:6ff). The mighty 'deed of salvation' upon which his kingdom is founded is the Creation, which is alluded to in a rather mythic guise (93:3f). His coming means the renewal of the life of nature—this being the reason why the poets exhort heaven and earth and sea, field and stream, trees and mountains, to rejoice at the coming of the king" (p. 118f). It is, besides, possible, he adds, that the day of Yahweh's epiphany (in the enthronement) was called "the day of Yahweh," i.e., the day of his cultic coming and revelation as king (Ho 7:5): "What will you do on the day of the appointed festival, and on the day of the (special) feast of the Lord?" (Ho 9:5). This feast was the harvest festival or the feast of Tabernacles in the autumn (cf. Ex 23:16; 34:22).

"It is quite clear, Mowinckel states, that already in pre-exilic times the harvest festival was also that of the new year." To sum up, then, Mowinckel's position, in his own words: "Our thesis will be that even on the basis of the special group of 'enthronement psalms' in the form-critical sense, we shall be able to prove that the enthronement festival of Yahweh, presupposed by them, could not be a separate, as yet unknown festival, but must have been the old festival of harvest and New Year, the 'feast of Tabernacles.' We have not here a newly discovered festival, not referred to elsewhere in the Old Testament, but a hitherto unheeded as-

To become King

The fact, admitted by Mowinckel, that in the Israelite view, Yahweh has always been king, does not, he holds, "prevent the view that Yahweh at a certain point of time became the king of Israel, i.e., at the election, at the exodus from Egypt (Ps 114:1f), or at the making of the covenant on Mount Sinai (Dt 33:5).... But in the cult the fact of salvation is re-experienced as a new and actual reality..." (p. 114f; cf. E. Lipiński in *Le Psautier*, p. 271). In Babylonia also, he adds, the god "Anu, or Enlil, or Marduk, or Sahur, *is* king; but the sources prove that the cultic feast celebrated him as the one *now becoming* king; the new year festival marked his enthronement. So also in Israel. In the rites and psalms belonging to the festival of the enthronement of Yahweh this idea was mirrored, or, rather, presented, expressed, and experienced. A main event was evidently the great festal procession, the victorious coronation entry of the Lord, to which reference is made in Ps 47:6. It must have had a strongly dramatic character, with playing, singing and dancing. The personal presence of Yahweh in the festive procession was most probably symbolized by his holy shrine (the ark). Both Pss 24 and 132 were probably connected with this procession; but our hypothesis is valid even without these witnesses" (I, 115).

Divergent views

Mowinckel's own insights and the studies they have provoked account for much of the progress registered in recent study of the psalms and of the Israelite cultic festivals. In the scholarly *Supplément au Dictionnaire de la Bible*, almost 100 columns are consecrated to the "New Year festival" in Israel and the Ancient Near East (vol. VI, Paris, 1959: also bibliography). The conclusion is given there that it would be a mistake to imagine that the Israelite and Babylonian festivals were conceived pect of the well-known and frequently mentioned feast of Tabernacles in its character of New Year festival.... The enthronement festival of Yahweh and the feast of Tabernacles and of New Year have in common the idea of Yahweh's 'appearance' and 'epiphany,' of the renewal of nature and creation, of the repeated 'work of salvation' to be performed by him, and of Yahweh's universal dominion over the earth (cf. Ps 65)" (I, p. 121).

on a similar pattern. The Israelite tradition has always been opposed to the cult practices of nature religions. It is striking, writes H. Cazelles (c. 645), that the Bible does not recognize the feast of the New Year. When the Israelite is requested "to appear before God," at the end of the year, it is for the harvest festival, not for the New Year. It is possible, however, that outside the bibical tradition proper a New Year festival did exist in Israel during the period of the monarchy, but no certainty can be obtained on this subject.

In his *Worship in Israel*, H.-J. Kraus questions some of Mowinckel's basic assumptions. It is true, he admits, that 2 S 15:10 and 2 K 9:13 suggest the idea of "becoming king" in the so-called "enthronement cry." But *mālak* means "to be king" in many passages in the Old Testament, particularly in 1 K 1:11, the meaning of which is clarified by verse 18: "And now, behold, Adonijah is king." Secondly, Mowinckel's theory implies an impossible theological context: the God of Israel being subject, like the vegetation deities to the natural rhythm of the seasons or to the death-resurrection cultic drama. Besides, the unchangeable and eternal kingship of Yahweh is emphatically extolled in Ps 93:2. H. Gross accepts an enthronement festival of Yahweh if it is understood as a Passover remembrance festival of the fundamental Israelite belief that "God is King." Furthermore, writes Kraus, those passages which describe a procession of the Ark and on which Mowinckel confidently bases his case for the reconstruction of the "festival of Yahweh's enthronement," have no connection with any such cultic act of enthronement. Ps 24:7ff speaks rather of an introduction of the divine throne into the temple: "There is no mention of Yahweh ascending the throne, but he comes in as 'King of glory,' and is therefore welcomed as the God who is already present above the divine throne of the Ark. The historical background of the Ark narrative as the *hieros logos* of Jerusalem makes it impossible for us to turn the God of Israel as he comes to Zion into a nature deity or to assume that Yahweh forfeited his sovereignty in any way" (p. 207f).

Deutero-Isaiah and "enthronement" psalms

Mowinckel willingly expresses his conviction that Deutero-Isaiah was influenced by the enthronement psalms. "The scene which these psalms take for granted and have for their background is the idea of the victorious king in triumph entering the city, which by his help has outfaced all storms, and from whose walls the heralds are proclaiming the ap-

pearance of the king in his victorious progress. Deutero-Isaiah uses the
picture to describe the coming return of the exiles headed by Yahweh and
the 'holy road'—*via sacra*—of the processions has become the wonderful
road to be built through the desert for the returning people; the call to
the heralds on the walls is here addressed to a city now in ruins, but to
be re-erected now that the king comes. And Yahweh's victory over the
primeval ocean and the dragon has been changed into the victory over
the Babylonians by Cyrus, and instead of the drying up of the waters of
the primeval ocean, of which the enthronement ideology and the psalms
speak, Deutero-Isaiah speaks about the wonderful springs of water which
shall well forth in the desert, wherever the exiles shall journey" (II, 148).
One could say, in other words, that Deutero-Isaiah has historicized the
myth.

Some remarks of C. Westermann are particularly relevant in discus-
sing the relations mutually affecting enthronement psalms, Deutero-
Isaiah and eschatology (cf. *The Praise*...pp. 142-151). It can scarcely
be accidental, he notes, that "the eschatological song of Praise" in the
form described by Gunkel is found most frequently in Deutero-Isaiah:
40:9ff; 42:10-13; 44:23; 45:8; 48:20f; 49:13; 54:1f. The following passage is typical:

> Break out together in song,
>   O ruins of Jerusalem!
> For the Lord comforts his people,
>   he redeems Jerusalem.
> The Lord has bared his holy arm
>   in the sight of all the nations;
> All the ends of the earth will behold
>   the salvation of our Lord (52:9f).

It can be assumed that in all probability these songs are a new development made by Deutero-Isaiah. They are, to some measure, "the echo
of the community to the promise of salvation which God had made"
(p. 144). It is true that similar themes may occur before Deutero-Isaiah:
cf. Dt 12:43; Is 12:4ff; Jr 20:13; 31:7; Jl 2:21; Na 2:1; Zp 3:
14f; Zc 2;14; 9:9f. But it cannot be asserted with certainty that any of
these passages are pre-exilic in origin, taking into account the possibility
of later additions. "It should not however be asserted as absolutely certain that this eschatological shout of jubilation could not also have been

raised before Second Isaiah or at the same period. Still, both historically and theologically and in respect to its occurrence it is finally anchored in the prophecy of Second Isaiah, in which, even apart from this form, the speech of the psalms and the words of the prophets came together" (p. 145).

It is written in Is 52:7: "How beautiful upon the mountains are the feet of him who...publishes salvation, who says to Zion, Your God reigns (*mālak 'elōhāyik*)." The inverted word order of the psalms' formula, Yhwh mālāk (cf. *Ps 93:1), presents a shift in emphasis, not a change in meaning. For the total understanding of the "enthronement psalms," notes Westermann, it is of decisive importance whether that cry has its origin in the Psalms or in Deutero-Isaiah. Six arguments are produced to prove the priority of Is 52:7f (p. 146f). This leads to other conclusions: Yahweh's enthronement then is not cultic, but a "historico-eschatological act"; the enthronement psalms do not constitute a category proper; their significance "lies in that a motif which was prophetic in origin, the eschatological exclamation of kingship, was absorbed into the *descriptive* praise of the Psalms" (p. 151; cf. above §7b). In the prophetic anticipation of Yahweh's coming kingship, explains Westermann, the expansion of the praise of Yahweh as Lord of history took on the characteristic form for Israel, which had become important and was subject to the great powers: "it is praise of the Lord of history—in expectation" (*ibid.*).

The dependence of the enthronement psalms [mainly 96, 97, 98] in respect to Deutero-Isaiah constitutes the main argument against the existence, proposed by Mowinckel, of an ancient pre-exilic festival of Yahweh's enthronement. Mowinckel writes, for example: "Deutero-Isaiah largely imitates the forms and ideas of the psalms of enthronement and harvest in order to express what was at hand" (I, p. 189). But the "mixed forms," of which the "enthronement psalms" are examples, cannot be as early as is claimed by Mowinckel. The first prophet, Westermann states (p. 142f), in whose work the prophetic oracle and the type of speech found in the Psalms come together strongly and unmistakably is Jeremiah. After a detailed study of the literary and doctrinal affinities existing between Pss 47, 93, 96-99 and Deutero-Isaiah, R. Bornert concludes: "these affinities suggest that the psalms of Yahweh's reign date from the period which followed the exile and that they sprang from a milieu close to Second Isaiah." On the positive side, Westermann expresses "thankful agreement" (p. 145, n. 99) with H.-J.

Kraus' interpretation of the royal motif applied to God. To this we now turn.

(b) *Mount Zion festival of the kingship of God*

It is a fact that the "kingship of God" was proclaimed on Mount Zion at a certain period. H.-J. Kraus, in his *Worship in Israel,* has examined with care the pre-history of the proclamation and its relation to the *Davidic covenant* and the royal festival on Mount Zion (pp. 179-222). A sketch of his views will help to understand also the background of the royal psalms and of others which involve historical motifs as well as pilgrimage themes.

From Shiloh to Jerusalem

Saul had been charismatically proclaimed king for an emergency, but David was appointed to a permanent covenant (*berît*) of royal authority by Nathan's prophetic utterance. Kraus writes (p. 181): "We can tell from the *royal psalms,* in which the *covenant with David* determines all that is said about the ruler, what a great influence this decisive development in the idea of kingship had in the Jerusalem cult (Pss 89:3ff; 132:12)." The descendents of David are described as "kings of Yahweh" (2:6; 18:50) and their relationship with God is thought of in terms of adoption (2:7; 110:3). The historical and prophetic election of David became the main basis of the cult in Jerusalem.

After conquering the Jebusite city and making Jerusalem the capital of his kingdom, David's next step was to restore the central Israelite sanctuary, which had collapsed with the fall of Shiloh, and to revive it in the form of a state cult. "The *hieros logos* of the Jerusalem Ark narrative [2 S 6] depicts the course of events.... By its installation in the city of David the Ark elevated Jerusalem to the status of an amphictyonic cultic center [i.e., of the pre-monarchic sacral tribe confederacy] and brought the ancient Israelite traditions and institutions of the tribal confederacy to *the chosen place*" (p. 152). An important question was asked: "who had authorized David to carry out an act which affected the sacred life of the tribal confederacy so deeply?" The main answer could only be: the election of David as king (2 S 6:21). In his refusal to grant David's wish to build a fixed sanctuary (2 S 7:5ff), Nathan was "an embodiment of the protest of the circles that sought to keep in mind their desert origins" (p. 183).

The transfer of the Ark to Jerusalem was recalled and re-experienced by cultic   repetition (cf. 1 K 8:3ff). Psalm 132 provides the decisive evidence for a "royal festival on Mount Zion" which actualized in worship both the "election of Jerusalem" and "the election of David" (p. 184). From 1 Kgs 8:1ff it can be deduced that the festival took place on the first day of the   feast of Tabernacles (Mowinckel disagrees with Kraus on many points: cf. II, p. 237ff).

The covenant with David and the Sinai tradition

Gerhard von Rad (II, 46) finds in the Nathan prophecy (2 S 7) a particularly revealing instance of the manner in which tradition has been continually reinterpreted during ancient Israel's history. Verses 11 and 16 would show the oldest strand: a prophecy aimed directly at David himself. Verses 12a, 14-15 would be later, as they focus the interest rather on David's son, or his descendants. "Then considerably later, the Deuteronomistic theology of history connected the whole prophecy with Solomon's building of the temple (v 13), while later still Deutero-Isaiah severed the tie with the house of David and applied the saying to Israel as a whole" (Is 55:3f; see on *Ps 105:15). Even after this, adds von Rad, the old reference of the promise to the seed of David himself is not wide enough for the Chronicler: he speaks of "the seed which shall come forth from thy sons," and thus adds a further stage in the prophecy's scope (1 Ch 17:11). "In this way," von Rad concludes "an oracle first spoken in the long distant past continued to have a present message considerably later than the exile."

David's role in relation to Jerusalem is also viewed differently in different periods. The new beginning in Bethlehem perceived by Micah (5:1ff), von Rad also remarks, "is bound up with the elimination of the old royal city, the total obliteration of Jerusalem from the pages of history (3:12), whereas... Isaiah looks for a renewal of Jerusalem. In both cases, the contemporary monarch or monarchs of the Davidic line are dismissed by the prophets. The fact that they so expressly look for salvation in the anointed one of the future is tantamount to saying that the contemporary descendants of David have lost the saving function so emphatically attributed to them in the royal psalms" (II, p. 171).

Other problems are raised by the connection between Sinaitic covenant and Davidic covenant, between the God-king relationship and the God-people relationship (cf. Kraus, *Worship...*, p. 190ff and bibliographical notes, *ibid.*). Kraus' long discussion cannot be even summarized here, but his main conclusion will be retained: "From the time of Solomon the Davidic covenant predominated in the official cult at Jerusalem. All the kings tried to exercise their rule on the basis of the promise expressed by Nathan as it was actualized in worship, but without recourse to the amphictyonic traditions. By this usurpation of the right of election the relationship of God and people was more and more undermined. Pagan gods and cults were introduced to Jerusalem, and only rarely was the Sinaitic covenant preserved on Zion as the basis for the Davidic covenant. But the reforms of the cult indicate a renewal of the Sinaitic covenant. Josiah was the first to include the Sinai traditions in the official Davidic cult as part of a general restoration. Of one thing, however, there can be no doubt: that the Sinai tradition was brought to Jerusalem along with the Ark, and that the cultic institution of the renewal of the covenant was something that was always held before David's successors in that monarchy that was rooted in the amphictyonic sacral order" (p. 200).

Jebusite-Canaanite influence

When it appeared in Jerusalem, the Ark tradition met with the Canaanite-Jebusite one firmly rooted in the holy place. Whereas, Kraus believes (p. 201), Ps 22 is a typical example of a song of Zion based upon the amphictyonic traditions, Pss 46 and 48 are typical expressions of a faith influenced by Canaanite-Jebusite language and ideas. Some elements of the ancient Canaanite-Jebusite cultic traditions were amalgamated in Yahwistic tradition. "The holy city, for example, the throne of the 'high God' and the heavenly source of all fertility, was thought of in mythology as impregnable. This idea is found in Ps 46: 5ff in the Old Testament (cf. also 2 S 5:6; Pss 87:5; 125:1f; Is 26:1). Mysterious forces rise against this place of imperturbable order and salvation (Pss 46:5f; 48:4ff; Is 17:12f), but the forces of chaos and the attacks of the nations are repelled with thunder and lightning, and the enemies are destroyed before the holy city (Pss 46: 6f; 48: 5; 76:3ff, etc.)" (p. 202f).

Recent research, involving especially the Ras Shamra texts (see

§9d), has shown "that the conception of Yahweh's kingship does not appear to have been a basic element in the original content of Israelite religion" (Kraus, *op. cit.*, p. 203, quoting A. Alt). "The conception of the deity as king was taken over by the Israelites from the Canaanites, who had received it from the great kingdoms on the Euphrates and Tigris and Nile, where it had been developed as early as ancient Sumerian times" (Mowinckel, I, p. 114; cf. *Ps 29). The title *melek*, "king," writes Kraus (*ibid.*), "could not be applied to Yahweh until the Canaanite sanctuary of the temple had become the place where he was present and where he dwelt." According to Canaanite belief, divine kingship and temple are inseparable. Furthermore, thinks Kraus, Yahweh received the title of "king," of *'el 'elyôn,* "the Most High" (cf. 83:18; 97:9), and other appellations proper to the "high God" when he had subdued the local deities. It is a fact that anciently the political changes were reflected in the divine world. Yet it is always the same Yahweh of Sinai worshipped under new names. He was now recognized as *'el 'elyôn,* king and creator of the earth, and reigning on Mount Zion. R. Rendtorff produces evidence to show that the designation of God in Genesis 14 as "El 'aeljôn" cannot be the expression of a common Canaanite picture of El... It unites the features of various deities.

The Jerusalem festival of *yhwh ṣᵉbā'ôt*

What has been said gives the general background of "the festival cult in Jerusalem." This festival most probably centered around the feast of the Tabernacles, although other cultic contexts provide some of their own elements. The cult festival is better understood in the context of a pilgrimage to Zion (Pss 42, 46, 48, 76, 84, 87, 122). The actual festival cult began with the solemn ascent of the Ark to the temple mount (cf. Pss 95 and 99). Cultic prophets and priests recalled the original event of the election of Jerusalem and of David. The transfer of the Ark to Zion was probably re-enacted in a cultic drama (cf. Ps 132). As the solemn procession moved close to the sanctuary the priests intoned the "Entrance Tôrâh" (cf. Pss 15 and 24:3-6), which was followed by the "Entrance Liturgy" (24:7-10).

The climax of the ceremony was, in Kraus' words, "the mighty official proclamation of the sacred cultic name of Yahweh. The exclamation of the name was an important act of worship" (p. 213). Yahweh is to be known and addressed as *yhwh ṣᵉbā'ôt,* "the Lord of hosts" (Ps 24:10), a title which recalls the cultic tradition of Shiloh: "So the people sent to Shiloh, and brought from there the ark of the covenant of *yhwh ṣᵉbā'ôt,* who is enthroned on the cherubim" (1 S 4:4; cf. 17: 45). The "king of glory" (24:7-10) worshipped in Jerusalem, under the influence of Canaanite-Jebusite cultic traditions, is still the *yhwh ṣᵉbā'ôt* that has come from Shiloh to Jerusalem. This festival of the installation of the Ark or of the "throne" (see on *Ps 93), writes Kraus, "is therefore to be thought of exclusively as an act of confession of the God of Israel and his first act of election (24:10). *Yahweh does not become King, but he comes as King.* The title *melek* is therefore merely the garment of *yhwh ṣᵉbā'ôt,* merely a title of honor, not something that affects the person or that influences the cult" (p. 214). The longer form of the title, MT *yhwh' ᵉlōhîm ṣᵉbā'ôt* (Ps 59:6; 80:20; 84: 9), is explained by Ugaritic scholars as "a construct chain with an interposed enclitic *mem.* Hence vocalize *'ᵉlōhēm ṣᵉbā'ôt* (Dahood, Psalms II, 68f).

The Ark in the Psalms

There is only one explicit reference to the Ark in the psalms: "Advance, O Lord, to your resting place, you and the ark of your majesty" (132:8; cf. Nb 10:35f). While Kirkpatrick finds at least ten (implicit) references to the Ark in the psalms (9:12; 15:1; 24: 7ff; 44:10; 47:6; 63:3; 68:2; 78:61; 96:6; 99:5. 101:2), Gunkel admitted only three, those of Pss 24, 68, 78. G. H. Davies notes that the idea of "strength" is associated with the Ark in Pss 78:61 and 132:8 and that the Ark is probably alluded to also in Ps 96:6 (cf. 1 Ch 16:27) and in Ps 105:4 (cf. 1 Ch 16:11), where the notion of "strength" recurs. This is true also of Pss 81:2 and 63:3. With reference to Nb 10.35, it is probable that the Ark must be associated with Ps 68:2: "God arises; his enemies are scattered, and those who hate him flee from him" (cf. also 3:8; 7:7; 9:20; 10:12; 17:13). As "before the Ark" means "before Yahweh" in 2 S 6:4f.; so also "before him" and "before the Lord" in Ps 96:6, 13 (cf. Ps 98:9) can refer to the Ark (cf. 56:14; 61:8; 63:3; 95:6; 116:9).

W. I. Wolverton accepts H.-J. Kraus' interpretation relating to a procession of the Ark of Zion but he adds his own suggestive ideas. David brought the palladium [the Ark] to Zion. His action "took on supernatural meaning. It was *mythologized,* i.e., it was construed to be an action on the part of the deity: *Yahweh had chosen Zion* as his dwelling place, or center of operations. A corollary event, the election of David by the tribe of Israel as king, was also mythologized: the line of David had been chosen by Yahweh.... By 'mythologized' we mean that a human action, particularly if it is a crucial one, is interpreted to be a divine action.... This form of thought presupposes a correspondence between events on earth and in heaven, so an important mundane event meant divine participation, indeed an act of God.... The mythologizing of historical events was a characteristically Israelite way of interpretation" (p. 24f). Wolverton reads mythologizing besides in Pss 74:2-3; 76:3-6; 102:13-20 [on the sacred Ark see also the studies of M. Haran, J. Maier, J. Morgenstern, H. Torczyner, R. de Vaux].

(c) *The Covenant Festival of Yahweh*

This festival has for A. Weiser the same importance as the festival of Yahweh's enthronement has for S. Mowinckel. Applying to both feasts what H.-J. Kraus (*Worship...* p. 8 and p. 209 note) meant of the latter one only, it can be said that they become a magnet which attracts the most varied elements, so long as they contain even a trace of the relevant material. Weiser has at least the merit of finding his evidence mainly in the biblical tradition itself. The substance of his argumentation can be read in his book, *The Psalms,* pp. 23-52.

Treaty and Covenant

"The designation of the actual feast of Yahweh as *Covenant Festival,"* Weiser writes, has been chosen in accordance with the characteristic form into which the religion of the Old Testament is cast" (p. 28, note). W. Eichrodt (p. 14) calls in fact the *covenant* "an epitome of the dealings of God in history." Its forensic and literary expression can be read in the "(Elohistic) Code of the Covenant" 20:22 to 23:19), in the "(Yahwistic) Code of Renewal of the Covenant" (Ex 34:14-26) and in the "Deuteronomic Code" (Dt 12-26).

"When the statement is made that religion is based on covenant," wrote G.E. Mendenhall, "it implies that a form of action which originated in legal custom has been transferred to the field of religion" ("Covenant Forms in Israelite Tradition," in *The Biblical Archaeologist,* XVII,

1954, p. 50). Working on this premise, he studied ancient legal documents and discovered striking similarities of pattern between the covenant forms of Israel and the forms of the Hittite suzerainty treaty by which a great king bound his vassals to faithfulness and obedience to himself. Mendenhall's pioneer and still fundamental study, *Law and Covenant in Israel and the Ancient Near East* (Pittsburgh, 1955), opened to scholars a fresh field of inquiry. More parallels have been found and the area of influence has been delimited and assessed (cf. D. J. McCarthy, *Treaty and Covenant. A Study in Form in the Ancient Oriental Documents and in the Old Testament*, Rome, 1963). An application of such parallels has been suggested in *Ps 3:4.

C. Westermann has drawn attention on what he calls *declarative praises* in the thanksgiving psalms which recount or report the *specific saving deeds* attributed to God. In the biblical tradition the Israelite *credo* is expressed by "confessing" the saving deeds of Yahweh (cf. Dt 6:20-24; 25:5-9). The main events of Exodus are recalled in the psalter, mainly in Pss 78, 105, 106, 111, 114, 135, 136 (see §14a). The poetic recital of history in these psalms and a few others, the declarative praises, correspond in a way to the Israelite "historical credo," an equivalent, it seems, of "the historical prologue" in the suzerainty treatises (or treatises of vassality). In this "prologue" the previous relations between the two partners are described, especially the benevolent deeds which the Hittite king has performed for the benefit of the vassal. As for the duties of the covenant people (cf. the decalogue), also recalled in the psalms, their role in the covenant has been compared to "the stipulations" section of the treatises, which enumerates the obligations imposed upon and accepted by the vassal.

Covenant — New Year festival

It is not to the Canaanite "agricultural religious festivals," A. Weiser suggests, that we must turn to understand the real *Sitz im Leben* of the psalms, but to the *Covenant Festival* as it was celebrated by the tribal (amphictyonic) confederacy of Israel, and also to the "cultic narratives" (*Festperikopen*) belonging to it (p. 27). In the different strata of tradition of the Old Testament, Weiser explains, *this autumnal feast celebrated at New Year* was regarded until a very late date as the main festival... so that it was simply described as "the feast": (Jg 21:19; 1 K 8: 2; 12:32; Ezk 45:25; Ne 8:14 (p. 28, note). "The cult of the feast of

Yahweh was in essence a *sacred action,* a 'cultic drama,' in the course of which the fundamental events in the history of man's salvation were re-enacted.... The theme of the Old Testament Covenant Festival is the continually renewed encounter of God with the people which has as its final aim the renewal of the Sinai covenant and of the salvation it promised" (p. 28f). The decisive part of the cultic act is the *actio Dei,* the action of God and the word of God, while the words offered by the congregation in prayer and in praise have the quality of a response to God's saving action.

The other elements of the Covenant Festival, as described by Weiser, include: the "theophany" (Yahweh's self-revelation in the presence of his people), "the proclamation of the name of God (cf. Nb 6:27) and of his will," the "idea of judgment," the "profession of loyalty" to Yahweh, the "renunciation of the foreign gods" and also perhaps the idea of the "kingship of Yahweh" and the "idea of creation." All these elements he describes in their original setting and whenever they occur in the psalms (which is naturally frequent!), they indicate the presence and the influence of the Covenant festival.

The festival and the psalms

Weiser has attempted to determine precisely *the place of the psalms in the cult of the covenant festival* (pp. 35-52). No proper ritual of the Covenant Festival of Yahweh, he admits, has been handed down to us, from Old Testament times. This can probably be explained, he thinks, by the fact that the ritual of the Covenant Festival was passed on by the priests by means of oral tradition. The description of the Qumran liturgy would point to the existence of corresponding elements in the Old Testament tradition (cf. e.g., Pss 78, 105, 106 and Dt 32; Ezr 9:6ff; Ne 9:1ff). "The liturgy which we find in Ps 50 is part of the order of the feast of the renewal of the Covenant which was celebrated at the Temple of Jerusalem. This follows incontestably from verse 5: 'Gather to me my faithful ones, who made a covenant with me by sacrifices!'" "This is furthermore corroborated," thinks Weiser, "by the references to the advent of Yahweh at Mount Zion (vv 2-3), to the judgment that Yahweh will pronounce on 'his people' (v 4), to the proclamation of his will and the self-predication of his name (v 7), to the profession of the congregation that they will be faithful to the Covenant and its commandments (v 16), and to the separation of the faithful (v 5) from the wicked (v 16) by executing judgment upon both (vv 22f)." In Ps 81:3ff, the traditional obligation to celebrate the feast of Yahweh would be recalled: "On our feast day [sic], for it is a statute for Israel, an ordinance of the God of Jacob. He made it a decree in Joseph, when he went out over the land of Egypt" (35f). We will not follow Weiser in his detailed examination of the occurrences of the Covenant Festival theme in the psalms. Most of his expositions are interesting in themselves, even independently of their relevance to the Covenant Festival. This is especially true of *theophany* (p. 38ff). About the festival, A. Gelin had this to say: "Every year perhaps Israel celebrates a feast of the covenant; or, more simply, every important feast has this significance..." (*The Psalms are our Prayers*, p. 41; see on *Ps 95 the fuller quotation). The main idea in A. Deissler's "Das lobpreisende..." is that Israel's praise in the psalms was addressed to the *Bundesgott,* the covenant-God.

(d) *Theophanies of the Psalter*

A. Weiser maintains (what C. Westermann denies) that the *theophanies of the Psalter* have a cultic character and are related to the Sinai theophany. The tradition of the theophany conceived Yahweh's epiphany in the sanctuary as God's coming down to his people from Mount Sinai (Jg 5:4f; Dt 33:2). For cultic purposes, Weiser writes (p. 29), the pillar of cloud in the Wilderness traditions (Ex 16:10; Nb 16: 42; Dt 31:15) was symbolized by the winged figures of the Cherubim on the mercy seat of the Ark (Pss 80:2; 99:1). The appearance of God was clothed in the heavenly light of glory (*kābôd*: Ex 24:10; Nb 14: 10) and accompanied by lightning, thunder and earthquakes. There are many good examples of the conventional language used to describe theophanic appearances of God: Dt 33:2f; Jg 5:4f; Jdt 16:15; Pss 18:8-16; 68:8f; 77:17-21; 97:1-5; Na 1:3-6. Important literarily is the theophany described in the prophet Habakkuk's canticle (3:1-19; cf. §5e). It was written about 600 B.C. and it uses Canaanite imagery to express authentic Israelite faith. Only a few verses can be quoted here:

God comes from Theman,
　the Holy One from Mount Pharan.
Covered are the heavens with his glory,
　and with his praise the earth is filled.
His splendor spreads like the light;

rays shine forth beside him,
   where his power is concealed.
Before him goes pestilence.
   and the plague follows his steps.
He pauses to survey the earth;
   his look makes the nations tremble.
The eternal mountains are shattered,
   the age-old hills bow low
   along his ancient ways (vv 3-6).

Another classical example is the theophany of Ps 18:8-16:

The earth swayed and quaked;
   the foundations of the mountains trembled
   and shook when his wrath flared up.
Smoke rose from his nostrils,
   and a devouring fire from his mouth
   that kindled coals into flame.
And he inclined the heavens and came down,
   with dark clouds under his feet.
He mounted a cherub and flew,
   borne on the wings of the wind.
And he made darkness the cloak about him;
   dark, misty rain-clouds his wrap.
From the brightness of his presence
   coals were kindled to flame.
And the Lord thundered from heaven,
   the Most High gave forth his voice:
He sent forth his arrows to put them to flight,
   with frequent lightnings he routed them.
Then the bed of the sea appeared,
   and the foundations of the world were laid bare,
At the rebuke of the Lord,
   at the blast of the wind of his wrath.

Yhwh $ṣ^eḇā'ôt$

In Ps 24:10 the "King of glory" is identified as $yhwh$ $ṣ^eḇā'ôt$, "the Lord of hosts" (cf. above). his appellation figures in other theophanic texts of the psalms: 46:8, 12; 48:9; 59:6; 80:5, 15; 89:9. It is is also used in Isaiah's inaugural vision (6:5). The name was known to the pilgrims of Shiloh: every year Elkanah used to go up from his town to worship and to sacrifice to *Yahweh Sabaoth in Shiloh* (1 S 1:3). "*Yahweh of armies,* writes *JB*: not only nor primarily the hosts of Israel, but the stars and heavenly powers too, and indeed all the cosmic forces (cf. Gn 2:1) under God's command. This ancient title is associated with the ark (cf. 1 S 4:3), the sacred emblem protecting Israel when Yahweh wages war with his people on the enemies. The title is used freely in the major prophets (with the exception of Ezekiel) and in the Psalms" (in 1 S 1:3).

In the ancient hymn sung by "Moses and the Israelites," to celebrate the miraculous crossing of the Red Sea, Yahweh is called a *warrior* (15:3; cf. Is 42:13; see §14b). A psalmist recalls the time when God went forth at the head of his people, marching through the wilderness: the earth quaked; it rained from heaven at the presence of God (Ps 68:8f; cf. Nb 14:14; Jg 5:4f). Other psalmists complain to God: "Now you have cast off and put us in disgrace, and you go not forth with our armies" (Pss 44:10; 60:12). Cf. F. M. Cross Jr., "The Divine Warrior in Israel's Early Cult," in *Biblical Motifs*. . .ed. A. Altmann: *Lown.* Inst., III (Cambridge, Mass., 1966), pp. 11-30.

Arise! Awake!

Another theophanic element can be traced back to the Exodus period. Whenever the ark is set out, in the desert, Moses would say: "Arise, O Lord, that your enemies may be scattered, and those who hate you may flee from you." And when it came to rest, he would say, "Return, O Lord, you who ride upon the clouds, to the troops of Israel" (Nb 10:35f *NAB*; *Ps 68:5). The cry "now I will rise up" became a conventional way of expressing God's theophanic intervention (cf. Is 33:10):

> God arises; his enemies are scattered,
>   and those who hate him flee before him.
> As smoke is driven away, so are they driven;
>   as wax melts before the fire,
>   so the wicked perish before God.
> But the just rejoice and exult before God;
>   they are glad and rejoice (Ps 68:2ff; cf. 59:5f; 74:22).

The phrase "shine forth!" belongs to the same context. In his book *Sakrales Königtum...*, G. Widengren assumes that the cultic shout "Awake!" (cf. 35:23; 44:24) has been borrowed by the cultic poetry of the Old Testament from the rite of the dying and rising king-gods, which was practiced in the royal ritual of the Near East. Such borrowing is unlikely and, Weiser points out, "the shout has at any rate now lost its former association with the resurrection of the god and has been applied to the encounter with God in the theophany" (p. 39). The psalmists do not cease repeating to God: "Hide not your face from us" (13:2; 22: 25; 27:9; 44:25; 69:18; 88:15; 102:3), "Let the light of your countenance shine upon us" (4:7; 44:4; 67:2; 89:16), even as in a refrain: "If your face shine upon us, then we shall be safe" (80:4, 8, 20). The origin of such language is also theophanic and can be traced back to the ancient liturgical benediction:

> The Lord bless you and keep you!
> The Lord let his face shine upon you,
>   and be gracious to you!
> The Lord look upon you kindly and give you peace! (Nb 6:24ff)

God's epiphany

According to C. Westermann (*The Praise...* p. 98f) three features usually represent the outline of God's epiphany:

1. God's coming from, or his going from....
2. Cosmic disturbances which accompany this coming of God.
3. God's (wrathful) intervention for or against....

The third element, however, is not often as explicit as in Habakkuk 3 and Isaiah 30, and has to be deduced from the context. In Micah 1: 3ff, God's intervention does not belong to the epiphany, but to the prophetic proclamation of doom which follows it. In all instances God appears to help his people. In most of the epiphanies the new intervention is related to the events that occurred at the beginning of Israel's history, above all to the events at the Red Sea. Yet "the clearly mythological language of the descriptions of epiphanies in the Psalms is to be explained on the basis of this background of other ancient religions" (p. 96). He quotes *inter alia* "the great hymn to Shamash" [=the sun god:

cf. §9b + *Ps 3]: "Shamash, when thou goest forth from thy great mountain" and a hymn to Adad in Ungnad: "When the Lord roars, the heavens tremble before him; When Adad is angry, the earth quakes before him; Great mountains break down before him...." E. Lipiński (*La royauté...*, p. 249) and H. Cazelles (*VT* 1966, p. 527) also believe that the descriptions of divine epiphanies do not come from the narration of the events of Sinai or of Horeb. This is indicated by the study of earlier Oriental hymns. J. Jeremias, in *Theophanie*...would admit that "the coming of Yahweh from his dwelling-place" arose from the unique encounter on Sinai, but one of his conclusions is that, generally speaking, all other Old Testament theophanies have evolved (*entwickelt*) from victory hymns of the pre-monarchic period, mainly from the ancient Deborah song:

> O Lord, when you went out from Seir,
>   when you marched from the land of Edom,
> The earth quaked and the heavens were shaken,
>   while the clouds sent down showers.
> Mountains trembled in the presence of the Lord:
>   in the presence of the Lord, the God of Israel (Jg 5:4f).

It is generally admitted that the so-called "Song of Deborah" (Jg 5:1-31) is the oldest remaining considerable fragment of Hebrew literature. [Other studies on the Theophanies include those of E. Beaucamp (Ps 50), J. M. Ruiz Gonzales, J. K. Kuntz, J. Lindblom, and J. Morgenstern].

§14. THE HOPES OF ESCHATOLOGY

Eschatology is the doctrine of "the last things" (Gr.: *eschata*). General eschatology is concerned with the future of the chosen people (national eschatology) or of the whole world (universal eschatology). These two conceptions are often merged together in the Old Testament. The object of individual eschatology is the final fate of the individual. "It does not yet come into view very much in the Old Testament; in any case, it is only slightly marked by belief in Yahweh," writes E. Jenni in *The Interpreter's Dictionary of the Bible* (New York, 1962, vol. II, p. 126). Some notions of Old Testament eschatology will be helpful to understand better the eschatology of the Psalter.

(a) Eschatology, judgment and salvation

According to Old Testament views, eschatology is "the part of the history of salvation which is still in prospect and which presses for realization." Yahweh is the Lord of history and his dominion will infallibly prevail. A radical change will occur in the world because Yahweh is coming to create everything new (Is 43:9; Rv 21:5). This coming is the central idea of Old Testament eschatology (see also §15b). It is described in the vivid colors of impending catastrophes. The same Lord who will reveal himself victoriously in the future has already manifested himself in history from time to time and still does. As a consequence the line is not yet clearly drawn in the Old Testament between history and eschatology.

The classical prophets, writes Jenni (p. 127), characteristically depict the final act of Yahweh as analogous to his earlier acts of salvation: deliverance out of Egypt (Is 10:24-27; 11:15f; 43:16ff; 51:10f; 52:11f); march through the desert (Is 48:21; Ho 2:16f); conclusion of the covenant on Mount Sinai (Jr 31:31-34; Ezk 37:26); victory over the Midianites (Is 9:3; 10:26); covenant with David (Is 55:3). Yet each one sees the eschatological event differently: "Thus Hosea foretells a new entry into the land, Isaiah a new David and a new Zion, Jeremiah a new covenant, and Deutero-Isaiah a new Exodus... with a difference in their various conceptions. For Isaiah the old saving acts and institutions are still valid enough to allow Yahweh to link his coming to them. This is true both of the new Zion (Is 1:26), and of the new David (Is 11:1). On the other hand, for Jeremiah and Deutero-Isaiah the break is so complete that Yahweh has to re-enact his former deeds—new covenant (Jr 31:31ff) and there is to be a new Exodus (Is 43:16ff). Isaiah could not have said, like Deutero-Isaiah, that the former saving history should be remembered no more" (Is 43:16ff) (G. von Rad, II, p. 117).

God's eschatological acts comprise, with regard to content, *both judgment and salvation*. In its broader sense, used here, "judgment" refers to the punishing and destroying intervention of God. "Yahweh *sits in judgment* over all that is ungodly, not in blind wrath, but to destroy sin: over the foreign gods (Zp 2:11), over the heathen nations (Jr 25:15ff; Ezk 25-32), but also over the sins of his own people (Am 3:2; 4:1f; Mi 6:1ff) and some of its representatives" (Jr 11:2-23; 20:1-6) (Jenni, *ibid.*). The apprehension of political catastrophes is not the decisive factor in the revelation of an impending judgment: especially in Amos, in Hosea, in the early teaching of Isaiah and Jeremiah. Yahweh is the central figure, and not only in the "Day of Yahweh."

The theme of the "Day of Yahweh" also combines judgment and salvation, for if the ungodly powers are destroyed deliverance comes to the Remnant (cf. §15a). Whether the saving or the punishing aspect predominates depends in part on the historical situation. Before the exile the prophecies of doom held the foreground: only a very dim light of salvation appears in Is 1:25f; 2:1-5; 9:1-6; 11:19; Ho 2:16ff; Am 9:11; Mi 5:1ff. But when the judgment has taken place, during or after the exile, then the prophecy of salvation is in the limelight (second Isaiah and Ezekiel), while the disaster theme is marginal (cf. Jl 3: 4f; Ml 3:5). In the prophecy of consolation also, Yahweh is the central figure. The initiative is His, not that of the people: "It is I, I, who wipe out, for my own sake, your offenses; your sins I remember no more" (Is 43:25). Features of the great change about to take place include a return to some conditions of Eden (Is 51:3), like long life (Is 65:20), peace (Ho 2:20; Is 11:6-8) and a renewed fertility of the land (Am 9: 13; Jl 3:18 to 4:18). "Still more often," writes Jenni, "salvation is depicted as an even *more glorious return* of the good old days of the people of God under Moses or David. Yahweh himself is Shepherd and King (Is 40:11; 52:7). The messianic king, usually represented as David or *David redivivus,* is considered by many, but not by all the prophets, to be a gift, among others, of the time of salvation" (p. 128). A special role is also assigned to Zion in the final drama.

The main events of Exodus are recalled in the Psalter, mainly in Pss 78, 105, 106, 111, 114, 135, 136 (cf. §13c). Real typology, however, can be read only, it seems, in Psalm 106 (Hebrew) and in Psalm 74 (Septuagint). Because mere repetition alone does not constitute typology. There must be a qualitative addition in the antitype (e.g., return from exile: cf. Ps 106:47) in respect to the type (e.g., the liberation from Egyptian servitude). This, within the Old Testament, can occur only in texts eschatologically oriented, pointing, that is, to events qualified by an absolute "plus." Salvation history knows no true return, only continuation. But the *magnalia Dei* of the past indicate what can be expected of the future ones. Typology is based on the unity of salvation history, teleologically oriented. This unity is expressed within the Covenant according to the promise-accomplishment pattern (cf. J. Harvey, "La typologie de l'Exode dans les Psaumes," *ScEcc* 1963, pp. 383-405). "The Exodus was at all times the type of God's intervention;

so it is not surprising that the felicity of Mosaic times should occupy more space in eschatology than truly paradisiacal felicity" (E. Jacob, p. 326).

(b) The "day of Yahweh" theme

It could seem strange that the "day of Yahweh" theme is included here for study when the expression does not appear even once in the psalms. In fact it is found as such only in the writings of the prophets. The theme has, on the other hand, been associated by Mowinckel with the "enthronement of Yahweh festival" which, he claims, constituted a primary setting for many psalms. It is known besides that the tradition of the "day of Yahweh" is related to the theophanic descriptions well repre-- sented in the psalms (cf. §13d).

The expression "the day of Yahweh" is absent from the older histori- cal literature of the Bible. The way it appears suddenly in Amos (5: 18) suggests that it was well known in his time (see, however, below). Originally associated perhaps with salvation, the day of Yahweh becomes with the prophets "darkness and not light" (Am 5:18). "The day of the Lord is near" repeat the prophets. It will be "destruction from the Al- mighty" (Is 13:6), "a slaughter feast" (Zp 1:7), "a day of clouds, dooms- day for the nations" (Ezk 30:3), "a day of retaliation" (Ob 15), "a day of ruin from the Almighty" (Jl 1:15), a "day of anger" (Is 13:13; Zp 1:15); it will take place "in the valley of decision" (Jl 4:14).

Mowinckel attributes a cultic origin to the "day of Yahweh." The "enthronement day of Yahweh," he believes, was originally called "the day of the Lord," "the day of the feast of Yahweh" (Ho 2:15; 7:5; 9: 5). That the "day" of Yahweh, he explains, "originally indicated the day of his festival becomes obvious from Amos 5:17ff, which does not refer to an eschatological day of Yahweh (as supposed by Gunkel, Gressmann, Sellin, Dürr and many others), but where the 'day' is clearly and distinct- ly imagined as a festival day" (I, p. 116, n. 35). Mowinckel's explanation of the "day of Yahweh" is subject to the same objections as his theory on the "enthronement day of Yahweh" (see §13a).

A more probable origin of the "day of Yahweh" theme has been ex- pounded by P. -E. Langevin in a well documented article:: *Sur l'origine du "Jour de Yahvé"* (*Sc Ecc* 1966, pp. 359-370). He believes that an historical rather than a cultic origin for the "day of Yahweh" seems war- ranted by a careful study of the texts and contexts. The eschatological "day of Yahweh" appears as an exceptionally important "holy war" (cf. G. von Rad, II, p. 123f). It will culminate the long history of Israel's "holy wars," whose description supplied much of the imagery proper to the "day of Yahweh" theme. In other words, the Israelite ideology of the "holy war" extended itself into the "day of Yahweh" ideology. In fact the historical "days of Yahweh" (probably: Is 13:6, 9; 34:8; Jr 46:10; Ezk 13:5; 30:3) are not always cearly distinguishable from the eschatological "days of Yahweh" (presumably: Am 5:18-20; Is 2:12; Zp 1:7-8; Ezk 7:19; Zc 14:2; Ob 15; Jl 1:15 to 4:14). In all the "days of Yahweh" the Lord fights against the enemies of Israel, or against rebellious Israel, with her conversion in view. But the "day of Yahweh" *par excellence* takes cosmic dimensions: it will affect all nations and fix their destiny for ever. It will be the last in a series of "days of Yahweh." The interpretation proposed respects the known character of Old Testament theology: the historical facts, interpreted by prophecy (cf. Is 48: 3-8), have taught Israel what to say about Yahweh.

In "The Origin of the 'Day of the Lord'—reconsidered" (*HUCA* 1966, pp. 29-60), M. Weiss is not disposed to accept without challenge the commonly held idea that the concept of the "Day of the Lord" is pre-prophetic in its origin. Nor will he easily follow G. von Rad's opinion that the concept derives from the tradition of the "holy war." About the well known Amos text, "Woe to those who yearn for the day of the Lord! What will this day of the Lord mean for you? Darkness and not light," Weiss denies that a pre-prophetic origin of the concept is implied, as if Amos was here dealing with a precise and generally known matter. It seems, on the contrary, plausible, that the phrase "day of the Lord" was coined by Amos, who uses it for the first time in his prophecy of 5: 18-20. The concept has its roots "in the ancient motif-complex of the theophany-descriptions," not in the "holy war" tradition. [On "holy war," cf. H.-J. Kraus, Psalmen, p. 957.]

Habakkuk's description of theophany includes the following: "The sun forgets to rise, the moon remains in its shelter" (3:10f). The same elements are found in the apocryphal *Assumption of Moses,* about contemporary with the earthly life of Christ: "And the horns of the sun shall be broken and he shall be turned into darkess; and the moon shall not give her light, and be turned wholly into blood. And the circle of the stars shall be disturbed" (10:5; tr. R. H. Charles; comp. Mk 13:24). Jörg Jeremias notes that these two texts represent a later expression of theophany, not included in the more ancient ones (*Theophanie,* p. 98ff).

The theme of the utter darkness then would have been added from the "day of Yahweh" tradition (cf. Is 13:10; Jl 2:10). It is possible, on the other hand, he thinks, that two motifs passed from the theophanies to the "day of Yahweh": the voice of Yahweh (Jl 2:11; 4:16) and the shaking of heaven and earth (cf. Jl 2:10; Is 13:13). The fact is that it is not always easy to know where the theophanies finish and the "day of Yahweh" begins!

(c) *Eschatology in the Psalter*

Israelite cosmogony is seen to have furnished the model for Israelite eschatology. As God has created the whole universe so also will his final intervention have cosmic repercussions. It is typical of eschatology that the disasters it predicts are entirely outside the previous experience of men, and that God displays in them an abnormal power. Besides, true eschatology is not merely national but universal. These aspects are illustrated in Ps 97:

> The Lord is King; let the earth rejoice;
>> let the many isles be glad.
> Clouds and darkness are round about him,
>> justice and judgment are the foundation of his throne.
> Fire goes before him
>> and consumes his foes round about.
> His lightnings illumine the world;
>> the earth sees and trembles.
> The mountains melt like wax before the Lord,
>> before the Lord of all the earth.
> The heavens proclaim his justice,
>> and all peoples see his glory (vv 1-6).

In other instances the wonderful deeds of the past seem to be cited as evidence of yet greater wonders to come or be hoped for (Pss 74:12-23; 114:3-8; cf. T. H. Robinson, "The eschatology...," p. 93f).

Eschatology or Restoration?

The metaphors used in Yahweh's kingship psalms (47, 93, 96, 97, 98, 99; cf. also 29, 68, 95, 100, 149) to describe the Lord's epiphany are generally related to the conventional forms of eschatology. For Mowinckel, however, these metaphors belong to the traditional style of cult theophanies. Indeed, he claims, the fundamental myth of the enthronement festival is the *myth of creation*: Yahweh has become the King of the world, because he has created it (I, p. 143; cf. Pss 74: 12-17;   89:10:13;   93:1-4;   104:5-9). He disagrees (II, p. 64) with those who, like Gunkel-Begrich (*Einleitung*...p. 329ff), T. H. Robinson and others, have sought to interpret quite a number of psalms, particularly "enthronement psalms" as "eschatological psalms." What should be said, Mowinckel asserts, is that there are psalms in which "the congregation among other things prays for the great *turning of the destiny of Israel* (cf. 14:7; 85:2; 126:4) to come soon, and there are prophetic psalms, psalm-like elements of the festal rituals, in which the cultic prophet also promises that this turning will take place: he beholds it already, as the extension of the new creation and salvation which the new year will bring about." *The re-establishment* of Israel was in fact expected through the miraculous intervention of Yahweh. But this faith in re-establishment is no original part of the religion of Israel: "it is concerned with the national, religious and moral re-establishment of the realm of David, which was destroyed in 587. It is this hope which in the course of 'post-exilic' days, partly under the influence of Persian ideas, developed into true eschatology" (II, p. 72).

In the words of H.-J. Kraus, Mowinckel, like Volz, sees the New Year-Yahweh festival as the *source* of old memories and expectations of deliverance...and even as the *origin* of Old Testament eschatology (*Worship...*, p. 9). In *Religion und Kultus* (Göttingen, 1953), however, Mowinckel states "that eschatology as a doctrine of last things did not grow out of the cult, but that, just as all that is living and dynamic in religion is expressed in the cult, eschatology become a vital force only in the cultic drama" (cf. E. Jacob, p. 317, note 1).

The eschatology of the psalmists

The authors of the introduction to BJ (*Les Psaumes*, p. 28ff) call "eschatological" the psalms of the kingship of Yahweh, which reflect ideas of Isaiah (cf. ch. 9, 11, 13, 24-27, 34-35, 65-66), of Ezekiel (38-39), of Zechariah (13-14), of Malachi (3), of Joel and of others whose oracles prelude to apocalyptic literature. Influenced by prophetical preaching, the hopes for Yahweh's epiphany and reign grew after the exile (587-538). Subject to pagan kings, threatened in its faith, harassed by its neighbors, having reaped mostly deceptions, the community of the repatriates deferred to a distant future the accomplishment of the splendid promises so poorly realized in the present. It was a major trend of post-exilic Judaism this attitude which also characterized the "poor of Yahweh," not strangers, as we have seen (§12a) to the inspiration of the psalms.

With the advent of God's reign the idols will disappear (96:5; 97:7) and the pagans be subdued (9:16; 18:44; 47:4; cf. Is 11:14): "Let the kings of the earth and all peoples, the princes and the judges of the earth...praise the name of the Lord, for his name alone is exalted" (149:11, 13). The terrified nations will unite with Israel in the praise of the only Lord (96:7; 97:6; 98:2; 99:1): "The princes of the peoples are gathered together with the people of the God of Abraham" (47:10; cf. 87:4-7; Gn 12:3). Similar universalist tendencies are already attested in the first part of Isaiah (2:2ff) and in Jeremiah (12:15f; 16:19ff). They would be accentuated by the Second Isaiah (Is 42:1-4; 45:14-25; 53:3-5)—the anonymous prophet who wrote chapters 40-55 about two centuries later than the eighth century prophet—and by other post-exilic writings (Zc 2:13; 8:20-23).

Deutero-Isaiah had also predicted that the universe would shake to its very foundations and be renewed (51:6; 65:17; 66:22). A psalmist has compared the transitory character of this world with God's eternal permanence:

Of old you established the earth,
    and the heavens are the work of your hands.
They shall perish but you remain
    though all of them grow old like a garment.
Like clothing you change them, and they are changed,
    but you are the same, and your years have no end (102:26ff).

To the universal convulsion will succeed an era of peace and happiness, as after the Flood (cf. Pss 29:11; 85:9-13; Is 54:9f). Psalm 29, an eschatological hymn, describes the might of Yahweh, Lord of the tempest. In *Ps 68:5 God is called "Rider of the clouds," the name of the Canaanite storm-god Baal (cf. Dt 33:26; Is 19:1). The thunderstorm imagery traditionally used to depict God's self-manifestation (Ex 19:16) or theophany, is a feature of the conventional style of eschatology, as inspired by the prophets.

Three canticles of Zion (46, 48, 76) are also eschatological in character, it is stated in *BJ*. They reflect mainly the oracles of Isaiah on the future glory of Zion, where the Great King is enthroned (cf. Is 25, 26, 60, 62 and 11:19; 49:14f; 51:17f; Jr 3:17; 14:21; Ex 43: 6). The central importance of Jerusalem, its God-given attributions were closely associated in some circles with the person of David (Ps 132:1ff), who, in some circles, enjoyed an eschatological status (cf. Ps 89:4f, 21f). This brings us to the threshold of messianic eschatology, to be examined separately.

Realized eschatology?

Reflecting on "Zion in the eschaton," W. I. Wolverton (pp. 28-33) recalls that Gunkel regarded the so-called enthronement psalms as eschatological... "But of late" W. I. W. writes, "there is a tendency toward a revision of Gunkel's position. The supposed eschatological features in the Psalms do not point to an end-time; it is a case of *realized eschatology*." Weiser writes: both "history and eschatology become in the cultic ceremony a present reality of actual significance, in which the festival congregation shares" (*The Psalms*, p. 375). In worship verbs frequently tend to take on a kind of liturgical present tense, something akin to the prophetic perfect. It is, indeed, to the prophets that we must look for that vision of Zion as the central stage of end-time events. Our psalmists seem rather to think of the events as taking place in the supernatural realm of which those which happen in the world, and especially in the cult, are somehow a reflection. Zion was the locale, they believed, where this wonderous interplay was enacted. [On eschatology in the Psalms, see also: R. Arconada, A. Feuillet, T. H. Robinson, R. Tournay]

(d) *Individual eschatology in the psalms*

There are three main characteristics of later eschatology: the prominence of the idea of judgment (cf. Pss 1:5; 7:7; 82:3); the appearance of the Messiah (see §15); greater attention paid to the future life of the individual. "In its most complete form the *Jewish apocalyptic* always contains, and indeed culminates in, the resurrection of the dead and the entry of the righteous into heaven, where they will remain for all eternity, while the wicked are doomed to endless torture in hell" (T. H. Robinson in *The Psalmists*, p. 103). But earlier eschatology, that of the main biblical period, had little to say about life beyond the grave. True, when the individual dies he does not cease to exist, yet existence in the other world was imagined as but a shadow of life on earth.

Sheol

In Sheol all the dead descended, to lead a colorless, diminished life, wrapped in silence (Pss 31:8; 115:17) and darkness (35:6; 88:7, 19; 143:3).

For it is not the nether world that gives you thanks,
    nor death that praises you;
Neither do those who go down into the pit
    await your kindness (Is 38:18).

Will you work wonders for the dead?
    Will the shades arise to give you thanks?
Do they declare your kindness in the grave,
    your faithfulness among those who have perished?
Are your wonders made known in the darkness,
    or your justice in the land of oblivion? (Pss 88:11-13).

Was Sheol considered as opposed, like death, to Yahweh, or simply neutral in relation to his sovereignty? The realm of Sheol, E. Jacobs believes, remained outside Yahweh's sphere of influence for quite a long time and was only gradually opened to his sovereignty (p. 304), presumably more or less like the watery abyss (cf. §11a), to which it is related (see below). The psalmists imagined that the dwellers of Sheol were generally abandoned by God, of whom they lost all remembrance: "For among the dead no one remembers you; in the nether world who gives you thanks?" (6:6).

Although Sheol is often described as a function, its *location* was also considered, in the setting of Hebrew cosmology. This J. A. Emerton has recently attempted to sketch, in connection with the statement of Ps 74: 15: "You released the springs and torrents; you brought dry land out of the primeval waters," "Originally," he writes, "there was a watery chaos; the earth existed, but it was covered by the all-embracing ocean. Yahweh set up the firmament to keep part of the ocean from pouring downwards. Below the firmament, dry land was created by driving the waters off the earth (Ps 104:6-9; Gn 1:9f). The world rested on pillars (Ps 75:4; Jb 9:6) in the great deep beneath (Pss 24:2; 136:6...). Sometimes Sheol was regarded as lying directly below the surface of the ground (cf. 16:31ff), but *sometimes it was thought that the way to it lay through the subterranean ocean* (Ps 18: 5f=2 S 22:5f; Jon 2:3ff). The seas of the world were joined to the great deep from which they were fed. The waters were forbidden by God to pass over their limits and to encroach upon dry land (Jb 38:8-11), but a certain amount of water was allowed to come up from the subterranean ocean through springs and fountains (Dt 8:7; cf. Gn 49:25)" (p. 124f). The illustration "The World of the Hebrews" supplied next to p. 4 in *NAB* is helpful to visualize what has just been said and what follows.

These notions of biblical cosmology may help to explain why the psalmists speak of Sheol as an abysmal swamp (69:3), a sort of quagmire (40:3; 69:15; see on *Ps 42/43), to which leads a dark and slippery way (35:6), through the gates of death (9:14; 56:13; 115:8). For the same reason, it seems, they ask God to prevent their foot from slipping (66:9; 94:18; 121:3) into the pit (28:1; 30:4; 40:3; 69: 16; 88:5; 143:7), to the nether world (30:4). With divine help their foot stands on level ground (26:12; 27:11; 143:10), high upon a rock (27:5; 40:3; 61:3; 62:5; 91:14), and their steps are made firm (37: 23; 40:3; 66:9), while the wicked are set on a slippery road (73:18). The relation of Sheol to the abyss explains also that death, Sheol's Shepherd (49:15), leads its flock down (30:4; 139:8) to the depths of the nether world (86:13; 130:1; 140:11; cf. Dt 32:22), into the depths of the earth (63:10; 71:20; 94:4; 139:15) and that rescue from death means going up (30:4; 86:13) from the depths of the sea (68:23; 69:3, 15; 77:17). On *'ereṣ*, "earth," as denoting Sheol, see on *Ps 18 (on the death-Sheol theme, cf. C. Barth, *Die Errettung...* and J. Zandee, *Death...*; on Sheol and *Mōt*, see *Ps 73).

Retribution

"You render to every one according to his deeds" (Ps 62:13). This doctrine of personal retribution, taught by the prophets, Ezekiel mainly (ch 18; *ScEcc* 1958, pp. 167-202), finds expression in other psalms also (28:4; 31:24) and in wisdom writings (Jb 24:12; 34:11; Si 16:14). To those whom the prosperity of the wicked scandalizes the author of Ps 37 (cf. *BJ*) recalls also wisdom teaching on retribution:

Pr 10:3; 23:17; 24:1; 16, 19; Jb 4:7f; 5:20; 21:7f, Eccl 8:11f. But the facts of experience did seem to contradict the traditional teaching and popular beliefs (see on *Ps 37, 49, 73). The just sometimes suffer while the wicked prosper. This prosperity, the psalmists answered, is shortlived and a terrible fate awaits the sinners (32:10). Many are the sorrows of the wicked (32:10), vice slays them, they pay for their guilt (34:22), like grass they quickly wither (37:2; 129:6; cf. Is 40:6-8), like smoke they vanish (37:20; cf. Ho 13:3), their day is coming (37:13), a little while and they are no more (37:10; cf. Pr 10:25). They seem to prosper (10:3; 37:34f; 73:4-12; 94:3), but their power will be broken (37:17), they will not live half their days (55:24; cf. Jb 15:32; Jr 17:11) and their final destiny is eternal destruction (73:17; 92:9; cf. Jb 8 and 20:17-35). The scanty store of the just is better than the great wealth of the wicked (37:16; 49:7ff). While the wicked leave no posterity (37:28), the inheritance of the just last forever (16:6; 37:18), for the righteous shall possess the land (37:29; cf. Dt 30:16; on "retribution," see also B. Hall, V. Laridon, E. Pax).

The book of God

Retribution is practiced according to the records of the book of God. The "book of God" contains the names of his intimate friends. From it Moses volunteered to have his own name erased for the sake of the people (Ex 32:32; cf. Rm 9:3). It lists also the just (Ml 3:15), those who enjoy life in communion with God. In an imprecation against the wicked a psalmist wishes that they be "erased from the book of the living" (69:29; cf. Rev 13:8), that is, excommunicated, expelled from the covenant, life's domain. In the book of God are also recorded the sufferings of the just (Ps 56:9), man's actions, whether meritorious (Rv 20:12) or sinful (Jr 17:1), and the divine dispositions concerning everyone (Ps 139:16; cf. *Ps 87). The elect of the Remnant (cf. §15a) were also noted down for survival (Is 4:3). For the second century b.c. author of the Book of Daniel those who will escape in the great day of Distress also have their names recorded in the book (Dn 12:1). Finally, for the authors of the New Testament, the elect have their names written in the divine book; they are predestined to eternal life (Lk 10:20; Rv 20:12): *Liber scriptus proferetur, in quo totum continetur, unde mundus judicetur* ("Dies irae").

Future life

So there was a difference between the just and the wicked in the manner of life and death. In Isaiah 14 and Ezekiel 32 can be read allusions to a different fate in Sheol itself, "but it is only from the second century B.C. that the division between the righteous and the wicked within Sheol will be taken up and developed in all its breadth" (E. Jacob, p. 305). A privileged afterlife seems to have been foreseen for the Servant of the Lord (Is 53:10ff; cf. Ps 22:23-32). The following passages of the psalms are usually quoted as indications of a persistent belief in some hope for the just after their death, even at the earlier levels of Old Testament thought:

Therefore my heart is glad and my soul rejoices,
    my body, too, abides in confidence;
Because you will not abandon my soul to the nether world,
    nor will you suffer your faithful one to undergo corruption:

You will show me the path of life,
    fullness of joys in your presence,
    the delights at your right hand forever (16:9-11).

But I in justice shall behold your face;
    on waking, I shall be content in your presence (17:15).

This is the way of those whose trust is folly,
    the end of those contented with their lot:
Like sheep they are herded into the nether world;
    death is their shepherd, and the upright rule over them.
Quickly their form is consumed;
    the nether world is their palace.
But God will redeem me
    from the power of the nether world by receiving me (49:14ff).

Yet with you I shall always be;
    you have hold of my right hand;
With your counsel you guide me,
    and in the end you will receive me in glory (73:23f).

In the detailed exposition of these texts, opinions will be discussed and conclusions drawn, whenever possible. It will be seen, for example, that M. Dahood has no difficulty in reading in Ps 17:15 clear belief in "the beatific vision" and in the resurrection (his elaborate presentation of the OT belief in afterlife in *Psalms* III, pp. XLI-LII, deserves serious consideration, but see on *Ps 63:5). R. Tournay, however, thinks it is "reasonable to conclude that none of the controversial texts of Pss 16, 17, 49 and 73 imply the idea of a future beatific life or of an individual resurrection" (*RB* 1949, p. 501). A. F. Kirkpatrick is for a qualified affirmative answer: "Some of the expressions which appear at first sight to imply a sure hope of deliverance from Sheol and of reception into the more immediate presence of God (e.g., 49:16; 73:24) are used elsewhere of temporal deliverance from death or protection from danger, and may mean no more than this (9:13; 18:16; 30:3; 86:13; 103:4; 138: 7). Reading these passages in the light of fuller revelation we may easily assign to them a deeper and more precise meaning than their original authors and hearers understood. They adapt themselves so readily to Christian hope that we are easily led to believe that it was there from the first" (*The Psalms,* I, p. LXXVII; cf. also the studies of J. Guillet ad A. Vaccari).

The Bible is in fact witness of the progressive revelation of the mystery of the resurrection of bodies to an extraterrestrial life. The origins of the doctrine are connected with a firm and constant belief in Israel from the beginning: the *living God* (cf. §10c) is stronger than death (cf. Dt 32:39; Lk 20:37f). He proved it by the assumption of Henoch (Gn 5:24; Wis 4:10f) and of Elijah (2 K 2:11; 1 M 2:58), and especially by the resurrections to temporal life as answers to the prayers of Eijah (1 K 17:17ff) and of Elisha (2 K 4:29; cf. 13:21).

To describe the *national restoration* the prophets often use the image of resurrection. Contemplating a valley filled with bones, Ezekiel hears God say: "Son of man, can these bones come to life?" (37:3). The word of God covered them with flesh and the spirit of the Lord put life into them. This eloquent symbol would suggest the possibility of an individual resurrection of the flesh, already less distant in that post-exilic oracle of Isaiah:

But your dead shall live, their corpses shall rise;
awake and sing, you who lie in the dust.

For your dew is a dew of light,
    and the land of shades gives birth (26:19).

Redacted toward the year 165 B.C. the Book of Daniel offers the first clear affirmation of individual resurrection to a life beyond the tomb. It is not yet stated that *all* men will rise, but the wicked do not seem to be excluded. A shining corporal glory (cf. Mt 13:43) is foreseen for one category of the risen:

Many of those who sleep
    in the dust of the earth shall awake;
Some shall live forever,
    others shall be an everlasting horror and disgrace.
But the wise shall shine brightly
    like the splendor of the firmament,
And those who led the many to justice
    shall be like the stars forever (12:2f).

A clear teaching on the resurrection of the just emerges from several texts of the *Second Book of the Maccabees,* an inspired work written in Greek for the Alexandrian Jews near the end of the second century B.C. (cf. 7:9, 14). As for the book of Wisdom, composed in Greek about 50 B.C. by a hellenized Jew, it does not exclude resurrection but it insists on incorruptibility (6:18) and immortality (3:4; 8:17). Paracanonical apocrypha of the last two centuries before Christ reveal a rather general hope in an eternally happy life for the just (cf Henoch: 58:3). The New Testament clearly testifies to the faith in the general resurrection. Jesus said to the Jews: "Do not wonder at this, for the hour is coming in which all who are in the tombs shall hear the voice of the Son of God. And they who have done good shall come forth into resurrection of life; but they who have done evil unto resurrection of judgment" (Jn 5:28f).

Imprecations

God's providential rule was interpreted (cf. §12e) as disposing that sinners be punished according to *lex talionis*: what they intended for others will be done unto them. This law of retaliation, "eye for eye, tooth for tooth..." (cf. Ex 21:23ff; Lv 24:17ff; Dt 19:21), was intended to prevent excessive revenge by laying down a punishment equal to the damage. It is progress compared to Lamech's talk of a sevenfold and seventy times sevenfold revenge (Gn 4:24). Jesus will use similar language to recommend forgiving an indefinite number of times (Mt 18: 21f).

In connection with *lex talionis* and the concept of retribution, it seems apposite to discuss a problem that has long been a worry to many, mostly Christian, interpreters of the psalms: *the imprecations of the psalmists,* these passionate appeals to divine vengeance against God's enemies or against the persecutors of the just.

Prayers and wishes

The Lord's *punitive justice* is implored in various ways against *the wicked*: "Punish them, O God...because they have rebelled against you" (5:11); let them be put to shame (31:18; 35:4; 40:15); smash their teeth in their mouths (58:7); may they disappear from the earth (104: 35), and be destroyed (139:19), reduced to silence in the nether world (31:18); "let them go down alive to the nether world, for evil is in their dwellings" (55:16). Sometimes *the psalmist's foes* are more directly concerned: "Turn back the evil upon my foes" (54:7; cf. 69:23; 140:10); "Let them be like chaff before the wind, with the angel of the Lord driving them on" (35:5) and "slay them" (59:12). Similar conventional language is used to curse *the enemies of Israel*: "O my God, make them like leaves in a whirlwind, like chaff before the wind" (83: 14). *Vengeance* as such is sometimes requested: "God of vengeance, Lord, God of vengeance, show yourself... How long shall the wicked glory?" (94:1-3; cf. Na 1:2); "Repay our neighbors sevenfold into their bosoms the disgrace they [the pagan nations] have inflicted on you, O Lord" (79:12); "Happy the man who shall repay you the evil you have done us!" (137:8; cf. Ps 58:11); "May he rain burning coals upon them; may he cast them into the depths, never to rise" (140:11). More disturbing still, perhaps, is the demand for a *refusal of mercy*: "Pour out your wrath upon them" (69: 25; cf. 59:14); "When he is judged, let him go forth condemned, and may his plea be in vain" (109: 7):

Heap guilt upon their guilt,
    and let them not attain to your reward.

> May they be erased from the book of the living,
>   and not be recorded with the just! (69:28f).

There is no doubt that the inspiration of these hopes and prayers indicates that a progress in the revelation was wanting to attain the degree of ethical standards divinely willed for man. This progress has been explicitly asserted by Jesus:

> You have heard that it was said, "Thou shalt love thy neighbor, and shalt hate thy enemy." But I say to you, love your enemies, do good to those who hate you, and pray for those who persecute and calumniate you, so that you may be children of your Father in heaven, who makes his sun rise on the good and the evil, and sends rain on the just and the unjust (Mt 5:43ff).

Fraternal love and hatred of enemies

There were laws in the Old Testament aimed at protecting the strangers, whom the Israelite had to love as himself (Lv 19:34), but the prescription against hatred had limits: "You shall not bear hatred *for your brother* in your heart. . . Take no revenge and cherish no grudge against your fellow countrymen. You shall love your neighbor as yourself. I am the Lord" (Lv 19:17f). The law of retaliation (Ex 21:23ff) and the institution of cities of refuge (Dt 19:1ff) were intended to mitigate and confine revenge, "but if someone lies in wait for his neighbor *out of hatred* for him". . .and kills him, he cannot escape the avenger of blood (Dt 19:11ff). God promised to Israel: "I will be an enemy to your enemies and a foe to your foes" (Ex 23:22). Israel will hate God's enemies in order to avoid imitating their conduct. This is the meaning of *ḥērem*, the "ban" or the rule of holy war: kill every man and animal and give the booty to the sanctuary (cf. Dt 20:10ff; Jos 6:17ff).

The spirit of vindictiveness can also be read in some of Jeremiah's wishes:

> Let my persecutors, not me, be confounded;
>   let them, not me, be broken.
> Bring upon them the day of misfortune,
>   crush them with repeated destruction (17:18).

Forgive not their crime,
  Blot not out their sin in your sight!
Let them go down before you,
  proceed against them in the time of your anger (18:23).

According to the more refined code of ethics requital is to be left to the
Lord (Pr 20:22;   Jb 31:29f). This notion was known already to Old
Testament wisdom (Pr 25:21f), quoted by St. Paul:

> Do not avenge yourselves, beloved, but give place to the wrath, for it is
> written, "Vengeance is mine; I will repay, says the Lord" (cf. Dt 32:
> 35f). But "if thy enemy is hungry, give him food; if he is thirsty, give
> him drink; for by so doing thou wilt heap coals of fire upon his head"
> (Pr 25:21f). Be not overcome by evil, but overcome evil with good
> (Rm 12:19ff).

Solutions proposed

Various explanations have been offered in respect to the *imprecations of the psalmists*. Some merit greater consideration than others (cf.
the special studies of J. Blenkinsopp, H. A. Brongers, J. Fichtner, H.
Junker, J. L. Lilly, J. L. McKenzie, O. Schilling, M. de Tuya, H. Ubbelohde, P. Van Imschoot, J. G. Vos). It has been already pointed out
that a progress in the revelation of ethical standards was to be expected.
"Under the Old Covenant, *retribution in this life* was still the rule;
against this background these appeals [for vengeance] betray simply a
hunger for justice" (*JB* in Ps 6; cf. Ps 7:9, 18). Secondly, it is also admitted by Christian theology that all sinners, *in respect of their guilt*, are to
be hated, although it is our duty to love in the sinner the prospective re-
pentant called to the beatific vision (cf. Thomas Aquinas, *Sum.Th.*
2-2,   25,   6). It can be said that what the psalmists desire is no more
than the satisfaction of divine retributive justice against the unrepen-
tant sinners. Yet the language of the psalmists is certainly excessive.
This can be ascribed in part to the spontaneous impulse of passion and
in part to the poetic nature of the expression. P. Van Imschoot makes
the observation that for Israelites and other ancient peoples as well, the
imprecation was a legitimate means of defense, sanctioned by custom.
He adds that Orientals are naturally violent in speech. On the psalm

imprecations see also N. Füglister, OSB, "Gott der Rache?", in T. Sartory, ed., *Entdeckungen im Alten Testament* (Munich 1970) 117-135.

Other observations spring from the literary viewpoint. Very few, if any, of the imprecatory optatives can be interpreted as prophetical futures like the following:

> God himself shall demolish you;
>   forever he shall break you;
> He shall pluck you from your tent,
>   and uproot you from the land of the living (52:7).

Gunkel termed Ps 109 the only pure example of imprecatory psalms in the Bible. It is generally considered as the worst offender of revealed ethics. It shall be seen, however, that the litany of imprecations may have been pronounced by the enemies. One of the most repulsive wishes would have been pronounced by the exiled community: "Happy the man who shall seize and smash your little ones against the rock!" (137:9). The imprecation, it seems, (see *in loc.*), reflects conventional speech. Besides, it is aimed at "little ones" as representing tomorrow's generation, called to perpetuate the enemies of God and of his people (Is 14:21). Sometimes the imprecations have to be read in the light of historical punishments wrought by God on Sodom and Gomorrah (Gn 19:23ff; cf. Ps 140:11), for example, or on Dathan and Abiram (Nb 16:33; cf. Ps 55:16). To safeguard the moral truth of the inspired word it has been proposed that what we read in the psalms is the record of the psalmist's past experiences, not subject to inerrancy, if the writer was not committal on their moral value. This explanation is unnecessary and founded on improbable subtleties.

The power of curse

" According to ancient opinion," writes Mowinckel, "*all* words were powerful in proportion to the 'power' of the speaker; evil words, curses, abuse, threats, sneers, evil wishes, 'the evil eye,' jealous thoughts, scornful or threatening gestures and looks and symbols—in the eyes of the Israelites and of all other ancient orientals, all such things were powerful, and would do harm to the soul and happiness of those against whom they were directed. All the powerful means of the gentile enemies their plans and threats and sneers, the 'curses' of their prophets and priests, and all their accompanying ceremonies, in short all their religious and cultic measures and acts and words, in the eyes of the Israelites seemed to be sorcery, '*āwen*; when used for the gods of the gentiles the word actually means 'demons,' 'devils,' 'trolls.' What to one person is cultus, to the person on the other side appears as sorcery. Such powerful words on the part of the enemy are 'falsehoods,' 'deceitful words,' because they call up the 'false,' pernicious power in life, 'the curse,' draining and laying waste blessings and happiness. But they are also 'falsehoods,' because they will make righteous people 'scoundrels,' and because, by Yahweh's help, they shall turn out to be unreal and of no effect, injuring only the mischief-maker" (I p. 199f).

"Prayers and wishes for the destruction of the enemy naturally claim much space in the national psalms of lamentation. Just as natural is that here, particularly, the ancient *formula of cursing* is used: 'may the gentiles be put to shame,' 'be destroyed,' 'may the culprit go to Sheol' (Hades), 'may Yahweh cut off all flattering lips! and so on. The last is a transition form to actual prayer. In some of the psalms these curses dominate the whole; see, for instance, the detailed curse in *Ps 58:5-10. And see, likewise, the prayer in Ps 83:14-17, where we only need to omit the reference to Yahweh and replace the imperatives by the subjunctive ('jussive') in order to get the wording of a cursing formula such as, for instance, the king of Moab would have had Balaam speak against Israel" (I, p. 202).

"The aim is to strike at the root of the disaster: the operative evil words and tricks and intrigues of the enemy; and so, by means of the cult and the ritual curses of the psalm, the congregation tries to parry the curse words of the enemy. But we are not justified in concluding from this that the psalmists thought that without the will and help of Yahweh the word of cursing by itself could deliver them from the enemy; at most we have the lingering remains of the old style. Rather more frequently than the directly cursing word, we find the prayer for Yahweh to slay the enemy by means of his 'ban': *his* operative word, his 'threats' shall destroy them. Even if corresponding thoughts *may* at any time be attached to the sacred words of religion, the laments can claim to be true prayer to God, and no magical formulas. Yahweh has to interfere, if the malice of the enemies is to be struck at the root, and brought home to themselves" (p. 202f).

Dissenting views

These rather extensive quotations were intended to give a fair picture of Mowinckel's conceptions. Most of what he says is important and suggestive. "It is entirely in keeping with Old Testament thought," G. W. Anderson believes, "to ascribe to the spoken word creative and destructive power. Such a conception, however, need not imply any reference to sorcerers..." (p. 25; see §12g). Mowinckel seems to have overstated the case as regards the presence in the psalms of magical cursing formulas (see also §8e, c. fi). There is repeated mention in the psalms, in the lament mostly, of "enemies" (cf. §12g) of the just, main-ly the "evildoers" (pō'alê-'āwen; cf. also Is 31:2; Jb 31:3; Pr 10:29; 21:15). It is stated in *BJ* (p. 19f) that "a theory" concerning them has been "solidly" refuted, the theory namely that they would be "magicians," whose sorceries the victim would oppose with incantations and ex-piatory rites. The evil words of "lying lips" and "deceitful tongue" (Pss 12, 52, ·64, 120, 140, etc.), *BJ* claims, are not incantations, they are insults, calumnies and blasphemies (59:8, 13; Si 28:13f). G. S. Gunn writes: "The least reliable and satisfying part of Mowinckel's great work on the Psalms is that in which he interprets the phrase *workers of iniquity* and kindred phrases in terms of sorcery and witch-craft" (p. 101).

Concluding his observations on the "Imprecatory Psalms," A. F. Kirkpatrick writes: the psalmists "set an example of moral earnestness, of righteous indignation, of burning zeal for the cause of God... Their fundamental motive and idea is the religious passion for justice; and it was by the Holy Spirit that their writers were taught to discern and grasp this essential truth; but the form in which they clothed their desire for its realization belonged to the limitations and modes of thought of their particular age" (*The Psalms,* I, p. LXXV).

§15. THE MESSIANIC HOPE IN THE PSALMS

For us who read the Old Testament in the light of its fulfillment, writes A. F. Kirkpatrick, "it is difficult to reatlize how dim and vague and incomplete the messianic hope must have been until the Coming of Christ revealed the divine purpose, and enabled men to recognize how through long ages God had been preparing for its consummation *The Psalms,* I, p. LVIII). But "the coming of Jesus Christ as a historical reality leaves the exegete no choice at all; he must interpret the Old Testament as pointing to Christ, whom he must understand in its light" (G. von Rad, II, p. 374). To understand better the messianic psalms and discern the messianic elements dispersed in the Psalter it is well to have some clear notions on messianism. What is suggested here can incite to further study.

(a) Messianism

Messianism is a notion more complex than most people imagine. Bent towards the future, A. Gelin writes, the messianic idea was "the longing for a definitive era coinciding with the movement of faith itself" (in *The God of Israel, the God of Christians*, New York, 1961, p. 199). So the Messiah belongs also to eschatology, being a figure of the last days. In an acceptable sense the word "eschatology" may allude either to the end of the world or to an important turning point in human history that somehow inaugurates a new era. Only by God's transcendent intervention does such an event happen. God's relation to history is conceived as a series of interventions that make its sweep unpredictable (cf. A. Gelin in *SDB*, vol. V. c. 1165f). An important current of biblical tradition assigns a decisive role to the Messiah in the unfolding of the most crucial turning points of world history.

"Messianism without a Messiah": such a phrase is sometimes used to describe a biblical tradition that concentrates on a basic expectation, that of the coming of *God Himself* to establish His rule and to ensure effective recognition of His royalty. God did come in the past: He delivered the Israelites from bondage in Egypt; He will come again to chastise the nations (Is 32:28), to re-establish Zion (Is 52:8), to judge the earth (Ps 96:13), or to save it (Ws 16:17). The theme of God's coming oriented the messianic hope towards the Incarnation.

The growth of messianism

Messianic expectation followed a trend perceptible in the first texts: the proto-evangelium (Gn 3:15), the promises to the patriarchs (cf. Gn 12:3; Rm 4:13), and the commitments to the Covenant (cf. Ex 19:5f). Derived from a Hebrew word meaning "to anoint" or "to rub with oil," the term *Messiah* (Gr: *Messias*) is usually applied to *the king* and to the ritual of his investiture (cf. 1 K 1:34). High priests (cf.

Ex 30:30) and even simple priests (cf. Lv 8:30;   10:7) were also anointed, although prophets were not. It is possible that, after the disappearance of the monarchy, the royal anointing was transferred to the high priest as head of the people and later extended to all the priests (cf. R. de Vaux, *Ancient Israel,* p. 105). A text, 1 K 19:16, is often cited to prove that some prophets were anointed. But it seems that there the term "anointing" is due to the context and is inexactly applied to the "consecration" of the prophets to God, as in Is 61:1 (cf. Ps 105:15). All three groups of leaders (king, prophet, priest) enjoyed messianic preferment in view of the roles they would play as founders of the Covenant.

Incorporating the Remnant

With the settlement in Canaan hopes focused on the king who, according to the biblical conception, embodies the whole people and appears as its natural mediator. In time the royal line will prove disappointing and drive the people to "messianism without a Messiah," the theme of Yahweh-King, found in Deutero-Isaiah (cf. 43:15;   52:7f), and in several psalms (93:1;   96:10;   98:6;   98:1). With the monarchy's disappearance and the collapse of national hopes came a new source of messianic promise: the Servant of Yahweh (*'ebed yhwh*) now embodies the vocation of the "Remnant" of Israel, called to self-sacrifice for the salvation of the world (cf. Is 53 and Ps 22; also Pss 31:6;   41:10;   69: 5, 22). In the fourth Servant Song (Is 52:13 to 53:12), the man of sorrows could represent the exiled generation, "taken away," "cut off from the land of the living" (=Holy Land), buried "among the wicked" in Babylon (Is 53:8f). It atoned for the sins of the "many" (the past generation) so that the "many" (the future generations) might live and prosper: "If he gives his life as an offering for sin, he shall see his descendants in a long life, and the will of the Lord shall be accomplished through him" (53:10;   cf. Ps 22:30ff; see on *Ps 51). The messianic-eschatological meaning of the Song is indicated by many allusions to it where the New Testament speaks of the atoning work of Christ (cf. L. Sabourin, *Rédemption Sacrificielle,* pp. 223-255 or W. Zimmerli-J. Jeremias, *The Servant of God,* London, 1965).

The Servant figure is linked to prophetic messianism and to the *Son of Man,* whose transcendence is still greater (cf. Dn 7:13;   Mk 14: 62;   cf. Pss 8:3-7;   16:8-11;   40:7-11). As for Ezekiel, he favored a post-exilic theocracy closely related to priesthood (ch. 40-48). Thus was sterngthened the concept of priestly messianism mentioned by a few texts (Nb 25:12ff; Jr 33:14-26; Zc 6:11f; Si 45:25) other than Ps 110:4: The Lord has sworn, and he will not repent: "You are a priest forever, according to the order of Melchizedek" (cf. Heb 5:6; 7: 21). The notion of the Remnant has just been mentioned. In the words of G. Pidoux, it supplied a theological requirement, the transition between the inevitable disaster and re-establishment (*Le Dieu qui vient*, p. 41). The theme of the Remnant is abundantly attested in Scripture: Gn 12:2; 18:26; 45:7; Ex 19: 6; 32:10; Lv 26:36, 39; Nb 14:12; 1K 18:22, 40; 19:17f; 2 K 19:31; 25:12; Am 3:12; 4:11; 5:15; 9:8f; Mi 2:12; 4: 6f; 5:2, 6f; Is 1:9; 4:2f; 6: 13; 7:3; 10:20-23; 11:11f; 14: 30; 15:9; 17:5f; 28:5; 30:17; 37:31f; Zp 2:7, 9; 3:12f; Jr 5:18f; 24:5ff, 31:2; 40:11, 15; 42:2, 15, 19; 43:5; 44:12ff, 28; 50:20; 51:50; Ezk 6:8; 9: 8; 11:13, 17; 14:22; 37:12; Zc 8:11, 15; 13:8f; 14:2; Ob 17; Jl 3:5; Ezr 9:15; Si 44:17; Rm 9:27; 11:5.

Trends in messianism

Père Daniélou detects, in Israel's expectation, two parallel trends: one concerns the *divine actions,* the glory of which will, at the end of time, make the former ones look pale; the other awaits the eschatological advent of *figures* which will reflect, at a higher level, those of the past. Prophecy is, in fact, not seldom the foreseeing of the recurrence of past events (cf. *Approches du Christ,* Paris, 1960, p. 94f; cf. §14a). Apologetics in the past strained its ingenuity by trying to draw "a premature portrait of the future" with details removed from their Old Testament context. Today we prefer to read in the messianic idea the continuity of God's intervention. In the Old Testament the chosen people was restored by victories over the enemy; in the New Testament all mankind is invited to become a chosen people. Seen in the light of the New Testament, messianism appears to be ancient history's most advanced expression of its inclination towards Christ and the Communion of Saints.

As the Christian era dawned, the longing for the Messiah was intensified, as it appears, for instance, in the apocryphal *Psalms of Solomon.* The inspiring ideas of Ps 17 center on the following theme: "See, O Lord, and raise up for them their King, David's son, in an age you, O Lord, know, so that he may rule over Israel, your servant, and gird him with strength to crush the unjust rulers." It is the accomplishment of this hope that rejoiced old Simeon, who "awaited the consolation of Israel" and who had been promised "that he should not see death before he had seen the Christ of the Lord" (Lk 2:25f).

(b) God-Who-Comes

Old Testament theology is dominated by the reality of God's intervention in world history, past, present and future. Sacred history is a drama extending from the beginning to the end of the world. The chief actor in this drama is one of many features, God-Who-Comes. Sometimes he is the "Lord of the Storm" (cf. Ps 29; Ex 19:16-25; Na 1:2-6), or the eschatological "warrior" (Pss 44:10; 60:12; Ex 15:3; Is 42:13). The God-Who-Comes is also represented as a *judge,* as for example in this royal psalm cited by 1 Ch 16 in connection with the levitical service before the Ark, Yahweh's mobile sanctuary:

Let the heavens be glad and the earth rejoice;
    let the sea and what fills it resound;
    let the plains be joyful and all that is in them!
Then shall all the trees of the forest exult
    before the Lord, for he comes;
    for he comes to rule the earth.
He shall rule the world with justice
    and peoples with his constancy (Ps 96:11ff; cf. Jl 4:1f).

Concerning opinions on messianism, A. Gelin writes: "It is surprising, Podechard liked to say, that, given the important place the preaching of the reign of God holds in the Gospel, even today more importance is given to the announcement of the Messiah-King than to the announcement of the kingdom of God. Surprising, too, that, given Jesus Christ is God and that in him God came upon earth, we fail to find in him the accomplishment of the promises which announced the coming of Yahweh upon earth to establish his reign there" (SDB vol. V, c. 1192). "The fact that God will come," writes G. Pidoux, "is the only permanent element in the Old Testament eschatology, all the colorings that describe His return are but secondary and impermanent elements" (Le Dieu qui vient, p. 53). For many Jews the expectation of the God-Who-Comes coincides with that of the Messiah. In the New Testament the messianic times do mark the beginning of the "last days," the era of God's eschatological intervention (cf. 1 Cor 10:11; Heb 1:2; 9:26), the advent of God-Who-Comes (Rv 1:4, 8; 4:8). Mowinckel's *He that Cometh* (Oxford, 1956) treats also generally of the messianic expectation.

(c) *Royal messianism*

In the psalms the term *māšiaḥ*, "anointed," designates the king-Messiah (2:2; 132:17), the king of Israel (20:7), the Davidic dynasty 89:39, 52), the high-priest (84:10; cf. Lv 4:3; 6:15) or Israel itself, the people of God consecrated to his service (28:8; 105:15; cf. Ex 19:6; Hab 3:13). In other books of the Bible also the king is called "the Anointed of God" (cf. 1 S 26:9, 11, 25), which is, equivalently, "the Christ of the Lord" (cf. Lk 2:26). As a candidate to the messianic dignity every Davidic prince was expected to embody the ideal Israelite monarch. "In the Old Testament perspective the reign of the Kingdom of God would be established in this world and temporal blessings accompany and attest spiritual values. The monarchy was infused with grace; its status was raised, its role was centered in the smooth functioning of the Covenant and became one of the basic factors in the perspective of salvation" (A. Gelin in *The God of Israel...*; p. 203). Consequently the enthronement of a Davidic king meant his divine adoption (cf. Ps 2:6-8).

The great messianic texts are in fact associated with royal figures: the oracle of Balaam (Nb 24:17); the prophecy of Nathan (2 S 7:1-16); the sign of the Emmanuel (Is 7:14); the advent of the just king (Is 11:1-9) and of the Bethlehemite Messiah (Mi 5:1); the messianic eruption of 520, evoked by Haggai (2:23) and Zechariah (4:9.14), where a scribe substituted the name of Joshuah, the high priest, to that of the Davidic Zerubbabel (v 11); and finally, the enthusiastic poem of Zechariah's disciple, describing the arrival of the humble and peaceful king (Zc 9:9; cf. Mt 21:5). Thus the royal dignity was a prominent feature among the principal attributes of the expected Messiah. Messianism was a tendency, a thrust forward, before becoming a precise hope. First a messiah was expected, than the Messiah. As J. Coppens writes, the Messiah in the Old Testament is often considered as a secondary figure. Attention concentrates on divine salvation, with or without a mediator (*Le Psautier...*, p. 55).

According to Gunkel most of the royal psalms are ancient and belong to the royal period (cf. §27). Those authors, mostly Catholic, who favor a messianic-eschatological interpretation of the royal psalms, would naturally assign a more recent, even post-exilic, date to a number of these psalms. The two conceptions are not irreconcilable. Read in the proper perspective the royal psalms can be both ancient and messianic. Was not messianism dynastic before becoming personal? Since Nathan's oracle (2S 7:1-17; 1Ch 17:1-5) each prince of the Davidic dynasty was a candidate to messiahship. The Messiah is not necessarily the *eschatological king*. Before becoming the last king of the privileged dynasty— the king whose reign would be eternal—the Messiah was considered as an ideal, modeled after the figure of David. This ideal would one day be incarnated in the actual Messiah (cf. J. Coppens in *L'attente du Messie*, Bruges, 1954, p. 35). Although the expectation of a Davidic Messiah was kept alive, every new hope ended in failure. In fact "the office of the *key of David* remained unprovided for until finally it could be laid down at the feet of Christ (Rv 3:7)" (G. von Rad, II, p. 373).

To conclude, directly the historical kings are meant in the royal psalms. But the successful reigns can have indicated the pattern of a reign properly messianic. Besides, by some traits the figure of the Davidic kings mentioned in the psalms appears as prophetic in the strict sense, even attaining beyond the level of typology. This could be verified especially in Pss 2, 45, 72, 110 (also perhaps 20 and 21). In Pss 132 and 89 the confirming and restoring of the messianic dynasty could be intended. Additional revelation has made it possible to discover in previous texts a fuller sense than that which had been apprehended even by the writer himself. The king's divine sonship, his "priestly" prerogatives, his role as judge, his spectacular victories, even over all the nations, the "eternity" of his reign, these were preparations for the definitive conceptions of messianism. Some conventional expressions of the extravagant court-style were to be used as patterns to formulate beliefs related to Christology (cf. J. Steinmann, *Les Psaumes,* Paris, 1951, p. 63).

Besides the messianic psalms based on Nathan's oracle, E. J. Kissane takes note of others based, he says, "on the written prophets, especially Isaiah, on the future glory of Zion" (I, p. XIX). These psalms, he thinks, generally belong to the period of the Exile. The theme is summarized in Ps 87: "Glorious things are said of you, O city of God!" For in the future there will be no distinction of nations, and all alike will be citizens of Zion. All the psalms of Yahweh's kingship can be said to be messianic, in as much as they proclaim the reign in Zion of God-Who-Comes.

In the introductions to each psalm individual messianic elements will be examined more closely. Others will be mentioned below (§16), where all the New Testament quotations from the psalms will receive notice. On messianism in the Psalter the studies of the following authors can be consulted, in addition to the commentaries: R. Arconada, L. Arnaldich, F. Asensio, E. Beaucamp, A. Bentzen, L. A. Colunga, J. Coppens, M. Gomes, A. Hanel, A. Luger, A. Miller, A. Robert, A. Rose, J. de Savignac, F. Segula, P. J. Smal, A. Strobel, P. Veugelers. It would take us too far to examine in detail the opinion of S. Mowinckel on the subject. Granted a qualified interpretation, especially of the reference to mythology, what he says in the following extract deserves proper attention.

"The kernel of truth in the messianic interpretation is, as we shall see, that it is ultimately the same common oriental mythologically conceived superhuman king-ideal, which underlies both the psalm-poets' description of the present king in David's city, and the prophet's description of the future king. Historically considered, the idea of the Messiah is derived from the same king-ideal that we have presented in the royal psalms. True enough, there is a great difference between what the poets have made of this traditional king-ideal, and what the prophets have made of it. The poets thought that the ideal was realized, or hoped that it would be realized, in the earthly king, seated before them on the throne. The prophets were not satisfied with anything which the present reality could offer, and looked hopefully forward to a new king, whom God would send 'in his own good time,' and who would be the realization of the ideal which the present kings did not appear to fulfill, because it was beyond human power. Thus both the psalmists' and the prophets' conception point beyond themselves, and are only realized in a figure of a totally different kind, in the Messiah Jesus who was both 'King' and 'Son of Man,' and the suffering and expiating 'Servant of the Lord.' To this extent the Church is right in taking the king in the royal psalms as a presage of Jesus, the Messiah" (I, p. 49).

§16. THE PSALMS AND THE NEW TESTAMENT

Christianity claims that the Old Testament is basically christological in its orientation. Salvation-history as a whole is inclined Christward, in the sense that it will attain its accomplishment in the fullness of time (Gal 4:4; Ep 1:10) and in the fullness of Christ (Ep 4:13). The admission of messianism in the psalms already favors their admission in Christian worship. The main objection against praying all the psalms has always been the presumed presence of so-called "unchristian elements" in them. But understood properly the "imprecations" do not seem to be a major obstacle (see §14d). There will remain, however, to examine more closely why and how the psalms can and should serve as Christian prayers. First we must see how Christ himself and the inspired Christian writers have used the psalms.

(a) *New Testament quotations of the psalms*

There are about 360 quotations of the Old Testament in the New. Of these one third are borrowed from the psalter. In the following list, hopefully complete, of the New Testament quotations from the Psalter, the main idea of the quotation is given as it appears in the New Testament. Significant allusions, with some identical words, are also listed. The psalm reference according to the Septuagint (and Vulgate) numeration (cf. §3a) is also given, in brackets, since the New Testament generally quotes the Greek Bible (cf. §2b). Of the 112 quotations 40 are found in Paul's writings, the Epistle to the Hebrews included. Acts and the Revelation have 11 each. Only a few quotations are used allegorically: 2:8f (Rv 2:26f); 19:5 (Rm 10:18); 47:9 (Rv 3:21); 69:23f (Rm 11:9f); 69:26 (Ac 1:20); 106:20 (Rm 1:23; applied to idolaters); 109:8 (Ac 1:20).

2:1-2	= Ac 4:25-26: the enemies conspire in vain against the Lord and his Anointed.
2:7	= Heb 1:5; 5:5; Ac 13:33: Christ's divine sonship.
2:8-9	= Rv 2:26-27. To him who overcomes. . .I will give authority over the nations. And he shall rule them with a rod of iron, and like the potter's vessel they shall be dashed to pieces.
2:9	= Rv 19:15: The Word of God will rule the nations. . .
4:5	= Ep 4:26: "Be angry and do not sin" (dominate your anger).
5:10	= Rm 3:13: Lying as attesting the univer-

	sality of sin.
6:4	= Jn 12:27: Jesus says: "Now my soul is troubled."
6:9	= Mt 7:23; Lk 13:27: On the Lord's day Jesus will declare: "Depart from me, you workers of iniquity."
7:10	= Rm 8:27: "He who searches the hearts knows what the Spirit desires."
7:10	= Rv 2:23: "I am he who searches desires and hearts, and I will give to each of you according to your works" (punishment).
8:3	= Mt 21:16: perfect praise from the mouth of infants.
8:5-7	= Heb 2:6-7: Jesus for a little while made lower than the angels.
8:8	= 1 Cor 15:27; Ep 1:22; all things made subject to Christ.
10(9):7	= Rm 3:14; Cursing and lying (see on Ps 5:10).
14(13):1-3	= Rm 3:10-12; Universality of sin.
16(15):8-11	= Ac 2:25-28, 31 (cf. 15:35, 37): Peter applies the verses to Christ's resurrection.
18(17):3+ 131(130):17	= Lk 1:69; in the *Benedictus*: "the horn of salvation."
18(17):50	= Rm 15:9; Let the "Gentiles" glorify God.
19(18):5	= Rm 10:18; The spread of God's word.
19(18):10	= Rv 16:7; 19:2; True and just are God's judgments.
22(21):2	= Mt 27:46; Mk 15:34; "My God, my God, why hast thou forsaken me?"
22(21):8	=Mt 27:39; Mk 15:29: The passers-by jeered at Jesus, shaking their heads.
22(21):9	= Mt 27:43; "He trusted in God; let him deliver him now, if he wants him."
22(21):19	= Jn 19:24 (cf. Mt 27:35; Mk 15:24): "They divided my garments among

	them; and for my vesture they cast lots."
22(21):23	= Heb 2:12; Jesus calls "brethren" those he saved.
23(22):1	= Rv 7:17; The Lamb will shepherd them, and will guide them to the fountains of the waters of life.
24(23):1	= 1 Cor 10:26; "The earth is the Lord's, and the fullness thereof" (cf. Ps 50:12). No forbidden food.
24(23):4	= Mt 5:8; Blessed are the pure of heart, for they shall see God.
31(30):6	= Lk 23:46: "Father, into thy hands I commend my spirit."
32(31):1-2	= Rm 4:7-8; About justification by faith.
33(32):3	= Rv 5:9; 14:3; A new canticle (cf. Pss 39:4; 95:1; 97:1; 143:8; 149:1).
33(32):6	= Jn 1:3; All things made by the Word.
34(33):9	= 1 P 2:3; If indeed, you have tasted that the Lord is sweet.
34(33):13-17	= 1 P3:10-12; In connection with fraternal charity.
34(33):15	= Heb 12:14; Strive for peace with all men.
34(33):21	= Jn 19:35; "Not a bone of him shall you break."
35(34):19	= Jn 15:25; "They hated me without cause" (cf. Ps 69:5).
36(35):2	= Rm 3:18; "There is no fear of God before their eyes" (see on Ps 5:10).
37(36):11	= Mt 5:4; "Blessed are the meek, for they shall possess the earth."
38(37):12	= Lk 23:49; All his acquaintances...were standing at a distance (of Jesus on the Cross).
40(39):7-9	= Heb 10:5-10; "Sacrifice and oblation thou wouldst not"...
41(40):10	= Jn 13:18; "He who eats bread with me has lifted up his heel against me."
41(40):14	= Lk 1:68; "Blessed be the Lord, the God

	of Israel" (*Benedictus;* cf. Pss 72:18; 89:53; 106:48).
42(41):6, 12+	= Mt 26:38; Mk 14:34 (cf. Jn 12.27):
43(42):5	the agony of Jesus.
44(43):23	= Rm 8:36; For thy sake we are put to death all the day long...
45(44):7-8	= Heb 1:8-9; Thy throne, O God, is forever and ever...
47(46):9	= Rv 3:21: He who overcomes, I will permit him to sit with me upon my throne; as I [the Amen] also have overcome and have sat with my Father on his throne.
47(46):9	= Rv 4:9-10; 5:1, 7, 13; 6:16; 7:10, 15; 21:5; About the One "who sits upon the throne."
51(50):6	= Rm 3:4; God is true; every man, in comparison, is a liar.
55(54):23	= 1 P 5:7; Cast all your anxiety upon the Lord.
56(55):10	= Jn 18:6; The enemies fell back (*eis ta opisô*) upon hearing the name.
62(61):13	= Rm 2:6; 2 Tm 4:14; "Who will render to every man according to his works."
68(67):19	= Ep 4:8; Ascension, captives, gifts (rather free application).
69(68):10	= Jn 2:17; The zeal of Jesus in cleansing the Temple.
69(68):10	= Rm 15:3; The reproaches of those who reproach thee fell upon me.
69(68):22	= Mt 27:34, 48; Mk 15:36; Lk 23:36; Gall, vinegar, thirst.
69(68):23-24	= Rm 11:9-10; All except the remnant blinded to the truth of the Christian revelation (cf. §15a).
69(68):26	=Ac 1:20; Application to Judas of "Let their habitation become desolate..."
69(68):29	= Ph 4:3; Rv 3:5; 13:8; 17:8; 21:27; the "book of life" (cf. §14d).

72(71).10, 15	= Mt 2:11; "Gifts of gold" to the child Jesus.
78(77):2	= Mt 13:35; "I will open my mouth in parables..."
78(77):24	= Jn 6:31; "Bread from heaven he gave them to eat."
82(81):6	= Jn 10:34; If the "judges" were called "gods"; *a fortiori* can the one "whom God made holy" be called the "Son of God."
89(88):4-5	= Ac 2:30; God has sworn to David...
89(88):11	= Lk 1:51; With the might of his arm he has scattered...
89(88):21	= Ac 13:22; I have found David...a man after my heart.
89(88):38	= Rv 3:14; Faithful and true witness.
91(90):11-12	= Mt 4:6; Lk 4:10; The devil quotes Scripture to make Jesus fall into presumption.
93(92):4	=Rv 19:6; The voice of the Lord like the voice of many waters.
94(93):11	= 1 Cor 3:20; Human wisdom, nothing to boast about.
94(93):14	= Rm 11:1; God has not cast off his people.
95(94):7-11	= Heb 3:7 to 4:11; Exhortation against heart hardening.
97(96):7	= Heb 1:6; Let all the "angels" adore him.
98(97):2-3	= Ac 28:28 (cf. Ps 67:3): "Be it known to you that this salvation of God has been sent to the Gentiles."
98(97):3	= Lk 1:54; He has given help to Israel, mindful of his mercy (*Magnificat*).
102(101):26-28	= Heb 1:10-12; The Son will outlast his creation (cf. with the angels).
103(102):8; 111:4	= The Lord is merciful and compassionate (cf. §11f).

103(102):13, 17	= Lk 1:50; And for generation upon generation is his mercy, to those who fear him.
104(103):4	= Heb 1:7; He makes his angels spirits, and his ministers a flame of fire (servants of the Son).
104(103):12	= Mt 13:32 + par.: the birds of the air come and dwell in its branches.
105(104):8+ 106(105):45	= Lk 1:72; Mindful of the covenant with the forefathers (*Benedictus*).
105(104):21	= Ac 7:10; He made him governor over Egypt and over all his household.
106(105):10	= Lk 1:71: Salvation from enemies.
106(105):20	= Rm 1:23; They have changed the glory of the incorruptible God...
107(106):9	= Lk 1:53: He has filled the hungry with good things (*Magnificat*).
107(106):20	= Ac 10:36 (cf. 13:26); He sent his word to the children of Israel (Peter's discourse).
109(108):8	= Ac 1:20; "His ministry let another take" (election of Matthias).
110(109):1	= Mt 22:44+par.; How is the Christ David's Lord and son?
110(109):1	= Mt 26:64 + par.; The Son of Man will sit at the right hand of God.
110(109):1	= Mk 16:19; Rm 8:34; 1 Cor 15:25; Eph 1: 20; Col 3:1; Heb 1:3; 8:1; 10:13; 12:2 (cf. Ac 2:34f): Christ, after the Ascension, sits at the right hand of God.
110(109):1	= Heb 1:3; Christ therefore is above the angels.
110(109):4	= Jn 12:34; Christ abides forever.
110(109):4	= Heb 5:6; 7:17; "Thou art a priest forever, according to the order of Melchizedek."
111(110):9	= Lk 1:49: Holy is his name.

112(111):9	= 2 Cor 9:9; The merits of fraternal charity.
113(112):7	= Lk 1:48; He has regarded the lowliness of his handmaid.
116(115):10	= 2 Cor 4:13; "I believed, and so I spoke."
116(115):11	= Rm 3:4; God's fidelity is accentuated by man's unreliability (cf. Ps 51:4).
117(116):1	= Rm 15:11; Let all nations praise the Lord.
118(117):6	= Heb 13:6; The Lord is my helper: I will not fear what man shall do to me.
118(117):22-23	= Mt 21:42 + par. (cf. Acts 4:11; 1 Pt 2:7); The stone which the builders rejected has become the corner stone...
118(117):26	= Mt 21:9 + par. + Jn 12:13: "Blessed is he who comes in the name of the Lord" (cf. §15b).
118(117):26	= Mt 23:39; Lk 13:35; Jesus explains the exclamation as meant for himself (cf. preceding).
119(118):32	= 2 Cor 6:11; Our heart is wide open to you.
130(129):8	= Mt 1:21; He shall save his people from their sins.
132(131):5	= Ac 7:46; About David's wish to build a dwelling place for God.
132(131):11	= Ac 2:30; God swore to David about his kingship (cf. Ps 89:4-5).
135(134):14	= Heb 10:30; God avenges and judges his people (cf. §14d).
140:(139):4	= Rm 3:13; Lying as sign of the universality of sin (cf. Pss 5:10; 10:7).
141(140):2	= Rv 5:8; 8:4; Prayer is like the incense of sacrifice.
143(142):2	= Rm 3:20; Gal 2:16; No human being shall be justified before him by works of the Law.
146(145):6	= Ac 4:24; The Lord, who made heaven and earth...

This impressive list of quotations is an indication of the importance attached to the psalms by the New Testament writers and the early Christians. The Psalter being a book of hymns and prayers, another question is raised: how will the Christian pray the psalms: to Christ or with Christ?

(b) *The psalms as addressed to Christ*

To his disciples, before the Ascension, Jesus said: "These are the words which I spoke to you while I was yet with you, that all things must be fulfilled that are written in the Law of Moses and the Prophets *and the Psalms* concerning me" (Lk 24:44). To the Jews he had said: "You search the Scriptures, because in them you think that you have life everlasting. And it is they that bear witness to me, yet you are not willing to come to me that you may have life" (Jn 5:39f). In some of the quotations listed above the New Testament applies to Christ, our Lord, what the psalms said of the Lord Yahweh (e.g., Ps 34:9 in 1 P 2:3; Ps 102:26ff in Heb 1:10ff). The Synoptics agree with John in citing and applying to the coming of Jesus a saying of Deutero-Isaiah, which announced the Lord's intervention: "A voice cries out: In the desert prepare the way of the Lord! Make straight in the wasteland a highway for our God!" (Is 40:3; Mk 1:3; Jn 1:23). The early Christians were "those who invoke the name of the Lord" (cf. Jl 3:5 and 1 Cor 1: 2; Ac 9:14, 16, 21f). In other New Testament texts Christ is directly called God (Rm 9:5; Col 2:2f; Tt 2:13; 2 P 2:1f; Jn 1:1; 20:28; 1 Jn 5:20). These examples are explained and others proposed in the exposition of the title "God" in *The Names and Titles of Jesus* (pp. 297-304; cf. K. Rahner, *Theological Investigations,* vol. I, London, 1961, pp. 135-148). In the divine Office for the feast of the Ascension the antiphons of the psalms of Matins seem to suggest that the Church prays these psalms to Christ the Lord. It is clear, however, that not all the psalms can be prayed in this way. Some are more appropriately addressed to God the Father while others are more suited for reflection.

(c) *Christ, the singer of the psalms*

No one has ever prayed as Jesus did. Saint Augustine called his Lord *iste cantator psalmorum,* "He, the singer of the psalms." There is no doubt that in his first pilgrimage to Jerusalem (Lk 2:41f) and on other occasions he sang the "pilgrim psalms" (cf. §3c). Each year he would presumably recite the great *Hallel*, *Ps 136, and the other *Hallel* (Pss 113-118). At the last Supper some phrases were particularly evocative of the occasion: "The cup of salvation I will take up" (116: 13); "Precious in the eyes of the Lord is the death of his faithful ones" (116:15); "I shall not die, but live" (118:22); "This is the day the Lord has made" (118-24). During the washing of the feet he quoted Ps 41:10 about Judas: "He who eats bread with me has lifted up his heel against me." On the cross he recited Ps 22, which spoke of him, and expressed both his distress and his trust in the completion of his work. Filial trust in the Father was also Jesus' last word: "Father, into thy hands I commend my spirit" (Lk 23:46; Ps 31:6).

Jesus, during his lifetime, had possibly ranked himself with "the poor," the 'anāwîm (cf. §12a), by saying, "Take my yoke upon you, and learn from me, for I am meek and humble of heart" (Mt 11:29). He had come, like the Servant of the Lord, to take away sin (Jn 1: 29; Mk 10:45; Mt 26:28), but clearly denied having ever committed any sin (Jn 8:46). Only a qualified answer can be given to the question: Can Christ pray the psalms called "penitential" (6, 32, 38, 51, 102, 130, 140) and others expressing repentance for sins? Non-Catholic authors have expressed the opinion that Christ made penance as representing sinful man. According to V. Taylor, "McCleod Campbell describes the representative ministry of Christ as 'a perfect confession of our sins' and R. C. Moberly as 'the sacrifice of supreme penitence'" (*The Atonement in New Testament Teaching*, p. 176). Taylor himself asserts: "Wherever and whenever sin has existed, the Son of God has borne its consequences upon His heart, voicing the penitence of the impenitent and the submission of the rebellious" (*ibid.*, p. 214). W. J. Wolf, however, rightly considers as impossible the concept of "vicarious repentance": "There are appealing features to this theory, but they are shipwrecked upon the simple fact of life that no one can really repent for the sins of another" (*No Cross No Crown*, p. 127). There exists an official decree of the Catholic Church forbidding in fact the use of the title: *Jesu poenitens, Jesu poenitens pro nobis* (ASS 26, 1893f, p. 319). About praying for the Messiah, see on *Ps 72:15.

Granted then certain restrictions, it is correct to say, with St. Augustine, that Christ being "the Brother of every man," when Christ prays the psalms, it is the whole Body which prays. The Church, following St. Paul's recommendation, prays God the Father, with Christ and through Christ. Christ is the unique Priest through whom passes the prayer of all men who are incorporated to him.

(d) *The psalms as Christian prayers*

Three reasons are offered for which the psalms can and should be popular Christian prayers: they are the very prayers that God himself has composed; they were the prayers that Jesus used; they provide an apt expression for all the sentiments our hearts contain (cf. B. Ahern, p. 121). This has been understood by the Church Fathers who, like Augustine and others, have given us such profound and spiritual expositions of the psalms, by the saints who have prayed the psalms with such ardent devotion, by the innumerable Christian commentators who have applied the best of their effort and knowledge to the understanding of the psalms. "When books of piety came to be composed, they were chiefly a compilation of psalms. Thus, from the thirteenth to the sixteenth century, the popular prayer book of the people was a primer that consisted of the Little Office of the Blessed Virgin, the Office of the Dead, the Fifteen Gradual Psalms, the Seven Penitential Psalms, the Litany of the Saints, and a few other devotions. This means that the greatest part of the ordinary prayer was drawn from the Psalter" (Ahern, p. 119). This is even more true of course of the breviary or Divine Office recited daily by priests and religious. In many Latin manuscripts of the Psalter Christian titles are added to indicate the message of each psalm. The oldest group of such *MSS* probably originated in the third century and reflects the language of Tertullian, but is better known as associated with St. Columba (cf. P. Salmon). In recent years the liturgical movement has done much to popularize the use of the psalms as Christian prayer. Exceptionally successful in that field was J. Gelineau's musical adaptation of the psalms to choral singing: cf. *The Psalms; a new translation from the Hebrew arranged for singing to the psalmody of Joseph Gelineau* (London, 1966), 255 pp. On the psalms as Christian prayer can be consulted the following authors: B. Ahern, L. Bouyer, H. Breit, H. de Candole, G. M. Castellini, B. Fischer, J. Fichtner, S. B. Frost, G. Garrone, A. Gelin, A. George, C. Hauret, M. F Lacan, J.A. Lamb, H. Lamparter, A. Miller, M. F. Moos, R. D. Richardson, A. Rose, R. B. Y. Scott, F. Vandenbroucke, T. Worden (see the titles in the bibliography).

IV.   The Hymns

A section of chapter II has been devoted to the "literary forms in the Psalter" (§7). There are indications, noted by C. Westermann (cf. "Zur Sammlung...") , that even the collections of the Psalter (cf. §3b) may have been arranged partly from a thematic viewpoint: the greater number of the laments are found in the first and second parts of the Psalter, while the hymns predominate in the two last parts. On the other hand, it is not easy to corroborate what is sometimes asserted, that the psalms of a collective type mainly belong to the collections of Core and Asaph. The classifying principles set forth above (§7) are applied in chapter IV and following. It is obvious that the present writer's precise classification does not claim the same degree of certainty for all the psalms. In some categories of the didactic genre the classification is made on the basis of predominant themes only. In some of the lists given after the general introductions brackets will indicate the doubtful cases. They are Pss 9/10, 12, 18, 22, 27, 36, 58, 62, 63, 65, 66, 68; 73; 77; 82; 91, 92, 94, 106, 107, 108, 115, 118, 121, 126, 129; 139; 144. Some authors would call such psalms *Mischungen,* that is, belonging to "mixed types." Several published studies tend to multiply the literary categories of the psalms. In this work the aim is to reduce and regroup them, to increase their usefulness without sacrificing objectivity. It is hoped that further study will confirm the validity of this attempt to set forth the present results of research. The literary structure of the main categories (hymn, lament, thanksgiving) is described somewhat dependently of H.-J. Kraus, *Psalmen,* pp. XLI-LII.

§17. THE HYMNS PROPER

(a) *General character*

The hymn or psalm of praise is represented outside the Psalter by two ancient lyrics: the canticle of Moses (Ex 15:1-21) and the song of

Deborah (Jg 5; cf. §13d). More recent hymns include the canticles of Hannah (1 S 2-10), of Hezekiah (Is 38:10-20), of Habakkuk (ch. 3), of the three young men (Dn 3:52-90), of Judith (16:1-7), Mary's *Magnificat* (Lk 1:45-55), Zechariah's *Benedictus* (Lk 1:68-79). The hymns reflect Israel's most disinterested form of prayer. As "confessions" (cf. §22a) they come closer to the thanksgiving category than when they are merely "descriptive," a quite common form of the ancient Oriental hymnology.

The majority of the hymns were, it seems, purposely composed for the liturgies of Israel's great feasts. They were sung with musical accompaniment, as it is often mentioned (cf. Pss 33:2f; 149:3; 150:3-5). The communal destination and use of these praises are also reflected in the refrains or acclamations which sometimes mark the rhythm. The exclamation "for his mercy endures forever" (cf. Pss 118 and 136 + §11f) is a praise mentioned for various occasions: first (1 Ch 16:34) and second (2 Ch 5:13) transfers of the Ark, temple dedication (2 Ch 7:3-6), Jehoshaphat's military campaign (2 Ch 20:21), oracle on the Restoration (Jr 33:11), building of the second temple (Ezr 3:11). The responsories "Amen!" (cf. Pss 41:14; 72:19; 89:53; 106:48) and "alleluia" (see *Pss 111 and 136) often expressed the final wish of the assembly: "And let all the people say, Amen! Alleluia" (1 Ch 16:36).

(b) *The literary structure* of the hymn generally corresponds to the following pattern:

1) *Introduction*: intention of praising God. The primitive nucleus of the hymn could have consisted of a simple cultic exclamation like "alleluia!", "praise the Lord!" The "introduction" expresses the intention of the psalmist himself (Ps 145:1f) or is an invitation addressed to the musicians and singers (33:2), to the servants (135:2) and the sons of God (29:1), to the righteous (33:1), to Jerusalem (147:12), to all the nations (117:1), to every living being (150:6) or even to all creatures (Ps 148). It can also consist of a simple statement (19:2), but it always specifies to whom goes the praise. The "introduction" is not always clearly distinct from the expression of motives.

2) *Main section (corpus hymni)* or development (often introduced by the conjunction *kî*, "for," "because"): the motives of the praise are made

known. These derive from the Lord's great deeds (creation, providence, redemption, legislation) or refer to his attributes: power, wisdom, fidelity, mercy (cf. §11). In the hymns especially, God is described both by what he has done and by what he is (cf. G. Pidoux, p. 31). The motives are generally expressed in relative (cf. Ps 8:2) or participial clauses (114:8). Thus, with the use of participles, creation appears as an action continuing in the present (Pss 104 and 136). The "joy" motif (cf. Pss 111:2; 145:7; 149:2, 5) is characteristic of the Israelite hymn, which in its purest form is also disinterested.

3) *Conclusion.* Figure among its most frequent elements: the partial (145:21) or total (8:10) resumption of the "introduction," a recapitulation of the motives (105:42-45), blessing formulas (29:11; 66:20; 135:21), requests or wishes (19:13ff; 104:35), sometimes an inference, as "trust" in the Lord (33:20f). The conclusion or ending is not always distinct from the *corpus.* It can be a simple "alleluia" (113:9; 148:14).

(c) The *hymns* are: Pss 8, 19 (combines two hymns), 29, 33, 100, 103, 104, 111, 113, 114, 117, 135, 136, 145, 146, 147; 148, 149, 150.

PSALM 8

The Majesty of God and the Dignity of Man

Through his inspired insight the psalmist sees the Creator in the transparency of creation. As in many other psalms, two main feelings fill his soul: awe of God and joy in his glory. His also is the pure reaction of the child (v 3) through whom God himself speaks and confounds his adversaries. The "babes and sucklings" could represent, according to Stamm, the ever growing Israelite generations which confound the plans of the enemies (cf. 1 S 12:22; Jr 31:35ff). But these two difficult verses (2b-3) are variously interpreted. A common trend is to refer the children's role to what precedes and not to what follows their mention. Generally admitted also (cf. *BJ*) is the meaning "fortress" or "stronghold" for *'ōz,* instead of "praise" (*CV*). God's fortress would be "heaven" (cf. Pss 31:22; 78:26; 150:1) or the "vault of heaven" (Gn 1:14-17). Introducing only vocalic changes Dahood translates the whole passage thus:

I will adore your majesty
   above the heavens,
With the lips of striplings and sucklings,
You built a fortress for your habitation,
   having silenced your adversaries,
   the foe and the avenger.

The building of God's habitation ($m\bar{a}'\hat{o}n$: cf. Ps 68:6; Dt 26:15) coincides with the "muzzling" of the enemies. This is elsewhere mythologically (cf. §11a) illustrated:

You have crushed Rahab with a mortal blow;
   with your strong arm you have scattered your enemies.
Yours are the heavens, and yours is the earth;
   the world and its fullness you have founded (Ps 89:11f).

In this psalm, as elsewhere in the Bible, human nature is not valued in itself, as in Greek culture, but as a gift from God. It is from God's will also, and not from conquest, that man rules the earth. He represents God, "the great king over all the earth" (Ps 47:3). The repetition of verse 2 at the end shows that the main concern is God's glorification. Like Ps 19A and probably also Ps 29, Ps 8 can be called a cosmic hymn (A. Deissler). In fact both Ps 8 and Ps 19 deal with a common theme, the majesty of God as revealed in the various phenomena of nature. Both psalms seem to have a direct literary contact with the first creation narrative (Gn 1:1-2:4). J. Morgenstern, who stresses the divergence between the two psalms, woud set the date of Ps 19A from 516 to 485 and that of Ps 8 more than a century later. Author C. Louis, on the other hand, maintains, in his thorough study, that Ps 8 could have been written by king David and that it involves messianic implications (cf. §16a). Instead of "than the angels" can be read in verse 6 "than the gods," since the reference is probably to the members of the heavenly court of God (cf. §10g). On Ps 8 see also B. S. Childs, *Biblical Theology in Crisis* (Philadelphia 1970) 151-64, and R. Tournay, "Le psaume VIII et la doctrine biblique du nom," *RB* 78 (1971) 18-30.

PSALM 19 (18)

God's Glory in the Heavens and in the Law

It is usually asserted that this psalm consists of two separate hymns.

In the first (*vv* 1-7), the firmament in general, then the sun, are sung as revealing the glory of God. The religious meaning of creation is stressed as in Ps 8, but with a greater artistic sense. That God's language is read in nature represents a theme known in Canaanite literature (cf. A. Jirku). This influence on the inspired writers could have increased with the arrival of proselytes from the North, shortly after the Captivity (cf. §9d), the period in which some date the origin of Ps 19A (see on *Ps 8).

It is quite possible though that Ps 19 was composed as one poem by the same author. This is favored by morphological indications and by the use, to describe the Law, of images applicable to the sun. The Israelite sages, notes R. Tournay ("Notules..."), easily passed from the physical to the moral world. In the ancient Orient the sun was currently represented as the Lord of justice and the Defender of the weak. If two distinct hymns existed originally, Weiser thinks, they were united for use in public worship and in the one poem they stress the idea of the divine order expressed in the creation and in the Law. Even if Ps 19 is a composite of two originally separate psalms, the combination of the two is very meaningful, H. Ringgren believes: "The heavens that tell the glory of God and the firmament that proclaims his handiwork, on one hand, and God's law that revives the soul, on the other, are actually two manifestations of one and the same divine will" (*The Faith...*, 104f).

If verses 8-15 are said to constitute a second hymn, then it is stressed that they differ from the first part in meter and belong to a more recent composition. Yet this second hymn belongs to an earlier type than Psalm 119, with which, moreover, it offers similarities. It is an invitation to find God in the Law, which is to be esteemed above all earthly values (v 10). Parallelism is improved by reading with Dahood vv 9b-10a: "The command of Yahweh is radiant, enlightening *my eyes*. The *edict* of Yahweh (*mir'at yhwh*) is pure, enduring forever." Dahood quite convincingly argues that *lᵉpānêkā* (CV: "before you") can mean "according to your will" (cf. 2 Ch 32:2; Gn 10:9), so that verse 15 would read:

May the words of my mouth
    be according to your desire,
And the thoughts of my heart
    according to your will,
O Yahweh, my Mountain, and my Redeemer.

In verse 14, *CV* has translated *zēdîm* by "wanton sin." Dahood suggests that in the present context it means "idols or false gods" or "the presumptuous ones" (cf. Ps 40:5). In Ps 119 (vv 21, 51, 69, 78, 85, 122), *BJ* notes, the word designates the wicked, offensively contemptuous of Yahweh's lowly faithful. Then Ps 19:14a can read: "And from pride preserve your servant, never let it dominate me" (*JB*=v 13). The second part of the verse is translated by Dahood: "Then shall I be blameless and innocent of the great crime." The "great crime" is "idolatry" (cf. Ex 32:21, 30, 31; 2 K 17:21; cf. Ps 25:11).

PSALM 29 (28)

God's Majesty in the Storm

This psalm lauds the majesty of God's theophany. High above the raging elements the King Lord thrones in sublime imperturbability (v 10): "Whilst the songs of the celestial choirs resound in the highest, the terror of God rages over the earth" (cf. A. Weiser). The distant voice of thunder (vv 3-4) announces the approaching storm, which comes suddenly close to the poet (5-6) and rages all around him (7-9). The third person form in addressing God is a sign of the genuine antiquity of the psalm.

It has been convincingly stated and repeated in recent years (Ginsberg, Gaster, Cross and others) that the poem derives from a prototype: an ancient Canaanite hymn praising Baal-Hadad, the weather god. Of Baal it was said: "And he gave forth his voice from the clouds" (Ugar. text 51, v. 70; C. H. Gordon, p. 171). B. Margulis claims that "the original subject of the poem was *Yahweh,* not Baal, and its author was a Yahwist" (*Bib* 1970, p. 346). On the Canaanite background of Ps 29 see also H. Strauss in *ZAW* 82 (1970) 31-67. The verse structure itself of Ps 29 (cf. E. Vogt), a form of "repetitive parallelism," points to a similar pattern attested in Ugaritic epics (see on *Ps 92:10). The difficult *behadrat qōdeš* (v 2; cf. Ps 96:9; 1 Ch 16:29) could be a theophany expression in Ugaritic (cf *Keret* 155; Gordon, p. 389), and Cross would translate Ps 29:2b: "Prostrate yourselves before Yahweh when he appears in holiness." A. Caquot qualifies this interpretation as an attempt to explain *obscurum per obscurius.* He in turn hesitatingly suggests another translation: "Prostrate yourself before Yahweh in giving him holy Majesty." Like "the glory due his name" (v 2a), "majesty" would be an attribute conferred on God by the adorer who proclaims it. A similar explanation is proposed for *Ps 110:3.

The parallel use of "Lebanon" and "Sirion" in verse 6 quite obviously refers also to a Ugaritic pattern (cf. §9d): when the palace of Baal was to be built, workers repaired "to Lebanon and its timbers, to Sirion and its choicest cedars" (t. 51:VI:20f; Gordon, p. 127). Dahood also points out that *mdbr qdš*, the "steppe of Kadesh" (others: "the holy desert") is mentioned in Ugaritic, whereas nowhere is the "wilderness of Sinai" called *midbar qādēš*. The expression could not therefore be adduced to associate the psalm with the theophany of the Sinai tradition (cf. §13 d.). Yet it is clear that this tradition draws from the storm imagery for its setting of God's revelation (cf. Ex 19:16ff). B. Margulis' attempt (*Bib* 1970, 340, 348) to read *Eilat* (="The Gulf of Aqabah") in v 9 can be classified as an exercise in fantasy. It is certain that *MT yᵉhôlēl 'ayyālôt*, "who makes the hinds writhe," is to be read, as in Jb 39:1. Others, after Lowth, read *yᵉhôlēl 'ēlôt*, "makes the oaks bend."

Canaanite religious texts certainly account for much of the literary background of Ps 29. Yet it is to be observed with Cazelles, that the original poem to a nature god has been reread ("une relecture") to praise the Israelite God of creation and salvation. "The sons of El," minor gods of the Canaanite pantheon, refer here (v 1), as elsewhere in the Bible, to the angels, servants and adorers of the Lord (cf. §10g). Cazelles believes, perhaps rightly, that the Canaanite "holy desert" has been reinterpreted in Ps 29:8 to mean the Sinaitic "desert of Cades" (cf. Nb 20:1) and thus recall the "saving deeds of Yahweh" (cf. §10f). The liturgical conclusion (vv 10f) transfers, it seems, to the Flood—and to the Covenant of grace (Gn 8:20ff)—what concerns the primeval abyss in other parts of the poem (v 3). Thus would Ps 29 praise both the God of creation and the God of salvation. The application of the title "king" to God in the present context would also reflect a Canaanite background (cf. §13b).

The psalm's main theological theme, E. Pax believes, is the revelation of God's holiness, expressing itsef in might and bestowing blessings. The glory of God is in fact the Lord's holiness seen manward (cf. §10 de). Theologically the theophany of Ps 29 is very close to Isaiah's famous inaugural vision (6:1-7). The cultic setting can be referred to a real liturgical theophany or to a deliberate literary form adopted by the author. A. Deissler would associate the psalm with the last day of the feast of Tabernacles, which came to assume an eschatological character (cf. §13).

PSALM 33 (32)

Praise of the Lord's Power and Providence

This psalm was apparently a festival hymn sung in liturgical worship to the accompaniment of musical instruments. It is a tribute to the Lord of Nature, of Creation (cf. §11a) and of History, to the Monarch who as trustworthy, powerful and kind fully deserves the confidence of his subjects.

Instructive philological features of the poem appear in Dahood's translation of verse 1: "Exult, you just, in Yahweh, in lauding, O upright, the Glorious One!" That the *lamedh* of *lay^{e}šarîm* is used as a vocative can be readily admitted, here as in Ps 3:9 (O Yahweh, salvation!) and elsewhere in the psalms (references in Dahood). The rendering of *nā'wâh* by *"in* lauding" is thus explained: "the preposition *b* with *nā-wâh* is forthcoming from *b-yhwh* in the first colon on the strength of the principle of the double-duty preposition" (cf. *v* 7 and Jon 2:4; here, however, the same preposition affects nouns in apposition, which is easier). *T^{e}hillâh* ("praise" in *CV*) is interpreted as a divine name, "the Glorious One" (compare *CV* in Ps 22:4). The noun would derive from the root *hll,* meaning "to shine." Besides Ugaritic, Habakkuk 3:3 is quoted as an example: "His splendor (*hôdô*) covered the heavens, and his glory (*ût^{e}hillātô*) filled the earth." Both *nā'wâh* and *t^{e}hillâh* are found in Ps 147:1 "How good it is to hymn our God, how delightful to laud (*nā'wâh*) our Glorious One (*t^{e}hillâh*)!" (cf. Ps 109:1).

We also learn from Dahood that *yaḥad* of verse 15, hitherto unexplained in this context, should be read *yeḥde* (also Ps 21:7) with the meaning "to see, gaze, inspect" in its Canaanite form *yeḥze*. Thus the verse should be translated: "The Creator inspects their intention, the Observer all their words." Perhaps equally striking is the new translation of verse 19: "To rescue them from Death, to preserve their lives from the Hungry One." The Hebrew *rā'ēb* or *rā'āb,* usually translated "famine" is used as a poetic name for Death, "the Hungry One" (cf. Dt 32: 24; Is 5:14; Jr 18:21; Hab 2:5; Pr 1:12; Jb 18:12). The preposition *b,* with the meaning "from," instead of "in," corresponds to *min* in *mimmāwet!* (cf. Ps 20:7 + §9d).

The author of Ps 33 drew much of his inspiration from biblical wisdom. The sapiential milieu is especially reflected in verses 13, 15b, 18a, 19. The poem's abundant literary borrowings could place its origin in the post-exilic period, when wisdom literature freely adopted the so-called anthological style (A. Robert's "procédé anthologique," cf. *SDB V*, c. 411), characterized by the re-use of words or expressions belonging to previous Scriptures. A. Deissler has shown that this literary genre is well represented in Ps 33 (cf. *Ps 119). Elements of Egyptian thought are discernible in the psalm, A. Barucq believes (p. 316), but prophetic teaching dominates.

PSALM 100 (99)

Processional Hymn

The verses of this entry psalm, seemingly antiphonal in structure, were presumably sung alternately by the choir and the congregation at the *introit* liturgy of the divine service (see also on *Ps 95). Some expressions of the hymn seem to reflect the atmosphere of a joyful thanksgiving procession. In v 3 read $w^e lô$, "to him," instead of $w^e lõ'$ (with aleph), "and not." According to the Masora, $lõ'$ is found fifteen times for $lô$ in the OT; for example Ex 21:8, 1 S 2:3, Is 9:2. In 1 S 2:16 and 20:2, $lô$ occurs instead of $lõ'$.

The psalm does not rank with the best from the standpoint of poetical art and it is little discussed by scholars. The doctrinal content, however, of its few verses is remarkable. *The Interpreter's Bible* finds that verses 3 and 5 summarize the creed of Judaism, contained in six capital statements: the Lord is God; he is our Creator; we are his people; the Lord is good; his kindness is everlasting; his faithfulness endures to all generations. The invitation to sing to the Lord is extended to the whole earth (v 1), by prophetic anticipation, according to St. Augustine (P.L. 37, 1271). Yet Gunkel denies that the verse has any eschatological import (cf. §14).

PSALM 103 (102)

Praise of Divine Goodness

Divine goodness is especially praised in this hymn, which draws its material from personal experiences of God's mercy and from the traditional acknowledgment in the cult of God's saving deeds wrought for "the children of Israel." The opening and closing verses respectively invite the psalmist himself and the heavenly choirs "to bless (*brk*) the Lord," that is, to praise and thank him for his graciousness and benefits. The statement of verse 8, "Merciful and gracious. . ." is part of the well known self-declaration of God on Mount Sinai (cf. Ex 34:6f and §11f).

Mowinckel (II, 38) cites Ps 103 as an example of a thanksgiving psalm turned into a hymn. This occurs when the gratitude of an individual for God's benefit to *self* passes on to the *unselfish* universal, to become a panegyric of God himself and of all his wonderful works in nature, history, and human life. The same author (II, 132) believes that three psalms, 23, 73, 103, among what he calls "the psalms of protection (cf *Ps 71) and thanksgiving," have moved so far from their particular style type that perhaps they ought to be classified in a special group of "psalms of confidence" (cf. §21). From both the religious and the poetic aspect, these psalms, he adds, rank among the best in the collection. They are good examples of compositions in which the psalmists write more independently of the conventional style pattern, to give better expression to an individual experience.

Psalm 104 (103)

Praise of God the Creator

In this hymnic confession the psalmist offers a poetic and colorful description of the marvelous universe as created by God and as governed and sustained by him. The majesty of the theophany Lord is celebrated in the beginning and at the end of the poem. The ministers of his epiphany (cf. §13d) are also in the picture. What foreign material could have been admitted in the poem, from Egyptian or Canaanite hymns (cf. §9cd), is well assimilated and the "mythical powers" appear amid subdued creatures (cf. §11a). To chaos cosmos has succeeded. This ordered universe is a religious one, in which even the wild beasts turn to God for their food (v 21).

Not the creation narrative itself of Genesis, but rather an underlying and older Israelite tradition seems to have inspired the author of Ps 104. The psalmist's view of the act of creation differs notably on several points from the Genesis presentation: the origin of light (v 2), the role of the winds (v 4), the disposal of the waters (v 6f). An Egyptian parallel to Ps 104 is often mentioned or quoted. It is the "long hymn" to the Aton, from the tomb of Eye at Tell-el-Amarna, where Pharaoh Amenhotep IV chose to have his capital. Having broken with the established religion of Egypt, this ruler instituted the worship of the Aton, the sun disc as the source of life, and reigned under the name of Akh-en-Aton (c. 1380-1362). His own attitude to god Aton is expressed in the famous hymn. The closest parallels are to verses 20-26, as it appears in the following extracts (cf. *ANET*, p. 370):

> When thou settest in the western horizon,
> The land is in darkness, in the manner of death. . .
> Every lion is come forth from his den;
> All creeping things, they sting.
> Darkness *is a shroud,* and the earth is in stillness,
> For he who made them rests in his horizon.
> At daybreak, when thou arisest on the horizon,
> When thou shinest as the Aton by day,
> Thou drivest away the darkness and givest thy rays. . . .
> All beasts are content with their pasturage;
> Trees and plants are flourishing. . .
> The ships are sailing north and south as well,
> For every way is open at thy appearance.
> [Thou] who givest breath to sustain all that he has made!
> Thou suppliest his necessities.
> How manifold it is, what thou hast made!
> O sole god, like whom there is no other!
> Thou didst create the world according to thy desire. . .
> Everyone has his food, and his time of life is reckoned.
> All men, cattle, and wild beasts,
> Whatever is on earth, going upon (its) feet,
> And what is on high, flying with its wings.
> The world came into being by thy hand,
> According as thou hast made them.
> When thou hast risen they live,
> When thou settest they die.

A. Barucq, an authority on the Egyptian parallels to the psalms, cannot decide if a direct influence of the hymn on the psalmist should be admitted or not (p. 316ff). G. Nagel (p. 402) opts for the negative because, he says, the differences exceed the similarities. It has been recalled (cf. §9) that a common poetic background can account for much of the supposed parallels between distant literatures. It has been argued also (§9c) that Egyptian influence more probably reached Israel by way of Phoenicia. Nagel goes on to explain that the psalm's affinity with Genesis 1 is so close as to exclude the necessity of seeking an Egyptian prototype. An "essential difference" has been pointed out: the sun-god's providence in Akhenaton's hymn is limited to the daytime; during the night evil forces prevail "until the appearance of the sun causes the dangers and fears of the night to disappear." But in Ps 104 "the night too is part of God's creation. According to God's plan it fulfills a definite role in the economy of the world"; cf. vv 20f and Ps 74:16: "Yours is the day, and yours the night" (cf. H. Ringgren, The Faith..., p. 119f). Some verses of the psalm (cf. 10-18) describe the activity of God in nature for the sake of living beings and ultimately to the benefit of man. This idea is reflected in the Egyptian hymn and also in Ignatius Loyola's "contemplation to obtain love" (3rd point; see *Ps 65). See also Huppenbauer's article and Griffith's.

A number of suggestions have been made to understand or improve some difficult passages of the psalm. Leaving unchanged the MT (cf. §2a) and understanding the words in their natural sense, Sutcliffe translates verse 8a: "They [the waters] go up the mountains, they go down to the valleys, to the place thou hast established for them." The psalmist would have meant the following: that water which naturally flows downwards, nonetheless gushes out (from springs) high in mountainous regions. In v 8 the primeval chaotic waters that flood the earth are involved: "They go up to the mountains, then down to the abysses." Compare with Ps 107:26, where "heavens" instead of "mountains" occur. In Dahood's view hārîm in v 6 designates mountains on earth, while in v 8 "the celestial mountains": "before God created the vault of heaven, all the waters were united upon the surface of the earth" (cf. Gn 1:7). For more comparative material see G. Leonardi in Bib 49 (1968) 238f. On the "Cosmic Mountain" and related questions see R. J. Clifford's study (Bibliography). A bit of philological reasoning brings H.F.D. Sparks to the substitution of Sirion for Yahweh in verse 16, which then reads: "The trees of Sirion have their fill (of rain), the cedars of Lebanon which he planted" (see on *Ps 29 and cf. Dt 3:9). As the text of verses 24-30 stands, notes G. R. Driver, the readers of the Old Testament are committed to the strange doctrine of the resurrection (cf. v 30) not only of man and of beast but also of Leviathan and of the "creeping" or rather "gliding things innumerable" which swim in the sea. In the new translation proposed by Driver the idea of (re)creation of God's creatures disappears:

When Thou hidest Thy face, they are troubled;
when Thou takest away their breath, they grasp.
When Thou sendest forth Thy breath, they recover health,
and Thou dost give fresh life to the whole earth (vv 29f).

The overall idea of vv 24-30 seems, however, simply to be the divine origin of life, as expressed in Job 12:10: "In his hand is the soul of every living thing and life breath of all mankind."

PSALM 111 (110)

Praise of God for His Goodness

Thought sequence is rather loose in this alphabetical psalm (cf. §6d), which is the faith testimony of an individual in praise of "God who acts." The mention of the "assembly of the just" and of the "covenant" (vv 1, 5, 9) suggests to Weiser that this hymn also was "composed for the purpose of its recital at the festival cult of the covenant community" (§13c). In fact, the psalmist seems to stand before "a great assembly" like the author of the second part of Ps 22 (cf. v 23). The psalm could equally be called a "Passover hymn" because of the statements: "A memorial (*zkr*) he made for his wondrous works" (v 4; cf. Ex 12:14); "He has sent deliverance to his people" (v 9). The Sinai tradition is represented by the reference to the covenant and to the miraculous feeding of the just (v 5). In Dahood's view "verses 2-9 are a compact version of the traditional recitals (cf. Pss 78, 105, 136), with references to the Exodus, Sinai, and the Conquest of Canaan." He thinks, besides, that the same author wrote Pss 111 and 112. Oesterley and Kraus, among others, assign to the psalm a post-exilic date, a time when the great deeds of God still constituted the great hymnal theme (cf. Ps 78:4, 11, 32; 106:7; Ne 9:17).

The liturgical acclamation *hallᵉlû yâh* (praise yahweh!) appears in the beginning of Pss 111 and 112, at the end of Pss 104, 105, 115, 116, 117, at the beginning and the end of Pss 106, 113, 135 and 146-150 (cf. Tb 13:22 and *Ps 136). The Septuagint and the Vulgate present a different textual tradition on *hallᵉlû yâh*. This indicates that the exclamation is an addition, obviously liturgical in origin. In the New Testament "alleluia" opens and accompanies the celestial acclamation after judgment has been passed on the "famous prostitute" (Rv 19:1-9). The phrase "with all my heart" in verse 1 would reflect the Deuteronomic hortatory style (cf. Dt 6:4). The psalmist's call "to delight" (*hps*, v 2; cf. Pss 1:2; 112:1 and §11g) in the Lord and in his work could be in reaction against the threatening effects of excessive traditionalism, which can degenerate into dogmatism and formalism. These moral ills are effectively kept in check by an attitude of wonder, constantly renewed, before God, his attributes and his deeds (cf. §10).

Psalm 113 (112)

Praise of the Lord for His Care of the Lowly

This hymn and the next two are part of the collection of the Hallelpsalms (113-118; cf. *Ps 136), especially related to the three pilgrimage feasts (Passover, Weeks, Tabernacles), to the Dedication and to the New Moon celebrations. The opening verse and a certain tone of solemnity in the psalm also reflects its use in cult worship. The "servants of the Lord" (v 1) probably refer to the priests on duty in the temple. The name of the Lord is to be praised "from the rising to the setting of the sun" (v 3), since this name is "glorious over all the earth" (Ps 8:2).

The praise of Almighty God, ruler of nature and of nations, stresses his concern for the lowly (see §11c). A special divine benevolence reaches down to the afflicted and to the barren wife (cf. Is 54:1), who were too often relegated to the fringe of human society. In fact, Kraus writes, Ps 113 delivers hymnically a message similar to that contained in Is 57:15: God's majesty and might appear in his mercy and in the way he extols the humble and the downcast. This divine behavior has been most clearly fulfilled with the temporal advent of the Son of God (Lk 1:51-53).

Psalm 114 (113a)

The Lord's Wonders at the Exodus

Four symmetrical strophes make up this psalm which in later Judaism was sung on the eighth day of the Passover festival. The beginnings of Israel's salvation history as a nation are recalled by a few striking events whose miraculous element is amplified. "Thus the receding of the sea on the occasion of the deliverance at the Red Sea (Ex 14:21f) becomes for the poet a flight from God as he draws near, and he changes the tradition of Joshua 3:14ff that the Jordan 'stood still' into a turning back of the river; again, he depicts the quaking of the mountain at the revelation of God at Sinai (Ex 19:16ff), as in Ps 29:6, with the grotesque word-picture of rams and lambs skipping on the pasture" (A. Weiser). When history is actualized in the cult, various incidents may be condensed into one event and described as present (cf. vv 5, 6). In our hymn, poetical tension is stressed by deferring until the end the mention of God. In the Greek and Latin versions, Pss 114 and 115 (Hebrew) are joined into the one Ps 113. But originally they were probably distinct.

"The designation in vs. 2 of all Palestine by political terms that were particularly significant in the period between the death of King Solomon in ca. 922 B.C. and the destruction of Israel by the Assyrians in 721 B.C. suggests a ninth-eighth century date of composition" (Dahood). The MT hapax *lō'az*, at the end of v 1, usually translated "to speak a foreign tongue" on the basis of Late Hebrew, is often given as evidence for a late composition of the poem. Dahood denies, however, the validity of this inference, since he thinks the term consists of emphatic *lamedh* and the word *'āz*, "strong, cruel, barbaric," as in Is 25:3, and translates 114:1: "After Israel went out of Egypt, the house of Jacob from a barbaric people." Even though *yām* designates the Dead Sea in Is 16:8 and Jr 48:32, and the Salt Sea is mentioned in Jos 3:16, this is a very weak basis for affirming that v 3 alludes "to a single historical event, the entry into Canaan across the Jordan River" (Dahood). See on *Ps 66.

PSALM 117 (116)

Doxology of All the Nations

Before the renewal of the covenant, God revealed his divine attributes to Moses, standing aside with the new tablets: "The Lord, the Lord, a merciful and gracious God, slow to anger and rich in kindness (*hesed*) and fidelity (*'emet*)" (Ex 34:6; cf. §11f). "Kindness" and "fidelity" are also the divine attributes proclaimed to the nations in Ps 117 (cf. §11e). This short hymn may well have been a formula introducing a covenant festival (cf. §13c) for which had gathered pilgrims from many peoples.

With a measure of imagination the term 'ēmîn, "frightful ones" (cf. Jr 50:38) may be understood to mean "gods" and give support to the following translation of Ps 117:1: "Praise Yahweh, all you nations, laud him, all you gods!" (Dahood). But does not this destroy the obvious parallelism between "nations" and "peoples"? So it seems preferable to accept the MT 'ummîm as an exceptional plural of 'ummâh, "clan, people" (instead of expected 'ummôt).

PSALM 135 (134)
Praise of God, the Lord and Benefactor of Israel

This psalm is generally considered to be late, its author having borrowed material from other psalms. Those "who fear the Lord" would then be proselytes of later Judaism. The scorn for the idols, expressed in verses 15-18, suggests to Mowinckel that this hymn also belongs to these psalms (96, 97, 115, 135) "which are marked by the spirit of early Judaism and its whole conception of God after the full victory of monotheistic thought" (I, 98). The phrase "greater than all gods" (v 5) would seem, however, to constitute an exception to pure monotheism (see § 10g). Weiser discovers in the hymn various features of his own "festival cult of the Israelite covenant community" (cf. §13c). The apparent borrowing can be accounted for, he believes, "by the psalmist's deliberate adherence to the fixed and stylized forms of the tradition which had their place in the cultus." The allusion to clouds, lightnings and rain (v 7) could actually reflect the atmosphere of the autumn festival and the beginning of the rainy season. The psalm praises once again the God of Creation and Redemption, by whose favor the election of Israel became a central element in the pattern of salvation history.

PSALM 136 (135)
Hymn of Thanksgiving for the Everlasting Kindness of the Lord

Much of what has been said of Ps 135 applies also to Ps 136, which in its present form is a sort of litany hymn with a refrain: "for his mercy endures forever" (cf. §11a+f). This antiphony appears else-

where, in the first verse of Pss 106,   107,   118 and in the account of
the dedication of the first and second temples (2 Ch 7:3; Ezr 3:11).
Six verses (17-22) of the psalm are almost identical with Ps 135:10-14.
The similarity may point to a literary borrowing or to dependence from
oral cultic tradition. "One type of hymn," Mowinckel notes, "simply
enumerates or points out God's lasting qualities and glorious deeds, a form
which may suit any cultic occasions, both daily and festal" (I, p. 85).
Psalm 136 belongs to this type and such "appositional style" appears
also in the book of Amos, "in the fragments of a hymn of praise about
Yahweh as Creator and ruler of the universe" (Am 4:13; 5:8). Psalm
136 has been compared to Dn 3:52-90 (cf. Si 51:1ff). It is called the
"Great Hallel" by the Jews, who generally join it to the "Hallel of
Egypt" (Pss 113-118; cf. *Ps 111), still recited on the feast of Hanukkah
and on Passover night. Pss 146-148 are also sometimes designated as a
Hallel (cf. *The Jewish Encycl.* vol. VI, p. 176).

PSALM 145 (144)

The Greatness and Goodness of God

A common source of inspiration, the cult community, could explain
that many phrases of this alphabetic hymn occur also in other psalms or
in other books of the Bible. The might of God is praised together with
his "terrible" deeds (v 6; cf. §10f), but the accent is laid on the loving
kindness which the Lord and King shows to all who look hopefully to
him (v 15). Verse 14 should be translated, "The Lord *lifts up* all those
who fall and raises up all who are bowed down" (cf. *NAB;* not "The
Lord upholds..." as *RSV* and others), since the meaning "lift up" for
the root *smk* is confirmed by the Arabic *samaka,* and the use of *bsmkt*
in UT 125:35 with the meaning "on the highlands" (courtesy M.
Dahood).

A careful study of the key-words of Pss 34 and 145 has revealed to L.
J. Liebreich that in these two psalms at least the alphabetical device (cf.
§6d) has not been detrimental to the art and skill of the poet. The key-
words of Ps 145 suggest the following division of the poem: Prelude (1-
2); I (3-6); II (7-9); Interlude (10); III (11-13); IV (14-20); Postlude
(21). It is observed that the root *brk,* "bless," is used in three significant positions within the framework of the psalm: at the beginning, in
the middle, and at the end. There is also progression in the thought: the

poet alone (v 1), then an elite (v 10), then "all flesh" *bless* the Lord (v 21). The *nun* verse, absent from *MT*, is preserved in 11QPs*a*, after v 13: "God is faithful in his words, and gracious in all his deeds." The Qumran scroll also carries a congregational response, "Blessed be Yahweh, and blessed be his name forever!", not found in MT. Dahood has not included these additions in his text because the problem of these transmissions has not yet been sufficiently clarified, also in connection with two other acrostic psalms: 25 and 34. He finds originality and warmth in the hymn, which, he writes, "may fairly be described as a litany of sacred names."

H. J. Kraus points out that *traditionsgeschichtlich* it is important to note that verses 11-13 speak of God's kingdom (*malkût*; cf. Dn 3:33; 4: 31) and not, as in the older psalms, of God as the King adored in the temple. The alphabetical device and the language (aramaisms) used also tend to confirm Oesterley's opinion that Ps 145 is one of the latest in the Psalter. The insistence on the kingdom of God preludes to one of the basic themes of the Synoptic tradition in the New Testament.

PSALM 146 (145)

Trust in God Alone

This simple hymn is a motivated invitation to put one's trust in God, who is always ready and able to deliver the oppressed, feed the hungry, free the captives, cure the blind and the cripple, protect the weak and the powerless (see *Ps 113 + §11c). As in other psalms of a later date (cf Ps 33), the structure of Ps 146 tends to adopt the alphabetical pattern (cf. §6d). It is compiled, writes Gunkel, from currently used hymnic motifs, and displays elements of the votive thanksgiving of an individual (cf. vv 2-4 and Ps 34).

Considering that in v 6c "who keeps faith forever" (*RSV, NAB*) breaks the parallelism with the following stichs and seems out of context, Dahood's reading deserves close attention. Schrewdly repointing *MT 'ōlām*, "eternity," to *'awūlīm*, "the wronged," he translates: "Who keeps faith with the wronged, who defends the cause of the oppressed...". But he supplies no other example of the root '*wl* used in that sense (*me'awwēl* in Ps 71:4 means "criminal," the usual connotation of the root).

PSALM 147 (146-147)

Zion's Grateful Praise to Her Bountiful Lord

Similar and additional aspects of God's providence (cf. §11b) are mentioned in this hymn, which consists of three parts, each of them beginning with an explicit invitation to praise God (vv 1, 7, 12). In the Greek and Latin versions the third part (vv 12-20) constitutes a separate psalm, in which Jerusalem is invited to praise her benefactor. By its contents Ps 147 is related to *Ps 33, to *Ps 104 and to the second (ch. 40-55) and third (55-66) parts of the Book of Isaiah. The Creator of the cosmos (§11a) is also the Savior (§11d) of Israel. The statement of verse 4 has a close parallel in Is 40:26 and also in the saying of Ahiqar (see on *Ps 141): "Many are the stars of heaven whose names no man knows" (VIII, 116: *ANET*, p. 429).

The allusions of verses 2 and 13 could point to a period following the (re)construction of the Jerusalem walls under Nehemiah (cf. Ne 12: 27ff). The theme of Israel's holy wars (cf. §14b) features mainly in verses 7-11. Great inspiration perhaps has come to many from Ps 147:9: "Who gives food to the cattle, and to the young ravens when they cry [to him]" (NAB; cf. RSV). This last statement is certainly not unworthy of God's benevolence, but the verse perhaps should be read: "Who gives to the cattle their grain, to the crows that which they gather" (Dahood in *Psalms III*). Quoting *VT* 3 (1953), p. 307, Dahood (on Ps 14:4) recalls that *qārā'*, "crying" (*NAB*), can mean also "collect, gather, harvest" (cf. Lv 23:2; 1 S 9:13; Am 5:8b). But young ravens do cry to God for nourishment, according to Job 38:41!

Dahood reasonably observes that the mention of snow and frost in vv 16-18 does not necessarily point to an exceptionally severe winter as the context of the psalm's composition but more likely confirms "that biblical poets often appropriated phrases and metaphors coined by their Phoenician and Canaanite colleagues further north where snow and frost were quite common."

PSALM 148

Hymn of All Creation to the Almighty Creator

In this post-exilic psalm "all creatures in the heavens (1-6) and on earth (7-10) are called upon to join in the hymn of praise that universal

mankind, and especially Israel, should sing to the Lord of all (11-14)"
(CV). The Greek and Syriac versions of Daniel have preserved a long,
mostly poetic, text (3:24-90) which includes in the *Benedicite* a good
part of our psalm. The nature imagery of four verses (7-10) draws
both from creation myths and from theophany themes (cf. §13d). It
is quite possible that v 7 should be read "Praise the Lord from the nether
world" (*'ereṣ* can mean this, see on *Ps 18:8), especially since the "sea
monsters," if they were not subterranean beings, would be listed with the
other animals in v 10. Lists of beings and elements as those proposed in
Ps 148, Jb 38, Si 43 and the Daniel *Benedicite* have much in common with the ancient encyclopedic knowledge of nature wisdom (*Die
Listenwissenschaft der Naturweisheit*: H.-J. Kraus, *Psalmen*, p. 962).
Amenope's Onomastikon belongs to this literary *Gattung* (cf. A. H.
Gardiner's *Ancient Egyptian Onomastica*, edited in 1947; cf. *VTSuppl.*
III, p. 293f). In the psalm the stress is on the name of God (cf. §10b).
The New Testament related the creation and the being of the universe
to another divine name, that of Jesus, our Lord (cf. Col 1:15f; Heb 1:
3f; Ph 2:10). R.A.F. MacKenzie has recently suggested, with full discussion, that Ps 148:14bc is a title-summary, composed for Ps 149 and
placed before it (*Bib* 1970, 221-24). In fact, the first bicolon of 148:
14 "and he has raised up a horn for his people" represents an effective
climax, and seems to be the end of the psalm. On the other hand, six out
of 7 words present in the last bicolon (v 14bc) occur in Ps 149, while
only one in Ps 148.

Psalm 149

Invitation to Glorify the Lord with Song and Sword

It is said of the second temple builders that each "had his sword
girded at his side" while working (Ne 4:18), and of the Maccabees
that they prayed in their hearts while they fought with their hands (2
M 15:27). The invitation of Ps 149, "let the high praises of God be in
their throats, and two-edged swords be in their hands" (v 6) draws its
inspiration from a similar tradition but the parallels are too general to
warrant any firm conclusion as to the date of the psalm's origin. It is
clear from the first three verses that the hymn was sung in the course of
a joyous liturgical festival celebrating the kingship of God. It was Gunkel's opinion that, in view of verse 6, Ps 149 was sung by sword-dancers.

It is an obviously good example of imaginative exegesis.

In this psalm praises of the Lord strangely intermix with warlike motifs and vengeful intentions (cf. §14bd). It will help here to recall that the nations' hostility was directed against Zion (Pss 2:1f; 9:20) and against God (Pss 2:10; 48:5), who from the holy city passed judgment on his adversaries (cf. Ps 46). It is also asserted (*BJ*) that in this national hymn the poet looks forward to an eschatological future (cf. Is 61:2f) and presents the Israelites as the avenger of divine justice (cf. Zc 9:13-16). The "written sentence" of verse 9 alludes to the "oracles against the nations" contained in the prophetic books (cf. Mi 4:13; Ezk 25:14; Jl 4:2; Zc 12:6. . .). Dahood sees in Ps 149 "a hymn sung and performed in the religious assembly on the eve of a battle against the heathen nations" and agrees with Weiser's suggestion that "the verdict written" of v 9 may allude to Israel's religious duty to destroy the pagan nations of Canaan (cf. Dt 7:1ff and 20:13).

PSALM 150

Final doxology with Full Orchestra

In this closing doxology to the entire Psalter "everything that has breath" is invited to praise the Lord with the help of the entire temple orchestra. Various musical instruments are also mentioned together with songs of praise at the dedication of the Jerusalem wall (Ne 12: 27). In Ps 150 imperative invitations to praise God have replaced or absorbed an important hymnal element: the evocation of God's great deeds (cf. §10f). The Lord to be praised is in his temple, but also "in the firmament of his strength," or, as Dahood would put it (see on *Ps 8:3), "in his vaulted fortress."

§18. PSALMS OF YAHWEH'S KINGSHIP

(a) General character

This is the most debated (sub) class of the whole Psalter, mainly because Mowinckel and others maintain insistently that these psalms form a special category, the "enthronement psalms," allegedly composed for a (special) cult festival in which God's enthronement was proclaimed. We need not repeat here, not even summarize, what has been said above on this subject (§13a). A. Weiser denies that a separate festival of enthronement existed. "In the psalms," he writes, "the enthronement of Yahweh was linked up with his theophany above the Ark, part of the tradition of the Covenant Festival" (*The Psalms*, p. 62; cf. §13c). The thesis of a separate Enthronement Festival is likewise refuted, he thinks, by the fact that the idea of Yahweh's kingship is to be found also in psalms which are not related to the act of enthronement: Pss 5:3; 8:2; 10:16; 22:29; 24:8ff; 44:5; 48:3; 59:14; 66:7; 68:25; 74:12; 84:4; 103:19; 145:1; 146:10; 149:2. In recent years Old Testament scholarship has shown, according to H.-J. Kraus, "that the conception of Yahweh's kingship does not appear to have been a basic element in the original content of Israelite religion" (*Worship in Israel*, p. 203). The idea is, however, already attested in Ex 15:18; Jg 8:23 and 1 S 12:12. W. Schmidt has attempted to show how the idea of Yahweh's kingship has been demythologized: "Die Geschichte des Königsprädikats hat sich als ein langsamer, aber tiefgreifender Prozess der Entmythisierung enthüllt" (*Königtum Gottes...*, p. 75). The Canaanite origin of the title can be detected, he thinks, especially in Dt 33:5, 26 and in Pss 18:8-16; 68:34; 104:3.

The priority of Deutero-Isaiah (cf. Is 52:7) in respect to the "enthronement psalms" has been quite convincingly defended by C. Westermann, as we have seen (cf. §13a, p.***f), and this is of course an important factor for the dating of these psalms (cf. §5). It seems preferable to adopt also Kraus's view that the psalms of Yahweh's kingship fit well in the context of what he described as the "Mount Zion festival of the kingship of God" (see §13b). The title *melek*, "King," applied to God would be closely connected with that of *yhwh ṣ⁀ebā'ôt*, "the Lord of hosts" (cf. Ps 24:10), a title which recalls the cultic tradition of Shiloh. Independently, it seems, of Kraus, J. P. Ross now writes on the meaning of "Jahweh Sᵉbā'ôt in Samuel and Psalms." He concludes: "What the title originally meant in Shiloh we can only guess. But we can be sure of this: that by the time Israel took it over, it had become the name of a god whose principal attribute was royal majesty" (*VT* 1967, p. 92).

Arguing from such phrases as "Absalom has become king!" (2 S 15:10) or "Jehu has become king!" (2 K 9:13), Mowinckel (cf. I, p. 107) states that *Yhwh mālak* (93:1; 96:10; 97:1; cf. 47:9) should be translated "Yahweh has become king." But this is far from certain (cf. Koehler's remarks on *Ps 93:1 and in §13a C. Westermann's conclusion from a comparison with Is 52:7). A brief survey of the recent controversy on "enthronement psalms" can be read in H. Ringgren, *The Faith...*, pp. XII-XIX. In his monumental *La royauté de Yahvé...*, E. Lipiński finds the background of the "enthronement psalms" in a festival of the period of the monarchy. For him Pss 93 and 99 could date back to the time of Solomon while Ps 97 would have been composed for the temple (re) dedication of 184 B.C. Lipiński has expressed elsewhere also his general support for the Mowinckel thesis, which, it seems, remains nevertheless confronted with basic unrefuted objections. The eschatological character of the psalms of Yahweh's kingship can hardly be put in doubt and from that point of view the authors of *BJ* have brought out the essential meaning of the compositions (see §14c). Other studies on these psalms include those of M. Didier, I. Engnell, A. Feuillet, H. Gross, A. S. Kapelrud, L. Koehler, D. Michel, J. Morgenstern, A. Neuwirth, N.H. Ridderbos, R.A. Rosenberg, J. Schreiner, T. de Orbiso, J. D. W. Watts, W. G. Williams (cf. bibliography). See also J. Coppens in *ETL* 47 (1971) 117-143.

(b) The Psalms of Yahweh's kingship are: Pss 47, 93, 96, 97, 98, 99.

PSALM 47 (46)

The Lord the King of All Nations

Although commentators are at variance in interpreting this psalm (see Caquot, pp. 311-314), it is generally admitted that the hymn is the most important of its category. A main event of "the festival of the enthronement of Yahweh," Mowinckel writes, "was evidently the great festal procession, the victorious entry of the Lord, to which reference is made in Ps 47:6" (I, p. 115). The ascent of Yahweh to his temple was probably represented by the procession with the holy ark (cf. §13b). Caquot explains that the celebration recalled mainly the Conquest and the past victories of Israel, associated with the ark and a specific type of shouting, the *terû'âh* (v 6; cf. Jos 6:5). A convenient date for such celebrations could have been, he adds, the period of David and Solomon, when these monarchs would have adapted to yahwism some oriental ideologies, that namely which made the king by right the master of the universe (cf. v 3). When the king conquers he represents God who brings nations under his feet (v 4). "The great king" (v 3) is a known expression in Ugaritic and Akkadian literatures (cf. Dahood, *Psalms I*, p. 284; cf. *Ps 48:3). In the "enthronement hypothesis" (cf. §13a), Yahweh became the king of Israel anew with the conquest of the Holy Land. The great event is actualized symbolically in the cult (v 9). Then the princes pay homage to the newly enthroned king (v 10).

Whereas the other divine kingship psalms speak simply of a "coming" of Yahweh (cf. 96:13; 97:3; 98:9), Ps 47:6 says that God "mounts his throne." What this divine action represents is variously explained: having saved his people, God ascends to heaven (Kissane, quoting Gn 17:22 and Ps 68:19); God's ascent is to be associated with solar worship (cf. G. May and §9b); *'ālāh* is a theological wordplay on the divine appellative *'elyôn*, "the Most High" (v 3; cf. A. R. Johnson, in *The Old Testament and Modern Study*, p. 66, n. 2). It is often maintained with Mowinckel that in this psalm God mounts upon his throne, the holy ark. We read in fact that David "brought up (*wayya'al*) the ark of God from the house of Obed-edom into the city of David with gladness" (2 S 6:12; cf. 6:15). It is possible that this event was reenacted in the cult, periodically (Mowinckel) or once only, to celebrate a great victory (Podechard). Yet much can be said in favor of Caquot's and Kraus' interpretation: Yahweh advances triumphantly *on the ark,* considered as a battle palladium. Eerdmans (*The Chasidim...*, p. 229f) speaks of a marching army, ready for campaign, led by the princes, "the shields of the earth" (v 10; cf. Ps 89:19).

Eerdmans notes also that the word *'ammīm,* "peoples," refers to Israelites in verses 2, 10 and to non-Israelites in verse 4. In Dahood's version verse 2 becomes: "All you *strong ones,* clap your hands, acclaim, you gods, with shouts of joy." This author's laudable efforts to prove that *'ammīm,* "peoples" (CV) often can and does mean "strong ones" (see on *Ps 18:28) will not convince everybody, even though *'ammīm* could be in Dt 33:3 "a deliberate substitution for *'ēlîm,* 'gods'" (cf. I: L. Seeligmann, p. 80). Less convincing still seems to be in verse 10 the substitution of "the God of Abraham is the Strong One" to the traditional "with the people of the God of Abraham." Yet it would be well to follow J. Muilenburg in keeping the MT *'am* and translating: "The princes of the peoples are gathered together, a people of the God of Abraham." E. Beaucamp cites Dt 33:5 as an example of a similar apposition: "The chiefs of the people assembled, tribes of Israel." Several indications, he believes, point to a very early date for the psalm. Its universalism could originate at the time of David. When the New Testament reads in

Abraham and Melchizedek the promise of a Christian oecumenism it is then based on one of the oldest and most authentic Old Testament traditions.

PSALM 93 (92)

The Glory of the Lord's Kingdom

A new "enthronement" is hardly meant in this psalm, which acclaims God's kingship as a permanent reality: "Your throne stands firm from of old; from everlasting you are, O Lord" (v 2). L. Koehler points out besides that in *yhwh mālak* (v 1) the accent being on the subject, the meaning is: It is Yhwh (and no one else) who is king (cf. Is 44:6; 45: 5). The same would be true of the other "so-called enthronement psalms" (cf. §13a): it is Yhwh (and not the other gods) who is the Lord of the nations (47:3-10), who has made the world firm (93:1), who contains the might of the sea (93:2), who guards the lives of the just (97:8-12), who provides and guarantees the norms of a moral world (99:4-7). In *mālak 'elohîm*, on the other hand (Ps 47:9), no one word is more accented than the other. The royal vestments (v 1) express the glory of God and his creative and saving deeds. The mention of the Lord's power over the floods (vv 3, 4) possibly depends on the creation narrative but other literary affinities have to be examined. In spite of what has been claimed for Ps 89:26, *nehārôt* in v 3 could well here have the meaning of "ocean currents," as explained in *Ps 24:2.

The throne (v 2), as symbolizing kingship, constitutes the unifying motif for the whole psalm. J. D. Shenkel (p. 402f) has presented clearly some aspects of the conceptual imagery of the psalm. "There is no need to demonstrate the intimate connection between kingship and throne in both Canaanite and Israelite religious literature. The throne of the deity was not only the symbol of his presence on earth, corresponding to his presence in heaven, but also the symbol of his victory over the forces of cosmic chaos, and in the case of Israel, over historic enemies as well. The earthly throne was the temple (Jr 17:12), and more specifically, the most sacred chamber or cell in the temple where the symbolic throne was to be found. In the Solomonic temple this room was the Holy of Holies, and the throne of Yahweh was conceived to be the outstretched wings of the Cherubim (cf. M. Haran). The temple-throne celebrated in these verses as the symbol of the deity's past victory and abiding presence served as a hymnic theme for the psalmist's profession of confidence in God." In the solemn and sonorous language of verses 3-4, Shenkel writes, "there is an echo of the combat between the storm god and the personification of the unruly waters, *Yamm*, by which the psalmist mythologically represents the imposition of order upon primordial chaos by God. The archaic poetic diction and imagery of these two verses, evocative of the most pervasive of Canaanite myths, well illustrate the indebtedness of this psalm to the conceptual imagery of Canaanite religious literature." On such affinities and other literary evidence H. G. Jefferson had previously concluded to a pre-exilic date of the psalm. Comparative material from the Bible itself suggests to some a date as early as the beginning of the monarchy (Kraus). H. Cazelles thinks that Ps 93 existed before Deutero-Isaiah (cf. *VT* 1966, p. 524). This is a debatable opinion (see §18a).

Verse 5, on the other hand, read "in the conventional translation," seems to reflect late compositions. It is the object of Shenkel's lucid study "to suggest a translation of verse 5 more in accord with the conceptual imagery of the remainder of the psalm." On the strength of Ugaritic and biblical parallels he first confirms with new evidence that *'d* can mean "throne" or "throne room," and suggests that *'dtk* be given the same meaning in Ps 93:5 (instead of "your decrees" in *CV*). It is fitting, he explains, "that the throne should be mentioned again in verse 5, and that its unshakable solidity should be again extolled as the basis of confidence, after the verses celebrating Yahweh's victory" (p. 409). The second stich of verse 5, "holiness befits your house" also calls for a new interpretation, based again (cf. *Ps 33) partly on the real meaning of *nāwâh tᵉhillâh* in two psalms: "Rejoice in the Lord, O you righteous. O you upright, *glorify the One worthy of praise*" (33:1); "How good it is to hymn our God, how pleasant to *glorify One worthy of praise*" (147: 1). Other biblical passages (Jr 17:14; Dt 10:21; Ps 22:4 are quoted to confirm that *tᵉhillâh* is a divine title. *Nā'wah* then does not mean "to be befitting" but "to glorify," as the Greek version of Ex 15:2b has long ago suggested. There remains only to show that *qdš*, meaning "the holy ones," is subject of the phrase, and Ps 93:5 can be translated:

Your throne has been firmly established;
in your temple the holy ones shall glorify you,
Yahweh, for length of days.

It is noted that with this new translation Pss 29 and 93 have four motifs in common: the thunder of the storm god, the kingship-throne, the palace-temple and the praise of the divine king by his heavenly court. E. Lipiński, however, believes (*La royauté*... p. 144ff) that *'ēdōt* in Ps 93:5 is synonym with *berît* and refers to the Davidic covenant (cf. *JBL* 1966, p. 499).

PSALM 96 (95)

The Glories of the Lord, the King of the Universe

In this psalm also God's kingship is praised and proclaimed at a liturgical assembly held in the sanctuary (vv 6, 10). The firmness of the world, originating at creation, is again asserted (v 10; cf. 93:1). The keynote of this psalm is (eschatological) joy, founded on the expected advent of God as judge or ruler of the earth, both now and at the end of the world. Salvation history extends from creation to judgment. Bornert lists Ps 96 with the eschatological psalms of Yahweh's kingship. Some elements of a Canaanite conceptual pattern can be detected in the hymn but the yahwist revision of Ps 96, in relation to a supposed prototype, has obviously progressed much further than in Ps 29: for example we have *mišpeḥôt 'ammîm* (v 7) instead of *benê 'ēlîm* (29:1; cf. F. M. Cross, "Notes...," p. 19, note 2). The translation of *be hadrat qōdeš,* "in holy attire" (v 9), has been discussed in relation to the same expression in Ps 29:2.

In 1 Ch 16:23-33 our psalm is abridged and linked to Ps 105 as part of a thanksgiving song meant to celebrate the arrival of the holy ark in Jerusalem (cf. §13b). The presence in 1 Ch 16:8-36 of a "new" psalm, composed of sections of existing psalms (105:1-15; 96:1b-13a; 106:47f) suggests to Mowinckel (II, p. 200) that on this special occasion a liturgy was composed by people who felt restricted to an existing "canonical" book of psalms. The addition "a ligno" (v 10: "from the wood") found in some Greek and Latin MSS is certainly not original, but it is ancient and means: Yahweh is King more than the wood, that is, than the idol (cf. J. Brinktrine).

A date as late as the fourth-third century can be proposed seriously for Ps 96, since the psalm is apparently dependent on the second and third parts of Isaiah. This dependence appears especially in verse 5 (comp. Is 40:17-20), in verse 11 (cf. Is 44:23;   49:13), in verse 12 (cp. Is 44:23;   55:12), in verse 13 (cp. Is 40:10;   59:19f;   60:1;   62: 11). The theme of God-Who-Comes (cf. §15b), also represented in the psalm (v 12f), has its natural setting in a period when the temporal monarchy has disappeared in Israel. There is an eschatological ring to the expression "new song" (v 1; cf. Pss 33:3;   40:4;   98:1;   144:9), just as the epithet "new" (*kainós*) belongs to the technical vocabulary of New Testament eschatology: new teaching (Mk 1:27), new wine (Mk 2:22;   14:25), new garment (Lk 5:36), new covenant (Mk 14:24; 2 Cor 3:6), new commandment (Jn 13:34), new dough (1 Cor 5:7), newness of life (Rm 6:4), newness of spirit (Rm 7:6), new name (Rv 2:17), new canticle (Rv 5:9), new heavens and new earth (2 P 3:3; Is 65:17;   66:22), new Jerusalem (Rv 21:2).

PSALM 97 (96)

The Divine King, the Just Judge of All

The first stanza of this "eschatological" (*BJ*) hymn (vv 1-6) is a theophany (cf. §13d) describing the coming of the Lord, king and judge. The rest of the poem declares what is the effect of the theophany on Israel and on the true and false worshippers. The image of the gods is so dimmed by Yahweh's appearance that the idol worshippers are put to shame and abandon the "graven things" (cf. Ps 135:15ff). Positively Zion and Judah rejoice triumphantly and for the just "light" is sown (*zr'*: v 11; but see below). Mowinckel (I, p. 109) reads in our hymn the main conceptual elements of "enthronement" psalms: the exhortation to praise, the mention of Yahweh's glorious presence and of the excellent deeds he has just performed or is about to perform. The themes related to "joy," "justice" and "judgment" could be added (cf. vv 2, 6, 8, 12 and §11e + 14a).

Instead of "light (*'ôr*) dawns for the just" in verse 11, Dahood proposes to read "a sown field (*'ûr*) awaits the just." The translation "dawns" (*zārah*) corrects in fact the MT *zārua°*, "(is) sown." But Dahood's view is closely associated with the postulate of a "field of life" proposed in connection with *Ps 36:10 (see in §20b). Verse 3 of Ps 97 is often quoted as an example for "the defeat of enemies," a supposed theophanic element of "enthronement" psalms: "Fire goes before him and consumes his foes round about" (v 3). Commenting on Ps 50:3,

Dahood, however, suggests the reading "A fire goes before him and flashes around his back." The Hebrew *sārāyw* ("his foes"): (CV) would be translated "his back," on the strength mainly of Ugar. *zr*, "back." But then is lost the relation to a basic text of God's epiphany: "Arise, O Lord, *that your enemies* may be scattered" (Nb 10:35; see §13d).

PSALM 98 (97)

The Lord, the Victorious King and Just Judge

A common liturgical setting and the drawing from the same treasure of traditional fixed forms explain sufficiently why this hymn is so similar to Ps 96 (see there the theme "new"). Salvation history themes are more explicit in Ps 98 and its universalism reminds one of the Deutero-Isaiah (cf. 41:5; 42:10; 45:22; 49:6; 52:10). The themes of God's salvation, justice, kindness, faithfulness have been explained in connection with the beliefs of the psalmists (cf. §11de), as also "his wondrous deeds" (§10f). Both *ṣedeq* in Ps 97:6 and *ṣᵉdāqâh* in 98:2 can be translated "justice," that is "saving justice," as it appears from the parallelism of Ps 98:2:

> The Lord has made his salvation known:
> in the sight of the nations he has revealed his justice.

This can be compared with Rm 1:17 and 3:21 (see on *Ps 143). The exultation of nature is stressed in both hymns (98 and 96). Psalm 98 pictures the rivers as clapping their hands (v 8), a metaphor applied to trees in Isaiah (55:12; same verb) and more properly to "peoples" in Ps 47:2 (different verb). What causes this excessive joy is a fundamental element of divine kingship: God comes and reveals himself (vv 2, 9). In this psalm also is recalled the gratuitous election of Israel, the nation in which the divine pattern of savation is made manifest to the whole world:

> The Lord has bared his holy arm
> in the sight of all the nations;
> All the ends of the earth will behold
> the salvation of our God (Is 52:10).

PSALM 99 (98)

The Lord the Holy King

In this psalm each of the three uneven stanzas concludes with the words "God is holy." The reference to God's holiness is explained in part by the themes of "justice" and "forgiveness" represented in the psalm. It can also be associated with the description of God's terrifying epiphany (v 1; cf. §13d). In ancient thought awe (cf. v 3) and *tabu* concepts (cf. God's inaccessibility) accompany the holy (cf. §10d). "The distinctive feature of the *tabu*-concept," writes Eichrodt (p. 407), "the idea of the divine reality as a specially restricted entity, remained decisive for the whole religious thinking of the priesthood." The holiness of God is stressed both in Leviticus (cf. 11:44f) and Deutero-Isaiah (cf. 41:14-20), but also in the first part of Isaiah (cf. 1:4; 5:19, 24...) The refrain "God is holy" could have been the liturgical answer to the divine theophany in the cult. The affirmation of divine holiness is also appropriate in a context which, as Weiser puts it, asserts that God has shown himself to be the God of grace, a grace which has transformed the history of Israel into a *Heilsgeschichte,* a salvation history. Psalm 99 was, it seems, originally linked with the covenant cult and had no eschatological implication. Perhaps it was composed during or shortly after Isaiah's preaching. To the faithfulness of the covenant God (*der Bundesgott*) must correspond the fidelity of the people of the covenant.

With the names of Moses, Aaron and Samuel are recalled in the third stanza the early days of the covenant people. This would indicate, Mowinckel believes (I, p. 156), that with God's (new) enthronement this glorious past is again present and that Yahweh will again answer and forgive "from the pillar of the cloud." "It is worth noticing," he adds (I, p. 117), "that in Ps 99, Moses like Aaron is included among those 'that call upon the name of Yahweh.' To 'call upon the name of Yahweh'... is a term used of cultic supplication, especially by the one who is performing the cult, a task in the first instance belonging to the priest (cf. Jl 2: 18). So even Samuel is here considered to be a priest, and this agrees with the earlier tradition, where he is a priestly 'seer' (*rō'eh*), whereas the later tradition describes him as a 'prophet'" (cf. 1 S 9:9).

The New Year festival, which, it is believed, the "enthronement" psalms reflect in part, was supposed to be a special occasion for God to forgive sins. Even an earthly king, Mowinckel notes (I, p. 128), would grant an amnesty on the day of his enthronement (cf. 1 K 1:51ff; 2 K 25:57ff). The accession of a new king could also mean destruction for his antagonists (cf. 1 K 2). This is sometimes referred to the "defeat of the enemies" as an element of the "enthronement psalms" (cf. Ps 2:8ff; 47: 4; 97:3; 110:5f).

The expression "his footstool" in verse 5 (cf. Ps 110:1) is thus explained by W. I. Wolverton: "In one of the Ugaritic texts the god Lutpan ('El, the 'kindly one') 'put his foot on the stool, and lifted up his voice and cried: I myself will sit down and rest' (cf. G. R. Driver, *Canaanite Myths and Legends*, p. 113). A footstool nearly always went with a throne in Near Eastern portrayals of seated monarchs. This was true of the gods as well. But as Israel was forbidden any plastic representation of deity it resorted to a poetic one. God was invisible, but he might have a visible footstool. In Ps 99 it is probably Zion itself that is so regarded, for in the post-exilic establishment the ark is gone from the temple. At one time, however, it was the ark (cf. 1 Ch 28:2). In Ps 132 it is difficult to say which it is, the ark or the temple (vv 7-8). It would seem that the deity was thought to be invisible and seated upon his throne just above the cherubim with his feet, still invisible, touching the ark, or else his throne was in the skies and his feet touched this holy place, i.e. the temple (cf. Lm 2:1; Is 6:1). It was a mythopoetic way of dealing with the problem of the transcendence and the presence of God, indicating that here was the point of contact between earth and heaven … Earth-pillar, paradisiacal stream [cf. on *Ps 46:4f], mountain of the Divine Assembly (cf. *Ps 48:2), and celestial earth footstool, such were the figures from pre-Israelite mythology which were associated with the sacred area, Zion" (p. 23).

§19. CANTICLES OF ZION

(a) *General character*

These poems extol Zion, God's "holy mountain" (48:2), Salem, chosen for his abode (76:3), "the city of God" (46:5, 48:2), "the city of Yhwh $s^eb\bar{a}'\hat{o}t$ (48:9; 84:2), "the holy dwelling of the Most High" (46: 5). To it the tribes go up, on pilgrimage (122:4); for the courts of the Lord the psalmist's soul "yearns and pines" (84:3). Non-Israelites also can find refuge there, because Zion is a mother to all (87:5). The Babylonian guards used to ask the exiles: "Sing for us the songs of Zion." Was the collection of the canticles of Zion known outside Israel, or was it introduced in Babylonia by the exiles?

The central role played by Zion in the political, cultural and religious life of Israel results from her choice as the seat of the Eternal King and the capital of the temporal monarchy. This choice was dramatized by the transfer of the sacred Ark from Shiloh to Jerusalem (see §13b). Prophet the tradition about David, this with qualifications, as explained by G. Isaiah's preaching was based on two traditions, the Zion tradition and von Rad: "The songs of Zion were based on the fact of Yahweh's past choice of Zion, and the royal psalms on Yahweh's past choice of David: Isaiah turned completely to the future—Yahweh is about to deliver Zion, he is about to raise up the anointed one, the new David. It is here, in the future event, and not in any historical event of the past, that Jerusalem's salvation lies" (II, p. 175).

The Canticles of Zion are of course different from the Pilgrim Songs (120-134) which do not constitute a distant category (cf. §3c). They have, though, some themes in common, mainly love for Zion and faith in God's presence in the midst of his people. The literary structure of the Canticles of Zion and of the Psalms of Yahweh's kingship does not differ significantly from that of the hymns proper. (On the praise of Zion see "Die Verherrlichung der Gottesstadt." in H.-J. Kraus *Psalmen,* pp. 342-345).

(b) The Canticles of Zion are Pss 46, 48,   76,   84,   87,   122.

PSALM 46 (45)

God the Refuge of Israel

In this first of the six hymns to Zion, "faith in God" is the key note and its particular object is expressed in the refrain: "The Lord of hosts is with us; our stronghold is the God of Jacob." The title *yhwh ṣᵉbā'ôt* (cf. §13b) could well be related to the sacred Ark upon which sat "the Lord of hosts" (2 S 6:2; 1 Ch 13:6), even to lead his people to the battle field. God is with Israel even when the world seems to dissolve in chaos (I). He is with Zion when the nations surge like waves against its stronghold (II). He is with us (*Immanuel*) forever as the God who has brought to earth universal peace and destroyed the instruments of war (III; cf. Ps 76:4; Is 9:4). God is the Lord of creation, of history and of eschatology.

Prophetic imagery, recasting certain mythological conceptions, contributed to the formation of the traditional cult language reflected in our psalm. It is in fact L. Krinetzki's conclusion that the psalm depends on the prophetic tradition. The import of the cultic tradition represented by Ex 15:1-18; Is 2:2-5 [=Mi 4:1-5] is not to be minimized, but these texts contain cult prophecies (cf. §5e). Unfortunately they cannot be dated precisely. The psalm carries in an historicized (demythologized) form some elements of Canaanite imagery. Such borrowings seem to have been a popular literary device shortly after the exile (cf. §9d). Krinetzki refers approvingly to this verdict of *The Interpreter's Bible* (IV, p. 241): "The psalm evidences a time when the psalmody of the temple was influenced by the prophetic spirit, and particularly by that of the later prophets with their visions of a warless world under the dominion of the Lord (cf. Is 8:9f; 17:12ff; 33:17-24; 59:15b-20; Ezk 6:7, 13; 11:10; Mi 4:3). In view of the extent to which the psalmist has assimilated the ideas preserved in a wide range of the prophetic literature, one is led to date the psalm in the late post-exilic period." Krinetzki's final word (p. 71) is that the psalm is definitely post-exilic. A greater precision cannot be established. In this context of "peace" literature, the following extract from (Ugaritic) *'Anat* (III:11-15; cf. M. Dahood on Ps 46:9) seems appropriate:

> "Banish war from the earth, put love in the land;
> pour peace into the bowels of the earth,
> rain down love into the bowels of the field."

Since it is difficult to understand that "there is a stream whose runlets gladden the city of God" (v 5a), any new interpretation of the passage deserves consideration. Verse 4 ends in the MT with *selah* (cf. §4c and *Ps 3:3). Dahood incorporates this word in the sentence with the meaning "to stand in a heap." With the following words it forms the phrase, "the river (and) its channels stand in a heap" (comp. Ex 15:8). The absence of the copula w^e, "and," before $p^e l \bar{a} g \bar{a} y w$, "its channels," is explained as a sort of ellipse well represented in other verses of the psalm. With other minor changes (explained in *The Anchor Bible*) verses 4 and 5 now read:

> Though its waters rage and foam,
> the mountain heave in its midst,
> the river and its channels stand in a heap.
> God brings happiness to his city,
> the Most High sanctifies his habitation.

Krinetzki, for his part, reads in Ps 46:5 a paradisiac motif (cf. Gn 2: 10ff). It is to make an allegory of a parable to ask the question: what river flows in Jerusalem? Much in the same vein H. Junker believes that the river in Zion is a symbol of the presence of God, who from the temple bestows security, prosperity and peace. The real, great river, by contrast, the pride of Babylon, did not provide long that city with the same gifts (cf. Is 8:6f). The river (*nahar*) in Jerusalem obviously reflects the poet's literary source of inspiration, perhaps Ezekiel's representation of the eschatological return of primeval conditions: "I saw water flowing from beneath the threshold of the temple" (47:1). In Deutero-Isaiah also, restored Zion is associated with the imagery of rivers and streams: "For thus says the Lord: Lo, I will spread prosperity over her like a river, and the wealth of the nations like an overflowing torrent" (66:12; cf. 33:21). Like Sinai (cf. Ex 19:12, 23) and other sacred mountains (cf. Is 2:2; Ex 40:2), Zion is described as a holy site and Jerusalem, where God dwells, takes its place among the sacred enclosures inaccessible to profane intrusion. W. I. Wolverton suggests that "the River of God" in Ps 46:4f preserves ancient mythological ideas about the city of '*El 'Elyon* (see on *Ps 48). In the Ras Shamra texts 'El's dwelling was located "at the springs of the (two) channels of the deeps" (texts 51:IV: 20ff and 49:I:5f; cf. C. H. Gordon, p. 171 and 167). See also S. Kelly, "Psalm 46: A Study in Imagery," JBL 89 (1970) 305-12.

Psalm 48 (47)

Thanksgiving for Jerusalem's Deliverance

The impregnability of Zion is again proclaimed in this psalm which describes an unidentified assault by a coalition of hostile kings. In such cases, writes Mowinckel (I, p. 85), where the epic-mythical tendency comes to the fore, "it presents Yahweh's superiority in the guise of one great mythico-historical victory over all enemies at once, as in Pss 46, 48 and 76." R. Tournay also associates these three psalms, in a different context (see on *Ps 76). Referring to Ps 87, Weiser writes that "the deliverance from the armies of Sennacherib (701 B.C.) was regarded as a visible proof of the inviolability of the sanctuary" (p. 581). Taken literally, the words "go about Zion, make the round" can allude to a liturgical procession, but in the context they are a simple invitation to tour the city, the better to admire its "ramparts and castles." In verse 15 the MT '*al mût,* "unto death" (not translated in CV) is probably a misplaced, textually corrupt, rubric belonging to Ps 49 (cf. Ps 9:1; 46:1; BJ and §4d). Yet Dahood would accept Krinetzki's (p. 73) proposal that *'ôlāmôt* is to be read in Ps 48:15 and the verse translated: "Our eternal and everlasting God—he will guide us eternally."

Zion is likened to the "mountain of the North" (cf. v 3), upon which Phoenician and Canaanite texts locate the residence of the gods (cf. J. Morgenstern and O. Eissfeldt, *Baal Zaphon*...), a tradition alluded to in other biblical texts (cf. Ezk 28:14-16; Pss 76:5; 87:1; cf. Bib 1933, pp. 41-67). In this connection Dahood notes: "Though *ṣāpôn* came to mean 'North' in Hebrew, there are three other [besides Ps 48:3] poetic passages where the ancient Canaanite sense as the name of a specific mountain is still preserved: Ps 89:13; Is 14:13...Jb 26: 7." If the psalm reflects, as it seems, an "archaizing age" of biblical literature (cf. §9d), then a likely date for its composition would be the end of the sixth century. The title "the great King" can allude to the supreme Phoenician deity, but an Assyrian or Persian monarch would also be referred to as "the great king" (cf. *Ps 47:3). M. Palmer would qualify the poem's theme as one of "theological geography" (cf. *Ps 133), the splendor and inviolability of Jerusalem, the royal city of Yahweh, the "joy of the earth." "The psalmist," he writes, "explicitly names the North and the East in the first two strophes, and then, having once established the pattern, introduces the South (*yāmîn*, v 11) and the West (*'aḥarôn*) by indirection in the last two strophes.... By mentioning the four Cardinal Points the poet has suggested that Jerusalem is also the center and naval of the world" (cf. Ezk 5:5; 38:12; cf. on *Ps 22:28). The second and third stanzas (vv 5-12) stress God's saving deeds with traditional *Heilsgeschichte* formulas. What spells disaster to the enemies is salvation for God's *protégés*.

Psalm 76 (75)

Thanksgiving for the Overthrow of Israel's Foes

Another God-given victory of Zion (=Salem) over the enemies is celebrated in this psalm. The first two strophes (vv 2-4; 5-7) refer to a past event, perhaps "to David's decisive victory over the Philistines at Baal-perazim (2 S 5:17f) which was gained near Jerusalem" (Weiser). But the account has "undergone cultic stylization and generalization." This, according to Weiser, "suggests the view that the historical events are viewed within the larger framework of the *Heilsgeschichte*, the representation and actualization of which were an essential part of the festival cult." The thoughts expressed in the other two stanzas (8-10; 11-13) would be eschatological in character (cf. the salvation judgment) and provide more direct evidence of the cultural setting of the psalm (v 12). R. Tournay (RB 1959, p. 321f) sees Ps 76 as an *'anāwîm* (cf. §12a) psalm depending on Isaiah and Jeremiah. It has affinities, he thinks, with Pss 46 and 48, related to Is 33. These psalms would reflect the Jewish mentality of the Persian period (5th-4th cent.), when the great liberations of the past were recalled to inspire confidence for the future.

Psalm 136 has been quoted as an example of the first of two types of hymns, recognized by Mowinckel. The second type, he writes (I, p. 85), a more special one, "more fully depicts one particular feature of divine activity, a single fundamental act of salvation... and appears... to belong to one particular kind of cultic festival...." Pss 46, 48, 76 and 114 are listed as hymns of this type. These special festal hymns, he adds (I, p. 87), may contain an almost epic description of the divine act of deliverance which is praised. Ps 76:3-7 is cited as an example. The cultic ceremonies with which many hymns were originally associated often involved a festal epiphany of Yahweh (cf. §13d). This revelation element, mentioned about Ps 98, features also in Pss 76:2 and 48:4.

Various interpretations have been proposed of the difficult verse 11. The following meaning can be given to the MT: "The wrath of man (*ḥamat 'ādām*) only adds to your glory, the survivors of your wrath will draw like a girdle around you." *JB* comments: "The image, taken from Jeremiah (cf. Ps 109:19), symbolizes close union. Like Terror (= the Terrible) in verse 11, the wrath of God is here apparently personified (cf. Ps 58:9). The helpless 'wrath' of man can only witness to the power and justice of God." According to *BJ* the imagery, borrowed from Jr 13:11, describes what close bond will unite God to those whom the judgment of God will have spared. A similar view is reflected in Weiser's translation: "Surely the wrath of men must testify to thee; he who has been spared death must extol thee." With a change in the vowels only of the two Hebrew words (see above), the new Latin Psalter and *CV* have read the proper names *Hamat* and *Edom*. Eissfeldt would, after others, read: "Hamat-Aram acknowledges thee, the remainder of Hamat celebrates thee." The allusion is to 2 S 8:3-12. This interpretation refers verse 11 to the time of David, like verse 3, which, it is believed, alludes to the transfer to Jerusalem of the ark of the covenant (2 S 6), like verses 4-7 also, where, it seems, David's victorious battles are recalled (cf. 2 S 5:17-25). In that case the *MT* could be maintained in verse 5 (cf. Montagnini) and translated: "Resplendent you came, O powerful one, from the mountains of (enemy) booty" (cf. v 6). Thus explained Ps 76 could well have been composed in the tenth century B.C.

PSALM 84 (83)

Desire for the Sanctuary

This hymn is a striking expression of the Old Testament devotion to the Jerusalem sanctuary. Though not explicitly listed as one of the "pilgrim songs" (cf. §3c) it is close to them in thought-content and in style, as also to Pss 42 and 43. A. Gelin calls Psalm 84 "le cantique par excellence du pèlerin." In three stanzas the poem sings the pilgrim's desire, journey and prayer. It was composed for the feast of the Tabernacles, as the mention of "the early rain" (v 7) would suggest (cf. Jn 7:37). Mowinckel (I, p. 6) would cite Ps 6 to illustrate the "living connexion" between the psalms, the temple and the cult. It supplies also a good example, he thinks (I, p. 88), of hymns in which Yahweh is praised more indirectly, namely by exalting "all that belongs to him: his temple, his holy city, and the blessings which flow from that place where the fountain of life is and where strength is to be found." "Quite characteristically," he will add (p. 186), these "outward things" and "not the Holy One himself" are described as the object of love which accompanies gratitude (cf. Ps 84:2ff and Ps 122). A peculiar translation of Ps 84:12 will be examined in connection with Ps 3:4. Quite probably $m^e\check{s}\hat{\imath}heka$, "your anointed," refers to the king, and not to the high priest (against JB). According to Dahood the king appears here as vassal of God the Suzerain, mentioned, he thinks, in the first word ($m^eg\bar{a}n\bar{e}n\hat{u}$) of the verse, which he translates: "O God, our Suzerain (see on *Ps 3), behold, look upon the face of your anointed" (cf. v 12). Dahood's translation of the following verse, "How much better is one day in your court than a thousand in the Cemetery!", will look convincing to those who are ready to admit that the last colon of the verse also refers to the nether regions: "How much better is one day in your court than a thousand in the Cemetery! To stand on the threshold of your house, my God, than to abide in the Tent of the Wicked One" ("The Wicked One" would be "death"; cf. Is 11:4; Pr 14:32). Not to mention the grammatical objections, it would seem that understood thus the preference of the psalmist is made so obvious as not to retain its intended meaning.

Psalm 87 (86)

Zion the Home of All Nations

Some assertions of this psalm are better understood if it describes Zion as seen during a feast attended by pilgrims from many nations, as on Pentecost (Ac 2:5-13). Zion is called to become the religious capital of all the nations. Egypt (Rahab), Ethiopia, Syro-Palestina (cf. Philistia, Tyre), Mesopotamia (Babylon), all the pagan neighbors of Israel are destined to know the true God and to provide proselytes (cf. Zc 2:15; 8:23; Ps 45:15). Such is the will of Yahweh expressed in this psalm in oracular form (vv 4-5). Isaiah also has described the maternal role of Zion, the fruitful bride of Yahweh (54:1; 62:4f). This *BJ* commentary can be supplemented by the remark that in ancient oriental myths the "fixing of fates" was a common feature, represented in the New Year festivals. To that corresponds more or less the biblical book of God (Ex 32:32), book of judgment (Dn 7:10; Ps 139:16) and book of life (Rv 20:12; cf. §14d).

Textual problems abound in the psalm. E. Beaucamp believes that some words have been accidentally misplaced: "This one was born there, and to Zion it is said..." (vv 4-5). The restitution of these to their proper place and a few other changes would result in the following translation (from the French) :

1. (Canticle to Zion) founded by Him on the holy mountains.
2. Because the Lord loves the gates of Zion
   more than any dwelling of Jacob,
3. What has been said of you,
   I shall evoke, O city of God:
4. "Rahab and Babel to whom that know me!"
   Here the Philistines, Tyre and Kush! (...)
5. How many men and men were born in her!
   Because the Most High establishes her.
6. Enrolling the peoples the Lord notes:
   "truly this one was born here!"

7. [and to Zion it is said]
   amidst dances and songs;
   in you are found our springs of life.

Weiser, for his part, suggests to place verse 6 before verse 4. Thus the general meaning would be clarified: whereas each has his own country, Jerusalem is their common home (cf. Is 55:5). Part of the text would then run as follows:

6. The Lord counts the peoples as he registers them
   according to the place in which they were born.
4. "Among those who profess me, I reckon Rahab and Babylon;
   and behold, there are Philistia, Tyre and Cush,
   people who were born there."
5. But of Zion he says, "Each one was born there."
7. They sing while they dance, "All my springs are in thee."

The MT phrase, kol-ma'yānay bāk, "all my springs are in thee," suggests to Mowinckel (II, p. 144), that the poet is under the effect of a mystical experience...suffused with 'holy' feelings and divine power." That "the psalmists well knew the ecstatic-mystical experiences (cf. §12f) attached to the cult" can be deduced also from expressions like "Yahweh is my power and my song" (Ps 118:14; Ex 15:2; Is 12:3).

PSALM 122 (121)

The Pilgrim's Greetings to Jerusalem

This simple Zion hymn, one of the "Pilgrim psalms" (cf. §3c), expresses in three stanzas what were the dominant feelings of the pilgrims about to leave Jerusalem: recollections of the joyful event, motives of the pilgrimage, prayer for the holy city. "The pilgrims halt at the gates and salute the holy city with 'Shâlôm!' (Peace!) [cf. vv 2, 8], alluding to the popular etymology of 'Jerusalem,' 'city of peace' (cf. Ps 76:2). This 'peace' plays a prominent part in the messianic hope (cf. Is 11:6; Ho 2:20). Affection for holy Zion (2 S 5:9) is a characteristic of Jewish piety, cf. Pss 48, 84, 87, 133, 137" (JB). The "decree for Israel" (v 4) need not refer to the Deuteronomic centralization law (Dt 12:5; 2 K 23) since already in Jeroboam's time the possibility existed that the people would go up to offer sacrifices in the house of the Lord at Jerusalem (1 K 12:27). Yet the following prescription is perhaps meant: "Three times a year, then every male among you shall appear before the Lord, your God, in the place which he chooses: at the feast of Unleavened Bread, at the feast of Weeks, and at the feast of Booths" (Dt 16: 16). In that case the psalm could not be earlier than the seventh century B.C.

Among the "Zion-hymns," Mowinckel writes (I, p. 90), "a special place is taken by Ps 122 with its deeply personal tone and its free treatment of motifs from other types of poetry, namely, the pilgrim song and the benediction." Grammatical particularities, he points out (II, p. 98), like the use of the relative particle *še* and its special construction with the proposition *le*, indicate that Pss 122 and 146 are among the latest of the Psalter. In Ps 122 at least, then, the heading *leḏāwîḏ*, "of David" (cf. §4f), does not shed any light on the authorship of the psalm.

Dahood notes, with other critics, that the relative pronoun *še* is "another of the dialectical elements that mark the Songs of Ascents," that "it was originally at home in North Israel and only later found wider extension" (on v 3). He renders thus verse 5: "Because there they sat on thrones of judgment, on thrones of the House of David"; "they" stands for the judges and the kings. Even in the more usual translations, "there thrones of judgment were/are set...," the initial because (Heb. *kî*) should not be omitted (as in RSV and NAB): Jerusalem must be prayed for because it is the religious and political capital of the nation.

V. Laments, Psalms of Confidence, and Thanksgivings of the Individual

According to the principles of the *Gattungsforschung* (cf. §7) great importance is attached to the original context of literary works. Prayers of or for the community generally originate from the cult and thus differ from compositions prompted by individual concerns. On the other hand, the three categories of the present family of psalms are related by a common interest: the situation of a man in distress. The lament and the expression of confidence accompany the crisis, while the thanksgiving describes its happy *dénouement*. That these three categories are in some way connected appears from their simultaneous presence in a few psalms (e.g. 22, 30, 31, 54, 56, 61).

§20. LAMENTS OF THE INDIVIDUAL

(a) The *structure* of these psalms generally includes the following elements:

1) *Introduction: Invocation of the name* (Yahweh or Elohim), followed by a cry for help (cf. 142:2), often in the imperative (cf. 5:2). This initial contact with God can be repeated or amplified. Like the hymn, writes A. Bentzen (I, p. 156), "the psalms of lamentation have a *'primitive call'* in a *cultic exclamation,* probably the *'ḥonnēnī Yahweh',* "Be gracious to me...," (51:3; 57:2; 86:3; cf. Lk 18:13), and probably the category has been called *tᵉḥinnā* ("supplication": cf. the superscription of Ps 102)." When the supplication proper mixes with the invocation, or when the complaint and the motives support the cry for help, it is not always easy to isolate the invocation (cf. Ps 5).

2) *Main section* (*corpus supplicationis*). It includes several elements, not always presented in the same order. They often intermingle or appear in successive stages. One or another is likely to be abridged.

(aa) *The complaint.* It is not always announced as in Ps 142:3: "My complaint I pour out before him; before him I lay bare my distress," or as in the heading of Ps 102: "The prayer of an afflicted one when he is faint and pours out his anguish before the Lord." These exceptional formulations reveal one of the common *motives* of the complaint: to relieve the heart. There existed in Babylonia a collection of psalms entitled: "complaint to appease the heart" (cf. *SDB*, vol I, c. 818f). But the complaint's main motive is to move God to act. Among these *Gebetserhörungsmotive the description of the man's distress* stands in first place. The danger of death is almost always involved, be it from natural causes (disease and calamities) or from human malice. So not the small *malaises* are the object of prayer but the dangers arising from the enemies of Life. Illness has a religious meaning: "for the biblical writer," writes G. Pidoux, "life was conceived as a power, of reduced strength in the sick and almost inexistent in the dead" (*Du Portique...*, p. 72). It is not surprising that the sick man felt himself to be at the mercy of hostile forces, if God had turned away his face from him. Hence his wish to see again the face of God (31:17; 42:), to enjoy again the community's fellowship (22:26): "I am sleepless, and I moan; I am like a sparrow *alone* on the housetop" (102:8). It is in the complaint especially that the individual traits of the lament are revealed, as distinct from the hymn, much less personal. Not all the expressions of the complaint are to be understood literally, however, since the suppliant draws also from a common stock of conventional formulas and semitic overstatements (cf. Ps 22:15f; 38:6-9). People in distress will likely depend for help on fixed religious patterns, which in turn can be reflected in the description of the need (cf. H. Ringgren, *The Faith...*, p. 62).

(bb) *The supplication.* It is a moving prayer requesting urgent help by people whom A. Gelin calls *"les tutoyeurs de Dieu,"* those who say *"tu"* to God. The familiar way of addressing God is also reflected in the frequent use of anthropomorphisms: "Listen to me!" "Open your ear!" "Look!" "Rouse yourself!" "Wake up!" "Hurry!" "Answer me?" "Save me!" "Return!" These repeated appeals, which generally spring from filial confidence, can also reflect moments of impatience: "How long, O Lord?... How long will you hide your face from me?" (Ps 13:2) But phrases like these also follow stereotyped patterns (see on *Ps 13). Some authors would propose that the Israelite prayer has been purified in a multiple-stage process: first God was blamed, then the enemy; the prayers with a request were replaced by pure penitential prayers, as in Ne 9. But in all periods one or another of these elements is likely to predominate.

(cc) *Who are the suppliants?* Psalm 102 is the prayer of an 'āni, a "poor" or an "afflicted" person (see on §12a-c). Modern scholars show interest in classifying the laments according to the distress involved (cf. J. Coppens in *Le Psautier*, pp. 17, 21, 29, 49, 77). There are psalms of the sick (6, 13, 28, 31B, 39, 61, 69, 70, 102, 109; cf. Is 38: 9-20), psalms of the accused (5 7, 13, 17, 25, 28, 38, 39, 54-59, 86, 88, 102; cf. H. Schmidt, *Das Gebet.. .*), psalms of the persecuted (13, 22, 31, 42/43, 109, 142, 143). No real evidence can be produced to support Mowinckel's suggestion that the majority of the suppliants are victims of sorcery (cf. §12g). Studying "Theophanies in holy places in Hebrew Religion," J. Lindblom discovered in Ps 3:6 evidence of "an incubation-oracle imparted in an incubation-dream. Thus the psalm was recited in the morning after the incubation-sleep." In Ps 17, however, the "incubation" leads to a real theophany (v 15), expected by the suppliant at his awakening. So the poet "is here thinking of an awakening from an incubation-sleep" (cf. p. 104f). A similar explanation is proposed for Ps 63:3. The theory is not convincing and is evidently based on extra-biblical postulates, like Mary Hamilton's *Incubation or the Cure of Disease in Pagan Temples and Christian Churches* (London, 1906), quoted by Lindblom. Other problems connected with the supplication have been examined elsewhere: are the suppliants individuals or representatives of the community (the "I" and "We" psalms; cf. 12g and 23a)? who are the "enemies" of the psalmists, who are the evildoers"? (cf. §12g); what about the "imprecations" of the psalmists? (cf. §14d, towards end). *Bible de la Pléiade*, vol. II, p. 122, distinguishes imprecations intended for (personal) "foes" (Pss 5, 35, 40, 41, 55, 58, 59, 69, 109, 140, 141) and imprecations pronounced against the enemies of the nations or of religion (Pss 14, 52, 59, 79, 83).

(dd) The expression of *trust in God* is rarely absent from the lament. When it predominates it becomes the main element of a special category of psalms, "the psalms of confidence." The motives of confidence vary: God's attributes and honor, the suppliant's urgent needs, his innocence (cf. *Pss 18 and 101) or penitence (cf. §12e). The worshipper's prayer often includes the vow to offer a sacrifice (Pss 22:26;   61:9; cf §8b).

3) There is no fixed *conclusion* of the lament, although it will generally end with a *blessing* (cf. 5:13;   26:12;   28:9), with a renewed expression of *trust* (cf. 17:15;   140:14), or with a thanksgiving (7:18;
13:6;   109:30). It is likely that the laments with a thanksgiving conclusion were written soon after the prayer had been heard, when the
psalmist's feelings were still alive with the bitter experience (cf. Ps 31).
The same can be said of those supplications ending on a tone of triumph
(cf. Ps 6:9-11). Another explanation is that the thanksgiving followed
the *Heilsorakel,* in which the suppliant had received the assurance that
his prayer was heard (see §8e). In some psalms a direct answer from
God seems to be expected: "My soul trusts in his word. My soul waits
for the Lord more than sentinels wait for the dawn" (Ps 130:5f); "Say
to my soul: I am your salvation" (Ps 35:3). If God listens the oracle
follows (cf. Pss 6:9f;   22:25;   28:6;   34:7;   66:19). Some authors
believe that the psalmic oracle is a simple literary device while others
claim it represents a real divine answer made known through direct revelation or ritual consultation. Several psalms seem to have been composed before the peril (17,   25,   38,   39,   42/43,   51,   55,   59,   61,
70,   109,   130,   141,   142,   143); others would have been written between the prayer and the rescue (5,   7,   35,   69,   71,   86,   102), while
a third group of psalms are rather reflections on a past danger averted
with God's help (6,   13,   22,   26,   28,   31,   54,   56,   57,   63,
64,   120,   140). A. Bentzen writes: "The psalms of lamentation have
been very much imitated by the prophets, especially Jeremiah (cf. Is 50:
4;   59:12ff;   64:5-7...). The Jeremianic lamentations are found in the
chapters 11-20" (I, p. 156). Other authors will prefer to give the priority to Jeremiah (on P. E. Bonnard's *Le Psautier selon Jérémie,* cf. §5d
and *Ps 6).

(b) The Laments of the individual are the following: Pss 5,   6,   7,
13,   17,   (22),   25,   26,   28,   31,   35,   (36),   38,   39;   42/43;
51,   54,   55,   56,   57,   59,   61,   (63),   64,   69,   70,   (=40:14-18);
71,   86,   88,   102,   109,   120,   130,   140,   141,   142,   143. [The
brackets indicate the psalms not as firmly classified as the others.]

PSALM 5

Prayer for Divine Help

This individual lament seems to have been uttered in connection with the *morning* sacrifice (vv 4, 8; cf. 2 K 3:20; cf. below). After the opening cry to God (vv 2-4), the psalmist reflects on the condition of admittance to the divine presence (5-7), as is usually done in the so-called "psalms of innocence" (cf. §12e). By admitting the defective spelling of the 1st person (cp. Ps 16:2) and a change of vowels, "you hate all evildoers," in verse 6, becomes "I hate all evildoers." This last statement, Dahood writes, "appears to be a *terminus technicus* employed in the formula of repudiation of false gods, when one was accused of idolatry" (cp. *Ps 31:7). Although admitted in God's presence, the suppliant still asks for God's guidance before invoking divine judgment on the enemies (cf. §12g), lest he deviate, like them, from sincerity and truthfulness (vv 8-9). The Lord is then petitioned to "punish" the treacherous and "cast out" the sinners, that God's judgment be manifested against those who rebel against him (10-11). In the last two verses the reassured psalmist includes all just men in his jubilant hymn to God who protects and blesses the righteous.

Quite obviously the suppliant of the psalm is a man falsely accused. "At dawn I will draw up my case" (v 4), he says, according to Dahood's translation (cf. Ps 50:2). His accusers are of course those "who speak falsehood" (v 7). That they accused the psalmist of idolatry has been indicated above. This assumption would find support also in Dahood's suggestion that in verse 7 'iš dāmîm (vocalization doubtful) be translated not "a man of blood" but "a man of idols" (cf. *Ps 26:9), the verb root being dāmāh, to be similar (cf. the latin *simulacrum*, used to designate an idol). In the same line of thought, the next word *mirmāh* would not mean "deceit(ful)" but "figurine," as in Jr 5:27: "Like a cage of birds, their houses are full of figurines (*mirmāh*)" (cf. 9:5). Read then in Ps 5:7b: "The man of idols and figurines Yahweh detests." The detractors are mentioned again in verse 10b: "their throats are yawning graves; they make their tongues so smooth ⟨ḥlq⟩" (JB). If Ugaritic ḥālāq, "to die, perish," applies here, as Dahood thinks, then good parallels certainly follow: "A gave wide-open is their throat, with their tongue they bring death."

When, in verse 5, the psalmist says: "At dawn you hear my voice," it may be simply because he usually addresses his prayers in the morning (Ps 88:14). Yet there is evidence that dawn or morning (cf. J. B. Bauer, J. Ziegler) were considered as the most auspicious time for prayer: "O Lord, be our strength every morning" (Is 33:2); "[The favors of the Lord] are renewed each morning, so great is his faithfulness" (Lm 3:23). The same theme occurs in several psalms: the kindness of the Lord is expected mostly in the morning (58:17; 90:14). God will help the holy city at the break of dawn (46:6; cf. 101:8), a probable allusion to the angel of the Lord's intervention against Sennacherib's army: "And when he arose early in the morning, he saw all the bodies of the dead" (2 K 19:35). One psalmist says: "My soul waits for the Lord more than sentinels wait for the dawn" (130:6). There may be an allusion to the "resurrection" theme when the psalmists speak of awakening in the presence of the Lord (3:4; 17:15; see §14d; cf. also R. Tournay's remark about *Ps 72:16). Much indicates, thinks J. Lindblom, that in Ps 17:15 "the poet is here thinking of an awakening from an incubation-sleep" ("Theophanies...," p. 105) "It might perhaps be obejcted," he adds, "that the only word 'awake' is insufficient for characterizing the Psalm as a ritual preparation for an incubation-sleep. But what we do not find in the text was, of course, completed by the *Sitz im Leben* of the Psalm, recited as it was as a liturgical introduction to the following ritual act." It is more likely that the morning, when awakening occurred, was simply considered by popular conviction as the time when God used to intervene for the benefit of his worshippers (cf. ZAW 59, 1942/43, p. 1ff; see also on *Ps 90; on the Lord and the night, see *Ps 104:20f and Ps 74:16).

PSALM 6

Prayer in Time of Distress

This lament is one of the seven "penitential" psalms (6, 32, 38, 51, 102, 130, 143; cf. §12e), although in it the suppliant's sinfulness is only implied by the statement on divine wrath (v 2), seemingly justified. In fact, whereas other suffering psalmists confess their sin (Pss 32: 1, 25; 38:4ff, 19; 39:9; 51:6), this suppliant refrains both from proclaiming, like others, his innocence (cf. Pss 7:4-10; 26:1f) and from confessing his guilt. He seems to solicit, from the first, a "paternal" punishment (cf. Jb 33:19-30; Pr 3:11f). The formula, "reprove me not in your anger" (v 2), is conventional; it recurs in Ps 38:2 and probably derives from Jeremiah: "Punish us, O Lord, but with equity, not in anger, lest you have us dwindle away" (10:24). Then the prophet suggests to God: "Pour out your wrath on the nations that know you not" (v 25; on God's wrath, cf. §11h).

Taken literally words like "I am languishing," "heal me," and the allusion to threatening "death" point to physical illness. The disease is aggravated by mental distress: the suppliant is convinced that God is angry against him. Yet all that is an ordeal of the past. Now that God has heard his plea (v 10) he doesn't dread any more the triumph of his enemies, for they shall be put to shame in utter terror (v 11). Among the motives put forth in his prayer, the psalmist had listed the following: "For among the dead no one remembers you; in the nether world who gives you thanks?" (v 6). The dead are unable to share in the praise of Yahweh, a characteristic aspect of Israel's worship (cf. §14d). If the suppliant dies God will have failed to manifest "his providential rule" (a favorite Weiser expression) in his life and the dead man will be in a hopeless state, severed body and soul from his lifeline, God's grace.

In his *Le psautier selon Jérémie*, P. E. Bonnard studies 33 psalms supposedly influenced by Jeremiah (cf. §5d). So Ps 6 would belong, with two other penitentials (38 and 51) to such a "Psalter according to Jeremiah." Bonnard would characterize Ps 6 as a post-exilic composition in the "anthological" style (cf. *Ps 33). The borrowings, mainly from Jeremiah, have been admitted also by Podechard, while Kissane remains unimpressed: "The supposed borrowings are mere commonplaces which any writer might have used!" Coppens reads in Pss 6 and 41 two formulas of prayers for the sick, presumably older than the Book of Jeremiah. Such literary forms, as individual complaints, were certainly known to the prophet.

PSALM 7

An Appeal to the Divine Judge

In spite of textual and literary problems, the unity of this psalm is to be maintained. In it a man pursued by an enemy takes refuge in God, and, in the temple, submits to "an oath of exculpation" (vv 4-6) that will establish his innocence and confound his adversary (cf. 1 K 8:31f), presumably a colleague who has betrayed him. The faults he mentions could reflect, according to one interpretation, the false accusations levied against him. Here, as in Job 31, these conditional statements are equivalent to "negative confessions," a literary genre known in the Near-East literature (cf. *Ps 101). Having cleared his conscience, the suppliant now invokes boldly God's judgment against his foes and the wicked. It belongs to the cultic tradition to consider God as the Holy One (cf. §10 d), the just judge, enthroned on high to pass judgment on the nations or on the wicked (cf. vv 8, 10, 12). When writing that the wicked "falls into the pit which he has made" (v 16) and the like (v 17; cf. Ps 5:11), the psalmist may allude to a legal maxim applied to slanderous accusers, but in speaking thus he also reveals that sin contains in itself its own judgment, to manifest God's righteousness (cf. §12e).

Other authors, like BJ, believe, that verses 4-5 reflect *lex talionis* (14d), "the tit for tat law" (Ex 21:23f). Verse 5 would then express a regret and, according to Driver, it should read: "...and I have rescued him that was for no reason mine enemy," that is: "If I have been so foolish as to requite a friend with evil or to do an enemy a good turn, may I be destroyed!". "The passage," he adds, "has been misunderstood owing to its un-Christian sentiment, which, however, is not unparalleled in the Psalter" (p. 151; cf. §14d, c.fi.). The same line of thought is followed by Kissane, who translates: "If I have done evil to my friend, and delivered one who had assailed me without cause," and comments: "There is only one charge—that he placated his enemy at the expense of his friend. If the psalm is Davidic, one can understand that he incurred the emnity of many of his friends when he spared the life of Saul (cf. 1 S 24:11; 26:18)."

The beginning of v 13 does not make much sense in the MT. BJ finds it necessary to supplement "the enemy" to the text. "When the enemy sharpens his sword..." would follow on v 6. But Dahood reminds us that *lē'* can mean "the Strong One," "the Victor." By vocalizing *'im lē' yāšūb*, verse 13 could sound like this: "O that the Victor would again sharpen his sword, draw and aim the bow!" (see *Ps 18:15). Other divine appellatives appear in verse 11: "My Suzerain is the Most High God, the Savior of the upright of heart" (see on *Ps 3:4 and *Ps 18:42). The first hemistich of verse 9 is probably a gloss (cf. Ps 96:10, Is 3:13) stressing that the "nations" (perhaps substituted for the "gods"; cf. *Ps 96:7) stand as defendants before God's tribunal, not as witnesses. (cf. BJ). J. Leveen has discussed omissions from the MT in verses 7, 9, 10, 12, 13. In verse 12 he retrieves a whole hemistich (cf. §6a) with the help of the Septuagint: "God is a righteous judge, *Mighty and slow to anger*: Yet a god who is also angry every day; *Yea, his anger will not turn back.*"

PSALM 13 (12)

Prayer of One in Sorrow

Both in the complaint (vv 2, 3) and in the supplication (4, 5) of this lament the thought goes first to God, then to the sick man and finally to the threatening enemy. There exist Babylonian parallels (cf. §9b) for the typical lament "how long?" or "Until when?", and for the idea, common in ancient cult tradition, that if the divine eye or face beholds the suppliant, his prayer has been answered (cf. E. Baumann, *ZAW* 61, pp. 125-131). It seems apposite to quote here extracts from the "prayer of lamentation to Ishtar," the goddess of valor and of war (cf. *ANET*, p. 383ff):

"O diety of men goddess of women, whose designs no
  one can conceive,
Where thou dost look, one who is dead lives; one who
  is sick rises up;
The erring one who sees thy face goes aright.
I have cried to thee, suffering, wearied, and distressed,
  as thy servant.
See me O my Lady; accept my prayers.
Faithfully look upon me and hear my supplication...
How long, O my Lord, shall my adversaries be looking upon me;
In lying and untruth shall they plan evil against me,
Shall my pursuers and those who exult over me rage against me?
How long, O my Lady, shall the crippled and weak seek me out?...
Faithfully look upon me and accept my supplication.
How long, O my Lady, wilt thou be infuriated so that
  thy face is turned away?
How long, O my Lady, wilt thou be infuriated so that
  thy spirit is enraged?
Turn thy neck which thou hast set against me; set thy
  face [toward] good favor.

Could the "enemy" mentioned in verses 3 and 5 be "the Enemy," Death personified. It is a fact, recalled by W. H. Brownlee ("Le livre grec...," p. 167), that death in the Old Testament was not always considered merely as a physical event. It was often looked upon as a Power (cf. Jr 9:20; 2 S 22:5f), comparable to god *Mot* in Ugaritic literature and to the Angel of death of more recent rabbinical writings (cf. 1 Ch 21:15). People afflicted by illness or caught in a peril were thought to be already in the power of Death or of Sheol. Brownlee then quotes Jon 2:2-9; Pss 16:10; 49:5; 71:20; 68:13; 116:3, 4, 8 as passages anticipating the later doctrine of resurrection (cf. §14d), by their affirmation of the power of the Lord to triumph over the powers of Death. Can it be, as Dahood suggests, that the psalmist's prayer to God is in fact: "Grant me immortality"? In verse 4 the phrase "Give light to my eyes" could mean "Restore my health" (cf. Ps 38:11) or "grant me immortality." "To see the light," Dahood believes, is idiomatic for "to enjoy immortality" (cf. Ps 36:9f). Other authors would agree with Weiser that "Give light to my eyes" is a prayer for the renewal of a faith that will attract divine grace (cf. v 6). If the enemy in the psalm is Death only, then the presence of *ṣāray*, "my foes" (governing a plural verb) in verse 5b has to be explained. The term, Dahood says, is a *plurale majestatis*. It means "the Adversary" and stands for *Mot*, "the psalmist's archrival" (cf. also J. Zandee, *Death as an enemy...*).

PSALM 17 (16)

Prayer against Persecutors

Here, as in Ps 7, the supplication is preceded by a negative declaration, denying the false charges brought against the accused (vv 1-5). It is God, the savior (*môšia'*, v 7; cf. §11d), present on the Ark, who is asked to protect the suppliant against the wicked, violent, cruel, ravenous enemies, lying in wait like lions (6-12). Then the prayer for rescue takes a tone of vindictiveness (cf. §14d) to ask (vv 13-14), according to Weiser, that the wicked be destroyed "by means of a mysterious food secretly stored up by God for future retribution, whereby they as well as their children and grandchildren shall be satiated" (other interpretations below!). As for the psalmist he will be satiated with beholding the divine form (*tᵉmûnâh*: v 15).

As in Ps 5, so here also, Dahood believes the psalmist has been falsely accused of worshipping idols. This assumption is confirmed by reading in verse 3: "Test me with fire, you will find no idolatry (*zimmātî*) in me." In verse 4 the accused would besides proclaim: "My mouth has not transgressed against the work of your hands" (reading here *'ādēm*, instead of MT *'ādām*, *'ādēm* being "the contracted Northern dual of *'ad*, 'hand,' a by-form of *yad*"; see Dahood, p. 95). Others speak of the wicked who "consider not the deeds of the Lord nor the works of his hands" (28:5). One psalmist tells God: "I meditate on your works; your exploits I ponder" (77:13). On the metaphor of "the shadow of the wings" (v 8), see §11b.

The obscurity of verse 14 has given rise to various interpretations. Two have been mentioned (CV and Weiser); three others are reflected in the following translations of (1) Pautrel, (2) JB, (3) Leveen:

(1) Anathematiza occidentes amicum tuum Domine,
   dele de terra partem eorum in vita.
   Et selectos tuos replebis, venter eorum saturabitur,
   et filii tradent reliquias suas parvulis suis.

(2) Rescue my soul from the wicked with your sword,
   with your hand, Yahweh, rescue me from men,
   from the sort of men whose lot is here and now.
   Cram their bellies from your stores,
   give them all the sons that they could wish for,
   let them have a surplus to leave their children!

(3) They that are perfect in thy ways will praise thee, O Lord:
   As for the perfect of this world, their portions is in this life;
   And for thy saints, thou wilt fill their belly,
   They will be satisfied with children,
   And shall leave their substance to their offspring.

In Dahood's translation, the psalmist then prophesies: "At my vindication I will gaze upon your face; At the resurrection I will be saturated with your being" (v 15). "At the resurrection," it is commented, seems to be the plain sense of *bᵉhāqîṣ*, when one compares it with the eschatological passage Is 26:19, "But your dead will live, their bodies will rise. Arise (*hāqîsû*) and sing, O you who dwell in the slime!", and Dn 12:2, "And many of those who sleep in the land of slime will arise (*yaqîṣû*), some to everlasting life, and others to everlasting reproach and contempt".... "In Ps 16:10f; 49:16; 73:23f," Dahood writes, "the psalmists express their conviction that they will be accorded the grace of assumption that was bestowed upon Enoch and Elijah." E. Podechard and others (cf. *BJ*) would reduce the psalmist's perspective: on waking he will be admitted again, so he hopes, in God's presence and will participate in the temple liturgy. In F. Asensio's view, however, this is not enough: what the psalmist tries to express is the hope for the just that after awakening from the sleep of death he will enjoy beatific vision (see also §14d and on Ps 17:15; cf. *Ps 5:4, and *RB* 1949, p. 489ff).

PSALM 22 (21)

Passion and Triumph of the Messiah

An extensive commentary would be appropriate for this important messianic psalm (cf. §16a), recited on the cross by Jesus (cf. Mt 27:46) and quoted in the Passion narrative (cf. Jn 19:24). The lament (vv 1-22) is followed by a thanksgiving (23-32), which may have been added when the worshipper obtained the assurance that his prayer had been heard. Some scholars believe, perhaps correctly, that the original psalm consisted of two sections: a lament (2-22) and a thanksgiving (23-27), both written out after the terrible experience had been lived through. Verses 28-32, they say, differ in style and subject-matter from what precedes. According to E. Podechard (p. 108), they would have been added later for use in the temple. In these verses the theme of the conversion of the nations is used to glorify the Lord, as in Ps 102:19-23. More precisely, writes A. Gelin, these verses, added about the end of the fourth century B.C., interpreted the whole psalm as concerning the future in a messianic sense.

The physical illness alluded to in the metaphors of verses 15-16 was aggravated by the sufferer's mental anguish at feeling himself forsaken by God. Figurative speech is also used by the poet when he describes his enemies as bulls, dogs or lions (vv 13, 14, 21, 22). The suppliant seeks comfort in recalling the saving deeds wrought for his people by God "enthroned on the praises of Israel (*yôshēb tehillôt yisrā'ēl*)" (vv 4-6), a peculiar designation of God "who is enthroned on the cherubim" (1 S 4:4; see below). He, on the contrary, feels himself to be put to shame, mocked, trampled underfoot, like a worm, by his adversaries (7-9). Is he not hoping for God in vain? The real sting of his suffering, Weiser believes, is the strain on his faith.

After a brief comforting recollection of his providential origin (10-11), the suppliant resumes his complaint (12-19) in terms even more pathetic. Fierce animals, his foes, surround him, his body disintegrates and he feels that God himself, his creator, has brought him down to the dust of death. But despite his extreme anxiety and suffering this great afflicted does not in his final prayer (20-22) call the judgment of God on his enemies but only asks to be delivered from their grip.

Somehow the suppliant's prayer has been heard and he is now participating in a communal thanksgiving service (23-27) where he recounts his experience, praises the Lord and invites the poor to share in the sacrificial banquet. The last part of the psalm (28-32), as it appears in our Psalter, is eschatological in character, and foresees the establishment of the kingdom of God. The first phase of eschatology has been realized with the advent of the messianic King, who through his death and resurrection brought salvation to the whole world (cf. §15). On vv 28-32 see O. Keel-Leu in *Bib* 51 (1970) 405-13.

It is noteworthy that the "just one" (*ḥāsîd*; cf. Ps 4:4) of this psalm makes no mention of his rights or of his sins and does not curse his adversaries. As both Gelin and Martin-Archard have pointed out, the original suppliant has been magnified by the liturgical use of the poem into an eschatological and oecumenical figure. So much so that some commentators, like G. Beer, have thought that the real subject of the psalm is "the people of Yahweh." It is said of this suffering *ḥāsîd* (cf. §12c) that he saved "many" *by his* "*sacrifice*," like the suffering servant of Isaiah 53 (cf. §15a), whose vicarious role is stressed throughout the whole poem (Is 52:13-53:12). Yet the conceptual pattern of Ps 22 follows the Deutero-Isaian thought-pattern: from failure and suffering to reinstatement and glory. Verbal reminiscences of Ps 22 did affect the Gospel narratives of our Lord's Passion (cf. J. Scheifler's + H. Gese's studies). The conclusion is not that the prophecy has brought about the "creation" of these narratives. It is rather that the evangelists have chosen to narrate those incidents of the Passion which were significant to the faith, the episodes namely that Old Testament prophecy was seen to have foretold (A. Gelin). The quotation of Ps 22 on the cross indicates that Jesus wanted to share the particular experience which God forced Israel to endure and which is echoed generally in the psalms of lamentation: the bitter experience of those who feel forsaken by God after having cast themselves entirely in his care and mercy (cf. G. von Rad, II, p. 377). Patristic writers, both from the East and from the West, have read in Ps 22:10a a prophecy concerning the special character of the birth of Christ (cf. J. A. de Aldana). The verse was associated with an

ancient belief of the Church: *virginitas in partu*. The relevance of the
association is more apparent in Dahood's translation: "Yet *you brought
me forth from the womb*, made me tranquil on my mother's breast."

Other remarks on the psalm concern philology rather than theology. Dahood reads in verse 4: "While you sit upon the holy throne
(*qādōš yošēb*), the Glory of Israel." *Qādōš*, "holy," becomes, by meto-
nymy, the name of the throne itself, as in Ps 114:2: "Judah became his
holy throne, Israel his kingdom" (cf. Ps 11:4). The same author translates verse 12: "Stay not far from me, for the adversaries (*sārāh*) are
near, for there is none to help." *Sārāh* ("distress" in *CV*) would be here
"an abstract form with a concrete meaning" (cf. Ps 13:5).

In v 17, the usual translation "they have pierced my hands and feet"
builds on a conjecture (others: "they have wounded"). *JB* notes that the
Passion narratives do not use the verse and translates verse 17c = 16c
(followed by 16c = 15c): "They tie me hand and foot and leave me lying
in the dust of death." A much more probable explanation is proposed by
Dahood in Psalms III, p. XXXI. The difficult *k'ry* would consist of the
conjunction *kî*, "because," followed by *'ry*: the verb *'ārāh*, "to pick,
pluck" (cf. Sg 5:1 and Ps 80:13) in the 3rd person perfect plural with
the final radical *-y* preserved ("as in Ugaritic regularly and sporadically
in Phoenician and Hebrew"). Thus Ps 22:17b-18 would read: "Because they picked clean (*'areyū*) my hands and feet, I can number all my
bones." This would be consonant with the description of the psalmist's
foes as dogs in v 17 and as devouring lions in vv 14 and 22. With these
Semitically conceived hyperbolic metaphors, to be understood figuratively,
the poet tries to convey to what physical and moral extremity his adversaries have reduced him. R. Tournay has just proposed independently
an explanation partly similar in *VT* 23 (1973) 111f. He vocalizes the
disputed MT *k'ry* as *ke'erô*, reading *waw* (infinitive construct) instead of
the final *yod*, and translates the whole term "comme pour déchiqueter
(mes mains et mes pieds)," "as if to tear into bits (my hands and feet)".
All considered, Dahood's presentation of the new interpretation seems
preferable. We also take note, however, of the solution very recently proposed by J.J.M. Roberts, "A New Root for an Old Crux, Ps 22, 17c,"
VT 23 (1973) 247-252. Basing his argumentation on a Semitic root
karû, "to be short," he reads in the verse a root *kārā(h)* V, "to be short,
shrunken, shrivelled," and translates: "My hands and my feet are shrivelled up, I can count all my bones."

The interpretation of verse 21 also is renewed in *The Anchor Bible*:

"Rescue my neck (*napsî*) from the sword, my face from the blade of the ax." *Nefes* (CV: "soul") does in fact mean "neck" in some biblical contexts (cf. Nb 11:6; Jb 7:15; Jon 2:6; Pss 69:2; 105:18) and the original meaning of Akkadian *napistu* is "throat." The *MT* of verse 21b offering a poor meaning, it is tempting to accept Dahood's interpretation, in which $y^e h \hat{i} d \bar{a} t \bar{i}$ ("my loneliness" in *CV*) would mean "my face." Compare with Is 40:5: "And the glory of Yahweh shall be revealed, and all flesh shall see his face (*yaḥdāw*)" (cf. *CBQ* 1958, pp. 46-49). In Ps 63: 11 $y^e d \bar{e}$ *ḥāreb* probably means "the edges of the sword," and sufficient evidence shows that consonantal *klb* "is a byform of *kēlappōt*, 'ax,'" which occurs in Ps 74:6." Both $k^e l \bar{o} b$ and *kēlūp*, "ax," are found in late Hebrew, Dahood adds (quoting G. Dalman, *Aramäisch-Neuhebräisches Wörterbuch*, Frankfurt a.M., 1897, p. 187ff), while Aramaic has *kūlbā*, "ax." "[Rescue] my face from the blade of the ax" offers certainly a better parallel to "[Rescue] my neck from the sword" than "[Rescue] my loneliness from the grip of the dog (*miyyad-keleb*)."

In v 22 the MT "from the horns of the wild oxen you have answered me (*ᵃnîtānî*, which Kraus retains)" gives no good sense. *NAB* reads (*ᵃniyyāti*, "my wretched (life)." It is probably preferable to follow Dahood, who parses *ᵃnîtanî* as precative perfect from *'ānāh*, "to conquer, triumph": "over the horns of wild oxen make me triumph" (see also Ps 18:36: "by your triumph you made me great").

More remarks on the text of this important psalm seems appropriate. Dahood proposes to read in verse 29: "For truly is Yahweh the king, and the ruler over the nations." The *lamedh* of *lyhwh* ("to the Lord") is here parsed as "emphatic *lamedh*" and its meaning expressed by "truly." A good parallel is quoted: *ke lyhwh mᵉgānēnū* (*MT māginnēnū*) *wᵉliqdōs yisrāēl malkēnū*, "For truly Yahweh himself is our Suzerain, the Holy One of Israel himself is our King" (Ps 89:19). As for *mᵉlūkāh* (*CV*, "kingdom") in our verse "it traces a semantic development much like that of Hebrew-Phoenician abstract *mmlkt*, 'royalty, kingdom,' which frequently denotes concretely, 'king.'" The biblical texts supplied as examples do not seem too convincing. Another instance of *lē'* (for *MT lō'*), meaning "the Victor" (cf. on *Ps 7:13), is offered by the last stich of verse 30, where instead of "and to him my soul shall live" Dahood reads: "For the Victor himself restores to life." Of the many examples cited, one is particularly striking:

"For he is the Victor from the East and from the West;

he is the Victor from the desert to the mountains" (Ps 75:7).

N. Airoldi would, however, use differently the emphatic *lamedh* and translate the last colon of v 30: "he himself *certainly* will live" (*Augustinianum* 1971, pp. 565-69). On Ps 22 and the priestly oracle of salvation see R. Kilian in *BZ* 12 (1968) 172-85. On Ps 22 and the New Testament see the study of J. R. Scheifler and also H. Gese in *Theology Digest* 18 (1970) 237-43 (from German *ZTK* 65, 1968, 1-22).

PSALM 25 (24)

Prayer for Guidance and Help

This rather peaceful lament of a pensive and solitary soul is laid down in an alphabetical psalm (cf. §6d) consisting of three almost equal stanzas. The psalmist is deeply convinced that it is a grace to follow always the path of the Lord, so he prays "God of his salvation" to make him walk in his truthfulness (v 5). Twice in the psalm (vv 7, 18) he asks to be forgiven his sins, especially those of his youth (cf. §12e). By the grace of God, who "shows sinners the way" (v 8), he has abandoned his evil ways. Wisdom concepts are represented even better in the second stanza, which contains a remarkable formulation of a basic *Heilsgeschichte* principle: "All the paths of the Lord are kindness (*hesed*) and constancy" (*'emet*; cf. Ex 34:6: "kindness and fidelity"; cf. §11f). This should apply also to the psalmist in distress, if only his sins are forgiven (16-21). The concluding verse does not fit in the alphabetical structure. It was apparently added later, when the psalm was adopted by the cult community.

The text of the psalm presents few problems. Instead of "guide me in your truth" (v 5) Dahood reads "make me walk faithful to you" (literally: "in fidelity to you"). If the psalmist's "great" sin (v 11; cf. Ps 19: 14) and the sins of his youth (v 7) refer to idolatry, as it is certainly possible, then comparison can be made with Ps 86:11: "Teach me, O Lord, your way that I may walk in your truth (*ba'amittekā*); direct my heart that it may fear your name." Here, says Dahood, *ba'amittekā* is employed "in the context of a profession of faith in Yahweh and a repudiation of the pagan deities" (cf. Ps 26:3). In verse 14, *CV* reads, correctly it seems, *sod* as meaning "friendship," which stands parallel to

b^erît, "covenant." That these two notions were associated comes out clearly in the three occurrences of the expression *'dy' wtbt'*, 'the treaty and the friendship,' in the Aramaic treaty texts of Sefire (cf. W. L. Moran, "A Note on the Treaty Terminology of the Sefire Stelas," *JNES* 22, 1963, pp. 173-6). Dahood also recalls on verse 21 that "integrity and uprightness" are "personified as two messengers sent by God to accompany and protect the psalmist." "Light and fidelity," "kindness and truth," "goodness and kindness" are similarly presented in other psalms (23:6; 43:3; 57:11; 62:8; cf. §11ef).

PSALM 26 (25)

Prayer of an Innocent Man

Falsely accused in the name of the sacral law, an innocent man willingly submits to an oath of exculpation (cf. *Pss 7, 26) and other purification ceremonies (cf. Dt 21:6; Ps 73:13), which includes negative confessions (vv 1-8; cf. *Ps 101). Yet he admits his fallibility and asks for moral preservation and even redemption (9-12). Some expressions in the psalm do in fact point to a "supplication": "Do me justice!" (v 3), "Gather not my soul with those of sinners" (v 9), "Redeem me, and have pity on me" (v 11). Not all commentators, as will be seen, admit that the psalm is a lament, since it is not clear what the psalmist is complaining about. But in Dahood's translation of verse 3 recurs the expression "to walk faithful to you" (cf. Ps 25:5). Here again this is taken to indicate that the psalmist has been accused of idol-worship (see on Pss 5:6f; 17:3; 19:14; 31:7). Other verses of Ps 26 would point to the same accusation. When, for example, the psalmist says, "I have washed my hands in innocence," his statement is that he has kept himself free of the sin of idolatry, "if the cognate expression of Ps 24:4 is exegetically relevant": "the clean of hands and the pure of heart, who has not raised his mind to an idol." The "sinners" and the "men of blood" (see on Ps 5:8) of verse 9 are "polytheists" and "men of idols" (cf. Ps 139:19). On their (left) hand are "idols" (*zimmāh;* see on *Ps 17:3) while their right hand is full of "bribes." M. H. Pope denies, however, that *zimmāh* means "idols" that could be held in the hand; it is a general term for wickedness, especially of a sexual nature, and can be used metaphorically for idolatry (*JBL* 1966, p. 458). It is claimed by some authors (cf. *ZAW*

1963, p. 91f) that *miškan* (v 8; tabernacle, *habitaculum*) is a Canaanite loanword in the cultic language of Jerusalem. As used for God's dwelling during the wilderness period (cf. Ex 26:1; 6f) the word could well be rendered "tent-shrine" (cf. *HUCA* 1961, p. 92).

A different interpretation of the psalm has been proposed by E. Vogt. A "protestation of innocence" (*Unschuldsbeteuerung*), he writes, need not be associated with laments (*Klagelieder*). It is in fact true, as we shall see, that such declarations belong also to the "liturgies of entry," as reflected in Pss 15 and 24 (cf. §32). It is Vogt's opinion that Ps 26 reflects the *Torliturgie* of a pilgrim. But it is not the priest's monition that is heard here, but the voice of the pilgrim, who declares that he has fulfilled all the conditions of admittance to the sanctuary. Yet he experiences sacred fear before the majesty and the holiness of God and his temple. This mixed feeling of joy and fear would explain that this innocent man prays for "justice" and "redemption." As Briggs writes (I, p. 230), "this profession of integrity is not so inappropriate as many moderns think. It is not self-righteousness. It is not so much self-conscious, as conscious of the divine presence and the requirements to invoke it." L. A. Snijders, for his part, observes that an affirmation of innocence is not a profession of absolute guiltlessness (cf. §12e). Its purpose is to destroy unfounded suspicions. If this is true, then Ps 26 could very well reflect a series of false accusations and be the lament of an accused. In connection with his category of "national psalms of lamentation" Mowinckel (I, 207) cites Pss 5, 7, 12, 26 to illustrate the following remark: "Even in the I-psalms where an individual is speaking on behalf of the congregation, we are often assured that he is 'guiltless,' 'has not transgressed thy commandments,' and that therefore the enemies 'hate him without cause' or even because of his piety" (cf. Ps 69:10).

Psalm 28 (27)

Petition and Thanksgiving

In this lament, as in Ps 26, the psalmist insists that he had nothing to do with evildoers (cf. Ps 43:1): perhaps an anticipation of a judgment of God expected in the cult. By means of the blessing and the curse, Weiser thinks, the members of the covenant community meant to express and even to effect their separation from the unworthy elements in their midst (cf. Dt 27:11ff). In the second part of the psalm (vv 6-9), the suppliant, convinced that the Lord has heard him, formulates his thanksgiving (cf. *Ps 6). His assurance, the mention of the "anointed" and the people, the *Heilsgeschichte* theme, all these elements indicate that his personal prayer was formulated in the framework of a communal cult celebration. "Psalm 28 is, in all probability, a psalm referring to the king's sickness, although it may be uncertain whether this psalm was originally made for this definite occasion or whether an older psalm has been adapted" (Mowinckel, I, p. 74). A psalm mentioning the king would have a pre-exilic origin. The welfare of the king was of course a concern for the whole people. This is reflected in verse 8: "The Lord is the strength of his people, the saving refuge of his anointed," as it is in King Hezekiah's hymn of thanksgiving (Is 38:9-20). A peril is threatening the "anointed" (cf. §15c) and the people, but it is neither specified nor past. These two elements combined suggest to Mowinckel (I, p. 219f) that Ps 28, like Pss 61 and 63, is at once "a royal psalm" and a "protective psalm" (cf. *Ps 103), this last type being related to the "national psalms of lamentation."

Dahood's translation of verse 8 runs as follows: "Yahweh is our stronghold and our refuge, the Savior of his anointed is he." In the phrase *yhwh 'ōz* (see on Ps 8:3) *lāmō umā'ōz* ("refuge"), the word *lāmō* must mean "for us" (cf. *lānū* in Ps 46:2) as in Pss 44:11; 64:5; 80:7; Is 26:16; 44:7; Jb 22:17. In Is 53:8 *lāmō* would mean "by us," not without theological implications: "for the crime of his people he was smitten *by us.*" The "Savior" translates *yešū'ōt*, here as in Pss 42:6, 12; 43:5; it is an abstract plural ("salvations") with a concrete meaning.

Psalm 31 (30)

Prayer in Distress and Thanksgiving for Escape

Here again a thanksgiving (vv 20-25) is added to the lament. Not a few elements in the psalm seem to indicate that the supplication was recited amidst the cult community after it had been answered (cf. v 21). The abundance of stereotyped forms in the psalm points to an exceptional familiarity of the author with the traditional vocabulary of the lament. The man seems to have been ill (vv 10, 11, 13), certainly he was persecuted (9, 12, 14, 16) and he worried a lot about his reputation (12, 14, 19, 21). "Into your hands I commend my spirit" (v 6): this phrase, immortalized on the Cross (Lk 23:46; cf. Ac 7:59), was form-

ulated, it seems, by the psalmist in the temple, where he had sought
refuge from his enemies and from his affliction (vv 1-9). Abandoned, as
he thinks, by his friends, he seeks relief in lament and prayer, opening his
burdened heart to the Lord and expressing his ardent trust in God (vv 10-
19). In the thanksgiving section (20-25) the psalmist lauds above all else
God's kindness and seems to recall that his faith wavered during his ordeal (v 23). Now he leaves his isolation for a fellowship with the community (24-25). The phrase: "in your justice (*ṣᵉdāqâh*) rescue me" (v
2) is one of several psalms' formulations which bring out the saving aspect
of God's justice (cf. §11e).

The *lamedh,* supposedly a kind of grammatical *passepartout* in Ugaritic, proves handy also in Hebrew. In Ps 31:2f the *lamedh vocativum*
appears again (cf. Ps 33:1) in *The Anchor Bible* to introduce a series of
divine names: "O Eternal One," "O mountain of refuge," "O fortified
citadel"! Its presence does not seem equally compelling in all the cases
enumerated by Dahood in the commentary of Ps 3:9. But it is well to
note this: "The bearing of the Ras Shamra tablets on biblical philology
is most widely felt in the study and interpretation of prepositions" (on
Ps 31:10). The *MT sānē'tî,* "I hate," seems acceptable in verse 7, as "a
terminus technicus used in the formal repudiation of idolatry or charges
of idolatry" (cf. *Ps 5:6). Thus, notes Dahood, the psalmist repudiates a
sin which among the Israelites was believed to be one of the chief causes
of sickness or other misfortunes. The repudiation of false gods was one
of the primary duties of the members of the covenant (cf. Dt 13:7-12;
17:2-5).

The dense consonantal Hebrew phrase *ydmw lš'l* (v 18), "let them
[the wicked] be reduced to silence in the nether world" (*CV*) becomes
in *The Anchor Bible:* "Let the wicked be humiliated, *hurled into Sheol!*"
On the strength of Ex 15:16, *yuddum* (encl. *mem*) *kā'eben,* "they were
hurled like a stone" (cf. Ne 9:11), one is justified, writes Dahood, in
vocalizing *yuddum lisᵉōl,* from the verb *nādāh,* "to hurl, cast," well
known from Akkadian and fully attested in Ugaritic. The final *m* is *mem
encliticum,* "a stylistic balance that recurs in Ps 109:13, 15; Jb 29;
36:15" (*Psalms I,* p. 34; cf. Dahood's art. of Bib 1956, p. 338ff; cf. on
*Ps 18). The Septuagint's *katachteiêsen,* "they are driven down," evinces
a similar understanding of the phrase, Dahood adds, "while Ps 55:16 and
Ezk 31:16 express equally unholy sentiments" (cf. §14d on "imprecations,") Another phrase, *be'îr māṣōr* (*CV* "in a fortified city") difficult
in the context, receives a plausible interpretation as read by Dahood:

"Praise to Yahweh, for he has shown me wondrous kindness *from the fortified city*" (v 22). The preposition *b* often denotes "from" in Hebrew poetry, and "the fortified city" would be "a poetic name for the heavenly abode of Yahweh" (cf. Pss 18:7; 74:20).

PSALM 35 (34)

Prayer for Help against Unjust Enemies

This is the lament of a man persecuted by enemies and former friends alike. "Unjust witnesses" have testified against him, they have repaid him evil for good. When they were ill he had compassion on them (11-14). They are "unprovoked enemies," "undeserved foes" (v 19). Using metaphorical language he calls on God to stand against them like a warrior (cf. §13d), to let his angel execute his judgment (1-6). Better yet, let evil produce its own punishment (cf. §12e): "Let the snare they have set catch them; into the pit they have dug let them fall" (v 8; cf. Pss 7:16; 54:7; 57:7; Pr 26:27; Si 10:8), and thus will the Lord be glorified (v 27). Between bursts of imprecations (cf. §14d) he manages twice to anticipate the victory God's help will provide: "I will rejoice in the Lord" (v 9); "I will give you thanks in the vast assembly" (v 18; cf. Ps 22:26). The final word of his passionate soul is also one of hope: "my tongue shall recount your justice" (*sedeq;* cf. §11e).

Dahood proposes to read in verse 6: "Let their destiny be Darkness and Destruction, with the angel of Yahweh pursuing them." "Darkness," "Destruction," he writes, are poetic names for the underworld. The first expression is used in 1 S 2:9; Ps 88:13; Jb 22:11, etc., while "Destruction" would stem from *ḥlq,* "to perish" (cf. Pss 5:10; 73:18). Jr 23:12 can be read in the same way: "And so their way shall be like Perdition to them; they shall be thrust into Darkness and fall into it." "Dark and slippery," however, are also appropriate expressions for describing the way to Sheol (cf. §14d). Mowinckel observes (II, p. 87) that "the quiet in the land" (v 20), a hapax legomenon, "does not mean a special social milieu, nor a special pious tendency or pious milieu, but is a poetical term for the congregation or people itself, which wants to live in peace with its neighbors and oppressors...." This could be correct but Dahood translates *rig'e 'āreṣ* as "the oppressed in the land": "For they do not speak of peace, but attack the oppressed in the land" (see on *Ps 30: 6).

PSALM 36 (35)

Human Wickedness and Divine Providence

Hans Schmidt divides the poem into two psalms: a prophetic word (vv 1-5 and 13) and a cultic hymn (6-12). But with Kraus, Weiser and others, it is better to maintain the unity of the psalm. The solution of *one* problem is sought: how to reconcile the reality of sin with the belief in God? The first part, sapiential in tone, describes the state of a man subject to evil (2-5). For him the voice of sin has replaced the word of God and there is no remedy to his delusion and hardness of heart. The best answer to human wickedness is the expression of faith in God's providence (6-10; cf. §11b). The worshippers "feast on the fat of the temple" in sacrificial meals symbolizing communion with God, fountain of life and light. But such a faith is also a gift and the psalmist asks for the grace to resist temptation: "Let not the foot of the proud overtake me nor the hand of the wicked disquiet me" (v 12). The peculiar form of the wording in the last verse (v 13), Weiser believes, seems to point to a judgment on the sinner, executed by means of a ritual act in the cult of the covenant. If this is true, the verse provides the *raison d'être* of the whole psalm, which, Mowinckel (II, p. 13) notes, is written "with all the traditional elements but with a rich and free formulation."

It is natural to assume that deep truths lie in the background of verse 10: "For with you is the fountain of life, and in your light we see light" (*CV*). To let the text yield a more satisfactory interpretation Dahood proposes "a distinction between the homographs *'wr* (*'ōr*), 'light,' and *'wr* (*'ūr*), 'field.'" In Ps 56:14 it would be possible to read: "to walk before God in the field of life (*beʾūr hahayyīm*)," in parallel with Ps 116:9: "I shall walk before Yahweh in the fields of life (*bearṣōt hahayyīm*)." In the poetic passages, it is argued, exists the motif of the *Elysian fields,* "the abode of the blessed after death." Some texts have to be understood accordingly:

Ps 36:10: "Truly with you is the fountain of life,
in your field we shall see the light."

Is 26:19: "Your dead shall live, their bodies will rise;
those who dwell in the dust will awake
and sing for joy:

For your dew is the dew of the fields,
but the land of the Shades will be parched."

Jb 33:30: "All these things God does,
twice or thrice over with a man,
To turn back his soul from the pit,
that he might be resplendent in the field of life."

It is worth noticing that in *'ūr kasdîm*, "Ur Chaldaeorum" (Gn 11:28, 31; 15:7; Ne 9:7). *'ūr* is always translated in the Septuagint by *chōra*, "land, region." Could it be that Abraham's homeland is not, after all, specified the way it was hitherto thought? Be it what it may, the teaching of Ps 36:10b would then be the following: "in your field we shall see the light," i.e., "the light of your face in the beatific vision" (cf. Ps 17:15). In Is 53:11, adds Dahood, the LXX reading has found confirmation in the Qumran text (*1QIsᵃ*): *yir'eh'ōr*, "he shall see the light" i.e., "the suffering servant will be rewarded with immortality for his vicarious suffering." Not unrelated with the "Elysian fields" is the theme *ṣᵉdāqāh*="meadow," which will be examined in connection with *Ps 143:10f.

PSALM 38 (37)

Prayer of an Afflicted Sinner

This is another penitential psalm (cf. *Ps 6). The heading "for remembrance" probably alludes to the "memorial sacrifice" (cf. Lv 2:2, 9, 16; 5:12; Is 66:3). The psalm has an alphabetic structure (22 verses, heading omitted) without the alphabetic acrostic. "The 22-verse structure is a literary convention which characterizes laments" (Dahood). In fact chapters 1, 2, 4, 5 of the Book of Lamentations have 22 verses. Whereas in Ps 6, which opens in much the same way, the psalmist does not confess or deny his guilt, the suppliant of Ps 38 feels overwhelmed by his iniquities (vv 4, 5) and openly acknowledges his guilt (v 19), although he also (cf. Ps 35:12) is repaid evil for good (vv 20f).

The disease mentioned in verse 6-11 is of a sort (perhaps leprosy) that was especially considered a punishment for sin (vv 2-4; cf. Ps 91:5) and for that reason also, the sufferer's friends turn away from him (v 12). Taking into account the psalm's Canaanite background, the illness could

also be identified as pestilence. The divine "arrows" of verse 3 would reflect a theme associated with the "Canaanite god of pestilence," called
"Resheph the archer" (Ugar. text 1001:3, Gordon, p. 214) or "Resheph
of the arrow" (4th century Phoenician inscription). The theme, Dahood
suggests, "has been adopted by Hebrew poets to express the belief that
illness comes from Yahweh" (cf. Dt 32:23f; Jb 6:4; 16:12f). More
probably perhaps, little can be known of the nature of the illness: its
description is couched in a rich display of conventional imagery and
hyperbolic semitisms (cf. Ezr 9:6). "Your arrows have sunk deep in me"
is, according to *BJ*, anthropomorphic language to designate God-sent
trials: Dt 32:23; Ex 5:16; Lm 3:12f; Jb 6:4.

Like the man of Ps 39 (vv 2, 3, 10) and like the suffering servant (Is
53:7), the character of Ps 38 bears patiently his terrible lot, opens not
his mouth (vv 14-15), and refrains from hurling imprecations at his
enemies. He breaks his silence only to say: "Forsake me not, O Lord; my
God, be not far from me! Make haste to help me, O Lord my salvation!"
(vv 22f) The psalm adapts itself easily for recitation in the Church's
choral office on Good Friday. So much so that some Greek manuscripts
and versions add: "They have rejected me, the loved one, like a hideous
corpse" (cf. Is 14:19), an allusion to the crucified Christ; the Coptic
version, still more explicitly: "They have nailed my flesh" (*JB*).

PSALM 39 (38)

The Brevity and Vanity of Life

In this, as in the preceding psalm, a man confesses to be justly afflicted by God (v 10) on account of his sins (vv 9, 12) and also en-
deavors to control his tongue (vv 2, 3, 10). Yet he cannot refrain from
applying to himself what Ecclesiastes teaches about the brevity and vanity
of life (vv 5-7). Having reduced himself to a "phantom," a "vapor," he
is in good standing to set his hope in God alone (v 8). While psalmists
generally say to God "turn toward me" (cf. 86:16), this "pilgrim" (v 13)
entreats the Lord: "Turn your gaze from me, that I may find respite ere
I depart and be no more" (v 14). *BJ* describes Ps 39 as an elegy similar
to Ps 88. Since one kind of illness was often considered as a divine
scourge (v 11; cf. Nb 12:9f), it can almost be assumed that the suppliant of Ps 39 had a "stroke" of leprosy (cf. Lv 13:2f). Commentators
A. Maillot and A. Lelièvre consider Ps 39 as singularly "original," a sort

of unconscious answer to Ps 37. The psalmist does not pretend to propose a teaching but tries to express his torment to the Lord.

PSALM 42 (41)

Desire for God and His Temple

PSALM 43 (42)

These two psalms (42 and 43) form one poem, of which the third stanza is Ps 43. This is indicated by the uniform subject-matter and by the recurrence of an identical refrain (42:6, 12; 43:5). In fine lyrical style the psalmist describes his homesickness caused by his being away from the temple, where he held a leading role in the liturgy (42:5). He is exiled in Northern Palestine, where cataracts roar down the Hermon (vv 7-8). But he finds renewed courage in his faith and he hears a voice saying: Hope in God! (v 12). The question, "Where is your God?", is one which characterizes the nature of disbelief in God in biblical times (see §10a). Psalm 43 was formerly alluded to at the Roman Mass by the priest, before he went up "to the altar of God" (v 4).

Mowinckel lists Ps 42-43 among those "I"-psalms, which, although apparently quite personal, are in reality national (congregational) psalms (I, p. 219). And he is careful to note: "Even if psalms like 23 or 51 or 42-43 are expressions of personal experiences and feelings and of a quite personal piety, we should not be justified in concluding that the psalms in question were not written to be used in the cult" (II, p. 20). And a note tries to explain how this can be adapted to the poet's situation: "During the monarchy cultic acts might be performed in any holy place; or any place might for the special occasion be sanctified for an act of Sacrifice, see 1 S 14:33f." Gunkel's deduction (Einleitung..., p. 262), he adds, that Pss 42-43, 55, 61 and 120 were composed "in the exile" is a deduction based on erroneous exegesis; the passages prove only that the psalm in question (i.e., 42-43) was composed for use somewhere away from Yahweh's city and temple.

If *'ālay* in Ps 42:6 means "before me," then v 6a (cf. v 12 and Ps 43: 5) can be translated: "Why are you so sad, O my soul? And why do you sigh *before me?*" Twice in Ps 42 (vv 6, 12) and once in Ps 43 (v 5) occurs the phrase *yᵉšû'ôt pānay wē'lōhay* (litt: "the salvation of my face and my God"). Some commentators read in *yᵉšû'ôt* the divine name

"Savior" (cf. §11d), morphologically explained as an abstract *plurale majestatis* with a concrete meaning (see on *Ps 28:8). Furthermore, *pānay* can be rendered "my Presence," Dahood thinks, and thus the psalmist would tell his soul in Ps 42:12b: "Wait for God, for I shall still praise him, my Savior, my Presence, and my God." The "Presence" is in fact what preserves the Covenant. The Covenant is severed when God withdraws (Ho 5:6; Ezk 10:2ff). A. Weiser reads Ps 42:3b as "When may I come and appear before the face of God?", giving a liturgical ring to the poet's visit to the sanctuary (cf. Ps 118:19; Is 1:12).

The geographical position of the poet is rather confusingly stated in Ps 42:7b: "From the land of the Jordan and of Hermon, from Mount Misar." G. Dalman thought he could identify Misar as a small hill N-E of Banyas on the Hermon slopes (cf. *Palästina Jahrbuch,* Berlin, 5, 1909, p. 101ff). The problem of identification is eliminated if the whole psalm is understood figuratively, that is, Dahood writes, as the biblical version of "The Dark Night of the Soul." The psalmist, who had enjoyed God's consoling grace, "finds himself in a state of extreme desolation because God has withdrawn his spiritual favors. He compares his wretchedness to the cheerless existence of Sheol." Sheol, in fact, is what is described in verses 7-8, according to Dahood:

> My soul before me is very sad
>   because I remember you,
> From the land of descent and of nets,
>   from the mountains at the rim;
> Where deep calls to deep,
>   at the peal of your thunderbolts;
> And all your breakers and your billows
>   pass over me.

This interpretation has a better chance of being true, of course, if personified Death is close at hand, as verse 10 would affirm it: "My prayer to my living God: I shall say: O El, my Rock, why have you forgotten me? Why must I go in gloom because of harassment by the Foe, because of the Assassin within my bones?" In that context "my Rock" is doubly relevant, for "Sheol was considered a vast quagmire with no firm footing" (Ps 69:3). Similar imagery, adds Dahood, is used in Ps 61:3 (his translation): "From the brink of the nether world to you I call, as faint grows my heart. From it lead me to the Lofty Mountain" (see on Sheol: §14d).

PSALM 51 (50)

The Miserere: Prayer of Repentance

The *Miserere* is quite a common feature in the Jewish as well as in the Christian penitential liturgy. Rightly so, since it describes, in moving terms, a true conception of penitence. After calling on the mercy of God (vv 3-4) the psalmist confesses his sin (5-8), then asks to be purified, renovated and cured (vv 9-14). Finally he promises to give thanks and to work for the conversion of sinners (15-21). The prayer of the *Miserere* reaches the depths of human nature itself and thus it belongs to all men. As such it was easily received in the Jewish and Christian communities as a collective lament and supplication.

The title (vv 1-2) ascribes the psalm to David, "when Nathan the prophet came to him after his sin with Bethsabee." But there is nothing in the psalm itself which directly supports this attribution, while some indications contradict it. The last two verses (20-21) point to the period which preceded the building of the second temple (520-515 B.C.) or of the Jerusalem walls (445 B.C.). But if, as it seems, they are later additions, the original psalm can be pre-exilic. L. Neve objects to Dalglish's thesis that the psalm was written to be "spoken by or for the king," namely Josiah, and rejects his main argument, that the Spirit (cf. v 13) was considered to be the permanent possession of the Davidides. Rather, he sees that what has only been promised for the future by Ezk 36:25-27, or by Jr 31:31-34 on the change of heart (cf. Ps 51:12), has been considered as realized in his own life by the psalmist" ("Realized Eschatology in Ps 51;" Exp T 80, 1968f, 264-68).

Not a few instructive statements on penitence are clearly expressed in the psalm: sins must be confessed; sin is primarily an offense of God; sin has deep roots in our human nature; contrition has more value than the offering of sacrifices; the grace of God is needed for conversion and for renewal of the heart and spirit. Our penitent does not say to God as the suppliant of Ps 32, "Forgive me because I confess my sin" (v 5), but "Purify me, because I am defiled" (v 9), an attitude founded on deeper humility. Nothing indicates that the man was a public sinner, but he has a deep sense of his innate corruption (cf. §12e). Remarkably the afflicted man is mainly concerned with moral cure, although physical cure may be hinted at in the phrase "the bones you have crushed shall rejoice" (v 10). Deliverance from physical peril could be prayed for if verse 16a is thus understood: "Save me from [premature] death, God my savior" (cf. *JB* and Ps 30:10; Pr 1:18). Psalm 51 shows affinities with Pss 6, 38, 40, but in contrast with these no other enemy is mentioned than sin, guilt and perhaps death. Not conversion or even purification is enough for our psalmist; sinners must be regenerated if future sins are to be avoided (v 12), because the remedy must reach as deep as the root of the evil. In the prophets (cf. Jr 24:7; Ezk 36:26) God took the initiative to renovate interiorly. Here the penitent asks for it. It will be the work of the "holy spirit" (v 13), source of moral life for the individual (cf. Ps 143:10) and the community (cf. Is 63:11).

In the last section of the psalm (vv 15-21) the penitent promises a thanksgiving, an essential duty of the biblical man visited by God. His cure itself will be a teaching which his word will confirm (vv 15-17). The psalmists often mention a sacrificial oblation in the ritual of thanksgiving (cf. Ps 66:13ff). The difficult passage, "for you are not pleased with sacrifices; should I offer a holocaust, you would not accept it," can be explained, like some prophetic sayings, as a "dialectical negation," in which "though the expression of condemnation is unconditional, it should be taken in a relative sense" (R. de Vaux, *Ancient Israel*, p. 454; cf. *VT* 1954, p. 385ff). Here it would mean: I prefer the sacrifice of a contrite spirit to ritual sacrifices. If verses 20-21 were added to the psalm after the exile, a ritually minded scribe would have attenuated the previous statement by his restricting observation. Apart from these two verses a terminus a quo (c. 800 B.C.) for the composition of the psalm seems implied in the teaching of the prophets: verses 12-14, on the purity of heart and on obedience, would reflect Jr 24:7; 31:33; Ezk 11:19; 36:25ff, while verses 18-19, on the relative value of sacrifice, remind of Am 5:22; Is 1:11; Mi 6:7; Jr 6:20.

Psalm 51 testifies, writes Mowinckel, (II, 17), to true personal piety, and was evidently written "by an individual who has grasped something very essential in the relationship between God and man. However, this does not prove that the reason for his prayer and confession of sin need be of a private nature." If the last two verses are to be included in the original composition, he adds, "it is more natural to think of a person in a condition much like that of Nehemiah when rebuilding the walls of Jerusalem, and of the hostility to which he was exposed on the part of political antagonists. And on the merits of the case the psalm will then have to be ranked among the public psalms, in which the whole congregation joins with the worshipper, while he officiates as the public religious spokesman of the congregation in a matter concerning them all." But perhaps the allusion to rebuilding the walls (vv 20-21) is too vague to warrant a personal connection with Nehemiah and Mowinckel's reasoning seems to miss the essential message of the psalm: the seriousness and significance of personal sin. Various elements of the psalm are eschatological in character, R. Press believes, and would reflect the exilic period, when sacrifices could not be offered, while the future was envisaged in a cultic setting (cf. Ezk 40-48). These eschatological realities include the "Holy Spirit" (v 13; cf. Jl 3:1ff; Tt 3:5; Ac 2:16), "blood" (v 16; cf. Ezk 38:22), and "clean heart" (v 12; cf. Ezk 36:16ff; 29ff). The "hyssop," mentioned in verse 9, is "a small bush whose many woody twigs made a natural sprinkler. It was prescribed in the Mosaic Law as an instrument for scattering sacrificial blood or lustral water on persons to be ritually cleansed. Cf. Ex 12:22; Lv 14:4; Nb 19:18. These ceremonies were mere symbols of purification; here the psalmist prays that God may effectively 'un-sin' him, as the Hebrew literally means" (NAB). Instead of MT harbeh, "much," it is possible to read with Dahood (vol. 2, 2nd edit.) the energetic hiphil hāribbāh, "rain down," which would form an inclusion with hētibâh, "make beautiful," in v. 20. Thus verse 4 would read: "Rain down, wash me of my guilt, and of my sin clean me." On this proposition see also Dahood, Psalms III, p. xxxi f.

Verse 7 is obviously important for Old Testament "hamartiology," theology of sin. The Jerusalem Bible translates it: "You know I was born guilty, a sinner from the moment of conception," and adds the comment: "Man is born in a state of impurity (Jb 14:4; cf. Pr 20:9), which is an implicit recognition of his tendency to evil (Gn 8:21). This basic impurity is here pleaded as a mitigating circumstance (cf. 1 K 8:46), which God should take into account. The doctrine of original sin will be proposed explicitly (Rm 5:12-21) in connection with the revelation of redemption by Jesus Christ." Mowinckel's translation of the verse, as it appears in Ap-Thomas' text, runs as follows:

'Twas stained with sin that I was born.
Sinful I was conceived in my mother's womb.

Neither any sinful disorder on the part of the progenitors, nor impurity in the conception, nor the doctrine of "original sin" are implied in this statement, comments Mowinckel. Rather "it is the strongest possible expression on the part of the author of the consciousness that as a weak and frail man he has never been without sin—from his very birth he has given offense in some thing or other. We must consider this against the background of the idea of unconscious sinning, which may happen to anybody at any moment" (cf. §12e). The commentator does not say what he means by "unconscious sinning." Would it be something approaching "the doctrine of original sin"? A. Feuillet believes that the affirmation in the verse of a native state of degeneracy affecting all men is a "serious preparation" for the Pauline doctrine of original sin, especially in view of the general context of the Old Testament. Yet neither explicitly nor implicitly does the verse affirm any connection between "the child's sin" and the Fall in paradise. Only by reading the verse in the light of the New Testament can this connection be seen and a meaning given, deeper and fuller than that perceived by the inspired writer.

According to E. Beaucamp's interpretation, the conceptual pattern of the first part of the psalm, in its primitive state at least, ran as follows: "Forgive me" (vv 3-4) . . . because I have sinned (vv 5-6a) . . . that you may be justified (v 6b). It is God's saving justice (cf. §11e) which is here in cause and not the vindication of any punishment, as the CV text implies. This problem will be examined more fully in connection with Ps 143:1, but the meaning of verse 6b seems to be the following: "That you may appear as just in your word and blameless in your judgment." The "word of God" here alludes generally to the often proclaimed disposition of God toward mercy (cf. Ex 34:6). When God punishes, it is to cure and thus is he blameless in his judgments, since they follow the path of mercy. Besides, as Lyonnet has pointed out, St. Paul, in Rm 3:5, gave to "David's confession" the traditional Jewish meaning of the "confessions of sins": in addition to repentance and humility the penitent expresses faith in God who fulfills *exactly* his promises of salvation.

In a recent study, A. Caquot again proposes that Ps 51 be interpreted as a collective lament of the exile period. The psalmist hopes that the sufferings of the exiled community will be accepted as a sacrifice worthy of God's pardon (vv 18f). His views are similar to those of Isaiah 53, interpreted collectively (see §15a and O. Kaiser, *Der königliche Knecht,* Göttingen, 1959). Verse 7 would refer to guilty Jerusalem (cf. Ezk 16: 1ff; 23:25), while the 'crushed bones' of verse 10 and the 'blood guilt' of verse 16 would allude to other themes of the exile prophets, mainly Ezekiel (cf. 7:23; 9:9; 37:1-14).

Dahood, however, solves otherwise the "blood-guilt" problem of verse 16a. He reads: "Deliver me *from the tears of death,* O God, my God," pointing *dammīm,* from *dāmam,* "to weep": cf. Psalms, I, p. 24 (on Ps 4:5: " upon your beds weep"!) and (*CBQ*, 1960, pp. 400-3): "Just as *māwet,* 'death,' can also denote 'the place of death, namely, Sheol' (e.g., Ps 6:6), so *dammīm* may have come to signify the place of tears par excellence... The connection between *dammīn,* 'tears,' and the nether world has been preserved in a misunderstood verse of Si 9:9: "Lest you permit your heart to succumb to her, and in tears you descend to the Pit" (*Psalms,* II, p. 8).

PSALM 54 (53)

Confident Prayer in Great Peril

Having been rescued from his distress (v 9) this persecuted man praises the name of the Lord and prepares to offer a sacrifice. Supplication is, however, the main theme of the psalm. The suppliant's cruel (*'ārîsîm*) enemies are called "strangers" (*zārîm*), mainly, it seems, because they are ungodly (v 5), while for the psalmist "God is my helper" (v 6). It seems that the suppliant had recourse both to a human court of justice (v 3) and to God's judgment (v 7) against his enemies. He wishes that they be destroyed, thus revealing the imperfection of his own religious sentiments.

The vow (cf. 8) being by its very nature a personal matter, it is found mainly in the "I"-psalms (cf. §23a). Of these, writes Mowinckel (I, p. 217), "a great many...are actually collective psalms in which an individual is speaking on behalf of the congregation. Ps 54 is one of these." Votive sacrifices are also mentioned in at least one of the collective thanksgivings (Ps 66). If the psalmist anticipates his rescue (v 9), it could be after learning somehow in the cult (see on *Ps 6) that his petition has been granted. The quotation in the heading, "David is hiding among us" (1 S 23:19), was apparently suggested by the similarity between "fierce men *seek my life*" (v 5) and 1 S 23:15: "And David was afraid because Saul had come out to *seek his life.*" Ps 112:8 and 118:7 offer good parallels to Ps 54:9.

PSALM 55 (54)

Complaint against Enemies and a Disloyal Companion

This suppliant also suffers persecution and the disorderly expression of his thoughts seems to reflect his restlessness. It is possible to read in the text allusions to at least two theologically significant events related in the Bible: the confusion of tongues round the tower of Babel (v 10; cf. Gn 11:1-9) and the punishment of Core and his company (v 16; cf. Nb 16:31ff). In the psalmist's sensitive soul two diverse sentiments alternately emerge: human vindictiveness and God-inspired trust in the Lord. Dahood denies that "the text seems distorted and in disorder." Besides he finds corroborated Gunkel's suggestion that the psalm was composed by an Israelite resident in a heathen city. His acceptable reading in v 24 "men of idols and figurines" (*'anše dāmîm ûmirmâh*; see on *Ps 5:7) would confirm that the psalm was composed on heathen soil. For B. D. Eerdmans (*OTS* IV, 1947) the author of the psalms was a trader who resolved to make a trip "to an oasis east of Palestine" (v 8). There he met a fellowman (v 14) who lived in the Jewish colony of "the Arabian city." A plot against the visitor was laid "in the house of Elohim" (v 15). The scanty evidence produced does not seem to substantiate the precise context suggested.

Instead of the difficult (*MT*) *'ārîd*, Dahood reads in v 3 *'ōrēd*, assumed to be an "aphel" imperative from *yārad*, "to descend," and he translates:

3. Heed me and answer me, descend at my complaint.
4. I shudder at the voice of the foe,
   at the stare of the wicked.

It is also admissible to translate *be'ēr šaḥat* (v 24) as "sludgy pit," in line with the description of sheol as a sort of quagmire (see above p. 146).

PSALM 56 (55)

Trust in God, the Helper in Need

This psalm is one of the laments pronounced after the prayer had been answered (v 14; cf. §20a). During the peril this persecuted man also had promised by vow to offer a thanksgiving sacrifice (vv 13f). Diverse metaphors illustrate that the sufferings of the just are not lost (v 9): his wanderings are counted by God, his tears stored in a divine flask and everything is recorded in the book of life (cf. §14d). In connection with *Ps 36, it has been suggested that Ps 56:14 could allude to the rescue from Sheol: "For you have rescued me from Death, my feet, too, from stumbling; to walk before God in the field of life" (cf. Ps 96: 9). Whatever happens to the psalmist in this life, the final word is not with the description of sheol as a sort of quagmire (see above p. 146). light.

The heading refers the psalm to the incident in David's life "when the Philistines held him in Gath." A subtle verbal affinity could have suggested the allusion: the root *hll,* occurring in the refrain (vv 5, 11), with the meaning "to praise" (*CV,* "I glory"), had been used in 1 S 21: 13: "And David feigned himself mad (*wayyithōlēl*) in their hands." Also in both Ps 56:4 and in 1 S 21:12 the idea of fear (with the same verb) is present (cf. vv 5 and 12). Dahood reads in v. 8b, "in your anger subject the peoples, O God!", an indication that the poem is a royal psalm (see Ps 57), but here, as elsewhere, a private individual may have prayed for the liberation of the Israelite nation from foreign domination (see our remarks on Ps 9/10). A liturgical derivation is also possible (see Ps 7:9; 22:28), as we shall see in Ps 59.

PSALM 57 (56)

Confident Prayer for Deliverance

This psalmist opens his supplication with the same words as in the preceding psalm. Dahood believes, moreover, that the composition "is of a piece with the royal psalms 54, 56, 58, 59," "is the lament of a king, harassed by malicious slanderers." In the present psalm this would be indicated by the presence of the words "Do not destroy!" in the superscription, "evidently connected with the prayer of Moses in Dt 9:26, so that the liturgist responsible for the psalm heading must have ascribed this lament to the king or to a religious leader of Israel." It remains more probable, in my opinion, that the psalm is an individual lament, just as Pss 54, 56, 59 and the others.

Perhaps the suppliant can be more precisely identified, even though the traditional phrases and images of a general character tend to blur the *Sitz im Leben.* The enemies are compared to bloodthirsty lions, armed with the sharp sword of their malicious tongue (v 5), who go hunting with net and pit (v 6). This conventional picture well suits the situation of victims of false accusations, H. Schmidt believes: cf. Pss 7:3, 16; 17:11f; 27:2f; 31:5; 35:7, etc. It seems, he explains, that the accused is in the temple for the night, with his adversaries (v 5; cf. Pss 3:6; 4:9; 5:4; 17:3), all waiting for God's judgment, which will decide where the guilt is. In one of the five apocryphal Psalms of David, known from Syrian manuscripts, a suppliant says: "I went to rest and slept, and dreamt, and help came to my rescue" (III:10; cf. *ZAW* 48, 1930, p. 10). After a night of "ordeal-incubation" (cf. 17:3), writes Kraus, comes, in the morning, the saving verdict of God (cf. Ps 130:5-6; see on *Ps 5:5).

Several noteworthy textual annotations are proposed in Dahood's commentary (II, pp. 51-53). Verse 3 he reads as follows: "I call to God, Most High, to the Avenger El, Most High." *Gōmēr ēl* is found elsewhere as a divine title (cf. Ps 7:10: "Avenge the treachery of the wicked...," and *art. cit.*), and is alluded to in verse 7: "May they fall into it." The title "Most High" recurs by reading *'ēlī* (root *'ālāh*, "go up"), instead of (*MT*) *'ālāy*, "on me." Other possible examples would be Pss 7:9; 13:6; 16:5-6; 32:5; 1 S 2:10; Lm 3:61 (cf. Dahood I, p. 45, and *art. cit.*).

"Kindness and fidelity," Dahood writes (cf. v 4), "are personified as two attendants to lead the poet to safety.... Since in Canaanite mythology the gods or dignitaries are often accompanied by two attendants, the present personification may tell us something about the identity of the supplicant. According to Philo of Byblos (see Eusebius, *Praeparatio Evangelica*, I, 10, 13), 'justice' and 'rectitude' were gods in the Phoenician pantheon. We may infer that 'kindness' and 'fidelity' also belonged to the larger Canaanite pantheon, but in Hebrew theology they were demythologized and reduced to attendants of Yahweh" (see also on *Ps 25).

The commentator of "Anchor Bible" also discovers three cases of "double-duty prepositions" (see on *Ps 33) in Ps 57: in verse 4, "He will send *from* (*min*) heaven to save me *from* the taunts (read *hārēp*) of those who hound me"; in verse 5 (*transeat!*); and in verse 7, to be read: "They spread a net *for* (preposition *l*) my feet, a noose *for* my neck! They dug a pit for my face, may they fall in it!" Consonantal *kpp* (*CV*, "to bow down") is identified with Akkadian *kippu* (m), "noose, snare." *Nefeš* can mean "neck" (see on *Ps 22:21) and this sense seems to me recommended here also. The metaphor "noose" is used elsewhere in the context of nets, pits, and traps (cf. Job 18:8-10). Continuity in metaphors does not seem, however, to require reading "for my face" instead of the more natural "before me" (*lepānay*).

The particular situation described above could help to explain that Ps 57 combines a lament (vv 1-6) and a thanksgiving (7-11), linked together by a refrain (vv 5 and 11). The two parts belong together, even though verses 7-11 reappear in Ps 108 with slight variations. Their juxtaposition. Weiser thinks, "is probably to be accounted for by the fact that the psalm was recited at a thanksgiving service where the lamentation and petition took the place of the otherwise customary 'narrative' of the deliverance of the worshipper."

PSALM 59 (58)

Against Bloodthirsty Enemies

The two symmetrical parts of this psalm end with a similar refrain (vv 10, 18) and the two half-parts open with an identical reference to the "enemies": "Each evening they return, they snarl like dogs and prowl about the city" (vv 7, 15). The supplant claims to be innocent, but his "enemies" or "adversaries" are mighty bloodthirsty evildoers. As in other "laments" (Pss 7:7; 17:13; 35:23f) and other psalms (44:24, 27; 10:12), God is called upon to "rouse" himself, to "awake," to "visit," that is, to punish all the nations (vv 5-6). This language, Weiser thinks, reflects the expectation of a cult theophany (cf. §13d), in which the just is vindicated and the enemies confounded. Communal liturgical use of the psalm has broadened its scope to include a prayer for a judgment on all nations (vv 6, 9).

If we admit that the communal liturgical use of the psalm has broadened its scope (see on *Ps 66) to include a prayer for a judgment of all nations (vv 6, 9), it is unnecessary to suppose, with Dahood, that the author is a king who complains about two different categories of foes, the nations in battle array (v 5), and his domestic defamers (vv 8, 11). Yet, according to Mowinckel (I, p. 226), where in a psalm God is represented as intervening against the nations, as here in vv. 6, 9 (cf. Ps 7:7f; 56:8), the indication points to a national lament, in which the speaker is the king of the people or one of the leading men of the congregation, such as the High Priest, or the governor, or the chairman of the council (the "prince" of Ezekiel 45). In the historical event referred to by the heading of Ps 59, Saul attempted in the *morning* to kill David who had fled during the night (1 S 19:11f). The association of the incident with the psalm could have been suggested (cf. *BJ*) by the use of a night-morning contrast (vv 7, 15, 17) and of the innocence motif (v 4; cf. 1 S 19:4) or by the mention of stray dogs (vv 7, 15; cf. 1 S 24:14). The idea of triumphing over enemies, mentioned in Ps 59:1 and 118:7, is represented also in the text of the Moabite Stone, in which king Mesha (cf. 2 K 3:4-27) relates the reconquest of Moabite territory from Israel around 830 B.C. (see *ANET* 320 f). The Mesha Stone is in the Louvre (Paris).

PSALM 61 (60)

Prayer of the King in Exile

The main trial of this suppliant is to be away from the temple (v 5), as for the psalmist of Ps 42/43, but it is not said that the sufferer of Ps 61 has been exiled or that he was a temple official. The phrase "from the earth's end" (v 3) does not necessarily point to the diaspora; it is probably a metaphor expressing how far the psalmist feels to be from the temple. The second stanza (vv 6-9) is mainly concerned with the fulfillment of vows (cf. Pss 54:8;   56:13f). Does the supplicant simply imagine himself back in the temple? Weiser believes that the recital of Ps 61 took place after the petition had been granted. Its author attends the ceremony of the covenant community of Yahweh, at which the "lots" of land were distributed amongst the members of the covenant (§13c), that is, among "those who fear thy name" (v 6). In that context it is natural that a prayer would be said for the king (v 7), the guarantor of the observance laid out by the sacral law.

In both Ps 61 and Ps 63, Mowinckel believes (I, p. 226), it is a king who prays (see on *Ps 28). In Ps 63 he "appears in the Temple to offer up sacrifices and prayers for help against the threatening enemies." "Ps 61, too, must be understood in a similar way, as a prayer accompanying the offering before the battle, far away from that capital and Temple which the king hopes to see again before long." In verse 8 it is said of the king: "bid kindness and faithfulness preserve him." These personified divine attributes (cf. §11e) will accompany the messianic king (Pss 85: 10f; 89:14, 24), as they protect the king (Pr 20:28) or the faithful Levite (Ps 40:11; cf. JB).

Dahood's rendering of Ps 61:3, quoted in connection with Ps 42:10 (cf. §11c), can be recalled: "From the brink of the nether world to you I call, as faint grows my heart. From it lead me to the Lofty Mountain." To understand that "from the brink of the nether world" (=Sheol) translates miqᵉṣēh ha'āreṣ (NAB: "from the earth's end"), it must be admitted that 'ereṣ, "land, earth," can also mean 'nether world" (see on *Ps 18:8 and Jr 10:13). "The Lofty Mountain" is possibly a poetic name of God's heavenly abode (see on *Ps 53:7).

PSALM 63 (62)

Ardent Longing for God

Supporters of the view that a great many psalms have been written in relation to the covenant celebration before the sacred Ark find in this poem elements of such a ceremony: for example, an allusion to the cherubim (v 8) and the prayer for the king (v 12). Whereas Weiser calls our psalm a hymn (see on *Ps 120), H. Schmidt believes it is a thanksgiving prayer (*Dankgebet*) and he reads its verses in the following order: 2, 3, 7, 8, 9, 5, 6, 4, 10, 11, 12b, 12a (p. 118). Mowinckel (II; p. 220) thinks Pss 28, 61, 63 are royal psalms, because the king is mentioned, respectively in verses 8, 7, and 12. It is, however, preferable to identify Ps 63 as a lament even if one reads in verse 8 "thou hast been my help" (*RSV, JB*) and not, "you are my help" (*CV, Osty*). Podechard reads the past tense and explains that the suppliant is a temple singer who recalls the time which preceded his unjust expulsion from his functions in the temple (cf. Ps 42/43). Weiser questions the way authors turn psalms into laments by translating perfect tenses as if they were presents (see on *Ps 120). For Kraus also the psalm is a lament: the suppliant has taken refuge in the temple and from there, he hopes, God's judgment will strike his enemies. In v 12 it is not clear whether "who swears by him" refers to God (Jr 12:16; Dt 6:13) or to the king. At any rate the original text presumably stated that God would declare blameless those who swore by him (Dn 13:42, 60). For the meaning of "the depths of the earth," cf. Nb 16:31ff, *Ps 18:8, *Ps 61:3 and §14d.

Dahood describes Ps 63 as "a king's prayer for the beatific vision in the heavenly sanctuary," and reads in v 3, "So in your sanctuary may I gaze upon you," parsing the Hebrew verb as a "precative perfect" (also *hāyîtā* in v 8). Coherently with this view, but not more convincingly, it seems to me, he reads v 5 thus: "So may I bless you throughout my life eternal, in your heaven raise my hands." Such precise belief in a beatific afterlife received expression only much later than most Psalms. But careful note should be taken of Dahood's more general argumentation in *Psalms* III, pp. XLI-LII, especially perhaps his analysis of Pr 15:24 (cf. *RSV*), on p. XLV.

Psalm 64 (63)

Treacherous Conspirators Punished by God

The psalmist, whose very life is threatened, implores God to shelter him from evildoers who "shoot from ambush at the innocent man" (v 5). Their tongues are like swords, their words like arrows. Although little can be drawn from these and other stereotyped metaphors, it would seem that he also is falsely accused before a tribunal. The judgment of God will pursue his enemies and, as is often the case in the psalms (cf. Ps 35:8; §12e) their sin will produce its own punishment: "He brings them down by their own tongues" (v 9; on God's "arrows" cf. *Ps 38:3). If the psalmist had wanted to speak in v 8 of "Exalted be the God of the Arrow!" (Dahood), would he not have written *yārûm* (with *w*), as in Ps 18:47. Besides, the usual translation gives a better sequence: "But God will shoot an arrow at them; they will be wounded suddenly" (*RSV*).

PSALM 69 (68)

A Cry of Anguish in Great Distress

The use of this psalm in the early Christian traditions (see § 16a) indicates that parts of it at least were considered as having a messianic import. One must be careful, however, not to apply the whole psalm to Christ, who was without sin (comp. v 6; cf. §16c) and who asked God to forgive (Lk 23:34) his enemies, not to punish them (comp. vv 23-29 of the psalm). Various metaphors designating deep waters are used here as elsewhere (cf. Ps 88:7, 18) to describe the suppliant's deep calamity (cf. below). Although admitting some faults (v 6) the man claims to have been zealous for the house of God and to have practiced penance (10-12). For that reason he is rejected by his own and mocked by drunkards (vv 9, 13). His presence was a condemnation of their vices and perhaps his words provoked their anger. He could certainly have been violent in his speech if we may judge from the collection of curses he has in store for his enemies (vv 23-29). The fact that he "broke down" (v 21) explains but does not justify recourse to such imprecations (cf. §14d). A better spirit moves him when in the next verses (30-35) his prayer turns to the praise of God. The last two verses may be an addition in which is foreseen the future restoration of Israel after the Babylonian exile.

The psalmist expresses the following wish with regard to his enemies: "Let their own table be a snare before them, and a net for their friends" (v 23). E. Vogt explains that a "table" could look like a "snare": when the fowler's trap or clap-net was set, its two semicircular flaps open, it looked like a table set for friends (cf. Ps 124:7). Dahood, however, translates the verse: "May their table before them be a trap and even their allies a snare" (on Ps 7:5). He quotes Ex 34:12 as a parallel and adds: the association of "ally" and "sharing one's table" recurs in Ps 41:10, which he translates: "Even my colleague in whom I trusted, he who ate my bread spun slanderous tales about me."

The Jerusalem Bible reads in verse 1 [=2:CV]. "Save me, God! The water is already up to my neck." It is true (cf. *Ps 22:21) that *nefeš* may have meant originally "neck" or "throat." If the expression "the water(s)" is taken metaphorically only, then *nefeš* was likely understood as meaning "soul." But "the water(s)," "the abysmal swamp," "the watery depths," "the flood" (vv 2-3), "the mire," "the floodwaters," "the abyss," "the pit" (vv 15-16) presumably refer also to the primeval watery chaos subdued by God (see §11a) and to Sheol considered as a location (cf.§ 14d). In that sense the psalmist may have imagined himself submerged (up to the neck!) by the enemy powers, mainly death and the nether world (cf. Jon 2:3-10). On the meaning of *ṣedāqâh* in v 28, see our comment on *Ps 143:10-11.

PSALM 70 (69)

Prayer for Divine Help

This short psalm is a lament almost identical with Ps 40:14-18 (see §22b).

PSALM 71 (70)

Humble Prayer in Time of Old Age

Persecuted in his old age (v 9) this man knows by experience (v 17) that God does not forsake anyone who trusts in Him. Consequently he firmly hopes to be rescued, delivered (2-4), revived by God (v 20). Self-control and faith prevent him from cursing his enemies. The numerous clichés of the psalm point to an unusual use of the traditional psalmic vocabulary and perhaps also to the closer connection of the poem with a particular cult ceremony.

Mowinckel lists Ps 71 among the "I"-psalms of the "protective" type (I, p. 220). In these "I"-psalms the speaker represents the community (cf. *Ps 129), the distress is not acute or the danger is only threatening. In Ps 71 it seems to be over: "How shamed and how disgraced are those who sought to harm me!" (v 24) In our category of individual laments Pss

7, 26, 28, 36, 54, 57, 61, 63, 64, 86, 140 are also listed by Mowinckel as "protective psalms."

Dahood translates v 16a "I shall enter your mighty house, O Lord," and this may be correct, although the same translation of *g⁰būrâh* by "mighty house" in v 18d has less to commend itself. As already noted in connection with Ps 18, and elsewhere, *'ereṣ,* "earth," can denote also the nether world and justify the reading in v 20: "from the depths of the nether world."

PSALM 86 (85)

Prayer in Time of Distress

Weiser maintains the originality of this psalm in spite of adverse opinions. It is certainly instructive to follow his reasoning. "The numerous borrowings from kindred passages in other psalms and the lack of straightforward development of thought lead most commentators to regard it as a late example of psalmody compiled from earlier prototypes and showing little importance or originality; but this view is hardly justified. First of all, the peculiar character of the individual laments does not lie in the originality of each example, but in the fact that their form and thoughts are both typical and generally valid, a fact which is to be accounted for by their association with the cultus. Moreover, we are not justified in regarding the affinity of the psalm with other songs as the result of borrowing from other literature in order to mask the author's own incompetence. On the contrary, we are here dealing with a liturgical style which is deliberately used to incorporate the personal concern of the worshipper in the larger context of the worship of the cult community and of the speech-forms and thought-forms proper to it" (p. 576). In a cultic setting it is not difficult to understand that three diverse literary types can appear together: a supplication (vv 1-7), a hymn of praise (vv 8-11) and a thanksgiving (12-14). This "anticipated" thanksgiving is followed by another supplication (15-17). Yet, according to *BJ,* the psalm is a recent anthology showing poor literary unity. It would reflect the piety of the *ḥasîdîm,* well represented in the Maccabean period (cf. §12c).

When the psalmist tells God in verse 17: "Grant me a proof (*'ôt*) of your favor," he is praying, suggests Mowinckel, for a "token for good." Ps 51:8 would allude to previous "omens and signs" which the priest (or the cult prophet; cf. §8e) has interpreted for the suppliant. Taken literally the verse can in fact allude to teaching revealed in dark and secret places. It would seem that the psalmist, God's servant (v 2), is especially concerned with renouncing idolatry. If '*ôt* in v 17 is taken in the sense of "miracle," then the poet had prepared this singular request in v 10 by praising God as Wonderworker. Commenting upon the expression "faithful to you" of *Ps 25:5, Dahood draws comparisons from verses 7, 10 and 11 of Ps 86. In this last verse he reads: "Teach me, O Yahweh, your way, that I might walk *faithful* to you" (cf. *Ps 26:3). For him also, Ps 86 "may justly be described as a royal letter addressed to God" following a pattern known from El Amarna royal correspondence and the Ugaritic letters of kings, in which the vassal ruler calls himself "your servant" while addressing his suzerain as "my lord." It is true that God's miraculous intervention on behalf of a private person can hardly be thought to produce the large-scale effects described in v 9, but this may be due to a later cultic orchestration (see on *Ps 66) or messianic reinterpretation (see Ps 22:28; Rv 15:4).

PSALM 88 (87)

Lament and Prayer in Affliction

This is a clear example of a sick man's lament. He is about to sink into the pit, into the dark abyss (2-7; on the relation between "abyss" and "sheol," see §14d). The wrath of God (cf. §11h) is upon him, he thinks (vv 8, 15, 17); seeing this, his friends have abandoned him (vv 9, 19; cf. Ps 38:12). This suppliant, like the one of Ps 6, recalls in his prayer that no thanksgiving to God, no praise of his will ever come from sheol, the world of the dead (vv 10-13). No firm hope or anticipation of joy is expressed by this sad man who wrote, "I am afflicted and in agony from my youth" (v 16). His analysis of suffering, like that of Job, does not reach the level where redemptive values are considered, as in the notion of Christian sacrifice.

The term "your terrors" in verse 17 "refers to the *demons of illness* serving as Yahweh's instruments of punishment." This statement of Mowinckel (II, p. 9) is related to his controversial idea that worshippers in the psalms often complain of evil enemies who cause illness by "their damaging words" (Pss 38:13; 41:6-9), their fatal witchcraft, that is, and their evil wishes (cf. §12g+14d c.fi.).

Whereas in JB the difficult *hammētîm hopšî* (v 6) is rendered "alone, down among the dead," it appears in CV as "my couch is among the dead," like in the new Latin Psalter. This translation is confirmed by Dahood with references to a Ugaritic text, to 2 K 15:5, Ps 139:8, Jb 17:13 etc. Other commentators are divided by the folowing debate: is a *leprosarium* a "house of liberation," because at the end of his life, the leper, considered as "dead," was liberated from Death, as a slave from his master (Jb 3:19)? Or is the *leprosarium* "a house of reclusion," as suggested in 2 K 15:5: from the day he became a leper, king Azariah was confined to a *bēt hahopšît* (could not the expression be a euphemism)? Then why not read with Grelot in Ps 88:6: "My commandment (is) among the dead"?

PSALM 102 (101)

Prayer in Time of Distress

Interpreters readily admit that in this penitential psalm (see on *Ps 6) two supplications have been united, one individual, the other collective. In the first (vv 2-13; 23-28), Canon Osty writes (p. 272), a sick man, burning with fever and insulted by his enemies, implores Eternal God to let him enjoy in peace the last few years of his life; in the second supplication (vv 14-23, 29) the community prays to God for the restoration of Zion and its establishment as the religious center of the world (cf. §14c. towards end). Verse 29 is a conclusion to both sections of the psalm.

For other commentators the structure of the psalm illustrates perfectly how an individual lament can become collective when adopted by the community for liturgical purposes. Kraus believes that hymnic elements have been normally added to the original individual supplication. Weiser maintains easily the unity of the psalm in the framework of a cultic ceremony. "Ps 102," writes Mowinckel, "is a fine example of such a forward-looking congregational lament, in which an individual is speaking on behalf of the community, as the person whose heart is especially loaded with the sufferings and the pressure of his time" (I, p. 221). The psalm could in fact be classified with the collective laments and the first part of the poem (vv 2-12) read as a figurative description of Israel in exile. In many verses (cf. 16, 23, 27) the tone is eschatological.

Instead of the traditional "I forget to eat my bread" in v 5b Dahood

proposes to read "I am utterly [*ki* emphaticum] wasted by the Devourer."
He refers to the parallel of 5a, "my heart is withered," and to Ugar. *tkḥ*,
"to wither." The meaning "be withered" is quite obviously indicated for
the root *škḥ* in Ps 137:5b (see *RSV*), where a translation like "may my
right hand be forgotten" (*NAB*) hardly makes sense. The Devourer
(*mē'ōkēl*) is of course Death, which Dahood finds thus personified also
in Job 18:12f. The difficulty in Ps 102:5 is the presence of *laḥmi*, "my
bread." Dahood transfers it to the next verse, which he translates: "My
jaws fester from my groaning, my skeleton clings to my flesh." This appears much less convincing, although the reasoning is too technical to be
discussed here.

Understanding '*ôyᵉbay* and *mᵉhôlᵉlay* as plurals of majesty, Dahood
sees in v 9 only one Enemy (Death) of the psalmist (see on *Ps 13).
Reading *nišbā'û*, for (*MT*) *nišbā'û*, to "swear" (the pre-Masoretic consonantal text used but one symbol for both *śin* and *shin*), he then proposes
the following translation, which, to say the least, is credible: "My Foe
taunts me, my Mocker feasts on me." The "all day long" is joined to the
preceding verses. In v 20 the psalmist lauds the rescuer of those destined
to the prisons of Death.

PSALM 109 (108)

Prayer against a Slanderous Enemy

This peculiar psalm could reflect in part a trial by ordeal (cf. Nb
5:22), called after the author of this lament had been accused of sorcery
and held responsible for the death of a poor man (v 16), presumably
caused by magically effective curses (v 17f). If this hypothesis, proposed
also by Weiser, is correct, the awful imprecations (vv 6-19; cf. §14d)
listed in the psalm could have been pronounced by the enemies during
the trial. This would also explain the use of the singular in these verses.
But in verse 20 the terrible words are applied to the adversaries: "May
this be the recompense from the Lord upon my accusers." Is it a wish
that what they said should happen to them, that they might fall in the
pit they have dug (cf. *Pss 35:8; 57:7; §12e) or more precisely, that
God bring them down "by their own tongue" (Ps 64:9)? Or else is it a
way of avoiding the effect of the curses (cf. §14d) by returning them
upon the adversaries? If they are genuine imprecations of the psalmist,
they reflect a religious standard yet unaware of the evangelical level of

forgiveness. Gunkel did call Ps 109 the oni͏̈ "pure" imprecation psalm. What exasperates this and other psalmists (cf. 35:16; 38:21) is the fact that ungrateful accusers repay evil for good and hatred for love (v 5). After the litany of imprecations, the prayer for help is renewed in moving terms: "I am wretched and poor, and my heart is pierced within me" (v 22). "Let them know, says the psalmist to God, that this is your hand; that you, O Lord, have done *this*" (v 27). Could "this" refer to the death of the poor man (v 16) the psalmist is accused of killing? Of course "divine action" can mean also an accident or a natural calamity.

Dahood's translation of v 6 deserves notice: "Appoint the Evil One against him, and let Satan stand at his right hand." He finds here another evocation of a judgment after death (cf. Ps 1:5; 17:15; 65:3-4; 75:3; 76:10-11), which his earthly prosecutor will have to face: "In vss. 6-19, the psalmist directs a series of dreadful imprecations against the venal judge (see vs. 31)" who has presided over the unjust trial. The translation of v 13 proposed by Dahood follows this line of interpretation: "May his future life be cut off, from the age to come his name erased."

In connection with v 30, Dahood presents more elaborately his theory that the common term *meʾôd*, "much," "greatly," should be at times repointed *māʾēd* and understood as a divine epithet, "the Grand": "I will thank Yahweh the Grand with my mouth, amid the aged (*sic!*) will I praise him." I see no reason to prefer this to the common translation: "With my mouth I will give great thanks to the Lord, I will praise him in the midst of the multitude" (cf. Ps 22:23). In fact Dahood's rendering damages the parallelism (*meʾôd—rabbîm*), instead of improving it. The existence of the Ugaritic adjective *mid*, "great, grand," does not constitute convincing evidence. The other alleged occurrences of the appellation "The Grand" (Ps 21:2; 58:7; 77:14; 92:6; see vol. 2, 2nd edit) do not seem to offer a better case than Ps 109:30. Besides, if we note that elsewhere (MT) *meʾôd* is split into the preposition *min*, "from," and *ʾēd*, "calamity" (on Ps 116:10), the credibility of these changes becomes overtaxed.

PSALM 120 (119)

A Complaint against Treacherous Tongues

This psalm figures among the "Pilgrim Songs" (cf. §3c) possibly because its author is away from Jerusalem, among barbarians represented by

Meshech (cf. Gn 10:2) "an ancient people of Northeastern Asia Minor," or Cedar (cf. Gn 25:13), "a tribe of the North Arabian desert" (CV). These names, referring to places far apart, are probably metaphorical, so that little is known of the real setting in life of the psalm. According to JB Meshech is "the country of the Moschor, a Caucasian people (Gn 10:2; Ezk 27:13), where God is later to be king (Ezk 38:2). The Arabs of Kedar lived in the Syrian desert. The psalmist makes 'Meshech' and 'Kedar' synonymous with barbarian."

"In my distress I called to the Lord, and he answered me" (v 1), writes the psalmist. What follows, "O Lord, deliver me from lying lip..." could be a hidden quotation recalling his prayer (cf. Ps 41:5) and the whole psalm would be a "testimony" (Weiser), recited during a cultic ceremony. Other authors read the first verse in the present: "When I am in trouble, I call to Yahweh, and he answers me" (JB). For Weiser, however, "it is unnecessary and hardly legitimate, though fashionable nowadays, to translate the perfect tenses by the present tense, thus making the whole psalm as a prayer of lament" (p. 742; see on *Ps 63). Whatever it is, a lament or a "recapitulated supplication," the poem seems to allude again to a trial by ordeal (cf. Ps 109) because of the mention of an oath in verse 3. By being untruthful the adversary works his own destruction. He will be hit by the arrow (cf. 7:13; 11:2; 57:4; 64:3) of his own "treacherous tongue" (cf. Ps 64:9) and burned with the charcoal (cf. *Ps 11:6) intended for others (cf. Pr 25:22; Rm 12:20). Dahood endorses Ehrlich's suggestion to read in v 7 l*emilḥamâh, with Lamed emphaticum, and translates: "As for me, peace indeed did I talk, but they, only war."

PSALM 130 (129)

Prayer for Pardon and Mercy

The De Profundis is both a "Song of ascents" (cf. §3c) and a penitential psalm (cf. *Ps 6). Martin Luther, reports Weiser, "has classed the psalm with the 'Pauline' psalms (Pss 32, 51, 130, 143) as the best psalms of the Psalter," also the best, presumably, in relation to his doctrines. Deeply affected by sin because of a God-given perception of its seriousness, the psalmist displays true repentance and hopes for forgiveness. The last two verses could be a later liturgical addition. If not, they express, as in other psalms, the psalmist's religious sensitiveness, toward fellowship in cult, belief and redemption (v 7).

The psalm is mostly associated in the Church, to the liturgy of the dead, because the mention of "depths" has suggested very soon the abyss in which popular representation places the abode of the souls in purgatory. Rather, perhaps the association arose from the idea of judgment: "If you, O Lord, mark iniquities, Lord, who can stand?" (v 3) In fact no one can live that hour without anguish unless he relies on God's mercy (v 4). Quoting verse 3 (cf. Ps 143:2), Mowinckel observes: "The psalmists agree with the author of the poem of Job that, face to face with God, all creatures are unclean and sinful" (II, p. 13). Š. Porubcan suggests that Ps 130 is a "pilgrim song" rather than a penitential psalm. Are not the souls of the dead pilgrims?

But this psalmist, who can be compared to the author of Ps 51 (the *Miserere*), "pleads for deliverance from sin that has plunged him into a spiritual abyss which he likens to the depths of the nether world" (Dahood). In Ps 130:5, as in *Ps 40:2, the root *qwh* can be given the meaning "to call" (In *RB* 1968, 343f, n. 99: "crier," "to yell"), and the verse is translated by Dahood: "I call Yahweh, my soul calls, and for his word I am waiting" (cf. v 1).

Psalm 140 (139)

Prayer for Deliverance from the Snare of the Wicked

This psalm has affinities with Psalm 64 in which also the "enemies" (cf. §12g) are slanderers armed with sharp tongues (v 4 in both psalms). As in Ps 120, so also in Ps 140 the accused prays that his enemies be destroyed by their own curses, the "burning coals" intended for the victim (vv 9-11; cf. *Ps 11:6). His hope is well founded: "I know that the Lord renders justice to the afflicted, judgment to the poor" (v 13).

Dahood divides the psalm into five stanzas (*NAB* has four): in the first (vv 2-4) the poet prays to be delivered from slanderers compared to serpents, in the second (5-6) he likens his foes to hunters in search of prey; the third stanza (7-9) contains the text of the poet's plea to Yahweh, while in the fourth (10-12) are found the imprecations uttered against his adversaries. In the final strophe (13-14) "the poet expresses his confidence that Yahweh will uphold the cause of justice by rewarding the persecuted and the poor in the future life." He reads in v 10 (*MT* unclear): "The mischief-makers who surround me—may the poison of their lips drown them." Arguing from parallels, he gives to *rō'š* (usually

"head") the meaning of "poison," as in Ps 69:22 (*RSV*; in *NAB* "gall").
He finds the mention of "hellfire" in v 11, as well as in Si 9:8 and Jb 15:
30. He does not find that this conflicts with the parallel mention of "the
Miry Bog" in the same verse (*RSV*: "pits"), because "the impassioned
curse aims to accumulate various types of punishment upon the wicked."

PSALM 141 (140)

Prayer of a Just Man To Be Saved from Wickedness

Little is known of the particular circumstance of this psalm, partly
because verses 6 and 7 are corrupt and obscure. Yet it seems that the
psalmist is plagued with temptation (vv 3, 4, 9) arising from the conduct of "evildoers" (vv 4, 9; cf. Ps 73:8-10). Prayer is remarkably
compared to incense and the lifting of hands, that is, supplication (cf.
Pss 28:2; 63:5; 77:3; 88:10; 119:48; 134:2; 143:6) to "evening
sacrifice" (v 2). Some authors see in this "a spiritualization and a deep-
ening of the idea of God and of man's intercourse with him which puts
the psalm in the same class with Pss 40, 50, 51, 69 and 71" (Weiser).
There will be more to say about that in connection with *"sacrificium
laudis"* of Ps 50:14.

The difficult verses 6-7 Weiser leaves untranslated (cf. *Ps 53:7). In
the 3rd edition of *Les Psaumes* Tournay makes a new attempt to interpret them. His translation would run in English as follows:

5. Let the just strike me as a friend, for my amendment,
   never let the oil of the wicked anoint my head,
   for my ornament is prayer in this corruption.
6. They are delivered to the grip of the Rock, their Judge;
   he will hear my words, for they are delectable.
7. As if he had dug and broken open the earth,
   their bones are strewn about the rim of Sheol.

Dahood reads, however, in verse 7: "Like one rent and riven in the
nether world, my bones are strewn at the mouth of Sheol." In fact the
Qumran scroll 11QPs^a has *'ṣmy*, "my bones," confirming perhaps that
in MT *'ṣmynw*, normally "our bones," can be understood as "my bones,"
like "my feet," instead of "our feet" in Ps 122: 2 where, Dahood thinks,
rglnw "may conceal an unrecognized morpheme first identified in Ugar.
anken, 'I,' that is, *ank* plus an affirmative -*n*."

The general meaning of Ps 141 is clear, Tournay wrote in 1959. The prayer of the faithful will be answered; it will hasten the punishment of the wicked, to whom *lex talionis* will be applied (cf. §12e, 14d). All evildoers will perish but the just man will escape unscathed from the temptations. The psalmist's only liking is for prayer, which he offers up, in fragrant fumes, like an evening sacrifice (cf. Pss 50:14; 51:19; 69:31f). The incense of his prayer wraps the worshipper up like a splendid ornament. The psalm, it is claimed, comes from a "didactic" milieu as the references to wisdom literature indicates. It shows special affinities with Pr 15:26-32 and the date of its origin can be set in the third century B.C.

Verse 5 can be compared with one of the sayings of Ahikar, from Eygptian wisdom circles. The Ahikar sayings have been found on eleven sheets of fifth century B.C. palimpsest papyrus recovered half a century ago in Elephantine (Aswan). Ahikar is mentioned in the Book of Tobit (1:22; 14:10 etc.); his presence and writings are associated with Assyrian Kings Sennacherib (704-681) and Esarhaddon (680-669). Ahikar used to say: "My son, let the wise man strike thee with many blows, and let not the fool salve thee with sweet salve" (II: 73 Syriac; in Charles, II, p. 738; cp. Eccl 7:5).

PSALM 142 (141)

Prayer of a Prisoner in Dire Straits

This persecuted psalmist (v 7) is cut away from his friends, isolated and perhaps kept in prison (vv 5, 8) by his enemies. Having lost all means of escape (v 5) his only hope lies with the Lord, who knows his path (v 4), that is, his past and destiny. The Lord is also the psalmist's "portion in the land of the living," a statement possibly related to a liturgical action. Among the *Heilsgeschichte* events experienced in the cult, those which belong to God's entire redemptive work in history (cf. *Pss 66), A. Weiser lists also the *redistribution* of the land (cf. Pss 16:5f; 25:13; 37:9, 11; 60:6ff; 61:5). According to Dt 31:9ff, he writes, "it was carried out every seven years in the autumn within the framework of the Covenant Festival and presumably followed the tradition of the conquest and distribution of the land" (*The Psalms*, p. 44; cf. §13b). In fact, for the Israelite believer the Covenant was life's domain and his "portion" was the Lord (cf. Pss 16:5, 11; 27:13; 73:26; 119:57; Lm 3:24). After his release by God's might the psalmist will rejoice in the fellowship of worshippers (vv 7-8; on the idea "God is my portion," see *Ps 73:26). For Dahood Ps 142 is the lament of an Israelite on his deathbed, who implores Yahweh to be his refuge at death, and to lead him after death from the dungeon of Sheol (v 8) into the land of life eternal (v 6). For the psalmist's foes are "Death and his emissaries."

PSALM 143 (142)

Prayer of a Penitent in Distress

The suppliant of this "penitential" psalm (see *Ps 6) is persecuted, perhaps on the verge of being brought to court by his powerful enemies (vv 3, 9, 12). He hopes to be heard in the morning (v 8), for sunrise symbolizes joy and hope (cf. Pss 90:14; 101:8; see on *Ps 5:4). His spirit is faint, failing (vv 4, 7), his heart appalled (v 4), presumably from fear. Having from the beginning noted the natural sinfulness of man and his impurity before God (v 2), he proceeds to ask for God's guidance to walk in the right path (vv 8, 10), firmly convinced that his moral deviations have brought him to this fearful state. Yet he boasts to be a "servant of God" and feels to be on good ground to ask for the destruction of his enemies and the annihilation of his foes (v 12).

It is noteworthy that in verse one God's justice is mentioned in parallel with his faithfulness. This explains why the psalmist can say: "In your justice answer me." The saving aspect of God's justice is implied in these statements. What problems this involved is discussed elsewhere (§11e). It is not difficult to see why the "absolution," a solemn prayer for the dead chanted after a mass of requiem, begins with the following words: "Enter not into judgment with thy servant, O Lord; for, save thou grant him forgiveness of all his sins, no man shall be justified in thy sight (Ps 143:2). Wherefore suffer not, we beseech thee, the sentence thou pronouncest in judgment upon one whom the faithful prayer of thy Christian people commends to thee, to be a doom which shall crush him utterly" (cf. Rm 3:20; Gal 2:16). Besides, not a few descriptive elements of Ps 143 are metaphors connected with darkness, death and pit (vv 3, 47), easily adapted to burials. In the Church's Latin Office, Ps 143 is recited at Lauds on Fridays, the antiphon being verse 9: "Rescue me from my enemies, O Lord, for in you I hope." With few corrections, mainly in verse 12, the psalm can be applied to the suffering Christ. In the Missal, the Gradual of Passion Sunday and the Offertory of Monday in the Holy Week are drawn from verses 9 and 10.

Commenting Ps 5:9 ("Lead me into your meadow"), Dahood had given to ṣᵉdāqâh, "justice," the meaning of meadow (the "Elysian Fields"; see on *Ps 36:10), also in Ps 143, reading in ⋎ 11b "grant me life in your meadow." In *Psalms III* he had the good sense of adopting a more traditional view: "For the sake of your Name, Yahweh, grant me life, in your justice deliver my life from my adversaries." Still in v 10b he has "With your good spirit lead me into the level land," which represents, for him, "the celestial abode of the just" (as he notes also at Ps 67:5). Others understand "lead me on a level path," which, according to the biblical notion of Sheol (see p. 146), can mean the same as "preserve my life" in v 11. This is not to deny that there might be a case for ṣᵉdāqâh meaning "eternal life" in Ps 69:28b, which *NAB* translates "let them not attain to your reward."

§21. PSALMS OF CONFIDENCE OF THE INDIVIDUAL

(a) *General character*

The "psalms of confidence" are in reality the "motives of confidence" from the corpus of the lamentation developed into independent psalms (A. Bentzen, *Introduction to the Old Testament*, I, p. 156). We read, for example, in a well known lament:

In you our fathers trusted;
  they trusted, and you delivered them.
To you they cried, and they escaped;
  in you they trusted, and they were not put to shame (Ps 22:5f).

Most of the elements constituting in fact the lament are found in the psalms of confidence, but here the confidence motif predominates. The idea of security (cf. 4:9; 16:8f; 27:1-5) and of peace, even during sleep (cf. 3:6; 4:5, 9; 16:7), is frequently mentioned. The joy which this quietude provides (cf. 4:8; 16:6, 9, 11; 23:6) is often associated with the temple, where God is likely to reveal himself (cf. 11:7; 16:11) and grant the prayers of his faithful (cf. 3:5; 11:4; 23:6; 27:4). In these psalms the personal tone is more apparent than in the thanksgivings. In her instructive study of the confidence motif in the psalms J. Thévenet has carefully examined also the vocabulary of "confidence" (cf. Ps 43-56) and even presented her findings in a four-column conspectus of words found in the Massoretic Text, with their equivalents in the Septuagint, the Vulgate and the new Latin Psalter (p. 116f). Some forty years previously J. Begrich had investigated the expressions of confidence of the Israelite (individual) laments and their Babylonian counterpart (see bibliog.).

(b) *These are the psalms of confidence of the individual*: Pss 3, 4, 11, 16, 23, (27), (62), (121), 131.

PSALM 3

Trust in God in Time of Danger

According to the ascription this psalm was composed by David when he fled from his son Absalom. There is no way of proving or disproving the value of this precision, but the psalmist could well have been a royal worshipper, imperiled as he is by so many adversaries (v 2), by "myriads of people" (v 7). Presumably, Weiser suggests, the psalm belongs to the royal ritual, in which the idea of Yahweh's warfare against enemies formed the *Heilsgeschichte* framework. It is true that the psalmist's absolute confidence in prayer rests on the saving deeds of the Lord experienced in the past.

Dahood finds in verse 4 the divine title "Suzerain," by reading *māgān* instead of *māgēn*, "shield" (CV). His argument proceeds from Ps 84:12 which, he says, "virtually defines a suzerain": "For Sovereign (*šemeš*) and Suzerain (*māgān*) is Yahweh; God bestows favors and honors." Shemesh (=Ugar. *špš*) was the title of the Pharaoh or of the Hittite overload, explains Dahood. As for "Suzerain" the root concept is *māgan*, "to give, bestow, hand over," frequent in Ugaritic and found also in Phoenician. In Pss 84:10 and 89:19, *māgān*, "Suzerain," would balance respectively the titles of "anointed" and "king." If one accepts to read *māgān* in Gn 15:1, then the title is associated with its root meaning, "to give": "Fear not, Abraham, I am your Suzerain who will reward you very greatly." The conceptual relationship between "suzerain" and "benefactor" comes out in Lk 22:25: "The kings of the heathen lord it over their subjects, and those in authority are called Benefactors." "In the historical prologues of suzerainty or vassal treaties," Dahood also notes, "emphasis was laid upon the past benevolent acts of the great king, and the advantages that would accrue to the vassal who accepted the treaty

10

were set forth. In other words, the great king represented himself as a
benefactor, so that the transition from māgān, 'benefactor,' to 'suzerain,'
may have occurred within this terminological framework" (cf. §13c).
These various associations are found in Ps 84:12: "For Sovereign and
Suzerain is Yahweh; God bestows favors and honors."

Other suggestions proposed by Dahood in connection with Ps 3 can
be usefully mentioned here. Read in verse 7: "I fear not the *shafts* of people, deployed against me on every side." The root *rbb* is understood as
signifying "to shoot arrows" and not 'myriads' (cf. Ps 18:44; Jb 16:
13). Verse 8 yields better meaning if *kî* is taken as an "emphatic particle
with the precative or optative perfect": "O that you yourself [O Yahweh]
would smite all my foes on the jaw!" (cf. Pss 9:5; 39:10 etc.) Smitten
on the jaw the adversaries will no longer be able to calumniate the
psalmist with their slanderous "shafts"!

Psalm 4

Joyful Confidence in God

If Ps 3 is a "morning hymn" because of verse 6, Ps 4 can be called an
"evening hymn" on account of verses 5 and 9. Verse 2, which does not
fit too well in the context, may have been altered somehow when the
psalm became a liturgical prayer of supplication. The central stanza of the
psalm (vv 3-6) would reflect a priestly exhortation to a group of influential people ("men of rank"), inviting them to avoid sin and trust in the
Lord. The supplication "lift upon us the light of thy face" (v 7:lit.) refers probably to ancient liturgical benediction (cf. §3c and Nb 6:25).
The "beds" of verse 5 (cf. Ps 149:5) could allude to the place of prayerful prostration: Ps 95:6 and Si 50:17 (cf. *BJ*).

Much could be said in favor or against Dahood's interpretation of the
psalm as "a prayer for rain" (cf. *JBL* 1966. p. 485f). "Drought is in the
land; the psalmist (a *ḥāsîd*; cf. §12c) is much distressed, while the pusil-
lanimous leaders of the people criticize Yahweh and seek rain from the
nature deities. The psalmist reminds those of little faith that Yahweh
will hear their prayer if they but examine their consciences, weep for their
sins, and offer legitimate sacrifices. The correct exegesis of some of the
phrases flows from the comparison with similar phrases and contexts in
the other psalms that are prayers for rain, such as 60:10-14, 67, 85." It
can be readily admitted that verse 3b translated, "how long will you wor-

ship inanities or consult idols?", refers to various practices of idolatry. The "prayer for rain" interpretation depends basically on the meaning of *ṭob* in verse 7. The claim is that the word means "rain" in this and other biblical texts:

Ps   4:7 : Many keep saying, "Who will show us rain?"
Ps 85:13: With a loud voice Yahweh gives his rain,
                    and our land gives its produce.
Dt 28:12: Yahweh will open for you his treasury of rain (*'oṣārô ḥaṭṭôb*),
                    the heavens, to give your land its rain in due season.
Jr 5:25: And your sins have withheld the rain from you.

That *ḥaṭṭôb* can be translated "the rain" in this last example is shown by comparing the statement with Jr 3:3, "So that the showers (*rebîbîm*) were withheld" and Am 4:7: "I withheld from you the rain (*geshem*)." In translating Ps 4:7b, "the light of your face has fled (*nāsâh*) from us (*'ālēnû*), O Yahweh," Dahood explains that *nāsâh*, from *nūs*, "represents an archaic third-person masculine singular of the Canaanite *qatala* type as in Ugaritic," and that in "Northwest Semitic" (*'al*) with verbs of fleeing can denote "from," as more than one study has shown. As consequence, he adds, *Ps 67 should also be classified as "a prayer for rain," because of verse 2: "May he make his face shine upon us." According to L. Dürr, the setting in life and the vocabulary of Ps 4 points to its being contemporary with the Book of Malachi (5th cent.).

PSALM 11 (10)

Unshaken Confidence in God

Advised by friends or disciples (vv 1-3) to flee from a great peril, the psalmist prefers to take refuge in the temple (v 4), for the Lord controls the destinies of the just and of the wicked (5-7), as the mention of the biblical figure of the cup suggests (cf. Pss 16:5; 23:5; 75:9; Is 51:17; Jr 25:15; Ezk 23:32; Hab 2:16). "Fiery coal and brimestone" probably refers to the Genesis stories about Sodom and Gomorrah (Gn 19:24; Ex 38:22; Jb 18:15). The phrase "see the face of God," Weiser explains, "is derived from the language of the cultus and refers to the theophany as the climax of the rites performed in the cult when the worshipper experiences the presence of his God with joy and trembling" (cf. Pss 24:6; 42:3). With reference to Ps 68:5 he asserts that in the cult theophany there is no clear distinction between the epiphany of God in the heavens and his appearance in the sanctuary. Thus Ps 11 declares: "The Lord is in his holy temple; the Lord's throne is in heaven" (v 4). This can be compared with Jesus' saying: "But I say to you, Do not swear at all, either by heaven, for it is the throne of God, or by the earth, for it is his footstool, or by Jerusalem, for it is the city of the great King" (Mt 5:34-35).

Are "the pillars" of verse 3 the foundations of "public order" (CV) or those of ethics and religion, entrusted to the rulers (BJ, referring to Is 19:10; Ps 82:5)? According to The Interpreter's Bible, "the supporters of the psalmist point out that his cause is tumbling to pieces, and he is about to be buried in the ruins." In Dahood's opinion, no "just man" is involved in the verse, but "the Just One," God himself: "When foundations are being torn down, what is the Just One doing?" The answer is given in the next verse. Ṣaddîq is a divine appellative which recurs in Pss 31:19 and 75:11 (cf. §11e+12b). "The complaint of the poet," Dahood writes, is not unlike the reasoning of the practical atheist in Ps 10:4-5, who was convinced that God in his heavens was too far removed to intervene in behalf of justice" (cf. §10a).

Quite striking also is Dahood's version of the last verse: "For the Just One is Yahweh, who loves just actions; Our face shall gaze upon the Upright one." He finds in it "the breakup of the stereotyped phrase (as in v 4) found in Dt 22:4...." "A God of faithfulness and without iniquity, the Just and Upright one is he." Dahood then comments: "The vision of God mentioned here is doubtless that of Pss 16:11; 17:15; 41:13; 49:16; 73:26, which suggests a belief in an afterlife in the presence of Yahweh. If perfect justice is not attained in this life, it will be in the next; this seems to be the ultimate motive for the psalmist's confidence." The difficulty of the Hebrew text (singular subject with plural verb) is attributed by BJ to an emendation introduced to avoid saying that God can be seen in this life (v 7). But, BJ suggests, the "theological scruple" (cf. Gn 32:30) was unfounded since the text merely states that the upright will stand in the presence of God like servants before a benevolent and generous master, to receive his favors: cf. 15:1; 16:11; 17:15; 24:6; 27:8; 105:4; Is 38:11; Gn 33:10; Jb 33:26.

PSALM 16 (15)

God the Supreme Good

The various historical interpretations of this psalm belong to three types. Some place the setting in life of the psalm soon after the return from the Babylonian captivity, mainly because of similarities with passages of Deutero-Isaiah (cf. §14c) regarding sacrifices to the gods, distributions of lots (vv 4-5; cf. Is 57:5ff; 65:3-7), atmosphere of joy (vv 9-11; cf. Is 62:4f). The psalmist's zealous opposition to idolatry would indicate, it is also thought, that he was one of the *hasidim* or "saints" (v3; cf. §12c) of the inter-testamental period. The psalm would reflect the conflict opposing Old Testament religion and new sects or cults of the Hellenistic age. A third interpretation is mainly represented by Weiser who discovered in this psalm also indications (cf. the renunciation of foreign gods) that its origin traces back to a pre-exilic cult of the covenant festival (cf. §13c). The poem would be the personal confession of a worshipper in which he sets forth what the encounter with God in the sanctuary means to him.

This psalmist, it seems, received less than his share of suffering. He is satisfied with his lot and he thankfully blesses the Lord (vv 5-7). With the Lord at his right hand he lives confidently soul and body, for, he adds, "thou will not abandon my soul to the nether world, nor will you let your saint (*hasîd*) see the pit" (8-10). The word *šahat*, "pit," may mean also "corruption," "decay"(cf. Jb 17:14), so that the Septuagint's text is not necessarily pioneering in the translation which the New Testament has applied to Christ's resurrection (Ac 2:27): "For thou wilt not abandon my soul to Hades, nor let thy Holy One see corruption" (cf. 13:35). This can be compared with *JB*'s rendering of Ps 16:10: "For you will not abandon my soul to Sheol, nor allow the one you love to see the Pit." An afflicted man, reflecting on the problem of retribution, also tried in Ps 73:24 to express his conviction that the last word is not to death: "With your counsel you guide me, and in the end you will receive me in glory." Other similarities link the two psalms (comp. Ps 16:7-8 and Ps 73:23-24). It is not excluded that what the psalmist hopes for is the privilege granted Enoch and Elijah (cf. Ps 49:16 and §14d).

Building on the premise that "the language and style of the psalm are peculiarly Phoenician," Dahood says of the psalm: "This profession of faith was composed by a Canaanite convert to Yahwism." The *professio fidei* (v 2) is followed by the abjuration of the false Canaanite gods ("the holy ones") once served (vv 3-4) and by the enumeration of the joys and blessings of the psalmist's new life (5-11). The belief in immortality (vv 10-11) was "well known among the Canaanites." In the very beginning the poet addresses himself to "*El*," "the ancient Canaanite and patriarchal designation of the chief deity." C. Schedl also admits that the $q^e d\delta\check{s}\hat{i}m$ (cf. §12d) and *'addîrê* of verse 3 are Canaanite deities. It would appear that Dahood's interpretation, served by his own translation, does fit in the context (but cf. §12b). Verses 1 to 4 are rendered as follows:

> Preserve me, O El,
>   for I have sought refuge in you.
> I said, "O Yahweh, you are my Lord,
>   there is none above you."
> As for the holy ones who were in the land,
>   and the mighty ones in whom was all my delight:
> May their travail-pains be multiplied,
>   prolong their lust.
> I surely will not pour libations to them from my hands,
>   nor will I raise their names to my lips.

According to R. P. Bierberg the last two verses of Ps 16 refer to Christ literally and exclusively, while the subject of the rest of the psalm is David literally (and Christ only typically). Other authors would prefer to say that the whole psalm in its literal sense refers both to David and to Christ, to David in a vaguer and less perfect way, and to Christ more clearly and perfectly (a case of *sensus plenior*). For A. Vaccari the words of verse 10 apply to both David and Christ in their proper sense, yet in a fuller sense to Christ who rose from the dead, while David's body knew corruption but will not be subject to *eternal* corruption. The psalmist's insight of the afterlife for the blessed is probably well rendered in Dahood's version of verse 11: "You will make me know the path of life eternal, filling me with happiness before you, with pleasures at your right hand forever."

PSALM 23 (22)

The Lord, Shepherd and Host

Childlike confidence in God, in peace and serenity, is the predominant note of this psalm, rightly considered to be one of the finest in the Psalter. Apparently the psalm expresses clearly a few simple ideas. Yet it is diversely interpreted, especially since it is not easy to determine the *Sitz im Leben* of the composition. W. E. Gössman remarks that the

various translations of the poem reflect men's different ways of understanding God. According to Weiser the author experienced during a
divine service what a blessing is communion with God. Recalling his
past life he saw it as spent under the vigilant care of the Lord, amidst all
kinds of perils. The divine service which inspired him could have been
a hymn praising Yahweh, the "shepherd of Israel" (Ps 80:1), who has
led the covenant people throughout salvation history (Is 40:11; 63:14;
Ezk 34:10ff; Pss 95:7; 100:3).

"It is a significant fact," notes Mowinckel (II, p. 127), "that this psalm
actually breaks all the patterns of 'form history.' Being a pure psalm of
confidence, it cannot immediately be classified under any of the 'categories' or 'types' of style history. A real poet using the traditional cultic
forms of style has here created a poem which has its own type. It is an
expression of the religious traditions of the people of the covenant. It is
also an expression of the conception of God with which they were entrusted, and of the personal experiences of God in their own lives and the
attitude to life created by these." Along the cultic line also, J. Eaton
suggests that "new force is gained by relating to the king's symbolic cultic
role the journey into the valley of the shadow of death, the restoration of
life or soul, the manifestation of righteousness and the greater glory of
God..." (cf. §8d). For A. L. Merrill the psalm would describe a royal
coronation ritual involving a procession which proceeds from the temple
to the spring and perhaps includes a "circumambulation of the holy city"
(cf. Ps. 48:13ff).

In a special study of the psalm, E. Vogt advances the opinion that Ps
23 is to be linked with a thanksgiving sacrifice offered by a pilgrim, presumably for a favor experienced very recently, perhaps as he passed
through a dark valley (v 4). Elsewhere in the psalms thanksgiving is
often followed or accompanied by the offering of a sacrifice (cf. 66:13ff;
116:17ff) or of a sacrificial meal (Pss 22:26f; 63:6). The temple itself
is called "the house of rest"(1 Ch 28:2) and "the place of rest" of the
Lord's ark (Ps 132:8, 14). "The waters of rest" in verse 2 of the psalm
and other indications could suggest that God the Shepherd is host to the
psalmist in his temple. Having guided him through difficult and perilous
paths he now "restoreth his soul," he feeds him (rōî) and his guests at
the sacrificial meal. If the "dark valley" of verse 4 is understood metaphorically, the calamity alluded to could be a false accusation in court.
Then the expression "paths of righteousness" (v 3b literally) could be
another confession of innocence (Pss 5:8; 28:11f; 143:8-10; cf. *Ps

101). The psalmist's slanderers, his "adversaries," happened to wander into the temple while he was celebrating and thus he could say: "You spread the table before me in the sight of my foes" (v 5). In the fourteenth century B.C. an official of the city of Irqata (='Arqah, N.E. of Tripoli, Lebanon) wrote to the pharaoh of El-Amarna (cf. §9d): "Let the king, our lord, listen to the words of his faithful servant and give a present to his servant, while our enemies see and eat dust" (Letter 100: S. A. B. Mercer, vol. I, p. 341). No precise date can be determined for the psalm's composition. Since however it seems to feature some of Deutero-Isaiah's description of the repatriation (cf. Is 40:11; 49:9f) and the (second) temple is (re)built the date could very well be the fifth-fourth century.

It has been suggested or restated by E. Power, and accepted by others (e.g., Morgenstern, Koehler), that the *sebet* and *miš'enet* of verse 4 are the two rods which are carried regularly by the Palestinian shepherd, the former as a weapon, the second as a guiding staff or as a weapon. E. Power believed that *šlḥn* ("table") owes its origin to a dittography of the initial letter of the following word *ngd*. So he reads *šelaḥ*, a word "used collectively for weapons in Joel 2:3." Thus he translated verses 4b-5:

> Thy club and thy staff,
>   they comfort me.
> Thou preparest arms for my defense
>   against my enemies.
> Thou anointed my head with oil;
>   my cup is full.

For Dahood "the psalmist is quietly confident that Yahweh is his shepherd, who will guide him through the vicissitudes of this life to the eternal bliss of Paradise" (cf. the theme of the "Elysian fields," on *Pss 1, 36, 143). Corresponding to this interpretation, the verbs of verses 2-3 are rendered as future rather than as present. Also "the house of the Lord" (v 6) is understood as "the heavenly dwelling of Yahweh" (cf. Pss 27:4; 31:3; 36:8; Is 6:4).

In his study of the psalm G. Rinaldi mainly stressed how the psalm reflects the biblical theme of "rest." *Mᵉnûhâ*, "riposo," he shows, was one of the great gifts of God to the covenant-people. A large number of biblical texts, in the two Testaments, treat the theme of the divine Shepherd: they are studied in my *The Names and Titles of Jesus*, pp. 65-71. Among the "admonitions of Ipu-wer," written in Egypt, probably before the time of Abraham, we read the following description of the ideal king: Men shall say, "He is the herdsman of all men, evil is not in his heart. Though his herds may be small, he has spent the day caring for them" (*ANET,* p. 443). "Just as Yahweh chose David to be 'the shepherd of his people,' writes Mowinckel (I, p. 56), so 'shepherd' is a standing attribute of the king of Mesopotamia. It is his calling to 'tend the blackheaded' (i.e., men). Hammurabi is 'the beneficent shepherd' (*re'u mušallimu*), and so likewise in Egypt."

PSALM 27 (26)

Trust in God

One proposed analysis of this psalm safeguards its unity: a man unjustly accused is away from the temple when he expresses his trust in God (vv 1-6); having reached the temple he formulates his supplication (vv 7-13) and obtains an answer: "wait for the Lord!" (v 14) The same desire of God's proximity is expressed in both parts (vv 4-5 and 8-9). Although he admits that the whole psalm is uniform in metrical measure, Podechard believes it really consists of two poems: a triumphant thanksgiving (1-6) and an anxious supplication (7-14). In the view of H. Schmidt the psalm reflects a judgment liturgy (*Gerichtsliturgie*).

E. Vogt has noted points of comparison between Pss 23 and Ps 27: 1-6. "Ps 23," he wries, "had its origin in the ceremony after thanksgiving: it is not itself a *Danklied,* but a general statement and expression of confidence phrased in the present tense. Ps 27:1-6 grew out of exactly the same situation; it is animated by the same sense of thankfulness and confidence, which is the result of a bitter experience" (p. 210). The only difference in the situation, adds Vogt, lies in the fact that the recital of Ps 23 followed the sacrifice, before or during the sacrificial banquet, while Ps 27 preceded the liturgy: "I will offer in his tent sacrifices with shouts of gladness; I will sing and chant praise to the Lord" (v 6). Ps 27:1-6, like Ps 23, uses present tenses and both speak of God in the third person. Different images express ideas in much the same phrase pattern:

Ps 23:1, "The Lord is my shepherd..."
   27:1, "The Lord is my light..."
   23:4, "Even though I walk in the dark valley I fear no evil..."

27:3, "Though an army encamp against me, my heart will not
fear..."

23:2f, "In verdant pastures he gives me repose; besides restful
waters he leads me; he refreshes my soul..."

27:5, "For he will hide me in his abode in the day of trouble;
He will conceal me in the shelter of his tent..."

23:5, "You spread the table before me in the sight of my
foes..."

27:6, "Even now my head is held high above my enemies on
every side."

23:6, "And I shall dwell in the house of the Lord for years
to come."

27:4, "One thing I ask of the Lord; this I seek: to dwell in the
house of the Lord all the days of my life."

In the second part of Ps 27 we read: "Show me, O Lord, your way, and
lead me on a level path" (v 11), while Ps 23:3 has: "He guides me in
right paths"—but the Hebrew words are different. In Ps 27:7-14 also the
"adversaries" use "false witnesses" (v 12) to attain their ends. H.-J. Kraus
considers verse 14 to be a priestly oracle (cf. §8e) linked to the psalm only
later.

In verse 4 Mowinckel (I, p. 6) thinks the rare verb *biqqēr* would allude to an "augural sacrifice" (cf. Ps 5:4). For him also, the worshipper
in Ps 27:1-6 "is no doubt a king in the typically bad situation of vassal
king" (I, p. 238; cf. §13c). To "behold the beauty of the god" (v 4:
nō'am, "pleasantness") Mowinckel writes (I, p. 238), is an old cultic
expression also found in Egypt (cf. *Ps 30), which originally meant the
corporeal vision of the unveiled statue of the god at the festivals, as the
highest religious experience. In Yahwism it has become a metaphor for
the more spiritual experience of the grace and benevolence of Yahweh
manifested especially at the festival of his personal "epiphany" in the
Temple. The verse obviously alludes to the position of the king as the
sacral leader of the festal cult; his highest desire is to hold this position
with its personal relation to Yahweh also in the future.

Verse 13 is translated by Dahood: "In the Victor do I trust, to behold
the beauty of Yahweh in the land of life eternal." We already know the
origin of the divine appellative "the Victor" (see *Pss 7 and 22). As for
the beauty" (*tûb* = "bounty" in *CV*) of Yahweh it is spoken of also in

Ex 33:19 and *ṭûb* equally designates "beauty" in Ho 10:11 and Zc 9:17. The concept of "life eternal" (see *Ps 21:5), notes Dahood, was known to the Late Bronze Age author who wrote: "Ask for life eternal and I will give it to you, immortality and I will bestow it upon you" (2 Aqht: IV: 27f).

PSALM 62 (61)

Trust in God alone

Repeatedly this psalmist calls God "my rock, and my salvation, my stronghold" (vv 3, 7). Again: "With God is my safety and my glory, he is the rock of my strength; my refuge is in God" (v 8). This language would come from a man who is in much the same situation as that of Ps 63. Persecuted by enemies he has found refuge in the temple where an oracle has reassured him (vv 12-13). In fact that sort of revealed assurance through an oracle (cf. §8e) is especially attested, writes Mowinckel (I, p. 219), in Pss 6, 28, 31, 62. The theme of trust and confidence, particularly of trust *in God alone,* dominates the whole psalm. Yet it is more explicit in the first part (vv 1-9), while the second part (10-12) recalls sapiential truths: the vanity of man and of wealth, the equity of God who renders to every one according to his deeds. This, Weiser thinks, illustrates the connection between cultic experience and hortatory "wisdom": "It is in the union of power and grace that the essential nature of the Old Testament belief in God is truly expressed; for power without grace does not admit of any trust, and grace without power is deprived of its ultimate seriousness." Before God, man is small but in his grace he can trust. All this is expressed in the form of the so-called "numerical proverb" (vv 12-13), frequent in wisdom literature (cf. Pr 6:16; Jb 5:19; Si 23:16).

In v 2 Dahood gives to *dûmiyyâh* the meaning of "mighty castle" (elsewhere "fortress"), although in Ps 39:3 he had admitted for the same word the more usual meaning "silence" (cf. Ps 22:3). Reading in Ps 62:2, "The God of gods alone is my mighty castle; my soul, from him will my triumph come," seems to suit the context well, but it remains disquieting to find that elsewhere the cognate word *dûmâh* denotes, in Dahood's view, the fortress of sheol (Ps 94:17; 115:17), on the basis of Akk.-Ugar. *dmt,* and Ezk 27:32.

PSALM 121 (120)

The Lord Our Guardian

This liturgy of blessing, Dahood notes, employs the "stairlike" pattern in which successive verses repeat words or ideas expressed in preceding lines. Although Jerusalem is not expressly mentioned, it is perhaps alluded to under the word "mountains" (v 1). Even supposing that *hārîm*, "mountains," is a plural of majesty, it is hardly probable that the psalmist thought of "Yahweh's celestial abode and Yahweh himself" (Dahood), in spite of what we have noted on *Ps 53, and in spite of Ps 18:32b: "And who is a rock (*ṣûr*), except Yahweh" (cf. 61:3). The whole poem is easily understood as a religious valediction. It is not surprising then that the psalm is one of the "pilgrim songs" (cf. §3c). In his farewell words the traveller asks: "I lift up my eyes toward the mountains; whence shall help come to me?" A priest, a friend, or a relative answers ("my" was probably added by mistake): "(my) Help is from the Lord..." (vv 2-8). Day and night God is the guardian of every man in their goings and comings (cf. §11bc), just as he has been in *Heilsgeschichte* the "guardian of Israel" (v 4). It is true that the ancients feared the action of the moon (cf. Mt 17:15, a "lunatic") as well as of the sun (Is 49:10; Jdt 8:3). But the mention of the "moon" in Ps 121:6 could have been required by parallelism (cf. Jos 10:12). For Mowinckel Ps 121 is a complex liturgy including a blessing addressed to an individual representing the congregation (II, pp. 50 and 76).

PSALM 131 (130)

Humble Trust in God

After perhaps many disillusions encountered in realizing ambitious projects, this psalmist has quieted his soul and obtained a more balanced state of mind with a good dose of humility. The implied statement that God is like a mother for the faithful is featured in the Deutero-Isaian hymn to Mother Zion (Is 66:7-13): "As a mother comforts her son, so will I comfort you" (v 13). In the same context God says: "Can a mother forget her infant, be without tenderness for the child of her womb? Even should she forget, I will never forget you" (Is 49:15). Humble trust in God, illustrated in this short poem, was obviously a major element in the inner life of the 'anāwîm and the ṣaddîqîm, the "poor" and the "right-eous," who presumably were natural candidates for psalm writing (cf. §12ab).

§22. THANKSGIVINGS OF THE INDIVIDUAL

The thanksgiving comes as the final act in the drama of a human situation. The prayer and trust of the suppliant have not been in vain. His request has been granted or at least help is assured. This assurance may have been delivered to him through a kind of prophetic revelation received in the cult (cf. §8e). If the deliverance is not yet a reality the suppliant's confidence rests on his faith in the word of God. This is the case, it seems, in these laments, like Pss 22 and 28, which end with a thanksgiving.

H. Gunkel expressed as follows what he thought distinguished the hymn from the thanksgiving: "The difference is that the songs of thanks shout for joy over the specific deed which God has just done for the one giving thanks, while the hymns sing the great deeds and the majestic attributes of God in general" (Einleitung. . .p. 276). C. Westermann has the following comment on this quotation: "Does not this observation say quite clearly that there exists between hymn and song of thanksgiving really *no* difference of type, or category, and the song of thanks, of the individual and of the people, is really another type of hymn? The result is then, that in the Psalter there are two dominant categories, the hymn (including the Psalm of thanks) and the lament" (The Praise..., p. 18; cf. §7b). As H. Ringgren remarks, "thanksgiving is not primarily an expression of gratitude to God, but rather the admission or acknowledgment that it is God who has acted and that the psalmist is entirely dependent on him. Thanksgiving is a confession [cf. the "confitebor" of the old Latin Psalter] and a proclamation of God as the one from whom all good gifts come. Thus thanksgiving is no less theocentric than the praise of God's greatness" (The Faith..., p. 77). Thanksgiving, he adds, is the proper response to God's actions, but it expresses itself in praise: "Thanksgiving is simply one way of praising God, and it is characteristic that the Greek translation of the Old Testament usually renders todah [=thanksgiving] as ainesis, i.e., praise" (p. 78). The difference between the "hymns" and the "songs of thanks," concludes C. Westermann, "lies in the fact that the so-called hymn praises God for his actions and his being as a whole (descriptive praise), while the so-called song of thanks

praises God for a specific deed, which the one who has been delivered recounts or reports in his song (*declarative praise*; it could also be called
confessional praise)" (p. 31; cf. §7b). Two thanksgiving psalms can be
read outside the Psalter, those of Hezekiah (Is 38:10-20) and of Jonah
(2:3-10). "It is characteristic of true piety that it not only turns to God
in time of distress, but also remembers to thank him in times of success
and prosperity" (H. Ringgren, p. 77). It is possible that copies of the
supplications of individuals were kept in the temple archives for further
use, H. Schmidt thinks (p. vii). Thus would the thanksgiving have been
joined sometimes to the lament, when at the thanksgiving ceremony the
two texts were handled together (cf. Pss 6, 7, 13, 30, 31, 40, 56,
57, 109).

(a) The *structure* of these thanksgivings consists normally of the following elements:

1) *Introduction*: in which the psalmist expresses his intention to thank
God (cf. 9:2; 138:2) or simply states: "It is good to give thanks to the
Lord." It is often noted where the thanksgiving takes place. "In the vast
assembly" (40:10; cf. 22:23, 26; 26:12), "in the assembly of the
people... in the council of the elders" (107:32), "in the gates of the
daugther of Zion" (9:15), "in the presence of the angels" (138:1; cf.
89:6), "at your holy temple" (138:2). The vast audience is typical of
the thanksgiving setting: "Sing praise to the Lord enthroned in Zion;
proclaim among the nations his deeds" (9:12); "I will give thanks to you
among the peoples, O Lord, I will chant your praise among the nations"
(57:10; cf. 67:3; 96:3; 105:1). The *introduction* is sometimes omitted
or replaced by wisdom sayings (cf. 32:1; 34:12-15; 40:9), which like
to infer doctrine from concrete examples (cf. 10:19; 30:6; 34:6-9). Descriptions contrasting the wicked and the just are not unusual (cf. Pss 10
and 92:7-15). Hymnic themes (cf. Pss 9:3-12; 30:5) sometimes occur
at the very beginning (cf. Ps 92:2f).

2) The *main section* consists essentially in describing the peril from
which the psalmist has been wonderfully delivered (cf. Ps 30:12). The
abrupt change of the situation must be proclaimed (Ps 40:6-11). "There
are some differences in the description of the distress according to its
character. If the danger has been caused by the *sins* of the subject of the
psalm this is of course mentioned. This is called '*positive confession*,' and
the *grace of God* in forgiving the sin and saving the people or the individ-

ual speaking in the poem from the sufferings, regarded as punishment for the transgressions, is emphasized. On the other hand, if the misfortune has been caused, not by the sins of the psalmist, but by the wickedness of enemies, we find the so-called 'negative confession': The prayer protests *innocence* and exalts the *justice of Yahweh* manifested in the liberation of the innocent from their distress. These two variations correspond to the two main forms of *psalms of lamentation,* viz, the *penitential* psalms and the psalms of *innocence"* (A. Bentzen, *Introduction...*I, p. 153). Every favor granted to the Israelite constitutes a testimony of God's faithfulness to the covenant-people. Hence the community is invited to take part in the thanksgiving song (cf. Pss 32:11; 107:1). In fact, as G. von Rad notes, it is as if the deliverance was granted to the individual mainly for the benefit of the community. The proper place for the proclamation of God's saving deeds is the community (I, p. 359). Sometimes the narration of the peril recalls the very words pronounced during the crisis: "I said, 'I confess my faults to the Lord,' and you took away the guilt of my sin" (32:5). If the transition is not indicated a lament seems to be involved (cf. 30:9). *'Amartî,* "I said," should be translated by "I thought" in several cases: Ps 30:7, 31:23, 82:6, 117:11, Is 49:4, Jr 3:19, etc. (cf. C. J. Labuschagne; already K. Budde in *JBL* 40, 1921, 39f). The recollection of the peril serves an additional purpose: to experience once again the effects of God's saving deed. Finally, the thanksgiving was the normal occasion to fulfill the vows made during the distress (cf. Pss 22:26; 116:14, 17). More will be said about the votive thanksgiving sacrifice in connection with the community thanksgiving (§25).

3) Only a few psalms of this category seem to have a distinctive *conclusion* or ending: invitation to praise (cf. 32:11), resolution (30:13), praise (138:8).

(b) The thanksgiving psalms of an individual are the following: (9/10), 30, 32, 40 (vv 2-12), 41, (92), (107), 116, 138.

Psalm 9 (9A)

Thanksgiving for the Overthrow of Hostile Nations

Psalm 10 (9B)

Prayer for Help against Oppressors

There is no need of repeating here why the Septuagint and the Vulgate are probably right in transmitting as one original psalm the double Hebrew composition. In favor of the original unity of this psalm is its acrostic character (cf. §6d), now partially lost in the poorly preserved text (CV). J. Enciso suggests that the division of the psalm, as transmitted in the MT, could have taken place after the Maccabean victory. This would explain that LXX preserved the unity of the psalm. A. Weiser considers as evident that the celebration of the feast of Yahweh's covenant (cf. §13c) was the occasion when "the psalm" was recited. The reference to God as to the King enthroned (9:5; 10:16) in Zion (9:12f) to pass judgment on the nations (9:5, 8f, 17f, 20f) could verily point to a cult festival. Besides, he thinks that an accurate consideration of the tenses used suggests that the "two psalms" represent a "prayer of supplication." Mowinckel (I, p. 219) classifies them as one of the "national (congregational) psalms" (cf. §23).

Yet it is better to read the composition as a thanksgiving, thus analyzed by E. Podechard: "The object of the psalm is the lot of the humble and of the faithful, oppressed by evildoers. The psalmist starts with a particular case, his own. After having expressed his joy and thanked God who has delivered him from his enemies, he offers higher and more general considerations on the misdeeds of the wicked. According to his petition, God's intervention will repress the evildoers and liberate their victims from persecution" (p. 49). Still more precisely, Podechard believes (p. 53), the so-called "nations" (the gôyîm: 9:6, 16, 18, 20f; 10:16; not the 'ummîm of 9:9 or the 'ammîm of 9:12) are the proud and arrogant, identified with the wicked, already by parallels (9:6, 16-18; 10:15f), explicitly in 10:2: "Proudly the wicked (rāšā') harass the afflicted..." The enemies are the same throughout both psalms; only the victims change. The psalmist considers himself first, victim already released (Ps 9), then the mass of the humble still persecuted (Ps 10; on evildoers see §12g).

Various names used in the psalms (9-10) refer to the same category; they are: the poor, the humble or the afflicted ('āni: 10:2, 9; 'aniwwîm: 9:19, 'anāwîm: 10:17; 'aniyyim 9:13; 10:12), the needy ('ebyôn: 9:19), the oppressed (dāk: 9:10; 10:18), the unfortunate (ḥlk: 10:8, 10), the innocent (nāqî: 10:8), the orphan (yātôm: 10:14, 18), and all those who seek God and cherish His name (9:11). One may ask, with Van der Berghe, if the 'āni is the weak, the humble (or humbled), the oppressed, the persecuted, the sick man or the poor. Does the term refer to individuals, to social categories or to the nations? We have attempted to find an answer to some of these questions (cf. §12abc) and also to determine in what sense God is the "avenger of blood" (9:13 cf. §11d). Another question raised by Ps 10 is that of the practical atheist (vv 4f, 11ff; see §10a).

According to R. Gordis the psalmist identified his own enemies with those of his group and, seeing his group of the "humble" and the "poor" as the authentic Israel, he identified the foes with the enemies of the nation. H. Junker believes that Ps 9/10 centers on the theme of the reign of God. In a first part (vv 2-13) the psalmist anticipated in a hymn the triumph of the justice and glory of God's eternal reign. Then he prayed for the advent of the reign (vv 14-21) and finally he complained about the delay of the reign of God (Ps 10). Parsing with M. Buttenwieser the verbs of Ps 9:5-7 as "precative perfects" (=optative perfects: cf. *Psalms* I, p. 39 and *Pss 4:8; 67:7), Dahood sees Ps 9/10 "as a lament throughout":

> Oh that you would defend my right and my cause,
>   sit upon the throne, O righteous Judge!
> Rebuke the nations, destroy the wicked,
>   blot out their name forever and ever.
> The foes — may they be destroyed,
>   a heap of ruins forever;
> Root out their gods,
>   may their memory perish (Ps 9:5-7).

The translation of *'ārîm* by "gods" in this context (v 7) is not at all required, it seems, even though that meaning can be maintained in Mi 5: 13: "And I will root out your *asherim* and will destroy your gods (*ārēkā*)." In this case *'ārîm* is related to a root *gyr*, meaning "to protect" in Ugaritic. Understanding *'ōlām* (CV: "forever") as referring to "primeval time" (cf. Pss 77:6; 92:9; 93:12; Is 51:9), and *le* as meaning "from," Dahood translates Ps 9:8: "Behold (*hmh* of v 7; cf. *CBQ* 1954, p. 16) Yahweh has reigned from eternity, has established his throne for judgment" (cf. Ps 29:10). Verse 13 he plausibly translates: "For he cares for those who mourn, their lament he remembers; He does not forget the cry of the afflicted." Parallelism is thus improved and the difficult "avenger of blood" is avoided. On the basis of Ugaritic *dmn*, parallel to *bky*, "to cry," *dammîm* for (MT *dāmîm*, "blood") is interpreted as "those who mourn." A similar use of the root *dmn* founds Dahood's version of Ps 4:5: "Be disquieted, but do not sin, examine your conscience, upon your beds *weep*." The translation Dahood proposes of Ps 10:3-5 cannot be discussed here, but it shows how differently a Hebrew text can be understood:

> For the wicked boasts of his desire,
>   and the despoiler worships his appetite.
> The wicked condemns Yahweh:
> "Since the Lofty One will not avenge his anger,
>   God will not upset his plans,
> And his wealth will last for all time."
> O Exalted One, your decrees are far from him,
>   with all his being he sniffs at them.

The proposed translation of verse 4, it is noted, "tries to make clear that the wicked man does not deny the existence of God but only his intervention in human affairs" (cf. §10a). Psalm 10 ends by this praise to God:

> The desire of the afflicted you hear, O Lord;
>   strengthening their hearts, you pay heed
> To the defense of the fatherless and the oppressed,
>   that man, who is of earth, may terrify no more (vv 17f).

One of the special titles of God is in fact to be the Defender of the lowly, of the orphan and of the widow, the Guardian of the little ones (cf. §11c).

PSALM 30 (29)

Thanksgiving for Deliverance from Death

This psalmist recovered from an illness which had taken him to the grave (vv 3-4). At the hour of danger he realized that he had falsely founded his security on human capabilities (v 8). The medicinal or educational character of the "wrath" of God is recalled (v 6; cf. §11h). According to the heading, the psalm was used for the Jewish feast of Dedication (cf. Jn 10:22). The *Hanukkâh* commemorated first the restoration of worship (1 M 4:59), interrupted when Antiochus Epiphanes desecrated the temple in 167, and then also the miraculous deliverance from

Syrian domination. To celebrate this event, notes Mowinckel (II, p. 199), "no new festival psalm was composed... but the most suitable psalm from the Psalter was chosen and given a new meaning, namely Ps 30. The Maccabees felt restricted to the canonical psalm collection."

In verse 2 Dahood reads *'ōyᵉbay*, "my Foe," as *plural excellentiae*, referring to Death, "the archfoe of the striken poet" (cf. on *Ps 13:3, 5). The same author concedes various meanings to the words derived from the root *rgʻ*. In *Ps 35:20 it was used to designate the "oppressed," in Ps 30:6 it denotes "death": "For death is in his anger, life eternal in his favor; In the evening one falls asleep crying, but at dawn there are shouts of joy." *Regaʻ* could also mean "Perdition," i.e., "the place of death," or Sheol, as in Ps 6:11 and Nb 16:21. Besides, "to fall asleep" is "symbolic language" for "to die." Then one may conclude that "dawn is a symbol of resurrection and immortality.... The psalmist is convinced that eternal life will follow" (on the meaning of "morning" see on *Ps 5:4).

Neb-Re, an artisan of ancient Egypt's nineteenth Dynasty (the Exodus period), composed a memorial prayer to Amon-Re after the god had cursed his son. His thanksgiving goes to "Amon-Re...the august god, he who hears the prayer, who comes at the voice of the poor and distressed (cf. Ps 10:18), who gives breath (to) him who is weak... May he grant to me that my eyes look at this beauty (cf. *Ps 27)... Thou art Amon-Re, Lord of Thebes, who rescued him who is in the underworld (cf. Ps 30:4)... He says: though it may be that the servant is normal in doing wrong, still the Lord is normal in being merciful. The Lord of Thebes does not spend an entire day angry. As for his anger—in the completion of a moment there is no remnant (cf. Ps 30:6), and the wind is turned about in mercy for us..." (*ANET*, p. 380). In this Egyptian thanksgiving also, recovery from serious illness is described as a deliverance from Sheol. References to similarities particularly striking have been added to the text. As a whole the Egyptian composition is notably inferior in inspiration as compared with the biblical psalm.

PSALM 32 (31)

Remission of Sin

In its literary structure this psalm is a true thanksgiving. It is also a penitential psalm (cf. *Ps 6), dealing mainly with the remission of sin. It reflects a past experience of sin, not a present one, as Ps 51. The psalmist had tried to cover up his guilt, but suffering having sharpened his moral sensitiveness (cf. Ps 119:67, 71) he confessed his sin (v 5). Thus he was "saved": he was forgiven, his "fault" taken away (vv 1-2; cf. Ps 25:18; Lv 10:17; Jn 1:29). This "beatitude" of the forgiven is quoted by Rm 4:6-8 as recited by David and is used by Paul to illustrate justice credited without works. This psalm carries also sapiential teaching and confirms a principle laid down by Proverbs: "He who conceals his sins prospers not, but he who confesses and forsakes them obtains mercy" (28:13). The doctrine is supplemented by the First Epistle of John: "If we say that we have no sin, we deceive ourselves, and the truth is not in us. If we acknowledge our sins, he is faithful and just to forgive us our sins and to cleanse us from all iniquity. If we say that we have not sinned, we make him a liar, and his word is not in us" (1:8-9; cf. §12e).

Psalm 32 is recited by the Church on All Saints day and in the Office for the deceased. Verse 11 is quoted in the liturgical texts in honor of the martyrs: "Be glad in the Lord and rejoice, you just; exult, all you upright of heart." In the Greek ritual the priest, after administering baptism, says three times with the faithful: "Happy is he whose fault is taken away, whose sin is covered" (v 1). The expression "covered" is a correct literal translation of the Hebrew $k^e s\hat{u}y$. The meaning is suggested by the parallel phrase "whose fault is taken away ($n^e s\hat{u}y$)". The verse is part of a "benedictory word" (vv 1-2) which serves as a means of instruction and exhortation. In the second part of the psalm (vv 8ff), addressed to "you" in the style of wisdom literature, the author warns against obstinacy of heart and calls upon the "upright of heart" to rejoice in the Lord. "Psalm 32," writes Mowinckel (II, p. 142), "voices strong and completely personal views about the happiness in recognizing and confessing one's sin; the traditional basic type is fairly well hidden behind the personal and didactic."

PSALM 34 (33)

Praise of God, the Protector of the Just

In this as in other alphabetic psalms (cf. §6d) the logical sequence of thoughts is not always observed. If verse 23 began, as it seems, with the (missing) letter waw (w^e), its place would be after verse 6. Most alphabetic psalms are believed by some to have originated in the sixth century B.C., like the Book of Lamentations. The hymnic introduction (vv 1-4) is followed by the psalmist's testimony in which he draws generalizing conclusions from his personal experience (vv 5-11). The sapiential pattern of presentation is even more apparent in the second part of the psalm (12-23), with its instructions and exhortations. The category of the "poor of Yahweh" encountered in Ps 9/10 is also represented in Ps 34. They are called the "poor" (*'anāwîm*: vv 3, 7), the "holy ones" (*q^edôšîm*: v 10), the "just" (*ṣaddîqîm*: 20, 22), the "servants" (*'abādim*) of the Lord (v 23). They are the humble clients of God, those who seek Him (v 11), who fear Him (8, 10), who take refuge in Him (v 9), when they are "crushed in spirit" (v 19; lit. "broken of heart"). The Psalter was the favorite prayer book of this *corpus piorum*, who would speak to God as "the generation of thy sons" (Ps 73:15; see §12a-d). The psalmist tries to communicate what experimental knowledge he has of retribution: security, prosperity and joy belong to the various protected or delivered by God, Savior and Redeemer (cf. §11d). At El-Amarna, in the tomb of pharaoh Ai (14th cent.), was found an inscription transmitting a text which corresponds word for word to Ps 34:13: "Which of you desire life, and takes delight in prosperous days?" (cf. M. Sandman, *Texts from the time of Akhenaten*: *Bibl. Aeg.* VII, 1938, p. 99). It is not known how the Egyptian phrase found its way to the Psalter (cf. *RB* 1950, pp. 174-179 and §9c).

The psalm heading alludes to an episode of David with Achish, the king of Gath (1 S 21:11-16). Perhaps the original heading read *'ākîš melek gat* (Akish, king of Gath) which, through scribal error, could easily have been shortened to *'ākîš melek*, then to *'abîmelek* (in the biblical story of 1 S 21, it was at the court of the Philistine king Achish that David feigned insanity after he had departed from the priest Ahimelek). By linking *ta'amû*, "taste" (v 9) and *tithallēl*, "let…glory" (v 3) of Ps 34 with *ta'mô*, 'his good taste" and (*w^e*)*yithôlēl*, "he feigned himself mad" of 1 S 21:14, a scribe, with a typically rabbinical touch, gave the psalm a davidic reference.

PSALM 40 (39)

Gratitude and Prayer for Help

The first section of this psalm (vv 2-11) is the thanksgiving of a man who has been rescued from the danger of death, while the second section (vv 14-18=Ps 70) is a typical supplication of one afflicted and persecuted.

In between there are two transition verses. For Weiser the whole psalm can be regarded as one unity, if one admits the presence, here as elsewhere, of a "tension between the possessing of the assurance of faith and striving for it." In the first section the worhipper would tell of past experiences (vv 2-11) which comfort and reassure him in face of a new calamity (12-18). Several phrases and thoughts of verse 14-18 recur in Ps 35:4, 21, 26f.

The psalmist's statement that obedience is better than sacrifice vv 7-9 follows a trend of thought expressed by Samuel (1 S 15:22) and other prophets (cf. Is 1:10-20; Mi 6:6-8). The problem is discussed in connection with *Ps 50:14 and 51:18. In the Epistle to the Hebrews, Ps 40:7-9 is quoted from the Septuagint and applied to Christ's sacrifice of perfect obedience: "Bulls' blood and goats' blood" are useless for taking away sins, and this is what he said, on coming into the world:

> You who wanted no sacrifice or oblation,
> prepared a body for me.
> You took no pleasure in holocausts or sacrifices for sin;
> then I said,
> just as I was commanded in the scroll of the book,
> "God, here I am! I am coming to obey your will" (10-5-7: JB).

The exact meaning of Ps 40:7-9 in the MT is still a matter of dispute. It is linked in part with a broader problem, that of the original structure of the psalm. This has been carefully studied by E. Vogt. It is beyond our scope to discuss in detail his proposals, which are radical enough. The text, he believes, suffers from a misplaced verse and additions. Verse 13 should be read after verse 2. The following lines were added later to verses 7-9:

> In volumine libri scriptum est id quo teneor,
>   aures fodisti mihi.
> Facere voluntatem tuam, Deus meus, volo,
>   et lex tua est in medio viscerum meorum.

In this marginal note to the psalmist's rather liberal views on sacrifice the "pious reader" had scribbled his wish to abide entirely by the law. N. H. Ridderbos maintains the unity of the psalm and considers verses 2-12 as an introduction to the rest of the poem. Following Eerdmans ("Essays...;

p. 268ff), he translates verse 8: "Then have I said: Lo, I come with the written scroll with me." The psalmist, supposedly the king, declares: "On the day of my coronation I presented myself before you with a copy of the law with me, symbolizing my intention of living according to thy will. I carry thy law in my heart."

A few of Dahood's sundry suggestions can be mentioned here. In verse 2, "Constantly I called Yahweh" makes better sense than "I have waited, waited for the Lord." *Qāwâh* (meaning II) does seem to mean "to call" (or "to proclaim") in other biblical texts, such as in Ps 52:11: "And before devoted ones I shall proclaim how sweet is your name" (cf. Jb 17:13). Knowing that "with the verbs of refusing, withholding, etc.," the preposition *l* denotes "from," as in Ugaritic, a more precise translation of verse 11b can be obtained: "I did not hide your kindness, nor your fidelity from the great congregation." "Kindness and fidelity" may be personified here (vv 11f) also (cf. Pss 23:6; *25:21), as "two attendants who protect the psalmist against sundry dangers—in the present context, against the danger of wild animals" (cf. v 13 and §11e). The meaning of verse 3 becomes clearer if read in the light of the interpretation of Sheol proposed above (§14d).

PSALM 41 (40)

Thanksgiving after Sickness

Didactic and hortative generalities (vv 2-4) introduce this thanksgiving psalm, which from verse 5 recalls the supplication expressed during a grave illness (vv 4, 9). The disease is described as "malignant" (v 9: "a thing of Belial"; cf. Dt 13:14; Pss 18:5; 101:3). Anciently sickness was generally considered as punishment for personal sins (cf. Pss 32:4; 38:3ff; 107:17 and Job, *passim*). Stressing the cultic setting of the psalm's origin, A. Weiser believes that the "lowly" (*dal*) of verse 2 is the psalmist himself, and that the "beatitude" is destined to those of the community who by "paying attention" to his praise will partake of the grace of the Lord.

Though he admits having been a sinner (v 5), the psalmist speaks of his "integrity" (v 13). His confession of innocence could refer only to the false accusations or insinuations of his adversaries (vv 8-9). To Mowinckel (II, pp. 6, 37), Ps 41 is good proof of his theory that the "enemies" of sick psalmists were generally those who by magically effective curses or evil words and wishes (cf. vv 6, 9; see §14d) increased illness and danger of death (but see §12g). Not being yet disciplined in the love for one's enemies (cf. Lk 6:27f), the psalmist all too humanly begs the Lord: "Raise me up, that I may repay them" (vv 11). The translation of verses 12-13 is crucial for the interpretation of the whole psalm. CV has understood that the man has been cured, and after recalling his supplication he now praises God (cf. also Weiser, Kraus, RSV et al.). L. R. Fischer's thesis is "that Ps 41 is an old Thanksgiving Psalm. It is probably related to a time when the king was ill and his enemies tried to overthrow him. Since he was healed and his enemies were not successful, the king's scribes changed the wording a little, and they used the psalm to teach loyalty to the king, to insure the dynastic line against the rebels." There would be a Ugaritic parallel for the thought pattern (UT 127:43-57; C. H. Gordon, p. 194).

Another opinion can be defended: the psalm is a supplication (cf. JB). Eerdmans ("Essays...," p. 274ff) translates verses 11-12: "But thou, O Jahu [=Yahweh], have mercy upon me and raise me up, that I may requite them. By this I will know that thou delightest in me if mine enemy will not exult over me and thou hast held me up in mine integrity and hast set me before thy face for ever." Eerdmans also suggests a setting in life which would explain the strange sapiential introduction of the psalm. "The psalm appears to be a prayer of a sick man lying down on his bed. Therefore it cannot have been said in the temple as is generally assumed. He was not alone. A visitor was with him. This man opened the prayer by reciting a dogmatic utterance, speaking of Jahu in the third person, as of the protector of those who consider the poor. From this we infer that he was a singer, who came to attend the patient, whom he knew as notorious for helping the poor. After this he turned to the patient and continued, addressing Jahu in the second person "Thou hast overturned him by his sickness."

Other remarks of Eerdmans are worth noticing. "In the subsequent prayer (vv 5-13) the sick man himself proceeds to ask Jahu for mercy, without describing the nature of the ailment. He is merely complaining of the fact that his visitors do not have any hope of his recovery. Therefore he called them names, enemies and haters they were to him. The only accusation brought against them was that they presumed his ailment to be incurable, saying 'when shall he die?' There is no proof of any malicious joy about his misfortune."

In this "prayer for healing," the psalmist, according to Dahood, tells the Lord: "Instead of putting me into Sheol after death, directly take me to yourself that I might encounter you face to face for all eternity" (cf. vv 3, 13). This is more easily understood if in verse 3 we read: "Do not put him into the maw (*nefesh*) of his Foe" (cf. Ps 16:10), a prayer for "the grace of assumption" (cf. *Ps 17:15). What Job hoped for in his distress was to have his innocence proved before God by a "mediator" who would stand as a witness:

> I know my vindicator lives,
> A guarantor upon the dust will stand;
> Even after my skin is flayed,
> Without my flesh I shall see God.
> I will see him on my side,
> My own eyes will see him unestranged,
> My heart faints within me (tr. *The Anchor Bible*).

PSALM 92 (91)

Praise of God's Just Government of Mankind

Various literary elements meet in this psalm, although the thanksgiving theme, which opens the poem, seems to be primarily intended. According to Mowinckel (II, 28, 29, 37), Ps 92 can be classified as a royal national (collective) thanksgiving psalm, like Pss 18 and 138. The "king-ego" style (cf. §23a) is presumably discernible here also and in verse 11 the psalmist says to the Lord: "You have exalted my horn like the wild bull's; you have anointed me with rich oil." The metaphor of the horn symbolizes power (Pss 75:5; 89:18; 112:9), that of the king especially: "The Lord will judge the ends of the earth; he will give strength to his king, and exalt the horn of his anointed" (1 S 2:10). The horn is also a symbol of Davidic descent (Ps 132:17; Lk 1:69). In given contexts, anointing with oil would, in itself, primarily refer to the king: "There Zadok the priest took the horn of oil from the tent, and anointed Solomon" (1 K 1:39). Not so much anointing in general (cf. Ps 132; Am 6:6; Ec 9:8) as anointing in public worship (cf. Ps 23:5) can also be read in Ps 92:11. The mention of musical instruments (v 4) also points to a liturgical setting for the psalm. Perhaps the psalmist spent one or more days in the temple (v 3; cf. Pss 55:17; 134:2).

In the second temple the Levitical choir chanted each day of the week a psalm to accompany the libation of wine (cf. Si 50:15ff) that followed the *tamid* (perpetual) offering (cf. *Mishnah*, "*Tamid*," 7:3-4). Of these "Levitical Psalms" (24, 48, 81, 82, 92, 94) only Ps 92 has in Hebrew a superscription to indicate its liturgical use. This would suggest, N. M. Sarna thinks, that it was the first of the group to be selected, the others having been chosen after the close of the Hebrew Psalter. In the Septuagint five superscriptions reflect the liturgical use: Pss 24 (23), 48 (47), 92 (91), 93 (92), 94 (93). Ps 92, Sarna claims, was selected for the Sabbath reading (cf. §8c) because its contents were felt to correspond to the two dominant themes of the biblical Sabbath, "the cosmogonic and the socio-moral." The presence of the first motif is indicated by a Ugaritic parallel:

> Now thine enemy, O Baal,
> Now thine enemy wilt thou smite,
> Now wilt thou cut off thine adversary (68:8f; Gordon, p. 180).

> For, behold, thine enemies, O Lord,
> For, behold, thine enemies shall perish;
> All workers of iniquity shall be scattered (Ps 92:10).

H. L. Ginsberg has pointed out (*Orientalia*, 1936, p. 180) that in the first two lines of each of these passages practically the same rhythm is present as in Ps 29:1, 5, 7, 8 (with some emendations). The parallel is more convincing, notes Sarna, if examined in the light of a known oriental and biblical device: express the evil deeds and punishment of the historical wicked in terms of the mythical conflict of God with the rebellious forces of primeval chaos (cf. §9b +11a). The overthrow of the wicked is in fact stressed in this psalm (vv 8-12). The cosmogonic theme is also represented by the creation motif alluded to in verse 6: "How great are your works!" (cf. Ps 104:1, 24) But the institution of Sabbath (cf. v 1) is conneced with creation (Gn 2:3; Ex 20:11). Besides, creation means order, passage from chaos *to* cosmos, also an effect of divine righteousness (cf. Pss 89:10, 15; 96:10), while the injustice of evildoers shakes the foundations of the earth (Ps 82:2-5). In this sense the "socio-moral theme" of Ps 92, the problem of the wicked and the righteous, can be related to the cosmogonic motif.

Some reflections of Ps 92 supposedly belong to the theme: *Gerichtsdoxologie,* in which the psalmists declare just the judgments of God, his intervention in favor of the just, against the wicked (cf. Pss 7:10ff; 11:6-9; 51:6; 119:75; 145:7, 13, 17). In Ps 101 that sense of justice is attributed to the pious prince, while Ps 139 praises divine knowledge, required to pronounce infallible judgments. The best example of such "doxology of judgment" is Achan's act of praise before his execution (Jos 7:19ff). "Through the doxology of judgment," writes G. von Rad, "the guilty person not only acknowledged the justice of his punishment; his confession also had a very concrete significance in sacral law, for the actions against him were thereby brought to an end (1 K 8:33; cf. Ezr 10: 7ff; Is 12:1f: *OT Theol.*, v 1, p. 358).

PSALM 107 (106)

God the Savior of Men in Distress

Although this psalm does reflect a community thanksgiving (v 32), recited before the offering of the sacrifice (v 22), it should be listed with the psalms of the individual because in it groups come in turn to thank God for personal favors. Some commentators find in the opening verses indications that a rather ancient private thanksgiving has been reread and applied to Israel. This application could follow the deeper theological insight which tends to set the particular favors in the general *Heilsgeschichte* pattern, since, as we have seen (§22a, 2), every grace bestowed to the individual confirms God's faithfulness toward the covenant-people. In this connection Weiser (p. 687) sees in the interchange of perfect and imperfect tenses an attempt to express the actualization of past events in the cult of the present. But Dahood understands "these *yqtl* forms as merely stylistic variants expressing the same time as the *qtl* verbs, namely the past" (see on *Ps 78).

Perhaps the psalm belonged to a *Dankfestliturgie* (a thanksgiving festival) inaugurating the thanksgiving season. The opening cry of praise "Give thanks to the Lord, for he is good, for his kindness endures forever!" frequently mentioned in the Bible (already: Jr 33:11; cf. §11f), belongs to the temple liturgy. Together with verses 2 and 3 it constitutes an introduction to the whole psalm. Yet it seems more true to say that verses 1-9 belong together and recapitulate, under one image, the innumerable instances of salvation: as the chosen people has been brought from the wilderness to the land of promise, thus from scattered places pilgrims have come to the Holy City to mingle in a common thanksgiving their various experiences. Verse 9, where *nefeš* occurs twice, could be translated: "For he satisfied the craving soul, and filled with good things the hungry throat" (see on *Ps 106:15). In the remaining stanzas there particular groups express their thanks for having been delivered from their respective afflictions: captivity or prison (10-16), grave illness (17-22), peril at sea (23-32). The presence of the refrain in verse 8 would favor the interpreters who read in verses 4-9 also a particular thanksgiving, in which God is praised as the rescuer of wanderers lost in the wilderness. The second part (vv 33-43) expresses in hymnic form the tribute of the community to the divine *Heilsgeschichte* deeds, now actuated in the cult. Verses 4-9 could allude to the exodus from Egypt and verses 10-16 to the return from the Babylonian captivity, the second exodus (compare Is 42: 10ff; 49:10f, 51:10f). Verse 16 is almost identical with Is 45:2 (cf. Is 61:1). There is an objective basis for claiming with Dahood that "the hymn in vss. 33-43 contains historical allusions and refers back to some of the earlier verses, so that the entire psalm is a unity composed by one psalmist." For example, the "princes" mentioned in v 40 can probably be referred "to the Canaanite leaders driven out of Canaan by the Israelites."

PSALM 116 (114-115)

Thanksgiving to God for Help in Need

This one Hebrew psalm appears in the Septuagint and Vulgate as Pss 114 and 115. Before offering the sacrifice he had promised (v 14) when his life was threatened (vv 3, 8, 15), the psalmist appears in front of the community (v 14) to give his thanksgiving testimony, which includes generalizing conclusions (vv 5, 6, 15), as well as personal recollections. If the psalm is rather recent, the "cup of salvation" (v 13) could refer to the Jewish wine libation (cf. *Ps 92). It may also refer to a judgment ordeal similar to the one mentioned in Nb 5:19-28. More probably the "cup of destiny" is meant (cf. *Ps 11:6) and perhaps, as in Ps 16:5, it alludes to what Weiser (p. 175) calls "the festival cup of Yahweh," which it is presumed, was passed around at cultic meals to signify the sharing of divine grace.

The personal or private thanksgiving psalm, writes Mowinckel (II: 31), belonged to the ritual of the thanksgiving feast. Some elements of the ceremony are preserved in Ps 116. "The psalm is sung where the sacrificial act is taking place, that is at the sanctuary, in the temple (Ps

116:19), before the assembled congregation, the 'god-fearing,' the righteous,' 'the worshippers of Yahweh' and so on. Probably before the sacrificial act itself (Ps 116:17ff; Jon 2:10), while it was being prepared, the offerer would appear with the 'cup of salvation' in his hand and empty the wine as a drink-offering upon the altar, while calling on the name of Yahweh (Ps 116:13); then the song of thanksgiving would follow, whether sung by himself or by one of the temple servants—most probably, no doubt, the latter." Elsewhere Mowinckel notes that it is in the thanksgiving psalms that "we perhaps meet with most deviations from the common style." Ps 116 in particular "is distinguished by the irregular, back and forth treatment of the traditional elements and by its Hebrew, which is anything but classical" (II, p. 142).

Dahood believes that the "poetic devices" attested in the psalm (as "enjambment," energetic -*nā*, double-duty particles, the use of *yqtl* verbs for past action) "bespeak a much earlier period of composition" than the post-Exilic period proposed by most critics. Instead of the usual translation of the first stich of v 1, "I love the Lord because he has heard..." (*NAB, RSV*), Dahood proposes to read "Out of love for me Yahweh did hear...." The reason given is that the *MT* strictly has: "I have loved, because Yhwh heard my voice, my supplications." He explains: *'āhabtî* should be repointed to the substantive *'ahabātî*, an accusative of cause, followed by the objective first person singular. This is somewhat subtle, but is worth noting.

PSALM 138 (137)

Hymn of a Grateful Heart

This liturgical prayer draws a lot on other psalms. The psalmist will sing his praise in the presence of *'elōhîm* (v 1). Is God meant by this word, or are these "divine" beings (cf. §10g) demythologized *'elōhîm* of the celestial phoenician court? (cf. Pss 58:2; 82:1, 6) The Greek and Latin Psalters read "angels" (cf. *Ps 8:6). *Neged 'elōhîm* can be translated also "in the face of the gods," with the meaning: despite the false gods (cf. Ps 96:5), or in the presence of the gods, understood as in *Pss 58 and 82. The psalmist speaks, as it seems, from the forecourt of the temple; he looks toward the sanctuary where he will prostrate and worship (cf. Ps 5:8). Already perhaps he has experienced in the cult theophany this "kindness and fidelity," once proclaimed by God himself at Sinai

(Ex 34:6) and so often recalled in the Pss: 40:12; 57:4; 61:8; 85:11; 89:15, 25; 115:1; 138:2 (cf. §11f).

Possibly, writes Mowinckel (II, p. 29), some apparently quite individual thanksgiving psalms, like Pss 92 and 138, must be interpreted in the same way as Ps 18, a pure royal psalm of thanksgiving. In some cases, he adds (II, 36f), "the terms used in the psalm seem to suggest that the worshipper is to be thought of as a person in high position, perhaps the king or governor, and that the distress had a more or less *political* character, as in Pss 18 and 138.... In the account of the distress *enemies* sometimes play a part. In the royal psalms, such as Pss 18 and 138, the case is clear: we have the political enemies of the king, and those probably foreigners, as a rule, as in the royal laments."

This poem, Dahood writes, "affords a paradigmatic example of the effects which can be produced by the application of Northwest Semitic philological principles to the biblical text." For example, these "principles" prove that F. Baethgen's pre-Ugaritic translation of *darkē Yhwh* by "dominion of Yahweh" in v 5 was correct (Dahood translates: "And they will sing of Yahweh's dominion"), since, as we have seen elsewhere also (see on *Ps 110:7), Ugar. *drkt* (probably pronounced *darkatu*) signifies "throne" or "dominion" (on *darkē* see *TS* 1954, pp. 629-31). Also in Ps 77:14 *darkē* and *gādōl*, "great," are found together: "O God your dominion is over the holy ones: What god is greater than you, O God?" Dahood's translation of v 6 seems more acceptable than the usual ones; he reads: "Though Yahweh is the Exalted, he regards the lowly one, and though the Lofty, he heeds even from a distance."

VI. Laments, Psalms of Confidence, and Thanksgivings of the Community

The literary structures in his family of psalms are similar to those of the corresponding categories related to the individual. Yet the situation is different: the distress to be removed, the favor obtained requesting a thanksgiving are now the concern of the community. The normal setting of collective prayer being the cult, these psalms of the community are likely to have originated in a liturgical milieu of feast and rites celebrated in the sanctuaries.

§23. LAMENTS OF THE COMMUNITY

(a) General character

Quite obviously these psalms are to be associated with days of humiliation, fast or prayer proclaimed for special occasions arising from national distress. Penitential rites of various kinds would accompany the national prayer for deliverance: cf. Jos 7:5-9; Jg 20:23, 26; 1 S 7:6; 1 K 8:33ff; Jr 14:2. These calls to repentance and prayer (cf. Jl 1:13f) were specifically intended to temper God's wrath aroused by grievous sins, to atone for them, to remove impurity from the midst of Israel or to move God to intervene for his people. It is not impossible, thinks A. Bentzen, that "an element of penitence has also been involved in the great *annual festivals*, already in pre-exilic days" (I, p. 155).

As "unquestionably communal or national laments" Mowinckel lists: Pss 12, 14, 44, 58, 60, 74, 80, 83, 89, 144 and Lm 5 (I, p. 194). These are national laments *in the we-form*, for which there does not seem to be any evidence in Babylonia, where the king spoke for the community in the I-form, even in public distress. Apart from the "national (congregational) psalms" proper which describes a disaster that has already taken place, Mowinckel identifies another series of psalms, in which Yahweh's protection is sought against a threatening danger. These are the protective psalms, which include: Pss 3, 5, 7,11, 20, 26, 27, 28, 36, 52, 54, 57, 61, 62, 63, 64, 71, 77, 83, 86, 139, 140, 144 (cf. I, p. 219f + *Ps 71).

Among the biblical "psalms of lamentation proper" there are some, Mowinckel believes (I, p. 219), which apparently are quite personal and yet are in reality national (congregational) psalms. Such national laments *in the I-form* would include: Pss 9-10, 13, 31, 35, 42-43, 55, 56, 59, 69, 94, 102, 109, 142 (cf. I, pp. 225-246). More probably, however, only one of them (Ps 94) is a national lament, the others being individual (private) laments or thanksgivings (Ps 9-10). In fact the debate on the *"ich"* of the psalms is an old one, but it has never been proved convincingly that in so many cases the psalmist speaking in the I-form is in reality the king or a leader of the people representing the community and expressing its collective interests (see on *Ps 59; cf. Pss 44, 77, 108). Already in 1888 R. Smend had strongly advocated the collective sense of the "I" in a large number of psalms. More recently A. Bentzen has expressed the opinion "that the line of demarcation between 'national' and 'individual' psalms must not be drawn too mechanically. For there is a possibility that the original connection of the psalms with the royal ritual must involve the conclusion that 'individual' psalms, originally to be used by the king, on account of the position of the king as 'incarnation' not only of God, but also of the nation, in reality are 'national' psalms" (I, p. 155).

The views of Smend and his followers are strongly opposed by Hermann Gunkel and by E. Balla, the latter arguing that of alleged "collective" *Ichpsalmen* of the Psalter, Ps 129 is the only example in which the people are poetically personified (p. 114). In his final conclusion Balla also warns against accepting an allegorizing interpretation of the psalms to the detriment of the obvious meaning expressed by the words (p. 150).

A few literary elements belong more clearly to the national laments then to the private supplications. The enemies referred to are non-Israelites, considered also as God's enemies. A salvation oracle (*Heilsorakel*) is usually expected, as often featured in the penitential services (cf. 2 Ch 20:14-19; Pss 60:8ff; 85:9). The negative oracle of Jr 14-15 could illustrate the background of many national laments. Gradually the Israelites learned to interpret even divine punishment as medicinal and the *Heilsorakel* was entirely replaced by the confession of sins and a begging for forgiveness (cf. Ezr 9:5ff; Dn 9:5f). National laments often appeal to the *magnalia Dei* of the *Heilsgeschichte* (cf. §10f) to motivate the request for God's intervention (cf. Pss 44 and 80). Our classification ascribes to this category a greater number of psalms than is usual (considering only the psalms in the "We"-form). The uncertain are indicated by the brackets and discussed in the respective introductions.

(b) The laments of the community are the following: Pss (12), 44, (58), 60, 74, (77), 79, 80, (82), (83), 85, 90, (94), (106), (108), 123, (126), 137.

PSALM 12 (11)

Prayer against Evil Tongues

Psalm 12 is identified by Mowinckel as a "national complaint" (I, pp. 200, 207), and described as "a promise about the rescue of Israel from the pressure of alien rule" (II, p. 216). The foreign nation is alluded to only in very general terms (I, p. 220f). Yet the main elements of the lament appear in the psalms: initial cry (Help, O Lord!), lament (vv 2-3), supplication (4-5), oracle (6), expression of confidence (7-8), lament again (9). It is the supplication of an individual (cf. v 6) who identifies his cause with that of the just, as opposed to the wicked. The prophetic tone is noticeable, especially in verse 2 (cf. Mi 7:2; Is 57:1; 59:15). Other commentators define our psalm as "a liturgy of some sort," which like Is 33, "is to be accounted for by its origin in the festival cult" (Weiser). These two interpretations are not incompatible if we admit Mowinckel's view that "the psalms of lamentation are in fact also cultic liturgies containing both the lament and the supplication itself, then Yahweh's promise of help through the temple prophet, and finally the thanksgiving or the confidence of being heard with a reference to the promise" (II, p. 76). Such a definition would apply especially to Pss 12, 60, and 108.

It is alleged that Ps 12 lends support to the opinion that the magic power of curses is attested in the psalms (cf. §14d). The masters of falsehood say: "We are heroes with our tongues; our lips are our own; who is Lord over us?" (v 5; cf. Jb 32:22; Jr 2:31; Ps 31:19) More convincingly it can be held that the psalm provides a good example of an *"oracle d'exaucement"* (cf. §8e), of an oracular assurance that the prayer has been heard: "Because they rob the afflicted, and the needy sigh, *now I will arise* (cf. §13d)," says the Lord; "I will grant safety to him who longs for it" (v 6). Previously the psalmist had noted sadly (v 2) that a generation was disappearing, that of the saints (*ḥasîdîm*) and the faithful (*'emûnîm*).

PSALM 44 (43)

Israel's Past Glory and Present Need

In this community lament God is reminded of his past favors to Israel (vv 2-9), as contrasting with the present situation (10-23), which requires the help of the Lord (24-27). Various afflictions constitute the national calamity: defeat in battle (v 11), deportation (v 12), loss of prestige (15-16), destruction of cities (v 20), divine indifference (vv 5, 10). Not a few elements of the descripion are traditional *clichés* (cf. Am 1:6-9; Jr 9:11; 10:22; 49:33; Is 13:22; 34:13; 63:7f) which may apply to any of the troubled periods of Israel's history: the Assyrian invasion (2 K 18-19), the Babylonian invasion (2 K 23:29 to 25:26; cf. Pss 74, 79, 80), "the national degradation of the Persian period." Religious persecution is not clearly alluded to even in verses 18-23, and there is no special ground for assigning the psalm to the Maccabean period. "The place of jackals" (*meqôm tannîm*) in verse 20 can mean devastation (cf. Is 34:13; Jr 9:10) or the desert where the Jews took refuge during the persecution of Antiochus Epiphanes (cf. 1 M 2:29; 9:33).

In verses 5-9 is proclaimed the saving inervention of God *acting alone,* the basic creed of the "holy war" (cf. §13d, 14b and Ps 35:1f). On the expression "my God" in verse 5 as relating to the God of Israel, see O. Eissfeldt (ZAW, 61, 1945-48, pp. 10-16). Not pharisaic theology in its initial stage but an excessive reliance on the covenant-bond seems to be reflected in verses 18-23. Some prophets, like Jeremiah, have to explain that Israel's infidelity can and must bring a break in the covenant, followed by disasters, even the exile.

Heilsgeschichte seen in the light of faith consists mainly in saving deeds wrought by the God of history (vv 2-9; cf. Ps 78:3; Dt 8:17f; Jos 24:12; 2 S 7:22f; Ho 1:7). For the same reason a national disaster is naturally ascribed to divine abandonment (vv 18-23). The opening verse, "O God, our ears have heard, our fathers have declared to us..." can refer to national tradition or to *Heilsgeschichte* recitals in the cult. The first person singular in verses 5, 7, 16 speaks for a leader who represents the nation (cf. §23a). Other national calamity psalms (74, 79, 80) deal with some of the themes exposed in Ps 44. For Mowinckel (I, 219) there are only three "national psalms of lamentation" proper: Pss 44, 74, 89. In them is found "a rather general description of the distress or disaster which the enemy has already brought upon land and people and king. . . . They were no doubt occasioned by a day of prayer and fasting after one or more lost battles, or perhaps the sack of the town."

The psalmist's question in verse 24: "Awake! Why are you asleep, O Lord?" is similar to Elijah's taunt addressed to the prophets of Baal in 1 K 18:27, "Perhaps he is asleep and needs to be awakened." Widengren in *Myth, Ritual, and Kingship*, p. 191, argues from this formula of Ps 44 to a dying and rising Yahweh (see §8d) but, as Dahood correctly notes, "a merely formal parallel does not permit one to infer a parallel meaning (cf. W. L. Moran in *Biblica* 1959, p. 1027). Mythical formulas must be interpreted in light of the dominating Hebrew concept of history, and vivid poetic images can scarcely be made the basis for serious theological discussion. The sleep of God, who really does not and cannot sleep (Ps 121:4), simply means that by remaining inattentive to the prayer of his people he gives the impression of being asleep."

PSALM 58 (57)

Against Unjust Judges

To understand this psalm and Ps 82 one must have in mind the "process whereby Yahwism came to terms with the local shrine-gods by means of the idea of divine judgment" (Weiser) on the wicked, delivered mostly in the cult. The gods of the Canaanite shrines were reduced to a lower rank and finally dispossessed completely of their power (cf. §10g). The court "gods" could be, here (v 2) and in Ps 82:11, degraded divinities still in a way responsible for certain spheres of human life. According to ancient belief divine behavior is reflected in the "affairs of men." In spite of the wholesale conversion to Yahwism something survived of the tension between Yahweh and the other gods. Mowinckel who notes this (I, 148) sees the evildoers of Ps 58 mostly as "the national enemies of Israel, or the heathen oppressors and their helpers within Israel" (I, p. 208).

The invocation is missing from this psalm, which starts with a lament in the form of an accusation directed against the gods of the oppressors (vv 2-3; cf. Mowinckel, I, p. 196). It is not sure, not even in this psalm, that curse (vv 5-10) is used as an operative power against the enemy. Imprecations were also part of the ritual for eliminating sinners (cf. Dt 27:11-26 and §14d). As perverted from the womb and astray from birth (v 3), the wicked lie outside the covenant fellowship. The wish for vengeance, expressed in verse 11, is better understood, if not justified, when read in that context.

R. Pautrel has proposed the following Latin translation of three difficult verses of the psalm (7-9):

Dissipentur sicut aqua quae recedit,
   calcabunt arenam et sitient.
Pereant sicut partus exiens in tabem,
   abortus mulieris qui non vidit solem.
Antequam oriantur spinae languescat rhamnus
   vivum tamquam siccum evellant eum.

A paraphrase in English can be attempted: "Let them disappear like a mirage, sand and thirst will be their lot; let them perish like a foetus in decay, like an untimely birth that saw no light; before the thorns grow, let the thorn-bush decay; uproot it green as if it had withered." All these metaphors illustrate one theme: the abortive destiny of the wicked.

Dahood proposes the following translation of v 11: "The Just man will rejoice when he beholds his victory; He will wash his feet of the blood of the wicked" (not "in the blood"). "Victory" instead of the usual "vengeance" may be here the meaning of *nāqām*, as also perhaps in Ps 18:48. On the use of *bᵉ* to mean "from" see Index at B. This is confirmed, adds Dahood, by 1QM 14:2-3 (Melchizedek scroll): "And in the morning they shall launder their garments and wash themselves clean of the blood (*mdm*) of the guilty corpses."

Psalm 60 (59)

Prayer after Defeat in Battle

It is not sure that all the sections of this psalm date from the same period and reflect the same historical situation. The divine utterance of verses 8-10 has a wider scope than the lament (vv 3-7) and not the same object. It probably reflects conditions of the Davidic era (comp. v 8 and

Nb 24:17). Yet later it was incorporated in the psalm, probably in pre-exilic times, when God would still be said to lead the people in battle (vv 12, 14; cf. Pss 44:10; 60:12; 68:8; Ex 15:3) as he did in the desert (Nb 4:14). Was the particular circumstance, as Weiser puts it, a military assembly rallied round the banner (v 6) of Yahweh (cf. Ps 20:6; Ex 17: 15f), perhaps during a campaign against the territory of Edom: "O Lord, when you went out of Seir, when you marched from the land of Edom, the earth quaked and the heavens were shaken, while the clouds sent down showers" (Jg 5:4; cf. Ob vv 1-21). Reading 'ir-m (enclitic mem) ṣor for (MT) 'ir māṣōr, Dahood translates v 11: "Who will bring me the Rock City? Who will offer me Edom's throne?"; "Rock City" would be another name for Petra ("rock"), the famous capital of the Nabateans. Edom's "throne" is obtained by comparison with Ugar. 'ad in UT 127:22-24 (see also on *Ps 93:5).

The oracle (vv 8-10) takes the form of a divine utterance borrowed from the sacred tradition of the distribution of the land (see on *Ps 142), in which is proclaimed once again Yahweh's ownership of the land of Canaan (Weiser). Yahweh's battle cry, "I will exult" (v 8), is sounded against Israel's frontier enemies. Victory is assured (BJ). Verses 7-14 are read again in Ps 108:7-14. From this Mowinckel concludes (II, p. 59) that "the same promise might reappear in different psalms, at different times... that oracles might be used over again... that they made up a permament feature of the liturgy itself, and that the wording would usually be rather stereotyped and according to pattern." Yet in Ps 60 the oracular promise, he adds, was formulated with reference to a definite historical situation: a war against Edom and other neighboring peoples. Yet the wording was re-used for a new situation (Ps 108).

PSALM 74 (73)

Prayer in Time of National Calamity

This psalm is concerned with a national calamity involving the temple. Its destruction by the Babylonians in 587 could be meant (cf. 2 K 25:9; Is 64:10): utter destruction, burning down and profanation included (vv 3-8). All this does not apply fully to the deeds of Antiochus Epiphanes who burned the doors of the temple (1 M 4:38; 2 M 1:8), then desecrated the sanctuary (1 M 1:23, 39; 2 M 6:5). But in this period the silence of the prophetic word (v 9) is more explicitly noted (1

M 4:46; 9:27; 14:41). Besides, ancient sources say Epiphanes was Epimanes, "the fool." Yet verse 22 may not allude to any one sinner: "Remember how the fool blasphemes you day after day." The phrase, "there is no prophet now" (v 9), could also refer to the absence of Ezekiel and Jeremiah or reflect a reality expressed in the Lamentations on Jerusalem: "Her prophets have not received any vision from the Lord" (2:9). Reference to the Babylonian invasion is also favored by the apparent indefinite duration of the temple calamity, whereas in the Maccabean events, the sanctuary was rededicated after only three years (1 M 1:54; 4:52). The opinion of J. Morgenstern is also worth noting: the allusion would be the defilement and devastation of the temple by the Edomites around 485 B.C. (see *HUCA* 27, 1956, p. 130f).

Instead of the more usual translation "direct thy steps to the irreparable ruins," which is quite close to the *MT*, Dahood reads in v 3 "raise up your own people from the total ruins," with the claim that *p* (=*pa*) in consonantal *p'mk* ("thy steps") is a conjunction "here serving an emphasizing function like *waw emphaticum*." Even if a case can be made for the existence of such a *pa* conjunction in Hebrew (see Dahood I, 292 and 329), its presence in our v 3 does not impose itself, and the rendering I have proposed is quite satisfactory. It introduces a description of the devastation by almost telling God: "See by yourself."

Even though *nēṣaḥ yiśra'ēl* does seem to mean in 1 S 15:29 "the Strength of Israel" or *triumphator in Israel* (Vulg.), it is no reason to translate in Ps 74:10 *lānẹṣaḥ* by "O Conqueror," instead of the normal "for ever" (the same applies to Ps 44:24, now translated by Dahood: "Be not angry, O Conqueror!", instead of "do not cast us off for ever!").

Having described the calamity, the psalmist recalls from the *Heilsgeschichte* tradition a series of divine saving deeds (vv 12-17): the crossing of the Sea of reeds (Ex 14:30), the defeat of the Egyptians (cf. Ezk 29:3; 32:4), the exodus miracles (cf Ezk 17:6; Nb 20:11), the miraculous crossing of the Jordan river (cf. Jos 3:15). In all this God's creative power was also active, especially against the watery chaos (cf. Ps 89:10f). With the mention of the water dragons and of Leviathan (vv 13f; cf. Ps 104:26; Is 27:1; Jb 3:8; 7:12), Canaanite mythical imagery is used for extolling God's supreme mastery of nature (cf. §9b, 11a and J. L. Mc Kenzie). Such divine grandeur, the psalmist concludes (vv 18-23), cannot tolerate the perpetuation of blasphemy.

The lament's aim is to move Yahweh to act in favor of the suppliant(s). The motivation often refers to his past deeds (cf. Ps 74: 12-17) and especially to his honor, by showing that Yahweh's cause is at stake. This will obviously be the case, if for example (as in Ps 74), the temple itself has been laid waste. In this context it seems less indicated to seek for the lament's motivation a precise historical setting. On the other hand, a purely cultic and dramatic setting cannot be admitted, although such an interpretation does contain elements of truth. The following views of F. Willesen illustrate well, it would seem, both the method and the excesses of a certain "myth and ritual" school of exegesis (cf. §8d).

"In the following pages," Willesen writes, "I hope to indicate that the psalms (=74 and 79) have no relation whatsoever to any historic occurrences, but are completely cultic. If this be true, the determination of their type as 'national psalms of lamentation' must fall, and it will come out that originally they were ritual laments with a fixed position in the cult drama of the New Year festival..." (p. 289). Then he attempts to prove that in the Semitic world the (cultic) profanation of the temple and the (ritual) death of the god are bound up inseparably. So the cultic weeping and lamentation accompanying the god to Sheol have been integrating parts of the act of temple profanation too. Texts would indicate "that the temple had to undergo a purification prior to the procession and the inthronization of the deity, and this postulates a preceding profanation ceremony. Would it be too audacious to interpret the purification of the postexilic Jewish Temple on the day of Atonement as a reminiscence of the ritual expulsion of the Chaos power from the house it had seized with the result of menacing misfortune to all creatures?" (p. 298) There is little doubt about the answer, but let us read the application to Ps 74.

"If this interpretation be consistent the verses are a decisive evidence partly of the presence of the cultic drama in Israel, and partly of the connection of Ps 74 with this cult. The course of the drama may then be this: After the introduction follow the rites representing the conquest of the sanctuary by the Chaos powers, viz., the roaring, the bringing in of signs followed by burning and complete ritual destruction. One of the sites, the disposition of the hostile signs, is explained by verses 5-6: the performing persons take the axes, Ba'al's insignia, into the sacred house after having removed Jahweh's signs, and this act is described further by an allusion to a—no doubt well known—mythic idea: it has to look like the behavior of Ba'al when felling Jahweh's forest, i.e., that the actors are cutting, hewing, and hammering with their tools on the wooden furniture destined for this purpose. After this casual flash on the sacred acts generally forgotten long ago the cultic text proceeds with the next picture, the burning of the ruined building" (p. 305). Dahood correctly observes that "Willesen unfortunately overlooks those historical psalms, such as Ps 89, which intersperse the description of historical occurrences with mythological motifs."

With less imagination it can be found that some aspects of Israelite cosmogony are reflected in verse 15: "You released the springs and torrents; you brought dry land out of the primeval waters." In connection with the description of Sheol (§14d) the views of J. A. Emerton have been mentioned. Applying these to Ps 74:15 he concludes that the whole verse "describes the removal of the primeval waters from the earth. God cleft open springs, so that the water might descend through them" and thus allow dry land to appear.

PSALM 77 (76)

Lament and Comfort in Time of Distress

It is not so much a past calamity as the precarious situation of the nation which constitutes the object of this lament. Mowinckel would classify it with the "protective psalms" (cf. §23a and *Ps 71), in which God's protection is sought against a threatening danger (I, p. 219f). Yet, as Mowinckel himself admits, it is possible that "the whole people has been struck by disaster" (p. 227). The speaker is the representative of the people, He lived in a difficult period, after the exile (JB). Considering, however, the archaic language used, Dahood thinks, "a tenth-century date for this composite psalm does not seem unlikely." In particular it could be inferred from v 17 that the psalm "must be older than Hab iii since it preserves the Canaanite metrical pattern which no longer appears in Hab iii." In addition, vv 14-16 recall Ex 15:11-13, while vv 17-20, which recall Ex 15:11-13, could be an ancient poem inserted into the psalm. Although the psalm has unity, it consists of two parts: a lament (vv 2-10) and a hymn (12-21). Verse 11 links both parts and expresses the main concern of the psalmist, the "intriguing" ways of God: "This is my sorrow, that the right hand of the Most High is changed." For sleepless nights he has brooded on that problem. Yet in the stylized form of the theophany tradition (cf. Ex 19: 18) he testifies to God's saving deeds (vv 14-23), in terms often similar to probably older writings, as Habakkuk 3:10-11:

Into streams you split the earth;
at sight of you the mountains tremble.
A torrent of rain descends;
the ocean gives forth its roar.

H. G. May believes that the "many waters" of Ps 77:20 are the waters of the Red Sea (cf. Hab 3:15), as in Ps 74:13f. John L. McKenzie, however, concludes his study of Ps 74:13ff with the following remark: "The weight of probabilities suggests that the phenomenon described in Ps 74: 13-15 are creative works, and not the historical events of Exodus; and that the imagery employed is derived from Semitic—principally Canaanite— mythology" (p. 282). The English translation refers twice to the "meditation" of the psalmist. In Hebrew two different words are used *śîaḥ* (v 7) and *hāgâh*. Their exact meaning has been explained (§12f). On reading "your dominion is over the holy ones" in v 14a see on *Ps 138:5.

PSALM 79 (78)

The Destruction of Jerusalem and Its Temple

The destruction of Jerusalem and of the temple, with the massacre involved, forms the historical background of this national lament. Yet in spite of the details provided, it is as little possible here as in Pss 44 and 74 to ascertain that the calamity described is the catastrophe of 587. At any rate the mention of "our neighbors" in verse 12 (cf. Pss 44:14; 80:7; 89:42) seems to indicate that verses 10-13 are directed against Moab, Ammon, Edom, who before (2 K 24:2) or after the fall of Jerusalem roamed in Judea to plunder (cf. Ezk 35:10; 36:5). No inference can be made on the psalm's date from the fact that vv 2-3 are used in 1 M 7: 17. The text of verses 6-7 occurs in Jr 10:25, and verse 5 is typically in style of national laments: "O Lord, how long? Will you be angry forever? Will your jealousy burn like fire?" (*Pss 13:2; 44:24; 74:1; 80:5; 89: 47) The avenging (*neqāmâh*) of innocent blood (v 10) is a theme well attested in the psalm (cf. Pss 18:48; 58:11; 94:1; 149:7) and is related to God's deeds as *gô'ēl* ("redeemer"; cf. §11d) of his people (cf. Pss 19: 15:13) and fully used in Deutero-Isaiah (cf. Is 43:1, 7, 15). Although

God is prayed to avenge "his servants' blood" (v 10), the "innocence motivation" is not proposed and allusion is made to the "iniquities of the past" (v 8). Finally, the image of the sheep and shepherd (v 13) serves to illustrate the relation of God with his people both at the end of this psalm and in the beginning of the next (cf. *Ps 23).

PSALM 80 (79)

Prayer for the Restoration of the Lord's Vineyard

The historical situation of this lament could have been similar to that supposed in Pss 44 and 60: whereas in the past the Israelites were led by God from victory to victory, now they are mocked by their enemies, threatened by their neighbors (cp. *Ps 79:12) and fed with the bread of tears (vv 5-8). The vine, which is Israel, has become a great tree (vv 9-12) and yet now it is abandoned to looting and destruction (13-14). It is high time for the Lord to arise with power (v 3) and hearken to the prayer of the refrain: "O Lord of hosts, restore us; if your face shine upon us, then we shall be safe" (vv 4, 8, 20). In this refrain the meaning of the whole psalm is condensed, as well as the main object of supplication in all the national laments: a return to normal relations between Yahweh and the covenant people. It will be brought about by God's initiative in restoring and reconverting the faithful (*hasîbēnu!*), in saving them by a theophany encounter. In the allegory of the vine (vv 8-14) the pattern of *Heilsgeschichte* appears in a traditional form (cf. Gn 49:22f; Is 5:1-7). There is an historical connection between the title "Lord of hosts" of the refrain and his "throne upon the cherubim" (see §11b). It can be recorded that the expression *ben 'ādām*, "son of man," used in v 18 had an equivalent in the Ugaritic *bnš*, vocalized (Dahood) *bu-nu-šu*, and composed of *bun*, "son," and *nōš*, "man."

For years the date of the psalm's composition has been the subject of debate among scholars. It is generally agreed that the *terminus a quo* is the period following king Solomon's death, since the mention of "Israel," of "Joseph," of "Ephraim, Benjamin and Manasse" (vv 2, 3) seems to suppose the divided kingdom. Dahood proposes the same date and adds: "The striking linguistic and conceptual similarities between this psalm and Ps 44 suggest a common provenance." From the tenth to the second century almost every possible date has been proposed. O. Eissfeldt would settle for one between 732 and 722. H. Heinemann has stated his proposal clearly. "Our contention is that the evidence points unmistakably in one direction: that the Psalm belongs to a much earlier period, preceding the division of the kingdom and, even more precisely, before the rise of Judah to predominance. Only thus can we understand why there is no mention of Judah, why 'Joseph' is used as a synonym for Israel and why special place is accorded to Benjamin. The psalm must have been composed in the time of Saul. Thus it becomes obvious why the author should think that the salvation of Israel depends on Benjamin, or rather on the *'iš yemini*—a phrase actually applied to Saul in 1 S 9:1 and 21:7. The situation of a country "wholly overrun by enemies (Kirkpatrick) is entirely in accord with conditions at the time of Saul, prior to his victory over the Philistines. Israel, at the moment reflected in the Psalm, is indeed going to war, and calls upon its God to lead it to victory, as He had done so often before. The memory of the Ark and its miraculous powers was still fresh."

More probably, Mowinckel believes (II, p. 152), Ps 80 originated from "some North-Israelite sanctuary, such as Bethel...and belongs in all probability to the last days of the Northern Kingdom." Having translated verse 18: "May your hand protect the man at your right, the son of man who has been authorized by you," *JB* comments: "Probable allusion to Zerubbabel (Hag 1:1; Esd 3:2) rather than to Benjamin ('Son of the right hand'), Amaziah ('Yahweh is trusty'; cf. 2 Ch 25:15), or Israel (cf. Ex 4:22)" (cf. Ps 132:10). Zerubbabel, high-commissioner in Jerusalem, began rebuilding the temple in 520 B.C. (cf. Esd 5:2).

PSALM 82 (81)

Judgment against Wicked Judges

Why is this world full of injustice? Because the judges themselves are wicked and easily bribed. This prophetic teaching (cf. Is 1:17f; 3:14f; Mi 3:1-11), eschatological in tone (cf. Is 24:21f), is presented in the psalm with a *mise en scène* (v 1) inspired by Canaanite mythology. The ancient literary themes involving assemblies of the gods, in judicial court, are used also elsewhere in the psalms (cf. Ps 58). For the greater part of the psalm, the divine judge speaks in the course of a cult theophany (vv 2-7; cf. §13d); the gods of the nations are doomed because they have failed to procure justice and have been imitated on earth by their human counterparts. A prayer follows the divine revelation: "Rise, O God;

judge the earth, for yours are all the nations" (v 8; on divine care for the lowly, vv 3f, see §11c).

Psalm 82 raises the problem of Israel's and the psalmists' monotheism. What status had the gods of the nations? The answer to that question has been attempted elsewhere (§10g). In Ps 82 also any existence or function independent of Yahweh is denied them. They are even sentenced to death like ordinary mortals (v 7). In *The Old Testament against its Environment*, G. Ernest Wright favors a literal interpretation of the psalm: the scene is a heavenly council, composed of the "gods of the nations" with Yahweh as the head of the assembly. Mowinckel (I, p. 150) adds that the idea of an assembly of gods belongs to the festival of new year and enthronement, when the coming year's destiny was determined. It was in such an assembly of "sons of gods" and "saints," i.e. divine beings, that Yahweh once portioned out the nations amongst the "sons of gods" whom he made governors over them (cf. Dt 32:8f; 33:2f). The *'elohim* can hardly be the human, Israelite judges, Wright thinks, in spite of Jn 10:34, nor Hasmonean kings (Duhm), nor the deified kings of the Hellenistic age (Buttenwieser). In his comprehensive and instructive study of the psalm, J. Morgenstern proposed that the *'elohim* were "fallen angels" and that the clue to the original indictment of the psalm was to be looked for in the well-known story of Gn 6:14. "There is no doubt," Wright declares, "that his reconstruction makes excellent sense, but in reality it is tearing a short composition to pieces on tenuous evidence in order to rebuild it according to one's own notions" (p. 32, n. 39).

R. T. O'Callaghan has related to Ps 82 extracts of a Ugaritic poem. In it, when King Keret is sick, his son, *Ilḥu,* queries of him: "Wilt thou die, then, Father, like mortals?" Then, when Keret has recovered, his son *Yṣb* is prompted to say to him (t. 127, 27-34; Gordon, p. 194): "Thou hast let thy hand fall into mischief, Thou dost not judge the cause of the widow nor adjudicate the case of the brokenhearted." Keret apparently neglects the welfare of his realm as a *result* of his mortal sickness, but in Ps 82 such neglect of justice is the *cause* of the sentence of mortality. O'Callaghan believes that in spite of the Ugaritic parallels it can still be maintained that the psalmist meant human judges in verses 2 and 6. A. González also rejects the determining character of the Ugaritic parallels and would set the date of the psalm's composition about Deutero-Isaiah's time. Owing to what he calls "the archaic quality of the language," Dahood would be inclined to set the origin of Ps 82 in the pre-monarchical period (agreeing with J. S. Ackermann's Harvard dissertation of 1966). He also proposes, correctly it seems, that in v 7 the pair men—prince forms a merism (division in categories) denoting all mortals. There would be no point in attempting to find who the princes are. On merisms see H. A. Brongers in *OTS* 14 (1965) 110-114. F. I. Andersen reads v 5 as follows: "Those who do not care and do not understand will walk around in darkness; all of them will totter in the lower structures of the earth" (*Biblica* 1969, 393f). On Ps 82 see now H. W. Jüngling, *Der Tod der Götter. Eine Untersuchung zu Ps 82.* SBS 38 (Stuttgart 1969), and M. Tsevat, "God and the Gods in Assembly, and Interpretation of Psalm 82," *HUCA* 40-41 (1970) 123-137.

PSALM 83 (82)

Prayer against a Hostile Alliance

Rather than a precise historical situation this psalmist has probably in mind the general state of tension which naturally opposes God-fearing Israel and the surrounding Gentile nations, supported by Assyria. From the silence on Babylon though, it may be assumed that the psalm was composed between the ninth and the seventh centuries (Weiser). Others believe, however, that the period of Nehemiah can be alluded to (cf. Ne 2:19; 4:1f; 6:1). In fact Israel has rarely been without hostile neighbors (cf. 1 M 5:3ff). In the first series of imprecations (vv 10-13) it is wished that the divine judgment in the cult will bring upon the present enemies of Israel the fate which fell upon her former enemies, during the period of Judges (ch 4). The God of history is also the theophany God (§13d) whose power can mobilize nature's forces against the enemies of His Name (vv 14-19). An ultimate result of the judgment will be, it is hoped, that men will seek God's name and acknowledge supreme divine dominion (vv 17, 19).

In some psalms, Mowinckel suggests (II, p. 51f), the original cursing word has been replaced by the prayer asking Yahweh to crush the enemy (cf. §14d). "But a prayer like the one in Ps 83:10ff, with its elaborate description of the disaster imprecated on the enemies of the people, is evidently connected with the ancient cursing formulas, such as seers and other 'divine men' (*'îš elōhîm*) and possessors of the effectual word would use against the enemy before the battle; with such words Balak expected Balaam to slay the Israelites for him" (Nb 23-24).

Reading *s^{e}pūnikā* as a singular noun with the genitive ending, and supposing it to mean "your treasure," to designate Israel, like *s^{e}gullāh*, "possession, treasure," in Ex 19:5, Dt 7:6, etc., Dahood translates, possibly correctly, v. 4: "Against your people they lay crafty plans, and conspire against your treasure" (*RSV* = v 3: "against thy protected ones"). He also proposes to identify Gebal in v 8 with the Phoenician city Byblos. Using the rhetorical figure known as inclusion the poet moves from north (Gebal) to south (Amalec), then again from the south (Philistia) to north (Tyre). Tyre and Byblos occur together in Ezk 27:8-9. On the other hand, it must be said, against Dahood, that En-dor, in v 11, as a locality, suits perfectly well the geographical context (near Mt. Thabor) of the victory wrought by Deborah and Barak (Jg 4-5). There is no need for the grammatical *tour de force* which would give to *b^e'ēn dō'r* the meaning "from the surface of the globe."

PSALM 85 (84)

Prayer for Complete Restoration

Some interpreters read in v 2 an explicit mention of the return from the Babylonian exile: "Thy favor, O Lord, is for thy land, you bring back the *captives of Jacob*" (*BJ*). Awkwardly following the Vulgate, the Douay version translates: "Lord, thou hast blessed thy land; *thou hast turned away the captivity of Jacob*." In better style, Msgr. Knox writes: "What blessings, Lord, thou hast granted to this land of thine, *restoring Jacob from captivity*, pardoning thy people his guilt. . . ." The majority of present interpreters, however, understand the expression *šabtā š^{e}bît ya'aqōb* as referring more generally to a restoration of "the fortunes of Jacob" (*RSV*, Weiser), of "the destiny of Jacob" (Osty), or of "the well-being of Jacob" (*CV*). Msgr. Kissane translates, "Thou hast shown favour to thy land, thou hast changed the fortunes of Jacob," then explains: "This psalm is a message of hope to the returned exiles who during the early years after the return from exile were discouraged because their condition fell far short of the glorious and happy state which had been foretold by the prophets." Deutero-Isaiah, especially, had depicted the restoration almost as a return to paradise (cf. 51:3). The content of the psalm is perhaps more accurately summed up by *BJ*: after a slow and difficult start, the repatriated will enjoy a happier period (cf. Pss 14:7; 80:4; 126:1-6), the one foreseen in Deutero-Isaiah, (45:8; 41:

5; 56:1; 58:8) and in Zechariah (8:12; 9:10). The first stanza of the psalm (vv 2-4) does reflect the atmosphere of the beginning of the "book of consolation" (Deutero-Isaiah):

Comfort, give comfort to my people,
    says your God.
Speak tenderly to Jerusalem, and proclaim to her
    that her service is at an end,
    her guilt is expiated;
Indeed, she has received from the hand of the Lord
    double for her sins (Is 40:1-2).

The second stanza, the complaint, is more dependent on the reflections of the prophets who lived the experiment of the Restoration (cf. §14 c): "You expected much, but it came to little" (Hag 1:9). The reason given is that they were not concerned with rebuilding the temple. In the same vein Zechariah writes: "O Lord of hosts, how long will you be without mercy for Jerusalem and the cities of Judah that have felt your anger these seventy years?" (1:12)

Some authors prefer to understand the psalm in the light of the tradition of the festival cult celebrated at the autumn feast, alluded to in verse 13b: "Our land shall yield its increase." With that interpretation the psalm could be pre-exilic. Weiser reads also in the psalm an illustration of his favorite theme: the necessary tension in genuine faith between what is possessed (*habender Glaube*) and what is expected (*harrender Glaube*). After the complaint a prophet from among the community "hears what God proclaims" and interprets it (vv 9-14): salvation is near, glory will dwell (cf. Hag 2:9) in the land, truth will spring out of the earth, and justice shall look down from heaven. In verse 11-14 the divine attributes and social virtues are poetically personified (comp. Pss 89:15; 97:2). Claiming here as elsewhere that *ṭob* means "rain" (see on *Ps 4) and *gam* "thunder" (instead of the usual "also") Dahood proposes to read in v 13: "With a crash will Yahweh give his rain, and our land will give its produce." Interpreters will more likely listen to what he has to say about "kindness and fidelity" ..."justice and peace" (v 11) being personified attendants of God (see on *Ps 25).

Psalms 85 and 126, writes Mowinckel (I, p. 223), "can most naturally be interpreted as prayers for peace and a happy year, and most probably they belonged to the festival of harvest and new year; at any rate they have the idea of a 'turning of the destiny' in common with this festival; for this term originally indicates the 'turning' which every new year means and is expected to involve. Especially in Ps 126 it is most natural to take the mention of sowing and reaping as referring to real life, and not merely as a metaphor for salvation in general, the hoped-for restoration.... Both psalms mentioned justify the prayer for a 'turning' by referring to a particular occasion known to everybody, on which God had turned the destinies of the people; this probably is a reference to the restoration after the Exile."

PSALM 90 (89)

God's Eternity and Man's Frailty

The psalm is ascribed to Moses by the heading, presumably because it contains material alluding to stories of Gn 1-3 and to Dt 32-33. Besides, the ascription is a precious witness of the high esteem in which tradition held the psalm. Although by its content the poem owes much to wisdom, its structure and main thoughts suggest that it is a community lament (cf. vv 12-17), not associated with any precise situation. Human life is reconsidered against the background of the eternal being of God. While God is from everlasting (v 2; cf. Ps 93:2; Hab 1:12; Pr 8:25), man has to return to dust (v 3; cf. Gn 3:19; Pss 89:48; 103:14; 104:29). Human beings disappear as grass in the Orient vanishes under the scorching sun (vv 5-6; cf. Pss 103:15f; 128:6; Is 40:6f). The brevity of human life is rightly explained by the judgment of God on sin (vv 7-11; cf. Gn 6:3, 13). In this reflection centered on the notion of time the psalmist has remarkably adapted sapiential maxims to the requisites of prayer.

Sometimes, Mowinckel notes (I, p. 91), a meditation takes a hymnal form: the introductory part of Ps 90 (vv 2-4) has become a song of praise to God's everlastingness as a background to a prayer of mercy towards short-lived man (see on *Ps 139). In fact it can be said that the description of the brevity of human life corresponds to the complaint of the lament. Yet the main point of Ps 90, Mowinckel writes, is not the hymn but "the prayer for the Eternal God not to overlook the short life of a man and let it pass away in misfortune, but to have mercy upon his congregation which consists of such short-lived people" (II, p. 75).

The insistence on the individual's personal claims precludes an early date for the psalm. Mowinckel (I, p. 221) attempts to characterize more precisely the original setting of Ps 90. "Later on, Judaism had a series of annual days of public penance and fasting in remembrance of the great disasters asociated with the fall of the kingdom and the destruction of city and temple (Zc 7:5; 8:19). On these occasions they would complain of the permanent distress, of the degradation of Israel and the oppression and dishonor of gentile supremacy and ask for deliverance, revenge and re-establishment. To this category probably belong for instance Pss 90 and 137." These psalms, he adds, (1, p. 222), including also, it seems, Pss 58, 82, 106, 123, 125 are closely connected—like the later ones of new year and enthronement —with the Jewish hope of future re-establishment: "The eyes of the poet and congregation are turned towards the future, praying for the fulfillment of Israel's hope, the turning of the fate" (see on *Ps 85). The Jewish penitential prayer of the fast days had a nocturnal character. This is perhaps reflected in Ps 90:5f and elsewhere (cf. Is 26:9; Ps 77:3), when God's answer is expected in the morning (see on *Ps 5:4).

PSALM 94 (93)

A Warning to Israel's Oppressors

There is a mixture of various literary elements in this psalm. The first part (1-11) is a prayer imploring the "God of vengeance" ('el n^{e}qāmôt) to pronounce judgment on the evildoers, and not to let the faith of the just be strained beyond limits. The second part (16:23) is a hymn of praise and thanksgiving, joined to the first part by a transition stanza (vv 12-15). Wisdom thought and expression is especially noticeable in the middle part of the poem (vv 8-15). Yet by content and style (cf. vv 5, 14) the psalm is mainly a national lament. With reference to *Ps 44 we have seen that Mowinckel (I, p. 219) links up Ps 94 in the series of I-psalms which also belong to the national psalms of lamentation. The psalmist, most likely the king, represents the congregation on the day of penance. Dahood claims that "the frequency of the yqtl verb form to express past time definitely suggests a pre-Exilic date of composition." He also thinks that "God of vindication" is a better translation in v 1 than "God of vengeance" (RSV): "By rescuing the oppressed and punishing the wicked, Yahweh has vindicated his law."

Two verses call for comment. If one accepts that dûmâh in v. 17 means "The Fortress" (of Sheol; see on *Ps 62:2), then he may translate the verse thus: "If the Lord had not been my help I would have soon dwelt in the Fortress" (*RSV*: "in the land of silence"). Verse 20 is notoriously difficult. A. Allgeier published in 1950 on the verse an article which is a history of its exegesis. It is in fact instructive to note how differently the verse could be rendered by scholars. Moreover there seems to be a deep theological thought involved, to be elucidated. In the following shorter review of mainly modern authors the Douay and *CV* versions represent respectively the Vulgate and the New Latin Psalter: (1) Douay, (2) *CV*, (3) *RSV*, (4) Briggs, (5) R. A. Knox, (6) Kissane, (7) Weiser, (8) Kirkpatrick, (9) *JB*, (10) Dahood.

(1) Doth the seat of iniquity stick to thee,
    who frames labor in commandment?
(2) How could the tribunal of wickedness be leagued with you,
    which creates burdens in the guise of law?
(3) Can wicked rulers be allied with thee,
    Who frame mischief by statute?
(4) Can the throne of engulfing ruin be allied to thee,
    Which frameth trouble by statute?
(5) What part have these unjust judges with thee?
    Thy punishments are for the breakers of thy law.
(6) Will He ally with thee, O throne of iniquity,
    That devisest trouble by statute?
(7) Can the throne of destruction be allied with thee,
    Which frames mischief on the basis of statutes?
(8) Shall the throne of iniquity have fellowship with thee,
    Which frameth mischief by a law?
(9) You never consent to that corrupt tribunal
    that imposes disorder as law...
(10) Can the seat of iniquity associate with you,
    the architect of disorder receive your protection?

All these translations, except the first and (?) last, refer to the wicked tribunal or throne, the verb *yōsēr*, "creates," "frames" (Latin: "fingere"). A typical comment is given by Kissane: "This verse takes up the thought of 16. Is God to make Himself accomplice of the wicked by condoning his crimes?" Much in the same line of thought, Kirkpatrick had written: "Though He may tolerate them for a time, it is inconceivable that Jehovah should let these rapacious judges shelter themselves under his authority."

On the contrary, Allgeier would, with the Vulgate, consider "God" as governing the participle *yōsēr* and translate verse 20b: "der du bildest Leid auf Grund eines Gesetzes." The verse, he comments (p. 28), touches a basic problem of theodicy (also discussed in Job): suffering is not contrary to faith in God. The fundamental motivation, however, of divine ordinations is ultimately beyond man's understanding. The expression *hoq yhwh* can mean a *Grundgesetz* which sets a divine pattern of conduct. Thus in Ps 2:7: "I will point out to you a *hōq yhwh*." So perhaps the following translation of Ps 94:20 could express the psalmist's idea:

Can the tribunal of iniquity be leagued with you,
who establishes suffering on the basis of a law?

PSALM 106 (105)

Israel's Confession of Sin

Although this psalm has much in common with the history Pss 78 and 105, "its basic mood is to be compared rather with a national penitential lament." Weiser notes also that according to the *Community Rule* the renewal of the Covenant at Qumran included the following ceremonies:

1. The praise of God in a hymn sung by the priest and Levites and the congregation's response, "Amen. Amen."
2. The recital by the priests of the divine saving deeds (*sidᵉqôt 'ēl*).
3. The recital by the Levites of the "sins of the Israelites."
4. The confession of sins of those who "enter into the Covenant," made in recognition of God's righteousness and mercy (cf. M. Burrows, *The Dead Sea Scrolls* II, pl. I, 18-II, 1).

In that context Ps 105 could be compared to the *Heilsgeschichte* recital, while Ps 106 would represent the Levitical recital of the sins. *BJ* sees in the first three couplets (vv 1-5) and the last (v 48) a liturgical frame. The enclosed "historical psalm," it adds, belongs to the literary category of national confessions: cf. 1 K 8:33f; Is 63:7 to 64:11; Ne 9:5-37; Dn 9; Ba 1:15 to 3:8. Mowinckel, on the other hand (II, p. 111f), describes Ps 106 as an "historical penitential psalm" and lists it as one of the non-cultic poems (cf. §8a). Ps 106 and Ps 1 deal with a favorite subject of "learned psalmography": Instruction about the destinies of good and evil people. D. G. Castellino, who holds that Pss 58, 77, 82 are community laments, classifies Ps 106 in the category he calls *liturgia della fedeltà jahvistica*: *Pss* 78, 81, 95, 105, 106.

To compare the historical account of Ps 106 with the extant biblical narratives makes interesting study in the longer commentaries. Independent treatment of the same matter usually responds to a theological intent. Thus, as Weiser remarks, the tradition of the Exodus (vv 6-23) "is considered from the point of view of the unbelief of the people who negligently pass by the wonderful works of God and rebel against his will." Verse 47a reads: "Save us, O Lord, our God, and gather us from among the nations." "This statement," notes Kirkpatrick (introduction to Ps 105), "which at first sight might seem to imply that no return had yet taken place, must be understood as a prayer for the completion of the restoration by the return of the Israelites from all the countries in which they were scattered" (see on *Ps 105). Verse 48 is a doxology seemingly added later to end the Fourth Book of the Psalter. It recurs in 1 Ch 16: 36 (see also on *Ps 96).

Two verses call for a special comment. The common translation of v 15, "he gave them what they asked, but sent a wasting disease among them" (*RSV, NAB*), can be referred to Nb 11:33, but does not adhere closely to the *MT* for the second colon, which has "and he sent leanness (*rāzón*) into their souls" (or "down their throats"; see on *Ps 22·21). Instead of reading *zārôn*, as these translations do, Dahood understands *be* as meaning "from," and thus obtains: "Yet he gave them what they requested, and cast out leanness from their throats," with a meaning similar to Ps 107:9, "and fills with good things the hungry throat." The solution can be proposed as a conjectural attempt to elucidate a sort of textual puzzle. Instead of understanding, as is more usual, v 28b as pointing to "the sacrifices of dead gods" (*NAB*), illustrated by Nb 25:2, it seems possible to read there a reference to "funeral banquets" (Dahood), in which the Canaanites upon their "high places" shared meals with their dead (cf. Dt 26:14).

PSALM 108 (107)

Prayer for Victory

At a period which is not anterior to the formation of the Elohistic collection (cf. §3b) an "editor" has apparently combined for liturgical purposes Ps 57:8-12 and Ps 60:7-14 into one psalm, our Ps 108. He may also have taken the texts from "ancient religious poems" (Dahood), which also served for the composition of the two other psalms mentioned. The first part (vv 2-7) is a thanksgiving, hymnic in form, which in *Ps 57 indicated that this lament had been written after the granting of the petition. The second part (vv 9-14) is an oracle of consolation introduced in the national lament (*Ps 60) explained above. Pss 12, 60 and 108 contain various elements typical of cultic liturgies (see *Ps 12).

Psalm 123 (122)

Israel's Prayer in Persecution

This short unpretentious yet moving poem, one of the "songs of ascents" (§13c), was recited by a genuinely pious and sincere man, in the name of the community. In it he stresses how dependent of God enthroned in heaven, is the company of the just, constantly in need, and satiated with humiliation. His interpretation of the right attitude of man towards God correctly combines reverential awe, which prevents undue familiarity, and trusting love, which is proper to sons and not to slaves. As expression of a humble feeling of dependence, Ps 123 can be compared to Ps 131. According to JB the psalm was "probably composed shortly after the return from exile or in the time of Nehemiah; the restored community was exposed to the contempt and hostility of surrounding pagans (cf. Ne 2:19; 3:36)."

Psalm 126 (125)

The People's Prayer for Full Restoration

This "pilgrim song" seems to reflect a situation similar to the one proposed for *Ps 85: the material and social conditions the poet witnesses fulfill very incompletely the splendid restoration promised by the prophets (cf. Ps 59:9-11). With the šibat of verse 1 recurs the translator's problems: should we read "When the Lord brought back the captives of Zion ..." (CV, Kissane, BJ, Osty, New Latin Psalter) or with Briggs, "When Yahweh restores the prosperity of Zion, we are like dreamers"? (also A. Weiser) According to Kraus also, we should read "Als Yahweh wandte Zions Geschick" ("When the Lord changed the fate of Zion") because, he says, *šibat* is obviously a scribal error. Ps 85:5 and Ps 126:4, he thinks, recommend reading either *šebut* (*Ketib*) or *šebit* (*Qerē*). Yet *šibat* may well be retained, as it is attested in an eighth century B.C. Aramaic suzerainty treaty from Syria (cf. *CBQ* 1958, pp. 449ff: verse 24 of the Beirut *Sefire* inscription; cf. J. A. Fitzmyer, p. 119f). Why not translate: "When the Lord brought about the return to Zion we were like dreamers"? And in verse 4 the meaning is quite certainly: Let the return of the "returnees" be like rushing streams in the Negeb. J. Morgenstern reads: "Restore our fortune, O God, even as the water-courses in the Negeb!" J. Strungnell, making explicit what is implicit in Hebrew, translates verse 1b: "Then were we as men who had been (were) healed" and refers to Jb 39:4; Is 38:16; Ho 6:11 to 7:1. But this reading is rejected by Kraus and by Dahood, who proposes: "When Yahweh restored the fortunes of Zion, we became like the sands of the sea" (*keḥōl-m yām*, with enclitic *mem*; cf. Gn 32:13). But no *Sitz im Leben* for such an interpretation is given, and v 4a is translated "Yahweh restored our fortunes" (against MT imperative "restore!"), with recourse to an assumed *qatala* verb *šābāh*, like *māšālâh* in Ps 103:19: "Though Yahweh set his throne in heaven, by his royal power he rules over all."

"Those that sow in tears shall reap rejoicing" (v 5) was probably a proverbial saying, which Jesus, according to the fourth Gospel, expressed otherwise: "Unless the grain of wheat fall into the ground and die, it remains alone. But, if it die, it brings forth much fruit" (12:24). In Ps 126:5, writes Mowinckel (I, p. 147), "we have a reference to the crops of the coming year, which are to be safeguarded by the harvest feast. But the thought goes further. The turning of destiny involves all conceivable happiness, in a moral as well as a material sense." The idea that rejoicing follows weeping (vv 5-6) finds expression also in the Fourth Gospel: "You shall weep and lament, but the world shall rejoice; and you shall be sorrowful; but your sorrows shall be turned into joy" (16:20).

PSALM 137 (136)

The Exile's Remembrance of Zion

The psalmist, a repatriated exile, recalls some features of the sad experiences of the Israelite captives in Babylonia. Ezekiel also had been with "the exiles who lived at Tel Abib by the river Chobar" and for seven days, he writes, "I sat among them distraught" (3:15). Their harps were idle, hung on the aspens. How could they sing in a foreign land the praises of God, who seemingly had abandoned them; how could they desecrate the holy hymns and their own souls by entertaining a pagan and mocking audience? A. Guillaume even feels quite certain that by tôleלîm (CV, "captors") in verse 3 "harsh, pitiless slavedrivers" are meant (on reading "let my right hand wither" in v 5, see on *Ps 102:5). The hated Edomites (cf. Is 34:5-15; Jr 49:7-22; Ezk 25:12ff) were allied with the Babylonians to bring about the "day of Jerusalem" (v 7), the catastrophe of 587-6 (cf. Lm 4:21f; Am 1:11f; Ob 2-9). They even seized that opportunity for settling in southern Judah.

The poet feels Babylon did not get the right treatment when spared by Cyrus. He lets himself be dominated by "his mounting rage" and "plunges into the abyss of human passion" (Weiser). Isaiah also, prophesying against Babylon proclaimed: "The bows of the young men shall be smashed, their infants dashed to pieces before their eyes" (3: 15f; cf. Jr 14:1). The prayer Mowinckel observes (II, p. 52), passes into a direct curse in a particularly refined form (in v 9), namely as a word of blessing on the person who shall inflict the most cruel revenge against the hated enemy. Yet "the little ones" of verse 9 could also mean the adults (cf. Lm 1:5); all the Babylonians being the "children" of the personified "daughter of Babylon" (cf. Ps 87:4f; Lk 19:44). The imprecation is directed against the future generation of enemies of God and of Israel. Among the calamities mentioned in the "admonitions of Ipu-wer" (see on *Ps 23) the following is mentioned: "Why really, the children of nobles are dashed against the walls. The (once) prayed-for children are (now) laid out in the highground..." (ANET, p. 442). So the fate of the little ones seems to have been used elsewhere also as one among conventional lament motifs. In Jeremiah's letter to the exiles God urged them to settle normally in Babylon and "promote the welfare of the city (LXX: 'country') to which I have exiled you; pray for it to the Lord, for upon its welfare depends your own" (Jr 29:7). Yet in another context the same Jeremiah described the coming "vengeance of the Lord" against Babylon (51:1-64). But this was a prophecy, not a wish! Dahood's translation of v 7b, "Strip her, strip her, to her foundation" (instead of "raze it, raze it...") finds support in Lm 4:21, where the same verb root 'rh is used in the description of Edom's future fate: "You shall become drunk [on the cup of Yahweh's wrath] and strip yourself bare."

According to J. Enciso, the psalms without heading were incorporated later in the Psalter, when the use of "titles" had ceased. For five of these,

Pss 1, 2, 104, 119, 137, the subject-matter pointed to their choice as introductory compositions to the respective collections they prelude to. In the third collection of David (137-145) the main theme would be prayers for help against the enemies, among whom Edom and Babylon occupied the first rank. Mowinckel (II, p. 130) also believes that "the psalm is considerably later than the 'return.'" The poet, he writes, was not among those carried away. This composer of psalms in Zion sees himself as a wandering harp-player. "Through his conventionalized, not realistic image, the poet has given an incomparably touching expression to the elegiac sentiment which grips him when he pictures to himself the emotions and situation of those who were forcibly evacuated to the land of the enemy." In this psalm as in many others traditionalism and personality merge successfully. On "The Structure of Ps 137" see D. N. Freedman in *Fs. W. F. Albright* (Baltimore 1971) 187-205.

§24. PSALMS OF CONFIDENCE OF THE COMMUNITY

(a) *General character*

Even in the private psalms the confidence motif has generally a collective bearing since the suppliant prays as a member of the covenant and the favor expected is for the benefit of the community (cf. §22a, 2). Biblical confidence relies on God alone (Is 30:15), any other support being excluded (cf. Is 31:1; Ps 40:5). This firm trust in the Lord is expressed both in urgent need and in normal situations of human life. The three collective psalms of confidence follow much the same pattern as the corresponding private poems. Psalm 46 is added by some to this category while Ps 115 is listed by others with the hymns. There are good reasons to maintain our classification. The key ideas of the three psalms include: the invitation to set fully one's trust in God (115:9ff; 125:1), rock of security (125:1f), source of blessing (115:15; 129:8) and peace (125: 5).

(b) The psalms of confidence of the community are: (115), 125, (129).

PSALM 115 (113B)

The Greatness and Goodness of the True God

The central idea of this psalm is found in vv 9-11, where the three classes of Israel, the laity of Israelite birth, the priests and "those who fear the Lord" express their confidence in God. This sort of litany, the benediction which follows (vv 12-15) and the hymn (16-18) featured, it seems, in a liturgy glorifying the name of God (vv 1-3). While the true "God is in heaven" (v 3), distinct from and infinitely above mankind, the idols are earthly and dependent on their human makers. Traditional formulas describe the powerlessness of the image of the gods (vv 4-8; cf. Ps 95:5; Dt 4:28; 1 S 12:21; Hab 2:18ff; Jr 10:3ff; 16:19f; Is 40:19f; 44:9f). Such descriptions presumably drew their stylized forms from their use in covenant liturgies which included the renunciation of the foreign gods (cf. Gn 35:2; Jos 24:14-25). Decisive against the gods is the fact that they are not alive. On earth human activity's highest living expression is the praise of God. When this is impossible, as in Sheol, life is at its minimum (cf. §14d). On *dûmâh* as the "fortress" of Sheol in v 17 ("go down to the Fortress") see on *Ps 62.

Mowinckel describes Ps 115 as a "liturgy for a day of penance" (II, p. 50) and believes it is also "marked by the spirit of *early Judaism* and its whole conception of God after the full victory of monotheistic thought" (I, p. 98). In these "younger psalms" (also Pss 135:15-18; 96: 6; 97:7), he adds, it is not the struggle against Canaanite influences which we face; it is the spirit of self-conscious "Judaism," feeling its superiority over the stupid polytheism of the surrounding "idolaters." Yet there is no compelling reason to classify the psalm as recent. "Judaism" began with Ezra and even in pre-exilic times there were "proselytes" (cf. Ex 18:9-12; 1 K 8:41ff; 2 K 5:17). Furthermore it is not certain that "those who fear the Lord" (v 11; cf. Pss 118:4; 135:20) are proselytes. The expression can designate the whole community of the just (cf. Pss 61:6; 103:17), although in New Testament times it did refer to those who sympathized with Judaism without accepting circumcision (cf. Ac 10:2, 22, 35; 13:16, 26). In the Greek and Latin versions Ps 115 is joined to Ps 114 to form one psalm (113), but originally they were probably distinct (see on *Ps 114).

PSALM 125 (124)

The Lord the Protector of Israel

Those who put their trust in God are immovable like Mount Zion, which was believed to be deeply rooted in the center of the earth (see on *Ps 46 and *Ps 48). The faith of the just is exposed to great temptations if "the sceptre of the wicked," foreign domination probably, remains too long upon the territory of the just (v 3; cf. §12b), Yahweh's holy inheritance (cf. *Ps 142:6). So a prayer for faith preservation is formulated (v 4). The call on the judgment of God to isolate the just from the wicked (vv 3, 5) and the allusions to the danger of apostasy seem to reflect an eschatological thought pattern already preluding to apocalyptic developments.

Repointing *yēšēb* to *yōšēb* and referrring to Pss 9:12; 99:1; 135:21, where he discovers (other) divine titles, Dahood translates v 1: "Those who trust in Yahweh are like the Mountain of Zion; never will be upset the Enthroned of Jerusalem," the Mountain of Zion being, like "the Enthroned of Jerusalem," a divine epithet describing Yahweh. But to say equivalently "those who trust in Yahweh are like Yahweh" lacks originality. It is then preferable to keep *yēšēb*, "to abide," "to be firm" (cf. Gn 49:24), and translate: "Those who trust in the Lord are like Mount Zion, which cannot be moved, but abides for ever" (*RSV*).

PSALM 129 (128)

Prayer for the Overthrow of Israel's Foes

This psalm also includes elements of a community lament (cf. vv 5-7), but the expression of confidence predominates: as in the past, Israel will survive (vv 1-3) and its enemies will be confounded (vv 5-8), under the just judgment of God (v 4). Weiser describes the psalm as a liturgical formulary of the Israelite covenant community (cf. §13c). Those "that hate sin" (v 5) could be, he thinks, Israelites of the Northern Kingdom, opposed to the Jerusalem cult. Cultic imprecations, recalled in verses 5-8, were employed against them. According to Mowinckel (I, p. 45), on the other hand, Ps 129 illustrates well that use of the I-psalms in which the singer represents the "corporate, greater I" of the congregation. The usage would be "normal, ancient, Israelite cultic style." Yet, according to E. Balla (p. 114), Ps 129 is, of all the *Ichpsalmen* of the Psalter, the only example in which the people are poetically personified (cf. §23a).

§25. THANKSGIVINGS OF THE COMMUNITY

(a) General character

These psalms praise God and thank him for his general favors. They celebrate his saving intervention on behalf of Israel or of the just, mainly the poor and the weak. Hymnic elements do appear in some of these psalms (see §23a). According to G. Pidoux the hymns celebrate Yahweh's interventions in Israel's early history, while the collective thanksgivings are concerned rather with recent deeds of deliverance (*Du Portique à l'autel*, p. 65). Postexilic eschatological prophecy will also express itself in a type of national thanksgiving (cf. Is 26:7-19; Zc 9:9-17).

It is likely that thanksgiving festivals constituted the original setting of the private and national thanksgiving psalms. Features of these liturgical ceremonies have been preserved, mainly in the thanksgiving psalms of the community. He who wishes to express his gratitude comes to the temple with a victim (66:13ff). Having been greeted by the worshippers present (32:1f), he announces his intention to praise God, "to declare all his wondrous deeds" (9:2), since his personal experience testifies to the merciful ways of divine Providence (30:6; 34:17-23).

The votive offering of a sacrifice (cf. Pss 65:2; 116:18) often accompanies the prayer of the thanksgiving: "I will bring holocausts to your house; to you I fulfill the vow which my lips uttered and my words promised in my distress" (66:13f; cf. 22:26; 76:12). Possibly some psalms were composed precisely to accompany the *tôdâh*, the thanksgiving sacrifice (cf. the heading of Ps 100), mentioned in various texts: Am 4:5; Jr 17:26; 33:11; Jon 2:10; Lv 7:12; 22:29. The same word *tôdâh* means in other texts "praise" (Jr 30:19; Is 51:3; Ps 26:7) of gratitude (Jos 7:19; Ezr 10:11; cf. *Ps 27:6). In Ps 50:14 instead of "Offer to God praise as your sacrifice" it is suggested to read "Offer to God a thanksgiving sacrifice" (cf. Pss 50:23; 107:22; 116:17). God does not condemn the offering of sacrifices (Ps 50:8-13), but the qualified value of animal sacrifice (see on *Ps 51:18) is sometimes recalled. As Ibn Ezra puts it: "The sacrifices are not useful to God, but to man" (see R. Pautrel, "Immola Deo...", p. 239; E. Podechard, *Le Psautier*, I, p. 226f; H.-J. Kraus *Psalmen*, p. 309f; S. Mowinckel, II, p. 90f).

Other elements of sacrificial rites are attested in the psalms (cf. §8b). In a lament the suppliant declares: "I wash my hands in innocence, and I go around your altar, O Lord, giving voice to my thanks, and recounting all your wondrous deeds" (26:6f). Processions around the altar could be an ancient rite of semitic religions. The "prophets of Baal," in Elijah's time, "limped about the altar which they had made" (1 K 18:26). The association of "innocence" with the altar reminds one of the purifying oath (*Reinigungseid*) described in 1 K 8:31f. In the second part of Ps

22 the thanksgiving says: "So by your gift will I utter praise in the vast assembly; I will fulfill my vows before those who fear him. The lowly shall eat their fill" (v 26f). It is probable that this thanksgiving (vv 23-32) was uttered during a ritual meal offered to the "poor" (cf. §12a), among whom the psalmist willingly counted himself (v 25). Some read in Ps 22:27 an allusion to the messianic banquet (Is 25:6; 55:1; 65:13; Pr 9:1f; Ps 23:5) rather than a ritual meal associated with the communion sacrifice (Lv 7: 15; Dt 14:29; 16:13). Ps 118 contains instructive indications concerning the thanksgiving liturgy: entry into the temple (vv 19f), exclamation of the worshippers (vv 22-26), procession (v 27), thanksgiving proper (5-18), and a responsory of a choir or of the congregation (vv 1-4 and 29). The main section includes a description of the distress (5-7; 10-13), particular (14-18) and general (8-9) deductions and finally the repetition of the psalmist's intention (28). As for the structure of these collective psalms it follows the same pattern as the similar psalms of the individual.

(b) These are the thanksgivings of the community: Pss (65), (66), 67, (68), (118), 124.

PSALM 65 (64)

Thanksgivings for God's Blessings

The statement in verse 2, "To you must vows be fulfilled, you who hear prayers," seems to imply that this community thanksgiving takes place after God had answered prayers for rain in a time of drought. The psalm could also have been sung at the harvest festival which, it is said, coincided with the New Year festival celebrated in the spring since the reign of Josiah. This "thanksgiving psalm of the harvest feast," writes Mowinckel, (I, p. 162f), is also one of the enthronement psalms (cf. §13a). Verses 6-9 celebrate the victory of God over the primordial ocean. "The dwellers at the earth's ends" are not remote nations but the "demonic powers of the $t^e h \bar{o} m$ around the earth," "the helpers of Rahab" (Jb 9:3), conquered at the moment of creation (cf. §9b, 11a). The regular return of the rainy season (vv 10-14) was an annual blessing resulting from the establishment of the "right order" in the beginning.

In Ps 65 the congregation thanks God for benefits of a general character: graces of the sanctuary (vv 2-5), mastery over natural elements

(6-8), blessing of fertility (10-14). Notions typical of the thanksgiving are featured: vows have to be fulfilled (v 2), God hears prayers (v 2), God answers in his justice (v 6). Temporal blessings of the community constitute the immediate object of the thanksgiving. This serves the psalmist as a starting-point for reviewing man's relationship with God. He reaffirms especially that only with God's grace can man overcome his sin and approach to God (vv 3-5). In this psalm, as throughout the Psalter, the divine purpose is seen achieving itself in history by divine rule which dominates the whole world from its very beginning (vv 6-9). To the retreatant wishing to acquire a greater love of God St. Ignatius Loyola suggests that he meditate on the way God is at work for us in the gifts of nature, including plant and animal life. A similar insight seems to have been in the psalmist's mind when he describes God himself as active in the fertility of the land (vv 10-14; cf. *Ps 104).

PSALM 66 (65)

Praise of God, Israel's Deliverer

The unity of the psalm can be maintained if we suppose, with Weiser, that the community thanksgiving festivals supplied the framework within which the worshippers' vows could be fulfilled (cf. 1 S 1:21; 2:1-10) and personal thanksgivings recited. For H. Schmidt Pss 66 and 106 are liturgies for the offering of votive thanksgiving sacrifices (cf. Ps 66:13).

The occasion for the festival in which Ps 66 featured was the deliverance from a great national danger, as it appears in verses 8-12, where the community thanksgiving recalls aspects of the calamity. This section of the poem is preceded by an hymnal introduction in praise of the *Heilsgeschichte* God (vv 1-7): "Come and see the works of God, his tremendous deeds among men" (v 5), sacred history actualized in the cult. "The psalm presents itself as the response of the cult community to the recital of the *Heilsgeschichte* tradition which has taken place in a previous cultic act; this was understood as a present action of God directed towards the members of the cult community themselves and causing all historical differences of space and time to disappear in face of the reality of God, so that participants in the cult, in facing God, faced the same situation in which the people of God had once found themselves at the time of the Exodus and their entry into the Promised Land" (Weiser).

When Dahood, on the basis of a frail Ugaritic parallel, claims that v 6 al-ludes only to the miraculous crossing of the Sea of Reeds and not (also) to the fording of the Jordan by Joshua, he fails to mention that nowhere else is the Sea of Reeds called *nāhār*, and that Ps 114:3 clearly attests a tradition which combined the two events. Although the notion of sheol as a slippery place is well documented (see above p. 146), no justifica-tion is apparent for turning *lammōṭ* (v 9) into a substantive meaning "quagmire," as Dahood does.

Mowinckel believes that the real thanksgiving occurs in the second part (vv 13-20) where, in "king-ego" style, a leading representative speaks in the name of the people. E. Podechard (p. 282) says that the leader of the nation illustrated with his personal *Heilsgeschichte* exper-ience what protection God provides to Israel. The influence of Deutero-Isaiah on the psalm could suggest a postexilic date.

Psalm 66 is a good example of the way dimensions of time and space are reduced to a present (cf. vv 3, 5) in the cult, and broadened to in-clude all peoples (vv 4, 8): the whole cosmos centers in the temple, where the singers are the stage-managers who orchestrate the worshipping praise of all nations (cf. §8b). Enlightened Christians believe that uni-versal *Heilsgeschichte* is re-experienced in their paschal liturgy. In the resurrection of Christ, the Head of renewed humanity, divine salvation concentrates. To this central event can apply Ps 66:12, especially in the German translation: "Du hast uns herausgeführt in die Freiheit" (Kraus, Lohfink): "You have led us out to freedom." Paschal themes related to the Exodus do in fact feature in Ps 66 (cf. v 6). In the Roman Missal verses 2, 3 constitute the Introit of the Third Sunday after Easter. In the LXX and Vulgate the title "psalm of the resurrection" is applied to Ps 66, presumably because of verse 9: "He has given life to our souls, and has not let our feet slip."

PSALM 67 (66)

Harvest Prayer That All Men May Worship God

This psalm featured as part of the harvest-thanksgiving festival cele-brated in autumn: "The earth has yielded its fruits; God, our God, has blessed us" (v 7). It is, like the majority of the psalms, very theocentric in thought structure. Its main concern is that God's salvation be revealed to the nations and be praised by all peoples. The Giver, not the gifts is central; not the blessing of the harvest (as in the fertility-rites) but the divine deed is celebrated in the Israelite cult. The tone of the psalm is firmly expressed in the refrain (vv 4, 6) and already felt in the opening prayer (v 2), similar to the "Aaronite blessing": "The Lord bless you and keep you! The Lord let his face shine upon you, and be gracious to you! The Lord look upon you kindly and give you peace!" (Nb 6:24ff) God's providential rule appears to concentrate on Israel's destinies. But divine intervention in this particular case discloses what pattern of salvation awaits the whole world.

Commenting upon some ideas involved in the "enthronement psalms" Mowinckel (I, p. 185) writes: "We shall not be able fully to realize the emotions of poet and congregation when, in Ps 93, creation is mentioned as the basis of kingship, unless we have also realized the actual re-experience of the saving work of creation through the growth of the crops of the blessed year, which is expressed by the authors of harvest festival thanksgiving psalms like 65 or 67." Parsing *nat^{e}nâh* as a "precative perfect" (see on Ps 4:8; cf. *Ps 3), Dahood translates Ps 67:7: "May the earth yield her produce, may God, our God, bless us." He can point to a parallel, Ps 85:13, to support his claim that the psalm is a prayer for rain, although rain is nowhere explicitly mentioned (see also Lv 26:4). He supplies additional proofs in *CBQ* 1970, p. 632f, for his view that *nat^{e}nâh* does not mean "has given," as is generally believed (cf. *RSV*, *NAB*). Although Tournay understands the past ("La terre a donné son produit") and calls the psalm "a thanksgiving hymn," he entitles its contents "collective prayer after the annual harvest." Technically v 7 can be understood as a precative perfect pointing to the future, but this is not required by the context of a psalm which includes both thanksgiving and prayer. Helen G. Jefferson notes that Ps 67 is one of four psalms (also 29, 93, 100) having 71% of its vocabulary paralleled by Ugaritic roots. In itself this statistic only shows that Ugaritic and Hebrew are related languages. But she concludes: "The cultic coloring of Ps 67, its vocabulary and style, all point to Canaanite influence. This supports the theory that Ps 67 is pre-exilic in origin." It can be doubted, however, that Canaanite influence does necessarily indicate such an early date (cf. § 9d).

PSALM 68 (67)

God's Triumphal Procession

The fact that the text is poorly preserved in some sections (cf. vv 12-15) renders even more difficult the interpretation of this psalm already obscured by brief allusions to too many scattered events. Yet the general real life setting of the psalm may well have been the autumn covenant festival (§13c). Two verses are especially significant in that respect.

Rain in abundance, O God, thou didst shed abroad;
thou didst restore thy heritage as it languished—(v 9=10:RSV).
Thy solemn processions are seen, O God,
the processions of my God, my King, into the sanctuary—(24=25: RSV).

At the heart of that festival, Weiser explains, is the revelation of God, who according to ancient thought, comes to his sanctuary from Mount Sinai and by his presence "actualizes" his redemptive work. This sacral act of salvation "is executed in a stylized pattern of sacred phrases and rites cast in a fixed form by tradition; and the psalm refers to this, though mostly only in brief hints." The main phases of *Heilsgeschichte* (salvation history) are celebrated in this triumphal hymn, which is introduced by the departure words of Moses addressed to the theophany God (§13d) on the sacred Ark: "Arise, O Lord, that your enemies may be scattered, and those who hate you may flee from you" (Nb 10:35; cf. Is 33:3). It could be the signal for the procession to leave.

BJ lists as follows the sequence of events evoked by the psalm: the exodus from Egypt, the wandering in the desert, marked by various incidents (rebellion, theophany, manna and quail), the victories at the time of the Judges (Deborah, Gideon) and the settlement in Zion (David, Solomon), the stories about Elijah and Elisha, the tragic fate of the Ahab family, the solemn pasch of Hezekiah. It seems that the unpleasant allusions to Egypt in verse 31 are more recent than the original psalm. The Deutero-Isaiah universalist views reflected in verses 29-33 could also point to a post-exilic re-edition of the psalm. The basic antiquity of the psalm seems to be indicated by its use of formulas like "rider of the clouds" (vv 5, 34). Other archaic expressions, *qōdeš*, "sanctuary" (vv 18, 25), *miqdāšîm*, "sanctuaries" (36) and "the voice of power" (34) suggest to Eerdmans that the psalm was composed during the reign of David. W. F. Albright has stated (p. 3) that "fully half of the unique words which strew Ps 68 may be elucidated by Ugaritic." He also believes that this psalm consists of a string of about thirty *incipits* (beginnings of poems) written not much later than the Solomonic period. A more likely interpretation would be that of H. Schmidt, for whom Ps 68 is a collection of short autonomous poems, sung on the same occasion: procession in honor of Yahweh (vv 25f) and of his enthronement at the New Year Festival (cf. §13a). It should be also recorded here that A. Caquot explains Ps 68 as a victory hymn probably composed at the time of King Hezekiah and for an enthronement celebration of Yhwh at the autumn New Year festival (in *Revue de l'Histoire des Religions* 178, 1970, 147-82).

Mowinckel writes that Ps 68 is an old originally North Israelite psalm later adapted for the epiphany festival in Jerusalem (II, p. 152). Ps 68, he also believes, is a procession psalm for the "festival of light" (cf. Ps 118:27). It celebrated Yahweh's triumphal entry as king at the feast of tabernacles (I, p. 170, 182). In fact, he says, Pss 24, 68, 118, 132 were written for festal processions (I, p. 5). Other authors suggest that Ps 68 reflects the cultic traditions associated with an ancient Israelite sanctuary at Mount Thabor. This would explain the attention given to the Deborah victory over Sisara (vv 13-17 and Jgs 4:12ff). As reported by Weiser, "Gaster (*Thespis*...p. 415ff) takes Ps 68 to be the libretto of the pantomime performed at the Canaanite New Year Festival, which in his opinion was worked over for liturgical use in the Yahweh cult; he believes that *bāšān* (vv 16, 23) alludes to the chaos dragon and corresponds to the Ugaritic *btn*, a designation that would fit in very well with the phrase *the depths of the sea* in verse 23." Weiser is probably right though in his opinion that the interpretation from Israelite tradition is the more natural one in view of the whole tenor of the psalm. (*Btn* in Ugaritic means "serpent, dragon"; on the destruction of *Bashan's* kingdom, cf. Nm 21:33ff.)

Because of the special character of this psalm it sems advisable to mention sundry suggestions made to help understand the more difficult passages (the numbers indicate the verses).

(5) "Extol him who rides upon the clouds." JB reads: "Build a road for the Rider of the Clouds," while the revised Latin Psalter has, "Lay a road for him who rides through the desert." "One and the same epithet is applied to Ba'l as *rkb 'rpt* (1 Aqht: 43:44) and to God as *rōkēb bā'arābôt* (Ps 68:5)" (C. H. Gordon, p. 292). "The expression *The Rider of the Clouds* as a divine epithet is very ancient, since it occurs in Chanaanite literature even before the time of Moses, and it is not uncommon in the Old Testament. Cf. Dt 33:26; Ps 18:10ff; 68:34; Is 19:1; Hab 3:8" (*CV*). Parsing *l* of *lē'lōhîm* as vocative *lamedh* (see v 33), M. Dahood translates: "Sing, O gods, chant, O his heavens, pave the highway for the Rider of the Clouds!"

(7) W. F. Albright proposed in *HUCA* the following improved translation of verse 7: "It is Yhwh who causeth the single to set up house, who setteth free prisoners with music, but who causeth rebels to tent in the wasteland" (cf. *Ps 113:9).

(9) Emending verse 9 with the help of Jg 5:4f and the Targum, E. Vogt finds the following meaning: "The earth quaked, the heavens swayed, the mountains shook before the Lord, before the Lord, the God of Israel." Instead of "[This is Sinai]" Dahood reads "The One of Sinai," and explains: "Because he created Sinai as his sanctuary (v 18), and because he appeared there to Moses at the momentous point in Israelite history, Yahweh received the epithet *zeh sīnay*, 'The One of Sinai' (also in Jg 5:5)."

(10) Whether we have a scribe's inspired misspelling or a rare Hebrew root, D. W. Goodwin believes, we need not alter the consonantal text in order to obtain a satisfactory translation of verse 10: "An abundance of rain will thou give freely, O God, a stream, subsided and exhausted, thou wilt restore it."

(12) Reading *'imrâh mebaśśeret*, R. Tournay translates verse 12: "The Lord gives an order, it serves notice of a vast army." With this would fall the allusion to female heralds.

(13) Having read in verse 13, "May the kings of the *host* bow themselves, bow themselves, the country's pasture land share the boon," Dahood explains that the "brighter stars" empty their contents upon Palestine.

(14) Various attempts have been made to elucidate verse 14. Even though the Rubenites had not cooperated, their Israelite brothers scored a great victory and collected a large booty of gold and silver (R. Tournay). The dove is Israel (cf. Ho 7:11; 11:11; Ps 74:19) or perhaps an object of art found in the booty: an image of the Phoenician goddess Astarte (cf. 1 K 11:5, 33), represented with a dove, symbolizing love (cf. E. Podechard, "Psaume LXVIII," p. 516).

(15) R. Tournay proposes that the snow which fell on Salmon was a rain of "salt" (cf. Jgs 9:45). Hoar-frost is compared to salt in Si 43:18f. But S. Iwry sees in the text no allusion to any miraculous event; Read: "When Shaddai scattered the kings, as snow dries up (*khtś ślg*) in Zalmon."

(18) According to Albright (*Fs Mowinckel*), the original text of verse 18 could have been "The chariots of Yahweh were two (?) thousand, two myriads the bowmen of my Lord, when they brought the Holy Ark(?) from Sinai." Reading also *šin'ān* as "archer," and *yābam*, as "creator," Dahood has the following rendering: "God's chariots were twice ten thousand, thousands the archers of the Lord, who created Sinai as his sanctuary." Cf. Ex 15:17; Ps 78:54.

(19) Instead of the rather queer idea that God "received men as gifts," one should probably read, with Dahood, in verse 19: "You received gifts from (*ba*) their hands ('*d*)" (see on *Ps 17:4).

(23) Completing suggestions advanced since 1959 at least, P. D. Miller amends the *MT* of verse 23 to read '*ešbam bāšān* and translates: "Said the Lord: I muzzled the Serpent, I muzzled the Deep Sea." The elucidation of the text is based on a Ugaritic parallel: "I muzzled *tannin*, I muzzled him. I smote the twisting serpent" ('*nt*: III:37f; cf. *JBL* 1961, p. 270f). F. C. Fensham relies also on Ugaritic to read in the same verse: *miḥōr bāšān 'ašib* and translates: God said: "From the hole of the snake I will bring back, I will bring back from the depths of the sea" (cf. Is 11:8). Other suggestions and discussions in Dahood's *Psalms* II, p. 145f.

(33) Dahood's translation: "O kings of the earth, sing! O gods, sing praises to the Lord!" This supposes the use of the vocative *lamedh* (cf. on *Ps 33 and VD 45, 1967,pp. 32-46) and the meaning "kings" given to *mamlekoth* ("kingdoms"), as in Phoenician and in biblical passages: 1 S 10:18; 1 K 10:20; 2 Ch 9:19; 12:8; Is 47:5; Jr 1:15; 25:26; Pss 79:6; 102:23; 135:11. But "kingdoms" fits also well in the context.

For a full discussion of these and of the other verses see now J. Vlaardingerbroek, *Psalm* 68 (an Amsterdam Dissertation in Dutch, with a short summary in English, dated 1973).

PSALM 118 (117)

Hymn of Thanksgiving to the Savior of Israel

Psalm 118 is very illuminating for the study of the ancient thanksgiving liturgy (cf. §25a). Mowinckel (I, p. 180f) attributes special importance to Ps 118, as illustrating what took place at the so-called "enthronement festival" (cf. §13a). Some of his remarks deserve attention. The psalm, like the procession, starts outside the "Gate of Righteousness,"

very likely the innermost temple gate, through which only "the righteous"
—the congregation in a state worthy of the cult—are allowed to enter. In
Babylonia also temple gates were named according to various blessings
supposedly received when entering (cf. H. Zimmern, in Z. d. Deutschen
Morg. Ges., 76, 1922, p. 49). The request to open the Gate of Righteousness (v 19-20; see on *Ps 24) is preceded by a thanksgiving (vv 1-18) in
which the king or the leader of the congregation testifies in the name of
the community that God has been the savior of Israel throughout the
ages. One "concentrated picture" recalls how, when Israel was encom-
passed about by the nations, the king destroyed them in the name of
Yahweh. Here, Mowinckel believes, the "saga has been conventionalized
on the model of the myth about *the fight of nations*" (p. 180).

Then follow a short thanksgiving (vv 21-25) and a prayer for prosperity (v 26), to which the priests answer with a blessing from the house
of the Lord on those who are now coming (in procession) in his holy
Name (v 26). What the priests say then, "The Lord is God, and he has
given us light" (v 27), could reflect the Aaronite benediction (N 6:
25) and allude to the "festival of light" of the feast of Tabernacles. The
invitation to join in a cultic "dance" around the altar, "with leafy boughs,"
could be in relation to an aspect of the Feast of Booths: "On the first day
you shall gather foliage from majestic trees, branches of palms and boughs
of myrtles and of valley poplars, and there for a week you shall make
merry before the Lord, your God" (Lv 23:40; cf. Ne 8:15; 2 M 10:7;
Mk 11:8). A third hymn concludes the psalm (vv 28-29). It includes
the thanksgiving of the king (v 28) and of the choir (v 29), probably
sung during the "festal dance."

When the representative of the people has ended his thanksgiving
(vv 5-21), the congregation, speaking in the third person, opens its
hymn with the following words: "The stone which the builders rejected
has become the cornerstone" (v 22). It alludes to various texts (cf. Zc 3:
9; 4:7; Is 8:14; 28:16) which have been interpreted in a messianic sense
and applied to Christ (Mt 21:42; Ac 4:11; Rm 9:33; 1 Cor 3:11; Ep 2:
20; 1 P 2:4f). The simile of the cornerstone could point to the restoration
of Israel when the temple was rebuilt after the exile (cf. Hag 1:9; Zc 1:
16). In the psalm itself "the parable illustrates the change that has taken
place in the fortunes of the saved man: he was rejected, despised and
persecuted by men, but was saved and honored by God and was entrusted by him with a particularly important task. The interpretation of
this saying in late Judaism as referring to David and to the Messiah. . .is

presumably based on the correct recollection that the king appeared in the cult in the rôle of David (cf. Ps 18) and that the royal cult entailed that at any given time the tradition of his ancestor was revived in the person of the actual representative of the Davidic dynasty" (Weiser).

According to *JB*, Ps 118 may have been used for the feast described in Ne 8:13-18 (cf Ezr 3:4; Zc 14:16; Ex 23:14). Ps 119 could then have been connected with the reading from "the book of the law of God." B. D. Eerdmans ("Foreign elements. . . , p. 130) thinks Ps 118 is pre-exilic. Among the indications he finds for that early date is the admission of the laymen into the inner-court of the temple, where the great altar stood. They are told (v 27) to bind their festal-sacrifices with cords to the horns of the altar. In the post-exilic period the laymen had to make their prostrations in the outer-court and attend to the offering of their sacrifices, standing on the threshold of one of the gates, leading into the innercourt, where priests and levites officiated. Eerdmans believes that the psalmist was a zealous missionary and that verses 10-12 allude to the circumcision of his proselytes. So he translates:

All the gojim [non-Israelites] compassed me about
    when I had them circumcized (*'amîlām*) in the name of Jahu.
They surrounded me, encircling me,
    when I had them circumcized in the name of Jahu.
They surrounded me like bees,
    they were quenched like the fire of thorns,
    when I had them circumcized in the name of Jahu.

Thus were the gojim appeased by their circumcision and incorporated "in the congregation of Jahu." Dahood offers a similar translation, and refers to 1 S 17:25-27, where David's hunt *for* Philistine foreskins is narrated. Reading in the psalm symbolical allusions to the king's encounter with death, he translates v 5 thus: "From Confinement I called Yah, Yah answered me from the Broad Domain." Here "Broad Domain," translating *merḥab*, would refer to Yahweh's celestial abode, although elsewhere it designates Sheol (cf. Ps 18:20; 31:9). Is this another tolerable inconsistency? (cp. with *dûmâh* in *Ps 62).

PSALM 124 (123)

The Lord the Rescuer of His People

The dangers and trials from which Israel has been preserved or liberated by the grace of God are evoked in such conventional and stylized metaphors that it is hardly possible even to suggest any specific historical circumstance as the background for this psalm. The adversaries have almost swallowed up Israel (v 3) as the dragon Babylon has swallowed Jerusalem (Jr 51:34). The metaphor of the raging waters (vv 4, 5; cf. Pss 18:5; 42:8; 69:2) can easily be linked with the mythical power of the primeval abyss (cf. §9b, 11a). Israel has also been saved from the teeth of the beasts of prey and from the fowler's snare (vv 6, 7). Salvation, revelation of the divine Name and creation (cf. v 8) are frequently associated in the cult. This and the initial notice, "let Israel say" (v 1), could indicate a liturgical use of the psalm.

Verse 7 borrows from the imagery of bird hunting. This seems also implied in our Lord's saying: "Take heed to yourselves...lest that day come upon you suddenly as a snare" (Lk 21:34f). Although biblical references for this comparison are available (cf. Hab 1:15; Is 24:17; Ho 7:12; Ezk 32:3), its origin can be traced to ancient Oriental representations. On the "stela of the vultures" can be seen a large human figure (the god Ningirsu or Eannatum, the king of Lagash) smiting with a mace human figures, with shaved faces and heads contained in a net. The limestone stela, from Tello in ancient Sumer, is now at the Louvre Museum (cf. ANEP, fig. 298, and A. Parrot, Terre du Christ, Neuchâtel, 1965, p. 102).

VII. Royal Psalms

§26. THEIR GENERAL CHARACTER

It has been said and repeated that the basic reality in human life was for the Israelite not the individual but the community. Within the nation the king was the representative of the whole. Mowinckel can even assert: "The covenant between Yahweh and Israel and between Yahweh and David is one and the same thing." Such being the importance of the king, it is no wonder that psalms have been composed in his honor. In truth, the unity of this category of "royal psalms" rests basically on one fact: they all concern the king. They have no special literary structure although some of the themes are predominant: divine adoption, the throne's stability, the prophecy of Nathan, prayers for the king, oracles promising him happiness and prosperity.

The traditional view which held that David wrote most of the psalms was inclined to increase considerably the number of "royal psalms." When the Davidic authorship was reappraised (cf. §4g) the opposite tendency came to the fore. Mowinckel tells us what happened next: "But in its earlier phase modern scientific study of the psalms tended to deny the presence of any royal figure in the psalms, and it was maintained that they had been largely composed in Jewish times, after the Exile, out of the private experiences of ordinary people in the joys and sorrows of daily life, and through impulses from certain individual prophets.... When we do meet a royal figure, as in the so-called 'messianic' psalms, this figure was interpreted as a personification of the people of Israel. Gunkel was the first to re-conceive of the royal psalms as real king psalms, and place this interpretation on a sure scientific foundation" (I, p. 46f). Conclusions should not be drawn too easily from the presence of themes of royalty, since motifs of royal psalms were sometimes taken over by private, unknown suppliants (cf. H. J. Kraus, *Psalmen*, I, p. 412). Mowinckel devotes in fact a whole chapter to the *"I" and "We" in the Psalms—the*

Royal Psalms (I, pp. 42-80). The problem of the *Ichpsalmen* has been examined above (§23a). It can be recalled here that unless the king is mentioned explicitly or implicitly it is usually difficult to prove that the "I"- speaker is a royal figure, when the context points to the interests of a private individual.

The cultic role of the king has been overemphasized by the so-called "Myth and Ritual School" (see §8d and G. E. Wright, p. 66f). J. L. McKenzie's statement of about ten years ago remains valid: "The arguments raised against this theory by many scholars I accept as decisive, and hence I interpret the messianic character of the Israelite king without any reference to his place in the cult" (*CBQ* 1957, p. 26). "Hebrew kingship and its ideology," he adds, "cannot be explained as a derivation or a borrowing from foreign ideologies because of its connection with the kingship of Yahweh, which is a distinctive Hebrew belief." The king has a "unique position" in the religion of Israel. "He is a charismatic officer, the successor of the judges.... To the king is attributed superhuman strength and wisdom and the possession of the spirit of Yahweh.... He is the incorporation of his people, and in him are recapitulated the covenant of Israel and the promises and obligations which flow from the covenant" (p. 36f; cf. J. De Fraine, *L'aspect...*, p. 371ff). Israelite kingship, observes Wright, "never achieved the sanctity of the absolutism which is encountered elsewhere.... The conception of Yahweh as the covenant-Lord of Israel, the Chosen People, prevented the Israelite monarchy from presuming too much and left independent religious leaders free to pronounce judgment on the kings for doing evil in the sight of Yahweh. It also permitted a people of Yahweh to survive destruction and exile, and attempt to rebuild a holy community without a king in the light of the wilderness period" (p. 67f). In his extensive study of ancient oriental king ideology, K.-H. Bernhardt rejects the "ritual pattern" theory (cf. §8d) and advocates an explanation of royal ideology based on the historical rejection of the kingship and on the traditions of the nomadic period (see especially his 3rd chapter: pp. 56-66). As for K. R. Crim, he agrees generally with H.-J. Kraus' explanation centered on the assumption of an annual festival in Jerusalem commemorating the election of David (see §13b).

The temporal monarch is in fact the delegate of Yahweh, the Eternal King of Israel: Ex 15:18; Nb 23:21; Jg 8:23; 1 S 8:7; 12:12; 1 K 22: 19; Is 6:5. For this reason the king's throne in Jerusalem is called "throne of the Lord" (1 Ch 29:23) or "the throne of the kingdom of the Lord over Israel" (1 Ch 28:5). The permanency attributed to the dynasty in the language of court etiquette was freely wished to the king himself: "He asked life of you: you gave him length of days forever and ever" (Ps 21:5). "Eternal duration" was a quality associated with kingship by the ancient conventional court-style. In the economy of divine revelation such hyperbolic language heralded the advent of messianism. It must be noted again that the line of division between individual and eschatological kingship is somewhat difficult to draw. "The historical king appears with traits which are sometimes superhuman, or very near it. He is, at least in the wildest sense, a messianic figure. The accession of a successor of David was a new sign that the national hope of a historical or an eschatological future persevered, that the blessing of Yahweh still rested upon the figure of Israel through the king" (McKenzie, p. 27; on "royal messianism," see §15c). W. H. Brownlee has recently suggested that the sacral kingship has been introduced in Israel and Judaism as belonging to an "angelic" category (cf. *RB* 1966, pp. 171-175). Four times David is compared to an angel of God: 1 S 14:17, 20, 27; 29:9. According to Zc 12:8, in messianic times the "houses of David shall be godlike, like an angel of the Lord..." (12:8). To king Ahasuerus Esther said: "My Lord, you looked to me like an angel of God, and my heart was moved with fear of your majesty" (Est 5:2; cf. Pr 16:14f).

§27. THE HISTORICAL SETTING

In Gunkel's classification, the royal psalms (2, 18, 20, 21, 45, 72, 101, 110, 132) form one of the five main categories (cf. §7a). The psalms deal with native Israelite kings of the pre-exilic period (Ps 45 which mentions a princess of Tyre, in verse 13, is presumably dedicated to a king of the northern kingdom). Various occasions of the official life of these Davidic monarchs constitute the historical setting of the royal psalms: enthronement (Pss 2, 72, 101, 110), royal wedding (Ps 45), songs related to the king's warring exploits (18, 20, 21, 144A), lament (Ps 89:47ff), and the anniversary of the founding of the Davidic dynasty and its royal sanctuary on Mount Zion (132; cf. Gunkel-Begrich, *Einleitung...*, p. 145f). This historical situation of the royal psalms will be more precisely investigated in the respective introductions. On the royal psalms can be consulted the studies of K. H. Bernhardt, K. R. Crim, J. De Fraine, G. B. Gray, A. R. Johnson, J. L. McKenzie, R. Nogosek, G. von Rad, K. H. Rengstorf, G. Widengren.

§28. INTRODUCTION TO THE ROYAL PSALMS

The royal psalms are: Pss 2, (18), 20, 21, 45, 72, 89, 101, 110, 132, (144).

PSALM 2

The Universal Reign of the Messiah

Pss 1 and 2 have no title. Both together would constitute, according to *BJ*, a sort of preface to the whole Psalter, by evoking some of its main moral and messianic teachings. Ps 1 begins and Ps 2 ends with a "beatitude." By its subject-matter, thinks J. Enciso (see on *Ps 137), Ps 2 is well adapted to fill its role as prologue to various collections: the first and second collection of David, the collections of Asaph, of the sons of Core and of the reign of God. These groups of psalms, it is thought, would have one theme in common: God's universal reign. Jewish and Christian traditions alike consider Ps 2 as messianic, like Ps 110, on which it likely depends. It is attributed to David by Ac 4:25 (see §16a for detailed references to the New Testament). Prominent literary and conceptual developments proper to the royal psalms find expression in Ps 2: the king as son of God, the stability of the Davidic dynasty, the divine oracles at the coronation ceremony, royal messianism.

A king of Judah recites this psalm at his own enthronement. The change of ruler should not be a signal for vassals to revolt (vv 1-3). God guarantees the perpetuation of the dynasty (4-6). After the divine proclamation instituting the new king (7-9), a warning is addressed to the rulers of the earth (10-12). Since Israel has ever been a modest kingdom, with no vassals worthy to be called kings, the world-wide setting of the psalm (see on *Ps 66) is partly literary and imitates the royal ceremonial pattern of the great oriental empires (see also below: the consequence of divine adoption). As a matter of fact, the divine installation of a kinglet is for the psalmist an occasion to dissert on God's universal dominion. While strife and ambition agitate the kings of the earth and the nations (cf. Is 17:12), the great Monarch smiles down serenely on this agitation from his heavenly throne (cf. Is 18:4) or terrifies the whole world with his thundering voice (cf. Is 17:13).

The divine proclamation (vv 7-9; cf. *Ps 19:4) is better understood against the background of ancient *royal protocol (cf. von Rad, "Das judäische Königsritual," *TLZ* 72, 1947, pp. 211-216). Yet here a new dimension is added, the eschatological one (cf. §14a), for this particular Davidic kingship is a prototype of the expected messianic kingship at the end of times, when the reign of God will be established in the whole world. In the last stanza (10-12) the Israelite king is out of the picture and the real intent of the psalm is again manifest: that all the rulers of the earth acknowledge with awe and serve with fear God as the universal Lord of the earthly kingdoms. The New Testament has applied to the messiaship and the divine sonship of Jesus the statements of Ps 2: cf. Ac 4:25ff; 13:33; Heb 1:5; 5:5. The same typology is verified whenever it is stated that Jesus is king, the son of David (cf. §15c).

Having recalled that the Israelite king had a role to play as mediator of the Covenant (cf. 2 K 23:3), G. H. Jones has the following to say about Ps 2:7: In proclaiming the "decree of Yahweh," "the king on his enthronement was accepting the Covenant of Yahweh, which had as its visible sign the decree which he was declaring." If it was not a written document, the "decree" certainly was fixed in content and form. At his enthronement the king would say: "I will repeat concerning the decree of Yahweh...." According to the Egyptian ritual of enthronement the reference was to a written document expressing the divine legitimacy of the king, his calling and enthronement by the deity, and the further destiny and "name" that will thereby be his. The "decree" or "edict" of Ps 2:7, adds Mowinckel (I, 62), is thus a confirmation of the covenant with David (2 S 7).

In verse 7-8, comments K. H. Rengstorf, an unidentified king of the pre-exilic period mentions at his accession the Royal Protocol or Oracle (*ḥōq*), which promises him dominion over the whole world. The phrase, "ask of me and I will give you," would be a peculiar feature of the Enthronement ritual of Jerusalem and Judea. J. Dupont has explained how the New Testament authors have given to the triumph of Jesus an enthronement setting: only after his Passion is Jesus declared Son of God, Lord and King. As man he had to "be born" to the glory he possessed eternally as the Son. In this sense it is said of Him in a paschal context: "Thou art my son, I this day have begotten thee" (Heb 1:5; Ps 2:7; cf. Rm 1:4).

Divine adoption is in fact one of the features of ancient coronation rites: "You are my son; this day I have begotten you" (Ps 2:7; cf. 89: 27f). Nathan's prophecy also declared: "I will be a father to him and

he a son to me" (2 S 7:14; cf. 1 Ch 22:10; 28:6). Following the revised
Latin Psalter (and the Septuagint), *CV* translates Ps 110:3: "Yours is
princely power in the day of your birth, in holy splendor; before the day-
star, like the dew, I have begotten you." But the Israelite king was in
no way divinized. The title *Elohîm* bestowed upon him by an obscure
text (Ps 45:7) is also attributed to less important officials (cf. Ps 58:2).
In Egypt and in Assyro-Babylonia the king was considered son of a god.
But in Israel divine adoption coincides with the coronation. The Israelite
king is not divine by natural generation (cf. M. Noth, "Gott, König,
Volk im Alten Testament" [1950], in *Gesammelte Studien zum Alten
Testament*, pp. 188-229). "*I beget you* is an audacious poetical hyperbole
which prepared the way for expressing supra-dynastic messianism. As
a result of divine adoption the king in Zion is entitled to a universal
dominion. The whole earth belongs to Yahweh, who makes his adopted
son his heir and his delight" (J. Steinmann, p. 28). The role of the
Israelite king then reflects in a way the universal dominion of the Lord
over the nation (Pss 47:3; 9; 89:12; Is 45:1; 52:10).

The "genuinely archaic flavor" of the psalm's language suggests to
Dahood "a very early date (probably the tenth century)." So this author
at least is not impressed by A. Robert's contention that "all the verses of
the Ps, 6 and 12 excepted, include terms characteristic of the post-exilic
language." "Nothing decisive can be said against a pre-exilic dating" of
the psalm, states Mowinckel (I, p. 65, n). B. Lindars finds some evidence
for assuming that "the men of Qumran... understood the psalm to be
concerned with Davidic kingship. Everything points to the conclusion
that they were right, once it is agreed that the acrostic is too insecure to
be accepted as the decisive factor" (p. 67). Already in 1885 an acrostic
beginning had been perceived in Ps 2 by G. Bickell (cf. *VT* 1967, p.
62). Developing a suggestion of R. H. Pfeiffer, M. Treves now finds
plenty of evidence to support his claim that the king of Ps 2 is one of
the Hasmoneans. Then he adds: any remaining doubt is dispelled by the
acrostic: the phrase in Hebrew formed with the first letter of each verse
can be translated: "Sing ye to Jannaeus the First and his wife." That,
Treves contends, was written at the accession of Jannaeus, in the year
103 B.C. Such a late date for the psalm is, however, very unlikely.

Other studies that merit consideration attempt to elucidate obscure
or difficult passages. The meaning "to forgather," applied to *rāgāš* (*CV*,
"rage") by Briggs ("consent together") is accepted by Dahood, who
notes that in Pss 55:15; 64:3, the word is associated with that meaning

to *sōd*, "council," represented by *nôsᵉdû* in Ps 2:2. The meaning of *yehᵉgû* (CV, "utter") in verse 1 is clarified by that of "to number," attested for *hāgâh* in a military context of a Ugaritic text (*Krt*: 90-91). If *rîq* (CV, "folly") can mean "troops" (cf. Gn 14:14), then sufficient evidence is produced to support the translation of verse 1-2 proposed by Dahood:

> Why do the nations forgather,
>   and the peoples number their troops?
> Why do kings of the earth take their stand,
>   and the princes make common cause
> Against Yahweh and against his anointed?

The following added comment seems equally relevant: "There is no point in trying to identify the kings historically. By the time of the composition of this psalm (probably tenth century) they had become stock literary figures who belong to the genre of royal psalms. They should be classed with the kings of Ps 48:5. If an historical background must be sought, the El Amarna correspondence (cf. §9d) offers graphic descriptions of the plottings and intrigues of the petty kings of Syria-Palestine against the Egyptian suzerain and against one another."

Some years ago A. Kleber applied to verse 9 known elements of the rite of the smashing of earthen vessels: at certain state functions of the Ancient East, vessels inscribed with the names of the hostile rulers or rebellious subjects, or of harmful things were ceremoniously dashed to the ground and broken with a stick or pounder, in order to give symbolic expression to the intention of destroying the objects of fear or hatred. In Revelation the "Son of God" says "to the rest of Thyatira: To him who overcomes and who keeps my works unto the end, I will give authority over the nations. And he shall rule them with a rod of iron, and like the potter's vessel they shall be dashed to pieces, as I also have received from my Father; and I will give him the morning star" (2:26ff).

Reading *nᵉšē qāber*, "men of the grave," instead of MT *naššᵉqû bar* (litt., "kiss the son"), Dahood translates v 11: "Serve Yahweh with reverence, and live in trembling, O mortal men!" This is followed by the remark: "The Yahwist king is portrayed as railing against the Canaanite concepts of divine kingship." But does not the "Yahwist king" also claim for himself a "divine kingship"? Besides, there is a kind of consensus among other scholars (Rowley, Closen, Weiser, Kraus, *BJ, Osty*) for accepting the textual emendation proposed by A. Bertholet a long time ago (*ZAW*, 1908, p. 58f; cf. *Bib* 1940, pp. 288-309; 426ff): unite differently the words of verses 11f and read *ûbir'ādâh naššᵉqû bᵉraglāw*: "with trembling kiss his feet." For this emendation accepted by him in 1925 A. Vaccari substituted in 1949: "Pay homage to him with trembling" (cf. *Liber Psalmorum* and *CV*). "Foot-kissing (Ps 2: 12; cf. Is 49:23) as a sign of subjection and homage was a general oriental custom, known both from Egypt, and Babylonia-Assyria" (Mowinckel, I, p. 55, with references).

PSALM 18 (17)

Thanksgiving for Help and Victory

This royal psalm of thanks describes how, when the king was already in the jaws of death, overwhelmed by the floods of Destruction, he called in his distress upon the Lord (vv 1-7), and the theophany God, revealing himself in his awful majesty, rescued his anointed (vv 8-20) on account of his loyalty and innocence (21-31). The account of the theophany follows the cultic pattern described elsewhere (§13d). By associating the king's deliverance with Israel's at the Red Sea (cf. v 16) the rescuing of God's anointed (v 51) is linked with the very foundation of the *Heilsgeschichte* tradition. The "protestation of innocence" (21-25) does not here derive from pharisaic self-righteousness but it is "an affirmation of faith in the covenantal faithfulness of God, which may be experienced by those who in obedience to God's ordinances keep their faith in him" (A. Weiser; cf. §12e). In the second part of the psalm God is praised and thanked for the "grace of kingship" (Weiser) renewed in Israel, and especially for having prepared the king for war (vv 32-35), given him victory over his enemies (36-43) and confirmed his ascendancy over the nations (44-46). Although the style remains somewhat grandiose in this second part, the cosmic background of the first part is replaced by a more plausible account of events dealing with war and political prisoners. Two hymnic stanzas of praise begin (2-4) and end (47-51) the psalm.

The ascription of the psalm to David by the heading (v 1) is confirmed in 2 S 22, where the text of the poem is thus introduced: "And David spoke to the Lord the words of this song on the day when the Lord delivered him from the hand of all his enemies, and from the hand of Saul." There exists no compelling reason to exclude the possibility that

David did compose the psalm. The parallels indicated from subsequent biblical texts may be dependent on the psalm or other common traditions. The so-called "Deuteronomic style in verses 21ff," writes Weiser, "is confined to phrases which are by no means characteristic only of the Deuteronomic literature." He indicates other features which seem to assign the psalm to an early date, as, for example, the king's archaic method of fighting on foot (vv 30, 34, 37). The expression $b^e n\hat{e}$ $n\bar{e}k\bar{a}r$, "the foreigners," is, however, found only in Ezk 44:7, in the last chapters of Isaiah (cf. 60:10), in Ne 9:2 and in Ps 144:7, 11, dependent on Ps 18 (cf. *BJ*). This does not favor a pre-exilic date of the psalm. Besides, the passage from Micah, parallel to verses 45b-46, is post-exilic: "They shall come quaking from their fastnesses, trembling in fear of you [the Lord]" (Mi 7:17b).

Not so much a single victory over the enemies as probably a series of providential saving deeds lie behind this enthusiastic praise, especially in the second part. The text may have suffered alterations during its long history. The cosmic dimension attributed to an event affecting a small kingdom indicates here again that the *prima intentio* of the psalm, in the first part especially, is the celebrating of the majesty of God which transcends the limits of time and place, while it manifests itself in some historical event (see on *Ps 66).

Dahood's annotations on Ps 18 began with the psalm's heading where he reads "from the hand of Sheol" instead of "from the hand of Saul." The poet's delivery from Sheol forms the subject-matter of verses 4-7. Not only that, Dahood observes, but "rescue from the grasp of all his enemies and from the hand of Sheol fairly summarizes the contents of the entire poem." An unpublished psalm in Akkadian, found at Ras Shamra, begins with the words, "Since the day you delivered me from the mouth of Death." The psalmist's interest in Sheol will of course appear even greater, if in verses 4, 18, 49 the "adversaries" are identified with "the Foe," Death personified (see on *Pss 30:2 and 13:3, 5) and if "the destroying floods (v 5)" are "the torrents of Belial," with the explanation that the word *Belial* derives from the root *bl'*, "to swallow" (hence "throat"). Add to this Dahood's reading of verse 20a: "He brought me out of the broad domain" (=Sheol; cf. Ps 31:9). Read also an allusion to Sheol in verse 8: "The nether world (*'ereṣ*) reeled and rocked, the foundations of the mountains shuddered." Other texts which place the foundations of the mountains in the underworld would include Dt 32:22; Is 24:18; Jr 31:37; Mi 6:2; Jon 2:7. Already in his

Schöpfung und Chaos in Urzeit und Endzeit (Göttingen, 1895), p. 18, n. 1, Gunkel had observed that in Ex 15:12, Is 14:12 and Eccl 3:21, *'ereṣ* denoted "nether world." In some biblical passages *'ereṣ* (usually= "land," "earth") does seem to mean "nether world." In Dahood's list the following references to psalms are given: 7:6; 18:8; 22:30; 41:3; *61:3, 10; 71:20; 95:4; 106:17; 141:7; 143:3; 147:6; 148:7 (on Sheol see §14 d).

Should the poetic "wings of the wind" disappear from verse 11? Dahood proposes to read: "He mounted the Cherub and flew, and soared on wings outstretched" (*kanᵉpē rewaḥ*: "the wings of broadness"; cf. Ps 104:3). In verse 43 also, Dahood notes, the Masoretes have erroneously read *'al pᵉnē rūᵃḥ*, "on the face of the wind," instead of *'al pᵉnē rewaḥ*, "upon the square": "I pulverized them like dust in the square, like the mud in the streets I trampled them." To this Dahood adds: "The image of God flying upon the Cherub of extended wings" is related to the widely mistranslated and misinterpreted phrases of Ezk 28:14, *kᵉrûb mimšaḥ hassōkēk*, "the overshadowing Cherub of wings outstretched" (cf. Vulg.: "Cherub extentus"). The use of *mšḥ* with the meaning "to measure, extend" is attested in Ugaritic (t. 76, 11:22-23; Gordon, p. 182): "Your powerful wings will Baal stretch out, Baal will stretch them out for flight." The more common meaning, "to anoint," attached to *mšḥ*, is not to be retained in Ezk 28:14: "With an *anointed* guardian cherub I placed you" (*RSV*).

If the "enemies" do not in fact appear before verse 18, then Dahood's translation of verse 15 gives a better meaning: "He forged his arrows and scattered them, he multiplied his shafts and dispersed them." The pronouns "them" refer to the arrows and the shafts. The latter are "bolts of lightning." The biblical poet, explains Dahood, ascribed to Yahweh the attributes of the Canaanite artisan-god Kothar. The point of the Aqhat (Ugaritic) legend is that the mortal Aqhat came into possession of a miraculous bow designed by Kothar for the huntgoddess Anath (Dahood, p. 115). The theme of the artisan-God forging the weapons of the psalmist recurs in verse 35: "Who trained my hands for battle, lowered the miraculous bow into my arms," and also in Ps 7:14: "O that he would create the weapons of death, make his arrows into flaming shafts." The effect of lightning is more apparent in Dahood's translation of verse 16:

The fountain heads of the sea were exposed,

and the world's foundations were laid bare.
At your roar, O Yahweh,
    at the blast from your nostrils.

Referring to a more traditional translation of verse 35 (cf. *CV*), S. Mowinckel (I, p. 54) points to other parallel sources: "When the king in Ps 18:34 says about Yahweh that 'he teacheth my hands to war, so that I can bend a bow of bronze,' this may be illustrated by an Egyptian picture of the God Seth teaching Pharaoh Thutmose to use a bow." "Of all the psalms, he adds (I, p. 72), Ps 18 is the one which has the most Egyptian style, and reminds one most directly of hymns to the 'god' Pharaoh, with their highflown descriptions of his majesty's overwhelming victories over all the wretched and wicked 'foreign' nations — poetical descriptions which are not always in accordance with the historical results of the 'victories.' One suspects the composer of Ps 18 of having studied the poetical art of Egypt, and that he too lays more stress on grandiose description and ebullient enthusiasm than on actual facts."

Arguing that the dative (double-duty) suffix, "to me," required with *tā'īr*, "to (cause to) shine," is to be supplied from *nērī*, "my lamp," Dahood reads in verse 29: "You shine for me; my lamp is Yahweh, my God illumines my darkness." In 2 S 22:29 we read in fact (*RSV*): "Yea, thou art my lamp, O Lord; and my God lightens my darkness." Compare with Ps 139:12 (Dahood): "Darkness is not too dark for you and the night shines for you like the day; as the darkness, so the light." — A better parallelism certainly results from translating verse 42 with *mošia'* understood as "Savior" (cf. §11d): "They implored, but the Savior was not there, the Most High Yahweh, but he did not answer them" (Dahood). This is how *The Anchor Bible* reads verses 44-46:

You delivered me from the shafts of people,
    protected me from the venom of nations.
An alien people must serve me,
    as soon as they hear, they obey me;
Foreigners cringe before me.
Foreigners shrivel up,
    and their hearts are seized with anguish.
May Yahweh live!
Praised be my Mountain!
And exalted the God of my triumph!

F. M. Cross and D. N. Freedman have published (*JBL* 1953, pp. 15-34) a detailed study of 2 S 22=Ps 18: "Both texts, they note, have been revised and modernized considerably in the course of transmission, but 2 S 22 preserves a number of archaic readings, which point to a minimal date in the ninth-eighth centuries B.C. for the written composition of the poem." Among the "archaic linguistic phenomena" can be mentioned here the use of the preposition *b* to mean 'from' and the presence of enclitic *mem* [cf. *Ps 31:18], both of which have been subject to editorial revision. Important also is the conclusion "that the imperfect form of the verb was the common, generally used verb form in old Israelite poetry, as in old Canaanite poetry, and that its time aspect was determined by the context, not the presence or absence of the conjunction" (i.e., "*waw consecutive*"). "It seems clear, these scholars add, that the author of the psalm drew on a number of older sources. The theophany in verse 8-16 with its Canaanite associations is of a piece with the ancient poetry of Israel, belonging to the period of the Judges and early monarchy. Similarly in verses 26-27, an old gnomic couplet with singsong rhythm and anthropopathic conceptions, apparently is quoted by the psalmist.... It remains a question as to whether the psalm is an amalgamation of two or more independent odes, or a single poem sharply divided into separate parts." The Davidic authorship of the psalm is not excluded since "a tenth century date for the poem is not at all improbable" (p. 20f). G. Schmuttermayer has now published a book on Ps 18 and 2 S 22; *StANT* 25 (Munich 1971).

Psalm 20 (19)

Prayer for the King in Time of War

It has been suggested, on good grounds, that various speakers intervene in this psalm: a priest (vv 2-4), the congregation (v 6), a priest or a cult prophet (v 7), the congregation again (vv 8-10). Perhaps the psalm was part of the sacrificial liturgy performed before the king departed for the battlefield (cf. 1 S 7:9; 13:9; 1 K 8:44; 2 Ch 20:18f). In that sense Ps 20 could be listed among the so-called "protective psalms" (cf. *Ps 71). Other commentators would associate the psalm with a fixed liturgy, namely that of New Year's day, when Yahweh was glorified as King. Accordingly Weiser translates verse 10: "O Lord, do help us, O King, who answers us in the day we call."

The aim of the cultic ceremony in which Ps 20 featured was to obtain that the "grace of kingship" be sent from Mount Zion (v 3), the usual site of God's epiphany (cf. Am 1:2). The assurance that the prayer has been heard (v 7) is variously explained: oracle, sacrificial evidence, prophetic pronouncement, cultic theophany, or, more simply, news from the battlefront. Yet the assurance is not too surprising to any one who takes seriously the promise that divine help is guaranteed to God's anointed (cf. Ps 18:5; comp. Pss 56:10; 60:8; 140:13). A different, perhaps better, translation of verse 7 is proposed in *The Anchor Bible*: "Now I know that Yahweh has given his anointed victory, has granted him triumph from his sacred heaven, and from his fortress has given victory with his right hand" (see on *Pss 8:2f and 78:26).

The prophets have consistently preached that it is not the will of God that Israel should compete with the other nations in resting confidence on the best weapons of war, like horse-drawn chariots (vv 8-9; cf. Dt 17:16; Ho 1:7; 14:4; Mi 5:9; Is 31:1; Zc 8:9; Pss 33:16f; 147:10 f). "Ps 20, as well as Ps 21, writes Mowinckel (I, p. 224), is partly addressed to the king himself, and in these psalms, as well as in Ps 72, the intercession is distinguished by piling up words of blessing; an evidence of the religious and style-historical connection between the prayer and the word of blessing, which is the cultic origin of the intercession)" (For the dating of Pss 20 and 21, cf. §5e).

PSALM 21 (20)

Thanksgiving and Prayers for the King

In this psalm again, blessings (*birᵉkôt*, v 4) and "saving help" (*yᵉšûʿâh*: vv 2, 6), proper to the "grace of kingship" are celebrated. They include, according to Weiser, such realities as convey terms like "glory," "splendor," "majesty," "sovereignty," "life," "length of days," "joy," "salvation," "victory." Perhaps the psalm was part of a coronation ritual (cf. v 4). Both the "cultic representation of the blessings" (vv 2-7) and the prayer (vv 9-13) may have been recited by a priest in the presence of the king, while verses 8 and 14 would be the congregation's antiphon (like Ps 20:6c). F. C. Fensham suggests that "Ps 21 may be an enthronement psalm which is closely connected to the renewal of the covenant.... A possible time of origin is during the reign of Hezekiah" (716-687). E. Beaucamp would deny that Ps 21 is a royal *Te Deum*. Should we not, he asks, consider verses 9-14 as addressed to Yahweh? The psalm is a "coronation liturgy" as could be also Ps 5, 16, 23, 27, 42-43, 61, 63, 84, 91, 101 etc. One of the blessings, "length of days forever and ever," has been interpreted in a messianic sense by late Judaism and by some commentators as referring to the everlasting reign of the Davidic dynasty. More simply, these hyperbolical expressions are quite common in ancient court etiquette, reflected also in the Bible (cf. 1 K 1:31; Ne 2:3; Is 53:10; Dn 2:4). Being God's anointed, his "vicegerent" (cf. *Ps 2), the king shares in a way divine fulness of life, as he does divine majesty and divine authority. The king was considered as the dispenser to the nations of the blessings he received: "for you made him a blessing forever" (v 7). Hence the great importance attributed to the "grace of kingship."

Alterations in the text may account for the fact that verses 9-13 refer partly to the king and partly to God (see below). In the ancient "song of Moses" already, God is called a "man of war" (Ex 15:3; cf. §14b), while the mention of "fire" evokes the "jealousy" of God (Ex 20:5), the Sinai theophany (cf. Dt 4:12; 5:5, 22-25; Ps 18:14f) and the eschatological day of judgment (Am 1:4-14; 2:2-5; Ml 3:2; 4:1). The psalm ends with a call which is also an element of the theophany in the cult: "Arise, O Lord!" (cf. §13d)

Dahood would entitle Ps 21: "A psalm of thanksgiving for the royal victory prayed for in the preceding psalm." Verses 9-13 describe the victorious battle: the subject is Yahweh and the imperfect forms are used to describe past narrative action (as in "archaic Hebrew poetry"; see on *Ps 18): "Your left hand overtook all your foes, your right hand overtook those who hate you..." etc. The favor asked for and granted as mentioned in verses 5-7, would be "eternal life" (see on *Ps 27:13; cf. Pr 12:28). Accordingly Dahood reads in verses 5a and 7b: "Life eternal he asked of you... you will make him gaze with happiness upon your face" (cf. *Pss 16:11; 17:15). The king, it is explained, was thought to receive the gift of immortality on the day of his coronation (cf. Ps 2:7). Another royal attribute is described as "splendor and majesty" (v 6). This corresponds to the Akkadian concept of *melammu*, denoting "a characteristic attribute of the gods consisting of a dazzling aureole or nimbus which surrounds the divinity. The king as representative and likeness of the gods also has such an aura, which constitutes the divine legitimation of his royalty. This *melammu* is bestowed upon him when he becomes king" (Dahood). Mowinckel, for his part, notes (I, p. 56) that the king's prayer for "life" and "length of days forever and ever" (v 5) often recurs both in Egyptian and Mesopotamian royal inscriptions. The "promising notes" of Pss 21 and 72, he believes, are probably not to be looked upon as direct oracles, "but as the words of an inspired psalmist, as echoes of such oracles inserted into the intercessions and blessing wishes the poet-singer puts into the mouth of the congregation. Once more they bring out the close relationship between temple prophet and psalmist, or rather, show that in fact the two would in many cases be one and the same person."

PSALM 45 (44)

Nuptial Ode for the Messianic King

This poem, Mowinckel thinks, is "the only example in the whole of Israelite psalm poetry of a true hymn to the king" (I, p. 74). It is not in fact a purely royal hymn, for the divine grace of kingship gets the real attention of the poet. Quite surprisingly Weiser offers no cultic interpretation of the psalm, which he calls "the only example of a profane lyric in the Psalter." It is, he adds, "a song of praise in honor of a young king and his consort, a princess of Tyre (v 13), which was composed and recited by a court-poet on the occasion of the ruler's wedding." The admonition served to the bride, "forget your people and your father's house," may be meant to avert the danger of other royal wives who would import idolatry and foreign customs into the kingdom of other Solomons or Ahabs. In fact the mention of a "princess of Tyre" (v 13) seems a reference to royalty of the northern kingdom of Israel, as would indicate also the allusion to "ivory palaces" (v 9; cf. 1 K 22:39; Am 3:15; 6:4). Such was the value of the hymn that it was soon interpreted as referring to the Messiah and as such was incorporated in the Psalter. To illustrate the superiority of Christ over the angels, the *Epistle to the Hebrews* states that in Ps 45:8-9 (LXX) it is written of the Son:

Thy throne, O God, is forever and ever,
and a sceptre of equity is the sceptre
   of thy kingdom.
Thou has loved justice and hated iniquity;
therefore God, thy God, has anointed thee
with the oil of gladness above thy fellows (1:8-9).

The *ho theos* is correctly understood by R. E. Brown (*TS* 1965, p. 562) as a vocative and *Hebrews* here unequivocally applies the title "God" to Jesus. The psalm may be read also in the typical sense as referring to Christ and his bride the Church (cf. Mt 9:15; 25:1-13; Jn 3:29; 2 Cor 11:2; Ep 5:21-32; Rv 19:7; 21:9). Other Christian interpreters consider Ps 45 as directly messianic, that is, written by the inspired writer himself as celebrating the sacred nuptials of the messianic King with Israel (cf. Ezk 16:13; Is 62:5; Sg 3:7, 11; 4:11) or with the Church. Since every Davidic king was a prospective Messiah (cf. §15c), it could well be that the very words of this lyric poem, written for an Israelite wedding, can now be read, in the fuller sense, as speaking of the "marriage of the Lamb" (Rv 19:7). From his thorough study of Ps 45, Philip J. King concludes (p. 129) that the poem is messianic in the typical sense: we promptly perceive in the person of the historical king (Solomon probably) of the royal psalm a prefiguring of the ideal sovereign of future times, the King-Messiah.

The king is handsome, notes Dahood, because God has favored him "from eternity" (v 3; see on *Ps 9:8), like other predestined individuals (cf. Ps 139:16; Is 49:1, 5; Jr 1:5; Gal 1:15). Considering the difficulty of telling the king, "Your throne, O God, stands forever and ever" (v 7), Dahood reads *kissē'ªkā* ("a denominative *piel* from *kissē'*, "throne") and translates: "The eternal and everlasting God has enthroned you!" This translation deprives of their main argument the proponents of an allegorical interpretation of the psalm. The poem does not any more apply to an earthly monarch an attribute strictly divine. Besides, one must always reckon with the figurative hyperbolic language of *Hofstil*, "style de cour" (cf. Ph. J. King, pp. 103-115 and R. Pautrel, "Le style..."). The divine vocative is maintained in *BJ* and qualified "titre protocolaire" In 2 S 14:17 the wise woman sent by Joab tells king David: "My lord is like the angel of God to discern good and evil." But this formula (cf. §26) is similar to God's reflection after the Fall: "Behold, the man has become like one of us, knowing good and evil" (Gn 3:22, *RSV*). According to B. Couroyer a king who would be a type of the Messianic King could have been called *elohim* (*RB* 1971, 233-41). On Ps 45 see also J. Mulder *Studies on Psalm 45* (Offsetdrukkerij Witsiers, Oss, Holland). Nothing that Ps 45 is a *maśkîl* psalm (v 1), a poem, he says, involving a symbolic meaning, C. Schedl would place the nuptial ode beside Isaiah's prophetic songs on the Messiah's birthday (Is 7:14) and enthronement (Is 9:1). To the same messianic cycle, he adds, belong Pss 2, 72 and 110. Finally *bᵉtûlôt*, "virgins," in verse 15, should be read in the singular, thinks Dahood, like Phoenician *btlwt,* "maiden" (cf. *ḥokmôt,* Pr 9:1) and verse 15 can be translated: "Let the maiden be led to the king, let her companions be brought to her."

PSALM 72 (71)

The Kingdom of the Messiah

Christian commentators entitle this psalm "The promised king" (JB) or "The Kingdom of the Messiah" (CV and the revised Latin Psalter). The Targum also has interpreted it as referring to the Messiah. Although the psalm is not quoted by the New Testament, it features in the Church's official prayers for Christmas, the Epiphany (com. vv 10, 15 and Mt 2:11), Holy Thursday, Christ the King and Holy Trinity. Almost half of the psalm consists of wishes that simply cannot be fulfilled in the world's present or foreseeable conditions. Even ancient Oriental court style (*Hofstil,* cf. *Ps 2) cannot account for all the hyperbolic expressions. Some commentators read in the psalm Israel's hope for the coming of *the ideal king* as the prophets have depicted him (cf. Is 9:5; 11:3; Zc 9:9f). In verse 15 it is written: "May he live... to be prayed for continually," and the whole psalm can be interpreted as an intercession for the king (cf. A. Barucq, *L'expression...,* p. 438). This has worried past literal messianists, since we do not pray for the divine Messiah, although we do for his coming. Yet we say to God: "Thy kingdom come!" (Mt. 6:10) Besides, messianic texts do not describe all the aspects of the future reality. Finally, "to pray for" can be equivalent to expressing a "wish," a "blessing" or a "prediction." Ps 72, Mowinckel writes (I, p. 69), "becomes [in the latter part] a formula of blessing which reminds one strongly of the promise of the prophets as it oscillates between blessing and prediction. The officiating priest who recites the psalm... speaks on behalf of the congregation and in the form of a petition. But he is also the representative of Yahweh and pronounces strong and effective words with a ring of certainty."

According to the "titles" mentioned in the Septuagint and some Hebrew manuscripts, Solomon would be the subject of the psalm, presumably because of verses 1, 2 and 10 (cf. 1 K 3:12ff, 28; 10:1-3). Perhaps Ps 72 featured, like other royal psalms (cf. 20 and 21), in the liturgy of the king's enthronement. Since the Israelite king was considered as God's representative, it is not too unexpected that attributes of the kingship of

God be drawn upon to express the hoped for prosperity and justice of the new reign. Again, since Nathan's prophecy (2 S 7:1-17), all Davidic princes were candidates for the Messianic promotion (cf. §15c), and thus could the celebration of their accession be illumined with the reality of the eschatological kingdom. It is generally thought that verses 18-19 represent a doxology concluding the second book of the Psalter. If this is not the case, if they belong to Ps 72, then the verses could shed light on the psalm's meaning: "The king's reign and its blessing are the reflection of the sovereign rule of God and of his salvation, and his fame is overshadowed by the 'glory' (*kābôd*) of God who alone does wondrous things" (Weiser). P. W. Skehan has shown that Ps 72 is a unity. It has five stanzas (the doxology excluded), each with four full lines of Hebrew verse (1-4; 5-8; 9-11; 12-15; 16:17).

Ps 72 is pre-exilic if it describes the reign of an Israelite king. The apparent allusions to post-exilic biblical passages can be explained of course as later editorial or messianic adaptations. Yet it could be, observes R. Pautrel, that the psalm is post-exilic and sings the glory of a non-Israelite king or kingdom. Does not Yahweh call Cyrus "my shepherd" and "his anointed"? (Is 44:28; 45:1) "It is worth noting, writes Mowinckel (I, p. 55), that when the Israelite psalmist wishes to express the king's universal sovereignty, he does so in images which are formed from the Babylonian point of view, and which originated there," as when he writes: "May he rule from sea to sea, and from the River to the ends of the earth" (72: 8; cf. 89:26; cf. §9b). R. Tournay reads in verse 16 an allusion to a myth, current in ancient Lebanon: the awakening of Melqart, the great Baal of Tyre, the god of vegetation, marked the appearance of spring (cf. 1 K 18:27). The allusion, he adds, would rather point to the post-exilic period. In verse 9 the difficult *ṣiyyim* is retained by JB with the explanation: "The word, meaning the animals or demons of the desert (Is 13:21; 34:14; Jr 50:39; Ezk 34:28), here refers to subjugated heathen states (cf. Is 27:1; Dn 7:3, etc.; Rv 13:1, etc.)." The first part of the verse is translated: "The Beast will cower before him and his enemies grovel in the dust."

PSALM 89 (88)

Prayer for the Fulfillment of God's Promises to David

The three sections of the psalm (vv 6-19; 20-38; 39-46) are preceded by an introduction (vv 2-5) which announces the themes of the second and third sections: the hymnic praise of the Lord (vv 6-19) and the divine promise to the royal Davidic succession (vv 20-38). A supplication (vv 47-52) at the end of the psalm follows the fourth section (39-46), which, in the form of a national lament, describes the present disastrous situation, setting a sharp contrast with the divine promises. The references usually supplied by Bible editions indicate the main allusions to other biblical material (for the New Testament quotations, see also §16a). If it is assumed, with most commentators, that the national and royal calamity described in verses 39-46 alludes to the destruction of Jerusalem in 586, then the psalm as a whole is not pre-exilic, although pre-existing material, like the theophany themes (vv 10-15; cf. Ps 18:8-16) could have been used in the composition.

It seems likely to A. Weiser that Ps 89 "was used in times of a grave national disaster (possibly pre-exilic) and was recited in the cult when the accession to the throne of both the heavenly King and the earthly king were (sic) celebrated together at the Covenant Festival." A cultic tradition also lies behind the prophecy of Nathan (2 S 7). According to Mowinckel (I, p. 63), the enthronement or anointment oracles, as recorded in Pss 2 and 110 or alluded to in Ps 89:20-22, have furnished "the material which the tradition used, when in the legend of Nathan, it makes Nathan pronounce such promises to David." It is not explained why what this author calls the "legend of Nathan" could not have provided the material to the oracles (see on *Ps 132:11f). According to J.-L. Mc Kenzie "Psalm 89, for those parts of the original oracle which it has preserved, represents the original source more exactly that 2 S 7:8-16 or 1 Ch 17:7-14. What characterizes the Psalm is the omission of all reference to the Temple... A third conclusion is the absolute priority of the original oracle, and its historical validity as a contemporary report. The dynastic oracle must be placed exactly where the literary tradition places it, in the time of David himself, and be understood as the root of the prophecies of the messianic kingdom" (TS 8, 1947, p. 217). In the published section of his thesis Ph. J. Calderone does not indicate his position on the problem just mentioned, but on other points his work has a basic importance: Dynastic Oracle and Suzerainty Treaty (2 S, 8-16). Ateneo University Publications (Manila 1966). See also our introduction to *Ps 132. In Weiser's setting, the various parts of the psalm appears as follows: a short hymn sung by a priest revealing God's character and providential rule (vv 2-5); jubilant response intonated by "the chorus of God's celestial attendants" (vv 6-8) and continued by the congregation (9-19); the king's answer (20-38); the community lament and supplication (vv 39-52). The psalmist could only express "the riddle of *Heilsgeschichte*" and hope for a solution. The solution seems to be that the Nathan prophecy was conditional and providential as regards the temporal Israelite monarchy, while the Davidic succession would endure through the Messianic King (cf. Lk 1:32f). Thus also the absolute promises made to Abraham were fulfilled in the new and eternal covenant: Jr 31:31; Ezk 16:60; 38:26; Is 54:10; 55:3; 61:8 (cf. Rm 4:16f; Lk 22:20). E. Lipiński believes that the primitive royal psalm consisted of vv 2-5 and 20b-35, composed by Ethan the Ezrahite towards the end of the tenth century. For an exposition and criticism of L.'s views, and the contribution of *4QPs 89* (cf. *RB* 1966, 94-104), see A. Fitzgerald in *CBQ* 1971, 442-45. On Ps 89 as enthronement ritual see J. B. Dumortier in *VT* 22 (1972) 176-96.

For Mowinckel (I, p. 70), Ps 89 is a lament, attributed to the king (v 39) on a day of penance and prayer, after lost battles. The lament is directed at Yahweh himself, who has allowed such calamities to happen. Doubt, however, remains as to whether the psalm must be dated from pre-exilic times (I, p. 118). In his very exhaustive study G. W. Ahlström classifies Ps 89 as a *maśkîl*, a psalm belonging to the annual renewal-of-life ritual. J. J. de Vault (*TS.*, 1960, p. 281) has clearly summarized Ahlström's views. "As a *maśkîl*, the Psalm belongs to those rites in which joy over the renewal of life is expressed, but to which are to be added also rites which represent suffering and death, dramatizing the (temporary) victory of the forces of chaos and the humiliation of the king. It is in this last significant ceremonial that the complaining words of the Psalmist are now heard (vv 39-46), words which ring out all the more clearly against the background of the earlier verses, in which Yahweh's victory over chaos and His great creative acts are hymned (vv 1-19), and in which the king is proclaimed Yahweh's song, supreme over the kings of the earth, and the great pact between Yahweh and David's house is concluded (vv 20-38). Verses 1-38, therefore, belong to the exultant ideology of the annual festival, and it is only with verses 39ff that the destructive activity of the enemy of God becomes apparent, so that the king's role turns to that of a suffering messiah whose task it is to assure the renewal of life through necessary suffering, portrayed as part of the cult ritual. In the closing verses the king in the first person turns to prayer, and the Psalm ends on a dark and somber note. It is at this point, says Ahlström, just as the Psalm ends, that a new phase of ritual began, a phase opening with a sacrifice and concluding with the ritualistic saving of the king from his (and God's) enemies and his resurrection from Sheol."

As an erudite attempt to understand the psalm, Ahlström's study had to be mentioned. It follows the tendency of the "extremists of the divine-kingship school" (including Engnell and Widengren), who assert that "the king represented the dying and rising nature deity in this cultic renewal ceremony." Others, adds J. M. Ward (*VT* 1961, p. 327), deny the currency in Israel of the dying-god myth while affirming the ritual humiliation of the king (e.g. Bentzen, Ringgren, A. R. Johnson). Still others deny the theory of ritual humiliation while assigning the royal psalms to pre-exilic ritual celebrations of the kingship (H. Schmidt, S. Mowinckel). Ward finally concludes (p. 336): "Without external controls against which to check the theory of a ritual humiliation, whether in the narrative portions of the *OT* or in the royal psalms, we are thrown back upon Ps 89 itself for an answer to the question of its liturgical background. And there is no ground in the psalm for supposing that the crisis is a mere sham, a dramatic device and nothing more. This is not to say that Ps 89 was not employed repeatedly in the national cultus, but rather to assert that the determining factor in bringing the ritual about was not the intention merely to demonstrate the king's dependence upon God, but an actual political experience, or series of experiences, of the nation." This seems to dispose of Ahlström's radical theory.

A few annotations of details. It seems possible to read in v 3 that God's fidelity is more steadfast than the heavens, as in Ps 119:89 (cf. Dt 1:28, and Dahood for a detailed reconstruction) and in Mt 24:35: "Heaven and earth will pass away, but my words will not pass away." On the "holy ones" (*qedôšîm*) who constitute the court of Yahweh, see C. H. W. Brekelmans, "The Saints of the Most High and Their Kingdom," *Oudtestamentische Studiën* 14 (1965) 305-29. Instead of the simple "the north and the south" in the beginning of v 13 *ṣaphôn* and *yāmin* should be read as denoting two of the four sacred mountains (the other two: Tabor and Hermon). Here, as in Job 26:7, Mt Saphon is the sacred mountain of Baal, the Canaanite weather-god. It is now called *Jebel el 'Aqra* and lies some thirty miles north of Ras Shamra-Ugarit. As for Mt Amanus (*yamîn*), known as Alma Dag (southern Turkey), it is also mentioned in Sg 4:8. On these four mountains see O. Mowan in *VD* 1963, 11-20. In v 26 the "sea" and the "river" (usually "rivers") "may well be mythical terms expressing worldwide dominion" (Dahood, who quotes *UT* 68). In this verse *nᵉhārôt*, "river," is supposed to be a singular feminine of the Phoenician type, but elsewhere it is presented by Dahood as a plural referring to the subterranean "ocean currents" (see on *Ps 24:2). Since (*MT*) *'ēd*, "witness" in v 38 hardly fits the context, it seems recommended to read *'ād*, "seat, throne" (see on *Ps 93) and translate: "Like the moon it (his throne, from v 37) shall be established forever, and (his) seat will be stabler than the skies."

Psalm 101 (100)

Norm of Life for Rulers

In this psalm a king of Judah reads a declaration, probably during a liturgical festival. His language is in part sapiential. The phrase, "when will you come to me?" (v 2; cf. Ex 20:24) could suggest that the Ark of the Covenant has not yet been transferred to Jerusalem (*BJ*). The "house" (vv 2, 7) of the king can be taken literally to mean his dwelling figuratively, as in 2 S 7:11-16, to mean the Davidic lineage. In that case the psalm would represent the "charter" or the "speech from the throne" of the Davidic kings, in which on the day of their enthronement or even annually, they would proclaim their resolution to rule according to the statutes of the covenant (cf. 1 K 23:3). The expression of this resolution shows affinities with so-called "negative confessions" known in Egypt. In the 125th chapter of the *Book of the Dead*, for example, a deceased individual makes a long "protestation of guiltlessness," upon "reaching the Broad-Hall of the Two Justices. . . ." A short extract illustrates the genre (*ANET*, p. 34).

I have not committed evil against men.
I have not committed sin in the place of truth.
I have not blasphemed a god.
I have not *done violence* to a poor man.
I have not done that which the gods abominate.
I have not defamed a slave to his superior.
I have not made (anyone) weep.
I have not killed.
I have not caused anyone suffering.
I have neither increased nor diminished the grain-measure.

I have not added to the weight of the balance.
I have not taken milk from the mouths of children.
I have not driven cattle away from their pasturage.
I have not built a dam against running water.
I have not stopped a god on his procession.

On the other hand, there exists no real proof that the king's declaration reflects the Babylonian enthronement ceremony at the New Year festival, when the king, by way of a confession before the god, would account for the way he had ruled his kingdom. H.-J. Kraus proposes to call the psalm *Loyalitätsgelübde des Königs* or *Reinheitsgelübde des Regenten* (see also K. Galling and F. Mand). Elements of such oaths of loyalty or of innocence are also found elsewhere (cf. Ps 18:21-27). It has been noted (cf. *Ps 31:7) that in certain contexts Dahood considers the term *śānē'tî*, "I hate," to be a *terminus technicus* employed in the formula abjuring idols and idol worship (see on *Ps 31). Accordingly, he would read in Ps 101:3: "I have never set before my eyes any worthless object; the making of images have I so detested it never clung to me." He also claims that the forms *yqtl* in vv 2c-8 describe past activity, and this of course could be more consonant with the "negative confession" pattern I have mentioned. On the other hand, "when will you come to me" in v 2 can hardly be interpreted as the king's complaint "that Yahweh has not adequately responded to his devotion and blameless conduct" (Dahood); has not the king expressed his intention to "sing Yahweh's love and justice" (v 1)?

PSALM 110 (109)

The Messiah: King, Priest and Conqueror

An ever increasing periodical literature is devoted to this important Messianic psalm. The best relevant material will here be exposed or alluded to. Subdivisions are introduced for clarity's sake.

a) An enthronement

Probably this psalm was also connected with the religious festival of the king's enthronement. Mowinckel thinks "it evidently belongs to the moment when the king is led forth to ascend his throne" (I, p. 63). He then explains that in the East the king's throne was looked upon as a symbol of the throne of the deity. Enough can be found within the biblical tradition itself to explain adequately the various elements of the psalm. E. Podechard's interpretation rests on the assumption that Ps 110 was composed to honor David, when the sacred Ark was transferred to Zion (2 S 6), or soon afterwards. Melchizedek, king at Salem, the Jebusite city, was priest of 'ēl-'elyôn (God-Most-High: Gn 14:18), worshipped by the Phoenicians and the Canaanites. In a way David installed Yahweh in Zion, to replace the former divinity. In return (cf. Ps 2:6) Yahweh proclaimed David king and priest according to the order of Melchizedek (Ps 110:4) and made with his family an eternal covenant (cf. also Pss 89:4, 5, 29, 30, 37; 132:11ff).

The invitation of the oracle, "Sit at my right hand" (110:1), could refer, adds Podechard, to the location of the palace in relation to the Tent of the Ark (2 S 6:17; 7:18). It is also possible that for the enthronement the king sat on a throne beside the Ark, seat of God's invisible presence (Kraus, p. 757). Parallels in the coronation ceremony in Egypt and to the following biblical text may serve to illustrate some aspects of both Ps 101 and Ps 110: "And the king (Josias) stood by the pillar and made a covenant before the Lord, to walk after the Lord and to keep his commandments and his testimonies and his statutes, with all his heart and all his soul, to perform the words of this covenant that were written in this book; and all the people joined in the covenant" (1 K 23:3; cf. 2 K 11:14; 2 Ch 23:13; 34:31; for Ps 110, cf. A. Barucq, L'expression..., p. 493ff). The king, it seems, had a special place "by the pillar" in the temple, perhaps at "the right hand" of the Ark. Figuratively David was the first king to sit at the right hand of the Lord since he was also first to come into close relationship with the Ark (or enemies as "footstools," v 1, see below).

b) *Divine adoption*

The first oracle (vv 1-3), presumably proclaimed by a temple prophet, certainly refers to the king's divine adoption (see on *Ps 2), although the text of verse 3 is obscure and poorly preserved. According to Mowinckel (I, p. 64) and G. Widengren, the "holy splendor" (haderē qōdesh) could refer to the royal robe of the enthronement ceremony ("Ps 110...," Uppsala Univ. Arsbok, 1941, 7, 1). In connection with verse 3 J. de Savignac has been looking for Egyptian parallels. Among the closest he found are the following extracts (*ANET*, p. 374) from the "hymn of victory" of Thut-mose III (1490-1436): "Words spoken by Amon-Re, Lord of the Thrones of the Two lands... I cause thy opponents to fall beneath thy sandals... They come, bearing tributes upon their backs, bowing down to thy majesty, as I decree... I have come that I may cause thee to trample down the great ones of Djáhi; I spread them out under thy feet throughout their countries. I cause them to see thy majesty as the lord of radiance, so that thou shinest into their faces as my likeness. I have come that I may cause thee to trample down those who are in Asia... I cause them to see thy majesty as a *shooting* star, sowing its fire in a flame, as it gives off its *steam*" (others understand "dew"). The results of the inquiry are rather disappointing (cf. Baruck, *ibid*).

The metaphor of verse 1, "till I make your enemies your footstool," occurs elsewhere also in the psalms: "Upon Edom I will set my shoe" (60:10); "Under God we shall do valiantly; it is he who will tread down our foes" (108:14; cf. 44:6). There exists several illustrations from the ancient world of enemies used as footstools. On a stela from Susa (now in the Louvre), Sargon's son, Naram-Sin of Agade, victor of the Lullubians, places his left foot upon the prostrate bodies of two enemies (cf. *ANEP*, n. 309 or H. Gressmann, *Altorientalische Bilden zum A. T.*, Tafel XVIII). On the sculptured rock of Zohab (Baghdad region) is an inscribed relief celebrating the victory of Anubanini, king of the Lullubians. In the middle of the upper register stands Inanna or Ishtar, vegetation and war goddess, with her left foot on the body of a prisoner (cf. *ANEP*, n. 524 and H. Gressman, Taf. CVIII; on the Lord's footstool, see on *Ps 99:5). The connections of the biblical imagery find another illustration in *UT* 51, V, 109-110: "A chair is placed and he is seated at the right hand of Triumphant (*Al'iyan*) Baal."

Verse 3 is notably difficult, possibly because the original text is not well preserved. Modifying slightly his previous proposition (1953), J. Coppens now offers a translation which in English would run as follows·

To you the princely power on the day of your birth!
On the sacred mountains
from the womb of dawn like dew
I have begotten you.

See his accompanying explanations in *Le messianisme royal*. Lectio Divina 54 (Paris 1968) 58. Verse 3 would be a sort of poetic commentary of Ps 2:7: "You are my son; this day I have begotten you." As for *behadᵉrê-qodeš*, "in holy splendor" of the same verse, it is closely related to a similar expression in *Ps 29:2. In his article "In splendoribus sanctorum," A. Caquot writes about Ps 110:3: *"Behadrēy-qōdāš* (ou plutôt *behadrï-qōdaš*) *merähäm"* could be translated: "*(tu es revêtu)* de Majesté sainte dès le ventre (de ta mère)." The meaning would be "You are clothed with holy Majesty from your mother's womb," that is, "chosen from your mother's womb," like so many outstanding biblical figures: cf. Jg 16:17; Is 49:1; Jr 1:5; Pss 71:6; 139:13; Lk 1:15; Gal 1:15. The glorious birth theme is also featured in the *NEB* translation: "At birth you were endowed with princely gifts and resplendent in holiness. You have shone with the dew of youth since your mother bore you."

c) *The order of Melchizedek*

Perhaps the main messianic significance of the psalm depends on the interpretation of verse 4: "The Lord has sworn and he will not repent: You are a priest forever, according to the order of Melchizedek" (cf. Heb 5:6; 7:21). In connection with this verse, H. H. Rowley would place the original setting of Ps 110 in David's time, when Gn 14 still had significance as an "aetiological story" legitimating for Israel Zadok's (formerly Jebusite) priesthood. "If the psalm is read in the light of this situation, it carries a clear meaning and the reference to Melchizedek is significant. In the opening verses Zadok addresses David, acknowledging that David's God had enabled him to conquer the city, and extolling the power of both God and king, and promising him the loyalty of the conquered but spared city. The phraseology with all its reminiscences of the cultic vocabulary of Ugarit, is precisely what would be expected in such circumstances.... In the first three verses the king is addressed by Zadok; in the fourth, Zadok is addressed by the king, who confirms Zadok in the priesthood" (p. 469f). If this is true, then we cannot say, with J. A. Fitzmyer (*CBQ* 1963, p. 308), quoting prevailing opinion: "Ps 110:4 thus presents the king as the heir of Melchizedek, succeeding him as priest forever." In fact the concept itself of priest-king would not be mentioned in the psalm. On v 4 see also A. Serina, *La figura di Melchisedec nel Salmo 110, 4. Il Sacerdozio e il Messianismo Sacerdotale del Re Davide* (Trapani 1970).

On the other hand, J. W. Bowker admits with Treves, that Ps 110 does not *necessarily* refer to a king and that David could hardly have been called a priest. Yet it is conceivable, he adds, that the king did act as priest on great occasions or in exceptional circumstances and this is perhaps precisely what Ps 110 envisages. For this reason also R. de Vaux questioned Rowley's solution in regard to verse 4. "The text, he writes, can be explained otherwise: it could mean that the king was a priest, but in the only way in which an Israelite king could be.... He was a priest in the same way as Melchizedek, who, it was thought, had been king and priest in that same Jerusalem where the new king was being enthroned" (*Ancient Israel...*, p. 114). Bowker concludes: "On general grounds, therefore, there is no reason why the Psalm cannot be understood as an attempt to justify the special sense in which David might be called 'priest' " (*VT* 17, 1967, p. 36).

The origin of the Genesis story (14:18-20) about Melchizedek has been investigated anew by R. H. Smith. Summarizing some of his conclusions, he writes (p. 137): "Thus far we have found that the situation to which Gn 14:18-20 alludes so laconically seems to be this: Abram comes to Melchizedek's city with an army and encamps threateningly. To avoid siege and possible desruction of his city, Melchizedek capitulates to Abram, coming out with bread and wine as tokens of hospitality for Abram and his men, making a speech of conditional surrender, and offering Abram a fixed tribute from the city if he will depart. Abram presumably agrees and departs with the tribute, leaving Melchizedek's city inviolate." The presuppositions, it is explained, of the Melchizedek's story are so similar to those of the Keret [Ugaritic] legend that the stories may be said to have approximately the same cultural milieu and have circulated between 1600 and 1200 B.C. For it is quite possible that the Melchizedek story originally concerned some figure other than Abram. Which was Melchizedek's city we cannot know with certainty: Jerusalem, Shechem, Hebron, Bethel, "The fact is," writes Smith, "that by its very nature the Melchizedek story could have happened at almost any Canaanite city" (p. 152).

Equally if not more hypothetical is the deletion from the psalm of any mention of Melchizedek. M. Dahood reads in verse 4 *malki ṣedeq*, "his legitimate king" (on Ps 18:18). In 1937 already, T. H. Gaster had rendered verse 4: "Thou art a priest forever, A king rightfully appointed, In accordance with Mine order." Rowley, who reports this translation (p. 466, note 6), comments: "Gaster holds that the formula is of high antiquity, antedating the Israelite régime, since it harmonizes with the earliest usage of the priest-king, which is not in accord with Israelite custom.

While I am doubtful whether any idea of a priest-king is rightly to be found in either Gn 14 or Ps 110, there is evidence that Israelite kings did on occasion exercise the priestly function, though later thought condemned such a practice (cf. 2 Ch 26:16ff)."

Two scholars conclude in the following manner their study of a Qumran scroll concerned with a Melchizedek: "The function of Melchizedek as heavenly deliverer who protects the faithful people of God and as chief of the heavenly hosts runs parallel with that of the archangel Michael in the Dead Sea Scrolls, and in late Jewish and early Christian literature. Michael and Melchizedek are, however, not identified explicitly in the Qumran text at our disposal. This identification is only found in certain medieval Jewish texts. ... Melchizedek was a priest of the Most High God (Gn 14:18; Ps 110:4). In some Jewish sources he is called high-priest. In the Babylonian Talmud a heavenly high-priesthood is assigned to Michael. The question whether *11Q Melch* provides any explicit or implicit references to Melchizedek's (high-) priesthood can only be answered with difficulty" (M. de Jonge and A. S. van der Woude, "11Q Melchizedek and the New Testament," *New Test. Stud.* 12 [1966], p. 305).

The traditional interpretation of the phrase "according to the order of Melchizedek" is faithfully represented by the *CV* commentary: It means "in the same way as Melchizedek was a priest. There are three main points of resemblance between Melchizedek, the prophetic type, and Christ who fulfilled this prophecy: both are kings as well as priests, both offer bread and wine to God, and both have their priesthood directly from God and not through Aaron, since neither belongs to the tribe of Levi. Cf. Gn 14:18; Heb 7." This can be completed by a note of *The Jerusalem Bible*: "The prerogatives of the Messiah, worldwide sovereignty and perpetual priesthood (cf. 2 S 7:1ff; Zc 6:12f), are no more conferred by earthly investiture than were those of the mysterious Melchizedek (Gn 14:18ff)" (for a detailed list of the N.T. quotations of Ps 110, see §16a). The views of the ancient Rabbis on Ps 110 are presented in H.L. Strack & P. Billerbeck, *Kommentar zum Neuen Testament aus Talmud und Midrasch,* vol. 4, pp. 452-65.

d) *The last verse*

In connection with the third oracular utterance (vv 5-7), and its belligerent tone (cf. Ps 2:9), JB remarks: "As the text stands, this is addressed to the Messiah: the Lord (Yahweh) is to be at his right hand.

Possibly the original text attributed the following act of judgment to the Messiah himself, and we should read 'At his (Yahweh's) right hand the Lord (the Messiah, as in v 1).' This text may have been corrected in order to reserve the functions of eschatological judge as described in the following lines. However this may be, Jesus, the Messiah and Son of God, claimed this right to judge as his own, Mt 24:30; 26:64; Jn 5:22; cf. Ac 7:56; 10:42; 17:31."

Perhaps the most difficult problem raised by Ps 110 is the meaning of the last verse: "De torrente in via bibet: propterea exaltabit caput" (*Vulg.*). Some of the solutions proposed are mentioned in a *BJ* note: Rather than a brook of blood (cf. Nb 23:24; 32:6; 39:17f; Is 34:7; Zc 9:15), the Messiah would drink from the torrent of trials (cf. Pss 18: 5; 32:6; 66:12) or of divine favors (Pss 36:9; 46:5; Jr 31:9, 12). This last meaning does suit the context. God sustains his Messiah and makes certain his victory over the enemies, the pagans, in the last days. In the allegorical sense the text would describe the zeal of the Messiah, who, certain of victory, pursues his enemies (cf. Jg 7:5; 15:18; 1 S 30:9; 1 K 17:4). Hence the application to Christ, suffering and glorious (Ph 2:7-11).

Instead of MT *minnaḥal,* "from the brook," C. Schedl reads in verse 7a *Manḥil,* "Erbvollstrecker" (executor of a testator's will), the one trusted with allocating (land) inheritance (*naḥalāh*: cf. Ps 78:55). Instead of MT *yišteh,* "he will drink," he reads *yᵉšîtēhû,* "he will place him." Assuming besides that *derek,* "way," has "*ein heilsgeschichtlicher Begriff*" (a saving history meaning), the verse could mean that Yahweh entrusts the Messiah with a mission broader in scope and yet similar to that of Joshua: "Be strong and of good courage; for you shall cause this people to inherit ('*attāh tanḥîl*) the land which I swore to their fathers to give them" (1:6; cf. Ps 2:8). This new Joshua, a royal figure, is on the way to take over the empire of the nations. The enemies have their heads down (v 1) but God will raise the head of the Messiah (v 7). Noting that in Ugaritic *drkt* (probably pronounced *darkatu*) means (religious) "rule" or "dominion," in parallel with "kingdom," P. Nober, in 1948 already, had "anticipated" part of Schedl's solution and proposed the Latin translation: "Distributorem dominii constituet eum et ideo Yahweh extollet caput ejus": [God will] entrust to him the apportioning of his domain; therefore his head he will raise. C. Schedl's translation would presumably run more or less as follows: "On the way he constitutes him to apportion (the land); therefore his head He will raise."

There is little doubt that *drk* (CV: "wayside") does in some biblical texts connote the meaning of "power" or "authority": cf. Nb 24:17; Ho 10:13; Jr 3:13; Jb 26:14; Pr 19:16; Ps 90:16; 138:5. Yet H. Zirker (*BZ* 1958, p. 293) does not believe that this notion of *drk* can be applied to Ps 110:7. Instead of "He has set him as ruler upon the throne," which he had first proposed (on Ps 1:1), Dahood now (in *Psalms III*) translates thus v 7: "The Bestower of Succession set him on his throne, the Most High Legitimate One lifted high his head." More than good will seems required to be persuaded that prosaic *'al kēn* ("therefore") can be promoted to mean "The Most High Legitimate One" (in Ps 119: 104 the same *'al kēn* is translated "Most High Honest One," and "the Reliable" in Ps 127:2 and 128:4!).

e) *Additional remarks*

Rowley and other authors would propose an early date for Ps 110. We have seen their reasons for doing so. At the other extreme M. Treves has recently proposed that Ps 110, like *Ps 2, is an acrostic, and that the only person "who fits the data of our Psalm" is Simon (143-134), the first civil ruler to become also high-priest. The acrostic would read: "Simon is terrible." The rehatched proposal will not likely gain more supporters than the original one made, almost a century ago, by G. Bickel and others. J. W. Bowker qualifies the acrostic theory as "extremely weak" and shows also the weakness of the other arguments presented by Treves. "Abstraction faite de ses multiples relectures" Tournay wrote (*RB* 1960, p. 38), Ps 110 seems to have been redacted about the time of Chronicles or Qoheleth, most probably before the rule of Antiochus III (223-187). His motives for assigning such a late date to the psalm cannot be discussed here, although they do call the reader's attention (e.g.: that period was one in which the claims of the priestly power were exceptionally great).

The claims of the psalm to be called messianic are self-evident and the more prominent aspects have been pointed out. Not all authors will, however, admit that the psalm is directly or in the strict sense messianic. True, Coppens notes (p. 22), royal messianism is expressed in this psalm, yet not messianim in its strict sense, because eschatology is not explicitly stated. This monarch, besides, rules by force, the ideal of his kingship has not reached beyond the lower level of typical messianism. His kingdom is still in this world.

Psalm 132 (131)

The Pact between David and the Lord

The transfer of the sacred Ark to Jerusalem (2 S 6; cf. §13b), alluded to in other royal psalms, is a central feature of Ps 132. Traditions related to the event belong to the essential background of this category of psalms. As Mowinckel puts it (I, p. 48), "in Ps 132 we meet the king as the leader of a religious festival play in remembrance of the time when David brought Yahweh's holy shrine up to Zion, and the king is here playing the part of David." Ps 132, would, he adds (I, p. 174), give us the "text" of a dramatic procession with Yahweh's ark. In 2 Ch 6:41f, Ps 132:8-11 forms the conclusion of the prayer offered on the occasion of the dedication of the temple. The annual commemoration of this event and the festival of the enthronement, Weiser assumes, coincided with the "Covenant festival of Yahweh" (cf. Ps 132:12, 15) celebrated in autumn (cf. §13c). The festival of the temple consecration, Mowinckel believes (I, p. 175), was at the same time the festival of the institution of the cult of Yahweh on Zion under David. The mention in this context of "the Mighty One of Jacob" (v 5) possibly reflects an attempt to merge Northern (cf. Gn 49:24) and Southern cultic traditions.

According to Dahood "the psalm divides into three stanzas: vv 1-5 contain David's promise to find a home for Yahweh in Jerusalem; vv 6-10 describe the procession and give the text of prayers asking God to come to Jerusalem, to bless his priests, and his king. The third stanza (vv 11-18) cites the text of Yahweh's oath to perpetuate both the Davidic dynasty and his own presence in Jerusalem." Whereas Dahood finds in Ps 132 a "concentration of archaic words, forms, parallelisms, and phrases" which, together with the contents, point to a tenth-century date of composition, D. R. Hillers finds one single example of archaism *š⁽ᵉ⁾nāt*, "sleep," in v 4 instead of *šinat;* (should it not be *šēnāt?*), and thinks the psalm "was probably written in the latter portion of the monarchy in Judah" (*CBQ* 1968, p. 51, note 12). But the main object of Hillers' article centers on his translation of v 8: "Arise, O Yahweh, *from* your resting place, You and your mighty ark." Although Dahood elsewhere likes to understand *l⁽ᵉ⁾* as meaning "from" (see on *Ps 40:11), he gives it here the usual sense of "to": "Arise, Yahweh, to your resting place, you, and the ark your fortress."

Verse 6 also alludes to the "changing fortunes" of the Ark of the

Covenant: "Behold, we heard of it in Ephrathah; we found it in the fields of Jaar." Ephrathah may refer to Bethlehem, David's birthplace (cf. Ru 4:11; Mi 5:1), or Shiloh (cf. 21:19), the sanctuary in Ephraim (1 S 1:1=Ephratha), where the Ark was stationed (cf. 1 Sm 2:12-17 and 1 S 3-4). Returning from Philistine territory the Ark passed from Bethshemesh to the house of Abinadab in *qiryaty^e'arîm* (1 S 6:21; cf. 1 Ch 2: 50). Nearby, "in the fields of *yā'ar*," the Ark *was found* (Ps 132:6). The cultic search for the Ark in Israel would correspond, Mowinckel suggests (I, p. 176), to a feature of the Babylonian New Year and enthronement drama: in Babylonia the other gods would go along with the king and the priests...in a cultic procession to search for and deliver the lost, dead or imprisoned god (cf. also W. Frankfort, *Kingship of the Gods,* Chicago, 1948, p. 321ff). More to the point is fact that Ps 132 is primarily "the *hieros logos* of the dedication of the Temple," including "a recital of the establishment of the sanctuary" (A. Weiser; cp. with § 13b). Ps 132, Wolverton remarks, presents "a thoroughly mythological interpretation" of the election of Zion and of the line of David. It has been explained (cf. §13b) that in Wolverton's view to "mythologize" is to interpret a human action as of divine action. Not the reenactment of the transfer of the Ark, Weiser believes, but the appearing of God from Sinai or from heaven (cf. §13d) is dramatized in verse 8: "Advance, O Lord, to your resting place, you and the ark of your majesty" (cf. Pss 18:8-16; 68:17, 25; Nb 10:35ff; Jg 5:4f; 1 K 8:10f; Is 6:1-5).

The two fundamental ideas of the psalm concern the prophecy of Nathan and the election of Zion as God's dwelling-place. They feature together also in 2 S 8 and in Ps 78:67-71. In Ps 132, however, God's promises (cf. 1 K 8:25; Ps 89:20f) are presented as the answer to an oath of David, not reported elsewhere. *The Oxford Annotated Bible* (p. 383) has this to say about 2 S 7:1-29: "This chapter is the only serious interruption of the Early Source in the entire book. Like 1 S 2: 27-36, it is a late theological commentary inserted into an early historical source, seeking to explain why David was not chosen to build the temple. It seems to have been based to some extent on Ps 89 (compare Ps 132: 11f). Nathan the prophet (vv 2, 3, 4, 17) is used as a mouthpiece of the author, though the historical Nathan does not appear in the Early Source until 12:1. Verses 4-17 are often referred to as The Prophecy of Nathan and verses 18-29 as The Prayer of David. In verse 6 the writer ignores the temple of Shiloh" (1 S 1:7; 3:3).

God's promise to the Davidic lineage was fulfilled with the advent of the messianic king (cf. Lk 1:32f; see §15c and *Ps 89:31-38). The "anointed" of Ps 132:10 is probably a reigning king of Judah, contemporaneous with the psalmist, although perhaps a post-exilic descendant of David, like Zerubbabel (cf. Ps 80:18) could be meant. To Zerubbabel's name that of Josue was substituted in Zc 6:11 (cf. Hag 1:1f). It is upon Zerubbabel, called "Sprout," "Shoot" or "Branch" (cf. Jr 23:5; 33:15) that the crown is to be placed (Zc 3:8; 6:11f). The same messianic theme occurs in Ps 132:17 (cf. Lk 1:69). In this verse 17, the expression 'rk nr, "set a lamp," is used, perhaps as an allusion to the lamp kept burning perpetually in the sanctuary (cf. Ex 27:20f; Lv 24:2ff). "My anointed" would be David himself (cf. Ps 18:50) rather than his successors. "The phraseology of verse 18," writes Kirkpatrick, "seems intended to suggest that David's representative will have high-priestly as well as royal dignity." The Hebrew word nezer, "crown," is also used for the high-priest's diadem (E 29:6) and the verb used for "shine" is cognate to the noun ṣiṣ which denotes in Ex 28:36 the plate of pure gold worn by the High-priest "upon the mitre" (Ex 28:37). On the plate were engraved the words: "Holiness to the Lord" (ibid). The messianic connotations associated with the "lamp" theme have been investigated by F. Asensio, for both Testaments. The promise to David of a lamp is reported in the Book of Kings (1 K 11:36; 15:4; 2 K 8:19). A lightless house is deserted (cf. Jr 25:10; Jb 18:5). As for the Messiah he will be "a light for the nation" (Is 42:6; 49:6; Lk 2:32; cf. BJ). On Ps 132 see also Mc Carthy's study mentioned in the bibliography.

PSALM 144 (143)

Prayer for Victory and Prosperity

The first part of this psalm (vv 1-10) probably featured in a royal liturgy which included hymnic elements (vv 1-2; 9-11) and a supplication (3-8). Its literary affinities with Ps 18 and other psalms are to be accounted for, Weiser thinks, by "a common and fixed liturgical tradition" rather than by direct borrowings from other sources. The second part (12-15) could constitute the "new song" announced in verse 9. It is an original composition which presents an idyllic picture of the messianic era (BJ), or reflects the grateful reaction of the cult community to the blessings of the "graces of kingship" (Weiser).

After stating that "the poem actually consists of two distinct psalms" (vv 1-11 and 12-15), Dahood calls Ps 144 "a royal psalm" which, like Ps 18, "may tentatively be ascribed to the tenth century B.C." He finds original features in it, like the hapax legomenon phrase *hereb rā'āh*, "the sword of the Evil One" (=Death) in v 10, and the use of six parallel pairs of words that have counterparts in the Ugaritic tablets (see on "Ugaritic-Hebrew Parallel Pairs": L. R. Fisher, ed., *Ras Shamra Parallels*, pp. 71-382).

VIII.   Didactic Psalms

In this family of psalms different categories join in a sort of unity based on a common interest, that of *teaching* in a variety of forms: sapiential reflections, lessons of history, prophetic exhortations, liturgical instructions. They follow no common literary pattern but they do reflect a tone inspired by their common purpose.

§29. THE WISDOM PSALMS

a) *General character*

The notion of "didactic psalms" applies first and best to the wisdom psalms. As *BJ* notes, the "spiritual guides" of Israel used the Psalms' literary genre to express their teaching or *tôrâ*. The scribes were both sages and poets. The "wise words of their teaching" they set down in rhythmical compositions (cf. Si 44:4f). The forms of expression and the thought patterns of wisdom literature are reflected in many psalms. Pss 127 and 133, for example, have preserved the proverbial form (cf. Ps 78:2). Admonitions and exhortative instructions, typical of sapiential and didactic poetry, are also represented in the Pss 34:12ff; 78:1-8; 81:9 (cf. Pr 8:4f). In the following passage some important characteristics of the wisdom psalm find expression (note the direct form of address: cp. Pr 22:17).

Hear this, all you peoples;
    hearken, all who dwell in the world,
Of lowly birth or high degree,
    rich and poor alike.
My mouth shall speak wisdom;
    prudence shall be the utterance of my heart.
My ear is intent upon a proverb;
    I will set forth my riddle to the music of the harp (Ps 49:2-5).

In wisdom poetry there exists a general tendency to substitute reflection to prayer and to insist on a *practical* wisdom of life: a religious basis is given for the practice of human virtues.

Several more common *themes* of the wisdom psalms can be pointed out. God's faithful willingly meditate on the *Law* (Pss 1:2; 37:31; 119: 15), with love (1:2; 119:47), for the Law is an inexhaustible source of benefits (Ps 119). The morality maxim; "turn from evil and do good" (Ps 37:27), is continually recalled in various ways. The ways and the final destiny of the wicked run contrary to that of the just (Pss 1, 37, 112). The happiness of the righteous 37:3f; 112:1), the domestic joys of the faithful (Pss 127, 128, 133) are emphasized. They will "possess the land" (37:9, 22, 29, 34), while the wicked threatened by God's judgment (1:4) are heading for ruin (Ps 37). The just man reflects and understands (3:16f); the wicked is senseless and foolish (49:21). Yahweh knows (1:6; 91:14; 139:1, 13ff, 23) and protects the just (Ps 91), who trusts entirely in him (37:5ff).

Retribution is a pressing problem for the sage. Its many aspects are featured in the wisdom psalms (cf. G. R. Castellino, *Libro.* . . . p. 729ff; see on "retribution": §14d). The testimony of experience is produced:

Neither in my youth, nor now that I am old,
    have I seen a just man forsaken
    nor his descendants begging bread.
All the day he is kindly and lends,
    and his descendants shall be blessed (37:25f).

On retribution the psalms reflect generally the traditional views: the righteous enjoy prosperity and happiness, the wicked harvest adversity and calamity (cf. Pss 1, 91, 112, 119, 127, 128). But the data of experience seemed to confirm the obvious shortcomings of temporal retribution. Some psalmists, faced with the prosperity of the wicked, profess to be scandalized and offended (cf. Pss 73:2-16; 139:19; cp. Ec 8:14). The idea that a different destiny awaits the just and the wicked in the other world was formulated only gradually. Insights and hopes involving extra-temporal values appear in a few statements: death is the shepherd of the worldly-minded, their dwelling is Sheol (49:15); the just, on the other hand, hope to be redeemed from the power of the nether world (49:16) and be received in glory (73:24), like Enoch (Gn 5:24) or Elijah (2 K 2:1-11).

The wisdom psalms do not follow a strict *literary pattern*. Three are alphabetical compositions (Pss 37, 112, 119; cf. §6d). The *mashal*, "proverb," "saying" or "sentence," represents the oldest and simplest mode of expression in wisdom literature (cf. A. R. Johnson in *SVT*, III, 1955, pp. 162-169; H.-J. Kraus, *Psalmen*, p. 889; A. Bentzen, *Introduction...*I, p. 167ff). The form of the *mashal* is either short (Pr 10:29) or elaborate (Pr 1-9). The word appears in Ps 49:5 and the "proverbial" form is not rare in the Psalter (cf. 62:12; cp. Pr 6:16), no more than certain typical expressions like "Happy the man..." (Ps 1:1; cp. Jb 5:17). Another peculiar feature of the wisdom psalmists is their more than usual recourse to the so-called "anthological style," characterized by the re-use of words or expressions belonging to previous scriptures (see on *Pss 33 and 119).

Introducing his lecture on "Psalms and Wisdom" (*SVT*, III, pp. 205-224), S. Mowinckel restated his conviction that "perhaps more than 140 of the 150 [psalms] of the Psalter, have not only been used as cult-poems, but have also been composed for that purpose" (p. 205: cf. §8a). The problem, in psalm exegesis, he said, is not the cultic psalms, but the non-cultic ones, which seem to belong to "learned psalmography," originated in the circles of the "wise men," the learned leaders of the "wisdom schools" (p. 206; cf. II, pp. 104-125). Five wisdom psalms (1, 37, 49, 112, 127) figure among Mowinckel's "non-cultic psalms" (the others: 19B, 34, 78, 105, 106, 111; cf. II, p. 111). In the latest psalmography, not related to definite cultic occasions, the learned writers try to adhere to the old rules of composition, but without much success and this would have brought "a dissolution of the style": the different modes and motives get mixed up ("Psalms and Wisdom," p 213). This is particularly marked, Mowinckel noted, "in what Jewish opinion held most skillful, viz., alphabetic psalms" (*ibid.*).

(b) The wisdom psalms are the following: Pss 1, 37, 49, (73), (91), 112, 119, 127, 128, 133, (139).

PSALM 1

True Happiness

Pss 1 and 2 form a sort of preface to the whole Psalter and bring out some of its moral and messianic ideas (see on *Ps 2). Ps 1 begins with a beatitude (*'ašrē*). This literary and religious category expressing a praise, a salutation, or a wish was adopted by the wisdom literature. It differs from the priestly blessing (*berākâh*), the counterpart of the curse. Yet Mowinckel suggests (II, p. 52) that the style pattern of the blessing and curse used in the "cultic rituals" has been imitated by the wisdom poetry, introduced in the prophetic admonitions, taken up by the "learned psalmography" and finally adopted by "private psalmography" (Pss 1 and 112) in the form of statements on "the two ways," the way of piety and the way of ungodliness, leading to life or to death (cf. Mt 7:13f). These number among Mowinckel's "non-cultic poems" (see §8a and 29a). A. Weiser though notes that the practical and educational wisdom proposed in Ps 1 and elsewhere "is based on a firm religious foundation the roots of which are firmly embedded *in the tradition of public worship.*" He remarks also that in contrast to some of Paul's views (cf. Rm 3:20; Gal 4:21-31; 1 Cor 15:56) the law in Ps 1 is not regarded as an irksome burden but as a source of joy (cf. Pss 19:8-11; 119:92; Dt 30:11). It is the *God revealing law* that Jesus has come not to abolish but to fulfill (Mt 5:17). The psalmist sees it as the expression of divine will, affording guidance under God's providential rule. In God's verdict, at the hour of judgment (vv 5, 6), the final issue of the two ways will confirm the pattern of retribution (cf. §14d). Ps 112 also ends with a pronouncement on the ruin of the wicked.

It has been observed by Kirkpatrick that the three clauses of verse one "denote successive steps in a career of evil, and form a climax: (1) adoption of the principles of the wicked as a rule of life; (2) persistence in the practices of notorious offenders; (3) deliberate association with those who openly mock at religion." Dahood believes that in verse 3 the final destiny of the just is alluded to: "So shall he be like a tree transplanted near streams of water," transplanted, that is, "to the Elysian Fields," the abode of the blessed after death (see on *Ps 36:10). As for the wicked they "shall not stand in the place of judgment" (v 5; cf. Dt 25:1). Dahood comments: "As the final judgment will take place in the heavenly council, to which the wicked will not be admitted, they will be condemned in *absentia*" (cf. Ps 82:1).

According to E. P. Arbez "the psalm gives a consistent solution of the problem of retribution." Without excluding eschatology, the thoughts expressed in verses 2-3 can very well apply to the temporal life of the man who is nourished by the word of God: "As a tree is nourished by constant supplies of water, without which under the burning Eastern sun it would wither and die, so the life of the godly man is maintained by the supplies of grace drawn from constant communion with God through his revelation": cf. Pss 52:8; 92:12; 128:3 (Kirkpatrick). Attentive as always to the "sacral king" motif (cf. §8d), I. Engnell characterized Ps 1 as a "word of blessing" connected with a literary type called "mirror of the prince" or "$s^e dak\bar{a}$-table," a "table of righteousness." This author also quotes rather unimpressing parallels which would associate the Tammuz god, the king, and the tree of life. Such explanations seem unduly *recherchées* and unnecessary, in view of the obvious clarity of the text.

Written for those "who fear God and walk in his ways," the inscriptions of the Petosiris tomb in Egypt (end of the fourth century b.c.; *BJ*, p. 51f and *RB* 1922, pp. 481-488) can be quoted in connection with this psalm: "I shall lead you to the way of life, the good way of he who obeys God; happy is he whose heart guides him to it. He who walks with a firm heart on the way of life is firmly established on earth. He who fears God greatly is very happy on earth" (Inscr. 62). In the "Instruction of Egyptian Amen-em-opet" (probably seventh-sixth cent. b.c.), can be read the following (*ANET*, p. 422):

As for the heated man of a temple,
He is like a tree growing in the open.
In the completion of a moment (comes) its
    loss of foliage...
(But) the truly silent man holds himself apart.
He is like a tree growing in a garden.
It flourishes and doubles its yield;
It (stands) before its lord [cp. Jr 17:5ff]

To conclude, a note on the metre of the psalm. Its peculiar character brings S. Bullough to suggest "that Psalm 1 is not in metre at all, but is plain rhythmic prose. Of course the metre is 'uncertain' (Kittel, *Bibl. Hebr.*) because it is no more than the free pattern of well-written prose" (*VT* 1967, see B.'s prose translation, p. 49).

PSALM 37

The Fate of Sinners and the Reward of the Just

In this collection of maxims loosely joined to form an alphabetic psalm (cf. §6d), a wise old man (v 25) repeats to the godly that in putting their trust in God they have chosen the right path. To those who become impatient about the ways of the Lord he says: "Wait and see!" (v 34) To the frail, exposed to temptation because the wicked are prosperous, he recalls the traditional doctrine of retribution (cf. §14d): "Criminals are destroyed, and the posterity of the wicked is cut off" (v 28). In this "noncultic poem" (Mowinckel; cf. *Ps 1), A. Weiser discovers various "references to elements of the tradition of the cult of the covenant": blessing and curse (v 22), (re)distribution of land (cf. *Ps 142), judgment and salvation (10f, 34, 37f). These references would allow the view that the psalm was composed and used in pre-exilic times. The *land,* so often mentioned in the psalm (vv 3, 9, 11, 22, 29, 34) is the Promised Land, Palestine (cf. Dt. 11:1-32), later considered as a type or figure of heaven (cf. Heb 11:9-16), or of the kingdom of heaven (cf. Mt 5:4).

It is a teaching frequently but diversely expressed in the psalms (cf. Ps 35:8+§12e), that the wicked perish by their own device: "Their swords shall pierce their own hearts" (v 15). It is an application of a more general religious truth that "sin is already in itself judgment" (Weiser). By divine disposition the sinner's sphere of life is bound to decay and ruin (cf. Ho 5:12; Jr 2:19; 5:25; 6:21, 30; 13:23; 18:17). For the just, adversity is medicinal and temporary. With God's assistance he will recover and lead a normal life (vv 23ff).

Some of the latest psalms, writes Mowinckel (I, p. 213), such as Pss 37, 49 and 73, present the more Jewish than Israelite conception of "the wicked": they are mainly "apostates," disregarding Yahweh's law and the claims of the covenant, and thus incurring "the chastising interference of Yahweh." The same author does not seem too particular about literary categories. Ps. 37, for example, he lists both among the "personal thanksgiving psalms" (II, p. 114) and among "the wisdom psalms" (II, p. 138).

PSALM 49 (48)

The Vanity of Worldly Riches

The traditional wisdom doctrine on retribution (cf. Pss 37 and 73+ §14d) is applied here to a specific problem: the riches of the wicked. Himself a potential victim of hostile wealth (vv 6-7), the psalmist has not let envy prevail in his heart (cf. Ps 73:2f), but by objective analysis he has carefully examined the riddle of the prosperity of the wicked. He presents his solution in proverbial form (*māshāl,* v 5): wealth cannot save from death (vv 8-10), decreed for all men (11-13); the wicked perish hopelessly but the just will be redeemed from the power of the nether world (14-16), because trust in God can overcome even death. The problem discussed being universal in scope, the sapiential consideration is addressed to all who dwell in the world. Yet it will be more beneficial to the poor, to those of lowly birth (v 3), as an encouragement in their distress and a protection against temptation. The psalm concludes with an exhortation (vv 17-21) which again stresses the vanity of riches and repeats the maxim: "Man, for all his splendor, if he have not prudence (i.e., sapiential understanding), resembles the beasts that perish" (v 21: cf. v 13).

The beginning of verse 9 is a *crux interpretum*. The root *yqr* usually denotes the idea of "costly." In some Palmyrene funerary inscriptions, P. Joüon (*Syria* 1938, p. 99f) attributed to *yqr'* the meaning "monument d'honneur." From this and other indications Dahood conjectures that somehow *yqr* in verse 9 and 13 must mean "Mansion," "another of the thirty-odd names of the nether world heretofore recognized in biblical poetry." Thus these verses would read:

But the Mansion shall be the redemption of his soul,
    and he shall cease forever.
For man in the Mansion will sleep indeed,
    become like beasts that cease to be.

Verses 14-15 which also involve difficulties, are rendered thus by R. Pautrel:

14 Haec est via eorum qui sperant in se
    et finis eorum qui ore suo delectantur.
15A Sicut oves in praedam ponunt,
    mors pascet eos et dominabitur eis.
15B Dociles in gregem includet,
    superesse inferno gloriantes.

Attention to the emphasizing particle *ki*, attested in Ugaritic texts, has brought about an improved translation of important verse 16: "But God will ransome me, from the hand of Sheol will he surely snatch me." Dahood adds the following comment: "What the psalmist is professing is his firm conviction that God will take him to himself, just as he took

Enoch and Elijah; in other words, he is stating his belief in 'assumption.' Most commentators find this meaning in the psalmist's words. ... The verb *lqh* is precisely that used in Gn 5:24; 2 K 2:3; 5:9; Si 42:15; 48:9; as well as in Ps 73:24" (*lqh* is, however, a very common verb!). The minimizing interpretations could be represented by *OABA*: "This might express the psalmist's assurance of his own immortality, but is perhaps better understood merely as confidence that he will be delivered from present trouble." Perhaps this is suggested by the three following parallel texts: "Great has been your kindness toward me; you have rescued me from the depths of the nether world" (Ps 86:13); "What man shall live, and not see death, but deliver himself from the power of the nether world?"; "Shall I deliver them from the power of the nether world? shall I redeem them from death?" Preservation from death rather than rescue from Sheol after death seems to be intended. It is hard to deny that Ps 49:16 expresses the belief that the just can hope for immortality (Pss 16:10f and 73:23ff are not clear). J. van der Ploeg thinks that the affirmation of the verse goes beyond a mere hope of being preserved from a premature death. He would not exclude that the psalmist had in mind the immortality of the person or, even more probably, bodily resurrection (p. 172). In contrast to the destiny of the just is that of the wicked "who shall never more see light" (v 20), i.e., enjoy immortality (see on *Ps 36:10). "The light of God's face in the fields of life will be denied those who put their trust in riches and boast of financial success" (Dahood; on Ps 49:16, cf. also *RB* 1949, p. 493ff).

PSALM 73 (72)

The False Happiness of the Wicked

How can faith in God survive against the background of the prosperity of the wicked? The psalmist himself had to resist the scandal and refrain the impulse of envy (vv 2-3). After having described the well-being, the apparent happiness and the arrogance of the wicked (vv 4-12), he compares their fortunate lot to the distressing state of the just, like himself. He was tempted to imitate the wicked but then a divine revelation showed him in a new light their final destiny (13-17). He suddenly understood that the prosperous sinner is really on the verge of ruin because his apparent security has no real foundation (18-22). In contrast, the psalmist's future rests on the firm basis of trust in God, the effects of which endure beyond death's frontier (23-28). If Luther's translation of verse 25 is correct, "as long as I have thee, I wish for nothing else in heaven or on earth," then communion with God, whether in heaven or on earth, is for the psalmist the supreme and, in a way, the only good (see §12f). This psalmist has expressed his views in the relation of a personal experience available for a general application.

Taking as starting-point the statement, "till I entered the sanctuary of God," recent authors link Ps 73 with the cult. The central character, representing Israel (v 1), would be the king (E. Würthwein), and the psalm has probably featured in the mythologizing New Year festival (H. Ringgren). H. Gressman discovered a royal rite in the affirmation: "You have hold of my right hand" (73:23; cf. Is 45:1). For H. Schmidt the psalm is the thanksgiving of an individual recited at a *Gelübdedankgottesdienst*. Mowinckel (II, p. 36) holds a similar view and describes the man's calamity as distress made more bitter by "travail of mind." There is much to be said in favor of these suggestions, some of which, however, depend too heavily on preconceived extraneous patterns of interpretation.

We read in verses 9-10:

They set their mouthings in place of heaven,
    and their pronouncements roam the earth:
So he brings his people to such a pass
    that they have not even water!

It is curious to read in this connection a text from the Ras Shamra tablets (cf. §9d), which states, Ringgren explains, "that some mythological beings, who obviously have some connection with chaos and death, put one lip to the sky and the other to the earth and drain the water in abundance" (*The Faith...*, p. 44f; cf. *VT* 1953, p. 265ff). The parallel is more apparent if the translation keeps closer to the Hebrew: "They set their mouths against the heavens, and their tongue struts through the earth" (*RSV*: Ps 73:9a). Other Ugaritic parallels are cited by R. T. O'Callaghan: "In the poem of the Gracious and Beautiful Gods, evidently of cosmogonic character, Dawn and Dusk are begotten by El and their ravenous appetites soon after birth are described: 'One lip is (stretched down) to earth, one lip (upward) to the sky...' (t. 52:61f; Gordon, p. 175). It is not impossible that the Psalmist used the wording of an early cosmogonic myth as a striking figure of speech to mark the colossal insolence of the impious. In keeping with the voracious appetite of

Dawn and Dusk we find a more forceful application of the same phrase to the god Môt into whose ravenous maw Baal will descend in the season of declining vegetation: 'One lip to earth and one lip to heaven, [He stretches his tongue to the stars], Baal enters within him, he descends into his maw' (t. 67, II, 2ff; Gordon, p. 178). Here the closest parallel is the biblical application to the extended gullet and insatiable hunger of Sheol, the most striking example being found perhaps in Is 5:14; cf. Hab 2:5; Pr 1:12; Ps 141:7" (*VT*, 1954, p. 169).

H. Birkeland's views on the "evildoing enemies" in the Psalms is known (cf. §12g). "Some revision of my exposition in *Die Feinde..*," he writes, "will be found implied in the following attempt at a solution of the chief problems of Ps 73:17ff." The identification of the *rᵉšā'îm* with the *gôyîm* is directly required in Ps 73:1, where it is said, in Birkeland's view, "that God is good towards Israel" (cf. v 10). The "I" of the psalm, he explains, is a representative of Israel. What solved the psalmist's doubt, Birkeland claims, was no divine revelation, but a visit to "the illegitimate places of worship," to the *miqdᵉšē-ēl*, mentioned in verse 17. This interpretation presupposes the centralization of the cult in one sanctuary, that of Jerusalem (cf. Dt 12:5ff; 2 K 22-23). "When the author came to (the remnants of) the illegitimate sanctuaries, which were destroyed, they became to him demonstrations of the fate of paganism and pagans, i.e., of gentile idolatry and the gentiles themselves: they flourished for a time, but were then demolished. And it was Yahweh who had destroyed them, so that they fell into ruins. . . . The devastated sanctuaries have made him realize the uselessness of idols and the eternal value of his own communion with Yahweh; he and his people are safeguarded under the protection of God." JB translates verse 17, "Until the day I pierced the mystery. . ." and comments: "Lit. 'the sanctuaries of God.' The psalmist is not referring to the Temple where God may have enlightened him, nor to divine mysteries (Ws 2:22), revealed to him, but to the teaching contained in the scriptures, dwelling place of wisdom (Pr 9:1f; Si 14:21f) and staple of Jewish piety (Si 39:1)."

As for verse 24, the text, in Birkeland's view, "simply contains the following meaning: Yahweh takes, i.e., leads the author on a path on which he is always after *kābōd* ("glory," "honor"), just as, for example, the shepherd is after the flock." The *kābōd*, in this case, consists "in real goods, for the time being communion with God, later on the restoration of the people." It is probably more true to say that the psalmist's intimate fellowship with God on earth has instructed him also on some secrets of the world to come. In accordance with parallel biblical passages (see on *Ps 49:16), Dahood would translate the verse: "Into your council lead me and with glory assume me." It is not easy to prove that he is wrong. The meaning of "glory" is thus explained by *JB*: "Probably not a reference to heavenly glory (Enoch, Gn 5:24; Elijah, 2 K 2:3). The versions translate 'with glory,' giving the word its usual sense when used of men; this interpretation suggests that God preserves the just man from an early and shameful death and will vindicate him, even though man dies while the wicked survive. Moreover, as in 16:9f, the psalmist yearns for unbreakable union with God; this is a milestone on the road to a formulated belief in resurrection and eternal life."

In verse 26 the psalmist affirms that God is his portion forever (see on *Ps 142:6). The apportioning of the inheritance (see on *Ps 110:7) can be generally related to the allocating of the land under Joshua who "had given the Levites no inheritance among the tribes" (14:3f); "Yahweh the God of Israel was their inheritance, as he had told them" (Jos 13:4). Yahweh had explained to Aaron: "You shall have no inheritance in their land, no portion of it among them shall be yours. It is I who will be your portion and your inheritance among the sons of Israel" (Nb 18:20; cf. Dt 10:9).

PSALM 91 (90)

Security under God's Protection

In Ps 46 the cult community expressed its unreserved trust in God "against the whole wide background of the *Heilsgeschichte* and of eschatology." In Ps 91, "springing from the same cultic source" (Weiser), it is a "personal and intimate relationship of trust in God" which is expressed and powerfully illustrated by various poetical metaphors. The first part of the psalm (1-13) was perhaps pronounced by a priest as an exhortation to the temple worshippers. Some authors (cf. G. Pidoux, p. 145) suggest that Ps 91 consists of liturgical fragments; others (cf. H. Schmidt) think it is one of the threshold dialogues (*Pfortengespräche*), like Pss 15 and 24A. It is perhaps easier to assume, with H.-J. Kraus, that the psalm was recited by a man who had taken refuge in the sanctuary. His thanksgiving takes the form of a confession (cf. Ps 34:12), in which the blessing of trust in God is impressed upon the listener(s) by the teaching of personal experience. According to Dahood the poem is "a royal psalm of trust or confidence composed by a court poet who here recites it before the king." It is observed that the verb ḥasâh, "take refuge" (v 4), "is frequent in royal psalms: cf. e.g. 212; 18:3, 32; 57:2; 61:5." But the hyperbolic statement of v 7 does not require a royal context, in spite of 1 S 18:7. See on Ps 91 the dissertation by P. Hugger published by offset at Münsterschwarzach, Germany, in 1971.

The mention in verse 1 of the divine names, "Most High," "Almighty," Caquot writes, could reflect the probable fact that the Israelite Yahweh replaced at a given time and place (Jerusalem) 'elyôn-šadday, the divinity of pre-davidic Zion (cf. v 9 and §13b). The central character meant throughout the psalm under the anonymity of the 3rd and 2nd persons could be the just *par excellence,* the Messiah himself, J. Magne thinks. This would be in a way confirmed by the gospel narrative: Satan quoted verses 11-12 when he tempted Christ to presumption against God's providence (Mt 4:6).

Various ancient versions, including the Vulgate (*"daemonium meridianum"*) read an allusion to "the noonday devil" in verse 6 (Hebr.: *yašûd,* "devastate") influenced, it seems, by the ancient Oriental representation of pestilence as a demon especially active during the night and the noon siesta. J. De Fraine has shown from biblical and non-biblical sources that a personal demonic power is meant even in the *MT.* Verses 5-6, he pointed out, refer to four manifestations of demonic power: during the night, in the morning, in the evening and at noon, embracing the whole day. Consequently divine protection is understood to accompany the just constantly. A. F. Kirkpatrick, on the other hand, would consider Pss 90, 91, 92 as a group, and conclude: "If now Ps 90 is the plea of Israel in exile, and Ps 92 its thanksgiving for deliverance, may not Ps 91 be the voice of faith assuring Israel that it will be safe in the midst of the calamities which are about to fall upon Babylon?"

The reading of "asp" in verse 13 follows the Greek, Syriac and Latin versions, but the Hebrew word *šaḥal* means "lion." What the psalmist has in mind, writes Weiser, is probably "the idea, widespread in the ancient Orient and handed down in the cultic myth, of the god killing a dragon and as a sign of victory over the monster putting his foot on its neck. And whereas the popular belief in Egypt led to the manufacturing of amulets with the picture of a god treading on a lion, and by its magic power giving protection against wild animals, in the Old Testament it is faith which supplies man with super-human, divine strength to overcome every kind of danger."

Psalm 112 (111)

The Blessings of the Just Man

Not only the opening words but the rest of the psalm as well show similarities with Ps 1 in subject-matter. In form and language Ps 112 can be compared to Ps 111, another alphabetic psalm, perhaps written by the same author Besides, some expressions said of God in Ps 111 are applied in Ps 112 to the just. Divine attributes are reflected in the works of the upright. Like God (cf. Pss 18:29; 27:1) the just man is a shining light (v 4; cf. Pr 13:9; Mt 5:16). The *ṣedeq* of both will endure forever (Pss 111:3; 112:3). In contrast there will be no other answer to the evil man's desire but powerless envy (v 10). Although it is probable that in v 4b not the just (*NAB*), but God is the subject, as in *RSV's*, "Light rises in the darkness for the upright; the Lord [not mentioned in the Hebrew text] is gracious, merciful, and righteous." Dahood's lavish name capitalizations do not seem to be called for: "In the Darkness [=the nether world] will dawn the Sun [cf. Ml 3:20] for the upright, the Merciful and Compassionate and Just One."

Psalm 119 (118)

Praise of God's Law

The longest psalm of the psalter comprises twenty-two stanzas of eight lines, each of which begins with the same Hebrew letter, assigned alphabetically to every strophe. The Akkadian "Dialogue about Human Misery," a poem sometimes called "The Babylonian Ecclesiastes," is composed in a similar framework (see *ANET*, 2nd ed., 438-40). Tedious repetitions, poor thought-sequence, apparent lack of inspiration reflect the artificiality of the composition. We must register here a different appreciation by Dahood, for whom a careful analysis of the Hebrew text reveals "a freshness of thought and a felicity of expression unnoticed and consequently unappreciated in earlier versions." For example, he adds, no other psalmist employs more frequently or more effectively the prosodic pattern labeled "the double-duty modifier," or "a type of zeugma." Reference is made to vv 43, 55, 62, 111, 140, 142, 144, 149, 160, 166, 169, 174, but I found that in five of these the same name Yahweh is the so-called "double-duty modifier" in "a chiastic or diagonal pattern," while in six of the other verses listed supposedly divine names, like the "Everlasting Grand One," present a debatable interpretation, which entails a questionable literary analysis. On the other hand, I see no difficulty in accepting the meaning "from" for *bā* in v 87 (in 11QPs^a it is changed to the regular *min* by writing *m'rṣ*) and the translation: "They nearly exterminated me from the earth, but I did not forsake your precepts."

Mowinckel (II, p. 78) believes that the long poem is a non-cultic individual psalm of lamentation (cf. vv 8, 61, 85, 95, 107, 110, 115, 150-154, 161) and that the numerous references to the author's own faithfulness with respect to the Law are intended as motivations of the supplication. The psalm can also be described as a hymn to the Law, mentioned under eight synonyms: law, statutes, commands, ordinances, decrees, precepts, words, and promises. The Law praised in the psalm should be understood as referring generally to divine revelation made known by the prophets and the messengers of God.

This great "Psalm of the Law," writes Kirkpatrick, "is based upon the prophetic (Ezr 9:11) presentation of the Law in the Book of Deuteronomy, with the spirit and language of which its author's mind was saturated. It represents the religious ideas of Deuteronomy developed in the communion of a devout soul with God. . . . The 'Law of God' which the psalmist describes. . .is not the law in the narrower sense of the Mosaic legislation or the Pentateuch. The Hebrew word *tōrāh* has a wider range of meaning, and here, as in Pss 1 and 19, it must be understood to mean all Divine revelation as the guide of life. This it is which kindles the psalmist's enthusiasm and demands his allegiance. It is no rigid code of commands and prohibitions, but a body of teaching, the full meaning of which can only be realized gradually and by the help of Divine instruction." In his detailed study of Ps 119, A. Deissler has stressed the author's intelligent use of previous scriptures (anthological style, cf. *Ps 33). He also maintains that the psalms' subject-matter seems to be deuteronomic *tōrāh*. To consider the "Word of God" as almost personified (v 89) helps to understand that it is a source of life (v 93). The psalm is later then Proverbs and Malachi but was written before Sirach and Maccabees, in the third and second century B.C. (on the "meditation" of the law, see §12f).

Additional views bring out the rich variety of the psalm's teaching in contrast with the apparent monotony of the expression. J. Enciso considers Ps 119 as a *Salmo-prologo* (see on *Ps 137) introducing the "Songs of ascents" (120-134; cf §3c). He finds that many verses of the Psalm reflect the context of a pilgrim's trip to Jerusalem. Some would allude to vexations endured when, coming form the North, the pilgrim passed through the territory of hostile Samaritans (cf. the *Caph* stanza: vv 81-88). The *Lamed* stanza (vv 89-96) is a kind of thanksgiving, marking the end (v 96) of the long trip. The following stanzas would describe the psalmist's state of soul during his stay in the Holy City, where he heard so much about the Law. Before leaving Jerusalem he prays God to "steady his footsteps" (v 133). During the return trip he suffers again in "distress and anguish" (v 143), is attacked by "persecutors" (vv 150, 157). The last two stanzas (vv 161-176) express the peace of mind and the gratitude of the pilgrim safely back in his country.

For H. Duesberg, on the other hand, Ps 119 has no concrete *Sitz im Leben*. This "mirror of the faithful," he believes, is a product of professional psalmography (see also Mowinckel II, pp. 104-125 and §29a); it could be a repertoire of pious sentences, collected for the spiritual training of the young scribes. M.-F. Lacan's view is that Ps 119 teaches us the alphabet of prayer, not in definitions, but in a prayerful dialogue with God. In the course of the dialogue several themes recur: the need of divine instruction to understand the mysterious Word of God (vv 12, 19, 66, 68); need of guidance (vv 28, 36, 37, 39, 59, 67); need of light (18, 34, 73, 105, 125, 144, 169); the lessons of trial (vv 67-71); prayer for fidelity (vv 5, 10, 44) in the face of wrongdoers (23, 46, 50, 53, 118f, 136, 158) and in the community of the just (1, 2, 38, 63); joy and satisfaction in the observance of the Law (14, 24, 35, 54, 92, 111, 131, 140, 143, 163, 167). As a result of the dialogue the attributes of God are revealed to the worshipper: his kindness (vv 41, 64, 76, 124), his fidelity (89ff, 140), his life-giving justice (40, 137f, 142, 144), the permanence of his Word (v 160), his salvation (vv 41, 81, 174). During prayer God lets his face shine upon the faithful (v 135), who reaps liberty, joy, light, wisdom, docility, humility and life (vv 32, 45-47, 88, 130, 141, 154). Did the psalmist exaggerate when he wrote: "I have more understanding than all my teachers when your decrees are my meditation"? (v 99)

Psalm 127 (126)

The Need of God's Blessing: His Gift of Sons

It is generally admitted that this is a unified psalm consisting originally of two expanded proverbial sayings. The "title" attributes the psalm to Solomon, for various possible reasons: he built the temple, he wrote proverbs (cf. 1 K 4:32), he is called *y^edîdyâh*, "God's beloved" (2 S 12:25), and in his sleep God appeared to him (1 K 3:5). Verses 1-2 present, clothed in imagery, a general truth expressed more concisely elsewhere.

It is the Lord's blessing that brings wealth,
and no effort can substitute for it (Pr 10:22).

Work is not condemned, but a godless attitude to work is, for "without God's blessing all human endeavor is futile" (*CV*). Trust in God's loving Providence was also insisted upon by Jesus (Mt 6:25-34). According to Pr 31:23, the husband of the "ideal wife" is prominent at the city gates as he sits with the elders of the land. His influence will be the greater if he has a large family. Like arrows in the hand of a warrior, sons defend the father. Human justice will not easily be denied to a large family protected by a row of robust and devoted sons. This is more clearly asserted in Dahood's translation of verse 5b: "He shall not be humiliated but shall drive back his foes from the gate" (*Psalms III*). In Amarna letter 76:38-41, Rib-Addi writes to the Pharaoh: "Send a large number of archers so that they might drive out the enemies of the king from the midst of his country." The meaning "drive out" of Akkadian *dubburu* seems preserved in the *y^edabb^erû* of Ps 127:5. In TS 1953, pp. 85ff, Dahood had proposed to read in verse 2b, instead of "for he gives to his beloved in sleep" (*NAB*): "Thus he gives to his beloved rich nourishment (*dōšen*: Mishnic Hebrew)," expressing a thought mentioned elsewhere: "He has given food to those who fear him" (Ps 111:5). In *Psalms III*, however, he understands *kēn*, "thus," "indeed," as a divine title meaning "the Reliable" (see on *Ps 110) and translates the phrase: "But the Reliable gives prosperity to his beloved."

PSALM 128 (127)

The Happy Home of the Just Man

The blessings of family life are also celebrated in this psalm, which may owe its origin to a liturgical benediction. Man is taught to acknowledge God's splendid gifts in the domestic joys and riches. Elsewhere the just himself is compared to "a green olive tree in the house of God" (Ps

52:10; cf. Ps 92:14). In line with the general tendency of wisdom teaching "the psalm deliberately confines itself to a strictly limited field of devout conduct in everyday life and should be understood within these limits" (A. Weiser). The final blessing (vv 5-6) is, however, broader in scope, and suggests that the prosperity of the nation itself rests on the foundation of a sound family life (see on *Ps 134:3).

PSALM 133 (132)

The Benefits of Brotherly Concord

This also is a song of ascents (cf. §3c) and, as in Pss 127 and 128, the poet extols the values of brotherhood, which perhaps are understood here in the broader national context. The psalm probably reflects a period when these values were in peril. In oriental taste scented oil dripping down to the collar through a long flowing beard is a telling expression of blessing, here the charm, beauty and internal value of brotherhood. After the daytime heat the refreshing dew of the night (Dt 5:2; Ho 14:6) is a special blessing. Mount Zion covered with Hermon dew is an expressive although idyllic metaphor (see on *Ps 48:3). Divine blessing assures long life on earth (Dt 30:20) and the inseparable union with God, source of life (Ps 36:10) and heritage of the just (Ps 73:26).

The connection between oil and dew may plausibly be illustrated by a Ugaritic text which speaks of "the dew of heaven, the oil of earth" (= the rain; see *UT 'nt,* IV, 87) and by early biblical usage, like Gn 27:28, thus translated by Dahood: "And may God give you of heaven's dew and of earth's oil" (cp. "...and of the fertility of the earth" in *NAB*). Dahood finds it also meaningful for our psalm that in Is 26:19 the dew "symbolizes the resurrection and immortality." In this connection he cites D. N. Freedman's observation that by omitting *ḥayyîm,* "life," in v 3, and substituting *šlwm 'l yśr'l,* "peace upon Israel," the Qumranic sect (see *11QPs^a*) may have wished to get rid of this obvious reference to eternal life. He adds that perhaps for the same reason the Septuagint translators have read "because of his integrity" instead of "at his death" in Pr 14:32: "For his evil the wicked will be flung headlong, but at his death the just will find refuge."

These three psalms of blessing (127, 128, 133) Kirkpatrick would assign to the Restoration period, when Nehemiah was trying to rebuild the Jewish community on a sound religious and civic basis, especially in Jerusalem (cf. Ne 11:1f). He also notes that "the running down upon the collar of his robe" can refer to the beard of Aaron, instead of the oil. In that same verse 3 seems to be recalled the scene of the consecration of Aaron himself (Lv 8), since sacred oil was not used in the time of the Second Temple. As for "dew," writes Kirkpatrick, it is "a symbol for what is refreshing, quickening, invigorating; and the psalmist compares the influence of brotherly unity upon the nation to the effect of the dew upon vegetation."

Instead of *ṣiyyôn* (v 3) some authors (Power, Zorell, Pascual) would read *śî'ôn*, mentioned in Dt 4:48: "Mount Zion, which is Hermon." As Power puts it: "Just as the sacred ointment descends from the head to the beard...so the heavenly dew descends from the highest summit to the lower peaks of the same mountain range." Less *recherchée* is the explanation that the psalmist follows popular belief: in some way the amount of dew falling on the Zion hills depends on Mount Hermon.

PSALM 139 (138)

The All-knowing and Ever-present God

This poem could, like Ps 90 with which it shows affinities, be classified as a supplication. Mowinckel (I, p. 24) believes that these two psalms really spring from a concrete situation, that of need; the reflection on God's eternity and omniscience (cf. §10c) would constitute a secondary accompaniment of divine intervention in the situation. The introductory section of both psalms is a hymn celebrating God's attributes. The most important part of Ps 139 is, in Mowinckel's opinion (II, p. 75), the prayer for the help of God against the "men of blood" (vv 19-24), perhaps "men of idols" (v 19; see on *Pss 5:7; 26:9). Yet this section could also reflect a rite of self-purification of the covenant community (separation from evildoers; cf. Pss 26:4; 31:7). Mowinckel admits (II, p. 131f) that "the profound consideration of God's omniscience and omnipresence in Ps 139 actually is a new form of the motif of innocence." In that respect also it is considered to be a "protective psalm" (see on *Ps 71).

In verse 24 CV reads "see if my way is crooked" ('*āqōb*). E. Würthwein, however, is for keeping the consonantal MT and for understanding '*ṣb* as referring to "idols" (cf. Is 48:5). As for *derek*, "way," it could mean *Kultübung,* "cult-practice" (cf. Am 8:14; Jr 2:23; 10:2; 12:16). Verse 24 then would be part of the psalmist's repudiation of idols: "See [O Lord] if I have taken part in idol worship"! In other words, a sort of "oath of exculpation" would be involved here as elsewhere (cf. *Pss 7 and 26). It is the Omniscient God described in verses 1-18 who is asked to "probe" the psalmist and testify to his innocence. Dahood characterizes Ps 139 thus: "A psalm of innocence composed by a religious leader (cf. vs. 21) who was accused of idol worship. Creating an inclusion, the psalmist begins (vs. 1) and ends (vss. 23-24) the poem with an appeal to Yahweh to investigate personally, on the basis of his omniscience and universal presence, the charges of idolatry brought against him." He also believes that the psalm belongs "to the same literary ambience as Job. In fact, the dating of the psalm, wrongly dated in the post-Exilic period by many scholars, will depend to a considerable degree on the date of Job, now correctly being ascribed to the seventh century B.C. by Pope in his introduction to *Job.*" The connection with Job is most striking if one compares v 2 with Jb 16:21, thus translated by Dahood: "Can mere man argue with God, or mortal discern his thoughts?"

It has been noted (cf. *Ps 92) that the praise of divine knowledge can be related to a theme called *Gerichtsdoxologie,* whereby the judgments of God are declared just and infallible. Yet such varying motifs as found in Ps 139 seem cast in a didactic and sapiential mould (cf. Si 42:18ff; Ps 94:8-11). It can be conceded to Castellino (p. 731) that in this psalm, as in Pss 17, 37, 49, 73, wisdom language tends to take a new tone, that of religious meditation. In one of the El-Amarna letters (cf. §9d), a Babylonian named Tagi tells his (divinized) king: "Whether we go up to heaven or go down to the earth our head is in thy hand" (tr. Mercer, II, p. 677; letter 264), while the Hebrew psalmist confessed: "If I ascend to heaven, you are there! If I make Sheol my bed, there you are" (139:8). Cp. also Amos 9:2.

God knows everything (vv 1-6), he is present everywhere (7-12), he can do anything (12-16), his thoughts and designs defy human reason (vv 17f). If this is so, he can destroy the wicked (19-22) and provide guidance (23f). The divine attributes of omniscience, omnipresence and omnipotence the poet does not express in abstract philosophical terms but in terms of I-Thou relationship. The first verses especially, as Weiser points out, "express the astonishment of a man who discovers that in all his ways he is involved in relations which remain hidden from the natural

eye; that he no longer belongs entirely to himself or lives his life exclusively for his own sake, because it points everywhere to those invisible
bonds which unite him to the reality of God." Here, as elsewhere in the
Psalter, God occupies the prominent place even in the construction of the
sentences. The whole psalm is an authentic expression of true faith in
God. "The consciousness of the intimate personal relation between God
and man which is characteristic of the whole Psalter reaches its climax
in Ps 139," writes Kirkpatrick. The ungodly the psalmist hates (vv 21f)
because they are God's as well as his own enemies. He does not understand that divine forbearance extends even to the wicked (Mt 5:45). It
is true that in biblical wisdom itself some problems concerning retribution
remained unsolved for a long time (cf. §14d+29a). Not all the sacred
authors saw a clear distinction between evil and evildoers (on the idea of
a "divine book," verse 16, see above §14d).

Having translated in v 15b, "when I was fashioned in the depths of
the earth," NAB explains the statement as "figurative language for the
womb." This is hardly possible if Dahood's reading is accepted: "I was
kneaded in the depths of the nether world." He thinks, against contrary
views expressed, that "an impressive number of texts take for granted that
men originated and pre-existed in the nether world; cf. Gn 2:7; 3:19;
Ps 90:3; Ec 3:20; 5:15; 12:7; Si 40:1; Jb 1:21. "But all these texts speak
of the dust or of mother earth to which all men appear to return in their
body."

With v 11, R. Lapointe believes, the proof of God's omnipresence
reached a climax: not even death can separate the psalmist from Yahweh:
"I told myself: 'Darkness certainly will crush me and Night will ensnare
me'!" The following verse shows that this will not be the case (see CBQ
1971, 397-402). Also in Gn 3:15 and Jb 9:17 the context suggests for the
root šûp the meaning "to crush." But is should be admitted that in the
psalm "Surely the darkness shall hide me" (NAB; cf. RSV) goes better
with the context, in which the psalmist imagines various possible ways
to escape God's omnipresence, and finds none. Finally we can mention
that H. Hommel, who studied the psalm religionsgeschichtlich half a
century ago, compared it with Vedic Atharvaveda IV, 16, as well as Greek
and non-biblical Semitic parallels (ZAW 1929, 110-24).

§30. THE HISTORICAL PSALMS

(a) General character

These psalms are hymnic narratives describing the significant events of *Heilsgeschichte* (saving history). They celebrate the *magnalia Dei*, mainly those traditionally preserved in what some call the "historical *credo*" (cf. Dt 6 and 26; see §13c). "It was above all in worship that Israel extolled Jahweh's acts in history. The hymns which take history as their subject obviously depend on a picture of the saving history which already possessed canonical validity at a very early time, and whose original form lies before us in the *Credo* of Dt 26:5ff or Jos 24:2ff. The simplest, and probably also the oldest, form of the hymn was the almost unconnected enumeration of the bare facts of creation and of the saving history which still lie before us as paradigms in Ps 136 (cf. Pss 77, 105, 114, 135). But in the course of an epic widening out of those facts, the poems did not confine themselves solely to enumerating and glorifying the acts of Jahweh, they also made Israel and her attitude, yes, and her failure as well, the object of their meditation (cf. Ps 106). In the process the hymn receives a somber tone, and in proportion as interest in the sin of Israel increased in them, their mood changed greatly, and they become somber confessions of Israel's failure and of Jahweh's judgment (Ps 78)" (G. von Rad, Old Testament Theology, I, p. 357).

In view of the importance of the historical tradition in Israel it is somewhat surprising that the Psalter does not contain a greater number of explicit references to the outstanding events of the Pentateuch. According to F. N. Jasper ("Early Israelite...," p. 50f), only Pss 44, 47, 60, 68, 77, 78, 80, 81, 99, 105, 106, 108, 114, 135, 136 "afford a recognizable link with the traditions of Israel's origins as a people. It is true that with a knowledge of the Pentateuch we can construct a coherent narrative from these Psalms. The people of Israel, the offspring of Abraham and Jacob (105:6), had gone down to Egypt by Joseph's invitation (105:16ff). God delivered them from oppression (77:15; 81:6) in Egypt (78:12; 81:10; 114:1; 136:11f) by Moses and Aaron (77:20; 99:6f, 105:26) after inflicting plagues upon their masters (78:44ff; 105:27ff; 135:8f; 136:10). He made a way for them through the Sea of Reeds in which the pursuers were drowned (77:16ff; 78:13, 53; 106:9ff; 114:3f; 136:13f). He guided and sustained them in the wilderness in spite of their rebellions (68:7f; 78:14ff, 52; 81:7; 105:39ff; 106:6f, 19ff, 28ff; 136:16). He gave them the land of Canaan as a heritage (44:2; 47:4; 60:7f; 78:54f; 80:8ff; 105:44; 135:10ff; 136:17ff), as he had promised the ancestors (105:9ff). But only in Pss 78, 105, 106, 135, and 136 is there an attempt to give a chronological record of the events. Jasper adds to his outline: "Apart from this, there are only occasional implicit references, which make no real historical contribution" (e.g., Pss 74:2, 12f; 91:6). Of the 15 "historical psalms" listed above he singles out five as "probably fairly late" in their present form: Pss 78, 105, 106, 135, 136: "earlier versions of them may have been used in pre-exilic times...but they now stand as the product of early Judaism," when the "separatist policy of Nehemiah and Ezra required that the traditions shared with the Samaritans" be not emphasized. The other ten psalms, however, belong to "the early, spontaneous group" which being already part of the established liturgy remained so, although the disappearance of the monarchy could have called for modifications (p. 59; on "The Psalms and History," cf. also S. du Toit).

A. Gelin has given striking expression to the biblical meaning of history. "The basic faith in Israel is that history is sustained by God, that it is an epiphany of God. God gives history its meaning because He is carrying out a design in it: God speaks through events. ... The Bible calls the setbacks and disappointments of history God's 'angers' (see §11h)." Among the "signs" of God (see §12f) on earth figure the *mirabilia Dei* visible in some privileged events: "Renew your *signs,* once more begin to work your *wonders*" (Si 36:5). "These wonders are the historical acts which launched the history of Israel: the exodus from Egypt, the desert of the Covenant, the entrance into the Promised Land. ... But this history is not a lifeless fossil. History lives again in the present of worship, history is made eternal, history is a mystery. ... The essential thing was to make the people understand that history is 'reactualized,' that it is not something past and gone, and that it is the liturgical 'today' which allows us to grasp history (cf. Ps 95:6-11). ... In worship we find history as a sign of God" (*The Psalms are our Prayers,* p. 28f; on the "actualizing" of history in the psalms, see also C. Westermann, "Vergegenwärtigung...").

S. Mowinckel calls Pss 78 and 105 "didactic hymns" (II, p. 112). Writing on "Psalms and Wisdom," he notes that "a didactic hymn may develop into a downright 'hymnal legend,' a synopsis of the holy history in the style of a hymn, as is the case with Pss 78 and 105. ... But history may also provide the material for a confession of sins and a prayer for restoration on the part of the congregation, and thus result in a *historical penitential psalm,* like Ps 106"(p. 214). Some authors would in fact list Ps 106 with the "historical psalms," while Pss 111, 114, 135, 136 are also considered by others for the same category. There are, however, sound objective reasons for limiting the group to two psalms.

(b) The historical psalms are Pss 78 and 105.

PSALM 78

God's Goodness despite Israel's Ingratitude

Other psalms contain some of the historical material offered here (cf. 105, 106, 114, 136). Yet Ps 78 is more interested in the interpretation of history than in its recital. The "mysteries (*ḥîdôt*, riddles) from of old" (v 2), the queer happenings of the past, follow the pattern "rebellion-punishment." The tribes of the North, Joseph/Ephraim, predecessors of the Samaritans, bear most of the blame. Verse 9 which seems to reflect a late antisamaritan trend did not necessarily belong to the primitive psalm. The favor of the Lord passed to the tribe of Judah and to David, who would preserve and perpetuate the sacred traditions. A. Weiser suggests that Ps 78, described as a *tôrâh* or *māshāl* (vv 1-2), could have been recited by a priest in connection with the covenant festival (cf. §13c). Its main thought-pattern reflects that of Deuteronomy, as expressed for example in ch 32:

The Rock—how faultless are his deeds,
how right all his ways!
A faithful God, without deceit,
how just and upright he is!
Yet basely has he been treated by his degenerate children,
a perverse and crooked race! (vv 4-5)

Think back on the days of old,
reflect on the years of age upon age.
Ask your father and he will inform you,
ask your elders and they will tell you. . . (v 7)

Surely, the Lord shall do justice for his people;
on his servants he shall have pity.
When he sees their strength failing,
and their protected and unprotected alike disappearing (v 36).

There is no compelling ground, however, for supposing that Ps 78 is later than the late seventh century Deuteronomy, since any presumed de-

pendence can be accounted for by a common older deuteronomic tradition. The psalm is often described as pre-exilic because it does not even
allude to the fall of Jerusalem. Ephraim's retreat "in the day of battle" (v
9) probably alludes to Saul's defeat at Gilboa and to the transfer of kingship from the tribes of Rachel to that of Judah. No clear mention is made
of the downfall of the Northern Kingdom. No real conclusion, in fact,
can be drawn, on the psalm's date, from the Davidic *terminus ad quem*
of the historical schema, since it probably reflects theological interests.
Dahood brings as evidence for the early date of the psalm its repeated
use of the *yqtl* (imperfect or future tense) form to express past time. But
this particularity, distinctive of Hebrew poetry (cf. P. Joüon, *Grammaire
de l'hébreu biblique* 303), as it is of Ugaritic poetry, can point to an
archaizing tendency, not necessary to an early date (see §9d, towards
end). The scholars who assign the psalm to a late period read in it the
Chronicler's Davidic ideology. C. Westermann has noted that "Deuteronomy 32 is the clearest example of how the historical Psalms pass over
into eschatological Psalms" (*The Praise...*, p. 141). Ps 78 is also a "descriptive psalm of praise" (cf. §22), he adds, "but the introduction here
is not an imperative call to praise; its place has been taken by an introduction in the style of wisdom literature."

The glorious deeds of the Lord must be proclaimed and a lesson
drawn from history, states the psalmist (vv 1-8): the "sons of Ephraim"
have been disloyal (9-11), like their forefathers, for whom God had
worked wonders at the exodus (12-16) and in the wilderness (17-31).
Their repeated rebellious acts were answered by new divine deeds intended to punish or to relieve the people (32-55), till finally God rejected the guilty tribes and turned to Judah, Mount Zion and the house
of David (65-72). From the wilderness people's fate follows a lesson:
God often grants extravagant requests but he will let their beneficiaries
perish in the midst of the satisfaction of their inordinate desires, when his
kindness does not lead to repentance but is followed by even greater avid-
ity. Thus are the grace and the judgment of God related to each other
(Weiser). On Ps 78 see also R. P. Carroll, "Ps 78: Vestiges of a Tribal
Polemic," *VT* 21 (1971) 133-50.

PSALM 105 (104)

God's Fidelity to His Promise

Like Ps 78, Ps 105 is a didactic hymn, a kind of synopsis of sacred
history in the style of a hymn. Mowinckel (II, p. 112) speaks in this re-

gard of "hymnal legends." They constitute, he explains, "a sort of theodicy," in which God's judgment is vindicated. In Ps 105, however, no mention is made of God's disfavor toward Israel on account of its sins. At a certain date at least the psalm was used in the liturgy, as it appears from the opening verses (1-6), and from the fact that in 1 Ch 16:8-22 the first 15 verses of the psalm are quoted (see on *Ps 96) as a festal hymn in connection with the transfer of the sacred ark to Mount Zion. The origin of Ps 105, C. Westermann believes (*The Praise...*, p. 140), can be explained thus: the "historical report" has been separated from the total unit of the "descriptive Psalm of praise" (cf. §22) and has become an independent psalm.

The successive periods of early Israelite history are represented in this *Heilsgeschichte* account (cf. *Ps 66): the patriarchs (vv 8-15), the story of Joseph (16-23), the call of Moses (24-27), the (seven) plagues in Egypt (28-36), the exodus and wandering in the desert (37-43), and finally the entry in Canaan (44-45; cf. 9-11). The opening words of the psalm are similar to those with which begin Pss 106, 107, 118, 136. They call upon the members of the covenant community to sing hymns of praise and thanksgiving to God. The main theological theme of the psalm is that God keeps his promises and fulfills his salvific plans in spite of or in the course of the apparently adverse or purposeless human interference or activities. On "The Plagues Tradition in Ps 105," see S. Margulis in *Bib* 50 (1969) 491-96.

Valuable reflections on the thought association of three psalms are offered by A. F. Kirkpatrick. "The two historical Psalms which stand at the end of Book IV are closely related. Ps 105 is a psalm of thanksgiving, recapitulating the marvelous works by which Jehovah demonstrated His faithfulness to the covenant which He made with Abraham. Ps 106 is a Psalm of penitence, reciting the history of Israel's faithlessness and disobedience. They present, so to speak, the obverse and reverse of Israel's history; the common prophetic theme of Jehovah's loving kindness and Israel's ingratitude. They have much in common with Ps 78, with which their author was evidently familiar; but that Psalm is distinguished by its didactic and monitory character, and it combines the two strands of thought which are here separated" (Introd. to Ps 105). Such a recital of the proofs of Jehovah's faithfulness as is contained in Ps 105, Kirkpatrick adds, was very suitable as an encouragement to the community of the Restoration.... The repeated call to "give thanks to Jehovah...to praise Yah" (cf. *Ps 11) corresponds exactly to the term in which the function of the Levites is described in the books of Ezra, Nehemiah, and Chronicles (Ezr 3:11; Ne 12:24; 1 Ch 16:4; see also *Ps 106).

G. von Rad reads in verse 15, "Touch not my anointed ones, and to my prophets do no harm," "the same reinterpretation in the collective sense" as the one apparent in Deutero-Isaiah, who did not "interpret Yahweh's promise concerning the throne of David and the anointed one of Israel in the traditional way, for he understands them to have been made not to David but to the whole nation" (*Theology*... II, p.240).

§31. THE "PROPHETIC" EXHORTATIONS

(a) *General character*

Of the psalmists it is said that they prophesy (1 Ch 25:1; 2 Ch 20:14). Some of them certainly utilized the prophetic writings, mainly Isaiah, whose style they adapted for a didactic purpose (cf. *BJ*, p. 27). The psalms of the present category, "prophetic exhortations," have in common a tonality and some "prophetic" literary elements, as the oracle and the exhortative speech, which include promises and threats.

"In the earliest period in Israel the priest was not originally in the first instance sacrificer but, as with the old Arabs, custodian of the sanctuary, oracle priest, 'seer' and holder of the effectual future-creating and future-interpreting word of power, the blessing and the curse" (Mowinckel, II, p. 53). At a certain period at least the priest was a "giver of oracles" (cf. §8e). To admit the prophetic role of the priest is to question the supposed fundamental rivality between prophecy and priesthood (cf. *Exp.T.* 1950, pp. 3-9; *ZAW* 1951, pp. 157-182; *TLZ* 1956, p. 339ff). Biblical evidence does suggest the existence in ancient Israel of "cult oracles" and "cult prophets" (cf. §8e). F. N. Jasper notes that "the reformation under Hezekiah as recorded by the Chronicler mentions Asaph, 'the seer'" (2 Ch 29:30). This almost certainly means that the Asaphite guild was originally a group of cultic prophets in Jerusalem who were later relegated to the position of Temple singers. Even if some of the Asaphite Psalms as they now stand are post-exilic, their original form might well reflect the part taken by the cultic prophets in Israel's worship during the monarchy" ("Early...," p. 54; cf. §3b). Ps 81, an Asaphite oracular psalm, "seems to be linked with a regular cultic practice rather than a specific event" (*ibid.*) and its Deuteronomic tone could point to a Northern background.

The association of divine revelation with the offering of sacrifices appears in the story about Solomon's dream at Gibeon (1 K 3:4ff). The deity's answer to a request could be obtained either by casting lots with the "Urim and Thummim" (cf. 1 S 14:41f) or by means of "looking for special signs in the sacrificial animal, and by interpreting them" (Mowinckel, II, p. 53). At a certain period at least the priest was a "giver of Israel's history prophetic inspiration became in a way institutionalized, that is, attached to a function rather than dependent on ecstatic experience or sudden revelations: "With the organized temple prophets, inspiration is rather what we should call an official, occupational inspiration, a permanent charismatic equipment belonging to the office itself. . . . Even at the time of Jesus, Judaism ascribed to the high priest an official prophetic inspiration" (ib. p. 57; cf. Jn 11:51).

In preceding paragraphs (cf. §5c, 13a) another problem has been discussed: have psalms been composed in the style of prophetic preaching or have the prophets taken over the psalmic way of expression? In any case, some psalms more than others deserve to be called "prophetic exhortations," as will be seen in the special introductions that follow. These exhortations were meant to teach the ways of God and the appropriate response expected of man; in that sense they can be classified as "didactic psalms."

(b) The "prophetic" exhortations are: Pss 14, 50, 52, 53, 75, 81, 95.

PSALM 14 (13)

A Lament over Widespread Corruption

This recension of the psalm seems to transmit more faithfully the original text than the other recension, Ps 53. Universal impiety (vv 2-3) is a theme known to the prophets:

Roam the streets of Jerusalem,
look about and observe,
Search through her public places,
to find even one
Who lives uprightly
and seeks to be faithful
and I will pardon her! (Jr 5:1; cf. 8:6; Is 64:6)

To prove by the Scriptures that Jews and Greeks alike are all under sin, St. Paul (Rm 3:10-18) combines various sources into one quotation (Pss 5:10; 140:4; 10:7; Pr 1:16; Is 59:7f; Ps 36:2). The Pauline text has been inserted in Ps 14 (after v 3) by the Vulgate and some Greek manuscripts. Micah (3:3) voiced complaints against the leaders of his time: "They eat the flesh of my people," and Habakkuk (1:13) writes: "The wicked man devours one more just than himself." The expression "devour my people" (cf. v 4) is also used about external enemies (cf. Is 9:11; Jr 10:25; see also below). Practical atheism (cf. §10a), more than metaphysical disbelief, is meant in the psalm (v 1), quite as in Jr 5:12: "They denied the Lord saying, Not he—No evil shall befall us, neither sword nor famine shall we see." It is also against the leading class of Israel that a prophetic threat is pronounced by the psalmist (vv 5-6), for these influential people know their duty, as Jeremiah would point out (5:5-6).

The meaning of the Hebrew phrase *beśûb yhwh śebût 'ammô* (v 7) has been discussed in connection with *Ps 85. It is understood by Mowinckel (I, p. 147) as a prayer of later times asking for the restoration of Israel's destiny, and Ps 14 would be, like Ps 85, a national supplication. More precisely, it is asserted, the phrase refers to a new "laying down of fate" to take place at God's enthronement on the New Year festival (cf. §13a). What the psalmist has in mind, Weiser believes, is probably the act of divine judgment firmly established in the ritual of the covenant cult at Jerusalem.

"Though commonly classified as a lament," writes Dahood, "Ps 14 has many points of contact with Wisdom Literature and could, with equal validity, be put in the category of Wisdom psalms." His translation of verses 4-5 being notably different from the CV is given here, with biblical references to support the changes: "Don't they know all the evildoers, that they who devour his people, devour the grain of Yahweh (Nb 14:9) they did not harvest (*Ps 147:9; Pr 27:16). See how (Ps 66:6) they formed a cabal (Pss 64:2; 91:5), but God is in the assembly of the just." That its enemies devour (the people of) Israel (like bread) is a prophetic expression, notes *BJ*: cf. Is 9:11; Mi 3:3; Jer 10:25; Hab 30:16; Hab 1:13 (cf. Pss 27:2; 79:7; Pr 30:14). Other commentators divide differently the *MT* and understand: "They eat the bread of God, but do not invoke his name."

The mention of the "assembly of the upright" in Ps 92:2 and of "the council of the upright" in Ps 111:1 would suggest that these two psalms have the same author as Ps 14. While the rest of Ps 14 is concerned with individuals, writes Eerdmans, the last verse refers to the people, to Israel. "Similar wishes for the restoration of the Jewish state occur at the end of other psalms. They are manifestly additions from a later period, when the psalms were recited in synagogical services" (*OTS* I, p. 260).

PSALM 50 (49)

The Acceptable Sacrifice

It can well be that the setting of this instructive admonition by Yhwh was the festival of the renewal of the covenant (cf. Kraus, Beaucamp). According to E. Osty the psalm fits well in the category which R. G. Castellino calls *"Liturgia della fedeltà yahwistica"* (Pss 78, 81, 95, 105, 106). It is cast, writes Mowinckel (II, p. 70), in the mould of prophetic speech, with a hymnal description of the glory of the theophany for an introduction (vv 1-6). Its central theme is the powerful experience of man's encounter with God and the conclusion to be drawn therefrom (A. Weiser). Also in line with the "decalogical tradition" is the insistence on the commandments of the covenant. The "cult prophet" (cf. §8e and *Ps 95) blames the community mainly for tolerating in its midst three sins: theft, adultery and slander (or sorcery). This admonition (vv 16-21) is addressed to the "wicked" in the present text. It is however, possible that the phrase, "But to the wicked man God says," was added later to shelter the faithful from the condemnation. For a similar reason, perhaps, verse 21c would have been shifted from verse 7, which reads (cf. *JB*):

Listen, my people, I am speaking;
Israel, I am giving evidence against you!
I charge, I indict you to your face,
I, God, your God.

M. Dahood describes Ps 50 as "a prophetic liturgy of divine judgment. In the tradition of the prophets, the psalmist stresses the futility of sacrifice divorced from true morality." In verse 14 it is possible to understand, "offer God a sacrifice of thanksgiving" (Pss 50:23; 107:22; 116:17, and R. Pautrel, p. 239). Sacrificial cult is not condemned, not even in Ps 51:18f, but it is sometimes recalled, as Ibn Ezra puts it, that sacrifices are not useful to God but to man (Ps 50:9-13). The strong words of the pre-exilic prophets (cf. Is 1:11-17; Jr 6:20; 7:21f; Ho 6:6; Am 5:21-27; Mi 6:6ff) have been related to a literary form called "dialectical negation": an absolute negation that can be interpreted relatively (see on *Ps 51:18). The offence reproved is disrespect towards God, shown by considering the sacrificial cult as influencing God, as making Him dependent on man. A sacrifice of thanksgiving, on the other hand, expresses man's dependence on God. The purpose of the psalm is to confront the worshipper with God as he is, to destroy the other image of God, that produced by wishful thinking (on "sacrificium laudis," see also G. Bornkamm).

The first line of verse 1 is translated by Dahood: "The God of gods is Yahweh." The expression 'ēl elōhîm recurs in Pss 62:2 and 77:2 (bis). It seems to be used as a superlative, like "the king of kings." In verse 4, Dahood explains, "heaven and earth are summoned by God to function as witnesses in his controversy with Israel. G. E. Wright, *The Old Testament against its Environment*, p. 36, has suggested that heaven and earth, invoked in the liturgy genus known as 'lawsuit,' can best be interpreted in the light of the divine assembly, the members of which constitute the host of heaven and earth." From some Ugaritic texts it can in fact be inferred that for the Canaanites Earth and Heaven were deities who formed part of the divine assembly. The term 'elôah, a poetic designation of God, is used in verse 22. It occurs normally in ancient poems (Dt 32:15, 17; Ps 18:32) and as an archaism in other texts, mainly in Job (41 times) but aso in Pss 114:7; 139:19; Pr 30:5; Is 44:8; Hab 3:3, Ne 9:17, Dn 11:38.

PSALM 52 (51)

The Deceitful Tongue

The historical circumstance (1 S 21:1-8; 22:6-19) proposed for this psalm by the "title" cannot be maintained. Doeg cannot be branded as a liar, since he told Saul the objective truth. Furthermore the psalm alludes to the temple (v 10), inexistent in Saul's time. A possible parallel would be Isaiah's threat against "Sobna, master of the palace" (Is 22:15-19), elsewhere called the "scribe" (36:3; 2 K 18:18). It is, however, doubtful that the "champion of infamy" refers to a specific character (see below). As in Ps 28, the original setting of Ps 52 could be the ritual expulsion of the evildoers by means of a curse pronounced by the covenant community. Yet the psalm quite clearly contains a prophetic judgment which exposes the crimes of the wicked and predicts their approaching doom (cf. Is 14 and 22). Deceit and lying are also the sins severely denounced by Jeremiah:

They ready their tongues like a drawn bow;
with lying, and not with truth,
they hold forth in the land...

Each one deceives the other
no one speaks the truth.
They have accustomed their tongues to lying,
and are perverse, and cannot repent (9:2, 4).

The translation of verse 3, "Why do you glory in evil, you champion of infamy?" follows the Latin and Greek versions. The Hebrew text is rendered in various ways:

Why do you boast of your malice, O mighty man?
The grace of God endures forever (A. Weiser).

Why do you boast, O mighty man,
of mischief done against the godly?
All the day you are plotting destruction (RSV).

Why do you boast of wickedness, O champion?
O devoted of El, why at all times
do you harbor pernicious thoughts? (Dahood).

In this last translation "O devoted of El" (*ḥᵃsîd 'el*) is sarcastic. Pretending to be one dedicated to El, the man is really a liar and scoundrel.

Strength, vitality and durability characterize the just who worship in the temple and trust in God. These attributes are symbolized by solidly rooted and healthy trees (Pss 1:3; 52:10; 92:14).

Why was the Doeg episode given as heading to the psalm? A "champion" is mentioned in verse 3. The same Hebrew word, *gibbôr*, is used for members of Saul's personal guard (1 S 14:52), to which Doeg in a way belonged (1 S 21:7). So when David, the presumed author of the psalm, complains of a *gibbôr*, it must have been Doeg! (cf. Mowinckel, II, p. 101) A powerful curse is pronounced against this *gibbôr*. According to A. M. Scharf's reading and translation of verse 7 it would cover three generations: "May God demolish you forever: make you fatherless (*yᵉhattēk*), pluck you from your tent and render you childless (*šērēš*) in the land of the living" (on "the land of the living," cf. *Ps 142).

PSALM 53 (52)

Lament over Widespread Corruption

Ps 53 differs from Ps 14 mainly in that it substitutes the divine name *'elōhîm* for the sacred tetragram. Some scholars conclude that Ps 53 is an Elohistic edition of an older Yahwistic song. H. Schmidt assigns the substitution to the Persian period and believes it anticipates the later Jewish tendency of not pronouncing the name of Yahweh. Eerdmans, however, has doubts about the existence of a collection of Elohim-psalms and notes that Ecclesiastes excepted the name "Yahweh" found in all proto-canonical books, even in the latest. More significant, he says, in verse 6, which would result from a deliberate alteration: He proposes the following translation:

> Ps 14:5f There they are in great fear,
> for Elohim acts righteously in the generation.
> The counsel of the poor was:
> Ye will put to shame, because Jahu was his refuge.
> Ps 53:5f There they are in great fear.
> It is no fear if Elohim scattereth the bones of him,
> that encampeth within thee;
> thou putteth to shame if Elohim rejecteth them.

"To have his bones scattered" means to be tired to death, as in Ps 141:7: "Our bones are scattered at the mouth of Sheol, like one, who has been digging and cleaving the soil." This verse reflects the oriental dislike of strenuous toil. In Ps 53:6 "he that encampeth within thee" is *spiritus malignus* (Lk 8:2): "Fever and illness were supposed to be caused by evil spirits which had penetrated into the body. Numerous amulets were worn to keep them off, and at a sick-bed sacred texts were recited to expel them." Verse 6 then "asserts that if Elohim has exhausted that evil power (has scattered his bones) there will be no fear. Then the sick man will be cured." Considering [all] these facts, Eerdmans concludes, we find no reason to attach importance to the use of the term "Elohim" in Ps 53. But Ps 53:1-6 reflects an adaptation of Ps 14:1-6 for the purpose of medical incantation. "To these psalms a final verse was added when they were recited for the sake of a restoration of the people, after Israel and Judah had been deported by the kings of Assyria in the last part of the eighth century B.C." (*OTS*, I, pp. 258-267). In Dahood's view, God's look from heaven (v 3) and salvation from Zion (v 7) may not refer to two different situations, since Zion may denote in some texts God's heavenly abode (cf. Ps 20:3; Heb 12:22), as "the Lofty Mountain" (Ps 61:3). See also Ps 18:47 and 43:3. A good parallel to v 5 is found in Jr 2:3, where Israel is called the first fruit of God's harvest, which may not be devoured with impunity. On Pss 14 and 53 see also R. Weiss in *Textus* 6 (Jerusalem 1968) 127-31.

Psalm 75 (74)

God the Just Judge of the Wicked

A prophetic judgment is also the central feature of this pattern, in which the oracle is set in a hymnal invocation and thanksgiving. The oracle, Mowinckel points out (II, p. 64), announces the coming of Yahweh to judge the pagan world and its unrighteous gods, under whose oppression Israel is now sighing and suffering. The judgment will come as an answer to the cult community's prayer for the reestablishment of Israel (cf. §14c). In these respects Ps 75 can be likened to Ps 82 and also to Pss 46, 48, 76, (cf. M., I, p. 151). More likely perhaps, what is announced is the proximity of a judgment against all the presumptuous evildoers (v 9) who dare oppose divine order and rule in this world. The judgment will surely come and at God's appointed time, as it becomes divine sovereignty. The "cup" (v 9) as symbolizing God's judgment is a metaphor frequently used by the prophets (cf. Is 51:17; Jr 25:15). In Ps 11:16, as in Ps 75:9, it is served to the wicked (cf. Ps 60:5). Hannah's song of praise speaks of God's free judgment in much the same way as Ps 75:

The bows of the mighty are broken,
but the feeble gird in strength...
The Lord kills and brings to life;

he brings down to Sheol and raises up.
The Lord makes poor and makes rich;
he brings low, he also exalts (1 S 2:1-7).

The psalm could be post-exilic since it seems to reflect Zc 2:1-14 and
Hannah's canticle, inserted later in the historical account (cf. *RB* 1958,
p 322).

In the last verses the psalmist "exults" over God's judgment revealed
by the oracle and considers himself instrumental in its proclamation or
execution. But Dahood finds no "exult forever" in verse 10, which constitutes for him a good example of ancient faulty reading. "An imperfect
knowledge," he writes, "of archaic divine appellatives will explain the repeated confusion between '*ēl*, '*ēlî*, 'the Most High,' and the prepositions
'*al and* '*ālay*, respectively: cf. Pss 7:9, 11; 16:6; 57:3; 68:30, 35; 106:7.
From this imperfect knowledge stems the erroneous division of consonants in Ps 75:10, when *MT* reads grammatically incongruent '*aggîd
l*e*ôlām* for '*a*gaddēl* '*ôlām,* 'I shall extol the Eternal,' parallel to 'I shall
sing to the God of Jacob.' In other words, the real parallelism intended
by the psalmist is between the God of Abraham, who in Gn 21:33 is
called '*el* '*ôlām,* 'El the Eternal,' and the God of Jacob (cf. *Ps 24:6).
The Masoretes missèd the historical allusion. The LXX experienced
difficulty with the consonantal division and read '*āgîl,* 'I shall rejoice';
many modern versions have opted, ill-advisedly in my judgment, for the
LXX emendation" (*Psalms* I, p. XXIII).

This brief psalm, Dahood notes, "contains twelve divine names—
hence more titles and names than the number of verses—five of which
have cropped up by applying the principles of Northwest Semitic grammar and lexicography" (v 1, p. 210). Among them figure "O Near One"
and "The Ancient Mountain." If such divine appellatives are accepted,
their list, I presume, could be extended indefinitely.

PSALM 81 (80)

Festive Song with an Admonition to Fidelity

The trumpet blast (cf. v 4) marked the beginning of the New Year
according to Lv 23:24 and Nb 29:1. The festival of Harvest and New
Year, celebrated in autumn (beginning of Tishri=October) became,

writes Mowinckel (I, p. 157), the festival of the renewal of the historical covenant (cf. §13a). Ps 81 would reflect the central theme of the festival: God's epiphany in the cult accompanies the renewal of the covenant and reaffirms the covenant's foundation, the keeping of the commandments (v 9). Verse 11 carries the ancient "formula of epiphany": "I, the Lord, am your God who led you forth from the land of Egypt." In the midst of a joyous feast a prophet would come forth to proclaim the requirements of "God present," using the covenant formula: 'ānōki yhwh 'elōhêkā, "I, the Lord, am your God" (v 11; cf. Dt 5:6, 9).

Pss 81 and 95 reflect, like Ps 50, the "decalogical tradition," but what they emphasize is the fundamental commandment, to worship Yahweh only. The "Meriba tradition," attested in the psalm (v 8; cf. 95:8), belongs to the Yahwist source and is seemingly pre-prophetic. This conclusion is also supported by the North Israelite basis of Ps 81, suggested by the use of "Jacob" and "Joseph" to designate the people. Mowinckel believes that the "prophetic element" in these psalms (50, 81, 95) belongs rather to the presuppositions of the "prophetic judgment" than to its consequences (II, p. 72). Yet the original compositions have been most likely "re-modeled" later in Jerusalem, in the Deuteronomic tradition (as regards Ps 81).

As in the so-called Deuteronomic writings of the Old Testament (Deuteronomy, Joshua, Judges, Samuel, Kings), Ps 81, writes H. Ringgren, "stresses the interaction of the people's religious attitude and their destiny: sin calls for punishment; repentance is the way to restoration. The essential point is that history is, so to speak, God's workshop. The history of Israel is a series of divine acts which began with the deliverance from Egypt, when God's victorious power was supremely manifested" (*The Faith of the Psalmists*, p. 99).

Instead of the usual "I tested you at the waters of Meribah" (v 8) Dahood proposes to translate "I was provoked by you near Meribah's waters," claiming that 'bḥnk should be vocalized as niphal 'ebbaḥeneka, "I was provoked," followed by the dative suffix expressing the agent. I do not wish to discuss here "the other examples of the dative suffix of agency" and the intrinsic merits of this grammatical category, but it is true that the majority of related texts do in fact speak of God being put to the test (cf. Ps 78:18, 95:9, 106:32; cf. Ex 17:7; Dt 6:16; 1 Cor 10: 9). Other texts, however, speak of God tempting Israel: Ex 15: 26 (see note in *JB*); 16:4; Dt 8:2; 13:3, but not explicitly about Meribah (except Dt 33:8).

PSALM 95 (94)

A Call to Praise and Obedience

This psalm opens the daily Divine Office of the Church. It consists of two parts: a hymn of praise (vv 1-7c) and a divine oracle (7d-11). Their setting was a liturgy which introduced the congregation into God's presence. The bowing down, or *proskynesis* (v 6) followed the acclamation of the King (v 3). Then an oracle, proclaimed by an authorized interpreter of the covenant, reminded the worshippers of their duties, mainly fidelity to the covenant. The prophetic element appears mainly in the second part, comminatory in tone (vv 7d-11). Was it a "cult prophet," as some authors suggest, who intervened in the liturgical festivals reflected by Pss 50 and 95? H.-J. Kraus prefers to speak of a special "covenant mediator" (p. 374). This procession hymn (comp. Pss 24, 68, 132) ends, BJ notes, with a divine exhortation to fidelity (cf. Pss 60 and 81), recited perhaps on the feast of the tabernacles (Dt 31:10f).

"Every year perhaps," writes A. Gelin, "Israel celebrates a feast of the covenant; or, more simply, every important feast has this significance: to relive, to actualize the event of Sinai, as in Christianity we reactualize Christmas. In this way the mysteries of the Old Testament are eternalized. In these feasts there is the grace of the recall, the grace of a new beginning. For the temptation of the people is to settle down in their possession, in their victories, in their institutions" (*The Psalms are our Prayers*, p. 41). Ps 95 would belong to one of these revivals, in which the believers experience anew the great events of the past. If verses 8-10 depend on the "Priestly" account of Nb 20:1-13 the psalm is post-exilic. But it must be reckoned with the older traditions reflected in Ex 17:1-7.

Mowinckel sees in the first part of Ps 95 an "enthronement hymn": "The king, Yahweh, creator of the world and of Israel, has come to take his seat on his throne and receive the homage of his people; in the second part of the psalm it is as a king renewing the covenant—through the mouth of the cultic prophet—that he recalls the first making of the covenant and the faithlesness of the people at Meribah and Massah, and warns against breaking the commandments of the covenant" (I, p. 156f). Leaving aside the "enthronement ideal" one views the setting of the psalm as an encounter between God and his people, in which "the ancient tradition of *Heilsgeschichte* regarding creation, election and the making of the covenant at Sinai is here renewed as a present sacral event"

(A. Weiser; cf. the "today" in v 7, Deuteronomic expression, as in Dt 4:4; 5:3). To the divine power and the divine grace revealed and released in the liturgical festival must correspond on the part of the faithful the decision, to be made "today," in regard to the observance of the commandments. In verse 7b the literal translation of *ṣō'n yādô*, "the sheep of his hand" (*RSV, BJ* and Latin Psalter) should perhaps be kept (cf. Ps 78:72): the expression makes a good parallel with "his voice" (7a), and evokes the "hands" of creation (v 5), as well as the tradition of "the hand of God": Ps 78:42; Ex 14:31; Dt 11:2; Jr 16:21. But Dahood translates "the flock of his grazing plot" and compares *yādô* with *mar'ītō*, "his pasture," in Jr 23:1 (in 2 S 19:44 and 2 K 11:7 *yādôt* means "parts, portions").

§32. LITURGIES

(a) *General character*

Liturgical fragments can be found scattered throughout the Psalter (see §8). Yet in three psalms the liturgical element is important enough to justify their classification as "liturgies." H. Gunkel described Pss 15 and 24 as *Tora-Liturgien* (cf. *Einheitung...* §11:14). "Another liturgy of an exceptionally brief but not altogether unrelated character may be found in Ps 134, which Gunkel explained as a combination of hymn and priestly blessing appropriate to the close of worship at one of Israel's festivals" (A. R. Johnson, "The Psalms," p. 178).

An important subject of priestly oracles, notes A. Bentzen, has been the treatment of the problems of cultic life (*Introduction...* p. 188f): "Especially must many people have asked for divine guidance concerning conditions excluding from the service in the temple." The solution of moral problems was also expected from the priests. A corpus of traditions allowed to find appropriate answers. Unusual problems could require that the oracle be consulted (cf. 2 S 21: 1ff; Hag 2:11-14; Zc 7:1-14). The *tôrâh-liturgies* are better understood against this background: in them are proclaimed the conditions for access to the sanctuary. They are also called "*tôrôt* of entry" and echoes of them can be found in the prophets (cf. Jr 7:1-10):

With what shall I come before the Lord,
and bow before God most high?

Shall I come before him with holocausts,
    with calves a year old?
Will the Lord be pleased with thousands of rams,
    with myriad streams of oil?
Shall I give my first-born for my crime,
    the fruit of my body for the sin of my soul?

(Mi 6:6f)

He who practices virtue and speaks honestly,
    who spurns what is gained by oppression,
Brushing his hands free of contact with a bribe,
    stopping his ears lest he hear of bloodshed,
    closing his eyes lest he look on evil—
He shall dwell on the heights,
    his stronghold shall be the rocky fastness,
    his food and drink in steady supply.

(Is 33:15f)

But the typical *Tora-Liturgien* are Pss 15 and 24 (see also *Ps 26). Related to these liturgies is the "Protestation of Guiltlessness" or the "Negative Confession," of which a good example is found in chapter 125 of the Egyptian *Book of the Dead* (see on *Ps 101). Lists of faults against the covenant rules were known and recalled (cf. also Ezk 18:5-9). Sometimes the confession is a very general one: "I have not transgressed any of thy commandments, neither have I forgotten them" (Dt 26:13; cf. Jb 31: 5ff); "From every evil way I withhold my feet, that I may keep your words" (Ps 119:101; cf. Ps 17:4f).

The decalogical tradition of Sinai expressed itself then also in a new form, that which belongs to the ancient custom of announcing the "sacred laws" of the sanctuary. These were not unknown among ancient Israel's neighbors. An inscription of an Egyptian temple warned: "He who enters here must be pure; purify yourself fittingly at the entrance of the great god's temple" (cf. A. Erman, *Die Religion der Ägypter,* p. 90). In Babylonia a man confessed: "I have always entered into the temple in a state of impurity; what displeases you most I have always done it" (cf. A. Falkenstein and W. von Soden, *Sumerische...,* p. 273; on the "Liturgies" see also the studies of K. Koch, K. Galling and J. Morgenstern, "The Gates..."). The *Tora-Liturgien* merit to take place among the *didactic* psalms, since in their own way they also teach the faithful the law of God.

(b) The "liturgies" are Pss 15, 24, 134.

PSALM 15 (14)

The Guest of God

The first verse identifies this psalm as a "liturgy of entry," in which the conditions for admission to the sanctuary are set forth, like "a moral catechism." The influence of the "decalogical tradition," Mowinckel notes (I, p. 158), is especially noticeable in Ps 15, in which *ten* "laws of entrance" are listed (vv 2-5). In the original cultic act perhaps the candidates for admittance clarified their status in regard to these laws. A more general response, "He who does these things shall never be disturbed" (v 5), would have been introduced later, when the psalm came to be used apart from its primitive setting. Dissociated from the cult the whole psalm, interpreted figuratively, refers to the spiritual relationship of the faithful with God. It is remarkable, as Weiser notes, that moral and social, not ritual, requirements are stressed. This reflects the prophetic attitude of disengagement from the sacrificial institution (cf. *Ps 51:18) and the gradual spiritualization of religion. "By attributing the 'perfection' of man's conduct and the 'righteousness' of his actions to the inward truthfulness of his conviction (v 2), Weiser notes, the psalmist has arrived at a conception of the moral law which is not very different from the basic moral truths taught in the Sermon on the Mount." As concerns the mention of the "reprobate" in verse 4, Weiser adds: "We shall have to understand this viewpoint of the psalmist as meaning that, where God has turned against a man, it does not befit the godly to go beyond that divine decision." On Ps 15 see also J. A. Soggin in *BibOr* 12 (1970) 70-108.

PSALM 24 (23)

The Lord's Solemn Entry into Zion

The middle section of this psalm (vv 3-6) is a *Tor(a)-Liturgie* which has much in common with Ps 15. Here also ethical, not ritual conditions are set. The *leges sacrae* regulating admittance to the sanctuary have been in part preserved in the *tôrâh* liturgies (see §32a), also called sometimes *Torliturgien*, "Gateliturgies." The first expression concerns the conditions of entry, the second one alludes to the place where the "liturgy" was performed (cf. G. Pidoux, *Du Portique à l'Autel*, p. 20).

In Ps 24, as elsewhere in the Old Testament (cf. 1 S 2:8; Pss 74:16f; 89:11f; 95:4f), creation is considered as the basis of God's universal sovereignty (cf. vv 1-2). An allusion to the victory of God on "the hostile powers of chaos" can be read in verse 8 if the third stanza (vv 7-10) is interpreted as referring to God's theophany in the sanctuary. More obviously these verses describe, as in Ps 118, the entry in the temple of the ark of the covenant, which bears the name Yahweh Sabaoth (2 S 6:2; 1 Ch 13:6;), the God of Hosts or Armies (cf. "mighty in battle," v 8). The "King of glory" is called "Yahweh Sabaoth' in verse 10, as in this passage "So the people went to Shiloh, and brought from there the ark of the covenant of the Lord of hosts, who is enthroned on the cherubim" (1 S 4:4). The association of "Yahweh Sabaoth" with the ark (cf. §13c) could reflect an attempt to "demythologize" the ancient title of "Yahweh Sabaoth" (cf. H.-J. Kraus, *Psalmen,* p. 201), originally connected perhaps with the mysterious powers of nature religions. W. Schmidt (*Königtum*...pp. 76-79) has studied the hypothesis of a Canaanite origin for the title "Yahweh Sabaoth."

Some psalms, mainly 24, 68, 118, 132, could be understood only in the setting of a festal procession, Mowinckel believes (I, p. 5). The three stanzas of Ps 24, he explains, were successively used on the way to the temple, before the gate and as the procession filed through the gates. Ps 132, on the other hand, describes "the beginning of the day's procession, as it started from a place outside the temple citadel, corresponding to the house of Obed-Edom, where the ark had stood for three months (2 S 6: 10f). H. Vilar's view is that Ps 24 was composed for the liturgy of the second temple, more precisely for the feast of Tabernacles (see on *Ps 118), when the return of the Glory of God was commemorated. In "The Gates of Righteousness" (p. 34) J. Morgenstern also mentioned the $k^e b \hat{o}d$ *Yhwh* passing through the "eastern gate" (cf. Ezk 10:19; 11:1).

Psalm 24:2 is translated by Dahood: "For he based it upon the seas, established it upon the ocean currents," that is, "the pillars upon which the earth rests have been sunk into the subterranean ocean" (cf. Jb 38:6; 1 S 2:8; Ps 75:4 and §14d). The meaning "ocean currents" ($n^e h \bar{a} r \hat{o} t$) is attested in a Ugaritic text (t. 68:12ff; cf. C. H. Gordon, p 180) and would recur in Pss 46:5; 89:26; Is 44:27; Jon 2:4. In verse 4 *napši* can be retained, with the meaning of *napšô,* "his mind" (*CV:* "who desires"), since Phoenician usage (cf. *JNES* 1951, p. 228ff) reveals the existence of a third-person suffix - y (See a full listing of the biblical examples in Dahood's commentary of Ps 2:6). Then Ps 24:4 should read:

"The clean of hands, and pure of heart; who has not raised his mind to an idol, nor sworn by a fraud" (cf. Pss 5:7; 16:4). This rendition could perhaps be related to the passages which call "virgins" those who have not worshipped the Beast of Idolatry (Rv 14:9; 20:4; cf. Ho 1:2). The divine name "Eternal" occupies a prominent place in Dahood's translation of Ps 24. In verse 6, as in *Ps 75:10, it occurs in parallel with the "God of Jacob": "The One of Eternity seek, O you who search for the Presence of Jacob" (cf. *Harv. Th. Rev.*, 1962, p. 238f). Then twice (vv 7 and 9) an acclamation goes to the "gates of the Eternal" (*CV*: "ancient portals"). On these two verses see P. -R. Berger in *Ugarit-Forschungen* 2 (1970) 335f.

In connection with the belief of the descent of Christ to the underworld (cf. 1 P 3:19; 4:6), writes A. Cabaniss, the early Christians are likely to have been struck by some words of Ps 24: "gates," "glory," "princes" (v 9; LXX: *archontes*), "king of glory." Mention can be made here of Col 2:15: "Disarming the Principalities and Powers, he displayed them openly, leading them away in triumph by force of it." Then, continues Cabaniss, "we may venture to assume, even without literary evidence and long before the preparation of the *descensus*-section of the Gospel of Nicodemus [fourth cent. apocryphal], that the early Christian Church was using the 24th psalm liturgically to commemorate the Lord's victorious conquest of Hades and death." A possible illustration of ceremonial use of Ps 24 could be, he adds, the well-known letter of Pliny the Younger to emperor Trajan, written in A.D. 113. The relevant section of it we quote here from D. M. Stanley's article, "Carmenque Christo quasi Deo dicere...":

> They [the Christians] insisted however that their whole crime or error came to this: they had the custom of meeting on a certain fixed day, before daybreak, to sing a hymn, alternating among themselves, to Christ as God; and to bind themselves solemnly by an oath, not with any criminal intent, but to avoid all fraud, theft, adultery, unfaithfulness to their promises, or denial of "the deposit" (cf. 1 Tm 6:20) if summoned to do so. After dispatching this business, it was their habit to disband, reassembling once more to take food, which is however of an ordinary and innocent kind... (*CBQ* 1958, p. 176).

The antiphonal hymn mentioned in this text applies well also to Ps 24 which has a dialogue structure and was probably sung by alternating choirs. The innocence motif is also found in both texts.

Psalm 134 (133)

Exhortation to the Night Watch to Bless the Lord

The last of the "Pilgrim Songs" preserves the remains of a night liturgy. It ends with a priestly blessing (v 3; cf. §3c). The first two verses are hymnic in character and could represent the answer of the congregation to the thanksgiving of an individual. Possibly also they are addressed to priests or pilgrims who participated in a vigil of prayers. Kissane observes, however, that the term "servants of Yahweh" includes all Israel (cf. Ps 135:1; 19f), and the phrase "who stand in the house of Yahweh" is not the equivalent of "who stand before Yahweh" as His ministers (cf. Dt 10:8), but merely "who are present in the temple" (Ps 122:2). The mention of "the night" is linked by LXX (and *Vulg.*), perhaps correctly, with verse 2: "Every night lift up your hands..." and "can refer to prayers offered outside the Temple by pilgrims who turn towards the Temple in prayer" (Kissane). The allusion in verse 3 to the divine title "Creator" stresses the validity and power of God's blessing (cf. Pss 24: 1f; 121:1-2; 124:8).

In his "Notes on Pss 68 and 134," Albright has called attention to the fact that a Canaanite text published by R. A. Bowman (*JNES* 1944, pp. 219-231) contains an exact parallel to Ps 134:3. It reads: "Baal from the North will bless you." In the same article he brings to notice the evidence (cf. *JBL* 1944, p. 4ff) of the ancient Canaanite divine title: "El, Creator of the Earth." This is reflected also in Ps 134:3. Albright concludes that verse 3 of Ps 134 "brings together two characteristic cola from pagan Canaanite literature, with slight modification to adapt them to monotheism and exilic or early post-exilic age" (p. 6). Similar reflections could be applied to Ps 128:5 (also a "Song of Ascents"), "The Lord bless you from Zion," and to Ps 118:26: "Blessed is he who comes in the name of the Lord; we bless you from the house of the Lord."

In v 1, as well as in Ps 113:1, and 135:1, it seems possible to read *ᵃbādē*, "the works of," instead of *MT* *'abdē*, "the servants of," and translate: "Come, bless Yahweh, all the works of Yahweh" (Dahood), making the latter the object, not the subject of the praise. It is recognized (cf. F. Zorrell, *Lexicon Hebraicum* 564) that this meaning is attested in Ec 9:1: "The just and the wise and their works (*ᵃbādēhem*) are from the hand of God."

Bibliography

Abrahams, I., "E. G. King on the Influence of the Triennial Cycle upon the Psalter," *JQR* 16 (1904) 579-583.

Ackroyd, P.R., "Some Notes on the Psalms," *JTS* 17 (1966) 392-399.
[about Ps 74:4; 93:1; *hadrat qōdeš*, Ps 118 at Qumrân]

Ackroyd, P.R. - Knibb, M.A., "Translating the Psalms," *The Bible Translator* 17 (1966) 148-162.

Ahern, B.M.; "Can the Psalms again be popular Prayers?" *Proceedings of the National Liturgical Week* (Esberry, Mo. 1954) 117-125. [cf. §16d]

Ahlström, G.W., *Psalm 89. Eine Liturgie aus dem Ritual des leidenden Königs* (Lund, 1959). [Uppsala School viewpoint; cf. *JBL* 1960, p. 68f + §7b]

A la rencontre de Dieu. Mémorial Albert Gelin (Le Puy, 1961). [cf. E. Beaucamp, P. E. Bonnard, H. Cazelles, R. Pautrel]

Albright, W. F., "A Catalogue of early Hebrew Lyric poems (Psalm LXVIII)," *HUCA* 23, 1 (1950f) 1-40.

Id., "Baal-Zephon," *Festschrift für Alfred Bertholet* (Tübingen 1950) 1-14.

Id., "Notes on Psalms 68 and 134," *Interpretationes ad Vetus Testamentum pertinentes Sigmundo Mowinckel Septuagenario missae* (Oslo 1955) 1-12. [see also §9d, 10g]

Aldama, J. A. de, "La naissance du Seigneur dans l'exégèse patristique du Psaume 21: 10a," *RSR* 51 (1963) 5-29.

Allegro, J. M., "A newly-discovered Fragment of a Commentary on Psalm 37 from Qumrân," *PEQ* 86 (1954) 69-75.

Allgeier, A., *Die altlateinischen Psalterien* (Freiburg 1928).

Id., *Die Psalmen der Vulgata. Ihre Eigenart, sprachliche Grundlage und geschichtliche Stellung* (Paderborn 1940).

Id., "Psalm 93 (94):20. Ein auslegungs-und bedeutungsgeschichtlicher Beitrag," *Fs. A. Bertholet* (Tübingen 1950) 15-28.

Alonso Schökel, L. *Estudios de Poética Hebrea* (Barcelona 1963). [cf. §6e]

Id., *Salmos* (Madrid 1966).

Id., "Psalmus 136 (135)," *VD* 45 (1967) 129-138.

Anderson, G. W., *Enemies and Evildoers in the Book of Psalms* (Manchester 1965). [from *BJRL* 48, 1, 1965 18-29]

Anders-Richards, D., *The Drama of the Psalms* (London 1968). [A Study of the development of psalm study during the last half-century]

Ap-Thomas, D. R., "An Appreciation of Sigmund Mowinckel's Contribution to Biblical Studies," *JBL* 85 (1966) 315-325.

Arbesmann, R., "The Daemonium meridianum (Ps 91:6) and Greek and Latin Exegesis," *Tradition* 14 (1958) 17-31.

Arbez, E. P., "A Study of Psalm 1," *CBQ* 7 (1945) 398-404.

Arconada, R., "La escatología mesiánica en los Salmos ante dos objectiones recientes," *Bib* 17 (1936), pp. 202-229; 294-326; 461-478.

Id., *Los Salmos, versión y comentario. Reajústan S. Bartína y F. X. Rodríguez Molero.* Biblioteca de Autores Cristianos (Madrid 1969). [cf. *CBQ* 1970, 463]

Arnes, A., *Die Psalmen im Gottesdienst des Alten Bundes. Eine Untersuchung zur Vorgeschichte des christlichen Psalmengesanges* (Trier 1961). [cf. *CBQ* 1962, p. 209 + §8c]

Id., "Hat der Psalter seinen 'Sitz im Leben' in der Synagogalen Leseordnung des Pentateuch?" *Le Psautier* [cf. R. De Langhe], 107-131.

Arnaldich, L., "Carácter messiánico del Salmo 16 (Vulg. 15)," *Verdad y Vida* 1 (1943) 251-286; 688-706; 2 (1944) 24-65.

Asensio, F., "Salmos Mesiánicos o Salmos Nacionales?" *Greg* 33 (1952), 219-260; 566-611. [Pss 2, 72, 22, 16]

Id., "Sugerencias del Salmista 'Peregrino y extranjero' (Salm. 39:13)," *Greg* 34 (1953) 421-426.

Id., "En torno al 'Sol-héroe' del Salmo 19," *Greg* 35 (1954) 649-655.

Id., "El *despertar* del justo en el Salm. 17:15," Greg 36 (1955) 669-675.

Id., "El Salmo 132 y la 'Lámpara' de David," *Greg* 38 (1957) 310-316.

Id., "Entrecruce de símbolos y realidades en el Salmo 23," *Bib* 40 (1959) 237-247.

Id., "Salmo 36. Su avance hacia la plenitud Luz-Vida," *EstE* 34 (1960) 633-643.

Id., "Teología Biblica de un triptico: Salmos 61, 62 y 63," *EstBib* 21 (1962) 111-125.

Id., "*El Yahweh mālak* de los 'Salmos del Reino' en la historia de la 'Salvación,' " *EstBib* 25 (1966) 299-315.

Auvray, P., "Le Psaume I. Notes de grammaire et d'exégèse," *RB* 53 (1946) 365-371.

Ayuso Maraguela, T., *La Vetus Latina Hispana. V, El Salterio* (Madrid 1962), vols. I-III.

Baillet, M., "Psaumes, hymnes, cantiques et prières dans les manuscrits de Qumrân," *Le Psautier* [cf. R. De Langhe] 389-405.

Balla, E., *Das Ich der Psalmen,* FRLANT 16 (Göttingen 1912). [cf. °Ps 129]

Bardtke, H., et al., eds, *Liber Psalmorum* of the *Biblia Hebraica* (R. Kittel) *Stuttgartensia* (Stuttgart 1969). [cf. *CBQ* 1970, 254f]

Barth, C., *Die Errettung vom Tode in den individuellen Klage-und Dankliedern des Alten Testaments* (Zürich 1947). [Pss 17:15; 18:17; 49:16; 73:23; cf. *RB* 1948]

Id., *Introduction to the Psalms* (New York 1966). [Tr. of the German edition, 1961; cf. *CBQ* 1964 140f]

Bartina, S., "Alabar, no 'Confessar' [en el Nuevo Salterio Latino]," *EstE* 30 (1956) 37-66.

Barucq, A., "La lode divina nei Salmi," *BibOr* 1, 3 (1959) 66-77.

Id., *L'expression de la louange divine et de la prière dans la Bible et en Égypte* (Le Caire, 1962).

Battle, J.H., *Syntactic Structures in the Masoretic Hebrew Text of the Psalms* (Diss. Univ. Texas 1969; cf. *DissAbstr* 30, 1970, 4434-A).

Bauer, J. B., "Incedam in via immaculata, quando venias ad me (Ps 100 [101]:2)," *VD* 30 (1952) 219-224.

Id., "Theologie der Psalmen," *BiLit* 20 (1952f); 21 (1953f); 22 (1954). [several articles]

Id., "L'aiuto divino al mattino," *RBibIt* 2 (1954) 43-47. [cf. °Ps 5]

Baumann, E., "Struktur-Untersuchungen im Psalter," *ZAW* 61 (1945-48) 115-176; 62 (1949f) 115-152. [Pss 4, 8, 13, 18, 26, 32, 36, 39, 40, 50, 56, 57, 59, 60, 72, 73, 84, 85, 110, 126, 135, 144]

Baumgärtel, F., "Der 109. Psalm in der Verkündigung," *Monatschrift f. Past. Theol.* 42 (1953) 244-253.

Id., "Zur Frage der theologischen Deutung der messianischen Psalmen," *BZAW* 105 (1967) 19-25.

Bea, A., "The New Psalter: its Origin and Spirit," *CBQ* 8 (1946) 1-35.

Id., "I primi dieci anni del nuovo Salterio latino," *Bib* 36 (1955) 161-181. [cf. *Liber Psalmorum...*]

Beaucamp, E., "Psaume 47. Verset 10A," *Bib* 38 (1957) 457-460.

Id., "La théophanie du Psaume 50 (49)," *NRT* 81 (1959) 897-915.

Id., "Le Psaume 21 (20), psaume messianique," *ColBibLat* 13 (1959) 35-66.

Id., "Justice divine et pardon (Ps 51:6b)," *A la rencontre...* 129-144.

Id., "Le problème du Psaume 87," *Liber Annuus* 13 (1962f) 53-75.

Id., "Des justices plein ta main, de redoutables exploits plein ta droite (Ps 45:5c)," *Bib* 47 (1966) 110-112.

Id., [also] *Bible et Vie Chrétienne*, N 22 (Ps 21), N. 24 (Ps 85), N. 28 (Ps 45) N. 29 (Ps 103), N. 63 (Ps 68), N 65 (Ps 67), N. 66 (Ps 74).

Beauchamp, P., "Plainte et louange dans les Psaumes," *Christus* 13 (1967) 65-82.

Becker, J., *Israel deutet seine Psalmen* (Stuttgart 1966).

Id., "Structures strophiques des Psaumes," *RSR* 56 (1968) 199-223.

Beer, G., "Zur Erklärung des 22. Psalms," Fs K. Marti, *BZAW* 41 (1925) 12-20.

Begrich, J., "Die Vertrauensäusserungen im israelitischen Klagenliede des Einzelnen und in seinem babylonischen Gegenstück," *ZAW* 46 (1928) 221-260.

Id., "Das priesterliche Heilsorakel," *ZAW* 52 (1934) 81-92.

Behler, G. M., "Der Herr als guter Hirt und milder Wirt (Ps 23)," *BiLit* 39 (1964f) 254-287.

Id., "Der nahe und schwer zu fassende Gott. Eine biblische Besinnung über Ps 139 (138)," *Bib* 6 (1965) 135-152.

Bentzen, A., "Der Tod des Beters in den Psalmen. Randbemerkungen zur Diskussion zwischen Mowinckel und Widengren," *Gottes ist der Orient, Fs. O. Eissfeldt* (Halle 1947) 57-60.

Id., *King and Messiah* (London 1955). [cf. §8a]

Id., *Introduction to the Old Testament*, I-II (Copenhagen 1957).

Bernhardt, K. -H., *Das Problem der altorientalischen Königsideologie im Alten Testament, unter besonderer Berücksichtigung der Geschichte der Psalmenexegese dargestellt und kritisch gewürdigt* (Leiden 1961). [rejects the "ritual pattern" theory and advocates an explanation of royal ideology based on the historical rejection of the kingship and on the traditions of the nomadic period. Cf. *RB* 1963 633f]

Bernimont, E., "De l'inégale valeur des Psaumes," *NRT* 84 (1962) 843-852.

Bernini, G., *Le preghiere penitenziali del Salterio* (Romae 1953), [especially Pss 19, 25, 32, 38-41, 51, 65, 69, 79, 85, 90, 103, 106, 130, 143].

414 THE PSALMS

Beyerlin, W., "*Die tôdā der Heilsverkündigung in den Klageliedern des Einzelnen.*" *ZAW* 79 (1967) 208-224.

Id., *Die Rettung der Bedrängten in den Feindpsalmen der Einzelnen auf institutionelle Zusammenhänge untersucht* (Göttingen 1970). [cf. *CBQ* 1971, 95f]

Bickel, G., *Carmina Veteris Testamenti metrice* (Oeniponte 1882).

Bierberg, R. P., *Conserva me, Domine (Ps 16)*, (Washington 1945). [cf. *CBQ* 1946 359-363]

Bileham, A., *El primer libro de los salmos* (Madrid 1966).

Bird T.E., "Some Queries on the New Psalter," *CBQ* 11-12 (1949f), a series of articles.

Birkeland, H., '*Ani und 'anaw in den Psalmen* (Oslo and Leipzig, 1933). [cf. §12a]

Id., *Die Feinde des Individuums in der israelitischen Psalmenliteratur* (Oslo 1933).

Id., *The Evildoers in the Book of Psalms* (Oslo 1955). [cf. *JBL* 1957, 162 + §12g]

Id., "The Chief Problems of Ps 73:17ff," *ZAW* 67 (1955) 99-103.

Blackman, A. M., "The Psalms in the Light of Egyptian Research," *The Psalmists* [cf. D. C. Simpson], 177-197. [cf. §9c]

Blenkinsopp, J., "Can we pray the Cursing Psalms?" *Clergy Review* 50 (1965) 534-538.

Blidstein, G. J., "Nature in Psalms," *Judaism* 13, 1964, 29-36.

Bloch, J., "The New Latin Version of the Psalter," *JQR* 38 (1947f) 267-288.

Boling, R. G., "Synonymous Parallelism in the Psalms," *JSS* 5 (1960) 221-255.

Bollegui, J. M., *Los Salmos. Oraciones inventadas por Dios para los hombres* (Barcelona 1967).

Bonkamp, B., *Die Psalmen nach dem hebräischen Urtext übersetzt* (Freiburg i.B., 1952). [is in part an attempt to study the Psalter with the contribution of Assyriological material; cf. *VT* 1953 202-208]

Bonnard, P. E., "Le vocabulaire du *Miserere*," *A la rencontre*. . .145-156.

Id., *Le psautier selon Jéremie* (Paris 1960). [see §5d + °Ps 6]

Bonnes, J. P., *David et les Psaumes* (Paris 1957). [cf. *RB* 1958]

Bornert, R., "Les Psaumes (Ps 97): Hymne pour la manifestation du Seigneur," *Assemblées du Seigneur* 17 (1962) 7-20. [cf. §13a]

Bornkamm, G., "Lobpreis Bekenntnis und Opfer," in *Apophoreta, BZNW* 30 (Berlin 1964) 43-63.

Botterweck, G. J., "Ein Leid vom glücklichen Menschen (Ps 1)," *Theologische Quartalschrift* 138 (1958) 129-151.

Bouyer, L., "Les Psaumes dans la prière chrétienne traditionnelle," *BiViChr* 10 (1955) (1955) 22-35.

Bowker, J. W., "Psalm CX," *VT* 17 (1967) 31-41.

Breit, H., "Die Psalmen in der christlichen Kirche," *Klerus Blatt* 45 (1965) 379-384.

Brekelmans, C., "Pronominal Suffixes in the Hebrew Book of Psalms," *JEOL* 17 (1964) 202-206.

Brethes, C., *Mon âme, bénis le Seigneur! Commentaire et traduction en vers des Psaumes* (Paris 1965).

Briggs, C. A., *A Critical and Exegetical Commentary on the Book of Psalms*, I-II (Edinburgh 1906f).

Brinktrine, J., "Dominus regnavit a ligno," *BZ* 10 (1966) 105-107. [cf. °Ps 96:10]

Brongers, H. A., "Die Rache-und Fluchpsalmen im Alten Testament," *OTS* 13 (1963) 21-42.

Id., "Ps 1-2 as a Coronation Liturgy," *Bib* 52 (1971) 321-36. 185. [cf. °Ps 13 + §26f]

Brownlee, W.H., "Ps 1-2 as a Coronation Liturgy," *Bib* 52 (1971) 321-36.

Bückers, H., "Die Sündenvergebung in den Psalmen," *Divus Thomas Freib.* 29 (1951) 188-210.

Id., "Zur verwertung der Sinaitraditionem in den Psalmen," *Bib* 32 (1951) 401-422.

Budde, K., "Zum Text der Psalmen," *ZAW* 35 (1915) 175-195.

Bulcke, M., "Le Psaume 67 (68), psaume de Pentecôte," *Rev. Clergé Afr.* 9 (1954) 569-582.

Bullough, S., "The question of metre in Psalm 1," *VT* 17 (1967) 42-49.

Id., "The Psalms," in *New Catholic Commentary on Holy Scripture* (London 1969) 439-99.

Buss, M. J., "The Psalms of Asaph and Korah," *JBL* 82 (1963) 382-392.

Buttenwieser, M., *The Psalms, chronologically treated, with a new Translation* (Chicago 1938).

Cabaniss, A., "The Harrowing of Hell. Psalm 24 and Pliny the Younger," *Vigiliae Christianae* 7 (1953) 65-74.

Calès, J., *Le livre des Psaumes,* I-II (Paris 1936).

Callan, C. J., *The Psalms, translated from the Latin Psalter in the light of the Hebrew, of the Septuagint and Peshitta versions, and of the Psalterium juxta Hebraeos of St. Jerome with introductions, critical notes and spiritual reflections* (New York 1944). [cf. *CBQ* (1946) 247f]

Cambe, M., "L'interprétation symbolique du Psaume XXIX (XXVIII) par les Septante. Note sur le verset 6," *Rev. Thom.* 65 (1964) 223-229.

Candole, H. de, *The Christian Use of the Psalms* (London 1955).

Caquot, A., "In splendoribus sanctorum," *Syria* 33 (1956) 36-41. [Ps 29:2; 96:9; 1 Chr 16:29]

Id., "Remarques sur le Psaume CX," *Sem* 6 (1956) 33-52.

Id., "Le Psaume XCI," *Sem* 8 (1958) 21-37.

Id., "Le Psaume 47 et la royauté de Yahve," *RHPhilRel* 39 (1959) 311-337.

Id., "Purification et expiation selon le psaume LI," *RHR* 169 (1966) 133-154.

Carmignac, J., "Précisions sur la forme poetique du Psaume 151," *RQum* 5 (1965) 249-252. [cf. §3a]

Castellini, G. M., "I Salmi, preghiera cristiana," *EphLitg* 72 (1958) 341-347.

Castellino, G. R., *Le lamentazioni individuali e gli inni in Babilonia e in Israele, raffronta riguardo alla forma e al contenuto* (Torino 1940).

Id., "Lamentazioni individuali Accadiche ed Ebraiche," *Salesianum* 10 (1948) 145-162.

Id., *I Salmi* (Torino 1955).

Id., "Salmo 73:10," *Studi Orient. G. Levi della Vida I* (Romae 1956) 141-150.

Cazelles, H., "La question du *lamed auctoris*," *RB* 56 (1949) 93-101. [cf. §4f]

Id., "Une relecture du Psaume 29?" *A la rencontre...* 119-128.

Id., "L'expression hébraïque *šûb šebût* viendrait-elle de l'accadien d'Assarhaddon?" *Groupe Linguistique d'Etudes Chamito-Sémitiques* 9 (1961) 57-60. [for Pss 14:7; 53:7; 85:2]

Id., "Note sur le Psaume 8," *Parole de Dieu et Sacerdoce, Hommage à J. J. Weber* (Paris 1962) 79-91.

Charles, R. H., *The Apocrypha and Pseudepigrapha of the Old Testament*, I-II (Oxford 1913).

Cheyne, T. K., *The Book of Psalms* (London 1888 and 1904).

Chouraqui, A., *Les Psaumes. Traduits et présentés* (Paris 1956).

Cilleruelo, P. Lope, "La mentalidad del salmo de Loanza," *Ciudad de Dios* 164 (1952) 533-552. [the sacrifice of praise]

Clark, D. L. -Mastin, B. A., "*Venite exultemus Domino*: Some Reflections on the Interpretation of the Psalter," *ChQR* 167 (1966) 413-424.

Clifford, R.J., *The Cosmic Mountain in Canaan and the Old Testament* (Cambridge, Mass. 1972).

Clines, D.J.A., "Psalm Research since 1955: I. The Psalms and the Cult," *Tyndale Bulletin* 18 (1967) 103-26 + II. "The Literary Genres" ibid. 20 (1969) 105-25.

Closen, G. E., "Gedanken zur Textkritik von Ps 2:11b +12a," *Bib* 21 (1940) 288-309.

Cohen, A., *The Psalms. Hebrew Text, English Translation and Commentary* (Hindhead 1945).

Colunga, L. A., "Jerusalén, la ciudad del Gran Rey. Exposición messiánica de algunos Salmos," *EstBib* 14 (1955) 255-279. [Pss 46ff, 87, 122, 137]

Condamin, A. *Poèmes de la Bible* (Paris 1933).

Cooper, C. M., "The Revised Standard Version of Psalms," *JQR, Seventy-fifth Anniversary Volume* (Philadelphia 1967) 137-148.

Coppens, J., "De torrente in via bibet (Ps 110:7), *ETL* 20 (1943) 54-56.

Id., "Les paralléles du Psautier avec les textes de Ras Shamra," *Le Museon* 59 1946) 113-142.

Id., "Trois parallèles ougaritiens du Psautier," *ETL* 23 (1947) 173-177 [Pss 110:3, 6b; 82:7]

Id., "La portée messianique du Ps 110," *ETL* 32 (1956) 5-23.

Id., *Het onsterfelijkheidsgeloof in het Psalmboek* (Brussel 1957). [Pss 16, 49, 73, including a summary, and a translation of these Pss in French]

Id., "Les psaumes des *ḥasîdîm*," *Mélanges bibliques...* 214-224. [cf. §12c]

Id., *Le Psautier et ses problèmes, Anal. Lovan.* 3, 19 (Louvain 1960).

Id., "Les Psaumes 6 et 41 dépendent-ils du livre de Jeremie?" *HUCA* 32 (1961) 217-226.

Id., "Les études récentes sur le Psautier," *Le Psautier* [cf. R. De Langhe] 1-71. [cf. §5e, 12cd]

Id., "Les Saints (*qedôšîm*) dans le Psautier," *ETL* 39 (1963) 485-500.

Id., "La date des Psaumes de l'Intronisation et de la Royauté de Yahve," *ETL* 43 (1967) 192-197.

Couroyer, B., "L'arc d'airain," *RB* 72 (1965) 508-514. [Ps 18:35]

Creager, H. L., "Note on Psalm 109," *JNES* 6 (1947) 121-123.

Crim, K. R., *The Royal Psalms* (Richmond, Va. 1962).

Cross, F. M., "Notes on a Canaanite Psalm in the Old Testament (Ps 29)," *BASOR* 117 (1950) 19-21.

Cross, F.M-Freedman, D. N., "A Royal Song of Thanksgiving: II Samuel 22= Psalm 18a," *JBL* 72 (1953) 15-34.

Crüsemann, F., *Studien zur Formgeschichte von Hymnus und Danklied in Israel.* WMANT 32 (Neukirchen 1971). [cf. *CBQ* 1971, 250f]

Culley, R. C., *Oral Formulaic Language in the Biblical Psalms* (Toronto 1967). See *CBQ* 1968 438f.

Dahood, M., "The root *GMR* in the Psalms," *TS* 14 (1953) 595-597. [see on °Ps 51]

Id., "Philological Notes on the Psalms," *TS* 14 (1953) 85-88.

Id., "The Divine Name '*ELI* in the Psalms," *TS* 14 (1953) 452-57. [see on °Ps 51]

Id., "The Language and Date of Psalm 48," *CBQ* 16 (1954) 15-19.

Id., "Enclitic *mem* and emphatic *lamedh* in Psalm 85," *Bib* 37 (1956) 338-40.

Id., "Vocative *lamedh* in the Psalter," *VT* 16 (1966) 299-311.

Id., "A New Metrical Pattern in Biblical Poetry," *CBQ* 29 (1967) 574-79.

Id., *Psalms* I, II, III. The Anchor Bible (New York 1966, 1968, 1970), and *Psalms* II, 2nd edition (1973).

Daiches, S., *Studies in the Psalms* (Oxford 1930).

Id., "The Meaning of 'Sacrifices' in the Psalms," *Essays in Honour of the Very Rev Dr. J. H. Hertz* (London 1944) 97-109.

Dalglish, E. R., *The Hebrew Penitential Psalms with Special Reference to Psalm 51* (New York 1951). [cf. §4e]

Id., *Psalm Fifty-One in the Light of Ancient Near Eastern Patternism* (Leiden 1962).

Daniélou, J., "Le Psaume 22 dans l'exégèse patristique," *ColBibLat* 13 (1959) 189-211.

Davies, G. H., "The Ark in the Psalms," *Promise and Fulfilment. Essays presented to Prof. S. H. Hooke* (Edinburgh 1963) 51-61. [cf. §13b]

Deaver, G. R., *An Exegetical Study of Psalm 24* (Dallas 1953).

De Boer, P. A. H., "Psalm CXXI:2," *VT* 16 (1966) 287-292.

De Fraine, J., *L'aspect religieux de la royauté israelite* (Rome 1954).

Id., "Quel est le sens exact de la filiation divine dans Psaume 2:7?" *Bijdragen* 16 (1955) 349-356.

Id., "Le démon du midi (Ps 91:6)," *Bib* 40 (1959) 372-383.

Id., "*Entmythologisierung* dans les Psaumes," *Le Psautier* [cf. R. De Langhe] 89-106.

Id., "Les nations païennes dans les Psaumes," *Studi G. Rinaldi* (Genova 1967) 285-292.

Deissler, A., *Psalm 119 (118) und seine Theologie. Ein Beitrag zur Erforschung der anthologischen Stilgattung im Alten Testament* (München 1955). [cf. *VT* 1958 441ff]

Id., "Der anthologische Charakter des Psalmes 33 (32)," *Mélanges Bibliques...* 225-233.

Id., "Der anthologische Charakter des Ps 48 (47)," *Sacra Pagina* I (Paris-Gembloux 1959) 495-503.

Id., "Mensch und Schöpfung. Eine Auslegung des Ps 103 (104)," *Oberrheinisches Pastoralblatt* (Freiburg i.B), 61 (1960) 15-22; 41-45.

Id., "Zur Datierung und Situierung der kosr ischen Hymnen Pss 8, 19, 29," *Lex Tua Veritas, Fs. H. Junker* (Trier 1961) 47-58.

Ib., "Das lobpreisende Gottesvolk in den Psalmen," *Seniire Ecclesiam. . .Fs. H. Rahner* (Freiburg 1961) 17-49. [cf. §13e]

Id., *Die Psalmen* (Düsseldorf 1963ff). [cf. *ETL* 1965, p. 219f; also a French Edit]

Id., *Le livre des Psaumes.* 1-75 (Paris 1966).

Id., "Das Israel der Psalmen als Gottesvolk der Hoffenden," in G. Bornkamm und K. Rahner, eds., *Die Zeit Jesu, Festschrift Heinrich Schlier* (Freiburg i. Br., 1970) 15-37.

De Langhe, R. (édit.), *Le Psautier. Ses origines, ses problèmes littéraires, son influence. Etudes présentees aux XIIes Journees Bibliques* (Louvain 1962). [cf. J. Coppens, A. Descamps, J. De Fraine, A. Arens, E. Lipiński, P. Van den Berghe, A. Rose, J. Dupont, M. Baillet, M. Delcor]

Delcor, M., "Cinq nouveaux psaumes esséniens?" *RQum* I: 1 (1958) 85-102.

Delekat, L., "Probleme der Psalmenüberschriften," *ZAW* 76 (1964) 280-297. [cf. §4de]

Id., *Asylie und Schutzorakel am Zionheiligtum. Eine Untersuchung zu den Privatpsalmen* (Leiden 1967).

Del Páramo, S., "El fin de las parábolas de Cristo y el Salmo 77 (cf. Mt 13:10-17)," *Sem. Bibl. Esp.* (Madrid 1954) 341-364.

Id., "El género literario de los Salmos," *EstBib* 6 (1947) 241-264; 450f.

De Pinto, B., "The Torah and the Psalms," *JBL* 86 (1967) 154-174.

Dequeker, L., "Les *qedôšim* du Psaume 89 à la lumière des croyances semitiques," *ETL* 39 (1963) 469-484. [cf. §12d]

Descamps, A., "Pour un classement littéraire des Psaumes," *Mélanges bibliques. . .* 187-196.

Id., "Les genres littéraires du Psautier; un état de la question," *Le Psautier* [cf. R. De Langhe] 73-88.

Didier, M., "Le Psaume II dans l'Ancien Testament," *Rev. de Namur* 11 (1957) 120-130.

Id., "Une lecture des psaumes du règne de Yahvé," *ibid.* 12 (1958) 457-470.

Donner, H. "Ugaritismen in der Psalmenforschung," *ZAW* 79 (1967) 322-350. [cf. §9d]

Drijvers, P., *The Psalms, their Structure and Meaning* (New York 1965).

Driver, G. R., "The Psalms in the Light of Babylonian Research," *The Psalmists* [cf. D. C. Simpson], pp. 109-176. [cf. §9b]

Id., "Textual and Linguistic Problems of the Book of Psalms," *Harv. Th. Rev.* 29 (1936) 171-195.

Id., "Notes on the Psalms," *JTS* 43 (1942) 149-160; 44 (1943) 12-23.

Id., "The Resurrection of Marine and Terrestrial Creatures," *JSS* 7 (1962), pp. 12-22. [see on °Ps 104:24-30]

Id., Psalm CX: its Form, Meaning, and Purpose," *Studies in the Bible presented to Prof. M. Segal* (Jerusalem 1964) 17-31.

Duesberg, H., "Le miroir du fidèle: le Psaume 119 (118) et ses usages liturgiques," *BiViChr* 15 (1956) 87-97.

Id., *Le psautier des malades* (Maredsous 1952).

Duhm, B., *Die Psalmen* (Tübingen 1899 and 1922).

Duplacy, J., "La lecture juive du Psaume 8," *BiViChr* 16 (1956) 87-95.

Dupont, J., "Filius meus es tu. L'interprétation de Ps 2:7 dans le Nouveau Testament," *RSR* 35 (1948) 522-543.

Id., "L'interprétation des Psaumes dans les Actes des Apôtres." *Le Psautier* [cf. R. De Langhe] 357-388.

Dürr, L., "Zur Datierung von Ps 4," *Bib* 16 (1935) 330-338.

Eaton, J., "Problems of Translation in Ps 23:3f," *BiTrans* 16 (1965) 171-176.

Eaton, J. H., *Psalms. Introduction and Commentary*. Torch Bible Comm. (London 1967).

Ebel, B., "Das Bild des Guten Hirten im 22. Psalm nach Erklärungen der Kirchenväter," *Fs. A. Stohr*, I (Mainz 1960) 48-57.

Eerdmans, B. D., *OTS* IV (Leiden 1947).

Id., "Essays on Masoretic Psalms," *OTS* I (Leiden 1942) 105-296: "On the Road to Monotheism"; "Foreign Elements in pre-exilic Israel"; "The Songs of Ascents"; "Thora-Songs and Temple-Singers in the pre-exilic period"; "The Chasidim"; "Psalm XIV-LIII and the Elohim-psalms"; "Psalms XL, XLI, LV, LXVIII." [cf. §12c + *Pss 41, 118]

Ehrlich, A.B., *Die Psalmen* (Berlin 1905).

Ehrman, A., "What did Cain say to Abel?" *JQR* 53 (1962f) 164-167. [cf. *Ps 4:5]

Eichrodt, W., *Theology of the Old Testament*, I (London 1961). [cf. *Ps 99]

Eissfeldt, O., "Psalm 80," *Geschichte und Altes Testament. Fs. A. Alt* (Tübingen 1953) 65-78.

Id., "Psalm 76," *TLZ* 82 (1957) 801-808.

Id., *Baal Zaphon, Zeus Kasios und der Durchzug der Israeliten durchs Meer* (Halle 1932).

Id., "Psalm 121," *Stat Crux, dum volvitur orbis. Fs. H. Lilje* (Berlin 1959) 9-14. [also in Kleine Schriften III, pp. 494-500]

Id., "Mein Gott' im Alten Testament," *ZAW* 61 (1945-48) 3-16. [in the Pss: 10-16]

Id., "Jahwes Verhältnis zu 'Eljon und Schaddaj nach Psalm 91," *Die Welt des Orients,* II (1945-59) 343-348.

Id., "Psalm 132," *ibid.*, 480-484.

Id., "Ein Psalm aus Nord-Israel," *Z.d. Deutschen Morg. G.* 112 (1962) 259-268. [cf. *ibid.* 115, 1965 14-22 = Mi 7:7-20]

Id., *Das Lied Moses Deut. 32:1-43 und das Lehrgedicht Asaphs Psalm 78...* (Berlin 1958).

Elbogen, I., *Der jüdische Gottesdienst in seiner geschichtlichen Entwicklung* (Leipzig 1913).

Emerton, J.A., "Melchizedek and the Gods: Fresh Evidence for the Jewish Background of John X:34-36," *JTS* 17 (1966) 399ff. [concerns also Ps 82; cf. *ibid.* 11 (1960) 329-332.

Id., "Spring and Torrent' in Psalm LXXIV:15," *Volume du Congrès, Genève 1965, VTSuppl XV* (Leiden 1966) 122-133. [cf. §14d]

Emmanuel, *Commentaire juif des Psaumes* (Paris 1963). [cf. RBibIt 1964 435f]

Enciso, J., "El salmo 67 (68)," *EstBib* 11 (1952) 127-155.

Id., "Indicaciones musicales en los titulos de los Salmos," *Misc. Bibl. B. Ubach* (Montserrat, 1953) 185-200.

Id., "Los titulos de los Salmos y la historia de la formación del Salterio," *Est Bib* 13 (1954) 135-166.

Id., "El Salmo 9-10," *EstBib* 19 (1960) 201-214.

Id., "Los Salmos-prólogos," *EstE* 34 (1960) 621-631.

Id., "Como se formó la prima parte del libro de los Salmos," *Bib* 44 (1963) 129-158. [cf. §4a + °Pss 2, 119, 137]

Engnell, I., *Studies in Divine Kingship in the Ancient Near East* (Uppsala, 1943 and 1967).

Id., *A Rigid Scrutiny. Critical Essays on the OT*, tr. from the Swedish by John T. Willis, with the collaboration of Helmer Ringgren (Vanderbilt Univ. Press, Nashville 1969), "The Book of Psalms", 68-122 (cf. §8d).

Id., "Planted by the Streams of Water'. Some remarks on the Problems of Interpretation of the Psalms, as illustrated by a detail in Psalm 1," *Studia Orient. Io. Pendersen* (Hauniae 1953) 85-96. [cf. §8d]

Eybers, I. H., "The Stems S-P-T in the Psalms," *Studies on the Psalms* 58-63.

Falkenstein, A. and W. von Soden, *Sumerische und Akkadische Hymnen und Gebete* (Zurich-Stuttgart 1953).

Farndale, W. E., *The Psalms in new Light* (London 1956).

Feinberg, C. L., "Old-Hundreth-Psalm C," *Bibl. Sacra* 103 (1946) 53-66.

Id., "Parallels to the Psalms in Near Eastern Literature," *Bibl. Sacra* 104 (1947) 290-297.

Id., "Are there Maccabean Psalms in the Psalter?" *Bibl. Sacra* 105 (1948) 44-55.

Id., "The Uses of the Psalter," *Bibl. Sacra* 105 (1948) 154-169. [cf. §8f]

Fensham, F. C., "Ps 68:23 in the Light of recently discovered Ugaritic Tablets," *JNES* (1960) 292f.

Id., "Widow, Orphan, and the Poor in Ancient Near Eastern Legal and Wisdom Literature," *JNES* 21 (1962) 129-139.

Id., "Psalm 29 and Ugarit," *Studies on the Psalms* 84-99.

Id., "Psalm 21 - A Covenant Song?" *ZAW* 77 (1965) 193-205.

Feuillet, A., "Le verset 7 du *Miserere* et le péché originel," *RSR* (1944) 5-26.

Id., "Souffrance et confiance en Dieu. Commentaire du Psaume XXII," *NRT* 70 (1948) 137-149.

Id., "Les psaumes eschatologiques du règne de Yahweh," *NRT* 83 (1951) 244-260; 352-363.

Fichtner, J., "Vom Psalmenbeten. Ist das Beten aller Psalmen der christlichen Gemeinde möglich und heilsam?" *Wort und Dienst* 3 (1952) 38-80.

Finkelstein, L., "The Origin of the Hallel (Pss 113-118)," *HUCA* 23, 2 (1950f) 319-337.

Fischer, B., *Die Psalmenfrömmigkeit der Märtyrerkirche* (Freiburg 1949). [also: *La Maison-Dieu* 27 (1951) 86-113]

Id., "Der Psalm *Qui habitat* in der *Quadragesima*," *ZfKatTh* 80 (1958) 421-429. [Pss 90-91]

Id., ed., *Ras Shamra Parallels. The Texts from Ugarit and the Hebrew Bible*, (1964) 20-38.

Fisher, L.R., ed., *Ras Shamra Parallels. The Texts from Ugarit and the Hebrew Bible,* vol. 1. AnalOr (Rome 1972), 1-70: "Literary phrases" (A. Schoors), 71-382: "Ugaritic-Hebrew Parallel Pairs" (M. Dahood & T. Penar), 383-452: "Flora, Fauna and Minerals" (J. M. Sasson).

Fitzmyer, J. A., *The Aramaic Inscriptions of Sefire.* Biblica et Orientalia, 19 (Rome 1967). [cf. *Ps 126:1]

Flashar, M., "Exegetische Studien zum Septuagintapsalter," ZAW 32 (1912) 81-116; 161-189; 241-268.

Forrester, W. F., "Sin and Repentance in the Psalms," *Clergy Rev.* 41 (1956), 663-674. [cf. §12e]

Franken, H. J., *The Mystical Communion with JHWH in the Book of Psalms* (Leiden 1954). includes a general study and a special analysis of Pss 16, 18, 25, 27, 31, 36, 63; cf. §12f]

Frethsim, T. W., "Psalm 132: a Form-Critical Study," *JBL* 86 (1967) 289-300.

Frost, S. B., "The Christian Interpretation of the Psalms," *CanJT* 5 (1959) 25-34.

Id., "Psalm 118: an Exposition," *CanJT* 7 (1961) 155-166.

Id., "Psalm 22: an Exposition," *CanJT* 8 (1962) 102-115.

Füglister, N., *Das Psalmengebet* (München 1965). [cf. *VD* 1966, p. 110]

Galdos, R., "La estrófica de los Salmos y su utilidad en la critica textual y en la exégesis," *EstBib* 5 (1946) 215--230.

Galling, K., "Der Beichtspiegel. Eine gattungsgeschichtliche Studie," ZAW 47 (1929) 125-130.

Garcia Cordero, M., *Libros de los Salmos,* I (BAC, Madrid 1963).

Garrone, G., *How to pray the Psalms* (Notre-Dame, Ind. 1965).

Gasnier, M., *Les Psaumes, école de spiritualité* (Mulhouse 1957).

Gaster, T. H., "Psalm 29," *JQR* 37 (1946f) 55-65.

Id., *Thespis, Ritual, Myth and Drama in the Ancient Near-East* (New York 1950). [cf. §8a]

Id., "Psalm 45," *JBL* 74 (1955) 239-251.

Gelin, A., "Les quatre lectures du Psaume 22," *BiViChr* 1 (1953) 31-39.

Id., "La prière du pèlerin au temple (Ps 84)," *BiViChr* 11 (1955) 88-92.

Id., *L'âme d'Israël dans le Livre* (Paris 1958) 46-68.

Id., "La question des 'relectures bibliques à l'intérieur d'une tradition vivante," *Sacra Pagina* I 203-215 [Ps 47; Ps 22 and Is 53; Zach 3:9; Ps 78; Ps 110:3 LXX]

Id., *The Psalms are our Prayers* (Collegeville, Minn.).

Gelineau, J., "Marie dans la prière chrétienne des Psaumes," *Maison-Dieu,* 38 (1954) (1954) 56ff.

Gelli, M., "Il Salmo del sacerdozio di Cristo (109/110)," *Ambrosius* 39 (1963) 197-212.

Gelston, A., "A Note on Yhwh mlk," *VT* 16 (1966) 507-512.

Gemser, B., "Gesinnungsethik im Psalter," *OTS* 13 (Leiden 1963) 1-20. [thought-morality in the Psalter]

George, A., "Jésus et les Psaumes," *A la rencontre...* 297-308.

Id., *Praying the Psalms. A guide for using the Psalms as Christian Prayer* (Notre-Dame, Indiana 1964).

Gese, H., "Zur Geschichte der Kultsänger am zweiten Temple," *Fs. O. Michel* (1963) 222-234. On Ps 22 see Id. in *ZTK* 1968 1-22.

Giavini, G., "La struttura letteraria del Salmo 86 (85)," *RBibIt* 14 (1966) 455-458.

Giblet, J., "Les Psaumes et la prière d'Israël," *ColMech* 42 (1957) 512-520.

Gierlich, A. M., *Der Lichtgedanke in den Psalmen. Eine terminologisch-exegetische Studie* (Freiburg i. Br. 1940).

Ginsberg, H. L., "A Phoenician Hymn in the Psalter," *Atti del XIX Congresso Internazionale degli Orientalisti* (Roma 1935) 472-476. [Ps 29]

Id., "Psalms and Inscriptions of Petition and Acknowledgement," *L. Ginzberg Jubilee Volume* (New York 1945) 159-171. [cf. §4b]

Id., "Some Emendations in the Psalms," *HUCA* 23, 1 (1950f) 97-104.

Glombitza, O., "Betende Bewältigung der Gottesleugnung. Versuch einer existentialen Interpretation der drei Psalmen 59; 94; 137," *NedTTs* 14 (1959f) 329-349.

Glueck, J. J., "Some Remarks on the Introductory Notes of the Psalms," *Studies on the Psalms* 30-39.

Goitein, S. D., "Ma'on - a Reminder of Sin" *JSS* 10 (1965) 52f.

Goldstain, J., *Le monde des Psaumes* (Paris 1964).

Gomes, M., *Salmo 18 (17). Unità, genere letterario e carattere messianico* (Romae 1956).

González, A., "El Salmo 75 y el Juicio escatológico," *EstBib* 21 (1962) 5-22.

Id., "Le Psaume 82," *VT* 13 (1963), 293-309.

Id., *El Libro de los Salmos. Introducción, versión y comentario* (Barcelona 1966).

González, Ruiz J. M., "Las teofanias en los Salmos," *EstBib* 13 (1954) 267-287.

Goodwin, D. W., "A rare spelling, or a rare root, in Ps LXVIII:10?" *VT* 14 (1964) 490f.

Gordis, R., "Psalm 9/10 — A textual and exegetical Study," *JQR* 48 (1957f) 104-122.

Gordon, C. H., *Ugaritic Textbook* (Roma 1965). [cf. §9d]

Gössmann, W. E., "Der Wandel des Gottesbildes in den Übersetzungen des 23. Psalms," *Münchener Theol.Z.* 5 (1954), 276-288. [the varying translations of Ps 23 reflect human ways of understanding God]

Goy, W. A., "Dieu a-t-il changé? Psaume 77," *Maqqel shâqédh... W. Vischer* (Montpellier 1960) 56-62.

Grail Breviary Psalter. The Daily Psalms, Canticles and Antiphons in Modern English (London 1966).

Gray, G.B., "The References to the 'King' in the Psalter, in their Bearing on Questions of Date and Messianic Beliefs," *JQR* 7 (1894) 658ff.

Gray, J., "The Kingship of God in the Prophets and Psalms," *VT* 11 (1961) 1-29.

Grelot, P., "Hofši (Ps LXXXVIII)," *VT* 14 (1964), 256-263.

Gressmann, H., "The Development of Hebrew Psalmody," *The Psalmists* [cf. D. C. Simpson] 1-22. [cf. §5c]

Griffith, L., *God in Man's Experience. The Activity of God in the Psalms* (London 1968).

Grosmann, W., *Poetic Devices in the Book of Psalms* (New York 1954). [cf. *JBL* 1956 160]

Gross, H., "Lässt sich in den Psalmen ein 'Thronbesteigungsfest Gottes' nachweisen?" *TrierTZ* 65 (1956) 24-40. [cf. §13a]

Gruenthaner, M., "The Future Life in the Psalms," *CBQ* 2 (1940) 57-63.

Gualandi, D., "Salmo 17 (16):13-14," *Bib* 37 (1956) 199-208.

Id., "Salmo 29 (28)," Bib 39 (1958), 478-485. [also *RBibIt* 1958 210-223: Pss 68, 141]

Guichou, P., *Les Psaumes commentés par la Bible*, I-III (Paris 1958f).

Id., "La prière de pèlerinage dans la Bible," *Rev. de Namur* 18 (1964) 347-368.

Guilding, A., "Some Obscure Rubrics and Lectionary Allusions in the Psalter," *JTS* 3 (1952) 41-55 [Pss 49:14b; 81:6; 32:6b; 110]

Id., "The Arrangement of the Pentateuch and Psalter," *The Fourth Gospel and Jewish Worship* (Oxford 1960) 24-44. [cf. §8c]

Guillaume, A., "The Meaning of *tôlēl* in Psalm 137:3," *JBL* 75 (1956) 143f.

Id., *Prophecy and Divination among the Hebrews and other Semites* (London 1938) 272-289.

Guillet, J., "L'entrée du juste dans Gloire," *BiVChr* 9 (1955) 58-70. [Ps 73:24]

Gunkel, R., *Schöpfung und Chaos in Urzeit und Endzeit* (Göttingen 1895).

Id., *Ausgewählte Psalmen* (4th ed.: Göttingen 1917).

Id., *Die Psalmen* (Göttingen 1926).

Id., "The Religion of the Psalms," in *What remains of the Old Testament and other essays*, transl. by A. K. Dallas (London 1938) 69-114.

Gunkel, H. and J. Begrich, *Einleitung in die Psalmen. Die Gattungen der religiösen Lyrik Israels* (Göttingen 1933). [cf. §7a]

Gunn, G. S., *God in the Psalms* (Edinburgh 1956). [cf. §11b]

Guthrie, H. H., Jr., *Israel's Sacred Songs: a Study of Dominant Themes* (New York 1966). [cf. *CBQ* 1966 505f]

Hall, B., "The Problem of Retribution in the Psalms," *Script.* 7 (1955) 84-92.

Haller, M., "Ein Jahrzehnt Psalmforschung," *Theol Rundschau* 1 (1929) 377-402.

Hanel, A., *Die Erlösergestalt in ausgewählten Psalmen* (Wien 1962). [typescript]

Haran, M., "The Ark and the Cherubim: their Symbolic Significance in Biblical Ritual," *IEJ* 9 (1959) 30-38; 89-94.

Hardy, E. R., "The date of Psalm 110," *JBL* 64 (1945) 385-390.

Häring, P., "Gross ist der Herr in unserer Gottesstadt: Ps 47 (48)," *Erbe und Auftrag* 36 (1960) 94-104.

Harmon, A.M., "Aspects of Paul's Use of the Psalms," *Westminster Theological Journal* 32 (1969) 1-23.

Harvey, J., "La typologie de l'Exode dans les Psaumes," *ScEcc* 15 (1963) 383-405. [cf. §5e, 14a]

Haspecker, J., "Ascendit Deus in jubilatione (Ps 46-47) und Himmelfahrt Christi," *GeistLeb* 28 (1955) 87-95.

Hauret, C., "L'interprétation des Psaumes selon l'école Myth and Ritual," *Rev. Sc. Rel.* 33 (1959) 321-346; 34 (1960) 1-34.

Id., "Un problème insoluble? La chronologie des psaumes," *RSR* 35 (1961) 225-256. [good survey of various opinions and methods in Psalm Chronology]

Id., *Notre Psautier* (Paris 1964).

Id., "Les ennemis-sorciers dans les supplications individuelles," *RechBib* 8 (Bruges-Paris 1967) 129-137.

Id., "Les Psaumes, études récentes état de la question," in *Où en sont les études bibliques?* (Paris 1968) 67-84.

Heinemann, H., "The date of Psalm 80," *JQR* 40 (1949) 297-302.

Hempel, J., "Mensch und König, Studie zu Psalm 8 und Hiob," *Forschungen und Fortschritte* 35 (1961) 119-123.

Herder's Commentary on the Psalms (Westminster, Md. 1961).

Hermission, H. -J., *Sprache und Ritus im altrisraelitischen Kult. Zur "Spiritualisierung" der Kultbegriffe im Alten Testament* (Neukirchen-Vluyn 1965).

Herrmann, J., "Der 103. Psalm: Dienst unter dem Wort," *Festgabe...H. Schreiner* Gütersloh (1953) 82-93.

Hesse, F., "Zur Frage der Wertung und der Geltung alttestamentlicher Texte Ps 109)," *Fs. F. Baumgärtel* (Erlangen 1959) 74-96.

Hjelt, A., "Sjukdomslidandet och fienderna i psalmerna," *Buhlfestskrift* 64-74. [cf. §12g]

Hofbauer, J., "Psalm 88 (89). Sein Aufbau, seine Herkunft und seine Stellung in der Theologie des AT," *Sacra Pagina* I, 504-510.

The Holy Bible (CV), III: *The Sapiential Books* (New Jersey 1955).

Hooke, S. H., (edit.), *Myth and Ritual. Essays on the Myth and Ritual of the Hebrews in Relation to the Cultic Pattern of the Ancient East* (Oxford 1933). [cf. §8d]

Id., (edit.), *The Labyrinth. Further Studies in the Relation between Myth and Ritual in the Ancient World* (London 1935).

Id., (edit.), *Myth, Ritual and Kingship. Essays on the Theory and Practice of Kingship in the Ancient Near East and in Israel* (Oxford 1958).

Hunt, I., "Recent Psalm Study," *Worship* 41 (1957) 85-98.

Huppenbauer, H.W., "God and Nature in the Psalms," *Ghana Bulletin of Theology* 3 (1969) 19-32.

Hurvitz, A., *The Identification of Post-Exilic Psalms by Means of Linguistic Criteria* (diss. Jerusalem 1967). [redacted in Hebrew]

Hyatt, C. M., *The Doctrine of Salvation in the Book of Psalms* (Fort Worth, Tex. 1952).

Inch, M.A., *Psychology in the Psalms. A Portrait of Man in God's World* (Waco 1969).

The Interpreter's Bible, IV, "Psalms, Proverbs" (New York 1955).

Iwry, S., "Notes on Psalm 68," *JBL* 71 (1952) 161-165.

Jacob, E., *Theology of the Old Testament* (London 1958). [cf. §11a]

James, F., *Thirty Psalmists: Personalities of the Psalter* (New York 1965).

Jänicke, H., "Futurum exactum. Eine Bibelarbeit über Ps 13..." *Evang. Theol.* 11 (1951f) 471-478.

Jasper, F. N., "Early Israelite traditions and the Psalter," *VT* 17 (1967) 50-59. [cf. §30]

Jefferson, H. G., "Psalm 93," *JBL* 71 (1952) 155-160.

Id., "Is Psalm 110 Canaanite?," *JBL* 73 (1954) 152-156.

Id., "Canaanite Literature and the Psalms," *The Personalist* 39, 4 (1958) 356-360.

Id., "The Date of Psalm LXVII," *VT* 12 (1962) 201-205.

Id., "Psalm LXXVII," *VT* 13 (1963) 87-91.

Jellicoe, S., "A Note on 'al mût (Ps 48:15)," *JTS* 49 (1949) 52f.

Id., "The Interpretation of Ps 73:24," *ExpTim* 67 (1955f) 209f.

Jeremias, Jörg, *Theophanie. Die Geschichte einer alttestamenlichen Gattung* (Neukirchen-Vluyn 1965). [cf. §13d, 14b]

Jiménez Gómez, H., "Los Generos Literarios en los Salmos," *Seminario Conciliar* 6 (1961) 9-25.

Jirku, A., "Die Sprache der Gottheit in der Natur," *TLZ* 76 (1951) 631.

Johnson, A. R., *The Cultic Prophet in Ancient Israel* (Cardiff 1944 and 1962). [cf. §8d]

Id., "The Psalms," *The Old Testament and modern Study* (H. H. Rowley, edit., Oxford 1951) 162-209.

Id., *Sacral Kingship in Ancient Israel* (Cardiff 1955).

Jones, G. H., "The decrees of Yahweh (Ps 2:7)," *VT* 15 (1965) 336-344.

Junker, H., "Unité, composition et genre littéraire des Psaumes IX et X," *RB* 60 (1953) 161-169.

Id., "Die Entstehungszeit des Ps. 78 und des Deuteronomiums," *Bib* 34 (1953) 487-500.

Id., "Der Strom, dessen Arme die Stadt Gottes erfreuen (Ps 46:5)," *Bib* 43 (1962) 197-201.

Id., "Salmos imprecatorios," *EncBib* VI (Barcelona 1965) 367ff.

Id., "Das theologische Problem der Fluchpsalmen," *Pastor Bonus* 5 (1940) 65-74.

Kaiser, O., "Erwägungen zu Psalm 101," *ZAW* 74 (1962) 195-205.

Kapelrud, A.S., "Nochmals *Jahwä mālāk*," *VT* 13 (1963) 229ff.

Id., "Scandinavian Research in the Psalms after Mowinckel," *Ann. Sw. Th. Inst.* 4 (1965) 148-162.

Kasser, R. (ed.), *Papyrus Bodmer XXIV: Psaumes 117-118* (Cologny-Genève 1967).

Kaznowski, Z., "Autor Ps 110 (109)," *Roczniki Teologiczno-Kanoniczne* (Lublin), 7, 3 (1960) 50-70.

Keel, O., *Feinde und Gottesleugner. Studien zum Image der Widersacher in den Individualpsalmen* (Stuttgart 1969).

Keet, C. C., *A Liturgical Study of the Psalter* (London 1928).

Id., *A Study of the Psalms of Ascents. A Critical and Exegetical Commentary upon Psalms CXX to CXXXIV* (London 1969). [see CBQ 1972, 83]

Kilian, R., "Ps 22 und das priesterliche Heilsorakel," *BZ* 12 (1968) 172-85.

King, E. G., "The Influence of the Triennial Cycle upon the Psalter," *JTS* 5 (1904) 203-213. [cf. I. Abrahams]

King, P. J., *Study of Psalm 45 (44)*, (Romae 1959).

Kirkpatrick, A. F., *The Book of the Psalms* I-III (Cambridge 1892-1903).

Kissane, E. J., *The Book of Psalms. Translated from a critically revised Hebrew Text with a Commentary* I, Ps 1-72 (Dublin 1953); II, Ps 73-150 (Dublin 1955).

Kleber, A., "Psalm 2, 9 in the Light of an Ancient Ceremony," *CBQ* 5 (1943) 63-67.

Kleist, J. A., "Toward a more rhythmical Rendering of the Psalms," *CBQ* 11 (1949) 66-75.

Knox, R., *The Psalms. A New Translation* (London 1947).

Koch, K., "Denn seine Güte währet ewiglich," *Evang. Theol.* 21 (1961) 537-544. [Pss 100, 106, 107, 118, 136]

15

Id., "Tempeleinlassliturgien und Dekaloge," *Studien zur Theologie der Altest. Über-lieferungen, Fs. G. von Rad* (Neukirchen 1961) 45-60. [Pss 15 + 24:4ff; Is 33: 14ff; Mi 6:6ff; Ez 18:5ff; cf. §32]

Koehler, L., "Jahwäh mālāk," *VT* 3 (1953), p. 188f. [cf. Ps 93:1]

Id., "Psalm 23," *ZAW* 68 (1956) 227-234.

König, E, *Die Psalmen eingeleitet, übersetzt und erklärt* (Gütersloh 1927).

Konus, W. J., *Dictionary of the New Latin Psalter of Pope Pius XII,* (Westminster, Md. 1959).

Koole, J. L., "Psalm 15 - eine königliche Einzugsliturgie?" *OTS* 13 (1963) 98-111.

Kragerud, A., *Die Hymnen der Pistis Sophia* (Oslo 1967). See *New Testament Abstracts,* vol XIII, p. 410.

Kraus, H. -J., *Worship in Israel,* tr. by G. Buswell (Oxford 1966). [cf. §7b, 13b]

Id., "Quelques remarques sur Psaume 139," *Studia biblica et semitica*: Fs. T. C. Vriezen (Vageningen 1966) 176-180.

Id., *Psalmen* (4th revised and bibliographically updated edit., Neukirchen 1972). [st edit. 1961]

Krinetzki, L., "Zur Poetik und Exegese von Psalm 48," *BZ* 4 (1960) 70-97.

Id., "Psalm 110 (109). Eine Untersuchung seines dichterischen Stils," *Theol. Blätter* 51 (1961) 110-121.

Id., "Psalm 30 (29) in stilistisch-exegetischer Betrachtung," *ZKatTh* 83 (1961) 345-360.

Id., "Der anth logische Stil des 46. Psalms und seine Bedeutung für die Datierungsfrage," *MüTZ* 12 (1961) 52-71.

Id., "Psalm 5. Eine Untersuchung seiner dichterischen Struktur und seines theologischen Gehaltes," *Tüb, Th. Qu.* 142 (1962) 23-46.

Id., "Jahwe ist uns Zuflucht und Wehr. Eine stilistisch-theologische Auslegung von Ps 46 (45)," *BiLeb* 3 (1962) 26-42.

Krings, H., *Der Mensch vor Gott. Die Daseinserfahrung in den Psalmen* (Würzburg 1952).

Kroeze, J. H., "Some remarks on recent trends in the exegesis of the Psalms," *Studies on the Psalms...* 40-47.

Kruse, H., "Fluminis impetus laetificat Civitatem Dei (Ps 45-46:5)" *VD* 27 (1949) 23-27.

Id., "Two hidden comparatives: Observations on Hebrew Style," *JSS* 5 (1960) 333-347.

Id., "Archetypus Psalmi 104 (103)," *VD* 29 (1951) 31-43.

Küchler, F., "Das priesterliche Orakel in Israel und Juda," *Fs. W. G. von Baudissin,* *BZAW* 33 (1918) 285-301.

Kühlewein, J., *Das Reden von Geschichte in den Psalmen* (Diss. Heidelberg 1966).

Knutz. J. K., *An Examination of Theophany in the Old Testament, with special reference to Theophanic contexts in the Psalter* (New York 1963). [microfilm]

Kunz, L., "Die formale Anklage des 95. Psalms," *MüTZ* 4 (1953) 349-356.

Id., "Die Gestalt des 84. Psalmes," *TGl* 45 (1955), 22-34.

Id., "Selah, Titel und authentische Gliederung der Psalmen," *TGl* 46 (1956), 363-369. [Ps 84]

Id., "Zur symmetrischen Struktur der Psalmen," *Misc. H. Anglés* I (Barcelona 1958-1961) 453-464.

Id., "Zur Liedgestalt der ersten fünf Psalmen," *BZ* 7 (1963) 261-270.

Labuschagne, C. J., "Some remarks on the Translation and Meaning of *'amarti* in the Psalms," *OTW* 5 (1962) 27-33. [cf. *Studies on the Psalms*]

Lacan, M. F., "Le mystére de la prière dans le Psaume 119," *Lumière et Vie* 23 (1955) 125-142 [677-694].

Id., "Les Psaumes, prière de l'Église," *Vie Spir.* 112 (1965) 519-530.

Lamb, J. A., *The Psalms in Christian Worship* (London 1962). [history of the Liturgical Use of the Psalms]

Lambert, W. G., "Three Literary Prayers of the Babylonians," *Archiv. f. Orientforschung* 19 (1959-60) 47-66.

Lamparter, H., *Das Buch der Psalmen übersetzt und ausgelegt*, I-II (Stuttgart 1958f).

Id., *Das Psalmengebet in der Christengemeinde. Eine Einführung in das Gebetbuch der Bibel* (Stuttgart 1965).

Laridon, V., "Psalmorum doctrina de retributione," *Col. Brug.* 44 (1948) 283-287.

Lattey, C., *The Psalter in the Westminster Version of the Sacred Scriptures* London 1945). [seeks to reconstruct the original metre: cf. §6]

Lauha, A., *Die Geschichtsmotive in den alttestamentlichen Psalmen. Acta Acad. Scient. Fennicae*, 56, 1 (1945).

Le Mat, L. A. F., *Textual Criticism and Exegesis of Psalm XXXVI. A Contribution to the study of the Hebrew Book of Psalms* (Utrecht 1957). [also treats of the "titles" of the psalms and of the "evildoers"]

Leonardi, G., "Note su alcuni versetti del Salmo 104," *Bib* 49 (1968) 238-42.

Leslie, E. A., *The Psalms. Translated and Interpreted in the Light of Hebrew Life and Worship* (New York 1949). [cf. *JBL* 1950 184ff]

Leveen, J., "Psalm 10 (Vulg. 9:II): a Reconstruction," *JTS* 45 (1944) 16-21.

Id., "A Note on Ps 10:17-18," *JBL* 67 (1948) 249f.

Id., "The textual problems of Psalm 17," *VT* 11 (1961) 48-54.

Id., "The textual problems of Psalm VII," *VT* 16 (1966) 439-445.

Id., "Textual Problems in the Psalms," *VT* 21 (1971) 48-58.

Liber Psalmorum cum Canticis Breviarii Romani, nova e textibus primigeniis interpretatio latina cum notis criticis et exegeticis cura Professorum Pontificii Instituti Biblici edita (Romae 1945). [cf. Foreword and A. Bea, J. Bloch, B. Steiert, T. E. Bird, J. C. M. Travers]

Liebreich, L. J., "The Songs of Ascents and the Priestly Blessing," *JBL* 74 (1955) 33-36. [cf. §3c]

Id., "Pss 34 and 145 in the Light of their Key-Words," *HUCA* 27 (1956) 181-192.

Id., "The Liturgical Use of Ps 78:38," *Studies A. A. Neumann* (Leiden 1962) 365-374.

Lilly, J. L., "The Sacred Duty of Hating and Imprecating," *AmER* 115 (1946) 271-277.

Lindblom, J., "Die Eschatologie des 49. Psalms," *Horae Soederblomianae*, I (1944) 21-27.

Linton, O., "Interpretation of the Psalms in the Early Church," *SPatrist* 4 (Berlin 1961) 143-156.

Lipiński, E., "Les Psaumes de la royauté de Yahve dans l'exégèse moderne," *Le Psautier* [cf. R. De Langhe] 133-272.

428

Id., "Yahweh mâlāk," *Bib* 44 (1963) 405-460.

Id., "Les Psaumes du Règne: l'Intronisation royale de Dieu," *AssSeign* 9 (1964) 7-22.

Id., *La royauté de Yahvé dans le poesie et le culte de l'ancien Israël* (Bruxelles 1965). [cf. *JBL* 1966 498f; RB 1966 420-25 and §18]

Id., "Juges 5:4-5 et Psaumes 68:8-11," *Bib* 48 (1967) 185-206.

Id., *Le poème royal du Psaume LXXXIX, 1-5. 20-38* (Paris 1967). [cf. *VD* 1967 366f.]

Id., "Macarismes et psaumes de congratulation," *RB* 75 (1968) 321-67.

Id., *La liturgie pénitentielle dans la Bible*. Lectio Divina 52 (Paris 1969).

Loewenstamm, S.E., "The Expanded Colon in Ugaritic and Biblical Verse," *JSS* 14 (1969) 176-96.

Lohfink, N., "Herausgeführt in der Freiheit," *GeistLeb* 38 (1965) 81-84. [Ps 66:1-12]

Louis, C., *The Theology of Psalm VIII. A Study of the Traditions of the Text and the Theological Import* (Washington 1946). [the psalm is messianic, but not in the strict sense]

Lovitt, H. B., *A Critical and Exegetical Study of Ps 139* (Diss. Columbia Univ., N.Y. 1964. Ann Arbor 1964, Univ. Microfilms).

Lowth, R., *De sacra poësi Hebraeorum praelectiones academicae Oxonii habitae* (Oxford 1753).

Lubsczyk, H., "Einheit und heilsgeschichtliche Bedeutung von Ps 114/115 (113)," *BZ* 11 (1967) 161-173.

Luger, A., *Der Messianismus der Psalmen* (Wien 1959). [typescript]

Lussier, E., "The New Latin Psalter: an exegetical Commentary," *CBQ* 9 (1947) to 12 (1950): a series of articles on Pss 1 to 33.

Luyten, J., "Het Zelfbeklag in de Psalmen," *ETL* 39 (1963) 501-538.

Lyonnet, S., "La notion de justice de Dieu en Rom III:5 et l'exégèse paulinienne du Miserere," *Sacra Pagina* II 342-356.

MacKenzie, R. A. F., *The Book of Psalms*, O. T. Reading Guide, 23 (Collegeville 1967. [a selection]

Maertens, T., *Jérusalem, Cité de Dieu (Pss 120-128)*, 2nd edit. (Bruges 1954).

Id., "La catéchèse des Psaumes," *Par. Lit.* 40 (1958) 257-294.

Maggioni, B., "Osservazioni sul Salmo 29 (28): Afferte Domino," *BibOr* 7 (1965) 245-251.

Magne, J., "Le texte du Psaume XXXV et l'hypothèse de sa transcription primitive sur deux colonnes," *RB* 54 (1947) 42-53.

Id., "Répétitions de mots et exégèse dans quelques Psaumes et le Pater," *Bib* 39 (1958) 177-197. [Pss. 1, 29, 51, 91, 123, 137]

Id., "Le texte du Psaume XXII et sa restitution sur deux colonnes," *Sem* 11 (1961) 29-41.

Maier, J., *Das altisraelitische Ladeheiligtum*, BZAW 93 (Berlin 1965).

Maillot, A.-A. Lelièvre, *Les Psaumes*, vols. I-II (Genéve 1962 and 1966). [Pss 1-100]

Mand, F., "Die Eigenständigkeit der Danklieder des Psalters als Bekenntnislieder," *ZAW* 70 (1958) 185-199.

Mannati, E. & E. de Solms, *Les Psaumes*, I-IV (Bruges 1966-68).

Martin-Achard, R., "La prière d'un malade: quelques remarques sur le Psaume 38," *Verbum Caro* 12 (1958) 77-82.

Id., "La prière des malades dans le psautier," *Lumière et Vie* 86 (1958) 25-43.

Id., "Notes bibliques: Remarques: sur le Psaume 22," *VerbC* 17 (1963) 78-87.

Id., *Approche des Psaumes* (Neuchâtel 1969).

Martindale, C. C., *Towards Loving the Psalms* (New York 1940).

May, H. G., "Some cosmic Connotations of *mayim rabbim,* many waters," *JBL* 74 (1955) 9-21.

Mayer, H. H., *The Modern Reader's Book of Psalms* (New York 1944).

McCarthy, C.B., *Ps 132: A Methodological Analysis* (Diss. Marquette Univ., Milwaukee, cf. *DissAbstr* 29, 1968, 3210f-A).

McClellan, W. H., "Obscurities in the Latin Psalter," *CBQ* 1 (1939) to 6 (1944): a series of articles.

McKeating, H., "Divine Forgiveness in the Psalms," *ScotJT* 18 (1965) 69-83.

McKenzie, J. L., "A Note on Ps 73 (74):13-15," *TS* 11 (1950) 275-282.

Id., "Royal Messianism," *CBQ* 19 (1957) 25-52.

Id., "The Imprecations of the Psalter," *AmER* 111 (1944) 81-96.

McNeill, J., *The Twenty-Third Psalm* (Westwood, N.J. 1965).

Meek, T. J., "The Metrical Structure of Psalm 23," *JBL* 67 (1948) 233-235.

Mélanges bibliques rédigés en l'honneur de André Robert (Paris 1957). [cf. J. Coppens, A. Deissler, A. Descamps]

Mercati, J., *Psalteri Hexapli reliquiae cura et studio Ioh. Card. Mercati editae*-I, (Bibl. Vaticana 1958).

Merrill, A. L., "Psalm XXIII and the Jerusalem Tradition," *VT* 15 (1965) 354-360.

Meysing, J., "A Text-Reconstruction of Ps CXVII (CXVIII):27," *VT* 10 (1960) 130-137.

Michel, D., "Studien zu den sogenannten Thronbesteigungspsalmen," *VT* 6 (1956) 40-68.

Id., *Tempora und Satzstellung in den Psalmen* (Bonn 1960).

Miller, A., "Gibt es direkt messianische Psalmen?" *Misc. Bibl. B. Ubach* (Montserrat 1953 201-209.

Id., "Die psalmen in christlicher Sicht," *BiLit* 24 (1956f) 134-140.

Miller, P. D., "Two critical Notes on Psalm 68 and Deuteronomy 33," *HarvTR* 57 (1964) 240-243.

Moeller, H. R., "Biblical Research and Old Testament Translation," *BiTrans* 13 (1962) 16-22. [Ps 8:2]

Möller, H. "Strophenbau der Psalmen," *ZAW* 50 (1932) 240-256.

Montagnini, F., "Illuminas te mirabiliter a montibus aeternis (Ps 76:5)," *VD* 40 (1962) 258-263.

Montgomery, J. A., "Recent Developments in the Study of the Psalter," *AnglTR* 16 (1934) 185-198.

Id., "Stanza-formation in Hebrew Poetry," *JBL* 64 (1945) 379-384.

Moos, M. F., *Les Psaumes, prières chrétiennes* (Paris 1956).

Morag, S., "Light is sown (Ps 97:11)," *Tarbiz* 33 (1963) 140-148.

Morant, P., *Das Psalmengebet. Neu übersetzt und für das Leben erklärt* (Schwyz 1948).

Moré, P., "Métaphores de la protection divine dans les Psaumes," *RClAfr* 10 (1955) 577-584.

Moreton, M. J., "The Sacrifice of Praise," *Church Qu. Rev.* 165 (1964) 481-494.

Morgenstern, J., "The Book of the Covenant," *HUCA* 5 (1928), 1-151. [the greater part is devoted to the Ark]

Id., "Biblical Theophanies," *Z.f Assyr.* 25 (1911), 139-193 and 28 (1914) 15-60.

Id., "The Gates of Righteousness," *HUCA* 6 (1929) 1-37. [Pss 24 and 118]

Id., "The Mythical Background of Psalm 82," *HUCA* 14 (1939) 29-126.

Id., "Psalm 48," *HUCA* 16 (1941f) 1-95. [cf. JBL 1945 285f]

Id., "Psalm 8 and 19 A.," *HUCA* 19 (1945f) 491-523.

Id., "Psalm 23," *JBL* 65 (1946) 13-24.

Id., "Psalm 11," *JBL* 69 (1950) 221-231.

Id., "Psalm 126," *Homenaje a Millás Vallicrosa* II (Barcelona 1956) 107-117.

Id., "The Cultic Setting of the Enthronement Psalms," *HUCA* 35 (1964) 1-42.

Mowan, O., "Quatuor Montes Sacri in Ps 89:13?" *VD* 41 (1963) 11-20.

Mowinckel, S., *Psalmenstudien* I-VI (Oslo 1921-1924).

Id., "Zum Problem der Hebräischen Metrik," *Fs. A. Bertholet* (Tübingen 1950) 379-394.

Id., "Traditionalism and Personality in the Psalms," *HUCA* 22 (1950f) 205-231.

Id., *Zum israelitischen Neujahr und zur Deutung der Thronbesteigungspsalmen* (Oslo 1952).

Id., "Metrischer Aufbau und Textkritik an Psalm 8 illustriert," *Studia Orientalia* I, Pedersen... (Hauniae 1953) 250-262.

Id., *Der achtundsechzigste Psalm* (Oslo 1954). [cf. *RB* 1956 129-132]

Id., "Psalm Criticism between 1900 and 1935. Ugarit and Psalm Exegesis," *VT* 5 (1955) 13-33.

Id., "Psalms and Wisdom," *Wisdom in Israel and in the ancient Near-East, Fs. H. H. Rowley, VTSuppl.* 3 (1955) 204-224.

Id., *Real and Apparent Tricola in Hebrew Psalm Poetry* (Oslo 1958).

Id., *The Psalms in Israel's Worship,* I-II (Oxford 1962): a translation by D. R. Ap-Thomas of the fully revised text of *Offersang og Sangoffer,* Oslo 1951. [will be quoted as Mowinckel I or II; see II 282f, for a complete list of M.'s works, and §5d, 7b, 8a, 13a, 14d on some of his views]

Muilenburg, J., "Psalm 47," *JBL* 63 (1944) 235-256.

Id., "A Study in Hebrew rhetoric, repetition and style," *VTSuppl* I (Leyden 1953) 128-149.

Müller, H.-P., "Die Gattung des 139. Psalms," *Zeitschrift der Deutschen Morgenländischen Gesellschaft Supplementa* I (1969) 345-55.

Munch, P. A., "Einige Bemerkungen zu den 'aniyyim und den resha'im in den Psalmen," *Le Monde Oriental* 30 (1936) 13-26.

Id., "Das Problem des Reichtums in den Psalmen 37, 49, 73," *ZAW* 55 (1937) 36-46.

Muntingh, L. M., "A few social concepts in the Psalms and their relation to the Canaanite residential area," *Studies on the Psalms* 48-57.

Murphy, R.E., "A New Classification of Literary Forms in the Psalms," *CBQ* 21 (1959) 83-87.

Id., *Seven Books of Wisdom* (Milwaukee 1960) 28-52.

Id., "Psalms," *Jerome Biblical Commentary* 569-602.

Nácar, E., "Rey y sacerdote. Salmo 110," *EstBib* 5 (1946) 281-302.

Nagel, G., "A propos des rapports du Psaume 104 avec les textes égyptiens," *Fs für A. Bertholet* (Tübingen 1950) 395-403.

Neusner, J., *The 89th Psalm; Paradigm of Israel's Faith* (London 1965).

Neuwirth, A., *"kis'akā 'elōhîm. Dein Thron, O Gott"* (Ps 45:7). *"Untersuchungen zum Gottkönigtum im Alten Orient und im Alten Testament"* (Diss. Graz 1963f).

Nicolsky, N., *Spuren magischer Formeln in den Psalmen*, BZAW 46 (Giessen 1927).

Nober, P., "De torrente in via bibet (Ps 110:7a)," *VD* 26 (1948) 351-353.

Nogosek, R., *The Royal Psalms in Form Criticism* (Paris 1961). [typescript]

Nötscher, F., *Die Psalmen* (Würtzburg 1947). [cf. *ETL* 1966 686f]

Obermann, J., "An Antiphonical Psalm from Ras Shamra," *JBL* 55 (1936) 21-42.

O'Callaghan, R. T., "A Note on the Canaanite Background of Psalm 82," *CBQ* 15 (1953) 311-314.

Id., "Echoes of Canaanite Literature in the Psalms," *VT* 4 (1954) 164-176.

Oesterley, W. O. E., *A Fresh Approach to the Psalms* (London 1937).

Id., *The Psalms translated with textcritical and exegetical Notes*, I-II (London 1939 + 1954).

Ohlmeyer, A., *Reichtum der Psalmen, Erschlossen von Heiligen aller Christlicher Zeiten*, I-II (Frankfurt 1965).

Osty, E., *Les Psaumes. Traduction nouvelle avec introduction et notes* (Paris 1960).

Ouellette, J., "Variantes qumrâniennes du livre des Psaumes," *RQum* 7, 25 (1969) 105-23.

Palmer, M., "The Cardinal Points in Psalm 48," *Bib* 46 (1965) 357f.

Pannier, E.-H. Renard, *Les Psaumes. La Sainte Bible, L. Pirot* (Paris 1950).

Páramo, S. del, *Libro de los Salmos, EncBib* VI (Barcelona 1965) 269-285.

Pascual, B., "Las dos comparaciones del Salmo 133 y su transcendencia doctrinal," *EstBib* 17 (1958) 189-197.

Paterson, J., *The Praises of Israel. Studies Literary and Religious in the Psalms* (New York 1950).

Patton, J. H., *Canaanite Parallels in the Book of Psalms* (Baltimore 1944). [cf. *CBQ* 1946 104f]

Pautrel, R., "Si dormiatis inter medios cleros (Ps 68:14)," *RSR* 33 (1946) 359-367.

Id., "Absorpti sunt juncti petrae judices eorum (Ps 141-140:6)," *RSR* 44 (1956) 219-228.

Id., "Essai sur le Psaume 57 (58):8ss," *RSR* 44 (1956) 566-572.

Id., "Immola Deo sacrificium laudis (Ps 50:14)," *Mélanges Bibliques...*234-240.

Id., "Sur le texte de Ps 17 (16):14," *RSR* 46 (1958) 78-84.

Id., "Le style de cour et le Psaume 72," *A la rencontre de Dieu...* 157-163.

Id., "La Mort est leur pasteur (sur le texte de Ps 49-48:14, 15)," *RSR* 54 (1966) 530-536.

Pax, E., "Studien zur Theologie von Ps 29," *BZ* 6 (1962) 93-100.

Id., "Studien zum Vergeltunsproblem der Psalmen," *Liber Annuus* 11 (1960f) 56-112.

Pedersen, J., *Israel, its Life and Culture*, I-II; III-IV (London-Copenhagen 1926 and 1940).

Peinador, M., "Los attributos 'misericordia,' 'justitia,' 'veritas' en los Salmos," *Virtud y Letras* 52 (1954) 228-241.

Id., *Los Salmos, plegaría de la Iglesia y de los fieles* (Madrid 1957).

Peters, J. P., *The Psalms as Liturgies* (New York 1922).

Petuchowski, J. J., *"Hoshi'ah na in* Ps 118:23 — A Prayer for Rain," *VT* 5 (1955) 266-271.

Pfeiffer, R. H., *Introduction to the Old Testament* (New York-London 1941, 1948). [cf. §5b]

Philonenko, M., L'origine esséniene des cinq psaumes syriaques de David, *Sem* 9 (1959) 35-48.

Piatti, T., *Il Libro dei Salmi. Versione omòfona dall'originale ebraico criticamente e metricamente ricostrutto, con introduzione critica sulla poesia e la metrica ebraica* (Rome 1954).

Pidoux, G., *Du portique à l'autel. Introduction aux Psaumes* (Neuchâtel 1959).

Pierik, M., *The Psalter in the Temple and the Church* (Washington 1957). [the musical adaptation of the Psalms]

Pinto B. De, "The Torah and the Psalms," *JBL* 86 (1967) 154-74.

Podechard, E., "Psaume LXVIII," *RB* 54 (1947) 502-520.

Id., "Psaume 110," *Etudes de critique et d'histoire religieuse, volume offert à L. Vaganay* (Lyon 1948) 7-24.

Id., *Le Psautier*, I: Pss 1-75. *Notes critiques. Traduction littérale et explication historique* (Lyon 1949). [also: Pss 95-100 + 110, Lyon 1954]

Porter, J. R., "The Interpretations of 2 Sm. VI and Psalm CXXII," *JTS* 5 (1954) 161-173.

Id., "Psalm XLV:7," *JTS* 12 (1961) 51-53.

Porubčan, S., "Il Salmo De Profundis (Sal 130)," *Aloisiana* 1 (1960) 3-17.

Power, E., "Sion or Si'on in Psalm 133 (Vulg 132)?" *Bib* 3 (1922) 342-349.

Id., "The shepherd's two rods in modern Palestine and in some passages of the Old Testament (Ps 23:4; Zc 11:7ff; 1 S 17:43)," *Bib* 9 (1928) 434-442.

Press, R., "Die eschatologische Ausrichtung des 51. Psalms," *TZBas* 11 (1955) 241-249.

The Psalms: Fides Translation (Notre-Dame, Ind. 1963).

The Psalms, A Prayer Book, also the Canticles of the Roman Breviary (Benziger, New York 1945). [cf. *CBQ* 1946 355-359]

Puukko, A., "Der Feind in den Alttestamentlichen Psalmen" *OTS* VII (1950) 47-65.

Quell, G., *Das kultische Problem der Psalmen* (Berlin 1926). [cf. §8f]

Rabinowitz, L. "Does Midrash Tillim reflect the Triennial Cycle of Psalms?" *JQR* 26 (1935f) 349-368.

Rabinowitz, I., "The Existence of a hitherto unknown Interpretation of Ps 107 among the Dead Sea Scrolls," *BA* 14 (1951) 50ff.

Rabinowitz, L. J., "The Psalms in Jewish Liturgy," *Historia Judaica* 6 (1944), 109-122. [cf. CBQ 1945 353]

Rad, G. von, "Erwägungen zu den Königspsalmen," *ZAW* 57 (1940-41) 216-222.

Id., "Gerechtigkeit' und 'Leben' in der Kultsprache der Psalmen," *Fs. für A. Bertholet* (Tübingen 1950) 418-437.

Id., "Hiob XXXVIII und die altägyptische Weisheit," *VTSuppl.* III (1955) 293-301. [for Ps 148]

Id., *Old Testament Theology,* I-II (Edinburgh-London 1962, 1965).

Rahlfs, A., *'Ani und 'anaw in den Psalmen* (Göttingen 1892). [cf. §12a]

Ramlot, M. L., 'Hymne à la gloire du Créateur, Psaume 104," *BiViChr* 31 (1960) 39-47.

Ravenelli, V., Psalmus 89 (88): *Textus-Compositio-Doctrina* (Romae 1957).

Reinelt, H., *Die altorientalische und biblische Weisheit und ihr Einfluss auf den Psalter* (Diss., Freiburg i. Br. 1966).

Rees, W., "The New Latin Psalter," *Scripture,* 4 (1950) 205-212.

Rendtorff, R., "El, Ba'al und Jahwe." Erwägungen zum Verhältnis von kanaanäischer und israelitischer Religion," *ZAW* 78 (1966) 277-292.

Rengstorf, K. H., "Old and New Testament Traces of a Formula of the Judaean Royal Ritual," *NT* 5 (1962) 229-244.

Rhodes, A. B., *Creation and Salvation in the Psalter* (Chicago 1952).

Richardson, R. D., "The Psalms as Christian Prayer and Praises," *AnglTR* 42 (1960) 326-346.

Ricotti, A. L., "I Salmi nel Culto Giudaico," *BibOr* 3 (1961) 161-174.

Ridderbos, N. H., *Psalmen en Cultus* (Kampen 1950).

Id., "Jahwäh malak," *VT* 4 (1954) 87-89.

Id., *De "Werkers van Ongerechtigheid" in de individuelle Psalmen* (Kampen 1939).

Id., *De Psalmen,* I: Pss 1-41 (Kampen 1962). In German, 1971 (BZAW 117).

Id., "The Psalms: Style-Figures and Structures (certain considerations, with special references to Pss 22, 25, 45)," *OTS* XIII (1963) 43-76.

Id., "The Structure of Psalm 40," *OTS* XIV (1965) 296-304.

Id., "Psalm 51:5-6," *Studia biblica et semitica: Fs. T. C. Vriezen* (Vageningen 1966) 299-312.

Id., *Die Psalmen: stilistische Verfahren und Aufbau mit besonderer Berücksichtingung von Ps 1-41* BZAW 117 (Berlin 1972).

Rinaldi, G., "Il Salmo 23 (Volg 22)," *BibOr* 3 (1961) 81-85.

Id., "Synagoga deorum (Ps 82)," *BibOr* 7 (1965) 9-11.

Id., "Al termine delle due vie (Salmo 1)," *BibOr* 9 (1967) 69-75.

Ringgren, H., "Einige Bemerkungen zum LXXIII Psalm," *VT* 3 (1953) 265-272.

Id., "Quelques traits essentiels de la piété des Psaumes," *Mélanges Bibliques...* 205-213.

Id., *The Faith of the Psalmists* (London 1963). [§8d, 12f]

Id., "Enthronement Festival or Covenant Renewal?," *Biblical Research,* 7 (1962) 45-48.

Id., *Psalmen* (Stuttgart (1971).

Rios, R., "A Call to Worship (Ps 94, Vulg.)," *Scripture* 1 (1946) 74-77.

Id., "Thirst for God (Psalms 41 and 42)," *Scripture* 2 (1947) 34-38.

Robert, A., "Considérations sur le messianisme du Psaume 2," *RSR* 39 (1951) 88-98. [see also above: *Mélanges Bibliques...*]

Id., "L'exégèse des Psaumes selon les méthodes de la 'Formgeschichte.' Exposé et critique," *Misc. Bibl. B. Ubach* (Montserrat 1953) 211-225. [cf. J. Coppens in *Le Psautier,* R. De Langhe edit. 31ff + §7b]

Robinson, H. W., "The Inner Life of the Psalmists," *The Psalmists* [cf. D. C. Simpson] 45-66.

Id., "The Social Life of the Psalmists," *ibid.* 67-86.

Robinson, T. H., "The God of the Psalmists," *ibid.* 23-44. [cf. §8d]

Id., "The Eschatology of the Psalmists," *ibid.* 87-108.

Id., "Basic Principles of Hebrew poetic form," *Fs. A. Bertholet* (Tübingen 1950) 438-450.

Robinson, W., "Psalm 118. A Liturgy for the Admission of a Proselyte," *Church Qu. Rev.* 144 (1947) 179-183.

Rodd, C. S., *Psalms 73-150. Epworth's Preacher's Commentary* (London 1964).

Roifer, A., "Psalm 73," *Tarbiz* 32 (1963) 109-113.

Rose, A., "L'influence des Psaumes sur les annonces et les récits de la Passion et de la Résurrection dans les Évangiles," *Le Psautier* [cf. R. De Langhe] 297-356.

Id., "Le Psaume 44 (45). Son interprétation chrétienne," *QuLitPar* 36, 4 (1955) 178-189.

Id., *Psaumes et prière chrétienne* (Bruges 1965).

Rosenberg, R. A., "Yahweh becomes King," *JBL* 85 (1966) 297-307.

Rosenstock, E.-E. Huessy, "Vivit Deus," *In memoriam Ernst Lohmeyer* (Stuttgart 1951) 250-260. [Ps 18:47]

Ross, J. P., "Yahweh Seba'ot in Samuel and Psalms," *VT* 17 (1967) 76-92. [cf. §18a]

Rowley, H. H., "The Text and Structure of Psalm 2," *JTS* 42 (1941) 143-154.

Id., "Melchizedek and Zadok (Gen 14 and Ps 110)," *Fs. für A. Bertholet* (Tübingen 1950) 461-472.

Id., *Worship in Ancient Israel* (London 1967) 173-212, "Psalmody and Music."

Sabbe, M., "Geborgenheid bij God, Ps 96," *ColBG* 7 (1961) 68-85.

Sabourin, L., *Un classement littéraire des Psaumes* (Bruges 1964). [= *ScEcc* 1964 23-58]

Sainte-Marie, D. H., de, *S. Hieronymi Psalterium juxta Hebraeos. Edition critique* (Libr. Edit. Vaticana 1954).

Salguero, J., "Quien es el 'desamparado' del salmo 22?," *CiTom* 84 (1957) 3-35.

Salmon, P., *Les tituli psalmorum des manuscrits latins* (Paris 1959). [cf. *TS* 1966 94f]

San Pedro, E., "Problemata philologica Ps. XIV," *VD* 45 (1967) 65-78.

Sanders, J. A., "The Scroll of Psalms (11QPss) from Cave 11," *BASOR* 165 (1962) 11-15.

Id., "Ps 151 in 11QPss," *ZAW* 75 (1963) 73-86.

Id., *The Psalms Scroll of Qumrân Cave 11 (11Psᵃ), Discoveries in the Judaean Desert of Jordan,* IV (Oxford 1965).

Id., "Variorum in the Psalms Scroll (11 QPsa)," *HarvTR* 59 (1966) 83-94.

Id., *The Dead Sea Psalms Scroll* (Cornell Univ. Press, Ithica, N.Y., 1967).

Sarna, N. M., "The Psalm for the Sabbath Day (Ps 92)," *JBL* 81 (1962) 155-168.

Id., "Psalm 89: a Study in inner Biblical Exegesis," *P. W. Lown Institute, Brandeis Univ., Studies and Texts* 1 (1963) 29-46.

Sauer, G., *Die strafende Gerechtigkeit Gottes in den Psalmen. Eine frömmigkeitsgeschichtliche Untersuchung* (Halle 1956).

Id., "I nemici nei Salmi," *Prot.* 13 (1958) 201-207.

Id., "Erwägungen zum Alter des Psalmendichtung in Israel," *TZBas* 22 (1966) 81-95.

Savignac, J. de, "Essai d'interprétation du Psaume CX à l'aide de la litterature égyptienne," *OTS* 9 (1951) 107-135.

Scammon, J. H., *Living with the Psalms* (Valley Forge, Pa. 1967).

Id., "Another Look at Ps 104," *The Journal of Hebraic Studies* 1, 1 (1969) 1-2.

Scharf, A. M., "Quaedam commentationes in Ps 52:7," *VD* 38 (1960) 213-222.

Schedl, C., "Aus dem Bache am Wege. Textkritische Bemerkungen zu Ps 110 (109): 7," *ZAW* 73 (1961) 290-297.

Id., "Die Pfade des Rechtsbrechers' orhôt-pāriṣ (Ps 17:4)," *BZ* 6 (1962) 100-102.

Id., "Psalm 8 in ugaritischer Sicht," *Forschungen und Fortschritte* 38 (1964) 183-185.

Id., "Die 'Heiligen' und die 'Herrlichen' in Ps 16:1-4," *ZAW* 76 (1964) 171-175.

Id., "Neue Vorschläge zu Text und Deutung des Psalmes XLV," *VT* 14 (1964) 310-318.

Scheele, P.-W., *Opfer des Wortes. Gebete der Heiden aus fünf Jahrtausenden* (Paderborn 1960).

Scheifler, J. R., "El Salmo 22 y la Crucifixión del Señor," *EstBib* 24 (1965) 5-83.

Schildenberger, J., "Zur Textkritik von Ps 45 (44)," *BZ* 3 (1959) 31-43.

Id., "Tod und Leben. Eine Auslegung von Ps 30 (29)," *BibKirche* 13 (1958) 110-115.

Id., "Bemerkungen zum Strophenbau der Psalmen," *EstE* 34 (1960) 673-687.

Id., "Psalm 78 (77) und die Pentateuchquellen," *Lex Tua Veritas, Fs. H. Junker* (Trier 1961) 231-256.

Schilling, O., "Noch einmal die Fluchpsalmen," *TGl* 47 (1957) 177-185.

Schmid, H. H., *Wesen und Geschichte der Weisheit. Eine Untersuchung zur Altorientalischen und Israelitischen Weisheitsliteratur*, BZAW 101 (Berlin 1966). [Wisdom in Israel: pp. 144-201; as personified: 149-154]

Schmid, R., "Die Fluchpsalmen im christlichen Gebet," *Theologie im Wandel. Fs. Kath. Th. Fak. Tübingen* (München-Freiburg 1967).

Schmidt, H., *Das Gebet des Angeklagten im Alten Testament*, BZAW 49 (Giessen 1928). [cf. also in *Old Testament Essays*, London 1927 143-155 + §20a]

Id., *Die Psalmen* (Tübingen 1934).

Schmidt, L., (ed.), *Die Psalmen, I. Halbband* (Stuttgart 1967).

Schmidt, W., *Königtum Gottes in Ugarit und Israel. Zur Herkunft der "Königsprädication" Jahwes*, BZAW, 80, 2nd ed. (Berlin 1966). [cf. 80-97, "Das Königtum Gottes in Israel."]

Schmidt, W. H., "Gott und Mensch in Ps 130. Formgeschichtliche Erwägungen," *TZBas*, 22 (1966) 241-253.

Schmuttermayr, G., "Um Psalm 87 (86):5," *BZ* 7 (1963) 104-110.

Id., *Studien zum Text der Ps 9-10 und 18. Probleme der Textkritik und Übersetzung und das Psalterium Pianum* (Diss. München 1966).

Schneider, H., "Die Psalterteilung in Fünfziger-und Zehnergruppen," *Universitas, Fs. A. Stohr*, I (Mainz 1960) 36-47.

Schollmeyer, A., *Sumerisch-babylonische Hymnen und Gebete an Shamash* (Paderborn 1912).

Schönbächler, V., *Die Stellung der Psalmen zum alttestamentlichen Opferkultus* (Freiburg 1941).

Schreiner, J., *Sion-Jerusalem, Jahwes Königssitz. Theologie der Heiligen Stadt im Alten Testament* (München 1963).

Schulz, A., *Die Psalmen und die Cantica des Röm. Breviers verdeutscht* (Regensburg 1939).

Schüngel-Straumann, H., "Zur Gattung und Theologie des 139. Psalms," *BZ* 17 (1973) 39-51.

Schwarzwäller, K., *Die Feinde des Individuums in den Psalmen* (Diss. Hamburg 1963. [typescript]

Scott, R. B. Y., *The Psalms as Christian Praise* (London 1958).

Seeligmann, I. L., 'A psalm from the pre-regal times," *VT* 14 (1964) 75-92. [Dt 33]

Segula, F., "Messias Rex in Psalmis," *VD* 32 (1954); 23-33; 77-83; 142-154.

Sellers, O. R., "The Status and Prospects of Research concerning the Psalms," *Willoughby, The Study of the Bible Today and Tomorrow* (Chicago 1947), pp. 129-143.

Sevra, R.M., "Nota critica," *Claretianum* 9 (1969) 413-46.

Shenkel, J.D.,"An Interpretation of Ps 93:5," *Bib* 46 (1965) 401-416.

Sievers, E., *Metrische Studien I-III* (Berlin 1904-1907).

Simpson, D. C. (edit.), *The Psalmists* (Oxford 1926). [cf. H. Gressmann, T. H. Robinson, H. W. Robinson, G. R. Driver, A. M. Blackman + §5c]

Simpson, W.G., "Some Egyptian Light on a Translation Problem in Ps 10," *VT* 19 (1968) 128-131.

Skehan, P. W., "Strophic Structure in Ps 72 (71)," *Bib* 40 (1959) 302-308.

Ib., "A Psalm Manuscript from Qumran (4QPs*b*)," *CBQ* 26 (1964) 313-322.

Ib., "Borrowings from the Psalms in the Book of Wisdom," *CBQ* 10 (1948) 384-397.

Smal, P. J. N., *Die universalisme in die Psalms* (Kampen 1956).

Smend, R., "Ueber das Ich der Psalmen" *ZAW* 8 (1888) 56ff.

Snaith, N. H., *Studies in the Psalter* (London 1934).

Ib., *Hymns of the Temple* (London 1951).

Ib., "Selah," *VT* 2 (1952) 43-56.

Snijders, L. A., "Psaume 26 et l'innocence," *OTS* 13 (1963) 112-130.

Soggin, J. A., "Appunti per l'exegesi cristiana della prima parte del Salmo 22," *BibOr* 7 (1965) 105-116.

Sonne, I., "The second psalm," *HUCA* 19 (1945-46) 43-55.

Ib., "Psalm Eleven," *JBL* 68 (1949) 241-245.

Sorg, R., *Hesed und Hasid in the Psalms* (St. Louis 1953). [cf. CBQ 1955 520]

Id., *Ecumenic Ps 87* (Fifield, Wisc. 1969). Also appendix on Ps 110:3 and Ps 87:4.

Sparks, H. F. D., "A Textual Note on Psalm 104:16," *JTS* 48 (1947) 57f.

Sperber, A., *A Historical Grammar of Biblical Hebrew* (Leiden 1966).

Stamm. J. J., "Ein Vierteljahrhundert Psalmenforschung," Theol. Rundschau 23 (1955) 1-68. [complete bibliog.: 1929-1954]

Ib., "Eine Bemerkung zum Anfang des achten Psalmes," *TZBas* 13 (1957) 470-478.

Ib., "Erwägungen zu Ps 23," *ÊÊvT* 44 (1966) 120-128.

Steiert, B., "Einführung in die neue römische Psalmenversion," *Anal. S. Ord. Cist.* 7 (Roma 1951) 91-166; 11 (Roma 1955) 199-324. [cf. A. Bea, *VD* 1956 321-326]

Steinmann, J., *"Les Psaumes"* (Paris 1951).

Stoebe, H. J., *Gott sei mir Sünder gnädig. Eine Auslegung des 51. Psalms* (Neukirchen 1958).

Ib., "Erwägungen zu Ps 110 auf dem Hintergrund von 1 Sam. 21," *Fs. F. Baumgärtel* (Erlangen 1959) 175-191.

Strobel, A., "La conversion des gentils dans les psaumes" (Roma 1949). [typescript]

Strugnell, J., "A Note on Ps 126:1," *JTS* 7 (1956) 239-243.

Id., "Notes on the Text and Transmission of the Apocryphal Psalms 151, 154 (= Syr. II) and 155 (= Syr. III)," *Harv. Th. Rev.* 59 (1966) 257-281.

Studies on the Psalms: Papers read at the 6th Meeting of Die O. T. Werkgemeenskap in Suid-Afrika (Potchefstroom 1963). [cf. S. du Toit, J. J. Glueck, J. H. Kroeze, L. M. Muntingh, I. H. Eybers, A. H. Van Zyl, F. C. Fensham]

Stummer, F., "Die Psalmengattungen im Lichte der altorientalischen Hymnenlitteratur," *JSOR* 8 (1924) 123ff.

Id., *Sumerisch-akkadische Parallelen zum Aufbau alttestamentlicher Psalmen* (Paderborn 1922).

Sutcliffe, E. F., "A Note on Psalm CIV:8a," *VT* 2 (1952) 177-179.

Szörenyi, A., "Quibus criteriis dignosci possit, qui Psalmi ad usum liturgicum compositi sint?" *Bib* 23 (1942) 333-368.

Id., *Psalmen und Kult im Alten Testament. Zur Formgeschichte der Psalmen* (Budapest 1961). [rejects as a myth the existence of a special feast of Yahweh's enthronement; cf. §8d]

Teófilo de Orbiso, "El 'Reino de Dios' en los Salmos," *EstFranciscanos* (Barcelona) 49 (1948) 13-35; 198-209.

Terrien, S., *The Psalms and their Meaning for Today* (New York 1952).

Ib., "Creation, Cultus, and Faith in the Psalter," in *Horizons of Theological Education*, Fs. C. L. Taylor, edit. by J. B. Coburn (Dayton, Ohio 1966) 116-128.

Thévenet, J., *La confiance en Dieu dans les Psaumes* (Paris 1965).

Thierry, G. J., "Remarks on various Passages of the Psalms," *OTS* 13 (1963) 77-97. [Pss 7:15; 10:3; 22:10; 23:3f]

Thomas, D. Winton, "*niṣṣab* in Psalm XXXIX:16," *Studies in the Bible presented to Prof. M. H. Segal* (Jerusalem 1964) 10-1ō.

Id., "Hebrew 'anî, Captivity," *JTS* 16 (1965) 444f.

Id., "Psalm XXXV:15f," *JTS* 12 (1961) 50f.

Toit, S. du, "Psalms and history," *Studies on the Psalms* 18-29.

Torczyner, H. *Die Bundeslade und die Anfänge der Religion Israels* (Berlin 1922).

Torrance, T. F., "The Last of the Hallel Psalms," *Evang. Theol.* 28 (1956) 101-108.

Tournay, R., "Le psaume LXVIII," *Vivre et Penser* 2 (1942) 227-245. [= RB]

Id., "Notes sur les psaumes," *Vivre et Penser* 3 (1945) 214-237.

Id., "Les psaumes complexes," *RB* 54 (1947), 521-542; 56 (1949) 37-60.

Id., "L'eschatologie individuelle dans les Psaumes," *RB* 56 (1949) 481-506.

Id., "Notules sur les Psaumes (Pss XIX:2-5; LXXI:15f)," *Alttestamentliche Studien F. Nötscher zum sechzigsten Geburtstage...* (Bonn 1950) 271-280.

Id., "Sur quelques rubriques des Psaumes," *Mélanges Bibliques...* 197-204.

Id., "Recherches sur la chronologie des Psaumes," *RB* 65 (1958) 321-357; 66 (1959) 161-190. [cf. §5e, 8b, 9a]

Id., "Le Psaume LXVIII et le livre des Juges," *RB* 66 (1959) 358-368.

Id., "Le Psaume 141," *VT* 9 (1959) 58-64.

Id., "Le Psaume CX," *RB* 67 (1960) 5-41.

Id., "Le Psaume 72:16 et le réveil de Melqart," *Trav. Inst. Cath.* 10 (Paris 1964) 97-104.

R. Tournay et R. Schwab, *Les Psaumes* (ed. 2, Paris 1955). [=*BJ*]

Travers, J. C.-M., "Le nouveau Psautier," *La Maison-Dieu,* n. 5 (1946) 60-65. [also in the same number, on the New Latin Psalter: 66-106, by various authors; see also *ibid.* n. 33 (1953) 72-92]

Treves, M., "The Date of Ps XXIV," *VT* 10 (1960) 428-434. [composed for the 25th day of Chisleu, 164 B.C.!]

Id., "Two acrostic Psalms," *VT* 15 (1965) 81-90. [Pss 2 and 110, related to the Hasmoneans!]

Tsevat, M., *A Study of the Language of the Biblical Psalms* — *JBL Monogr. series,* Vol. IX (Philadelphia 1965). [cf. §9d]

Tur-Sinai, H. H., "The Literary Character of the Book of Psalms," *OTS* 8 (1950) 263-281. [cf. H. Torczyner]

Id., "On some obscure passages in the Book of Psalms," *Fs. A. H. Silver* (New York 1963) 1-35.

Tuya, M. de, "El problema biblico de las 'imprecaciones,'" *CiTom* 78 (1951), 171-192; 79 (1952) 3-29.

Ubbelohde, H., *Fluchpsalmen und alttestamentliche Sittlichkeit* (Breslau 1938).

Vaccari, A., "Antica e nuova interpretazione del Salmo 16 (Volg. 15)," *Bib* 14 (1933) 408-434.

Id., "Il Salmo della Risurrezione," *La Redenzione* (Roma 1934) 165-190. [Pss 16-15]

Id., "I salteri di S. Girolamo e di S. Agostino," *Scritti di erudizione e di filologia* (Roma 1952) 207-255.

Id., *I Salmi tradotti dall'ebraico con a fronte la nuova versione latina approvata da Pio XII. Seconda edizione completamente rifatta* (Torino 1953).

Id., "Il salmo 108 (109)," *RBibIt* I (1953) 55-60.

Vagaggini, G., *Bibbia e spiritualità liturgica con particolare riferimento ai Salmi* (Roma 1964).

Vanbergen, P., "Le psaume 117 (118). Une Eucharistie qui éclaire l'Eucharistie de Jésus," *QLitPar* 45 (1964) 65-81.

Vandenbroucke, F., "Le psautier, prophétie ou prière du Christ?" *QLitPar* 33 (1952) 149-161; 201-213.

Id., *Les Psaumes et le Christ* (Louvain 1955).

Id., "Le Dieu des Psaumes," *Vie Spir.* 74 (1946) 625-640.

Van den Berghe, P. "'ani et 'anaw dans les Psaumes," *Le Psautier* [cf. R. DeLanghe], 272-296. [cf. §12a]

Van der Ploeg. J., *De Psalmen uit de grondtekst vertaald en van korte inleidingen en aantekeningen voorzien* (Roermond/Maaseik 1963).

Id., "Psalm XIX and some of its problems," *JEOL* 17 (1964) 193-201.

Id., "Notes sur le Psaume XLIX," *OTS* 13 (1963) 137-172.

Id., "Le Psaume XCI dans une recension de Qumrân," *RB* 72 (1965) 210-217.

Id., "Réflexions sur les genres litteraires des Psaumes," *Studia Biblica et semitica: Fs. T. C. Vriezen* (Vageningen 1966) 265-277.

Id., "L'étude du Psautier 1960-67," *Donum natal. J. Coppens* 1 (Gembloux 1969) 174-91.

Van der Weijden, A. H., *Die "Gerechtigkeit" in den Psalmen* (Nimwegen 1952).

Van der Woude, A. S., "Zwei alte Cruces im Psalter," *OTS* 13 (1963) 131-136.

Van Imschoot, P., "De psalmis imprecatoriis," *ColGand* 27 (1944) 89-93.

Van Zyl, A. H., "Psalm 23," *Studies on the Psalms* 64-83.

Vaux, R. de, "Les chérubins et l'arche d'alliance. Les sphinx gardiens et les trônes divins dans l'Ancient Orient," *Mél. Univ. St.-Joseph* 37 (1961) 93-124 = *Bible et Orient* (Paris 1967) 231-259.

Id., *Ancient Israel*, vol. I: *Social Institutions*; vol. II: *Religious Institutions* (New York 1965).

Vénard, L. "L'utilisation des Psaumes dans l'Epître aux Hebreux," *Melanges E. Podechard* (Lyon 1945) 253-264; cf. *SDB* II, cc 23-51.

Veugelers, P., "Le Psaume LXXII, poème messianique?" *ETL* 41 (1965) 317-343.

Vilar, Hueso, "El Salmo 24: unidad literaria y ambiente histórico," *EstBib* 22 (1963) 243-253.

Vogt, E., "The 'Place in Life' of Psalm 23," *Bib* 34 (1953) 195-211.

Id., "Der Aufbau von Ps 29," *Bib* 41 (1960) 17-24.

Id., "Ihr Tisch werde zur Falle (Ps 69:23)," *Bib* 43 (1962) 79-82.

Id., "Psalm 26, ein Pilgergebet," *Bib* 43 (1962) 328-337.

Id., "Gratiarum actio Psalmi 40," *VD* 43 (1965) 181-190.

Id., "Die Himmel troffen (Ps 68:9)?," *Bib* 46 (1965) 207-209.

Id., "Regen in Fülle (Psalm 68:10-11)," *Bib* 46 (1965) 359-361.

Id., "Die Wagen Gottes, zehntausendfach, Tausende *šin'án* (Ps 68:18)," Bib 46 (1965) 460-463.

Id., "Psalmus 44 et Tragoedia Ezechiae regis," *VD* 45 (1967) 193-200.

Volz, P., "Psalm 49," *ZAW* 55 (1937) 235-264.

Vos, J. G., "The Ethical Problem of the Imprecating Psalms," *Westm. Th. J.* 4, 2 (1942) 123-138.

Vosté, J.-M., "Sur les titres des Psaumes dans la Pešittā surtout d'après la recension orientale," *Bib* 25 (1944) 210-235.

Wächter, L., "Drei umstrittene Psalmstellen (Ps 26:1; 30:8; 90:4-6)," *ZAW* 78 (1966) 61-68.

Wanke, G., *Die Zionstheologie der Korachiten in ihrem traditionsgeschichtlichen uusmmenhang, BZAW,* 97 (Berlin 1966). [Pss 46, 48, 84, 87 are post-exilic]..

Ward, J. M., *A Literary and Exegetical Study of the 89th Psalm* (Ann Arbor 1958). [microfilm]

Id., "The Literary Form and the Liturgical-Background of Psalm LXXXIX," *VT* 11 (1961) 321-339.

Watts, J. D. W., "Yahweh Malāk Psalms," *TZBas* 21 (1965) 341-348.

Weber, D. R., *Le Psautier Romain et les autres anciens Psautiers latins. Edition critique, ColBibLat,* X (1953).

Weber, J., *Le psautier du bréviaire romain. Texte et commentaire* (Paris 1937).

Weiser, A., "Zur Frage nach den Beziehungen der Psalmen zum Kult: die Darstellung der Theophanie in den Psalmen und im Festkult," *Fs. für Alfred Bertholet* (Tübingen 1950) 513-532.

Id., *The Psalms* (London 1962). [cf. §13c]

Weiss, M., "Wege der neuen Dichtungswissenschaft in ihrer Anwendung auf die Psalmenforschung," *Bib* 42 (1961) 255-302.

Welch, A. C., *The Psalter in Life, Worship and History* (Oxford 1926). [cf. §8f]

Werbeck, W., Art. "Psalmen" (Im AT), *RGG*, IV 3rd. edit., cf. 672-686. [with bibliogr.]

Westermann, C., "Struktur und Geschichte der Klage im Alten Testament," *ZAW* 66 (1954) 44-80.

Id., *Gewendete Klage. Eine Auslegung des 22. Psalms* (Neukirchen 1955).

Id., "Zur Sammlung des Psalters," *Z. d. Morg. Ges.*, III (1961) 388f.

Id., "Vergegenwärtigung der Geschichte in den Psalmen," *Zwischenstation, Fs. K. Kupisch* (München 1963) 253-280.

Id., *The Praise of God in the Psalms*, tr. by K. R. Crim (Richmond, Va. 1965). [cf. §7b, 13ad and 22]

Id., *Der Psalter, Bibl Seminar im Calwer Verlag* (Stuttgart 1967).

Wevers, J. W., "A Study in the Form Criticism of Individual Complaint Psalms," *VT* 6 (1956) 80-96.

Whitelocke, L.T., *The rib-Pattern and the Concept of Judgment in the Book of Psalms* (Diss. Boston Univ. Graduate School 1968; cf. *DissAbstr* 29, 1968f, 1950f-A).

Widengren, G., *The Accadian and Hebrew Psalms of Lamentation as religious Documents, a comparative Study* (Uppsala 1936). [new edit.: Stockholm 1937]

Id., *Sakrales Königtum im Alten Testament und im Judentum* (Stuttgart 1955).

Willesen, F., "The Cultic Situation of Psalm LXXIV," *VT* 2 (1952) 289-306.

William, P. R., *The Perfect Law of Liberty* (Ps 119), (London 1952).

Williams, W. G., "Liturgical Problems in Enthronement Psalms," *JBR* 25 (1957) 118-122.

Wolff, H. W., "Der Aufruf zur Volksklage," *ZAW* 76 (1964) 48-56.

Wolverton, W. I., "The Psalmists' Belief in God's Presence," *CanJT* 9 (1963) 82-94.

Id., "The Meaning of the Psalms," *AnglTR* 47 (1965) 16-33. [cf. §13b, 14c + on *Pss 46, 99] [on Pss 78, 105, 106 see also *idem* in *CanJT* 10, 1964 166-176]

Worden, T., *The Psalms are Christian Prayer* (London 1962). [Key patterns of Israelite thought and expressions are explained; also two themes often recurring in th, Psalms: "the Redemption of Israel," "Yahweh the Conqueror of Israel's Enemies"]

Wright, G. E., *The Old Testament against its Environment* (London 1950) 30-41.

Würthwein, E., "Erwägungen zu Psalm 73," *Fs. für A. Bertholet* (Tübingen 1950) 532-549.

Id., "Erwägungen zu Psalm CXXXIX," *VT* 7 (1957) 165-182.

Young, E. J., *Psalm 139: a Study of the Omniscience of God* (London 1965).

Zandee, J., *Death as an Enemy according to Ancient Egyptian Conceptions* (Leiden 1960).

Id., Hymnal Sayings addressed to the Sun-god by the High-priest of Amün Nebwenenef, from his tomb in Thebes," *JEOL* 18 (1964) 253-265.

Zbik, F., *De sensu filiationis divinae in Ps 2* (Romae 1951f).

Zeneboni, M. I., "Il Salterio e la gioia," *RAscMist* 27 (1957) 374-389.

Ziegler, J., "Die Hilfe Gottes 'am Morgen,'" *Alttestamentliche Studien* (Fs. Fr. Nötscher: Bonn 1950) 281-288. [see on *Ps 5:4]

Zink, J. K., "Uncleanness and sin. A Study of Job XIV, 4 and Psalm 51:7," *VT* 17 (1967) 354-361.

Zirker, H., *Die kultische Vergegenwärtigung der Vergangenheit in den Psalmen* (Bonn 1964). [cf. *CBQ* 26, 1964 518f]

Zolli, E., "In margine al *Miserere,*" *Sefarad* 9 (1949) 142-151.

Id., *Il Salterio* (Milano 1951).

Id., *I Salmi. Documenti di vita vissuta* (Milano 1953). [cf. *CBQ* 1954 487f]

Zorell, F., "Einführung in die Metrik und Kunstform der hebräischen Psalmendichtung, (Münster 1914).

Id., *Psalterium ex Hebraeo Latinum* (Romae 1928).

Indices

II. LIST OF THE PSALMS: NUMERICAL ORDER

(The number within parentheses is that of the Septuagint and the Latin Psalter; the symbols give the category; the page indicates the beginning of the "title and introduction" to the psalm).

1 (1) p. 371 W	42 (41) p. 239 LI	82 (81) p. 307 LC
2 (2) p. 338 R	43 (42) p. 239 LI	83 (82) p. 309 LC
3 (3) p. 265 CI	44 (43) p. 298 LC	84 (83) p. 211 CZ
4 (4) p. 266 CI	45 (44) p. 349 R	85 (84) p. 310 LC
5 (5) p. 219 LI	46 (45) p. 206 CZ	86 (85) p. 254 LI
6 (6) p. 220 LI	47 (46) p. 197 YK	87 (86) p. 212 CZ
7 (7) p. 221 LI	48 (47) p. 208 CZ	88 (87) p. 255 LI
8 (8) p. 177 H	49 (48) p. 374 W	89 (88) p. 352 R
9/10 (9) p. 279 TI	50 (49) p. 397 Ex	90 (89) p. 312 LC
11 (10) p. 267 CI	51 (50) p. 241 LI	91 (90) p. 379 W
12 (11) p. 297 LC	52 (51) p. 298 Ex	92 (91) p. 289 TI
13 (12) p. 223 LI	53 (52) p. 400 Ex	93 (92) p. 199 YK
14 (13) p. 395 Ex	54 (53) p. 245 LI	94 (93) p. 313 LC
15 (14) p. 407 L	55 (54) p. 245 LI	95 (94) p. 404 Ex
16 (15) p. 268 CI	56 (55) p. 246 LI	96 (95) p. 201 YK
17 (16) p. 224 LI	57 (56) p. 247 LI	97 (96) p. 202 YK
18 (17) p. 342 R	58 (57) p. 299 LC	98 (97) p. 203 YK
19 (18) p. 178 H	59 (58) p. 249 LI	99 (98) p. 203 YK
20 (19) p. 346 R	60 (59) p. 300 LC	100 (99) p. 183 H
21 (20) p. 347 R	61 (60) p. 249 LI	101 (100) p. 356 R
22 (21) p. 226 LI	62 (61) p. 275 CI	102 (101) p. 256 LI
23 (22) p. 270 CI	63 (62) p. 250 LI	103 (102) p. 183 H
24 (23) p. 407 L	64 (63) p. 251 LI	104 (103) p. 184 H
25 (24) p. 230 LI	65 (64) p. 324 TC	105 (104) p. 392 Hi
26 (25) p. 231 LI	66 (65) p. 325 TC	106 (105) p. 314 LC
27 (26) p. 273 CI	67 (66) p. 327 TC	107 (106) p. 291 TI
28 (27) p. 232 LI	68 (67) p. 327 TC	108 (107) p. 316 LC
29 (28) p. 180 H	69 (68) p. 252 LI	109 (108) p. 257 LI
30 (29) p. 282 TI	70 (69) p. 253 LI	110 (109) p. 357 R
31 (30) p. 233 LI	71 (70) p. 253 LI	111 (110) p. 187 H
32 (31) p. 283 TI	72 (71) p. 351 R	112 (111) p. 381 W
33 (32) p. 182 H	73 (72) p. 376 W	113 (112) p. 188 H
34 (33) p. 284 TI	74 (73) p. 301 LC	114/115 (113) p. 188,
35 (34) p. 235 LI	75 (74) p. 401 Ex	320 H:CC
36 (35) p. 236 LI	76 (75) p. 209 CZ	116 (114/115) p. 292 TI
37 (36) p. 273 W	77 (76) p. 304 LC	117 (116) p. 189 H
38 (37) p. 237 LI	78 (77) p. 391 Hi	118 (117) p. 331 TC
39 (38) p. 238 LI	79 (78) p. 305 LC	119 (118) p. 381 W
40 (39) p. 285 TI	80 (79) p. 306 LC	120 (119) p. 258 LI
41 (40) p. 287 TI	81 (80) p. 402 EX	121 (120) p. 276 CI

III. SUBJECT INDEX